MW00647206

# Curtiss Aircraft

## 1907–1947

The tiny F9C-2 Sparrowhawks achieved fame out of all proportion to their numbers and performance because of their unique function as auxiliaries to the US Navy airships *Akron* and *Macon*. Although open-cockpit biplanes in the old tradition, they were representative of the new era in being the first production Curtiss aeroplanes of all-metal construction.

# Curtiss Aircraft

## 1907–1947

Peter M Bowers

**Naval Institute Press**

BY THE SAME AUTHOR

*Boeing Aircraft since 1916*

© Peter M. Bowers 1979
Printed in Great Britain for
Putnam, an imprint of
Conway Maritime Press Ltd,
24 Bride Lane, Fleet Street,
London EC4Y 8DR
Published and distributed in the United States of
America and Canada by the Naval Institute Press,
Annapolis, Maryland 21402
Library of Congress Catalog Card No. 87–62882
ISBN 0–87021–152–8
This edition is authorized for sale only in the
United States and its territories and possessions,
and Canada
*First Published 1979*
*Reprinted 1987*

# CONTENTS

# Introduction

## Organization of this Book

Because of several changes in the aeroplane designation systems used by Curtiss, the overlap of many long-production models, and the desirability of treating certain large 'families' of aeroplanes separately from their contemporaries, this book does not present the Curtiss aeroplanes in strict sequential order. The easily recognized chronological and technological periods that divide the history of aviation make the organization of this book along similar lines logical and simple. Presentation of the material within the chapters varies according to the nature of the subject; some aeroplanes are presented alphabetically by Curtiss name or letter designation, some are in sequence of Curtiss model number, while others are in the sequence of US Army and Navy designations. Where applicable, the aeroplanes are identified by both Curtiss and customer designations.

Non-technical data such as registrations and serial numbers, and approved type certificates, appear in appendices.

## Aircraft Technical Data and Sources

The presentation of aeroplane specifications and performance figures that follow the text are not uniform throughout nor are complete data presented for every basic model and variant listed. Structural and armament details are presented only when necessary to point out significant transitions. Space and cost considerations of this volume due to the great numbers of similar models covered are only partial reasons for abbreviating data and reducing near and actual duplication of data. In the matter of specifications and performance, photographs and the aeroplane's place in time often make the type of construction and the equipment obvious.

Complete data were seldom accumulated on experimental and custom types in the very early days and to the end of World War I. In some cases, parts of two existing machines would be put together to try a new configuration; a single test flight might then prove the combination undesirable and it would be abandoned with no data being recorded. Some custom variations of standard models incorporated changes that altered

1

the original performance considerably. However, the criterion of the time was that a desirable change was accomplished; the precise degree of the change was relatively unimportant. In other cases, complete data accumulated on some experimental and early production types were never released, either by Curtiss or the military customer, and the data have since been lost. This was particularly true to the end of World War I.

Differences from previously published data will be found at times even for some well known standard military models. This is because of differences in procedures, conditions, etc, between factory and military testing. In some cases, US Navy test reports have noted differences resulting from the use of 'West Coast' or 'East Coast' petrol. Some of the performance data in this book are from Curtiss sources, including documents in the possession of old employees, some are from military publications, and some are from aviation magazines and reference books of the time.

For many standard military models, performance decreased during the production and service life of the model as extra equipment was added and weight and drag increased without power increase. Available data for only the basic model is presented in such cases, as the US Army P-6. The very minor performance difference for the P-6A is not given, but those for the racing variants, the turbo-supercharged P-6D, and the notably different P-6E are. In some cases, noteworthy differences from the basic model are mentioned in the text rather than being presented in the standardized table following the text.

# Photographs and Acknowledgements

The photographs used throughout this book have been gathered from many sources, many of which are acknowledged beneath each individual photograph. While a great number of the photographs were taken by Curtiss photographers at Curtiss factories, not one of these was obtained directly from Curtiss sources for use in this book. Since the closing of the aeroplane division of the Curtiss-Wright Corporation in 1947, such material has been in storage inaccessible to researchers. The Curtiss factory photos used are copies made by the US Army, Navy, or National Air Museum or are original photographs in the hands of private collectors and former Curtiss employees.

Particular mention should be made of the remarkable series of glass plate negatives made of Aerial Experiment Association and Curtiss activities from 1907 to 1914 by Mr E. T. Benner. These independent photographs provide the principal record of the work done during that period.

This results in the reappearance of some familiar photographs, as only one or two views of certain old aeroplanes are known to exist and the same views have been used to illustrate the particular aeroplanes for many years.

For this book photographic quality has occasionally been sacrificed to a small degree in order to present a different view of a single aeroplane that has previously been represented only by its one 'best' photograph.

Photographic coverage by other agencies improved in the late 1920s as aircraft came into the hands of private and commercial organizations that had occasion to make photographic records for their own archives. In the early 1930s, the hobby of aeroplane picture collecting by amateur photographers began to develop on a national scale and opened up a new and extremely valuable source of material.

From the very beginning, Curtiss photographers endeavoured to obtain studio-quality photographs of test aircraft and most standard production models in the configuration of the first deliveries. However, modifications and marking changes made in the field after delivery escaped the company photographers. Similarly, such customers as the armed forces and the airlines take good photographs of early delivery models for their own archives but do not always keep running photographic records of minor modifications, changes of colouring and unit markings. These differences from the initial configuration usually appear in official photographs only when a particular machine is photographed later in its life for some other reason. Consequently, many of these interesting and sometimes significant changes, which were regarded as routine matters at the time but which now form a priceless historical record, were recorded only by the zealous amateur photographers to whom the slightest change in colouring or other external detail was a valid reason for re-photographing the same aeroplane. While their entirely unofficial chronicle of changes is by no means complete, it does fill in many gaps in the official records.

Unfortunately for historians, no hard and fast rule has existed, either at Curtiss or in the armed services, to photograph every variant that was produced. Neither the factory nor the Army, as far as can be determined, ever photographed the XP-21, a modified P-3A 'Hawk' used to test a new engine. This aeroplane lost its identity as XP-21 when it was converted to a P-1F at the conclusion of the tests. In other cases, aeroplanes not photographed officially have been 'saved' by the amateur photographers, as in the case of the O-1F. This was a minor variation of the standard O-1E observation aircraft with armament omitted. The amateurs were able to identify this one-off variant and record it.

Whenever possible, photographs have been credited to their original source, whether Curtiss, customer agency, or private individual. The practice, both in industry and in government archives, of copying and distributing photographs originating elsewhere has made absolute accuracy in crediting some of these pictures impossible. Many photographs taken in bygone years are no longer available from the original sources. In cases where the only known print of such a photograph is in the hands of a private collector, it has been credited to him since he is now the only source. The fact that he did not actually take the picture is acknowledged by crediting it to *The Collection of . . .* or *Courtesy of. . . .*

Apologies are extended to those private photographers who may find that their original photographs have been credited to someone else. It is a widespread practice among the collectors to exchange negatives among themselves, with the result that one negative may pass through several hands before coming to a final owner. This makes it impossible to give proper credit to the originator. Except in those cases where the actual photographer is known to the author, illustrations made from other collectors' negatives have generally been credited to the person who provided the negative, or a print from it, for use in this book. Prints made from acquired negatives in the author's personal collection have been credited to the originator whenever possible.

While considerable detailed information relative to the careers of various aeroplane models is available from the manufacturer's published material or from its customer, there is more that has escaped the official recorder. Many of the fascinating incidents that form parts of the overall story are preserved only in the memories of the people who were directly involved with the story as it developed or are stored in the attics of those who happened to retain a particular record or bit of data that would otherwise have been lost to the researcher of later years.

The assistance of the following individuals, mostly collectors, authors, or former Curtiss employees, is greatly, if inadequately, acknowledged:

*Authors and Publishers*
Joe Christy; Joseph P. Juptner; William T. Larkins; Paul Matt; Kenn C. Rust; F. Gordon Swanborough; John Underwood; Ray Wagner.

*Curtiss Employees and Associates*
Frank T. Courtney, Consultant; Robert Darby, Engineer; Herb Fisher, Test Pilot; Maximilian Garavito, Colombian AF Inspector; Paul Hovgard, Test Pilot; Peter Jansson, Factory Manager; Charles F. Willard, US Pilot No.4.

*National Air Museum Staff*
Walter J. Boyne, Curator of Aeronautics; Louis S. Casey, Curator of Aircraft; Don Lopez.

*Photographers, Collectors*
Dustin Carter; James H. Dilonardo; Harry Gann; Daniel P. Hagedorn; Merle Olmstead; Boardman C. Reed; Richard Seely; Frank Strnad; Gordon S. Williams.

*Specialists*
Harold M. Andrews, US Naval Aviation; John C. Barbery, civil aircraft registrations; Gerry Beauchamp, Model 75; Carlos Dufriche, Brazilian serial numbers; Robert Garrard, US Army inventories; Eric H. Hart, P-40; William Lloyd, civil aircraft registrations; David W. Menard, USAF

4

historical research; Ken M. Molson, Canadian history; E. D. Weeks, Pioneer aviation; Norbert F. Yaggi, Military serial numbers.

*Special Mention*
In addition, special appreciation is expressed to the following: Robert B. Casari, publisher of the historical series, US Military Aircraft, for allowing the use of some of his original research and copyright material on early US Army aviation in advance of his own publication; George A. Page, Curtiss employee since 1917 and last Chief Engineer of the Airplane Division, who provided technical data and photographs from his personal files and filled many details of history and model development from his fantastic memory; Victor D. Seely, for the use of his extensive technical data files, many hours of darkroom work in printing photographs from the author's negative files, and organization of reference material, military serial numbers, and civil registrations; George S. Shairer, Vice President of The Boeing Company and son-in-law of John P. Tarbox, Curtiss's patent attorney and later Director of Engineering, 1913–23. Mr Shairer made some of the Tarbox photographs and papers available to the author and provided a tape recording of Tarbox reminiscences; and finally, no words can express my appreciation of the support and encouragement of my wife Alice and daughter Alison, who patiently sacrificed many normal family activities to the time requirements of this book.

# Designations

A better appreciation of Curtiss aeroplanes, their usage, and periods of service can be had from an understanding of the company aeroplane model and serial number designation systems, the equivalent systems of the two principal US military services and the Royal Air Force, and the constantly changing military markings. These are all described in this introductory section rather than being presented throughout the book as they occur.

## Manufacturer's Model Designations

Throughout its existence, Curtiss has used a variety of designation systems to identify its aeroplanes. No system at all was involved at first— the product was simply the Curtiss (actually Herring-Curtiss) aeroplane. Individual names, official or otherwise, were sometimes applied, as *Reims Machine* or *Albany Flyer*.

When standardized models were offered to the public through catalogues, it became desirable to identify the product and its optional variations. Consequently, an alphabetical system was established that was to run on into 1918. The first advertized models were the D and E, with

5

powerplant and other variations identified by numbers, as Type I, II, etc. Unfortunately for the historian, there were many experimental and custom models developed outside of this system for which no recognized designations exist.

The alphabetical system did not hold to strict sequence nor were all letters actually used. Some Curtiss models, known to have been undesignated in their time, seem to have been given unused letter designations appropriate to their design sequence at considerably later dates as part of an attempt to bring order, but not necessarily accuracy, to a confusing historical situation.

Merger of some established designs resulted in two-letter designations, as JN for a combination of the Models J and N. Major modifications were also reflected, as HS, for a single-engine variant (hence the S) of the Model H twin-engined flying-boat. At first, variants of a basic letter-model were indicated in the designation, as D-75 for a D with 75 hp engine. Later, successive developments of the basic models were identified by number, examples being JN-2, N-9. Further developments of the numbered sub-types again used letters, as JN-4A, JN-4B. Some out-of-sequence letters were used to identify variations in powerplant, as JN-4H and N-9H for versions of those models with the Hispano-Suiza engine and R-4L for an R-4 with Liberty engine replacing the original Curtiss.

Designations from 1917 into 1919 were very inconsistent. Two-letter identifications were sometimes keyed to the aeroplane origin or function, as NC for flying-boats designed jointly by the Navy and Curtiss, and CB for Curtiss Battleplane. The application of HA to the Dunkirk Fighter seems purely arbitrary, but the MF of 1918 was a modified or modernized F.

The experimental Garden City factory used separate project numbers in 1918, as Experimental 502 for a model that was to become the 18-B (for biplane; there were also 18T-1 and 18T-2 triplane variants).

After World War I most Curtiss civil aeroplanes were marketed under the names of birds rather than numbers, but there were engineering model numbers for internal use only. The famous Falcon line carried the designation L-113 while the earlier CR (Navy designation for Curtiss Racer) was L-17. The Robin of 1928 was L-910, after which the L-system seemed to die out. All publicity and sales literature relative to civil models was strictly by name; publicity and company records and photographs relative to military models used either the popular name or the actual Army or Navy designation.

In 1930, the St Louis branch adopted a designation system of its own that started with CW-1 (for Curtiss-Wright) and reached CW-25 by World War II. However, for publicity and marketing, names (not necessarily of birds) were preferred to numbers; examples being Junior and Sedan.

In 1935, the Buffalo factory adopted a new numerical system. With the intention of applying it retroactively to all earlier models but the St Louis CWs, it was started at 75. It fell considerably short, however, with Model 1 going to the JN-4A of 1917. Many of the earlier letter-type and undesignated experimentals were left out, as was a number of later World War I developments. Because of its convenience in establishing model sequence, this system is used in the organization of this book starting with The Postwar Decade on page 167. Too many first-war models were overlooked for the system to be effective for that chapter.

The new numeric system used sequential letters and additional numbers to identify variations, as 75-A, 75-A1. Later, prefix letters were added, as H87-A3. When the model numbers passed 99, they were switched to a continuation of the CW numbers to avoid going to three-digit basic designations that were incompatible with the machine record-keeping system then in use.

## Military Model Designations

Shortly after World War I, the US Army and Navy, principal customers for Curtiss military aircraft, adopted systematic but different aircraft designation schemes. These are described here briefly to familiarize the reader with the symbols used. Specific identification of most symbols used appears in the text under the appropriate aircraft heading.

# US Army (later US Air Force) Designations

In 1920, the Army adopted a Type-Model-Series system that told much about an aircraft. As originally adopted, the initial letter of the designation PW-8B indicated the type of aircraft as Pursuit. The second letter indicated that it used a Water-cooled engine, while the 8 indicated that it was the 8th model of the PW type. The B indicates the second variant, or improved version, of the original PW-8 model. The system was simplified in 1924 to delete the second letter, and the series started anew with the Curtiss P-1. Another change was made at that time to indicate the status of the aeroplane. The letter X was added to the designation as a prefix to identify an experimental, usually prototype, model. There was the XO-1, and the initial production O-1. A significant change resulted in O-1A, and so on to O-1G.

Sometimes new features were tested on a later series of an established model and justified an X-designation, as XP-1C. In 1929, the prefix Y was adopted to indicate the Service test status of a new model ordered into production in limited quantity for evaluation, as YA-8. If the aircraft were procured with F-1 funds instead of from the regular Service appropriations, the prefix was Y1, as Y1A-8. The letter Z was adopted to designate obsolete types still in service. Usually, X and Z prefixes were permanent while Ys could be deleted upon completion of the Service test.

Before World War II, practically every minor variation in armament or structure resulted in a new series letter. These changes became so numerous by wartime that the Army adopted a block number system to keep track of minor changes without changing the series letter. There were, for example, P-40N variants from P-40N-1 to P-40N-40. This does not mean that there were actually this many variations; the numbers were assigned by the Army in blocks of five, starting with -1, then -5, -10, -15, etc. The intermediate numbers were saved for changes made at modification centres. A P-40N-10 with such a change could have become -11 or -12.

In 1942, when a number of factories or even different firms were building the same type of aeroplane under a single military designation, the Army added manufacturers' code letters to the basic designations to identify the actual manufacturer and the plant. Curtiss C-46As built at Buffalo were C-46A-CU. Those built at Louisville, Kentucky, were C-46A-CK while those built at St Louis were C-46A-CS. C-46As built by Higgins in New Orleans were C-46A-HI.

Usually, the military designation is assigned when a purchase contract is negotiated. In the 1930s, an existing company-owned aeroplane being tested by the Army on a Bailment Contract was frequently given an experimental project number during the test. The Curtiss experimental fighter known as the Swift was tested by the Army as XP-940 before being purchased as the XP-31 and assigned an Army serial number. A model developed on an Army contract or at Army request carries the military designation and serial number from its inception.

## US Navy Designations

The Naval aircraft designation system adopted in 1922 was similar to the Army system in designating by type, but the model number was determined by the sequence of models from a particular manufacturer. Originally, the manufacturer was designated just by a letter, as C-for-Curtiss. The type was also identified by letter, as CR for Curtiss Racer, CS for Curtiss Scout. The initial configuration was identified by number, as CR-1. The first variation was CR-2.

In 1923, the system was revised to put the type letter first. By this time a second Curtiss Navy racer model was being ordered, so this became R2C-1; a third became R3C-1, then R3C-2, -3, etc. This system continued with little change throughout World War II except for the addition of dual-purpose type letters in 1934, as BF for bomber-fighter (Curtiss BFC-2, XBF2C-1). The prefix X-for-Experimental was adopted in 1927, and suffix letters to identify special missions or equipment, as SB2C-1C with cannon armament, came along during the war.

When one manufacturer's aeroplanes were built by another in World War II, the Navy changed the designation. Curtiss SB2Cs built by Fairchild were SBF; those built by Canadian Car & Foundry were SBW. The Naval designation was applied to both sides of the rudder starting in 1928 and remained there throughout World War II.

# Royal Air Force Designations

The Royal Air Force, which used large numbers of Curtiss aeroplanes in both world wars, used manufacturer's designations during the first war, as Curtiss H-12, but switched to a given name system shortly afterward. Curtiss models used in World War II were usually identified by their previously-given US 'popular' names except in cases where none existed; an example is the Curtiss Model 75A (US Army P-36) being named the Mohawk by the RAF. Variants were identified by mark numbers, as Mohawk II, etc.

# Popular Names

While most aircraft manufacturers assign actual model numbers to their products, many are marketed under a popular name rather than a number. Curtiss used names for both civil and military models from 1919 even though the customer might have his own designations for specific versions of a general model like the Curtiss Hawk.

Starting in October 1941, the US government encouraged the use of popular names rather than specific numbers for general reference to a particular model, ostensibly as a security measure so that unauthorized persons could not determine the production or development status of a particular model that would be indicated by a designation such as P-40K. Manufacturers were given the option of choosing the names themselves, subject to official approval, or the Aircraft Production Board picked one for them. This was easy for most Curtiss military models, which were already named, but a few were assigned that did not fit the Curtiss tradition of bird names, as Commando for the Army C-46 and Caravan for the C-76.

The popular name system was not too well received by people closely associated with the aircraft, and actual model designations with accurate series letters were preferred.

# Powerplant Designations

The engines in civil aircraft use the engine manufacturer's own name or model number, as did military engines until 1926. At that time, a Type-Size-Series system similar to Army aircraft designations was adopted by both Services. A letter identified the type, as R-for-Radial (air-cooled) and V-for-Vee (liquid-cooled). The size was indicated by the displacement to the nearest 5 cubic inches. Series was originally designated by letter, as V-1150C for a third military variation of the Curtiss D-12, a twelve-cylinder Vee type of 1,150 cu in displacement. This was changed in the late 1920s to a numerical suffix assigned in sequence of development. 'Even' dash numbers indicated Navy engines, while 'odd' dash numbers indicated Army, as R-1820-39 for an Army version of the Wright Cyclone radial. Inter-Service transfers of aircraft and/or engines resulted in Army aircraft carrying Navy engines, and vice versa. In some cases, letter prefixes were used to indicate experimental status or special features, as G for geared and S for supercharged. This Type-Size-Series system is still in use for reciprocating (piston) engines.

# Manufacturer's Serial Numbers (C/Ns)

At present, every aeroplane manufacturer applies to each aeroplane he builds a serial number (called c/n for constructor's number by historians and data enthusiasts) that is separate from any military serial number (s/n) or civil registration number (r/n) applied. However, this has not always been a mandatory practice, particularly with Curtiss. Because Curtiss records have been unavailable for research since the closing of the Airplane Division in 1947, known c/ns used in this book have been obtained mainly from civil aircraft registration records, aeroplane name plates, and other outside sources.

There is no indication that Curtiss used sequential c/ns until the end of World War I. Since most orders to that time were military, the military s/ns of the individual aeroplanes served the purpose of keeping track of production, points of detail change within production batches, etc. This is borne out by the frequency with which the former military s/n, rather than a c/n, appears in civil registration records for surplus World War I Curtiss aeroplanes.

There is evidence to show that sequential c/ns were applied to all military airframes built at Buffalo from 1919 until the Curtiss-Wright merger of 1929 and possibly beyond. These included production military models built at Garden City. Numbers reached by early 1929 (2439 for an O2C-1) indicate that this run of c/ns must have included all of the first war surplus types reconditioned at and sold by the Buffalo plant. However, civil and demonstrator Falcons built at Buffalo from 1928 were serialized within the model from c/n 1 to 20. Change of the system in the early 1930s is indicated by the c/n 11894 assigned to a demonstrator Hawk III, NR14703, which is higher than the known total of all Curtiss aeroplanes then built.

The Garden City plant, at least from 1925 on, identified individual civil aeroplanes by c/n only within the production range of a single model, the c/n sometimes being preceded by the letter G for Garden City, as G-1 to G-3 for the three Carrier Pigeon IIs and G-1 to G-6 for six Condor transports. If production was transferred to Buffalo, as for the Fledglings, the same system was followed but the c/n was preceded by a B-for-Buffalo. From this time on, the number-within-model system was applied to civil and export versions of such long-established military models as the Hawk and Falcon.

The Curtiss-Robertson plant at St Louis started a new sequential line of c/ns when production of the Robin began there in 1928 and carried it into other models produced there until the plant closed in 1932. The system was resumed when the plant reopened. C/ns assigned to the former Travel Air and Moth designs continued their original c/n sequence but later models given CW designations from 12 on were assigned c/ns within each model, as CW-15-2001.

World War II saw further changes. C/ns assigned to the first C-46s built at Buffalo in 1941–42 were higher than the total of Curtiss aeroplanes built to that time while the c/ns of C-46s built at the new Louisville plant in 1943 started at 26, following twenty-five C-76s. Yet the prototype of the C-46, the CW-20 transport built at St Louis, had c/n 101.

In this book, the expression c/n: 2929/2945 indicates Curtiss serial (constructor's) numbers 2929 to 2945, inclusive.

# Military Serial Numbers (S/Ns)

Both US military Services use their own serialization systems, which are entirely separate from c/ns and are used for operational identification, maintenance, procurement, and technical-change effectivity.

# US Army Serial Numbers

Army serialization began in 1908 and reached the 68000s by 1921. At that time, the system was changed to a fiscal year basis, aircraft 22-1 being the first one ordered in the fiscal year of 1922 (1 July, 1921, to 30 June, 1922). This system is still in use. The Army serial appeared in various forms on both sides of the fuselage during the 1920s but was confined to the Technical Data Block on the left side of the nose after 1931. After the Japanese attack on Pearl Harbor, it reappeared in large figures on both sides of the tail, but without the first digit of the fiscal year. P-40B 41-5205 showed the tail number as 15205. No conflict with a later aircraft 51-5205 was anticipated as military aircraft were not supposed to last ten years. Since the last four digits of the serial were used as radio call signs, short numbers were built up to a minimum of four digits. The tail serial number of P-36A 38-6 thus became 8006. When World War II aircraft began to exceed 10 years of service, the prefix letter O was added to the tail serial, as O-2107294 for C-46H 42-107294.

# US Navy Serial Numbers

The Navy numbered aircraft consecutively within types or classes as it did with ships, starting in 1911. After several changes in the system, serial numbers were separated from type designations early in 1917 and the existing aeroplanes were issued new serial numbers starting at 51. S/ns were prefixed with the letter A-for-Airplane from 1917 to 1930. The total reached 9,999 in 1934, so was restarted. Increased rate of procurement threatened to reach the second 9,999 by 1940, so the system was short-circuited at 7303 to prevent duplication of late numbers in the first series. The third series started with five digits, 00001, in November 1940, and has now grown to six. Navy serials were originally painted in large figures on the fuselage or hull, then were standardized on the vertical fin, starting in 1923 and continuing through World War II.

# Royal Air Force Serial Numbers

The principal customer for Curtiss military aeroplanes outside of the USA was Great Britain, whose purchases started early in the 1914–18 war and were on a large scale early in World War II. The Royal Flying Corps and Royal Naval Air Service (which merged to form the Royal Air Force in 1918) shared a sequential-numerical system which, upon reaching 9999, adopted a letter prefix (A, B, etc.) to succeeding blocks of 9999 numbers. Upon reaching Z early in World War II, the system adopted two-letter prefixes (AA, AB, etc.) and used only three-digit serial numbers. Throughout the years, these have traditionally appeared on each side of the rear fuselage and occasionally in additional locations.

# Military Markings and Colouring

Both US military Services and the Royal Air Force had standard colour schemes that varied widely over the years for different classes of aircraft and for different missions. This subject is worthy of a book by itself, and remarks on the colouring of individual Curtiss-designed aircraft are confined to the appropriate aircraft descriptions in this book.

# US National Markings

Over the years, there have been many changes in the application of national markings to US military aircraft. To save discussion in the text, the important changes are described here.

Shortly after US entry into World War I, standardized national markings were adopted in keeping with the schemes then in use by the major allies. On 17 May, 1917, wing markings were adopted in the form of a white star on a blue disc, with a red disc in the centre of the star. The tail marking duplicated that of France and Britain, with three vertical stripes of red, white, and blue, in equal width, on the rudder, the red being at the trailing edge. In January 1918, a change was made from the star to a tricolour circle that was more in keeping with the circle markings of the other allies. The colour arrangement was that of the former Imperial Russian forces, a red outside circle, a blue inner circle and then a white centre. The order of rudder stripes was reversed at the time to place the blue at the trailing edge. This marking remained official until August 1919, at which time the star and the tail stripe order of 1917 were readopted.

The tail stripes remained in use by both Services until the end of 1926, at which time its use became less frequent by the Navy, which began to use solid-coloured tail surfaces to identify squadrons of aircraft by unit, assigned aircraft carrier, or station. The US Marines retained rudder striping until the adoption of camouflage in 1941. In November 1926, the Army deleted the vertical red and white stripes and substituted thirteen alternating red and white horizontal stripes based on the arrangement of the American flag. All military rudder striping was deleted in May 1942, after having been removed from camouflaged aircraft starting in February 1941. The Navy temporarily adopted 'Army' rudder stripes but without the blue from January to May 1942, for camouflaged aeroplanes.

From 1917 the star (or circle) marking had been used on both wings only, but with the readoption of camouflage for Army and Navy aircraft in 1941, the marking was unbalanced by being used on the upper surface of the port and lower surface of the starboard wing only and on each side of the fuselage. By the middle of 1943, this arrangement had been standardized for all Army and Navy aircraft, camouflaged or not.

A major change was made in May 1942, when the red centre disc was eliminated because of similarity to the Japanese aircraft marking. In July 1943, another change was made to increase the visibility of the marking. A white rectangle, equal in length to the radius of the basic circle and having a height of half the radius, was placed on each side of the circle and the whole was surrounded by a red border having a width one-eighth of the radius of the circle. Two months later this red border, again because of similarity to Japanese colour, was changed to blue. No further changes were made until January 1947, when a red bar was added to the centre of each white rectangle. This marking is still in use.

# US Army Colouring

Until 1918, US Army aeroplanes were in natural finish, that is clear-doped or varnished fabric. In 1918, camouflage was adopted for tactical military types, consisting of khaki-brown on top surfaces and part-way down the fuselage and clear-dope or cream for lower sides and under surfaces. By late 1918, this changed to khaki-brown all over and was extended to trainers then in production. This remained standard for all Army types until 1927.

In mid-1927, all Army models adopted chrome-yellow wings and tail surfaces as a peacetime safety measure. The khaki fuselage, now called olive drab (O.D.) was retained until the mid-1930s, when the olive drab was replaced by blue. A few of the new all-metal models introduced in the 1930s were left in natural metal.

The imminence of United States' participation in World War II saw the readoption of olive drab camouflage for tactical types, this time on all top surfaces and the fuselage sides, with grey undersurfaces. The Curtiss P-40 was the first US Army production model delivered with this new colouring. This was declared inessential for all but a few specified models late in 1943 and most military types were delivered in natural metal finish thereafter.

## US Navy Colouring

Like those of the Army, Naval aeroplanes were 'natural' until 1918. The Navy then adopted overall light grey for camouflage and it remained standard into 1920, at which time overall silver became the basic colour. Wooden-hulled flying-boats kept the hulls grey to 1928, and metal parts on most fabric-covered aeroplanes were painted grey.

In the early 1920s, chrome yellow began to be applied to the top surfaces of upper wings and the top of horizontal tails for increased visibility and remained standard to World War II. New all-metal fuselages from 1930 to 1935 were painted a light grey, after which they were painted silver.

Overall light grey camouflage was readopted early in 1941, soon changed to sea-green tops and sides with grey undersides, and then graduated to blue tops and sides with white undersides. This was supplemented late in 1944 by overall dark blue for some types. The dark blue became the standard in 1946 and remained until 1956, well past the Service life of the last US Navy Curtiss aeroplane.

## Civil Colouring and Markings

The colour schemes for civil aircraft were, of course, an individual matter. Each airline preferred a standardized scheme for all of its machines as a matter of public identification, while private owners could specify their own colouring for a price or take whatever pattern the factory happened to use.

From the appearance of the Oriole early in 1919, Curtiss used a distinctive arrangement of orange fuselage and yellow wings for production models and demonstrators. Some demonstrators that were minor variations of production US Army models were finished in the Army olive drab and yellow.

## Civil Registration Numbers

Registration of US civil aircraft was not required until January 1927, although unofficial attempts had been made earlier to use the international system adopted by the Versailles Convention of 1919, which used a single

14

letter to identify the nation and four letters to identify the individual aeroplane. The US system of 1927 used two letters, the letter N assigned to the USA at Versailles, followed by another letter to indicate the status of the aeroplane, X for experimental, R for restricted, and C for commercial or fully licensed. These were followed by a sequential number to identify the aircraft. If no letters preceded the number, the aircraft was merely registered but was not licensed. When the numbers passed 10,000 in 1929, they were shortened to one, two, or three digits with a suffix letter added, but soon went to five digits. The registration number does not change with the status of the aeroplane. The prototype NX-1234 became NC-1234 upon certification. The second prefix, or status letter, was deleted in 1948.

Registration numbers are usually assigned in blocks to a manufacturer, and a single large production run of aircraft will generally have consecutive registrations, usually progressing in step with the c/ns. From 1927 to the late 1950s, the registration was applied to the upper starboard and lower port wings, and to each side of the fin or rudder. Since then, it has appeared in figures a foot high only on each side of the fuselage, which is hardly large enough to be read from much beyond the wingtip of a large aeroplane. In spite of the changes in the marking regulations, the Federal Aviation Administration has allowed the use of the old two-letter prefixes to the registrations and the use of the old wing and tail locations on restored antique aircraft that date to before 1933.

Most other nations adopted the Versailles scheme of 1919.

## Trademark

Trademarks have long been a standard means for a manufacturer to identify his product. While still in the motorcycle business in 1906, Glenn Curtiss adopted as his trademark the rather fancy script word 'Curtiss', written on a diagonal as shown. Starting in the 1920s, the Wright Aeronautical Corporation used an aeroplane-like device as its trademark.

In spite of the Curtiss-Wright merger of 1929, the two divisions continued to use their original trademarks well into World War II, although there was an exception in the form of a 'Curtiss-Wright' trademark used on St Louis-built aeroplanes in the late 1930s.

## Nameplates

Essential data on a particular aeroplane, such as the name and address of the manufacturer, the basic model and sub-series, the serial number, the date of manufacture of the specific airframe, and sometimes such additional data as make, model, and power of engine are incorporated on a metal nameplate affixed to the aircraft in a location where it is available for ready reference.

Nameplate made up specifically for the Curtiss Robin series. Model is C 1, engine is No.67, and serial number is 558. No date is given.

Standard nameplate of Curtiss Aeroplane & Motor Co, with Naval designation N2C-2 steel-stamped in. Navy symbols V for Aeroplane and N for trainer appear in class block, along with Navy serial number A-8543. Factory serial number is 18, and the date is 15 December, 1930.

*Manufacturers' Nameplates*—These have taken many forms over the years, and have often been patterned after the distinctive company trademarks. Curtiss aeroplanes used a variety of nameplate forms from 1909 to 1947. In the years immediately preceding World War II, the Manufacturers'

This plate for Curtiss Aeroplane Division of Curtiss-Wright identifies the aeroplane as Customer Model Y1P-36, Manufacturer's Model designation 75E. Serial numbers are AC 37-70 for the Army and 12242 for Curtiss. Class is Pursuit, and delivery date is 3 March, 1937.

Aircraft Association sought and largely achieved standardization of manufacturers' nameplates among the member aircraft firms. In addition to the basic information covering the aircraft, the plate contained a statement to the effect that the machine was built using patents covered by the cross-licensing agreements of the Association.

Wartime nameplate for Airplane Division at St Louis proclaims association with Manufacturers Aircraft Association. Military designation of the aeroplane does not appear, only Curtiss Model 25 (the AT-9). Date of manufacture is 3 December, 1942, engines are Lycoming R-680s, and engine serial numbers are 7841 and 7821. Since this is a military design, nothing appears in the block for the ATC number. Number 77842 in the bottom block is the number of the nameplate within the Manufacturers Aircraft Association.

*(Nameplate photographs courtesy William T. Larkins)*

*Military Nameplates*—Originally, aircraft built for the military used the manufacturer's nameplate with the military designation stamped on it instead of and sometimes in addition to the manufacturer's model number. The Army standardized on nameplates of its own, however, and these were installed in the aircraft in addition to the manufacturer's plates. Military plates carried the military designation of the aircraft, the military serial number, the delivery date, inspector's stamp, and the number of the contract under which it was built.

18

# Licences and Approved Type Certificates

To the end of 1926, there was no government supervision or regulation of civil aviation in the United States. Neither aeroplanes nor pilots were licensed, although unofficial licensing of pilots was started by the Aero Club of America in 1909. Glenn Curtiss received US Licence No.1.

## The ATC

Starting in 1927, following passage of the Civil Aeronautics Act of 1926, the government, through the Bureau of Air Commerce within the Department of Commerce, stepped in with licence and airworthiness requirements and air traffic rules. To be eligible for Commercial operation, aeroplanes had to qualify for an Approved Type Certificate (ATC), which was obtained only after extensive engineering analysis, static and flight tests, and the use of an approved powerplant. The first Curtiss aeroplane to have an Approved Type Certificate was the OX-5 Robin, which received ATC No.40 in May 1928.

A major production alteration of an ATC'd aeroplane, such as a change to a more powerful engine, greater seating capacity or increased weight, usually required re-analysis and test and the issuance of a new ATC, as the Robin B with ATC No.68 with 90 hp OX-5 engine becoming the Robin C-1, ATC No.69 with 185 hp Challenger engine. Once issued, the ATC remained in effect for the production life of that version of the aeroplane and all production articles were inspected for conformance. Unapproved changes invalidated the ATC for that particular aeroplane.

## Category 2 Approvals

Some aeroplanes, either factory-new or altered from ATC'd model by subsequent owners, were still considered suitable for commercial operations without meeting full ATC requirements. These were issued Category 2, sometimes called Memo Approvals, on an individual aeroplane basis. In some cases, Memo Approvals issued to new models were superseded by full ATCs. The most common reasons for downgrading an ATC'd aeroplane to Category 2 was a change to a different engine or a weight change that altered the load factor. Some Memo Approvals were obtained by individual owners long after the aeroplane model was out of production.

## Experimental and Identified Aeroplanes

Purely experimental aircraft, or prototypes anticipating issuance of an ATC, are issued experimental licences for the period of their testing. In the period of Curtiss production, these were identified by the letters NX or X preceding their registration numbers. Restricted licences for special-purpose aeroplanes were identified by the letters NR or R.

From 1927 to World War II, some aeroplanes were allowed to fly without benefit of licence because they could not meet ATC or Category 2 requirements. These were issued registration numbers unadorned by any prefix letters and were merely identified, not licensed. These were primarily pleasure or personal-type craft severely restricted regarding revenue operations and use of the Federal Airways. The majority of the World War I surplus Curtiss types such as the JN-4, HS-2L, and MF Seagull, and a few mid-1920s model built before the ATC requirements, operated through the late 1920s and even into the early 1930s as identified types. However, a few HS-2Ls, MFs, and even some JN-4s were allowed to operate commercially and carry NC registrations without either ATC or Category 2 approvals on the basis of individual inspection under a Grandfather Clause of the regulations.

## Limited Licences

A new licensing category appeared in 1946 to cover surplus military designs that had limited civil use but which could not qualify for full ATC or Category-2 licences. Others that could not even meet NL Licence requirements were forced to operate under straight experimental certificates with attendant restrictions.

A full listing of all ATCs, Category 2, and Limited approvals issued to Curtiss aeroplanes from 1927 to 1957 will be found in Appendices 1–3.

## Aeroplane Costs

Wherever possible, the cost of Curtiss aeroplanes has been included with the descriptions. For civil models, this is usually the advertized price of a ready-to-fly machine.

From 1917, most US military aircraft have been sold as airframes only, with such equipment as powerplants, instruments, and armament supplied by the government but installed by the aeroplane manufacturer for flyaway delivery. Such material is called government-furnished equipment, or GFE. Most published figures of military aircraft purchases show airframe cost less GFE. Wherever possible, the distinction between complete costs and costs less GFE is made in this book.

The exact costs of military aeroplanes are sometimes difficult to determine because a price might be established for a production batch that included spare parts, crew training, and company service support for the aeroplanes in the field.

Military prototypes usually show costs far in excess of the production versions because all research, engineering, and tooling have been charged to a single machine rather than being amortized over a production run.

A grim-visaged Glenn Curtiss sits in the *Silver Dart*. Note the belt-driven propeller and individual carburettors for each cylinder of the 50 hp V-8 engine.

# Glenn H. Curtiss and the Aerial Experiment Association (AEA)

Glenn Hammond Curtiss was born in Hammondsport, a small wine-producing community in western New York State, on 21 May, 1878. As a child, he was inventive and showed a keen interest in competition and in speed, particularly racing. To improve his performance on ice skates on adjacent Lake Keuka, for example, he devised a kite-like sail. At the age of 12 he moved with his parents to Rochester, NY, and obtained after-school work as a telegraph messenger. This work gave him an opportunity to study electricity and he soon built a crude communication system of his own. Full-time employment was soon found at the famous Eastman Kodak Company. After assembling Kodaks for a while, he was able to build his own cameras, too.

It should be pointed out that Curtiss's association with Kodak gave him a profound respect for the recording capability of the camera; practically every variation of the early AEA and Curtiss aeroplanes was faithfully recorded on film even though accurate drawings may never have existed.

In 1897, Curtiss returned to Hammondsport on his own and went to work in a bicycle repair shop. Three years later he left to go into business for

21

himself, and in September 1901, he established the G. H. Curtiss Manufacturing Company to build bicycles.

As a result of his constant quest for more performance, he soon adapted a small petrol engine with a carburettor of his own invention to one of his bicycles. This led to increasing interest in motorcycles and motorcycle racing, and the little factory was soon converted to motorcycle and motor manufacture. Curtiss also became the local agent for several different automobiles.

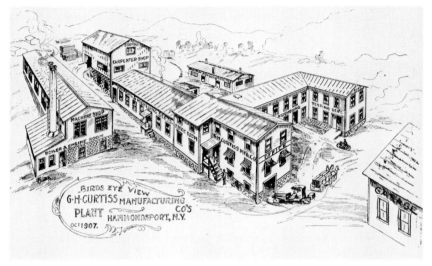

An artist's drawing of the G.H. Curtiss Manufacturing Company plant as it appeared in October 1907. From 1907 Curtiss catalogue.

In addition to Curtiss winning many personal prizes, the cycles themselves, with their Curtiss-designed and built air-cooled motors, won awards for their quality. On 24 January, 1907, Curtiss became the 'fastest human' by setting a world's record with the unprecedented speed of 137 mph on the hard sands of Ormond Beach, Florida.

The high power-to-weight ratio of Curtiss's motorcycle engines soon drew the attention of early balloonist Thomas Scott Baldwin. 'Captain' Baldwin was originally a circus acrobat who elevated his act with balloons and became the world's first parachute jumper. He established a balloon factory in San Francisco, and by 1904 was trying to develop a small dirigible airship based on the existing Santos-Dumont principles.

In response to a telegraphed order, Curtiss provided a custom-built engine, which Baldwin used with great success in his *California Arrow*, making the first circular flight in America on 3 August, 1904. A close association soon developed; Baldwin moved his works to Hammondsport after the San Francisco fire of 1906 and Curtiss collaborated with him on

'Captain' Thomas Scott Baldwin and Glenn H. Curtiss with the 'wind wagons' used to test propellers for Baldwin's airships. *Below* Glenn Curtiss in an air-driven iceboat.

the propulsion problems of airships. Experimental propellers were proved out on the ground in three-wheeled 'wind wagons' and in runner-equipped iceboats.

Baldwin was not afraid of competition and did not object to Curtiss supplying engines to other American airship builders. In 1906, all airships in America are reported to have been powered with Curtiss engines. On 15

Glenn Curtiss (*left*) and Thomas Baldwin (*right*) aloft in a Baldwin-built dirigible. Note the advertizing for Curtiss 'motocycles'.

August, 1908, a Baldwin airship piloted by Baldwin, with Curtiss aboard as mechanic, completed its Army tests and became the US Army's first aircraft. Purchase price was $6,740.

The success of his airship engines brought Curtiss a degree of fame in aeronautical circles. This, plus the proximity of Hammondsport to Baddeck, Nova Scotia, summer home of telephone inventor Alexander Graham Bell, brought Curtiss an invitation to join Bell's new Aerial Experiment Association (AEA). This was formally organized on 1 October, 1907, as a time-limited association 'for the purpose of constructing a practical aerodrome, driven by its own motive power, and carrying a man'.

The other members were Dr Bell, J. A. D. McCurdy (a Canadian), Lt Thomas Selfridge of the US Army, and F. W. 'Casey' Baldwin (not to be confused with 'Captain' Baldwin). Curtiss was named Director of Experiments.

Following a period of research into the existing state of the art, it was decided that each member would design an 'Aerodrome' (contemporary term for aeroplane) which the AEA would build. Bell had already been experimenting with unconventional man-carrying tetrahedral kites and continued with them to the point of adding power. While this procedure was followed, no AEA machine could be fully credited to one man since all contributed ideas. A fifth machine not generally recognized in accounts of AEA activities was a hang glider patterned on the established Chanute and Pilcher designs that was built before the numbered aerodromes. Actually, several gliders were built, the first by Glenn Curtiss to specifications mailed from Bell's home in Baddeck.

While associated with AEA, Curtiss continued his work at the G. H. Curtiss Manufacturing Company, which had been incorporated in 1905, and developed engines for the AEA machines. Curtiss's major contribution to AEA was his experience and ingenuity; he did not put up cash. The association was financed by Mrs Bell, wealthy in her own right, who contributed $35,000.

One of several hang gliders built by AEA before construction of the numbered 'Aerodromes'.

The initial activity of AEA from 1 October, 1907, was the accumulation of aeronautical experience leading to the design and construction of the aerodromes. Valuable data were obtained from the construction of kites, the hang gliders, and further propeller and powerplant research with wind wagons. A point of historical controversy arose from the fact that Curtiss had visited the Wright brothers during a trip to Dayton with Baldwin for an air show. Charges were made later that some details of the AEA machines were the result of information gleaned on this visit. Curtiss's interest in the Wrights was to sell them engines; he did not seek nor was he given aircraft details although propellers were discussed.

Four successful aerodromes were built in 1908 and a man-carrying tetrahedral kite was completed in 1909. Because of Curtiss's large contributions, the aerodromes are generally lumped into the overall view of 'Curtiss' aeroplanes even though that line did not begin until 1909. The accumulated AEA experience was reflected in the first independent 'Curtiss' aeroplane of 1909, developed with the knowledge and approval of AEA.

The major research work of the AEA was completed by early 1909. Since production was not an objective, the association was dissolved on the previously-scheduled date of 31 March. The many patents applied for by the AEA were turned over to a trustee and remained the joint property of the founders.

The four AEA 'Aerodromes' are detailed in the following paragraphs in the order of their construction:

**Aerodrome No.1,** *Red Wing* The first AEA aeroplane was named *Red Wing* because of the colour of its fabric covering. It was a biplane with a movable elevator ahead of the wings and a fixed stabilizer behind. A movable rudder was provided, but no means of lateral control. Since it was to be flown from ice, it used skids for an undercarriage. The 'sponsor', or principal designer, was Lt Selfridge.

AEA Aerodrome No.1, the *Red Wing*. The pilot's semi-enclosed nacelle is the crude triangular structure on the left.

The first of two flights was made by Thomas Baldwin on 12 March, 1908, since Selfridge was absent on Army business. The flight covered a distance of 318 ft 11 in (97 m) and ended in a crash landing. This has been represented as the first public aeroplane flight in the United States, and figured in the subsequent controversies with the Wrights. The second flight, on 18 March, also ending in a crash, covered only 40 yards and proved the need for lateral control.

Span 43 ft 4 in (13·2 m); wing area 385 sq ft (35·76 sq m); gross weight 570 lb (258 kg); powerplant Curtiss 40 hp air-cooled V-8.

AEA Aerodrome No.2, *White Wing*. This was the first aeroplane to have a three-wheeled undercarriage.

**Aerodrome No.2,** *White Wing* The second AEA aeroplane was *White Wing*, sponsored by Baldwin. It was very similar to *Red Wing*, except for the substitution of three wheels for the ice runners, and used the same engine. The most important innovation was the addition of movable lateral control surfaces on all four wingtips that later came to be called ailerons. In principle, these had the same effect as the Wright's wing-warping, but Curtiss claimed mechanical and control differences. The method of control reflected Curtiss's motorcycle experience—a yoke embraced the pilot's shoulders—when he wanted to bank for a turn, he leaned in the desired direction and the proper control movement was automatically applied.

*White Wing* made four flights, the first on 18 May, 1908, again with Baldwin at the controls. Distance was 93 yards (85 m) at a height of 10 ft (3 m). Longest flight was the third, at 339 yards (310 m) with Curtiss flying. *White Wing* crashed on 23 May after McCurdy had flown 183 yards (167 m).

Span 42 ft 3 in (12·87 m); wing area 408 sq ft (37·9 sq m); gross weight 605 lb (274 kg).

Glenn Curtiss aloft in Aerodrome No.3, *June Bug*, most successful of the AEA aeroplanes.

When equipped with twin pontoons, *June Bug* was renamed the *Loon*.

**Aerodrome No.3,** *June Bug* The *June Bug*, a further refinement of *White Wing*, was sponsored by Curtiss and was eminently successful with the same engine. First flown on 21 June, it made numerous flights, including a straightaway run of 1,140 yards (1,042 m) on the seventh flight. On 4 July, Curtiss made a pre-arranged flight to win the first task, or 'leg', of the Scientific American Trophy, which called for a straightaway flight of one kilometre (3,281 ft). After a couple of false starts, he won this with ease by flying over a mile (1·6 km) at a speed of 39 mph (62·76 km/h).

Span 42 ft 6 in (12·95 m); wing area 370 sq ft (34·37 sq m); gross weight 615 lb (279 kg).

*Loon*—In November 1908, the *June Bug* was put on twin wood-frame pontoons covered with cloth and was renamed *Loon*. Attempts to fly from the water were unsuccessful due to the high hydrodynamic drag of the pontoons.

**Aerodrome No.4,** *Silver Dart* The *Silver Dart* was less famous than *June Bug* but was a far more successful flying machine. Sponsored by McCurdy, it had a 50 hp Curtiss water-cooled V-8 engine, biplane forward elevators, and no rear stabilizer. Instead of being connected directly, the engine drove the propeller by a chain and sprockets.

First flight was at Hammondsport on 6 December, 1908, with McCurdy flying. It was moved to Baddeck where it made the first flight in Canada on 23 February, 1909, again with McCurdy piloting.

Span 49 ft (14·93 m); wing area 420 sq ft (39 sq m); gross weight 860 lb (390 kg).

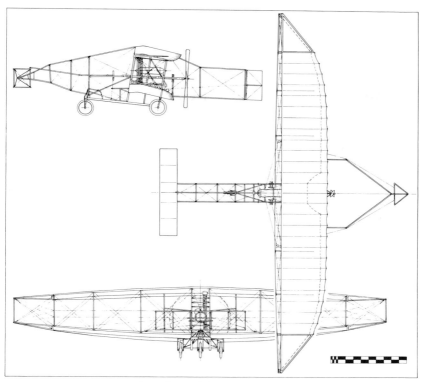

Aerodrome No.4, *Silver Dart*

AEA Aerodrome No.4, the canard *Silver Dart*, was built at Hammondsport but did most of its flying in Nova Scotia, where it became the first aeroplane to fly in Canada.

This 1911 drawing shows the great expansion of the Curtiss Aeroplane Company plant at Hammondsport to that time.

# Curtiss Companies
# and Accomplishments,
# 1909–14

Following the dissolution of the AEA on 31 March, 1909, Glenn Curtiss undertook the design and manufacture of aeroplanes on his own at Hammondsport. In the period 1909–14 covered by this chapter, this remarkable man engaged in a fantastic amount of personal activity— designing, building, and testing new models, making exhibition flights, instructing, forming new companies and establishing new flying fields, defending lawsuits, writing books and magazine articles, and conducting a brisk domestic and export trade, almost any one of which would have been a full-time job for an ordinary man.

Two major production models evolved in separate periods of this era, the Curtiss pusher from 1909 into 1913 and the single-engine pusher flying-boat from 1912 to 1914. Other experimental types were introduced but nothing else reached production status before 1915. Early in 1911, the landplane pusher was fitted with pontoons and became the world's first successful seaplane.

One of the major moves of 1909 was the affiliation of Glenn Curtiss and his G. H. Curtiss Manufacturing Company with Augustus M. Herring, a self-styled aviation pioneer of great reputation but no recognized accomplishment. Herring's contribution to the Herring-Curtiss Company, announced on 4 March, 1909, was to be patents allegedly held by him that would help Curtiss defeat the impending Wright patent suit. Herring contributed nothing to the partnership, which was eventually dissolved, but was to keep Curtiss embroiled in litigation until his death in 1930.

The first sale of a Curtiss-built aeroplane, and the first in the United States to a civil owner, was to the New York Aeronautical Society. While other machines were subsequently built to private order, the principal source of income to the fledgling company was exhibition flying by Curtiss himself and selected company pilots. To formalize this business, the Curtiss Exhibition Company was formed on 30 July, 1910. This organization also took on the operation of Curtiss flying schools.

Early triumphs for Glenn Curtiss personally as well as for his products were his second winning of the Scientific American Trophy in the *Golden Flyer* in 1909, the winning of the first International Gordon Bennett Race in France in August of that year, and his third win and permanent possession of the Scientific American Trophy for a 150-mile (241 km) flight from Albany, NY, to Governor's Island in New York Harbor in May 1910. He was the first recipient of the Collier Trophy in 1912 for the development of the hydro-aeroplane, or seaplane, and won it again in 1913 for his development of the flying-boat.

Curtiss soon recognized that his principal aeroplane customers would have to be the US armed forces. However, the tradition-bound Army and Navy had little real interest in flying. By 1909 the Army had bought one Wright aeroplane and had operated a Baldwin airship since 1908. The Navy did not buy its first aeroplane until 1911.

In the face of this apathy, Curtiss set out to create a market by demonstrating the value of the aeroplane to the armed forces, particularly the Navy. Through the co-operation of sympathetic senior officers, he was able to make some very convincing demonstrations.

On 10 November, 1910, Curtiss pilot Eugene Ely flew a 50 hp Curtiss pusher from a wooden platform on the forward deck of the cruiser USS *Birmingham* anchored in Hampton Roads, Virginia, and landed safely ashore.

On 18 January, 1911, Ely landed a pusher on another platform built on the after deck of the cruiser USS *Pennsylvania* anchored in San Francisco Bay. The landing run was shortened by a hook on the aeroplane engaging a simple form of arrester gear. Ely then took off over the stern and returned to shore.

On 17 February, 1911, Glenn Curtiss alighted in a seaplane alongside the *Pennsylvania*, now anchored in San Diego Bay, and he and the seaplane were hoisted aboard. Man and machine were then lowered to the water and flew back to the beach.

An early Curtiss promotional effort resulted in pilot Eugene Ely making the first take off of an aeroplane from a ship, on 10 November, 1910. This is the second take off, made after landing on the USS *Pennsylvania*, on 18 January, 1911.

In an earlier effort to stimulate Navy interest, Curtiss had written to the Secretary of the Navy on 14 November, 1910, and offered to teach one Naval officer to fly free of charge. The campaign paid off—the first Navy man to undergo flight training reported to Curtiss's San Diego School on 23 December, 1910, and on 8 May, 1911, the Navy initiated purchase orders for two Curtiss aeroplanes. Similar offers of free instruction were also made to the US Army and were accepted.

On 3 January, 1910, the Wright brothers injunction against Curtiss was granted. Curtiss tried in many ways to invalidate the patent by proving prior development by others, even to building complete aircraft to old designs, but was not successful.

In January 1914, former Curtiss exhibition pilot Lincoln Beachey remarked that it was too bad that the Langley aerodrome of 1903 didn't fly. The Smithsonian Institution, whose secretary, Samuel Pierpoint Langley, had built the machine following successful flights of a steam-powered scale model in 1896, proclaimed it to be 'the first man-carrying machine capable of flight'. The fact that it did not fly on either of its two attempts was attributed to its snagging the catapult during launch. Beachey's idea was to have Curtiss rebuild the wreck to show that it was capable of flight, thereby proving prior application, and to this end he contacted the Smithsonian on his own.

Curtiss was somewhat surprised and embarrassed by the action, but agreed to carry it through. On 28 May, 1914, the restored Langley, using its original engine and modified only to the extent necessary to fit pontoons, made a successful flight at Hammondsport.

The Langley Aerodrome of 1903 as restored by Curtiss in 1914 with its original powerplant and propellers but with Curtiss-built pontoons.

The Wright interests kept close watch on this activity and filed a vehement protest itemizing many changes from the original 1903 configuration of the machine, including a change of powerplant and rearrangement of the wing structure and bracing. Curtiss acknowledged the changes, but insisted that the first flights were made with the machine unmodified except for pontoons; the later alterations were to make the aerodrome a more suitable vehicle for a research programme on tandem wings.

In 1914, another major patent suit was filed against Curtiss, this one by Albert S. Janin, who claimed that Curtiss's 1912 flying-boat infringed a patent applied for earlier by Janin. Janin had applied for a patent on a flying-boat design in 1911, but had never built one. Although Curtiss built a Janin hull in 1918 to prove the Janin claim unworkable, the Janin case dragged on and was not resolved in Curtiss's favour until 1921.

The restored Langley Aerodrome in flight in 1914 after Curtiss powerplant and single propeller were installed.

The harsh winters in western New York State proved a handicap to Curtiss's expanding school and aeroplane development activities, so suitable sites for winter operations were sought. A branch school was set up at Miami, but the principal winter school and experimental manufacturing operation was established on the barren but level North Island in San Diego Bay. Curtiss obtained a three-year lease on the entire island and moved in late in 1910. The season for the school was from 25 November to 25 April.

In November 1912, Curtiss sub-leased a portion of the island to the US Army for its new flying school; in 1917, Naval Aviation moved in to share the island. Joint Army–Navy use continued until 1932, when the Navy took over completely.

Although the Herring-Curtiss Company was established in 1909, it never really functioned as a joint venture. Curtiss continued development and activity as an individual, and formed new companies to handle specialized work. The companies owned by or affiliated with Curtiss were: The Curtiss Exhibition Company—30 July, 1910, The Curtiss Aeroplane Company—1 December, 1910, and The Curtiss Motor Company—19 December, 1911.

It should be noted that a contemporary organization, the Burgess Company and Curtis (one s) had no connection. The nearly-similar name has resulted in confusion to later historians, particularly since Burgess became a Curtiss subsidiary in 1916.

By the end of 1912, both Curtiss and the Wright Company had worked themselves into the same untenable technological position—they had continued to refine their basic landplane and hydro pusher designs to the limits of their capabilities while other designers had introduced new and

Curtiss seaplanes on Lake Keuka, Hammondsport, NY, in 1914. (*Paul Matt collection*)

34

much more efficient tractor designs. The military quickly became dissatisfied with pusher-type trainers and so advised Curtiss and Wright. The pushers carried on for a while, but all were grounded in February 1914.

Unfortunately, neither firm had experience with the more advanced tractors, but both tried them with notable lack of success. This failure was to end the production of original-design Wright aeroplanes, but Curtiss, recognizing his firm's lack of talent in this particular design field, filled the important gap by importing proven talent. During a trip to England in 1913, he hired a British engineer, B. Douglas Thomas, who had helped design very successful tractors at both Sopwith and Avro. Thomas started the design of the Curtiss Model J while still in England and made major contributions to other Curtiss models, notably the Model N and the *America*, at Hammondsport.

The aeroplanes in this chapter are presented in approximate chronological order within four separate groups: Evolution of the Curtiss Pusher, Seaplane Development, Flying-boat Development, and Miscellaneous Aeroplanes – 1910–14.

# Evolution of the Curtiss Pusher

In the period 1909–12, the major Curtiss design and manufacturing effort was directed to the development of a basic model that historians later called 'The Curtiss Pusher'. This was a direct descendent of the final AEA design, the *Silver Dart*. The major change was redesign of the wings to simple rectangular shape with no dihedral and relocation of the ailerons to the mid-points of the forward wing struts. The aileron relocation was done partly for efficiency but mainly to separate those surfaces from the wing in an attempt to avoid infringement of the Wright patent.

The earliest models were all single seaters, with the pilot seated slightly ahead of the wing. The single water-cooled Curtiss engine of 26 to 90 hp was mounted between the wings behind him, driving a single propeller. Forward elevator controls were carried on bamboo booms ahead of the pilot while a fixed stabilizer and movable rudder were carried on booms behind. The ailerons were operated by shoulder yoke, the pilot leaning in the direction he wished to bank, a 'natural' function for Curtiss, the former motorcycle champion. As on the AEA types, the wings were originally covered on the top surfaces only.

Logical improvements such as more powerful engines and double-surfaced wings improved performance and made a practical vehicle of the pusher by allowing two people to be carried. Curtiss then developed a throw-over control column whereby the single control wheel could be moved from one pilot to the other. This was an improvement on the contemporary Wright brothers' system, where two pilots shared one-and-a-half sets of controls, and developed into recognized 'left-seat' and 'right-seat' Wright pilots.

No designations were assigned to the early Curtiss models, which were merely identified according to their purchaser or the specific purpose for which they were built. As custom-built machines, each incorporated differences from its predecessor, and then took on additions that have further complicated the historians' recognition problems. Improved models illustrated in contemporary publications were identified only as 'The New Curtiss' or 'The XX Horsepower Curtiss'.

Even after the assignment of official model designations, positive identification of individual Curtiss pushers of the 1910–13 era was impossible. A number of close copies were built by outsiders, who either used Curtiss-built machines as a guide or built from the workable plans that appeared in contemporary books and magazines and made various changes. Also, special features of aeroplanes custom-built by Curtiss, plus modifications and the use of parts from other models, further complicate the identity problem.

From 1909 into 1911, however, the major evolutionary changes in the pusher resulted in the recognition of the four distinct 'Types' listed here:

Type I—Single-seat machine with single-surface wings, biplane forward elevator on long forward booms, and fixed horizontal stabilizer located with rear rudder on long rear booms.
Type II—Single-seater similar to Type I except double-surfaced wings, ailerons relocated to rear struts.
Type III—Single- or two-seater with monoplane forward elevator on shortened booms, elevators added to horizontal stabilizer.
Type IV—Military model of Type III with wings built in short interchangeable sections to facilitate breakdown to small units for transport on Army wagons.

The Curtiss pushers started with a basic design and improved upon it, so the four definitive types seen from 1909 into 1911 can be regarded as developmental or evolutionary rather than experimental.

An oddity in the evolution of the pusher is inconsistency of later application of the forward elevator, which started as a biplane surface and then was simplified to a monoplane type before disappearing altogether. The one contribution that Augustus Herring is credited with making to Curtiss aeroplanes is the small forward vertical fin used on some of the 1909–11 models.

The need for the forward elevator was originally questioned by stunt pilot Lincoln Beachey, who successfully eliminated it from his exhibition machine late in 1910. While several experimental models subsequently flew without forward elevators, production aeroplanes continued to be delivered with them into 1912. On some Model Es, where the short forward booms formed an essential part of the bracing, the booms were retained after the elevators were removed subsequent to delivery.   Four significant developmental pushers are now described:

36

The first Curtiss aeroplane, the *Golden Flyer* built for the Aeronautical Society of New York.

**Curtiss No. 1,** *Gold Bug* or *Golden Flyer* The first Curtiss-built aeroplane designated as such was the single-seat model ordered by the Aeronautical Society of New York on 2 March, 1909. The purchase price of $5,000 included instruction for two Society members. With no designation, No.1 was initially called *Gold Bug* because of the golden tint of the varnished fabric but later officially became the *Golden Flyer*. Although built after the Herring-Curtiss affiliation, Curtiss specifically excluded No.1 from the inventory of the new company.

**Curtiss-Herring No.1,** *Reims Racer* At the urging of the Aeronautical Society of New York to represent it in the 1909 Gordon Bennett Cup Race in France, Curtiss built a larger version of No.1 and installed a new 60 hp V-8 engine, which was a carefully-guarded secret until the racer was set up in France in August.

Glenn Curtiss and Curtiss-Herring No.1, the aeroplane with which he won the 1909 Gordon Bennett Cup at Reims, France.

37

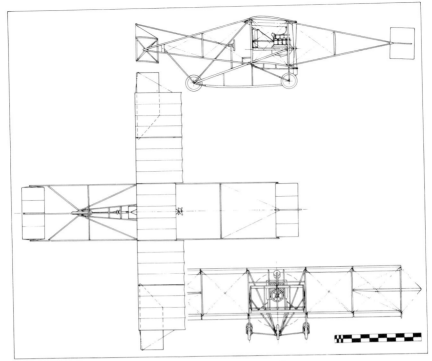

Curtiss-Herring No.1 *Reims Racer*

Flying against the clock rather than other aeroplanes, Curtiss completed the 20 km closed course at a world's record 43·35 mph (69·76 km/h). The *Reims Racer* was later used by Curtiss and his pilots for exhibition work and other record flights in the United States.

***Hudson Flyer*** In 1909, Glenn Curtiss decided to try for the $10,000 prize posted by the New York *World* newspaper for the first flight between Albany, the capital city of New York State, and New York City. After many delays due to weather, the record 156-mile (251 km) flight was made on 29 May, 1910. The start was at Albany, with a refuelling stop at Poughkeepsie and a precautionary stop within the northern city limits of New York before the final landing on Governor's Island.

The *Hudson Flyer* was a stock model Curtiss of the period, modified for the flight. Since the entire route was over the Hudson, emergency flotation gear was added. To preclude nosing over on alighting on water, a hydro-vane was installed ahead of the nosewheel at the suggestion of Charles Willard, who had made two unintentional alightings in the *Golden Flyer*. To carry the weight of the extra equipment and fuel, the area of the upper wing was increased by adding strut-braced extensions to the tips.

The *Hudson Flyer* in which Glenn Curtiss won $10,000 for a flight from Albany to New York City in May 1909. The extended upper wing supported the weight of the emergency flotation gear used for the 156-mile overwater flight.

Early Curtiss single-seat Model D.

**Beachey Special** Curtiss exhibition pilot Lincoln Beachey, whose early fame came from dirigible racing, was the leading American stunt pilot of the 1911–14 period and was the first American pilot to perform a loop. He could have been the first in the world, but when he proposed the idea to Curtiss in 1912, Curtiss said it couldn't be done and forbade him to try.

In 1911, to improve Beachey's performance, Curtiss built him a special extra-strength and higher powered showplane. As requested, this did not have forward elevators since Beachey had already proved that the standard model could do without them. Beachey used his Special to set the world's altitude record of 11,642 ft (3,548 m) on 20 August, 1911.

By mid-1911, when Curtiss pushers were pretty well standardized and being manufactured in what could be considered production quantities, Curtiss began to use specific designations in its advertizing. The following descriptions of officially-designated D and E models are reproduced verbatim from the 1911 Curtiss Aeroplane Company catalogue. The Curtiss A to C designations, if used at all, cannot be correlated to specific aeroplanes or configurations; the designation Model C is seen on some photographs of *June Bug*, apparently added by later misguided historians.

The Model E was a two-seater, but with only 40 hp, the US Army's Aeroplane No.6 of 1911 was rigged as a single-seater.

## Model D

*Width*—Planes, over all, 33 feet, 4 inches.

*Length*—Front to rear control, 25 feet, 9 inches.

*Height*—From ground to highest points, 7 feet 5½ inches.

### DESCRIPTION AND PRICES

*Model D-4*—Equipped with a 4-cylinder, 40 H. P., water-cooled Curtiss motor. An excellent machine for exhibition work, endurance, etc. Speed, 45 miles per hour. Weight ready for flight, 550 pounds. Weight, packed for shipment, 950 pounds. Price, complete for shipment . . . . . . . . . . . $4,500

*Model D-8*—Equipped with an 8-cylinder, 60 H. P., water-cooled Curtiss motor. Entire outfit identical with that used by the famous aviators of The Curtiss Exhibition Co. The safest machine, and the most suitable for a confined space. Speed 60 miles per hour. Weight, ready for flight, 650 pounds. Weight, packed for shipment, 1,000 pounds. Price, complete for shipment . . . . . . . . . . . $5,000

*Model D-8-75*—Same as Model D, but equipped with an 8-cylinder, 75 H. P., water-cooled Curtiss motor. Capable of developing a speed of 70 miles an hour. For speed and cross-country races. Weight, ready for flight, 700 pounds. Weight, packed for shipment, 1,050 pounds. Price, complete for shipment . . . . . . . $3,500

## Model E

SPECIFICATIONS

*Width*—Planes, over all, 35 feet, 4 inches.

*Length*—Front to rear control, 25 feet, 9 inches.

*Height*—From ground to highest point, 8 feet.

### DESCRIPTION AND PRICES

*Model E-4*—Equipped with a 4-cylinder, 40 h.p. water-cooled Curtiss motor. This machine is a slow, strong flying aeroplane, especially suitable for aviation schools and beginners. It is also available for high, dry altitudes. Speed, 40 miles per hour. Weight, ready for flight, 600 pounds. Weight, packed for shipment, 1000 pounds.

Price, complete for shipment . . . . . . . . $4,500

*Model E-8*—Equipped with an 8-cylinder, 60 h. p. water-cooled Curtiss motor. A machine that combines speed with the advantages of weight-carrying. Equipped with the Curtiss alternating dual control system. A machine that makes aviation a sport. Speed, 55 miles per hour. Weight, ready for flight, 700 pounds. Weight, packed for shipment, 1050 pounds.

Price, complete for shipment . . . . . . . . $5,000

*Model E-8-75*—The same as model E-8, but equipped with an 8-cylinder, 75 h. p. Curtiss motor. The surplus power gives greater speed as well as more weight-carrying possibilities. Speed, 60 miles per hour. Weight, ready for flight, 750 pounds. Weight, packed for shipment, 1,100 pounds.

Price, complete for shipment . . . . . . . . $5,500

### DESCRIPTION AND PRICES

*Model D-8*—Exhibition type with hydro equipment, in addition to the regular chassis.

Price, complete . . . . . . . . . . $5,500

*Model E-8-75*—The "triad" passenger carrying hydroaeroplane, which is identical with Model E when the hydro is not attached. This machine is equipped with a 75 h. p. motor.

Price . . . . . . . . . . . $6,000

41

Triplane adaptation of Curtiss Model E with monoplane forward elevator.

With standardized Curtiss pushers in production and being advertized world-wide, business was brisk by 1912. The aeroplane and engine factories were enlarged and licences were issued for the manufacture of pushers in other countries.

While a basic design was sold, there were special custom variations. Aviatrix Ruth Law, for example, had learned to fly on a Wright aeroplane with its peculiar control system and could not make the transition to the Curtiss system. Consequently, her custom-built Curtiss D was fitted with Wright controls.

Between them, the US Army and Navy bought twelve Curtiss landplane pushers in 1911 and 1912, and these are now discussed.

The US Army's second aeroplane was an existing model ordered on 13 March, 1911, for $6,000 and was delivered the same month. Identified as Signal Corps Aeroplane No.2, this was a single-seat Model D powered with a 60 hp Curtiss engine. The engine was soon replaced with a 40 hp model and the front elevator was removed some time later. No.2 ended its days as a 'Penguin' ground trainer after the Army grounded all of its pusher trainers in February 1914. Rebuilt to original configuration, it is now in The National Air Museum of the Smithsonian Institution.

Three two-seat Curtiss Es also went to the Army—S.C. numbers 6, 8, and 23. The original 40 hp engine of No.6 was exchanged for the 60 hp model of the smaller S.C. No.2, S.C.8 was eventually converted to a seaplane, and S.C.23 was sold out of the Service after the pushers were grounded.

The poor safety records of both the Wright and Curtiss pusher trainers at the Army's North Island school brought about a demand for safer tractor-type equipment and led directly to the development of the Curtiss J and N models that culminated in the immortal JN series.

42

*Top*, famous aerobatic pilot Lincoln Beachey seated in his special Curtiss pusher fitted with standard controls, including shoulder-yoke for the ailerons. *Below*, aviatrix Ruth Law learned to fly on a Wright aeroplane and had to have this entirely different control system installed in her Curtiss.

Of eight Curtiss pushers bought by the US Navy between 1911 and 1913, only one was delivered as a landplane, and it was soon converted to a seaplane.

Shortly after World War I, a special 1912-style Curtiss pusher was built under Glenn Curtiss's personal direction at Garden City, evidently for nostalgic reasons. Such minor refinements as improved fittings and a revised control system featuring a rudder bar and wheel control for the ailerons were incorporated. Long a fixture at Curtiss Field, this machine was in the Roosevelt Field Museum until World War II and is now at The National Air Museum.

A true replica of a 1912 Curtiss pusher built by Glenn Curtiss and associates at Garden City after World War I. Powerplant was a war-surplus Curtiss OX-5.

## Seaplane Development

The first American attempt to fly from the water was made by the AEA in 1908 with the *Loon*, but it was unable to take off. In June 1910, Curtiss successfully alighted on Lake Keuka in a Type III pusher with a canoe secured beneath it; however, the aeroplane would not take off for the same reason as the *Loon*—the high hydrodynamic drag of the rounded canoe hull prevented the machine from reaching flying speed.

Curtiss soon realized that a flat-bottomed float could plane over the water, offering less drag and consequently more speed for a given power. A long series of experimental pontoons, or floats, was then developed and tried on standard Curtiss pushers at San Diego during winter 1910–11.

Although the Frenchman Henri Fabre had successfully taken off from water in a powered aeroplane on 28 March, 1910, Curtiss is recognized as the inventor of the practical seaplane. The original short Curtiss floats had flat bottoms for their entire length; later, long designs featured the hydroplane step, located slightly behind the aeroplane's centre of gravity, that Curtiss had developed for his flying-boat in 1912, combined with V-bottoms.

The single main float with wingtip floats standardized by Curtiss early in 1911 remained in use on most US Navy seaplanes to the end of their service in 1960; the twin-float arrangement of the 1908 *Loon* is in universal use on civil seaplanes today.

# Experimental Hydros, 1911

The first successful flight of what was originally called a hydroaeroplane or simply hydro, but is now known as a seaplane, was made on 26 January, 1911. It used a clumsy tandem-float arrangement featuring a main float six ft (1·82 m) wide by five ft (1·52 m) long under the centre section, a smaller float forward, and a hydrofoil ahead of that to keep the bow from submerging at high speed. The wide design of the main float served two purposes. By being wide it was expected to function as an auxiliary wing to generate useful lift; also, its width would keep the spray pattern well outboard of the pusher propeller. Being short, it did not provide longitudinal stability on the water thus necessitating the forward float.

By 1 February, a new arrangement was introduced, comprising a sled-shaped single float 12 ft (3·65 m) long, two ft (60 cm) wide and a foot (30 cm) deep, under the pilot and engine to provide longitudinal stability; small floats for lateral stability were under the wingtips.

At first, the main float was not compartmented. On a flight at Hammondsport, Curtiss took off in a hydro but a considerable amount of water had got into the float and as he nosed down to alight, all the water ran to the bow of the float and made the machine so nose heavy that Curtiss was unable to raise the nose and crashed into the lake. He recognized the problem as soon as it appeared and fortunately survived to correct it.

An early refinement of the hydro was to eliminate the booms that supported the forward elevator and place a monoplane elevator on the bow of the float. As on contemporary landplanes, the hydro's forward elevators were soon eliminated.

The first successful Curtiss seaplane of January 1911 had tandem floats and a forward hydrovane. (*Paul Matt collection*)

45

The second Curtiss seaplane had the engine forward and the pilot aft. Glenn Curtiss used this machine to fly from North Island to the cruiser *Pennsylvania* anchored in San Diego Bay.

**Tractor Hydro** The second Curtiss hydro was a notable exception to the standard pusher design. The un-named machine that Curtiss used for his flight from North Island to the cruiser *Pennsylvania* was an otherwise standard Type III pusher airframe with the engine installed ahead of the wing as a tractor to keep the propeller out of the spray. The pilot was seated behind the wings and the forward elevator was eliminated. Curtiss didn't like the arrangement mainly because of the discomfort of sitting in the propeller blast and engine exhaust; the problem of spray on the propeller on subsequent pusher seaplanes was reduced somewhat by the addition of horizontal spray deflectors to the top of the main float ahead of the propeller.

**Triad** With the conventional landplane converted to water operations by the substitution of pontoons for wheels, it was only natural to develop an aeroplane to operate from both elements. Curtiss achieved this by adding

Glenn Curtiss demonstrates the *Triad*, the first successful amphibian, at San Diego in February 1911.

46

retractable wheels under the lower wings of a hydro and adding a nosewheel to the bow of the float. The resulting amphibian, named *Triad* by Curtiss, was successfully demonstrated at North Island on 25 February, 1911.

Although still in use today, the popularity of amphibious floatplanes has always been limited by the double weight handicap of the floats and the necessary wheel-retracting mechanism. The most popular amphibians have all been flying-boat types.

The third wing on this mid-1911 Curtiss hydro generated 200 lb of additional lift. (*Paul Matt collection*)

**US Navy A-1** The Navy's first aeroplane, a 50 hp Curtiss Model E seaplane costing $5,500, was tested by Glenn Curtiss on 30 June, 1911, and turned over to Navy pilot T. G. Ellyson at Hammondsport the same day. On 7 July, the 75 hp V-8 engine originally intended for the A-1 was installed. The A-1, later AH-1 under the 1914 Naval designation system, operated as a straight seaplane, as a *Triad* amphibian, and as a landplane.

Among the experiments undertaken with A-1 were take off down an inclined wire, with a groove in the bottom of the float to maintain alignment, and the Navy's first attempt to launch an aeroplane from a compressed-air catapult. After sixty flights totalling 285 hours, plus numerous rebuilds, A-1 is believed to have been struck off charge on 16 October, 1914.

By the autumn of 1911 Curtiss was advertising hydros on the open market. The standardized float gear was available for an additional $500 when buying a standard Model D or E landplane. The hydros were nearly as popular as the landplanes and were licensed to overseas manufacturers in 1912.

47

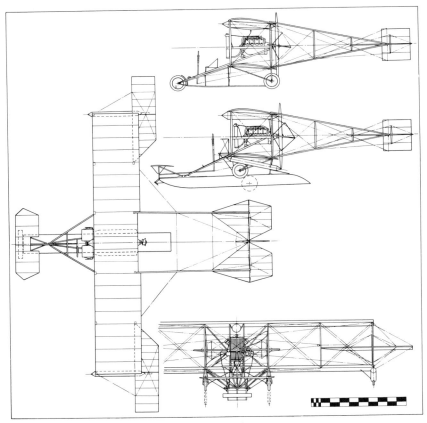

A-1, *Triad*

The standard Curtiss hydro of late 1911 still had the forward elevator, but the forward booms were no longer used and the elevator was mounted on the float. (*Paul Matt collection*)

48

The forward elevator had been eliminated from Curtiss landplane and seaplane pushers alike by the time the US Navy bought the AH-13.

The US Navy bought fourteen pushers with detail variations between 1911 and 1914. The combined Navy Type I serial numbers were A-1, A-2 (delivered as a landplane but converted to hydro), A-3, A-4, AH-8, AH-9, and AH-11/18. AH-8 was turned over to the Army, was still in Army hands in 1919, and was then stored. It was refurbished for a brief flight on 10 February, 1928. AH-9 was rebuilt and redesignated as an AH-8 type, Navy serial No.A-83.

## Flying-boat Development

Following the perfection of the hydro aeroplane or seaplane, which was simply a landplane with floats substituted for wheels, Curtiss sought to develop a true flying-boat. The distinction lay in the fact that the boat-like hull formed an integral part of the structure rather than being an interchangeable accessory as on the hydro. Although others were working on the same idea concurrently, Glenn Curtiss is recognized as the inventor of the aeroplane configuration known as the flying-boat. The basic layout that he developed in 1912 became the world standard for single-engined flying-boats and is still being used.

**Flying-boat No.1** The first Curtiss flying-boat, tried at San Diego on 10 January, 1912, was more a hydro than a true boat. A wide hull, only slightly longer than the standard Curtiss pontoon, was attached under the lower wing of the de-engined airframe of the tractor seaplane. A single 60 hp engine was mounted in the hull and drove two tractor propellers through chains in Curtiss's only deliberate adaptation of a Wright brothers' feature. There were two side-by-side seats in a cockpit behind the wing.

Although No.1 was unable to take off, the experiment did indicate that the flying-boat concept was practicable. Subsequent developments were made at Hammondsport.

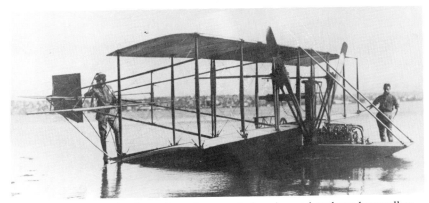

The first Curtiss flying-boat, featuring a central engine and outboard propellers, was not a success but proved that the concept of a hull-borne seaplane was practical. (*Courtesy Harry Gann*)

**Flying-boat No.2,** *The Flying Fish* The first successful flying-boat, built at Hammondsport, featured a full-length flat-bottomed hull that supported both the wings and tail. To keep the horizontal tail surfaces out of the water, they were sited part-way up the long vertical fin.

The engine was a 75 hp Curtiss Model O installed between the wings as on standard pushers. An indication of the fact that Flying-boat No.2 was built quickly and cheaply to prove a concept rather than to achieve optimum performance is shown by the initial use of an old set of 1910-style single surface wings. Forward elevators were also fixed to the bow at a time when they were being omitted from production aeroplanes. Flying-boat

The first successful Curtiss flying-boat was assembled and flown at Hammondsport using an old set of single-surface wings and a forward elevator.

No.2 underwent considerable modification and refinement within a short period, ending up with double surface E-75 wings and no forward elevators. In this configuration, it was widely publicized as *The Flying Fish*.

At first, Flying-boat No.2 would not leave the water; the hydrodynamic drag of the hull prevented it from reaching flying speed. After observing the difficulty from an accompanying motorboat, Curtiss suggested breaking the smooth line of the bottom with a step just behind the centre of gravity.

Incorporation of the hydroplane step had two beneficial effects. First, it removed nearly half the length of the hull from contact with the water at near-take off speeds; second, it permitted a degree of rotation at take off speed to allow the wings to reach the higher angle of attack needed for take off. Too much rotation, however, put the rear of the hull back in the water and the added drag killed the take off speed. The step worked so well that Curtiss patented it, along with vents that allowed air to bleed into the water cavity behind the step to further reduce drag at take off speed.

Fitted with the step, Flying-boat No.2 made its first flight in July 1912.

## Other Experimental Flying-boats

Several other flying-boats were built immediately after No.2 to try different hull designs, engine positions and other features. They carried no known designations and their constant modifications have complicated the identification problem. Three are described here.

**Freak Boat/C-1/AB-1** Identified only as 'Freak Boat' in later Curtiss photographic records, this 'boat had a full-length hull but the pilots were in the open as on the standard hydro. The close gap of the equal-span wings lowered the upper wing to the top of the pusher engine. The horizontal tail was mounted on struts above the hull and the square rudder was used without a vertical fin.

The Freak Boat of 1912 had such a small wing gap that the engine had to be mounted near the upper wing. After extensive modification, this machine was sold to the US Navy as C-1.

After extensive modification that included entirely new tail surfaces and shorter unequal-span wings, this 'boat was sold to the Navy in November 1912, and designated C-1. In March 1914, the designation was changed to AB-1. As C-1, it made the first successful catapult launch of a flying-boat on 12 December, 1912, at Washington Navy Yard. Its last flight was on 1 April, 1914.

A later and more refined Curtiss flying-boat, known only as the *Tadpole*, taking off at Hammondsport.

**Tadpole** Identified only as *Tadpole*, this flying-boat is representative of several that had their hulls built in the form of elongated main hydro floats with the area between the top of the float and the wings built up with a light fabric-covered superstructure. On *Tadpole*, the tail surfaces were carried above the hull on struts. The wing assembly pivoted about the rear spar to provide a variable-incidence feature; the pusher engine was stabilized by a tie rod between the end of the propeller shaft and the tail surfaces.

**A-2/OWL/E-1/AX-1** The A-2 was the Navy's second aeroplane, a Curtiss Model E delivered as a landplane on 13 July, 1911. The original engine was a four-cylinder 50 hp model, soon changed to a 60 hp V-8.

The A-2 was converted to a seaplane in June 1912. It was further modified at Hammondsport in October 1912 to enclose the crew in a fabric-covered superstructure between the float and the wings, eliminating the interchangeability feature and making the A-2 a short-hull flying-boat. Further experimentation added retractable wheels to give amphibian capability; the unofficial designation of OWL was applied to signify operation 'over water and land'. The Navy designation was changed to E-1 in September 1913 and finally to AX-1 in March 1914. It was wrecked on 27 November, 1915, after 91 flights.

Testing of the experimental flying-boats of 1912 soon resulted in a marketable design. The earliest production versions, which were undesignated, had hulls with strong lower structure and a light upper superstructure filling the underwing gap and enclosing the two-man crew. Wings, with interplane ailerons, were sometimes of equal span and

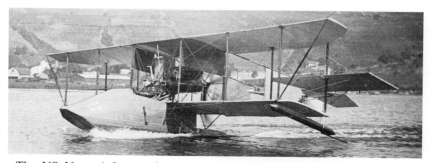

The US Navy A-2 started as a conventional landplane pusher, then was converted to a seaplane, and finally had the forward superstructure added to make it resemble a flying-boat. Subsequent designations were OWL, E-1, and AX-1. (*Bowers-Williams collection*)

sometimes had extended upper wingtips. The design culminated in the Model F, which was immediately popular and enjoyed wide sale to private owners in the United States and to foreign governments.

**US Navy C-1/C-5 (AB-1/5)** The Navy bought five early flying-boats from Curtiss and designated them Navy Type C. Numbering was in sequence of delivery, but the 'boats were not identical, ranging from one of the experimentals modified to near-production standard (C-1/AB-1) to the stock F-boat. On 30 August, 1913, the C-2 flew at Hammondsport under the complete control of a Sperry gyroscopic automatic pilot. The C-boats were redesignated as ABs with the same sequential numbers on 25 March, 1914.

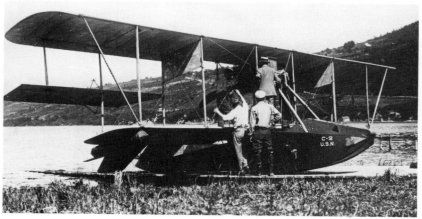

The Navy C-2 was essentially a stock Curtiss Model F flying-boat with extra span added to the top wing. This was used for early automatic pilot experiments in August 1913.

The AB-3 became the first US military aircraft to see action. It was transported with AH-3 to Vera Cruz, Mexico, aboard the cruiser *Birmingham*, arriving on 21 April, 1914. On 25 April, Lt P. N. L. Bellinger piloted AB-3 on a reconnaissance mission over the city of Vera Cruz and surveyed the harbour for mines. AB-3 later had its wings shortened and was used as a non-flying 'Penguin' taxying-trainer.

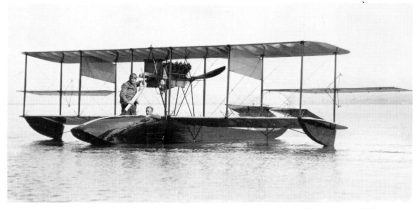

The standard Curtiss Model F of 1913 was used by the US Army and Navy, by civil and foreign owners, and remained in production into 1918. This is Army serial number 34. (*Air Force Museum*)

**US Army 15, 34, 49** The three Curtiss flying-boats delivered to the Army between November 1912 and December 1915, were identified in service only by their Signal Corps numbers. In detail they ranged from composite-hull 'E-boat' (No.15) to the standardized 1914 model mahogany-hull F-boat (Nos 34, 49).

## Model F
**1913 Model** The 1913 Model F used the early composite hull construction and what were essentially Model E-75 wings with strut-braced extensions of the upper wing. Because of its many 'old' features relative to the 1914 F-boat, the 1913 model has sometimes (and erroneously) been referred to by historians as the E-boat in disregard of the recognized Curtiss Model E landplane and the Navy's E-designation.

### Model F (1913)
Two seats.
Span 41 ft 8 in (12·69 m); length 27 ft 4 in (8·33 m).
Gross weight 1,760 lb (798 kg).
Maximum speed 54·8 mph (88·19 km/h); climb 1,200 ft (365 m) in 7·6 min; endurance 4 hr.
Powerplant 75 hp Curtiss O.

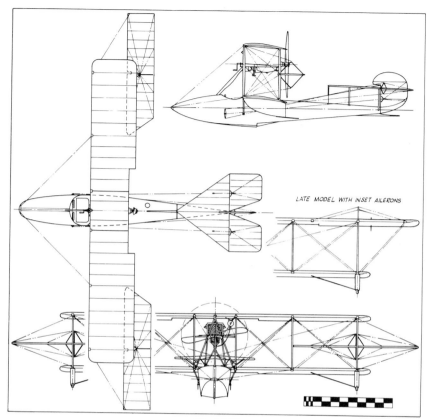

Model F

**1914 Model** The standardized Model F of 1914 differed noticeably from the 1913 versions, particularly in having equal-span wings with rounded tips projecting beyond the end struts and a hull with full-depth primary structure and a rounded wood veneer foredeck. On some civil models, the foredeck hinged forward to form a gangplank for crew movement to or from a beach. An additional feature was a diagonal strut from the engine mount to the lower forward hull structure, intended to protect the crew from a falling engine in a crash. This became known as the Goodier strut since it was installed as the result of Army Lt Lewis Goodier's crash in the Army's first F-boat, S.C.15.

While producing the standard F-boat for the open market, Curtiss also built custom-designed 'boats to special order. These were usually named to the preferences of their owner rather than being given Curtiss designations.

***McCormick Boat*** In 1914, Curtiss delivered a special five-seat tractor flying-boat to Harold F. McCormick, who used it for business and to

The Curtiss McCormick flying-boat of 1914 was built as a tractor but was soon modified to have the engine at the rear and the pilots and passengers ahead of the wings. (*Smithsonian Institution*)

commute from his Lake Michigan home to his Chicago office, a trip of 28 miles (45 km).

The McCormick 'boat was considerably larger than the F, with the cockpit behind the wing and the engine ahead of it as on the 1911 tractor hydro. McCormick's 'boat was eventually rebuilt to put the cockpit and powerplant in the standard F-boat arrangement. Original specifications:

Span 38 ft 4 in (11·68 m); span across ailerons 41 ft 8 in (12·69 m); length 24 ft (7·31 m). Powerplant 100 hp Curtiss OXX.

**Model M (Morris) Flying-boat** It is not known whether the M designation identifies the 1913 monoplane flying-boat built for Raymond V. Morris in the Curtiss letter designation system or is M-for-Morris; the 'boat, which

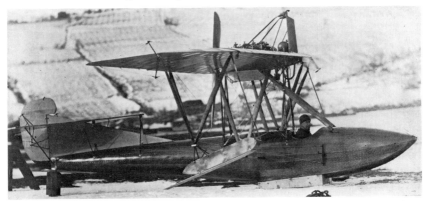

This single-seat Model M was built in 1913 for Raymond V. Morris, a Curtiss employee, to use in his work.

The performance of the Model M as a monoplane was marginal so it was converted to a biplane in Curtiss's San Diego shops. (*Air Force Museum*)

predates both the J and N models, was referred to mostly as 'The Morris Boat'.

The high and swept-back wing was fitted to a narrow single-seat hull covered with mahogany veneer in the manner of later F-boats and the 90 hp pusher engine was carried at the level of the wing. The stabilizing floats were carried on the ends of trusses that also formed the wing bracing.

Morris took the M-boat with him to San Diego when he became Curtiss's manager there. Its performance as a monoplane was unsatisfactory so a lower wing was added at San Diego. Monoplane specification:

Single-seat.

Span 34 ft (10·36 m); length 25 ft (7·62 m); height 10 ft 10 in (3·3 m); wing area 120 sq ft (11·14 sq m).

Powerplant 90 hp Curtiss O.

**Model H *America*** The Model H twin-engined flying-boat originated at the request of Rodman Wanamaker, wealthy owner of department stores in New York and Philadelphia, who sought to win the £10,000 (then 50,000 US dollars) prize offered by the British newspaper *The Daily Mail* for the

The first twin-engined American aeroplane, the Model H, was built for an attempted Atlantic crossing in the summer of 1914 and was named *America*. This became a class name for many of its direct descendants.

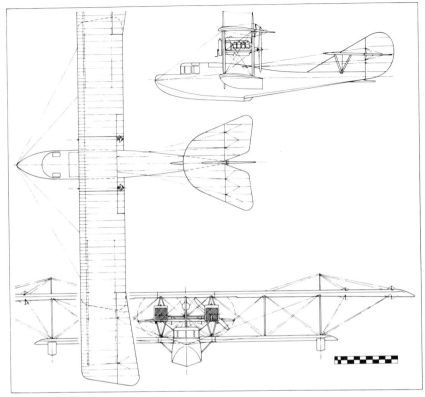

Model H, *America*

first aerial crossing of the Atlantic Ocean. The Curtiss organization was the logical one to develop the required aeroplane, which the patriotic Mr Wanamaker had already named *America*, and an order for two machines was placed in August 1913.

In form, the Model H followed the layout of previous Curtiss flying-boats, but it was enlarged in order to carry the fuel needed for a flight of 1,100 miles, the longest leg of the proposed transatlantic flight, and had two 90 hp Curtiss OX engines mounted as pushers. To increase their comfort, the two pilots and the mechanic were seated in an enclosed cabin. The wings, with two bays of struts on each outer panel, had tapered ailerons built into the upper wing, which also had a large overhang. The wings, which became the pattern for subsequent multi-engined flying-boats and their British-built counterparts for the coming war years, were designed by B. Douglas Thomas. Thomas was assisted to a considerable degree by another Briton, Lt John C. Porte, then on leave from the Royal Navy, who was selected by Wanamaker to pilot the *America*.

Since the Wright patent suit was active at the time, Curtiss sought to avoid duplicating certain details of the Wright system. The ailerons were hooked up so that only one worked at a time, one being pulled down by the action of the pilot's foot instead of both being moved in opposite directions by a control wheel. The wheel control was used to operate the rudder.

Following naming ceremonies on 22 June, 1914, the *America* began an extensive test programme. One of the early troubles was the tendency of the bow to submerge as power was applied to the engines. The high thrust-line of the engines applying forward force and the water drag on the hull acting in the opposite direction created a downward force on the bow. This phenomenon had not been significant in the past because of the relatively low power available in the smaller single-engined flying-boats.

The need for more forward buoyancy in the hull was met first by adding planing surfaces to the sides of the hull forward of the step. These were soon replaced by additional structures that Curtiss called 'fins' attached to each side of the hull, above the chines, that increased the volume and buoyancy of the hull as well as adding planing area. This Curtiss-developed feature was to be used on many other flying-boats into the 1930s but were called sponsons rather than fins.

With its take off problems solved, the *America* still could not carry the required fuel load for the distance, and the lifting capacity was then increased by adding a third engine to the top of the wing in a tractor position.

With the *America* finally considered to be ready, the oft-postponed flight was scheduled for 5 August, 1914, with Lt Porte as pilot. The starting point was to be St John's, Newfoundland, with intermediate stops at Fayal and San Miguel in the Azores and on to Portugal. Crews had actually been dispatched to some of these points when the flight was cancelled by the

Unable to lift the fuel required for the Atlantic crossing in its original configuration, the first *America* was given a third engine.

59

outbreak of what was to become the Great War, or World War I to later historians.

Lt Porte was recalled to duty in the United Kingdom and was able to persuade the Admiralty to purchase the *America* and its sister ship. These were to become the prototypes of a long line of twin-engined biplane flying-boats that would serve Britain and the US Navy well into World War II. The original *America*, in fact, gave its name to the class, and later developments up to H-16 sold to Britain became known as Small Americas and Large Americas.

### Model H *America*

Three crew.

Span 74 ft (22·55 m) upper, 46 ft (14 m) lower; length 37 ft 6 in (11·43 m); height 16 ft (4·87 m).

Empty weight 3,000 lb (1,360 kg); gross weight 5,000 lb (2,268 kg).

Maximum speed 65 mph (104·6 km/h); range 1,100 miles (1,770 km).

Powerplant two 90 hp Curtiss OX.

RNAS serial numbers: 950, 951 (Curtiss prototypes), 1228/1235 (8, Aircraft Manufacturing Co, UK), 1236/1239 (4, Curtiss), 3545/3594 (50, Curtiss).

## Miscellaneous Aeroplanes, 1910–14

In addition to the principal pusher and flying-boat designs, Curtiss produced others within this period. While not all were designed by Curtiss, their construction provided additional experience.

While not a Curtiss design, the design of the unique Pfitzner monoplane drew heavily on Curtiss experience and was built in Curtiss shops.

**Pfitzner Monoplane** Late in 1909, Alexander L. Pfitzner, who occasionally helped Curtiss with powerplant problems, undertook the building of a monoplane of his own design in the Curtiss shops at his own expense, although Curtiss employees built some of the parts. While it owed much to the layout of the contemporary Curtiss biplane, it had one unique feature. Mindful of the Wrights, Pfitzner achieved lateral control by means of telescoping wingtips, extending one tip to increase the lift on that side.

Pfitzner's monoplane was barely successful, flying on 21 December, 1909, but it did earn him the distinction of flying the first American monoplane.

The Ely monoplane was built to the special order of Curtiss exhibition pilot Eugene Ely and was not a true Curtiss design. (*Smithsonian Institution*)

**Ely Monoplane** In 1910, Curtiss exhibition pilot Eugene Ely ordered a monoplane to be built by Curtiss. While this was essentially a single-wing version of the current Curtiss biplane, it was Ely's concept and should not be considered a Curtiss design.

**Model G Tractor** The first Curtiss aeroplane designed as a tractor was the Model G, developed late in 1912 in response to US Army interest in the type. Two were built and sold to the Army in 1913.

The first, which became Signal Corps No.21, was a side-by-side two-seater with a 75 hp Curtiss Model O engine driving a three-blade propeller through a chain reduction system. The aeroplane sat on a tricycle undercarriage and the unequal span swept-back wings used interplane ailerons. First flown at San Diego in February 1914, S.C.21 was accepted by the Army on 12 June after change to a direct-drive propeller, extended

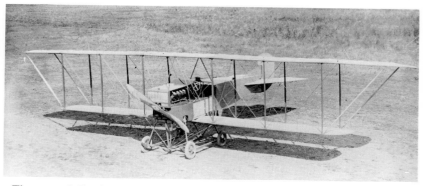

The second Curtiss Model G, built for the US Army in 1913, was a great improvement over the first but was still not a notable success; Curtiss had no previous experience with tractor-type landplanes.

61

wing span, upper-wing ailerons, and conventional tailwheel undercarriage. Purchase price was $5,500. The Army later added floats for operation in Hawaii and sold the barely-adequate aeroplane out of the Service in mid-1914.

The second G, Signal Corps No.22, was similar to S.C.21 except for 90 hp direct-drive OX engine, four-wheel undercarriage, and longer equal-span wings. It was accepted by the Army on 1 December, 1913, with shorter lower wings and upper-wing ailerons. Intended as a Service type, it too was inadequate and served as a trainer until condemned in October 1914.

### Model G

Two seats.
Span 41 ft (12·49 m); length 25 ft (7·62 m); wing area 390 sq ft (36·23 sq m).
Gross weight 2,400 lb (1,088 kg).
Maximum speed 53·5 mph (86 km/h).
Powerplant 90 hp Curtiss OX.
US Army serial numbers, 21, 22.

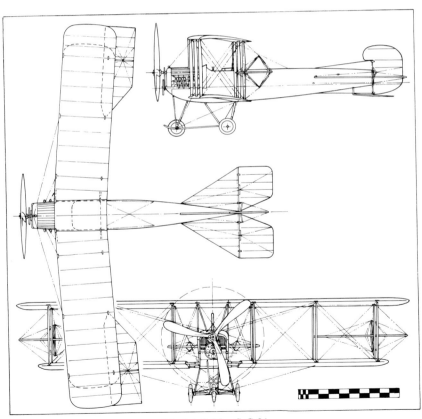

Model G No. S.C.21

The second Curtiss tractor landplane design was an aerobatic machine designed to the requirements of exhibition pilot Lincoln Beachey. It was not a success and Beachey went elsewhere for a tractor. (*Paul Matt collection*)

**Beachey Tractor** Although he had left the Curtiss Exhibition Company in 1911 to do his own air show work, Lincoln Beachey retained a preference for Curtiss aeroplanes. Believing that the tractor type would be advantageous in his work, Beachey collaborated with Curtiss early in 1913 on the design of a single-seat open-fuselage tractor biplane powered with a 90 hp Curtiss OX engine.

The tractor did not perform as expected, and Beachey had a scaled-down Curtiss pusher type built by Warren Eaton and later a tractor monoplane by Glenn L. Martin. He was killed when the Martin broke up in the air at San Francisco on 14 March, 1915.

**Model J** The Model J tractor was the first aeroplane designed for Curtiss by his imported British engineer, B. Douglas Thomas, and logically bore a great resemblance to the established British Sopwith and Avro tractor designs.

The first successful Curtiss tractor, the Model J of early 1914, was designed by B. Douglas Thomas, an experienced designer imported by Curtiss for that particular purpose.

When the Model J was tried as a seaplane, the span of the upper wing was increased to carry the added weight of the floats.

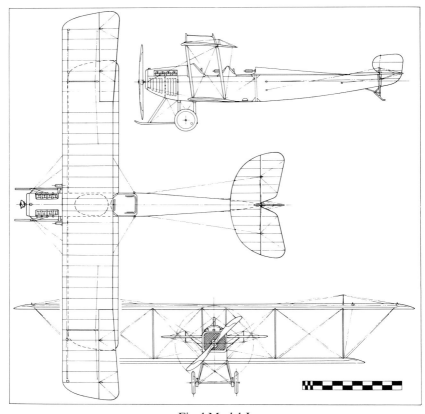

Final Model J.

Two Js were built and demonstrated desirable characteristics from the start. The 90 hp Curtiss O engine fitted behind a new nose radiator and the crew sat in tandem cockpits equipped with shoulder-yoke aileron controls. The ailerons were built into all four panels of the original equal-span wings, which used a modified French Eiffel 36 aerofoil. In an attempt to avoid infringement of the Wright patent, the ailerons of the Model J operated independently and moved only upward from the neutral position.

Flown in the spring of 1914, the first J was tried both as a landplane and a single-float seaplane. The upper wing span was soon extended to help carry the added weight of the float and the lower wing ailerons were removed. The longer wings were retained when the US Army bought both Js for $6,725 each and assigned them Army serial numbers 29 and 30.

The key features of the Model J were combined with the Model N to create the immortal JN design described later.

### Model J

Two seats.
Span 40 ft 2 in (12·24 m); length 26 ft 4 in (8·02 m); wing area 340 sq ft (31·58 sq m).
Empty weight 1,075 lb (487·6 kg); gross weight 1,635 lb (741·6 kg).
Maximum speed 70 mph (112·65 km/h); climb 3,000 ft (914 m) in 10 min; endurance 4 hr.
Powerplant 90 hp Curtiss OX.
US Army serial numbers: 29, 30.

Also designed by Thomas, the Model N was identical to the J except for wing details. (*US National Archives*)

**Model N** The Model N was a parallel design to the Model J of 1914, differing from it mainly in the use of an RAF 6 aerofoil instead of the Eiffel 36. In 1915, the best features of the J and N models were combined to produce the JN.

The original Model N was a two-seat biplane with equal-span two-bay wings and a 100 hp Curtiss OXX engine in the nose. The nose radiator duplicated the J installation but the N's ailerons were between the wings. The Curtiss shoulder-yoke aileron control system was used. The prototype N was evaluated by the US Army at North Island, was accepted at a price of $7,500, and given Army serial number 35.

During its Army trials, Curtiss repossessed the model at North Island to further his defence of the Wright patent suit. He locked the ailerons and rigged in the exceptionally high dihedral angle of seven degrees to prove that full three-axis control was not essential to safe flight.

After a period of service in the original configuration, its wings were modified to incorporate the ailerons in the upper wing.

The Model N was later rebuilt in Curtiss shops on North Island to a side-by-side two-seater and fitted with a 90 hp British Beardmore engine. The greater weight of the new engine in a longer nose just compensated for the balance change of moving the former front-seat occupant aft.

### Model N

Two seats.
Span 41 ft 6 in (12·64 m); length 27 ft 2 in (8·28 m); wing area 371 sq ft (34·46 sq m).
Empty weight 1,300 lb (589·6 kg); gross weight 1,800 lb (816·46 kg).
Maximum speed 82 mph (131·96 km/h); climb 4,000 ft (1,220 m) in 10 min; endurance 4 hr.
Powerplant 100 hp Curtiss OXX.
US Army serial number: 35.

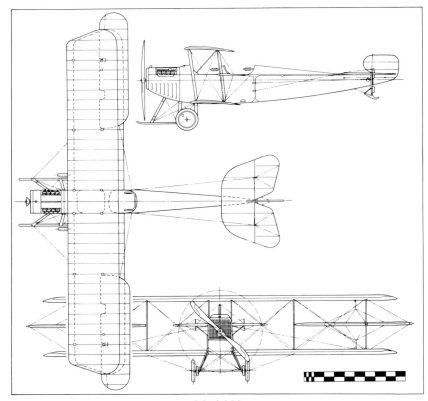

Model N.

The Model O was either a new aeroplane or a redesignation of Model N when it was rebuilt as a side-by-side two-seater. (*Air Force Museum*)

**Model O** Not known to be an official Curtiss designation, but seen occasionally in reference to the rebuilt Model N with side-by-side seating and Daimler engine. It is logical that such extensive changes would justify a new designation.

**Loening-Milling Tractor Biplane** Late in 1914, when the Army's pusher-type trainers were proving so unreliable, the Army's civilian engineer Grover C. Loening and Army Lt T. D. Milling jointly designed a new tractor biplane that was structurally and aerodynamically far behind the earlier Curtiss Models J and N. Since this was designed at North Island, Loening and Milling arranged for Curtiss to build it in his North Island factory.

The work was done largely by Curtiss students and the tractor was delivered on 30 December. It was unacceptable and was not purchased by the Army.

The Loening-Milling biplane was not a Curtiss design but was built in the Curtiss shops at North Island and fitted with a Curtiss Model S engine.

# World War I

Although World War I started in August 1914 and ended in November 1918, the effective 'World War I Period' of aircraft development can be regarded as mid-1915 to the end of 1919. The first few months of the war saw little change in aircraft design and many of the combat types designed in 1918 were not completed and tested until well into 1919.

The warring powers, uniformly inexperienced in the use of aviation as a military arm, went into action with a motley collection of types dating from 1912 to 1914. There was no distinction at the time between aeroplanes built specifically for the military and those built for civilians. While occasional experiments had been made in prewar years with firing machine-guns and dropping bombs from aeroplanes, they were regarded by the military principally as scouts—a new form of cavalry with only limited tactical application.

Civil aviation, at least in Europe, came to a halt as soon as the war started. Many sportsman-pilots offered both themselves and their machines to the military and were accepted while numbers of career officers in various traditional arms of their Services took flying lessons at their own expense in order to qualify for the new air arm.

As operational needs developed in the first year of the war, specialized aeroplanes were quickly developed to meet them. All of the emphasis on the military requirements of performance, strength, and servicing suppressed the characteristics that were desirable for purely civil flying such as inherent stability, comfort, simplified control and tricycle undercarriages. Aircraft design made enormous advances in World War I, but the military considerations became so thoroughly established that the 'World War I design concept' dominated almost all aspects of postwar aviation and only began to fade in the very late 1920s.

The European demand for aeroplanes was of immediate benefit to American manufacturers, particularly Curtiss. However, the majority of orders placed in the United States up to 1917 were for relatively low-performance types—trainers, unarmed reconnaissance two-seaters, and slow patrol flying-boats. The warring countries developed their high-performance combat types on their own and weren't about to share their design advances with a neutral power. Consequently, the United States entered World War I in April 1917 without a single combat-worthy military aeroplane. The few Service types on hand were mostly trainers and minor refinements of basic 1914 designs.

Curtiss aircraft, particularly the F-boats, had become well-known in Europe before the war and European orders began to pour in to Hammondsport after the war started. The original *America* boats were bought by the Royal Navy immediately and orders were placed for improved versions. With large orders for JN trainers and Model R scouts following, Curtiss soon found that Hammondsport could not support such a rapidly-growing industry. A new plant was established in Buffalo, New York, 100 miles (160 km) northwest of Hammondsport. Buffalo is a large industrial city, located on the shores of Lake Erie, and it possessed labour market, power, and transport facilities necessary to a large manufacturing operation that were not available at Hammondsport. Initial Curtiss operations at Buffalo took place in a leased portion of the Thomas Power Building. The Hammondsport facilities were retained and used throughout the war years for engine production.

Air view of the Curtiss North Elmwood plant in Buffalo, NY, which was the world's largest aeroplane factory in 1917.

Continued British war orders resulted in rapid growth at Buffalo. The Power Building soon proved inadequate so an entire new factory with 110,000 sq ft (10,220 sq m) of floor space, known as the Churchill plant, was started on 10 March, 1915, and by 15 May, 1915, it was turning out complete aeroplanes. Soon after, the Century Telephone Building was taken over and, used for engine manufacture, was named the South Elmwood plant. Two more plants, one on Austin Street and one on Bradley Street, were also acquired. America's entry into World War I resulted in the biggest aeroplane factory in the world being added to the Curtiss complex—the North Elmwood plant. This covered 72 acres (29 hectares), with 71 acres under one roof. Started in July 1917 it was in operation three months later and cost $4,000,000.

The rapid expansion of company activity that followed the move to Buffalo soon brought about a need for reorganization. On 13 January,

1916, the two major Curtiss companies were brought together in a single organization known as the Curtiss Aeroplane and Motor Company. Some of the companies retained separate identity but were now under the control of the parent company, namely Curtiss Aeroplane and Motors Ltd, of Canada; the Curtiss Exhibition Company, which continued to operate the flying schools at Buffalo, Hammondsport, Miami, and San Diego; and the Atlantic Coast Aeronautical Station, Newport News, Virginia. A month later, Curtiss acquired the stock of the Burgess Company of Marblehead, Mass. This was one of the oldest American firms and had been doing sub-contract work for Curtiss on pontoons and flying-boat hulls. Curtiss later made it a subsidiary plant and it became the principal supplier of N-9 Navy training seaplanes in 1917–18.

Flight testing facilities were also established at Buffalo, but because of the severity of the winter weather in the area, some testing of new models was undertaken at the Curtiss flying school in Virginia. While experimental scouts were developed on speculation for the Army in the absence of first-hand combat experience, the development of commercial, sporting, and exhibition models continued past America's entry into the war until civil flying was shut down for the duration.

The Wright patent litigation continued after the outbreak of war. Curtiss was still trying to invalidate the patent and as late as 1917 was still building reproductions of pre-Wright designs to prove prior application.

The patent situation had its effect on war production. To assure the manufacture and delivery of American aeroplanes for military purposes, the British government bought manufacturing rights to both the Wright and the Curtiss patents, paying $75,000 to Wright and $20,000 to Curtiss. Upon US entry into the war, Congress appropriated the sum of $1,000,000 for the purchase of the Wright, Curtiss, and other patents that were essential to war production.

This appropriation was never used. Instead, the industry set up a patent pool known as the Manufacturer's Aircraft Association. Formed on 24 July, 1917, this included the major manufacturers of the time and allowed use of the key patents by all members with royalties to be paid to the holders. This organization was subject to severe criticism during the postwar congressional investigations of the war effort. Charges were even made to the effect that it had been formed with the intent of capitalizing on the patent situation by adding a royalty of $100 to $200 to the price of each aircraft sold to the government. The fact that Curtiss and Wright each received approximately $1,000,000 in royalties when Congress had appropriated only $1,000,000 for their purchase and Britain had obtained the rights for only $95,000 were big points in the charges.

However, while the formation of the Association did not resolve the patent problem permanently, it did clear the way for wartime production.

US entry into World War I was a traumatic experience for the Curtiss Aeroplane and Motor Company and for Glenn Curtiss personally. While Curtiss was the country's largest aeroplane manufacturer at the time, no

American aircraft firm was really big business. In fact, it was pointed out in the postwar investigations of the aviation industry that of 16 firms given orders by the War Department in April 1917, *Only Six Had Built More Than 10 Aeroplanes*!

Curtiss had expanded from a tiny motorcycle shop, and while it could manage the sizeable British war orders of 1915–16, it could not cope with the enormous expansion sought by the US government in 1917. A good example of the prevailing situation upon American entry into the war is given by Major H. B. Hickham, writing of the early mass-production problems during the postwar investigations:

'In the Curtiss JN-4 we had an elementary training plane which had given satisfaction, and except that many important shop practices were not on record but existed only in the minds of certain executives of the Curtiss Company, the knowledge for production was at hand.'

Along with the new plant expansion, new management talent was brought in. This was drawn mainly from the automotive industry, which was well experienced in mass-production methods as applied to motor cars. Because of their common use of wood-frame bodies and petrol engines, aeroplanes and cars were considered by the planners of the time to be so similar that established motor manufacturing and management techniques could easily be applied to aircraft production.

This assumption proved to be one of the great fallacies of all time. The aircraft industry of the time was much more closely related to the small boat business, with its high percentage of hand work, minor variations between consecutive units in a small production run, and individuality of the finished product. In spite of this, motor manufacturing tycoons virtually took over the American aviation industry and established an image that persists to this day. The general public still equates aeronautical and motor production methods and cannot understand why aeroplanes aren't stamped out like cars.

The new management, with John North Willys, formerly of Willys-Overland Motor Co as president, immediately began to run the Curtiss factories like big car plants, to the great chagrin of the original Curtiss personnel. These, with their limited educational and managerial backgrounds, plus their 'cut-and-try' development procedures, were a serious handicap to the new order. To the satisfaction of all concerned, an entirely separate experimental plant was set up, far removed from Buffalo and the efficient production operation that was expected to function there. This was the Curtiss Engineering Corporation, with Glenn Curtiss in charge, and was located adjacent to the Army's Hazelhurst Field at Garden City on Long Island. Here, Curtiss and some of the other old timers, aided by qualified engineers and up-to-date research facilities, were able to concentrate on new designs while the motor experts took care of mass production in Buffalo.

Unfortunately, very few of the early 1917 predictions of 'skies black with American warplanes' came to pass. Although built up to a work force of

The experimental plant of the Curtiss Engineering Corporation at Garden City.

18,000 people in the Buffalo plant alone, some Curtiss plants had a war record of 60–70 per cent idleness, a percentage unfortunately shared by other manufacturers. This, however, was a situation beyond company control.

Soon after US entry into the war, the War Department set up an aircraft production board (APB) to control the industry's war effort. Recognizing the fact that the US was way behind Europe in combat aircraft design, a military commission was sent to Europe to study the latest designs and pick the most suitable of a variety of types for mass-production in American plants. It was expected that this production would get under way quickly and result in up-to-date combat aircraft being available sooner than European combat experience and design advances could be assimilated by US engineers and then translated into all-new American production models.

As a result of this policy, American firms were forbidden to develop new models on their own initiative. Curtiss was given large orders for models already in production, notably the JN Army trainers, plus Navy N-9 trainers and the F- and H-series flying-boats. An order for 3,000 French Spad XIII single-seat fighters was placed with Curtiss by the APB on 19 September, 1917, but was cancelled on 7 November. This was followed by an order for 2,000 British Bristol Fighters, two-seaters that were originally powered with the 250 hp Rolls-Royce Eagle engine but which were to be redesigned to take the new 360–400 hp American Liberty engine. Curtiss delivered 26 of these unfortunate adaptations before the contract was cancelled in July 1918.

Further orders for European designs were placed with Curtiss, one for 500 Italian three-engined Caproni bombers, later cancelled, and another, placed in April 1918, for 1,000 British S.E.5 fighters. Only one aeroplane was built under this order but the impression of more exists because Curtiss assembled 56 British-built S.E.5s that were delivered to Buffalo from Army warehouses.

The insignia change of January 1918, resulted in some interesting mixtures when stored components carrying old markings were installed on newer aeroplanes. The grey-painted Curtiss N-9C at the right has 1917 wing stars and 1918 rudder stripes, N-9C 2382 has 1918 circles and 1917 stripes, while 2363 and 2384 are correctly marked for 1918. *(Edgar Wischnowski)*

Early in 1918, the APB finally realized the folly of trying to adapt European designs that were now obsolete to American manufacture and allowed the industry to design its own. New prototypes appeared in quantity by mid-year, but were hardly through their test programmes, much less ready for production, at the time of the Armistice. Earlier, the existing Curtiss models ordered into production could not be produced in the desired quantities in the facilities allotted to them, so additional firms were selected by the APB to build them under licence. Similarly, production of the Curtiss OX-5 engine was assigned to several motor firms that built the majority of the 9,255 produced under the APB contracts. The quantities of Curtiss aeroplanes built by other firms are given under the individual model descriptions later.

Out of approximately $640,000,000 appropriated for the aviation programme from July 1917 to March 1919, Curtiss received approximately $90,000,000 and delivered 5,221 complete aeroplanes (approximately 33 per cent of total US wartime production) and 5,000 engines. The major production models produced by seven Curtiss factories are as follows:

**PRODUCTION AEROPLANES DELIVERED BY CURTISS UNDER
AMERICAN WARTIME CONTRACTS, JULY 1917–MARCH 1919**

| Model | Quantity Ordered | Number Delivered | Cost |
|---|---|---|---|
| Bristol Fighter . . . . | 2,000 | 26 | $4,968,173 |
| F . . . . . . | 144 | 144 | — |
| F-5L* . . . . . | 60 | 60 | — |
| H-12 . . . . . | 20 | 20 | — |
| H-16 . . . . . | 125 | 125 | — |
| HS-1, 2, 3 . . . . | 678 | 678 | — |
| JN-4 Primary Trainer* . . | 1,899 | 1,410 | $6,742,489 |
| JN-4, 6 Advanced Trainer . . | 1,965 | 1,965 | $8,550,667 |
| L (Army, Navy) . . . | 15 | 5 | — |
| MF** . . . . . | 53 | 22 | — |
| N-9*** . . . . . | 569 | 569 | — |
| R-4 (Army) . . . . | 43 | 8 | $82,220 |
| R-6/R-9 (Navy) . . . | 188 | 188 | — |
| S.E.5 . . . . . | 1,000 | 1 | $544,716 |

\* Excluding Canadian and Naval Aircraft Factory production
\*\* Excluding Naval Aircraft Factory
\*\*\* Including Burgess

Costs per unit are not given because more than just airframe cost is involved. Also, it should be noted in the case of Army aircraft purchases, the price included the cost of the installed engine on aeroplanes up to and including the JN-4B. Where realistic unit costs can be determined, they appear in the individual aeroplane descriptions.

In addition to the cancellation of practically all wartime production orders, the end of the war brought unprecedented congressional investigation of military procurement policies and practices related to aircraft. Everything from the decision to build European rather than American designs to the Army's harvesting of aircraft-grade spruce trees was investigated. Flagrant examples of conflict-of-interest, profiteering, and the placing of incompetent people in key positions were uncovered.

The aircraft companies themselves looked bad at first when the numbers of airframes they delivered were compared to the enormous sums paid to them. However, they were largely cleared of the charges of profiteering, featherbedding, and incompetence when it became evident that they were under tight government control and were actually following orders. Testimony given before a congressional committee by Curtiss's first postwar president, C. M. Keyes, readily confirmed the high percentage of idleness. It also pinpointed the reasons for it and revealed the company's protestations of the *status quo* and its efforts to use the staff and facilities for new work that the company was qualified to do.

While the investigations of the wartime aircraft programme made much of the fact that not a combat-worthy aeroplane of American design and manufacture reached the front, and this statement is widely accepted as gospel 50 years later, it should be pointed out that this referred to Army aviation. Little publicity has been given to the fact that single- and twin-engined flying-boats built by Curtiss and its licensees were operated from US Navy bases in France, the United Kingdom and Italy and that JN trainers were delivered to AEF training bases in France.

The aeroplane descriptions in this section have been arranged alphabetically by the first letter of their name or letter designations—Autoplane, Bristol Fighter, BT, F, FL, F-5, etc. Numerical designations, as 18B and 18T, follow the alphabetical, and model numbers in the 1935 system are included when they apply.

The Curtiss Autoplane of early 1917 had an automobile body with detachable wings from a Model L triplane.

### Autoplane (Model 11)

The Autoplane, known only by that name, was a unique winged car that Curtiss developed quickly for display at the Pan-American Aeronautic Exposition of February 1917. Basically, the design consisted of a set of standard Curtiss Model L triplane wings fitted to an aluminium-body three-seater motor car designed and built by Curtiss. A 100 hp Curtiss OXX engine in the standard car position turned a drive shaft to the rear; belts then turned the pusher propeller mounted on a shaft at the top of the car. The tail surfaces were carried on two wire-braced booms spaced 9 ft (2·74 m) apart to clear the propeller and a small auxiliary surface was attached at the extreme nose. The pilot-chauffeur sat in the front seat at conventional Deperdussin controls and two passengers sat side by side in the rear seat.

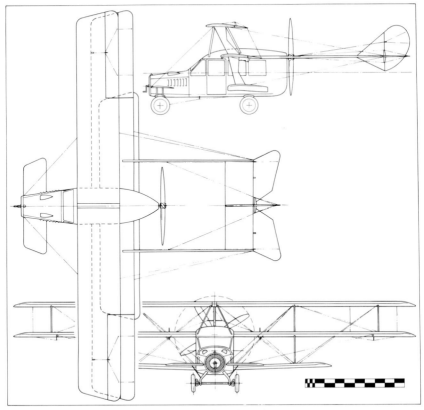

Autoplane (Model 11).

The unique feature of the Autoplane was that the wings and tail could be removed as a unit to permit the car component to operate as a conventional road vehicle. The Autoplane is reported to have made only a few short straight-ahead hops before development was abandoned upon US entry into the war.

Span 40 ft 6 in (12·34 m); length 27 ft (8·22 m); height 10 ft (3·04 m).
Speed range 45–65 mph (72·4–104·6 km/h).
Useful load 710 lb (322 kg).

## Model BA (Models 13, 14)

The BA flying-boat was a logical development of the F and K models intended to replace the F as the standard US Navy trainer flying-boat in 1918. The unusual use of a third letter in the Curtiss designation, BAT and BAP, is apparently an afterthought intended to distinguish between two configurations of the same aeroplane.

76

The Model BA was intended as a replacement for the F-Boat. The designation was changed to BAT to distinguish the tractor version from the later pusher (BAP) configuration. (*Smithsonian Institution*)

The final form of the BA served as the prototype for the 1918 Model MF and the postwar Seagull series.

**BAT (Model 13)** In its original form, the BA used a 100 hp Curtiss OXX engine mounted as a tractor (T) in the style of the 1914 McCormick Boat and the two-man crew sat behind the wings. This arrangement was unsatisfactory and the aeroplane was converted to a pusher.

**BAP (Model 14)** With the engine now installed as a pusher (P) and the crew moved forward, the BA became a satisfactory design. A simplified hull and minor refinements in the production version resulted in the new designation of MF.

The BAP was the pusher version of the BAT and became the prototype for the later Model MF. (*Smithsonian Institution*)

The Curtiss-built version of the British Bristol Fighter failed because the American Liberty engine was too heavy for it. (*Paul Matt collection*)

## Bristol Fighter

One of the successful European combat aeroplanes selected by the Bolling Commission for mass production in the United States was the Bristol F.2B, better known as the Bristol Fighter. The US government owned the rights to the design and assigned the official designation of USAO-1 as an observation type, but the Bristol Fighter name stuck. This was to be Americanized to the extent of having parts dimensions altered to be compatible with standard American tooling and altering the front end to accommodate the new 400 hp Liberty engine in place of the original British Rolls-Royce Eagle. Curtiss was given a contract for 2,000 in October 1917.

Production lines were set up in the new Elmwood Plant in Buffalo, and the first Liberty-powered Bristol was ready for flight in April 1918. The Liberty engine installation was troublesome from the start. It was both too heavy and too powerful for the relatively standard Bristol airframe and there were cooling problems. Because of the size of the Liberty, the original neat nose radiator of the Bristol could not be used; several arrangements of side and belly radiators were tried as well as fixed and movable units in the upper wing centre section.

Following several serious crashes of early test models, the Curtiss contract was cancelled after 26 Bristols had been completed (US Army serial numbers 34232/34257). This did not kill off official US interest in the design, however. While Curtiss tried to develop its own version of a Bristol replacement, the CB, the Air Service Engineering Division at McCook Field developed lower-powered versions with 300 hp Wright-Hispano engines and new laminated wood monocoque fuselages. Thirty of these were eventually produced by the Dayton-Wright Aircraft Company under the designation of USXB-1A.

## Bristol Fighter (USAO-1)

Observation aircraft. Pilot and observer/gunner.

400 hp Liberty.

Span 39 ft 4 in (11·98 m); length 27 ft 1 in (8·25 m); height 10 ft 2 in (3·09 m); wing area 416 sq ft (38·64 sq m).

Empty weight 2,245 lb (1,018·3 kg); gross weight 3,500 lb (1,587·57 kg).

Maximum speed 125 mph (201·16 km/h) at sea level; climb to 10,000 ft (3,048 m) 7·05 min; absolute ceiling 25,000 ft (7,620 m); endurance 2 hr.

Armament—two fixed Marlin and two flexible Lewis machine-guns.

## Model BT

The unique BT originated early in 1917 following discussions between Glenn Curtiss and US Coast Guard personnel concerning the possible use of aircraft to deliver lifeboats from shore stations to ships in distress beyond the breakers or at sea. Having a conventional aeroplane carry a boat was ruled impractical. Curtiss then designed what was essentially a winged lifeboat, with a hull more boat-like than on previous flying-boats.

The BT had two unconventional features. The 200 hp Curtiss V-2-3 engine was installed in the hull and drove two tractor propellers through shafts and gears, and the triplane wings and boom-mounted tail surfaces could be jettisoned if necessary to allow the hull to operate as a pure boat driven by a marine propeller and a small auxiliary motor. The pilots sat in a side-by-side cockpit behind the wings.

The power transmission system of the BT proved unworkable from the start. The engine was then installed ahead of the middle wing and turned a single direct-drive tractor propeller. The US Navy bought the modified BT in December 1917 and assigned Navy serial number A2277.

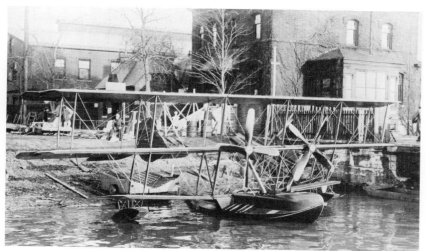

The BT was a flying lifeboat with the engine in the hull. Its wings could be jettisoned after alighting at sea, after which it proceeded as a motorboat.

79

The BT was modified with external powerplant, as shown, and the jettisonable-wing feature was discarded. (*Smithsonian Institution*)

The BT was of no use to the Navy, which encountered problems of hull strength, spray protection for the crew, the proximity of the propeller to the relocated front cockpit, and the danger of hand-starting engines in seaplanes. The BT was surveyed* on 9 June, 1919.

Span 57 ft (17·37 m); length 40 ft (12·19 m); height 16 ft (4·87 m).

**Model C-1 Canada**

The Canada of 1915 was the first twin-engined Curtiss landplane designed as such. It was an adaptation, however, as the wings and 160 hp Curtiss V-X powerplant installation were similar to those of contemporary

* Surveyed is a US military term meaning written off and ordered to be scrapped.

The Curtiss C-1 Canada was built in Canada and America flying-boat wings were adapted for the landplane bomber. Struts bracing the upper wing overhang were added in Britain.

Curtiss flying-boats. The name resulted from the fact that design and construction of this large aeroplane were entrusted to the new Curtiss plant in Toronto. The official designation was C-1.

Design work began in May 1915, and the prototype was completed in July. The early flights were made with Curtiss OX engines because the desired V-X models were not then available. Unconventional features of the three-seat Canada were the short fuselage, with the tail surfaces carried on booms, and the tandem-wheel-pair arrangement of each undercarriage unit.

The Canada showed great promise, and 102 were ordered by the RNAS. However, all but one were cancelled. The prototype was delivered to the United Kingdom in November and received RNAS serial 3700. Eleven others were built but their disposition is unknown. The prototype was based at Farnborough, where it was modified and used for test work. The wing overhang was now braced with struts instead of the original wires and the C-1 was the first aeroplane to fly with the new streamlined interplane wires (actually tie-rods), developed by the Royal Aircraft Factory, that came to be known as RAF Wires.

Span 75 ft 10 in (23·11 m) (upper), 48 ft (14·63 m) (lower); length 33 ft 4¾ in (10·17 m); height 15 ft 6 in (4·72 m).
Empty weight 4,700 lb (2,132 kg); gross weight 6,300 lb (2,858 kg).
Maximum speed 90 mph (144·83 km/h); range 600 miles (965 km).

The CB Battleplane was Curtiss's attempt to replace the unsatisfactory Bristol with another Liberty-engined two-seat fighter. (*Harold Andrews*)

## Model CB

One example of the CB, the letters believed to mean Curtiss Battleplane, was built at Buffalo early in 1918. This was a two-seat fighter type intended to be Curtiss's successor to the troublesome Liberty-engined Bristol Fighter. The fuselage was an early example of Curtiss ply construction, where two layers of two-inch wide wood veneer strips were cross-laminated over a form to build up a monocoque fuselage shell.

Unusual features of the CB by contemporary practice were the installation of the radiators under the leading edges of the upper wing near the fuselage, where they had a very detrimental effect on airflow over the wing and into the tail, and the lowering of the upper wing to the top of the fuselage. While this provided the rear gunner with a fine field of fire and the pilot with good upward visibility, the pilot's view forward and down was impaired, although small windows in the side of the fuselage gave some help. The main disadvantage of the lowered wing was the aerodynamic penalty of the very narrow wing gap that resulted.

The CB crashed early in the test programme and no further development was undertaken.

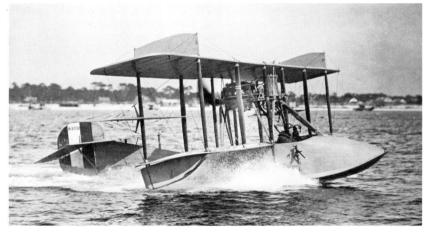

The Model F of 1913 became the standard Navy flying-boat trainer and remained in production into 1918. Increased upper wing span and Deperdussin controls were the principal changes.

## Model F (Revised)

The basic single-engine pusher-type F-boat of 1913–14 was ordered in small numbers by the Navy to the end of 1916. After US entry into the war in 1917, orders were increased when the design was chosen as the Navy's standard primary training flying-boat; 144 were procured after April 1917 and production continued into 1918 until replaced by the MF, yet the F was overlooked in the 1935 redesignation.

The 1917–18 Model Fs were greatly improved over the 1914 model, the principal change being redesign of the control system to delete the shoulder-yoke aileron control, both Services having agreed to standardize on the Deperdussin system in August 1916. Various wing modifications were tried on a few examples, among them extension of the upper wing span to 45 ft 1⅜ in (13·75 m) and transfer of the interplane ailerons to the upper wing. Several F-boats were fitted out as aerial ambulances, with provision for a litter to be carried on top of the hull behind the cockpit. Powerplant was the

100 hp Curtiss OXX-3.

Costing $7,500, less GFE, new, surplus F-boats came on the postwar market priced at $1,750 and saw relatively wide use by private owners. US Navy serial numbers: A145, A146, A386, A387, A390/393 (4), A408, A752/756 (5), A2279/2281 (3), A2295/2344 (50), A3328/3332 (5), A4079/4108 (30), A4349/4402 (54), A5258

### Revised 1917 Model F

Trainer flying-boat. Two pilots.

100 hp Curtiss OXX-3.

Span 45 ft 1⅛ in (13·75 m); length 27 ft 9¾ in (8·47 m); height 11 ft 2¹³⁄₁₆ in (3·42 m); wing area 387 sq ft (35·95 sq m).

Empty weight 1,860 lb (843·68 kg); gross weight 2,460 lb (1,115·83 kg).

Maximum speed 69 mph (111 km/h); climb to 2,300 ft (701 m) 10 min; service ceiling 4,500 ft (1,372 m); endurance 5·5 hr at cruising speed.

Fitting Model L wings to a Model F hull to produce the Model FL is representative of Curtiss's method of developing new models quickly.

## Model FL (Model 7)

The single FL is a good example of Curtiss innovation—the mixing of major components of two existing models to form a new one. A set of stock Model L wings on the hull and powerplant of the Model F flying-boat resulted in the entirely logical designation of FL for the single experimental model produced in 1917. It was owned by the American Trans-Oceanic Corp and was advertized for sale in September 1919 at $6,000.

## Model F-5L

Although it clearly showed its ancestry in earlier Curtiss twin-engined flying-boats, the F-5L did not carry a Curtiss designation. Actually, it was not even a Curtiss design; it was one of several established European models chosen for production in the United States in 1917.

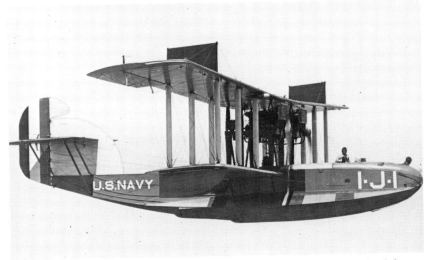

The F-5L was an Americanized version of the British F.5 that evolved from earlier Curtiss H models. This is the first Curtiss-built version, shown with postwar tail modification in July 1927.

The F-5L evolved from the original *America* of 1914 after Lt Porte, one of its designers, returned to England after the war began. For the Royal Naval Air Service he developed improved versions of the *America*, the several H-boats called Small Americas, and the H-12 Large America that Curtiss supplied to the RNAS. The first of the production British-built developments was the F.2, the F standing for the government aircraft plant at Felixstowe.

The wings, empennage, and powerplant arrangement of the British F-boats were essentially Curtiss; Porte's principal contribution to the design was an improved hull. Porte's F.5 model was a parallel design to Curtiss's H-16. While the British F.5s used 345 hp Rolls-Royce Eagle engines, the American versions, redesigned to American standards by the US Navy, were built with Liberties, hence the letter L in the designation. The principal recognition points between the F-5L and the improved Liberty-engined H-16 was the horn-balanced parallel-chord aileron and balanced rudder of the former, and its noticeably different hull lines and open cockpits instead of the enclosed cabin of the H-16. Although the F-5L design belonged to the US Government, its well-known Curtiss ancestry, plus the fact that some were built by Curtiss, has caused it to be widely regarded as a Curtiss. Curtiss built sixty F-5Ls, Canadian Aeroplanes Ltd built thirty, and the US Naval Aircraft Factory built 138. After the war, redesigned vertical tail surfaces were introduced by the Navy on the two of the last three Navy-built F-5Ls which were redesignated F-6. These new tails were then retrofitted to all F-5Ls in service.

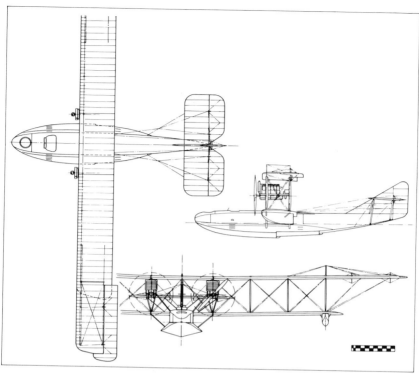

Model F-5L.

Curtiss installed tandem engines in one F-5L to test the concept before making modifications to the first two NC boats. (*Edgar Wischnowski*)

When the Navy adopted an aircraft designation system in 1922, aircraft already in service retained their original designations but the F-5Ls unofficially became PN-5 (P for Patrol, N for Navy, regardless of actual manufacturer). Two F-5L hulls were fitted with entirely new wings and 525 hp geared Wright T-2 engines in 1923 and became PN-7s. Duplicate models with the hull built of metal instead of wood were PN-8s. Further Navy-designed variants continued up to PN-12, with production versions of the PN-12 being built by Martin as PM-1 and -2, Douglas as PD-1, Keystone as PK-1, and Hall as PH-1, -2, and -3 in the late 1920s and early 1930s. The Halls served into 1943 to carry the direct descendants of the *America* through two World Wars.

Early in 1919 F-5L A3864 was modified by the Navy to a tandem-engine design to test the concept of one tractor and one pusher engine in a single nacelle for possible modification of the existing NC-1 and NC-2 three-engined flying-boats. This variant survived to March 1925.

A number of surplus F-5Ls were converted to 16/20-passenger transports by several overwater airlines in the 1920–24 era. Postwar price direct from the Navy was $12,400 while new prices for Navy-built F-5Ls ranged from $56,099 less engines for the first to $20,495 for the last.

### F-5L

Patrol flying-boat. Four crew.

Two 400 hp Liberty 12A.

Span 103 ft 9¼ in (31·62 m); length 49 ft 3¾ in (15·03 m); height 18 ft 9¼ in (5·72 m); wing area 1,397 sq ft (129·78 sq m).

Empty weight 8,720 lb (3,955·3 kg); gross weight 13,600 lb (6,168·85 kg).

Maximum speed 90 mph (144·83 km/h); climb to 2,200 ft (670 m) 10 min; service ceiling 5,500 ft (1,676 m); range 830 miles (1,335 km).

Armament—6–8 flexible ·30-in machine-guns, four 230 lb (104 kg) bombs.

Serial numbers: Canadian Aeroplanes—A3333/3362 (30); Naval Aircraft Factory—A3559/4035, 4038 (343 of 480 cancelled); Curtiss—A4281/4340 (60); Naval Aircraft Factory F-6L—A4036, 4037.

## Model G (1916)

The Curtiss G designation is confusing, for it seems to have been applied to both the first Curtiss tractor model delivered to the Army in 1913 and to a nacelle-type pusher based on 1915–16 European practice and using existing Curtiss Model R wings and tail and the 150 hp Curtiss V-X engine. Curtiss photographs of this single 1916 model have been labelled both Model G and Pusher R, which see. Photographs indicate that the 1916 model originally had equal-span wings with interplane ailerons and that the upper wing was then extended and incorporated the ailerons.

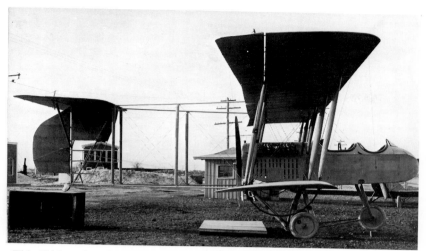

This 1916 pusher design has been identified as the Model G and has also been referred to as a Pusher R.

## Goupil Duck

The odd-looking Duck of 1916–17 was the result of further Curtiss attempts to invalidate the Wright patent. The design was originated and patented in 1883 by a Frenchman, Alexander Goupil, and showed

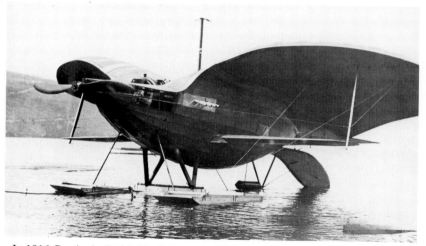

In 1916 Curtiss built this Duck from the 1883 design of Alexander Goupil in his continuing effort to invalidate the Wright patent. It was first flown as a seaplane at Hammondsport.

The Goupil Duck was transferred to the Curtiss facility at Newport News and continued its flights there as a landplane. (*Paul Matt collection*)

surprisingly modern lines and features. While Goupil did not build his design because of lack of a suitable powerplant, he clearly recognized the need for three axes of mechanical control. Lateral control was by means of auxiliary surfaces that functioned exactly like latter-day ailerons.

Working from Goupil's patent drawings, Curtiss Project Engineer N. W. Dalton revised the design only enough to make it structurally sound and added a conventional undercarriage in place of Goupil's skids. The Duck was powered with a Curtiss OXX engine buried in the fuselage at the centre of gravity and drove a tractor propeller through an extension shaft. Built in Buffalo, the Duck was first tried at Hammondsport on the old Langley floats. Barely able to hop off the water with their weight, it was shipped to Newport News, fitted with wheel undercarriage, and flew successfully on 19 January, 1917.

### Model GS

In 1917 the Navy gave Curtiss a contract for five single-seat seaplane scouts to be powered with the American-built version of the 100 hp French Gnome rotary engine. This was the first Curtiss design laid down from the start with a rotary engine and was given the designation of GS for Gnome Scout. The designation was altered to GS-1 and GS-2 when a contract for one additional GS was received.

The aeroplane designated GS-1, Navy serial number A868, was the sixth GS. It was a triplane that drew heavily on Curtiss experience with the S-3 to S-6 and other triplanes. Other than the three wings, the unusual feature of the GS-1 was the incorporation of shock absorbers in the struts between the fuselage and the main float. Seaplanes with their rigid truss between float and fuselage had always taken a beating during rough-water take-offs and alightings, but the GS-1 seems to have been the first aeroplane on record in

The GS-1 of late 1917 was the last of a Navy scout order and was completed as a triplane. (*Paul Matt collection*)

which something has been done about it. Unfortunately, the scheme didn't work well. The flexibility in the rigging allowed the trim angle of the float to change at high speed on the water and induce undesirable porpoising of the entire aeroplane. The GS-1 was nicknamed 'Flying Door Knob Control' by Curtiss pilots because of the detail of one of the controls on the tricky carburation system of the rotary engine.

The first five Navy Gnome Scouts were completed as GS-2 biplanes; these were the only Curtiss aeroplanes designed from the start for rotary engines. (*George Page*)

The GS-1 was delivered to the Navy in Florida on 1 January, 1918. After demonstration by a Curtiss test pilot, the Navy acceptance pilot made several flights but damaged the machine beyond repair on a landing on 1 April.

The first five Gnome Scouts, Navy serial numbers A445/449, were biplanes. These were not merely two-winged versions of the GS-1 but were entirely different designs. Little is known of these beyond photographs and Curtiss test pilots' comments on their tail heaviness. First acceptance was on 14 February, 1918, and the last was on 9 August. A447 was sold as surplus in August 1920 and A449 was struck off charge in November 1923.

## Model H Series (Model 6)

The Curtiss twin-engined flying-boat line that started with the *America* in 1914 continued into 1918 with designations in the H-series up to H-16. Only seven of the designations from H to H-16 are known to have been carried by existing aircraft. In the 1935 system, Model 6 applied to H-4, 6, 7, 8, and 10, but details are not available.

Until the introduction of the H-12, the only customer was Britain's Royal Naval Air Service. Curtiss's lead in large flying-boat development was a notable exception to the state of American aviation in the 1915–17 period, when European designs made great advances under the stimulation of war requirements while America, isolated from these developments, fell farther and farther behind.

Even so, the design of the Curtiss hulls demonstrated notable structural and hydrodynamic deficiencies in British wartime service. Late in 1915, Lt Porte, now back in uniform, designed and built improved hulls and fitted them with standard Curtiss wings and tails. The improvements proved desirable, and the F-series of large flying-boats was produced with the new hulls and British-built Curtiss wings to become the standard patrol/bomber flying-boat of the RNAS and the later Royal Air Force. The final F-5 model was to be built in the United States by Curtiss in 1918 in parallel with Curtiss's own Model H-16.

H-4 (Model 6)—The designation H-4 was assigned to the original *America* after modification in Britain. Subsequent production versions were identified in RNAS service as the Small Americas. As built by Curtiss, the powerplants were two 90 hp Curtiss OX installed as tractors. These were not favoured by the RNAS, which substituted ten-cylinder 100 hp French Anzani air-cooled radial engines or two 130 hp British Clerget rotary engines for the water-cooled Curtiss types.

Curtiss built sixty-two H-4s including the prototypes and another eight were built in the United Kingdom by the Aircraft Manufacturing Company (Airco) and Saunders.

RNAS serial numbers: 882, 883, 950, 951, 1232/1239*, 3454/3594

* Built by Aircraft Manufacturing Company and Saunders.

The H-4s were production versions of the 1914 *America*. The Anzani radial engines shown were installed in Britain. (*Imperial War Museum*)

The H-10 was a further tractor development of the *America*.

The prototype Curtiss H-12 flying-boat with circular radiators and counter-rotating propellers.

H-12As were H-12s with their 200 hp Curtiss engines replaced in Britain by 275 hp Rolls-Royce Eagles.

H-8—No data available other than published photographs that show it to be a twin pusher slightly smaller than the *America* and powered with the same Curtiss OX engines.

H-10—A twin-engined flying-boat larger than the H-8 and having the Curtiss OX engines installed as tractors. On the H-10, two booms were used to connect the engine nacelles to the horizontal tail.

H-12 (Model 6A)—The H-12 of late 1916 was a considerably enlarged version of earlier H-boats and was powered initially with two 160 hp Curtiss V-X-X engines. Eighty-four went to the RNAS, which named them Large Americas. Again, Britain was dissatisfied with the underpowered Curtiss engines and substituted 275 hp Rolls-Royce Eagle I engines in their H-12s, later replaced by 375 hp Eagle VIIIs.

With US participation in the war becoming imminent, funds for the expansion of Naval aviation became available and the Navy was at last able to buy twin-engined flying-boats. The first of twenty H-12s was delivered in March 1917. Engines were the 200 hp Curtiss V-2-3, later replaced with Liberties.

US Navy serial numbers: A152, A765/783

H-12A (Model 6B)—Original H-12s re-engined in Britain with 275 hp Rolls-Royce Eagle I engines and later Curtiss versions altered at the factory for engines to be installed in the United Kingdom. For the H-12A model at least, some hulls were built by the Niagara Motor Boat Company of Tonawanda, NY.

RNAS serial numbers: 8650/8699 (50), N1160/1179 cancelled (20), N1510/1519 (10).

### H-12A

Patrol-bomber flying-boat. Four crew.

Two 275 hp Rolls-Royce Eagle I.

Span 92 ft 8½ in (28·25 m); length 46 ft 6 in (14·17 m); height 16 ft 6 in (5·02 m); wing area 1,216 sq ft (112·96 sq m).

Empty weight 7,293 lb (3,308 kg); gross weight 10,650 lb (4,830·75 kg).

Maximum speed 85 mph (136·79 km/h) at 2,000 ft (610 m); climb to 2,000 ft (610 m) 3·3 min, to 10,000 ft (3,048 m) 29·8 min; service ceiling 10,800 ft (3,292 m); endurance 6 hr at cruising speed.

Armament—four flexible ·303-in Lewis machine-guns, four 100 lb (45 kg) or two 230 lb (104 kg) bombs.

H-12B (Model 6D)—Believed to be H-12s and H-12As re-engined with 375 hp Rolls-Royce Eagle VIIIs.

RNAS serial numbers: N4330/4353 (24).

H-12L—The US Navy followed the British lead in refitting its H-12s with more powerful engines. When the 360 hp low-compression Liberty became available late in 1917, the H-12s on hand were fitted with these new V-12 engines and were redesignated H-12L. The last H-12Ls were withdrawn from squadron service in July 1920.

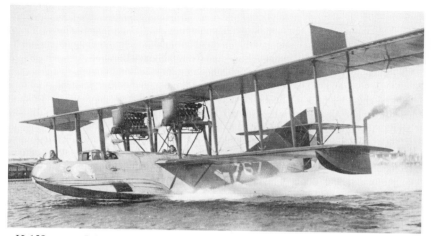

H-12Ls were US Navy production versions of the H-12 fitted with the 360 hp low-compression Liberty engine. Navy wartime colouring was grey overall.

H-14—The H-14 was a smaller twin-engined flying-boat than the H-12 and reverted to the pusher engine arrangement of the original *America*. The US Army ordered sixteen examples, serial numbers 396/411, before the prototype was completed late in 1916. This did not come up to expectations and work on the Army machines was halted.

In mid-1917, the prototype was converted to a single-engined type with 200 hp Curtiss V-X-3 engine and was redesignated HS-1 (H-model with single engine). The Army having cancelled its order, the sixteen former H-14s were completed for the Navy in the HS-1 configuration and delivered with Navy serial numbers A800/A815 and new Liberty engines that resulted in the designation HS-1L.

The H-14 was a small twin-engined flying-boat that was converted to a single-engined type with a more powerful engine. The example in this photograph has also been identified as the H-8.

93

**H-14**

Powerplant two 100 hp Curtiss OXX-2.

Span 55 ft $9\frac{5}{32}$ in (16·99 m) (upper), 45 ft $9\frac{5}{32}$ in (13·94 m) (lower); length 38 ft $6\frac{5}{8}$ in (11·75 m); wing area 576 sq ft (53·51 sq m).

Empty weight 3,130 lb (1,420 kg); gross weight 4,230 lb (1,919 kg).

Maximum speed 65 mph (104·6 km/h); climb 2,000 ft (610 m) in 10 min.

H-16 (Model 6C)—The H-16 was the final model in the Curtiss H-boat line and was built in greater quantities than any of the other twin-engined Curtiss flying-boats.

It was a logical development of the H-12 and was originally intended to use the 200 hp Curtiss V-X-X engine. However, the Liberty became available before the first H-16 was completed so all 124 H-16 deliveries to the US Navy were made with the 360 hp low-compression Liberty. These were replaced by 400 hp Liberty 12As in postwar years. The sixty British versions were shipped without engines and were fitted with 345 hp Rolls-Royce Eagles on arrival in the United Kingdom.

The H-16, with twin Liberty engines and enclosed pilot's cabin, was the final Curtiss H-Model. Also built under licence by the Naval Aircraft Factory.

In addition to 184 built by Curtiss, 150 H-16s were built at the Naval Aircraft Factory in Philadelphia. Originally, the Navy-built models were to be identified as Navy Model C, but all were operated as H-16s. The first Curtiss-built H-16 was launched on 22 June, 1918, while the first Navy-built model had come out of the factory on 27 March. H-16s were shipped overseas to US bases in Britain in 1918; H-16s remained in postwar service with the F-5Ls until May 1930. Prices for Navy-built H-16s ranged from $55,547 less engines for the first example down to $21,680 apiece for the last thirty.

Postwar passenger conversion of an H-16. The pilot's cockpit was relocated between the wings and the entire forward hull converted to a passenger cabin. (*Western Airlines Photo*)

Because of their great similarity, identification problems between the H-16 and the F-5L were inevitable. The distinctive features of the H-16 were originally the unbalanced ailerons with significant sweep back toward the tips as on the *America* and H-12, and the enclosed pilots' cockpit. The rudder was unbalanced, but could not be distinguished from early F-5L outlines because the balance area of the F-5L rudder was below the horizontal tail at that time. In postwar years, some H-16s were fitted with F-5L ailerons, had the pilots' enclosure removed, and were given added balanced area to the top of the rudder, further complicating the identity problem.

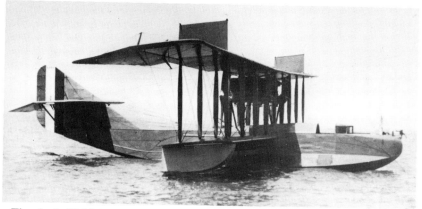

The single H-16-1 was a standard H-16 with the engines installed as pushers. (*Edgar Wischnowski*)

US Navy serial numbers: (Curtiss) A784/799 (16), A818/867 (50), A1030/1048 (19), A4039/4078 (40). (NAF) A1049/1098 (50), A3459/3558 (100).

RAF serial numbers: N4890/4949 (60) (4950/4999 cancelled).

H-16-1—One H-16 had its engines turned around and was completed as a pusher. No advantage accrued; the adaptation proved to be excessively tail-heavy.

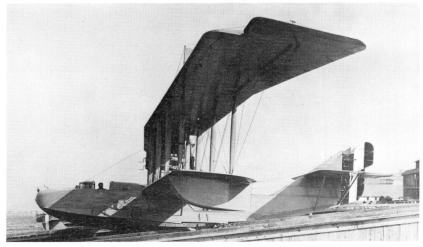

The H-16-2 had additional rudder area and the wings were swept back to overcome the tail heaviness of the pusher engine installation.

H-16-2—A second pusher H-16 (A839) was produced by Curtiss with more consideration for the change of balance. Wings of slightly increased span were swept back $5\frac{1}{2}$ degrees. Straight-chord ailerons used with F-5L-type horn balance brought the revised span to 109 ft 7 in (33·27 m). The increased wing area required additional rudder area in the form of two auxiliary rudders mounted on the tailplane.

### H-16

Patrol-bomber flying-boat. Four crew.

Two 400 hp Liberty 12A.

Span 95 ft $0\frac{3}{4}$ in (28·97 m); length 46 ft $1\frac{1}{2}$ in (14·05 m); height 17 ft $8\frac{5}{8}$ in (5·4 m); wing area 1,164 sq ft (108·13 sq m).

Empty weight 7,400 lb (3,356·58 kg); gross weight 10,900 lb (4,944·15 kg).

Maximum speed 95 mph (152·88 km/h); climb 4,700 ft (1,432 m) in 10 min; service ceiling 9,950 ft (3,033 m); range 378 miles (608 km).

Armament 5–6 flexible 0·30-in Lewis machine-guns, four 230 lb (104 kg) bombs.

## Model HA (Model 16)

The HA series of 1918 had no connection with the H-series flying-boats that originated in 1914. The HA was not even a Curtiss design; it was designed by Captain B. L. Smith of the US Marine Corps, and the Curtiss Engineering Corporation at Garden City was given a contract to build a prototype in December 1917. Two others were ordered later. Powered with the new Liberty engine, the two-seat seaplane was named Dunkirk Fighter because it was intended to establish Allied air superiority over the Belgian coastal area around Dunkirk, then held by the Germans.

Construction of the first HA, Navy serial A2278, was conventional wood and fabric, but there were several notable departures from standard configuration. The Liberty engine was entirely buried in the nose of a fat fuselage that was rounded out by formers and stringers outside of the basic rectangular structure. The nose was tipped with a large-diameter spinner. The single main float was mounted on two centreline struts and was stabilized by bracing wires running out to the inner bay of wing struts. The wing arrangement was unusual in that the upper wing, which had its roots resting on the top of the fuselage, was rigged with dihedral while the lower wing was rigged with anhedral. The pilot in the forward cockpit sat in a large cutout behind the rear spar of the upper wing while the gunner had a conventional cockpit and two-gun Scarff ring.

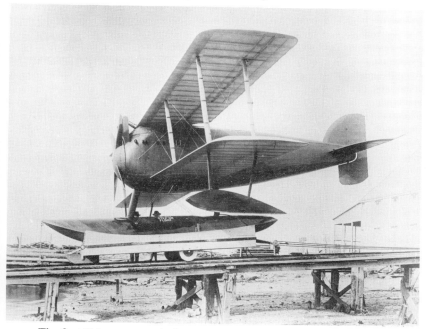

The first HA was excessively tail heavy and crashed on its first flight.
(*Paul Matt collection*)

97

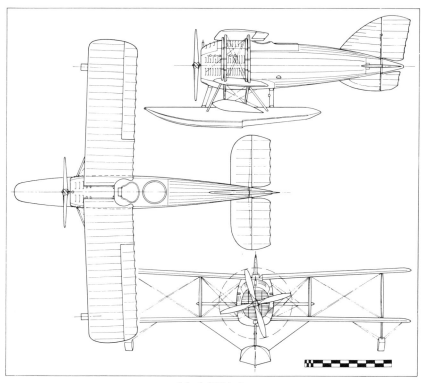

Model HA-1.

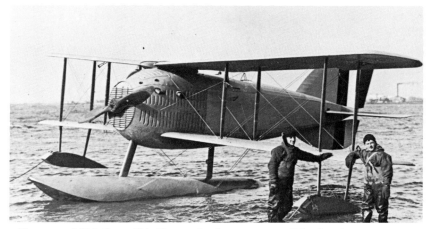

The second HA (later HA-1) contained some parts of the first but was a new
aeroplane with a later Navy serial number.

98

The first HA was ready for flight on 21 March, 1918. It was so tail heavy as to be almost unmanageable in the air and Curtiss's best pilot Roland Rohlfs managed to bring it down in a series of swoops to a crash landing that destroyed the aeroplane.

HA-1—Curtiss was then given a contract for two additional HAs, Navy serials A4110 and 4111, and some parts of the first one were incorporated into a considerably revised second prototype designated HA-1. Main changes were redesigned vertical tail surfaces with fixed vertical fin area above and below the fuselage, a more rearward location for the wings, and deletion of the spinner in favour of a nose radiator installation. Price less GFE was $42,900.

The performance of the A4110 was greatly improved, but it caught fire in the air. Pilot Rohlfs got it down safely but A4110 was a total loss.

The HA-2 differed from the HA-1 mainly in wing and engine cowling detail.

HA-2—The third HA was fitted with entirely new wings and became the HA-2. The new wings were of two-bay type with no dihedral on either panel. A centre section for the upper wing was held above the fuselage on conventional struts. The Armistice ended further military development of the HA design but the speed of the surviving example encouraged the Navy to enter it in the postwar Curtiss Marine Trophy Race for Service seaplanes. Cost was $42,900 less GFE.

HA Mail—In 1919, Curtiss developed a landplane version of the HA-1 into a single-seat mailplane for the Post Office Department, which was then operating the US Air Mail service. The pilot was moved to the former rear cockpit location and the front cockpit was converted to a mail and cargo compartment. After trying one with single-bay wings, Curtiss sold three two-bay HA mailplanes to the Post Office for $12,000 each less engines.

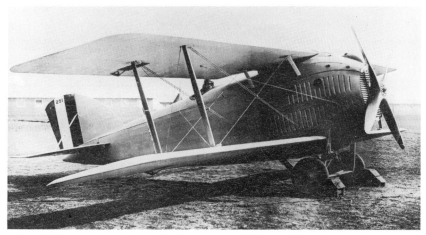

The HA was tested on wheels as a mailplane. The short wings were unsatisfactory and two-bay wings of the HA-2 type were installed on the three sold to the US Post Office.

### HA-1

Fighter seaplane. Pilot and gunner.

360 hp Liberty.

Span 36 ft (10·97 m); length 30 ft 9 in (9·37 m); height 10 ft 7 in (3·22 m); wing area 387 sq ft (35·95 sq m).

Empty weight 2,449 lb (1,110 kg); gross weight 3,602 lb (1,634 kg).

Maximum speed 126 mph (202·77 km/h); climb 9,000 ft (2,743 m) 10 min; service ceiling 19,000 ft (5,791 m); endurance (full throttle) $2\frac{1}{2}$ hr.

### HA-2

Fighter seaplane. Pilot and gunner.

360 hp Liberty.

Span 42 ft (12·8 m); length 30 ft 9 in (9·37 m); height 11 ft 5 in (3·47 m); wing area 490 sq ft (45·52 sq m).

Empty weight 2,946 lb (1,336 kg); gross weight 3,907 lb (1,772 kg).

Maximum speed 118 mph (189·89 km/h); climb 7,900 ft (2,408 m) 10 min; endurance (full throttle) $2\frac{1}{2}$ hr.

Armament (both types)—two fixed and two flexible machine-guns.

## Model HS Series (Model 8)

In mid-1917, Curtiss converted the three-seat H-14 twin pusher flying-boat into a single-engined model and assigned the new designation of HS for Model H, Single-Engine.

With the US now involved in the war, the Navy ordered a modified version of the HS into largescale production. Existing Curtiss plants were overloaded and Curtiss couldn't meet the Navy's requirements for the HS.

100

The first HS-1 was converted from the twin-engined H-14; the letters HS stood for a Model H with a single engine.

Consequently, five other manufacturers were given Navy contracts to build HS-boats under licence from Curtiss. Of the 1,092-aeroplane total, Curtiss built 675. Production ended when contracts were cancelled after the Armistice; only aeroplanes in an advanced stage of construction were completed in 1919. The type remained in Navy service into 1928 and in civil use in the US and Canada for a few years longer.

HS-1—A traditional pusher flying-boat with 200 hp Curtiss V-X-3 engine driving a three-blade propeller, converted from the unsuccessful H-14 airframe.

On 21 October, 1917, the HS-1 prototype was the test bed for the first flight of the US Government's new 360 hp twelve-cylinder Liberty engine and was later converted to HS-1L standard.

HS-1L—Significant changes were made in the production version of the HS-1, which was designated HS-1L because of the Liberty engine

The HS-1L was the production version of the Model HS, with the letter L identifying the use of the Liberty engine.

The HS-2L had 12 ft greater wingspan than the HS-1L and four bays of outer wing struts instead of three. This one is in the postwar colours of grey hull, silver wings and tail, and yellow on the top surface of the upper wing.

installation. The most noticeable difference from the prototype was the use of horn-balanced ailerons on both wings—these were the first used by Curtiss on a production aeroplane—and two degrees of dihedral in the outer wing panels. Up to 360 lb (163 kg) of bombs or depth charges could be carried on underwing racks and the defensive armament was a pair of ·303-calibre Lewis machine-guns on a Scarff-ring around the front cockpit. Colouring was the new overall light grey adopted as standard Navy camouflage into 1920.

The exact number of HS-1Ls flown is not known because some ordered as HS-1L were completed as HS-2L and others were converted later. Of the six builders of HS boats, only Curtiss and L.W.F. delivered HS-1Ls. Approximately 163 HS-1Ls were delivered to France in 1918, where they operated from ten US Naval Air Stations. The first ones arrived on 24 May and the first patrol was flown on 13 June.

In 1920, the Naval Aircraft Factory fitted stock HS-1L wings to fifteen new tractor-type aeroplane fuselages to create the PT-1 torpedo seaplane (serials A6034/6048).

The HS-3 was essentially the HS-2L with redesigned hull and vertical tail surfaces.

HS-2L—The 180-lb (82 kg) depth charges carried by the HS-1Ls proved to be ineffective against submarines; heavier charges (230 lb/104 kg) were needed but the HS-1L could not carry them. This deficiency was overcome by the old Curtiss trick of increasing the wing span; a new centre-section 12 ft (3·65 m) wider was fitted and one 6 ft (1·82 m) panel was installed between each lower wing panel and the hull to create the longer-span HS-2L. The vertical tail was also enlarged and balance area was added to the rudder.

The contract quantities and actual deliveries of HS-boats from the six manufacturers are listed here. Average unit cost was $30,000.

| Model | Manufacturer | Ordered | Delivered | US Navy serial numbers |
|---|---|---|---|---|
| HS-1L/HS-2L | Curtiss | 675 | 675 | A800/815, A1549/2207* |
| HS-1L/HS-2L | L.W.F. | 300 | 250 | A1099/1398** |
| HS-2L . . | Standard | 150 | 80 | A1399/1548 |
| HS-2L . . | Gallaudet | 60 | 60 | A2217/2276 |
| HS-2L . . | Boeing*** | 75 | 25 | A4231/4255 |
| HS-2L . . | Lougheed | 2 | 2 | A4228, 4229 |
| HS-2L . . | Assembled by Navy from spare parts in postwar years | — | 25 | A5564/5569, A5615/5619, A5787, A5808, A6506, A6507/6513, A6553/6556 |

   * HS-2Ls start at A1820.
  ** HS-2Ls start at A1223.
 *** The Boeing-built HS-2Ls could be identified by the absence of lower wing ailerons.

At least nineteen of the 182 HS-boats delivered to France were the HS-2L model. Some HS-2Ls fitted with improved 400 hp Liberty engines remained in Navy service until September 1928. After 1920, standard colouring was grey hull with silver wings and tail and chrome yellow on top surface of upper wing and horizontal tail. Thirty surplus HS-2Ls were sold

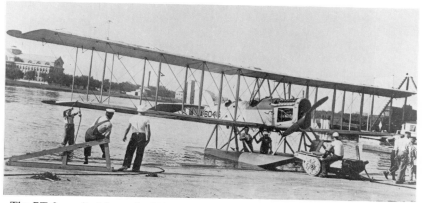

The PT-2 resulted from the US Naval Aircraft Factory fitting standard HS-2L wings to a conventional two-seat fuselage to create a twin-float torpedoplane.

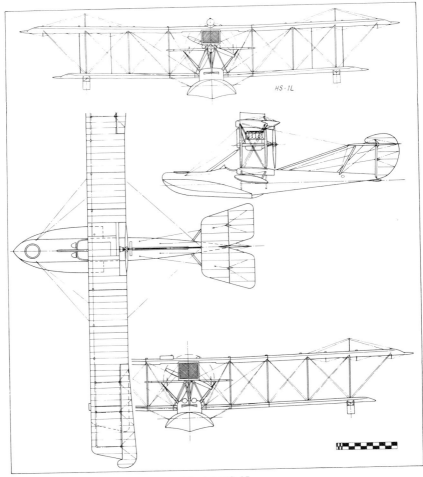

Model HS-2L.

to the Canadian Air Force and eventually came into civil use into the 1930s.
Others were used for short-haul airline work in the US in the late 1920s.
The US Navy fitted HS-2L wings to more tractor-type fuselages to create
eighteen PT-2 torpedo aircraft (A6326/6343).

HS-3—The HS-3 was a major redesign of the HS-1L/HS-2L that fitted
HS-2L wings to a completely new hull and vertical tail design developed
jointly by Curtiss and the Navy. The major change was widening the hull to
eliminate the sponsons. The Armistice ended official interest in the HS-3 as
a Service type and only four were completed by Curtiss (A5459/5462) and
two by the Naval Aircraft Factory (A5590, 5591) at $23,570 each less
engines.

## HS Series

Patrol flying-boat. Two or three seats in two cockpits. 360 hp low-compression Liberty 12.

|  | HS-1L | HS-2L | HS-3 |
|---|---|---|---|
| Span . . . . . | 62 ft 1 in (18·92 m) | 74 ft 1 in (22·58 m) | 75 ft 6 in (23·01 m) |
| Length . . . | 38 ft 6 in (11·73 m) | 39 ft (11·88 m) | 38 ft 7 in (11·76 m) |
| Height . . . . | 14 ft 7 in (4·44 m) | 14 ft 7 in (4·44 m) | 14 ft 7 in (4·44 m) |
| Wing area . . . | 653 sq ft (60·66 sq m) | 803 sq ft (74·59 sq m) | 824 sq ft (76·54 sq m) |
| Empty weight . . . | 4,070 lb (1,846 kg) | 4,300 lb (1,950 kg) | 4,550 lb (2,064 kg) |
| Gross weight . . . | 5,910 lb (2,680 kg) | 6,432 lb (2,917 kg) | 6,432 lb (2,917 kg) |
| Maximum speed . . . | 87 mph (140 km/h) | 82·5 mph (132·76 km/h) | 89 mph (143·22 km/h) |
| Climb in 10 min . . | 1,725 ft (526 m) | 2,300 ft (701 m) | 3,120 ft (951 m) |
| Service ceiling . . . | 2,500 ft (762 m) | 5,200 ft (1,585 m) | 6,500 ft (1,981 m) |
| Endurance . . . . (full throttle) | 4·2 hr | 4·5 hr | 5·3 hr |
| Armament . . . . | One flexible 0·30-in Lewis machine-gun (all models), two 230 lb (104 kg) bombs (HS-2L and HS-3) | | |

## Janin Patent Boat

This aeroplane was unique in that it was built solely to prove that it would not fly. In 1917, Curtiss was involved in a continuation of the Janin patent infringement suit (*see page* 33). To prove that the Janin patent was unworkable and should therefore be invalidated, Curtiss built a twin-engine flying-boat that was conventional in all respects except in the areas affected by Janin's patent. The special flying-boat, completed early in

The Janin Patent Boat of 1918 was built to prove that the flying-boat patent issued to Albert Janin was unworkable.

1918, proved Curtiss's points of contention but the patent suit was not settled in Curtiss's favour until after the war.

## Judson Triplane (Model 7)

This undesignated triplane is an example of several one-only aeroplanes developed by Curtiss to the specific requirements of the customer. It was built late in 1916 or early in 1917 for a Mr Judson as a slightly enlarged triplane version of the standard Curtiss F-boat using the 150 hp Curtiss V-X engine.

Refurbished after the war and fitted with a 400 hp Curtiss K-12 engine, the Judson Triplane was used for exploration in South America.

The Judson Triplane of late 1916 was a development of the Model F into a larger and more powerful flying-boat. (*John W. Underwood collection*)

## Model K (Model 4)

The Model K of 1915 was a logical development of the popular Model F flying-boat. It was larger, more refined in detail, and was powered with a 150 hp Curtiss V-X engine in the now traditional between-wings pusher location. Other than size, the distinctive differences between the F and the K were the heavy stagger of the K wings, the use of ailerons inset into the upper wing, and a V-bottom for the hull.

106

The Model K of 1915 showed the influence of both the F and J designs.

The K-boats did not sell well in the US but enjoyed a brisk export trade. Some, sold to Russia and delivered after many delays, were unseaworthy when set up because they had lain in their shipping crates so long that their wooden hulls had dried out and opened up numerous cracks.

### Model K
Three-seat military flying-boat. 150 hp Curtiss V-X.

Span 55 ft 9⅞ in (17·01 m); length 31 ft 5¼ in (9·58 m); wing area 592 sq ft (54·99 sq m). Empty weight 2,700 lb (1,225 kg); gross weight 3,900 lb (1,769 kg).

Maximum speed 70 mph (112·65 km/h); rate of climb 150 ft/min (0·76 m/sec); range 364 miles (586 km).

## Model L (Model 9)

The Model L triplane was a late 1916 development intended as a side-by-side two-seater suitable for training and for operation by private owners. The use of three wings was not unusual for the time. However, the extremely wide gap-chord ratio of the Model L wings compared to contemporary biplanes led Curtiss to develop a different wing strut pattern. Span of the two upper wings was equal while the bottom wing was short. The wider-than-standard fuselage terminated in a horizontal, rather than vertical, knife-edge at the tail.

The Model L became a production aeroplane, some being sold to individuals while others were used in the Curtiss flying schools. After the US entered the war, both the US Army and Navy bought limited quantities.

The Model L was a side-by-side two-seater and a contemporary of the JN-4.

The L-1 was a refinement of the Model L.

The L-2 originally had the short lower wing of the L and L-1 but the span was increased to carry the extra weight of the floats.

L—The original civil two-seater with 90 hp Curtiss OX engine.

L-1—An improved L with revised tail and strut details. This was the first time that the first variant of a designated Curtiss model was given a -1 designation instead of being designated -2 for the second configuration. The US Army acquired one when it bought three different triplane models from Curtiss and assigned Army serial number 473 to the L-1.

L-2—A single-float seaplane version with 100 hp OXX engine used by both the US Army and Navy. The first Navy model was flown with the original short bottom wing of the previous versions but this was soon enlarged to the span of the other wings to add needed lifting area to the heavier seaplane.

US Navy serial numbers: A291/293; US Army serial number: 475.

### Model MF (Model 18)

The MF was a greatly improved two-seat training flying-boat that was evolved from the Model F through the experimental BAT and BAP models. The designation stood for Modernized F. Structurally, the MF was more like the HS design than the F, but it was in the weight-power-size class of the F and was intended as a replacement for it.

A very prominent feature of the MF was the use of sponsons on each side of the forward hull as introduced on the *America* and used on many subsequent flying-boats. Initial powerplant was the 100 hp Curtiss OXX-3 but experimental installations were made with the 150 hp Wright-Hispano and the 150 hp Curtiss K-6, a new six-cylinder inline engine that was essentially half of the 400 hp K-12 developed for Curtiss by Charles Kirkham.

The MF was the production version of the Model BAP and the letters stood for Modernized F. The Naval Aircraft Factory also built MFs.

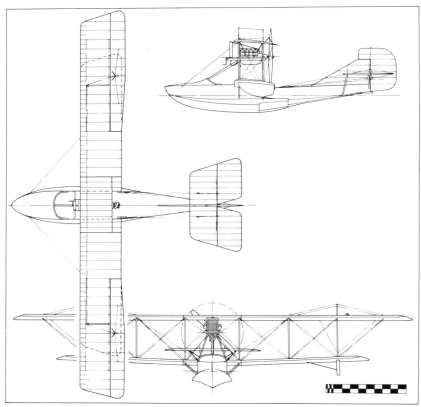

Model MF (Model 18).

Curtiss built six MFs at Garden City on one Navy order and sixteen of 47 on a second order that was cancelled by the Armistice. The Navy built 80 more in the Naval Aircraft Factory at a cost of $5,821 each less engine for the first 20 and $3,771 each for the last 20. After the war, Curtiss continued limited production of the MF for the civil market under the name of Seagull and also converted former Naval MFs to Seagulls for civil use. Other Curtiss and Navy-built MFs that became surplus were acquired by the Cox-Klemin Aircraft Co of College Point, Long Island, which rebuilt them for the civil market in the early 1920s.

**MF**

Trainer flying-boat. Two pilots. 100 hp Curtiss OXX-3.

Span 49 ft 9 in (15·16 m); length 28 ft 10 in (8·78 m); height 11 ft 7 in (3·53 m); wing area 402 sq ft (37·34 sq m).

Empty weight 1,850 lb (839 kg); gross weight 2,488 lb (1,128 kg).

Maximum speed 72 mph (115·87 km/h); climb 2,400 ft (731 m) in 10 min; service ceiling 4,100 ft (1,250 m); range 345 miles (555 km).

The N-8 was developed for the US Army. This is the prototype with its original long-span wings which were later removed.

## Production Model Ns (Models 1D, 5)

The expansion of US aerial forces in 1915–16 resulted in later versions of the Model N being produced independently of the JN series. Models designated N-1 to N-7 are not known to have been built; the known production models are the N-8 and N-9 described below.

N-8 (Model 1D)—In April 1915, the Army bought four N-8s (serial numbers 60/63) that were essentially duplicates of the contemporary JN-3 except for the 90 hp OX-2 engine, RAF 6 aerofoil, and retention of the shoulder-yoke aileron control. The first one had the wing span increased 10 ft (3 m) for better altitude capability by using a longer-span centre section and two 5 ft (1·52 m) extra sections for the lower wings inboard of standard-size outer panels. The increased span was soon deleted.

The N-8s were assigned to the Mexican Punitive Expedition of 1916 but were not operated over Mexican territory before being transferred to training duties.

The second N-8, with standard two-bay wings. The number 61 on the fuselage is the US Army serial; no national markings were in use at the time.

111

### N-8 (standard wing)

Observation aircraft. Pilot and observer. 90 hp Curtiss OX-2.
Span 43 ft (13·1 m); length 27 ft (8·22 m); wing area 350 sq ft (32·5 sq m).
Empty weight 1,335 lb (606 kg); gross weight 1,932 lb (876 kg).
Maximum speed 70 mph (112·65 km/h); endurance 4½ hr at cruising speed.

N-9 (Model 5)—The N-9 of late 1916 was essentially a JN-4B fitted with
the 100 hp Curtiss OXX engine, a single float, a lengthened centre section,
and 5 ft (1·52 m) lower wing extensions on each side of the fuselage in the
manner of the prototype N-8 in order to carry the additional weight of the
floats. The control system was the Deperdussin type with the control wheel
operating the ailerons and a foot-bar controlling the rudder. The prototype
used JN-4B vertical tail surfaces and oversized ailerons; the vertical fin was
enlarged on production models.

The Curtiss N-9 was the standard US Navy primary trainer of World War I and
early 1920s. Early models with Curtiss engines were retroactively identified as
N-9C to distinguish them from later N-9H models with Hispano-Suiza engines.

The US Army made limited use of the N-9, ordering fourteen early in
1917; the Navy was the principal user, ordering a total of 560 as primary
trainers. Of these, only 100 were built by Curtiss; the rest were from
Curtiss's wholly-owned subsidiary, the Burgess Co of Marblehead, Mass.
Fifty additional airframes were built up at Navy bases from spare parts in
the early 1920s; N-9s remained in US Navy service into 1927.

N-9C—Two designations were applied to the Navy N-9s. N-9C was not
official but came into use after the later N-9H appeared in order to
distinguish the original Curtiss-powered N-9s from the later versions. The
principal identification point of the N-9C was the exposed cylinder banks
of the distinctive Curtiss OXX engine and the use of a nose radiator
enlarged slightly over that of the JNs and the N-8 by having a curved area
added at the bottom.

US Navy serial numbers: (Curtiss) A60/65 (6), A85/90 (6), A201/234 (34),
A294/301 (8), A342/373 (32), A2285. (Burgess) A409/438 (30), A999/1028
(30), A2351/2409 (59).

US Army serial numbers: 433/446 (14).

## N-9C

Trainer seaplane. Two pilots. 100 hp Curtiss OXX.

Span 53 ft 4 in (16·25 m); length 29 ft 10 in (9·09 m); height 10 ft 10½ in (3·31 m); wing area 496 sq ft (46·07 sq m).

Empty weight 1,860 lb (844 kg); gross weight 2,410 lb (1,093 kg).

Maximum speed 70 mph (112·65 km/h); climb in 10 min—2,000 ft (610 m); range 200 miles (322 km).

N-9H—The N-9H designation was official, the letter identifying the 150 hp Wright-Hispano engine.* This installation differed considerably from the N-9C. The cylinder banks were exposed as on the N-9C but were different in appearance. The use of a large spinner over the propeller hub precluded the use of a nose radiator, so the cooling was done by a large column-like radiator that projected well above the wing. The Navy tested some N-9Hs with the 150 hp Curtiss K-6 engine but did not adopt the new powerplant. Cost was $10,050 less GFE.

US Navy serial numbers: (Curtiss) A2286/2290 (5). (Burgess) A2410/2572 (163), A2574/2650 (77). (NAS Pensacola postwar assembly) A6528/6542 (15), A6618/6633 (16), A6733/6742 (10), A7091/7100 (10).

An N-9H with 150 hp American-built Hispano-Suiza engine and unique tower radiator. Burgess built N-9s under licence and the US Navy assembled many others from spare parts.

## N-9H

Trainer seaplane. Two pilots. 150 hp Wright A.

Span 53 ft 4 in (16·25 m); length 30 ft 10 in (9·39 m); height 10 ft 11 in (3·32 m); wing area 496 sq ft (46·07 sq m).

Empty weight 2,140 lb (971 kg); gross weight 2,750 lb (1,247 kg).

Maximum speed 78 mph (125·52 km/h); climb in 10 min—3,240 ft (987 m); service ceiling 6,600 ft (2,012 m).

* Also known as the Wright A and the 'Hisso'.

113

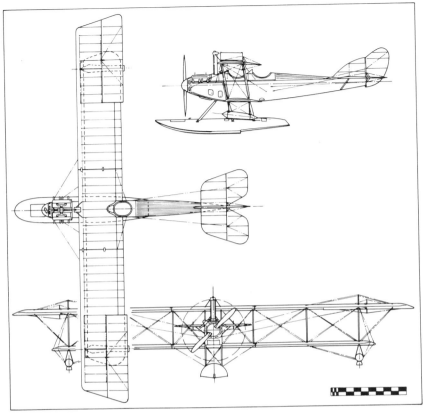

Model N-9H.

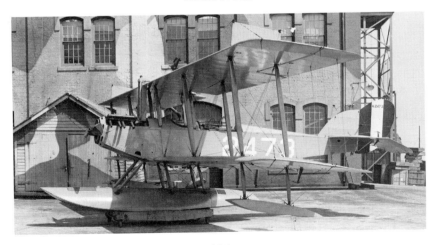

N-10—The N-10 was not a new design in the Curtiss N-series. The two known examples were one Curtiss N-9C (A365) and one Burgess N-9H (A2473) fitted with shortened equal-span two-bay wings to produce a faster aeroplane for other than primary training duty. The Curtiss model was later refitted with the Wright-Hispano engine.

## The NC Boats (Model 12)

The famous NC flying-boats were the result of a design co-operation between the US Navy and Curtiss, hence the designation NC. As the JN designation became Jenny, so the NC became Nancy but while that term was used in contemporary times, it soon died; the fame of the NC series rests on the accomplishments of a single example, the NC-4, the first aeroplane to fly across the Atlantic ocean.

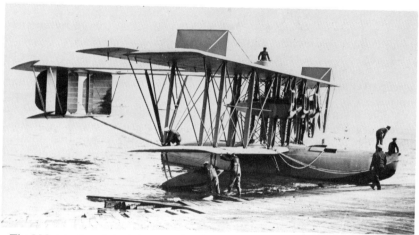

The NC-1 in its original three-engined configuration with upper wing gunner's position.

The concept of the NC boats originated with Rear Admiral David W. Taylor, Chief of the Navy's Bureau of Construction and Repair, who was concerned about aeroplanes *en route* to France by ship being lost to German submarines. He thought that aeroplanes should be developed that could fly across and be ready for duty on arrival. Navy engineers led by Commanders G. Conrad Westervelt and Jerome Hunsaker began design studies in September 1917.

As the only experienced builder of large flying-boats in America, Glenn Curtiss was called to Washington for consultation. He returned to Buffalo

Two N-10s were standard N-9 airframes fitted with shorter-span wings for livelier performance as gunnery trainers.

and was back in a few days with two versions of a short-hull flying-boat with a wingspan of 140 ft (42·67 m). One had five of the Navy's new 360 hp Liberty engines and the other had three. The short hull was primarily a weight-saving device; Curtiss had previous experience with the type on the earliest flying-boats and the BT of 1916. Curtiss's original designation for the design was TH-1, for Taylor-Hunsaker.

Taylor's group chose the three-engined design and Commander Holden C. Richardson was called in to do the detail design of the hull. Curtiss was to design the wings, empennage, and other details, finally receiving a contract for this work on 24 November. In December, it was decided to give Curtiss a contract to build four of the new flying-boats. Later, the new Naval Aircraft Factory was ordered to build six more.

No official designation for the new type existed at the time. Suggestions to call it DWT for Admiral Taylor were vetoed and Curtiss's TH-1 was not adopted because the Navy felt that it was primarily a Navy, not a Curtiss, project. The final NC for Navy-Curtiss was a logical compromise.

Virtual flying ships, the NCs followed the Naval custom of numbering the individual ships within a class. The assigned designations of NC-1 to NC-4 were not separate model numbers; they were individual aeroplane numbers for NC-class aeroplanes. Like series-built ships, the NCs showed individual differences as a result of construction experience and different approaches to design problems, particularly powerplant arrangement. Two official variations of the NC designation appeared in 1919: NC-T— a configuration using four tandem-pair engines in two nacelles, applied only to NC-2, and NC-TA—four-engined aircraft configured in the modified form of NC-1 and equipped for the transatlantic flight of May 1919.

Under the revised Naval designation system of 1923, all the NCs became P2N-1 for the Navy's second patrol design, at least on paper. The original designations remained in common use.

With the Buffalo plant expanding for largescale production, Curtiss's design work on the experimental NCs got low priority from the new management. Not until the project was transferred to the new Experimental plant at Garden City did work really get under way although construction of NC-1 had started in Buffalo in December 1917.

The existing Curtiss Garden City plant was too small for such an enormous construction job, so the Navy built a greatly enlarged shop area there. It also built a new hangar capable of housing two assembled NCs at the Rockaway Naval Air Station, 20 miles (32 km) from Garden City. The NCs were first assembled at the factory, then dismantled, trucked to Rockaway, and reassembled for flight there.

Curtiss also had a manpower problem. All available skilled help was already employed in other aircraft plants in the New York area, so most of the actual construction of the NCs was farmed out to established boat builders and woodworking firms in the New England area. After the first four NCs were completed, Peter Jannsen, the Garden City shop manager, was hired by the Navy to supervise construction of the final six at the Naval Aircraft Factory. Average cost of the NC boats, less GFE, was $125,000.

The war ended soon after completion of NC-1 and the requirement for transatlantic delivery vanished. For a while, it looked as if the remaining NCs would be cancelled. However, with other nations preparing to go after the renewed *Daily Mail* prize for the first transatlantic flight, the Navy decided to be the first to make the crossing—not for the money but for the prestige of the US Navy. The project received official status on 4 February, 1919.

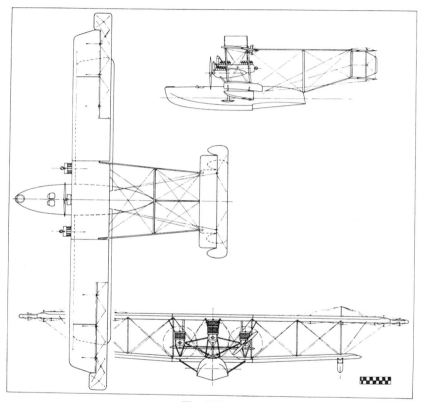

The NC-4.

Briefly, the plan was to use NC-1, 3 and 4, collectively known as Seaplane Division One, departing from Rockaway for Trepassy Bay, Newfoundland, 950 miles (1,529 km) away, in May. From there, there was a nonstop flight of 1,381 miles (2.222 km) to Horta in the Azores, a short 169-mile (272 km) hop to Ponta Delgada, then a 925-mile (1,489 km) leg to Lisbon and a 500-mile (805 km) leg to Plymouth.

Commissioning ceremonies were held at Rockaway on 3 May, and the three departed for Trepassy on 8 May, with departure for the Azores scheduled for 16 May. A string of Navy ships was stationed along the route to provide radio communication and necessary emergency assistance. Due mainly to the problems of navigating in fog, only NC-4 completed the record 3,925-mile (6,317 km) trip, reaching Plymouth on 31 May.

NC-1—The NC-1 (serial A2291) was a tractor three-engined aircraft powered with the 360 hp low-compression Navy version of the Liberty. Each engine was in an individual nacelle and all were at the same level and in line with each other longitudinally. Pilot and co-pilot were in a cockpit in the centre engine nacelle and a gunner was located in a nest on the upper wing above the centre engine. Other gun stations were in the extreme bow and near the rear of the hull.

The NC-1 had the only Curtiss-built hull; the wings, with the now-traditional RAF 6 aerofoil, were built by the Locke Body Company of New York City, a builder of car bodies. The first flight, with Commander Richardson as pilot, was made on 4 October, 1918. On 27 November, NC-1 carried a record load of 50 passengers and crew plus one stowaway.

Test results showed that the three-engined NC-1 could not lift enough fuel for the transatlantic flight, so an extra engine was added. This was accomplished by raising the centre nacelle and modifying it to accommodate two engines in tandem. To prevent tail-heaviness from the new rear engine, the centre forward engine was moved ahead of the unchanged side engines. The pilots were relocated from the nacelle to a conventional side-by-side cockpit in the forward hull.

On the transatlantic flight, NC-1 alighted at sea short of the Azores; the crew was taken aboard a ship and the flying-boat was sunk.

NC-2—As launched on 3 February, 1919, NC-2 (serial A2292) was a three-engined aircraft differing from NC-1 in having the centre engine

The NC-2 was also three-engined, but with the centre engine installed as a pusher and the pilots' seats in the forward part of the centre nacelle.

118

NC-2 was converted to have four engines in two tandem nacelles. The control nacelle in the centre was soon eliminated in favour of a conventional pilots' cockpit.

installed as a pusher. The pilots rode in the front of the centre nacelle. With no centre tractor propeller between them, the side nacelles were closer together than on NC-1. This fact complicated the subsequent conversion to four engines—the revised NC-1 arrangement could not be used without the major structural work of moving the side nacelles further outboard. The problem was solved by arranging the engines in two tandem pairs in the side nacelles, hence the NC-T designation. The pilots remained briefly in the now engineless centre nacelle, which was later removed in favour of a conventional cockpit in the hull. The hull was built by Lawley & Sons, boat builders of Boston. The NC-2 was wrecked when blown ashore in a storm and parts were used on the other three NCs.

NC-3—The construction of NC-3 (serial A2293) was far enough behind NC-1 to benefit from its test and modification programme. As launched and flown on 23 April, it duplicated the four-engined NC-1 pattern and was the first NC-TA built as such. Like NC-2, NC-3's hull was built by Lawley. NC-3 was chosen by Commander John H. Towers, commander of the flight, to be his flagship. It made a precautionary alighting at sea some 200 miles (322 km) short of the Azores. Unable to take-off again, it taxied to Horta.

NC-4—The NC-4 (serial A2294), with hull built by the Herrescholl Company of Bristol, Rhode Island, duplicated NC-3 and was launched on 30 April. Under the command of Lt-Commander A. C. Read, it departed with the others for Trepassy, but was forced down by engine trouble and taxied 60 miles (96 km) to the Naval Air Station at Chatham, Mass. Following an engine change, it arrived at Trepassy on 10 May.
After an uneventful flight of 19 hr 23 min, NC-4 reached Horta on 17 May. It then made the short flight to Ponta Delgada to wait for word from the missing NC-1 and NC-3. It arrived in Lisbon on 27 May and reached Plymouth on 31 May after an emergency stop at Mondego in Portugal, just

north of Lisbon, and an overnight stop at Ferrol in Spain, due to the delay. The hull of NC-4 was put on display in the Smithsonian Institution. In 1969 the entire machine was rebuilt for outdoor display in Washington on the 50th anniversary of the flight. It is now to be seen fully assembled in the Naval Aviation Museum at Pensacola, Florida.

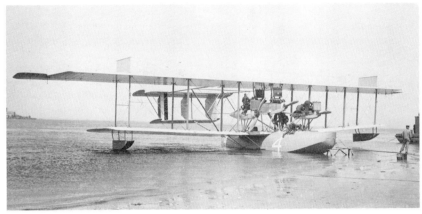

NC-3 and NC-4 were completed in the four-engined configuration of the modified NC-1. NC-4, *illustrated*, made the first aerial crossing of the Atlantic in May 1919.

### NC Flying-boats

Long-range flying-boat. Five crew. Three 400 hp Liberty 12A (NC-2), four 400 hp Liberty 12A (NC-4).

Span 126 ft (38·4 m); length 68 ft 3 in (20·8 m) NC-2, 68 ft 2 in (20·77 m) NC-4; height 24 ft 5 in (7·44 m); wing area 2,441 sq ft (226·76 sq m).

Empty weight 14,100 lb (6,396 kg) NC-2, 16,000 lb (7,257 kg) NC-4; gross weight 23,000 lb (10,433 kg) NC-2, 28,000 lb (12,700 kg) NC-4.

Maximum speed 85 mph (136·79 km/h); climb in 10 min—2,200 ft (670 m) NC-2, 2,000 ft (610 m) NC-4; service ceiling 4,500 ft (1,372 m) NC-2, 2,500 ft (762 m) NC-4; endurance 14·8 hr at cruising speed.

## Model R Series (Model 2)

Following Curtiss's acquisition of designers experienced with tractor-type aeroplanes, the company sought to develop larger and more advanced models than the J and N for military use. The first such effort was the two-seat Model R, a tandem two-seater introduced early in 1915 and powered with the new 160 hp Curtiss V-X engine that was essentially an enlargement of the well established O and OX models. The Model R was not notably successful but, thanks to having no significant competition, enjoyed brisk sales to both the US Army and Navy from 1915 until the end of the war and remained in Navy service into 1926. Early models were also bought by Britain's Royal Flying Corps.

The prototype Model R was essentially an enlarged and more powerful Model N. It had a single cockpit with two seats in tandem.

R—The prototype R could be regarded as an enlarged version of the original Model N, with equal-span wings, RAF 6 aerofoil, no dihedral, and shoulder-type aileron control. The most noticeable differences, other than the size, were the extremely heavy stagger of the wings and the use of a single long cockpit for both occupants. Although heavier than the N, the R was still light enough for its balance to be affected by crew location, so the pilot occupied the rear seat. The presence or absence of the observer in the front cockpit, located on the centre of gravity, did not affect the balance of the aeroplane. The single company-owned prototype was soon modified by the addition of dihedral and tested both as a landplane and as a single-float seaplane.

The Model R was also tested as a single-float seaplane.

121

The R-2 had unequal span wings and integral ailerons. Number 71 is the US Army serial and the red star on the rudder was the earliest US Army aeroplane insignia.

R-2—The R-2 model that appeared late in 1915, was an extensive refinement of the original Model R. The crew was now accommodated in two separate and widely-spaced cockpits, the tail was redesigned to use a fixed vertical fin and unbalanced rudder, and the undercarriage was redesigned. The wings took on the appearance of the JN-3 and short-wing N-8 by having the upper wing span increased to 45 ft 11½ in (14 m), having the ailerons in the upper wing, and dihedral. Experiments were conducted on one example fitted with a propeller spinner and dual radiators installed on the side of the fuselage. The production versions retained the nose radiator and had an enlarged vertical tail with balanced rudder that established the shape for subsequent R-models into 1918.

Twelve of the improved R-2s were sold to the US Army in 1916 for $12,000 each and some saw service with the Mexican Punitive Expedition. One hundred others were sold to the RFC; the original Curtiss V-X engines were replaced by 200 hp Sunbeam Arab IIs.

US Army serial numbers: 64/75. RFC serial numbers 3445/3544.

**R-2**

Observation aircraft. Pilot and observer. 160 hp Curtiss V-X.

Span 45 ft 11½ in (14 m) upper, 38 ft 4⅞ in (11·7 m) lower; length 24 ft 4⅜ in (7·42 m); wing area 504·88 sq ft (46·9 sq m).

Empty weight 1,822 lb (826 kg); gross weight 3,092 lb (1,402 kg).

Maximum speed 86 mph (138·4 km/h); climb 4,000 ft (1,219 m) in 10 min; endurance 6·7 hr at cruising speed.

R-2A—The R-2A was a parallel development with the R-2 but was completed first. Again, the crew was in two separate cockpits and the tail and landing gear were redesigned, but the wings were equal-span and retained the interplane ailerons and no-dihedral rigging. In August 1915, Curtiss pilot Raymond V. Morris overloaded the R-2A and set an American altitude record of 8,105 ft (2,470 m) for pilot and three passengers.

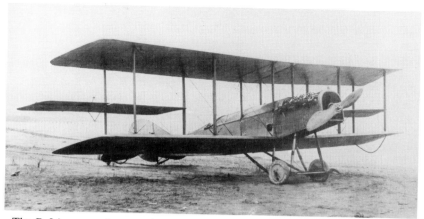

The R-2A was an improved R with two separate cockpits. The front cockpit, beneath the upper wing, is seen covered.

R-3—Two R-3s delivered to the US Navy in 1916 were fitted with twin floats and 160 hp Curtiss V-X engines. Generally similar to the production R-2s, the R-3s had their wing spans increased to 57 ft $1\frac{1}{32}$ in (17·39 m) by the addition of a longer-span centre section for the upper wing and the insertion of extra panels on each side of the fuselage inboard of the standard-length outboard lower wing panels in the manner of the N-9. The wings were rigged without dihedral.

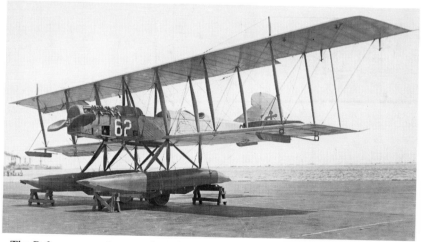

The R-3 was a seaplane version of the R-2 with longer wings to carry the added weight of the twin floats. The blue anchor on the rudder and under the lower wingtips was the first US Navy aeroplane insignia. The figures 62 were part of Navy aeroplane designation AH-62. (*Edgar Wischnowski*)

123

The original Navy identification/serial numbers for its two R-3s were AH-62 and AH-65 in the system adopted in March 1914; after 18 May, 1917, these became A66 and A67 in the new sequential serial number system and operated under their Curtiss model designations.

Eighteen R-3s were ordered by the US Army in 1916 for delivery in 1917, but these appear to have been completed as improved R-6s and R-9s.

R-4—Fifty-three R-4s ordered by the Army in 1916 were improved versions of the Army R-2s using later 200 hp Curtiss V-2-3 engines. Two more were purchased in 1917. Except for a redesigned tailskid in a more forward position and strut-connected ailerons in both wings, the R-4s were hard to distinguish from the R-2s. Some R-4s also entered Mexico with Gen Pershing's Punitive Expedition. Additional Army R-4s were ordered after the US entered the war but most were cancelled to allow maximum delivery to the Navy.

US Army serial numbers: 177/192 (16), 218/316 (36), 469, 2157, 37932

R-4s were improved R-2s and were in production from 1916 into 1918. This is a special white-painted ambulance conversion with covered litter behind the cockpit.

R-4L—Late in 1917 several of the large single-engined aeroplanes on hand in the Army and Navy were used as test beds for the US Government's new twelve-cylinder Liberty engine. An Army R-4 was among these and, when it was found that the new engine improved the characteristics of the aeroplane, a number of other R-4s were fitted with the Liberty and redesignated R-4L (L for Liberty). Twelve production R-4Ls were then ordered. Principal recognition feature, other than the larger engine, was the enlarged nose radiator similar to that used on the famous de Havilland 4.

US Army serial numbers: 39362/39367 (6), 39954/39959 (6)

In 1918 a number of R-4s were re-engined with the Liberty to become R-4Ls and some others were built as such.

R-4LM—After the US Army started to fly the new US Air Mail on 15 May, 1918, a need for aeroplanes with greater load capacity than the JN-4Hs then being used became apparent. At Army request, Curtiss converted six R-4Ls to R-4LM by adapting the front cockpit to a mail compartment with a capacity of 400 lb (181 kg).

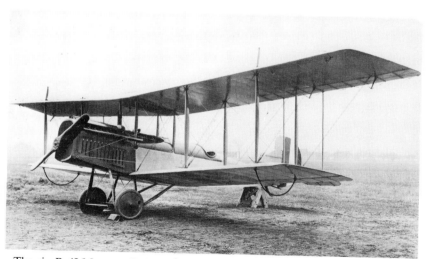

The six R-4LMs were R-4Ls converted to single-seat mailplanes for the Post Office.

## R-3 and R-4

R-3—Observation seaplane. Pilot and observer. 160 hp Curtiss V-X.

Span 57 ft $1\frac{1}{32}$ in. (17·39 m); length 30 ft $11\frac{1}{2}$ in (9·43 m); wing area 609·7 sq ft (56·64 sq m).

Empty weight 3,000 lb (1,361 kg); gross weight 3,837 lb (1,740 kg).

R-4—Observation landplane. Pilot and observer. 200 hp Curtiss V-2-3.

Span 48 ft $4\frac{5}{32}$ in (14·73 m); length 28 ft $11\frac{3}{4}$ in (8·83 m); height 13 ft $2\frac{1}{4}$ in (4·02 m); wing area 504·88 sq ft (46·9 sq m).

Empty weight 2,275 lb (1,032 kg); gross weight 3,242 lb (1,470 kg).

Maximum speed 90 mph (144·83 km/h); climb 4,000 ft (1,219 m) in 10 min.

R-4LM—Single-seat mailplane. 400 hp Liberty.

Span 48 ft $4\frac{5}{32}$ in (14·73 m); length 29 ft (8·83 m).

Maximum speed 120 mph (193·11 km/h); range 350 miles (563 km).

The R-6 differed mainly from the R-3 in having a more powerful engine and three degrees of dihedral on the outer wing panels.

R-6 (Model 2A)—The R-6 of early 1917 was a long-wing seaplane like the R-3 and differed from it mainly in use of the 200 hp V-2-3 engine and three degrees of dihedral in the outer wing panels. All but one of the seventy-six R-6s delivered to the US Navy had twin floats, serial number A193 being fitted with a single float. Army R-6s were delivered both as landplanes and as twin-float seaplanes. The US Army ordered 18, but most are believed to have been released to the Navy before Army acceptance.

Navy R-6s became the first American-built aeroplanes to serve US forces overseas in World War I when a squadron was assigned to patrol duty in the Azores in January 1918. Average cost of the R-6 and similar R-9 was $15,200 less GFE.

US Navy serial numbers: A162/197 (36), A302/341 (40). US Army serial numbers: 504/521

126

One R-6 was fitted experimentally with a single main float.

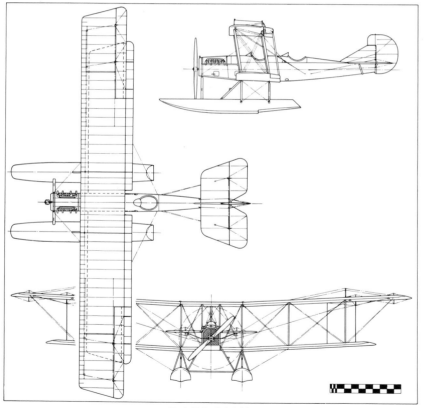
R-6 (Model 2A).

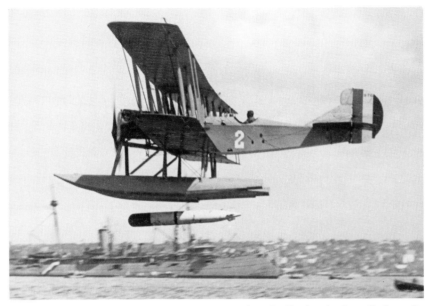

Most US Navy Curtiss R-6s were converted to R-6Ls by the installation of Liberty engines and were used as torpedoplanes after the war.

R-6L—Forty of the Navy's R-6s were converted to R-6L in 1918 by the installation of 360 hp low-compression Liberty engines in the manner of the R-4Ls of the Army. R-6Ls were used for the renewal of Navy torpedo-dropping experiments in 1920 and a number as Service torpedo aircraft until replaced by later equipment. The last R-6Ls were condemned in 1926. An additional fourteen R-6Ls were created by converting the R-9s with serial numbers A919, 920, 925, 943, 956, 958, 963/966, 970, 976, 991, and 994 to R-6 configuration.

### R-6L

Observation and torpedo seaplane. Pilot and observer. 360 hp Liberty.

Span 57 ft 1$\frac{3}{16}$ in (17·4 m); length 33 ft 5 in (10·18 m); height 14 ft 2$\frac{1}{32}$ in (4·31 m); wing area 613 sq ft (56·94 sq m).

Empty weight 3,513 lb (1,593 kg); gross weight 4,634 lb (2,102 kg), or 5,662 lb (2,568 kg) with torpedo.

Maximum speed 100 mph (160·93 km/h); climb in 10 min—6,000 ft (1,829 m); service ceiling 12,200 ft (3,718 m); range 565 miles (909 km).

Armament—one 1,036 lb (470 kg) torpedo.

R-7—A long-wing landplane that appears to be a development of the R-3 because of similar strutting. Powerplant was the same 200 hp Curtiss V-2-3 used in the R-4. The designation appearing in contemporary publications was in quotation marks as though it were in doubt; Curtiss identified the machine only as 'New York Times' since the single example

R-7 is an unconfirmed designation applied to this special aeroplane built for the *New York Times* in 1916.

had been sold to that newspaper. Flown by Curtiss test pilot Victor Carlstrom, it attempted a nonstop flight from Chicago to New York City in November 1916. The flight ended just short of the half-way point due to a fuel leak but still set a new US nonstop record of 452 miles (727 km). This date puts the 'R-7' ahead of the military R-6 model chronologically.

R-9—The R-9 airframes for the Navy were bomber versions of the R-6 with the controls rearranged to place the pilot in the front seat and the observer/bombardier in the rear. Ten (A883/887, A901/905) were transferred to the US Army in February 1918.

US Navy serial numbers: A873/984 (112). US Army serial numbers: 39033/39042 (10)

The R-9s were structurally identical to the R-6s but the pilot was in the front seat. The Navy serial number verifies this as an R-9 but the photograph shows wheel control in the rear cockpit.

Twin R—Early in 1916 Curtiss converted an R-2 airframe to an experimental twin-engined type. No official designation is known beyond the reference to a 'twin-engine R'.

Pusher R—In 1916 Curtiss made an attempt at reviving US Army interest in the landplane pusher configuration by fitting a pod, containing tandem cockpits and a pusher engine, with early Model R wings and new vertical tail surfaces to create a pusher in the 1914–15 European style. Longer-span R-2 wings with inset ailerons were soon installed. While performance reportedly matched that of the contemporary R-models, there was no official support for the design. This model also appears in Curtiss records as a second Model G.

The Curtiss Model S-1 was the smallest aeroplane that could be built to accommodate the 90 hp Curtiss OX engine.

## Model S (Model 10)

The first Model S of 1916 was a single-seater built to the concepts of what European builders had called a Scout in 1914. This was a single-seat tractor biplane originally used for the work its name implied—the scouting of enemy activity. Early scouts were unarmed but new designs were soon fitted with fixed forward-firing machine-guns; even though they then became fighters or pursuit planes, the term Scout stuck to the single-seaters almost to the end of the war.

Curtiss developed several different Scout models in its S-series of 1916–17, but succeeded in selling only a few to the US Army and Navy. The inadequacy of these aeroplanes cannot be blamed on lack of skill among the Curtiss designers; rather, it showed how far the US aviation industry had fallen behind that of Europe, which was operating under the immediate requirements of the European war. American designers were almost completely cut off from the latest European advances and had to progress from the 1914 designs on their own without the stimulus and largescale financing of a war economy.

The original 20-ft wing of the Model S-1 was inadequate so the upper span was increased and braced with diagonal struts. (*Paul Matt collection*)

The Curtiss S-2 was named Wireless because the unique strut bracing system eliminated the need for conventional wires.

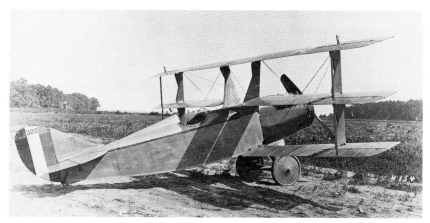

The four US Army Curtiss S-3s of early 1917 carried the new US national aeroplane markings but did not carry guns although they were classified as Scouts, which was synonymous with Pursuit at the time.

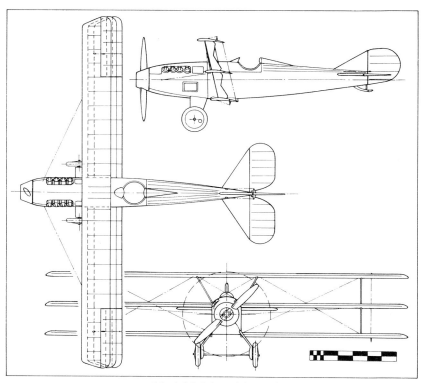

Model S-3 (Model 10).

S-1 Speed Scout—Also called Baby Scout, the original Model S-1 was the smallest aeroplane that Curtiss could build around the 90 hp OX engine. Construction was thoroughly conventional for the time, but the 20-ft (6·09 m) span of the single-bay wings was inadequate. The upper wing was lengthened and the strut arrangement was altered to two spanwise Vs. The S-1 did not sell, and Curtiss kept the modified prototype for its own use.

S-2 Wireless—The S-2 was essentially the Model S-1 fitted with new wings and a strut arrangement that eliminated the need for wing bracing wires, hence the name Wireless. The problem of fitting shock absorbers in the undercarriage when the wing struts were anchored to the ends of the cross-axle was solved by using the new Ackermann Spring wheels, which featured curved spokes made of flat spring steel that served that purpose; these wheels did not have good resistance to side loads, unfortunately, and were not widely used.

Powerplant: 100 hp Curtiss OXX-2. Span 21 ft 10 in (6.65 m) (upper), 11 ft 3 in (3·42 m) (lower). Aerofoil Eiffel 32. Empty Weight 805 lb (365 kg). Maximum speed 119 mph (191·5 km/h).

S-3 (Model 10)—The only 'production' models of the S-series were four S-3 triplanes sold to the US Army early in 1917 (serial numbers 322/325). These used the basic fuselage, engine, and tail of the S and S-2 fitted with single-bay triplane wings using the RAF 6 aerofoil. These were the Army's first single-seat Scouts, but they were still more than two years behind equivalent European types.

### S-3
Speed Scout. Single-seat. 100 hp Curtiss OXX-3.
Span 25 ft (7·62 m); length 19 ft 6 in (5·94 m); height 8 ft 7 in (2·61 m); wing area 142·6 sq ft (13·24 sq m).
Empty weight 970 lb (440 kg); gross weight 1,320 lb (599 kg).
Maximum speed 115 mph (185 km/h); climb—9,000 ft (2,743 m) in 10 min.


S-4 (Model 10A)—This was a triplane similar to the S-3 intended as a seaplane Scout for the US Navy (serial A149). This was Curtiss's first experience with the twin-float configuration. As with other Curtiss seaplanes, it became necessary to increase the span of the S-4 to carry the extra weight. The front float struts collapsed during a heavy alighting in January 1918 and the aircraft was struck off charge.

S-5 (Model 10B)—This was similar to the S-4 except for being fitted with a single main float and small wingtip floats. Navy serial number A150, struck off on 6 August, 1919.

S-6 (Model 10C)—The S-6 was an improved version of the S-3 and was the first American Scout fitted with twin forward-firing machine-guns. This may have been only an inoperative test installation intended to check weight, balance, and location, for the guns were gas-operated Lewis models which were not used for synchronized fire through the propeller. The Army ordered twelve early in 1917 but only one, serial number 492, was delivered.

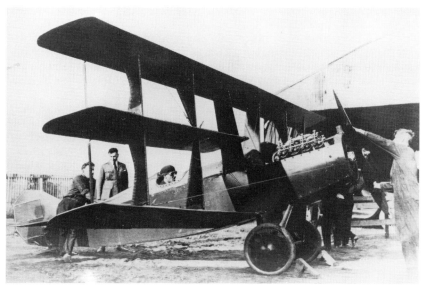

Although tested as a landplane, the S-4 was intended to be a seaplane and had longer wings than the similar S-3 to carry the weight of the floats.
(*Courtesy Dustin Carter*)

The S-6 was slightly larger than the S-3 and was the first US Army single-seater to carry machine-guns.

# S.E.5

The S.E.5 was one of the leading British fighters of 1917 and was one of two European single-seaters chosen by the Bolling Commission for mass production in the United States. It was designed and built at the Royal Aircraft Factory and the letters stood for Scouting Experimental, Model 5. Powerplants were direct-drive and geared versions of the 180–200 hp French Hispano-Suiza and a British-built copy known as the Wolseley Viper.

Curtiss completed only this one of 1,000 British S.E.5 fighters ordered but assembled 56 others that had been built in Britain.

Curtiss was given an order for 1,000 S.E.5s, but only one example was built (US Army serial 43153). Fifty-six others, sometimes referred to as Curtiss SE-5s, were British-built airframes sent to Curtiss for assembly. These were flown as trainers in the US under their original British serial numbers and markings. The single Curtiss-built SE-5, using the Americanized Hispano-Suiza engine as built by Wright-Martin, was delivered to the Army for test in September 1918, and was carried on Army books at a value of $544,716.

Additional British S.E.5s, delivered to American pursuit squadrons in France, were brought to the US when those squadrons returned home after the Armistice. These were first-line pursuit aircraft until replaced by new American designs in 1920. In 1923, fifty S.E.5s were sent to Eberhart Steel Products Company for rebuild as SE-5Es (for Wright E engine, the American-made 180 hp Hispano-Suiza) and served with other SE-5s as advanced trainers until 1927.

This special single-seat aerobatic aircraft was built for Katherine Stinson by fitting a Model S triplane fuselage with new biplane wings.

### Stinson Special

In early 1917, before the wartime ban on private flying in the US, the famous aviatrix Katherine Stinson commissioned Curtiss to build her a single-seat exhibition aeroplane. The result was a quick adaptation of an S-model triplane fuselage to new two-bay biplane wings, a 100 hp OXX engine, and modified JN-4 tail surfaces.

Miss Stinson, exempted from the ban on civil flying because of her use of the aeroplane in fund-raising activities, gave many exhibitions in the US and Canada in 1917 and 1918. The aeroplane underwent several minor modifications at the hands of its owner as the result of repairs or desired improvements.

### Model T (Wanamaker Triplane, Model 3)

At the time of its construction in 1915–16, the Curtiss Model T flying-boat, which was instigated by Rodman Wanamaker of *America* fame, was the largest seaplane in the world. It was also the first four-engined aeroplane built in the United States. An unusual feature was the arrangement of the engines—four 250 hp Curtiss V-4 tractors in a straight line, a feature used successfully up to that time only by the Russian Sikorskys and the single German Siemens-Forsman. Because of marginal directional control under one-engine-out conditions, designers usually grouped engines as close to the aeroplane centreline as possible to minimize the turning couple of an unsymmetrical power condition. A favourite procedure was to pair two side engines in tandem installations in a single nacelle, which Curtiss did on the NC-2 in 1919.

The *America*-type control cabin was equipped for two pilots and an engineer. The control forces were so great that an early form of power boost was provided. Small windmills installed on the wings were connected to the aileron cables by electrically-operated clutches. The power of the windmill was imparted to the cable to aid the pilot. Similar devices were used for the tail controls.

The Model T triplane was too big to be assembled and flown at the Curtiss Buffalo plant so was shipped to Britain, where it was assembled and fitted with French Renault engines. (*Jack Bruce*)

The T was designed to requirements of the British Admiralty, which ordered 20 examples, RNAS serial numbers 3073/3092. While the first T was assembled inside the Buffalo plant, it was not flown in the US because the V-4 engine was not developed in time. The aeroplane was shipped to Britain without engines and 240 hp French Renaults were installed there.

The big triplane was not put into service and the remaining 19 on order were cancelled. The basic design concept was retained, however; the Curtiss Model T was the direct predecessor of the five-engined Felixstowe Fury triplane that Cmdr Porte designed for the Admiralty.

### Model T Triplane

Patrol Bomber flying-boat. Crew included two pilots, one engineer, and gunners. Four 240 hp Renault.

Span 134 ft (40·84 m) (top), 100 ft (30·48 m) (centre), 78 ft 3 in (23·85 m) (lower); length 58 ft 10 in (17·93 m); height 31 ft 4 in (9·55 m); wing area 2,812 sq ft (261·23 sq m).

Empty weight 15,645 lb (7,096 kg); gross weight 22,000 lb (9,979 kg).

Maximum speed 100 mph (160·93 km/h); climb to 4,000 ft (1,219 m) 10 min; endurance 7 hr.

The Model X-1 was similar to the JN-4B except for nose details and the use of triplane wings.

## Model X-1

The single X-1 of early 1917 was a contemporary of the L-1 triplane, using the same wings and engine installation but a different fuselage, undercarriage, and tail. The most noticeable differences were the use of a two-cockpit tandem-seating fuselage much like that of the JN-4, with vertical tail post, and a JN-4 type vertical tail. The US Army bought one, serial number 474.

### Model 18 Series (Model 15)

In March 1918, the Navy authorized Curtiss to build two two-seat fighter triplanes designed at Garden City by Curtiss engineer Charles Kirkham, Navy serial numbers A3325 and A3326. Unit prices were $55,400 less GFE. Although these were identified in service as Model 18T (for triplane) and were also known as Curtiss-Kirkhams, they carried the Curtiss engineering designation of Experimental 502.

The 18 was designed specifically for the 400 hp Curtiss-Kirkham K-12 engine, a water-cooled geared V-12 type of somewhat unorthodox construction developed late in 1917. The K-12 gave the Model 18 world-record performance in 1918 and evolved into the C-12 and eventually into the D-12 and the Conqueror.

The fuselage was a well-streamlined structure featuring a combination of previous Curtiss flying-boat practice and German laminated wood veneer construction in a new process called Curtiss ply. The nose was kept as streamlined as possible by mounting the radiators on the sides of the

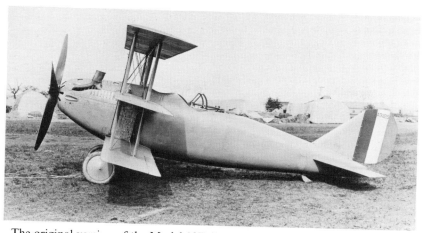

The original version of the Model 18T (for triplane) Wasp was tail heavy with the unswept wings shown.

fuselage. Armament was a pair of ·30-calibre Marlin machine-guns on the nose, a pair of ·30-calibre Lewis guns on the rear cockpit Scarff ring, and a single Lewis firing out of the belly.

18T-1 Wasp—Kirkham chose the triplane configuration for his new fighter because the shorter span would enhance the manoeuvrability. The -1 was added to the designation after alternate wings of longer span became available on a -2 version. In all configurations, the 18T was known as the

The prototype 18T had its wings swept back five degrees to correct the tail-heaviness problem. With a speed of 163 mph, it was briefly the fastest aeroplane in the world.

139

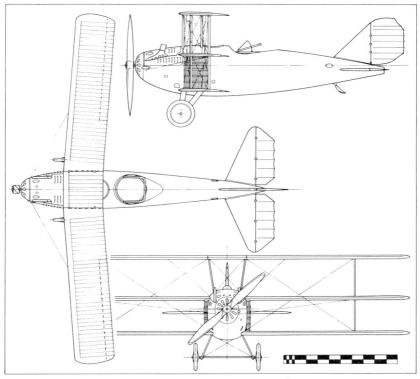

Model 18T Wasp.

Wasp but, because of the sound of its wires during landing approaches, it was known around Garden City as Whistling Benny.

For its first flight, on 5 July, 1918, the 18T had straight wings; tail heaviness was soon corrected by sweeping the wings back five degrees. The Army became interested in the design and arranged to borrow the first one from the Navy. Tests with full military load in August 1918 produced a top speed of 163 mph (262·3 km/h), making the 18T the world's fastest aeroplane at the time even though the record was not recognized. The Army then ordered two 18Ts of its own with Army serial numbers 40054 and 40059.

No Navy production orders were received for the 18T; its hand-built engine was more experimental than the aeroplane itself and the end of the war killed any requirement for it as a Service type.

The speed of the 18T-1 was put to good use, however, since the Navy entered both examples in postwar air races. Both were flown in the 1920 Pulitzer Trophy Race but dropped out because of engine trouble. As single-float seaplanes, both were entered in the 1922 Curtiss Marine Trophy Race.

A3325 (painted green, Race No.5) dropped out with engine trouble and A3326 (painted yellow, Race No.4) was in the lead when it ran out of fuel just short of the finishing line. As landplanes again, both were entered in the 1923 Liberty Engine Builder's Trophy Race for Service two-seaters. A3325 crashed during a trial flight and A3326 (Race No.3) broke its crankshaft during the race and was destroyed.

The first of the two Army 18T-1s was delivered to McCook Field for static test in February 1919.

When fitted with longer wings as either a landplane or seaplane, the Curtiss Wasp was designated 18T-2. The short-wing version became 18T-1 retroactively.

18T-2—Since the Navy had no urgent need for both 18s after the Armistice, A3325 was left at Garden City for further testing. A longer set of wings, with two bays of struts and a span of 40 ft 7½ in (12·25 m), was fitted, creating the 18T-2 designation. On 18 September, 1919, Curtiss test pilot Roland Rholfs set a new world's altitude record of 34,910 ft (10,640 m) with this aircraft. Fitted with floats, A3325 also set a world's seaplane altitude record.

In 1919, Curtiss built a fifth 18T as a civil aeroplane. Fitted with long wings, it was sold to Bolivia, where it became the first aeroplane to fly from the capital city of La Paz at an elevation of 13,500 ft (4,115 m). After consistent performance there it crashed on 19 May, 1921.

18B Hornet (Model 15A)—After introducing the 18T, Curtiss offered the same design with more conventional two-bay biplane wings and designated it 18B. This was known as Experimental 510 but was publicized as the Hornet. The Army ordered two in August 1918, with Army serial numbers 40058 and 40064. The first was delivered for static test in June 1919; the flight test aircraft crashed soon after delivery.

The Curtiss 18B (for biplane) was named Hornet and was identical to the Wasp except for the use of biplane wings.

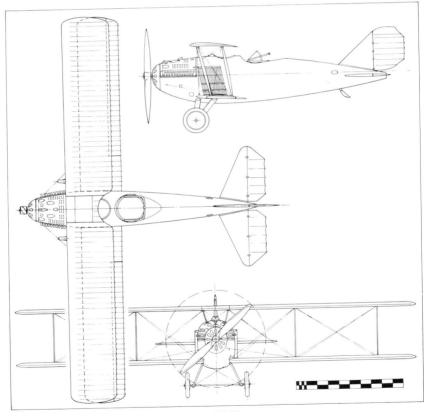

Model 18B Hornet.

Model 18T-1—Fighter/Observation landplane. Pilot and gunner/observer. 400 hp Curtiss K-12.

Span 32 ft (9·75 m); length 23 ft 4 in (7·11 m); height 10 ft 2 in (3·09 m); wing area 288 sq ft (26·75 sq m).

Empty weight 1,980 lb (898 kg); gross weight 3,050 lb (1,383 kg).

Maximum speed 163 mph (262·31 km/h); climb in 10 min—12,500 ft (3,810 m); service ceiling 23,000 ft (7,010 m); endurance 5·9 hr.

Armament—two fixed Marlin and three flexible Lewis machine-guns.

Model 18T-2—Fighter/Observation seaplane. Pilot and gunner/observer. 400 hp Curtiss K-12.

Span 40 ft 7½ in (12·25 m); length 28 ft 3⅞ in (8·63 m); height 12 ft (3·65 m); wing area 400 sq ft (37·16 sq m).

Empty weight 2,417 lb (1,096 kg); gross weight 3,572 lb (1,620 kg).

Maximum speed 139 mph (223·69 km/h); climb in 10 min—10,400 ft (3,170 m); service ceiling 21,000 ft (6,400 m).

Armament—one fixed Marlin and one flexible Lewis machine-gun.

Model 18B—Fighter/Observation landplane. Pilot and observer/gunner. 400 hp Curtiss K-12.

Span 37 ft 6 in (11·43 m); length 23 ft 4 in (7·11 m); wing area 306 sq ft (28·42 sq m).

Empty weight 1,690 lb (766 kg); gross weight 2,867 lb (1,300 kg).

Armament—two fixed Marlin and two flexible Lewis machine-guns.

# The Jenny

The Curtiss Jenny, to apply the popular name to the entire production JN series, was a design that achieved immortality through circumstances rather than by the normal criteria of competitive performance or a spectacular combat record.

The long production life of this model, its step-by-step evolution, its status as the principal American and Canadian primary trainer of World War I, and its unique position in the early postwar years of American civil aviation justify the devotion of a separate section of this book to this particular design.

The JN series began with the merging of the better features of the J and N models of 1914 into a new design. The name Jenny was an entirely logical phonetic corruption of the model designation JN. By coincidence, it was also a name eminently suited to that particular aeroplane. As with boats, aeroplanes are regarded by their crews as having feminine characteristics and Jenny was exactly right for the personality of the aeroplane.

The N series continued to develop separately but the Model J was dropped in favor of the JN. There was no officially designated JN or JN-1 model. The first JNs were ordered by the US Army late in 1914 as Service observation types; however, their successors were trainers. It has been said that over 95 per cent of the US and Canadian pilots trained during World War I flew a JN in some phase of their training. The JN-4 series became Model 1 in the 1935 designation system starting with the JN-4A.

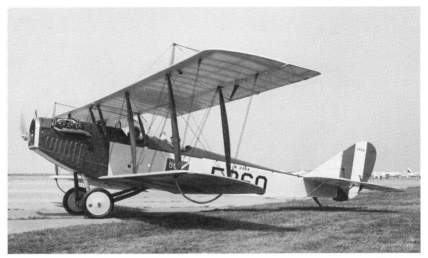

The JN-4D was the principal US Army primary trainer of 1917–18. This is a perfect restoration completed in 1967 by airline pilot Dan Neumann. (*Peter M. Bowers*)

With a good tractor trainer in production in America, it was logical for Britain to order the same model for its rapidly-expanding war training programme. The relatively largescale production that followed naturally led to rapid step-by-step refinement of the basic design. By the time the United States entered World War I in April 1917, the Jenny had reached the JN-4D model. Thanks to increasing US and British military orders, plus sales to neutral nations and American private owners, the Curtiss JN-4 was built in greater numbers than any other American model up to the time the US entered the war. Increased demand from Britain resulted in the establishment of a Canadian subsidiary, Curtiss Aeroplane and Motors, Ltd, in Toronto. This plant built JN-3s for Britain prior to being taken over by the Canadian Government and being renamed Canadian Aeroplanes, Ltd. The Canadian-built JN-4s became known as Canucks to distinguish them from the American built Jennies.

When the build-up of American airpower began after the country entered the war, the JN-4 was the only proven domestic design ordered into immediate mass production. A total of 6,070 Jennies, JN-4 to JN-6H, was delivered to the US Army out of 7,166 ordered after April 1917. These orders were placed with Curtiss, which delivered 4,895, and with six other firms. While the US Navy acquired 134 Jennies during the war and others after, most of the Navy's were transferred from the Army and are presumed to be included in the Army figures.

The price of a Jenny dropped steadily as the production rate increased, but rose again when larger engines were installed. Also, costs were different for similar models built by different manufacturers in 1917–18. Direct cost

144

comparisons between early and late models are invalid because the cost of the engines, instruments, and other government furnished equipment was not included in the contract price of Army aeroplanes ordered after the JN-4B.

The following JN-4 costs, taken from the *Congressional Record*, were established after the postwar investigation of aircraft procurement and the final settlement of the war contracts:

| | |
|---|---|
| JN-4, 4A, 4B | $8,160 (with engine, etc) |
| JN-4Can | $4,250 (airframe only) |
| JN-4D | $4,750 " |
| JN-4D-2 | $3,500 " |
| JN-4H, 6H | $4,750 " |

Contrary to current belief, the era of the cheap war-surplus aeroplane did not begin right after the war. The Army and Navy did not put their surplus aircraft on the open market immediately; instead, considering the condition of some of the machines, the government invited bids for their purchase from the manufacturers and other responsible organizations with overhaul and repair facilities. Under this arrangement, Curtiss bought $20,000,000 worth of aeroplanes and engines, mostly Jennies and OX-5s, for $2,700,000, or approximately 13 cents in the dollar.

Starting in mid-1919, Curtiss launched an advertizing campaign that emphasized the skillful factory reconditioning or overhaul of these aircraft that made them safe for public use. Jennies advertized as brand-new were sold by Curtiss for $4,000 late in 1919 and new OX-5 engines were priced at $1,000. Prices quoted by other organizations selling the same items were comparable or slightly lower.

The first JNs available to the American public from sources other than Curtiss were Canadian JN-4 Canucks exported from Canada by two firms, one was John Ericson, designer of the Canuck and the other was a new sales organization established after the war by the leading Canadian war aces William A. Bishop and William G. Barker. Late 1919 prices for Canucks in as-new condition were $2,600–$3,000.

Curtiss prices dropped only slightly in mid-1920, following largescale dumping efforts by firms disposing of British war surplus. Unused JN-4Ds were $3,250, rebuilds were $2,000 to $2,750, and Canucks reconditioned by Curtiss were $1,500. Rebuilt OX-5 engines were $750 and used OX-5 engines were $300 to $500 depending on condition. While the Jenny price was close to the original selling price, it was still relatively low compared to the only comparable postwar models then in production, the Curtiss Oriole at $8,000, down from $9,850, and the Laird Swallow at $6,500.

The day when an interested purchaser could go to a government warehouse and acquire a surplus Jenny for a few hundred dollars was still in the future and did not play a large part in the early postwar sales picture. Most of the surplus aeroplanes reached their first civilian operators through organizations that had bought in quantities with the intention of reselling. Toward the end of their days, Jennies were changing hands among the private owners for $500 to as little as $50.00. Unused OX-5s dropped to a standard price of $250 by 1928.

After the war, Jenny had two careers, one civil and one military. The military use resulted in additional designations being applied to existing aeroplanes, which are identified later in this section. The civil operations produced no new designations but did result in uses and configurations undreamed of by the original manufacturers. These two careers are described separately.

After the war the Army decided that the 90 hp Jennies were marginal even for primary training and quickly withdrew them from those military schools that were still in operation. The higher-powered JN-4H and JN-6H models with 150 hp American-built Hispano-Suiza engines were retained and few of these reached civil owners. Some 216 were transferred to or purchased by the Navy in the years 1920–23.

The Hisso Jennies remained the Army's principal primary trainer until new designs began to enter the inventory in 1925. Because funds were limited for new equipment but were available for maintenance and reconditioning, many JN-4H and 6H models were put through rebuilding programmes, conducted mainly at Army Air Depots that gave them the status of new aircraft even to the extent of sometimes receiving new Army serial numbers.

Basic differences between JN-4H and JN-6H models were eliminated during these programmes, from which they emerged with the new designation of JNS. This modification and rebuilding continued to the end of 1925, when the JNSs still formed the backbone of the National Guard Aviation Programme. The last US Army Jennies were withdrawn from service and scrapped in September 1927.

Jennies in the US Army inventory dropped from 3,285 in 1919 to 37 in 1927, their last year of service. The Navy, which had 76 in November 1919, ended 1926 with 22 examples on hand.

This transfer of a man from a speeding car to a JN-4C Canuck along the straight of a racetrack is representative of some of the Air Circus stunts performed during the Jenny Era of 1920–25.

The most memorable reputation of the Jenny was earned at the hands of civil pilots in the years 1920–26. This was the Barnstorming period of American aviation. Former military pilots, as well as some who had learned to fly after the war, bought surplus trainers by the hundreds and set out through the country to earn money by carrying passengers, putting on aerial circuses and doing other work. Since the Jenny was the most plentiful of several similar surplus models available, this period has since been referred to as The Jenny Era. Certainly the first aeroplane that a large segment of the American public ever saw, or got close to, was a Curtiss Jenny. The term Barnstorming resulted from the close parallel between these gypsy fliers, moving from pasture to pasture in search of customers, and the old travelling theatrical troupes that held their performances in suitable barns along their route.

Further antics of the Jenny Era. Gladys Ingle, a lady daredevil, transfers from the upper wing of one JN-4D to the lower wing of another. The kingposts on top of the wing were essential to her stance. The other Jenny has had the kingposts removed and the upper wing overhang braced with struts instead of wires.

The Jenny, along with the similar Standard J-1, was the world's best stage for the wing-walker's act. It had a handy maze of struts, a straight-across axle between the wheels, wingtip skid bows, low airspeed, and most important, king-posts on top of the upper wing. Without these posts, moving from one aeroplane to another and most above-the-wing performances would have been impossible.

While systems of aircraft registration and airworthiness requirements were adopted by most aviation user nations in 1919, the United States did not sign the agreement. Consequently, there was no required licensing or inspection of American aircraft or pilots until 1927. Pilots who had just soloed could and did carry passengers for hire on their next flight, and in machines so decrepit that they well deserved the appellation of Crate that was frequently applied to them.

The owners had an absolutely free hand in the matter of structural modification, too, and many weird adulterations of the Jenny were to be seen. A popular one was the fitting of upper wing panels in place of the short-span lowers. This had its practical aspects; the attrition rate of lower wings in cow-pasture operations was considerable and sometimes caused local spares shortages. It was easy to reverse the strut fittings on an upper wing, add a set of struts to replace the overhang wires, and have a long-wing Jenny.

Recognizing the fact that most of the drag of the Jenny was in the wings, several small firms developed replacement wings in the early 1920s. Some of these were biplane sets that attached to the original fittings while using deeper-section aerofoils and fewer struts while others were parasol monoplane wings that were of necessity attached a little aft of the original upper wing position. Some owners took a course opposite to the Long Wing and clipped the overhang from the upper wing.

The Jenny Era began to wane in 1925, when efficient new production designs were finally able to get a foothold in the market that had long been dominated by the cheap war surplus types. The final blow was administered by the adoption of Federal licensing requirements for both aeroplanes and pilots at the beginning of 1927. The Jennies could not meet the new airworthiness requirements. Some did qualify individually for C licences while others continued to operate as unlicensed but legally registered aircraft. As the various States fell in line with the Federal regulations, the horizons of the Jenny became more and more limited until by 1930 it was downright illegal in almost every part of the country.

A handful pursued legal careers after that date in Hollywood, when they performed in period aviation films. Some of these were extensively modified to look like other models that were not available for film work.

The birth of the antique or vintage aeroplane movement in the 1950s led to a renewed life for the few surviving Jennies that were not in museums or still in the Hollywood Squadron. Four were known to be airworthy in 1976, more than half a century after the peak of Jenny production. Even though they are in far better condition now than when they were new, they are not

A Long Wing Jenny, a JN-4H with the standard lower wing panels replaced by upper wing panels. Such alterations were made often by ingenious private owners. (*Taylor Maxey*)

Short-span Hi-lift wings were provided for Jennies by various builders. This JN-4D operated as a seaplane in Alaska into the early 1930s. (*A. Elliott Merrill*)

A Sikorsky monoplane wing fitted to a JN-4D. Sperry offered a similar installation. The registration's C prefix meant that the aeroplane was licensed for commercial operation but could not fly outside of the United States. (*Courtesy William T. Larkins*)

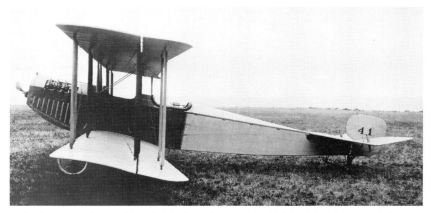

The first aeroplane with a JN designation was the JN-2 of 1915. The US Army bought eight with the equal-span two-aileron wings shown. The shoulder yoke for aileron control can be seen in the rear cockpit.

used in the old Jenny role of trainer or sporting aeroplane; they operate under experimental licences primarily for exhibition purposes.

Starting with the JN-2, the Jennies are presented here in ascending order of JN designation concluding with the Twin JN and the JNS. Since performance of models with the OX engines is so similar, the technical data table for the JN-4D is representative of all.

JN-2—Eight modified Js were ordered by the Army in December 1914. Since Curtiss considered these as having significant features of the model N, the type was eventually designated JN-2. Deliveries to the First Aero Squadron began in April 1915. The JN-2s moved with the squadron from San Diego to Fort Sill, Oklahoma, and then to the Mexican border, where

The Army's remaining JN-2s were all fitted with JN-3 wings of unequal span having ailerons on the upper surfaces only. (*Boardman C. Reed collection*)

early in 1916 they became the first US Army aeroplanes used in tactical operations.

The JN-2s had equal-span wings with the Eiffel 36 aerofoil and four strut-connected ailerons with shoulder-yoke control. Performance was poor and drew criticism from all levels of the Army. Curtiss improved matters somewhat in late 1915 by progressively updating the six survivors with JN-3 wings and then 100 hp OXX engines. In spite of certain obvious differences, the refurbished JN-2s were thereafter regarded as JN-3s.
US Army serial numbers: 41/48

A JN-3 used by the Royal Naval Air Service in 1915–16. The four-blade propeller was not standard.

JN-3—The JN-3s were evolutionary improvements of the JN-2 and featured a return to the unequal-span wings of the original modified J with upper-wing ailerons only. The control system was improved by a change to Deperdussin control featuring a wheel for aileron control and a foot bar for the rudder.

Britain bought 91 JN-3s starting in March 1915 and the US Army bought two in August. To expedite production for Britain, Curtiss established a branch factory in Toronto and twelve of the estimated 99 JN-3s were built there.
RNAS serial numbers: 1362/1367, 3345/3423 (Curtiss), 8392/8403 (Canada)
US Army serial numbers: 52, 53

JN-4—The JN-4, virtually identical to the JN-3, appeared in July 1916. While some were used by the US Army for observation, most became trainers. Britain acquired approximately 105 JN-4s; others were sold to private owners and some equipped the Curtiss flying schools. At unit prices of $7,750, the US Army bought a total of 21 JN-4s on six contracts prior to US entry into the war in April 1917.
US Army serial numbers: 76/81, 120/125, 130/135, 318/319, 468, 2265, 2266, plus one unknown

The first Curtiss JN-4 was virtually indistinguishable from the JN-3.

RNAS serial numbers: 3424/3444, 8802/8880, 8901, N5670/5673
British records show a total of 160 mixed JN-3, JN-4 and JN-4A, transferred from the Royal Naval Air Service to the Royal Flying Corps. These got new RFC serial numbers as follows:
JN-3/JN-4 5404/5408, 5624/5639, 5722/5728, 5910/5915, 6121/6124, 7310, A614/625, A898/903, A1254/1260, A5160/5168, A5215/5224, A5492/5524
JN-4 A3276/3280
JN-4/JN-4A A5492/5496, B1910/1950
JN-4A A4056/4060
JN-4A (Model 1)—The JN-4A of November 1916 was a major refinement of the JN-4 initiated at British request that crystallized the Jenny

The JN-4A was a later aeroplane than the JN-4B and used B-type tail surfaces. Distinguishing features were the engine down-thrust and increased wing dihedral.

152

configuration. Prominent external changes were new and enlarged tail surfaces, revised fuselage lines, six degrees downthrust for the OX-5 engine, four degrees dihedral for the wings instead of one, ailerons on both wings, and the trailing edge of the upper wing centre-section cut away to the rear spar. Two JN-4As (1262 and 1527) were fitted with 100 hp Hall-Scott A-7A engines as prototypes for a re-engined series.

An estimated 87 JN-4As were built by Canadian Aeroplanes as part of US Army and British JN-4 contracts. Six hundred and one of the 781-unit JN-4A total went to the US Army for $4,753,874. The Navy acquired five.
Known US Army serial numbers: 1057/1656 (600), 3925
Known Canadian serial numbers: C501/560 (60), C1015/1051 (37)
Known RNAS serial numbers: 8802/8901 (100)
Known RFC serial numbers: A4056/4060 (5)
US Navy serial numbers: A388, A389, A995/997 (5)

The JN-4B of 1916 was sold to both private owners and the US Army.

JN-4B (Model 1A)—The JN-4B was actually an earlier design than the JN-4A and introduced the revised fuselage and tail of the JN-4A. It had a level OX-2 engine, ailerons on upper wings only, and an uncut centre section. Introduced late in 1916, the JN-4B enjoyed brisk sales to civilians, and 76 went to the US Army for $8,000 each, including engine, propeller, and military equipment. Subsequent purchases were for airframes only, the government buying the engines, etc, separately. The US Navy acquired three direct from the factory and an additional six late in 1917 from the Curtiss Exhibition Company.
US Army serials: 141/176 (36), 229/264 (36), plus four in the 541/556 range.
US Navy serials: A157/159 (3), A4112/4117 (6)

JN-4C—Only two JN-4Cs were built as such by Curtiss. These were JN-4B airframes fitted with experimental wings using the RAF 6 aerofoil of the N-series in place of the JN's Eiffel 36. Both of these, fitted with Curtiss OXX-3 dual-ignition engines, went to the US Army in June 1917.
US Army serials: 471, 472

JN-4Can (Canuck)—The Canadian JN-4 evolved from the Canadian-built JN-3 independently of the Curtiss-built JN-4. Britain wanted more Canadian Curtiss trainers but was dissatisfied with certain features of the JN-3. The requested changes were made by F. G. Ericson, Chief Engineer of the newly-designated Canadian Aeroplanes Ltd, and the improved model, which flew in January 1917, was designated JN-4. Noticeable differences were a revised metal-frame empennage, strut-connected ailerons on both wings, and the use of stick for control instead of the JN-3's Deperdussin system.

Canadian JN-4 production was divided between Canada and the US Army, which acquired 680. Approximately 50 were transferred to the US Army from the winter flying schools that Canada had established in Texas in 1917. Some of these subsequently flew with a mixture of US and Canadian markings.

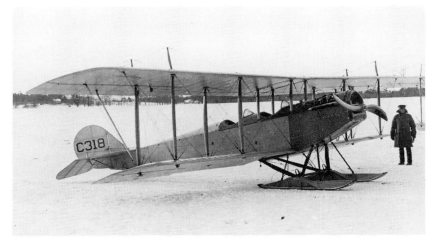

The JN-4Can Canuck follow-on to the JN-3 was developed in Canada. This one was the first aeroplane to fly on skis in Canada. The C-number on the rudder is the Royal Flying Corps Service number and should not be confused with US civil C-registrations issued from 1927.

Because of their Canadian origin and certain structural and control system differences from the American built models, these were given the designation JN-4 (Can) when purchased by the US Army. In paperwork this was often (and incorrectly) shortened to JN-4C. However, the pilots and mechanics promptly named them Canucks and the distinction was retained by civil pilots in the postwar years.

The exact number of Canadian-built JN-4s is unknown because some unfinished Curtiss-built JN-4As were completed in Toronto and some Canadian wings were fitted to JN-4A fuselages in Canada. The accepted figure is 1,260 JN-4 aeroplanes delivered as such, to which should be added

154

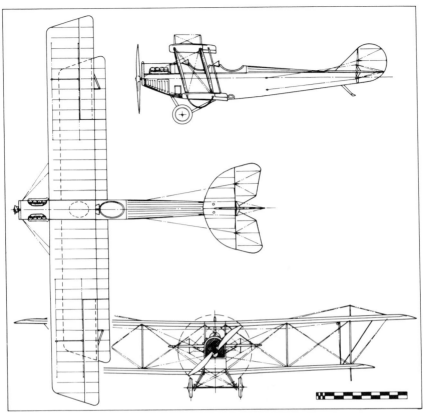

JN-4 Can (Canuck).

87 JN-4As for a total of 1,347. The spare parts produced would raise the total to the equivalent of 1,611 complete aeroplanes.

A few Canucks remained in Canadian Air Force service into 1924 and surplus models served Canadian civil aviation into the 1930s. John Ericson sold approximately 120 reconditioned or assembled from spares up to 1927 and adapted some to three-seat Ericson Special Threes. Bishop-Barker sold approximately 42 Canucks and Hoffa Brothers of Vancouver converted a number to single-float seaplanes.

Canadian military serial numbers assigned to Canucks are: C-101/500 (400)***, C-501/1450* (950)***, C-1451-1500** (7)

US Army serial numbers: 38533/38632 (100), 39062/39361 (300)

*C-501/550 (50), C-1015/1051 (37) are reported as JN-4A
** C-1457 is highest number known to be built
*** 280 random numbers to US Army

155

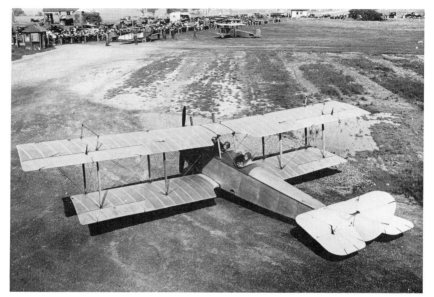

The prototype JN-4D of 1917 differed from the production models only in having ailerons fitted to upper and lower wings.

JN-4D (Model 1C)—The JN-4D was introduced in June 1917 and combined the stick control of the Canadian JN-4 with the lines and down-thrust of the JN-4A. The prototype had ailerons on both wings but the production models had them on the upper wing only. A distinctive feature was the curved cut-outs of the inner trailing edges of all four wing panels.

Deliveries of 2,812 JN-4Ds to the US Army began in November 1917 and continued to January 1919. Surplus JN-4Ds were the principal JN-4 models that established The Jenny Era.

While some Army JN-4Ds were adapted to gunnery and bombing trainers, no designation changes were involved; the only designated JN-4D subtype was the JN-4D-2.

Since Curtiss could not fill the demand, Army contracts for JN-4Ds were given to six additional manufacturers, including the already-producing Canadian Aeroplanes, which delivered some JN-4Cans on JN-4D contracts. The following table shows orders, actual deliveries, and costs, and identifies the variously-built JN-4Ds by serial number.

### JN-4D

Primary trainer. Two pilots. 90 hp Curtiss OX-5.

Span 43 ft 7⅜ in (13·29 m); length 27 ft 4 in (8·33 m); height 9 ft 10⅝ in (3·01 m); wing area 352 sq ft (32·7 sq m).

Empty weight 1,390 lb (630·49 kg); gross weight 1,920 lb (870·89 kg).

Maximum speed 75 mph (120·69 km/h); cruising speed 60 mph (96·55 km/h); climb to 2,000 ft (610 m) 7·5 min; service ceiling 6,500 ft (1,981 m).

The improved JN-4D-2 was intended to replace the JN-4D, but only this single example was built before the cancellation of war orders. The only outward difference was the level position of the engine relative to the downthrust of the JN-4D.

### JN-4D Production

| Manufacturer | Ordered | Delivered | Total cost | Army serial numbers |
|---|---|---|---|---|
| Curtiss Aeroplane & Motor Corp | 1,400 | 1,400 | $4,417,337 | 2525/3924 |
| | 3 | 3 | 27,653 | Navy A995/A997 |
| | 1 | 1 | — | 12876 |
| | 400* | 1 | 4,015 | 47816 |
| Fowler Airplane Corp, San Francisco | 50 | 50 | $ 323,166 | 2405/2454 |
| Liberty Iron Works, Sacramento | 100 | 100 | $ 450,206 | 3976/4075 |
| | 100 | 100 | 400,385 | 47415/47514 |
| | 100 | 0 | 151,775 | |
| Springfield Aircraft Co, Springfield | 400 | 400 | $1,981,736 | 4976/5375 |
| | 275 | 185 | 1,086,402 | 44257/44531 |
| | 300 | 0 | | |
| St Louis Aircraft Co, St Louis | 450 | 450 | $2,137,500 | 33775/34224 |
| | 200 | 0 | | |
| US Aircraft Corp, Redwood City | 50 | 50 | $ 326,170 | 39868/39917 |
| Howell & Lesser Co, San Francisco | 75 | 75 | $ 300,000 | 47340/47414 |
| | 100 | 0 | 94,121 | |

* JN-4D-2

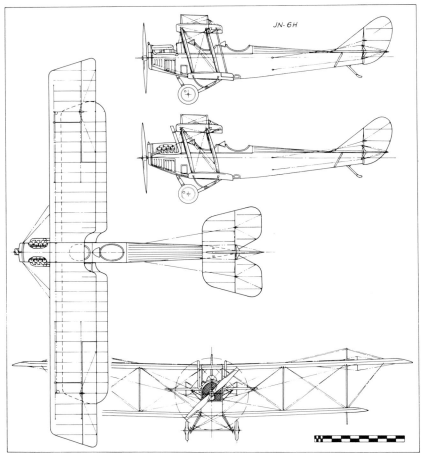

JN-4D and JN-6H.

JN-4D-2—At Army request, Curtiss made many minor structural and control system improvements on the JN-4D. The only noticeable outward change was elimination of the engine down-thrust. The first JN-4D-2, US Army serial number 47816, was delivered to Dayton for Army test in September 1918. Previously, orders totalling 1,100 production aircraft had been placed with the five firms then building JN-4Ds and were to follow them. All were cancelled at the Armistice before any but the first Curtiss example were built.

Curtiss marketed a few civil JN-4D-2s immediately after the war but ended production when the new Oriole became available early in 1919.

JN-4H (Model 1E)—As a wartime production expedient, the US Army decided to re-engine the JN-4D with a more powerful engine to make it an advanced trainer rather than develop entirely new models and then build new factories for their production.

The adaptation was easy for Curtiss, and the improved model was designated JN-4H, the suffix letter indicating the 150 hp Wright-built Hispano-Suiza engine instead of sequential sub-type development. Structural strengthening was undertaken, the fuel capacity was increased from 21 to 31 US gallons (79·5 to 117·3 litres), and a larger nose radiator resembling that of the N-9C was installed. Fuel capacity was increased further on some by converting the upper wing centre-section to an auxiliary

In the JN-4H series the 90 hp Curtiss OX-5 engine was replaced by the 150 hp Wright-Hispano. Note the enlarged radiator. This is the JN-4HB bomber-trainer version.

tank. The delivery of 929 JN-4Hs to the Army, all built by Curtiss, began in January 1918 and continued until the Armistice. Special-purpose variants were as follows:

JN-4HT—Four hundred and two of the JN-4Hs were delivered as dual-control JN-4HT, but this proper designation was not normally used. The Navy acquired 203 from the War Department between 1918 and 1923.
US Army serial numbers: 37933/38332, plus two from 42122/42125
US Navy serial numbers: A3205/3234, A6193/6247, A6271/6288

JN-4HB—Bomber trainer with flight controls in the front seat and fitted with racks for up to five 25-lb (11·3 kg) bombs under the fuselage. One hundred delivered from June 1918.
US Army serial numbers: 38433/38532

JN-4HG—Single-control gunnery trainer with either machine-guns or camera guns. The pilot's single Marlin machine-gun was synchronized to

159

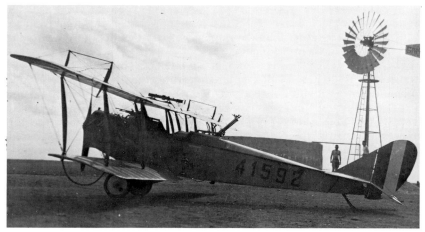

The JN-4HG was used for gunnery training. This example has a synchronized Marlin machine-gun for the pilot, two Lewis machine-guns in the rear cockpit, and a fixed camera gun on top of the upper wing.

fire through the propeller arc while his camera gun was often mounted on the top of the wing. The gunner-observer had the standard Scarff ring around the rear cockpit and one or two Lewis machine-guns or a camera gun. Delivery of 427 JN-4Hs to the Army began simultaneously with the JN-4HBs. The Navy got 90 of these in 1918 and assembled another from spares in 1923.

US Army serial numbers: 38333/38432 (100), 41411/41735 (325), plus two
US Navy serial numbers: A4128/4217 (90), A6545

Postwar Rebuilds—After the war, at least sixty JN-4Hs were rebuilt in Army depots as JN-4Hs and were given the following new Army serial numbers: 22-529/572 (44), 23-492, 557, 605/650 (46 mixed JN-4H, 6H)*, 937 (4H or 6H), 24-152/161 (10)

* 23-605/625 (21), 631/636 (6) rebuilt again as JNS-I with later serials.

### JN-4HG

Gunnery trainer. Pilot and gunner. 150 hp Wright-Hispano A.

Span 43 ft 7⅜ in (13·29 m); length 27 ft 4 in (8·33 m); height 9 ft 10⅝ in (3·01 m); wing area 352 sq ft (32·7 sq m).

Empty weight 1,625 lb (737 kg); gross weight 2,269 lb (1,029 kg).

Maximum speed 91 mph (146·44 km/h); cruising speed 75 mph (120·69 km/h); climb to 2,000 ft (610 m) 3·3 min; service ceiling 7,500 ft (2,286 m).

Armament—one fixed Marlin and one or two flexible Lewis machine-guns.

JN-5H—There were two short-term uses of the JN-5 designation. The first was an unofficial Curtiss designation for the model that came to be known as the Twin JN. The second was for an improvement of the JN-4H that would have sufficient speed and manoeuvrability to serve as a truly advanced trainer.

The JN-5 was a JN-4H fitted with short-span wings for improved performance but was not a success. The example illustrated is seen with experimental metal-frame JN-4H wings.

One JN-4H, Army serial number 38124, was taken from the Curtiss production line for conversion. Since this model was the subject of a separate contract, it was given the new serial number 41358. The aeroplane was inadvertently delivered with the JN-4H number painted on it.

As delivered in March 1918, the JN-5H had equal-span wings shortened to 30 ft (9·14 m) and a revised vertical tail shape. Two sets of wings, one with the RAF 15 aerofoil and one with the Eiffel 36, were supplied. The JN-5H was beaten by the Vought VE-7 in the fly-off competition, after which it was reconverted to JN-4H configuration and given its correct serial number.

Redesignated JN-4H, the former JN-5H served at McCook Field as a test bed, at one time being fitted with an experimental set of steel-frame wings (still with the JN-5 rudder) and later fitted with a 180 hp Wright-Hispano engine and a JN-4H rudder.

The JN-5 was reconverted to a JN-4H and used for test work at McCook Field. Here it is fitted with an early controllable-pitch propeller and an experimental rudder that incorporates a steerable tailskid.

161

The JN-6H models could be distinguished from the JN-4Hs mainly by the addition of ailerons to the lower wing. This first JN-6HB bomber-trainer is one of a very few to use the JN-5 form of fin and rudder.

JN-6 (Model 1F)—The JN-6 designation was applied to improved versions of the special purpose JN-4H trainers instigated by the Army through the JN-5. Principal outward difference was the use of strut-connected ailerons on both wings. Altogether, 1,035 JN-6s were delivered to the Army by Curtiss. Navy records show five plain JN-6Hs transferred from the Army (Navy serial numbers A5830/5833, A5859). All Army models had the following sub-designations:

JN-6HB—Single-control bomber trainer. The first of 154 delivered from July 1918 had the R-type balanced rudder of the JN-5, all others were as JN-4H.
US Army serial numbers: 41736/41885 (150), 44243/44246 (4)

JN-6HG-1—Dual-control gunnery trainers with a single flexible gun in the rear cockpit. Deliveries of 560 simultaneous with JN-6HB. Thirty-four went to the Navy.
US Army serial numbers: 44728/45287
US Navy serial numbers: Including A5470, A5471, A5581/5586

JN-6HG-2—Single-control gunnery trainer with one gun each for pilot and gunner/observer. Delivery of 90 began in October 1918.
US Army serial numbers: 44153/44242

JN-6HO—Single-control observation trainer. Delivery of 106 simultaneous with JN-6HG-2.
US Army serial numbers: 41886/41985 (100), 49117/49122 (6)

JN-6HP—Single-control pursuit trainer. Delivery of 125 was simultaneous with JN-6HG-2 and HO.
US Army serial numbers: 41986/42110

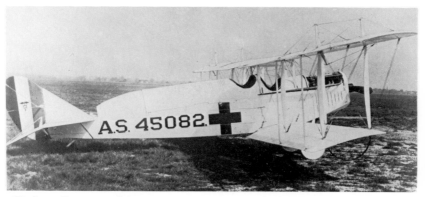

Various Jenny models were converted to ambulances with varying configurations. This one with raised housing for a stretcher case is a former JN-6HG-1 gunnery trainer. (*Courtesy John Amendola*)

Postwar Rebuilds—A number of JN-4Hs and JN-6Hs were rebuilt as such after the war in Army depots and were assigned the following new Army serial numbers: 23-554/556 (3), 23-605/650 (46 mixed JN-4H, 6H)*, 23-937 (JN-4H or 6H), 24-41/48 (8), 164/180 (17), 186/195 (10).

\* 23-605/625 (21), 631/636 (6) rebuilt again as JNS-I with later serials.

### JN-6HG-2

Gunnery trainer. Pilot and gunner. 150 hp Wright-Hispano A.

Span 43 ft 7⅜ in (13·29 m); length 27 ft 4 in (8·33 m); height 9 ft 10⅝ in (3·01 m); wing area 352 sq ft (32·7 sq m).

Empty weight 1,886 lb (855·47 kg); gross weight 2,580 lb (1,170·26 kg).

Maximum speed 81 mph (130·35 km/h); cruising speed 65 mph (104·6 km/h); service ceiling 6,000 ft (1,829 m).

Armament—one fixed Marlin and one or two flexible Lewis machine-guns.

This JN-6H-I was fitted with a 150 hp Wright-Hispano I engine and used for test work at McCook Field. Here it is seen equipped to launch an aerial gunnery target glider.

Starting in 1923, over 200 wartime JN-4s and JN-6s were rebuilt and standardized under the designation of JNS. Absence of lower wing ailerons made them resemble JN-4H models. (*Courtesy Henry R. Palmer Jr*)

JNS—The JNS designation appeared in 1923 and was applied to obsolescent JN-4H and 6H models modified and rebuilt by US Army Air Service Depots until 1926. The letters stood for JN Standardized and were sometimes followed by the letters A, I, or E to indicate use of the 150 hp Wright A or I engines or the 180 hp Wright E. These were all American-built versions of the French Hispano-Suiza given letter designations after Wright-Martin was reorganized as Wright Aeronautical Corporation in 1919. Outwardly, the JNS was indistinguishable from the JN-6H except that it had ailerons on the upper wing only.

The total of 247 JNS aeroplanes derived by adding up known serial numbers is only an approximation since some were rebuilt a second time and acquired new serials while others became JNS without a change of Army serial. The last JNS models in US Army service were scrapped in September 1927.

US Army serial numbers:
23-473/480 (8), 485, 486, 488/490 (3), 493, 494, 532/551 (20); 24-57/49 (3), 92, 93, 101/108 (8), 134, 135, 226, 227, 231/245 (15), 255/274 (20); 25-1/44 (44), 53, 56/68 (13), 74/77 (4), 84, 90, 129, 134/160 (27), 165/200 (36), 447; 26-1, 2, 4/14 (11), 16/20 (5), 22/28 (7), 31/35 (5).

The prototype Curtiss Twin JN was essentially a JN-4 enlarged to a twin-engined type. The propellers rotated in opposite directions. (*Courtesy Gordon Swanborough*)

The production Twin JNs differed greatly in detail from the prototype. This was the first for the US Army, Serial No.102.

Twin JN (Model 1B)—The Twin JN of April 1916, tentatively designated JN-5, was an enlargement of the new JN-4 model to a twin-engined type for observation work. Wing span was increased by use of an 11 ft 4 in (3·45 m) centre section for the upper wing and the installation of short panels between each lower wing and the fuselage. The standard JN-4 outer wing panels had one degree of dihedral outboard of the flat centre-sections on the prototype and $3\frac{1}{2}$ degrees on the production versions.

The need for increased tail area was met by installing a Curtiss R-4 rudder and an enlarged fin on the prototype and a modified R-4 fin on the production versions. Directional control was still marginal but was improved somewhat by modifying the starboard Curtiss OXX-2 engine to rotate in the opposite direction to that in the port side unit as was done on earlier Curtiss twin-engined flying-boats.

In spite of the two engines, the Twin JN was still only a two-seat machine and crew efficiency was greatly handicapped by the wide separation between the pilot's cockpit aft of the wing and the observer in the nose.

The US Army acquired eight Twin JNs in 1916 and early 1917, seven by direct purchase and one a donation to the Militia by private citizens. These saw very brief service on the Mexican border in 1916. The US Navy acquired two examples, which were operated as twin-float seaplanes.

Although delivered to the US Army in 1917 under the designation Twin JN, Serial No.428 appears to be an earlier and less refined design than the other Twin JNs.

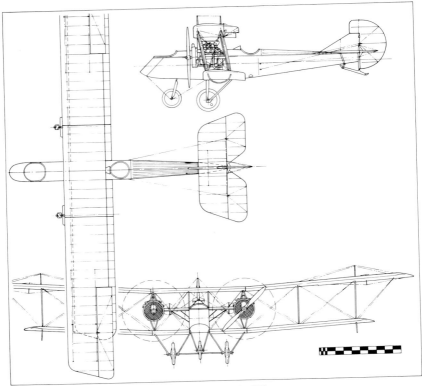

Production twin JN.

One Army model, serial number 428, differed greatly from the other Twin JNs. It was so retrograde in both aerodynamic and structural detail that in the absence of other evidence the author believes it to be an entirely different and somewhat earlier aeroplane, possibly the rumoured 'Twin R'. Since its general configuration was similar to the Twin JN, Curtiss doubtless found it easier to sell this existing aeroplane to the Army as a modified Twin JN than as a new and entirely separate design.
US Army serial numbers: 102/107, 428, 470 (delivery of 470 doubtful). US Navy serial numbers: A93, A198

### Twin JN

Reconnaissance aircraft. Pilot and observer. Two 90 hp Curtiss OXX-2.

Span 52 ft 9⅜ in (16·08 m) (upper), 43 ft 1¾in (13·15 m) (lower); length 29 ft (8·83 m); height 10 ft 8¹¹⁄₃₂ in (3·26 m); wing area 450·28 sq ft (41·83 sq m).

Empty weight 2,030 lb (921 kg); gross weight 3,110 lb (1,411 kg).

Maximum speed 80 mph (128·74 km/h); climb to 3,500 ft (1,067 m) 10 min; service ceiling 11,000 ft (3,353 m).

One example had a Lewis machine-gun.

# The Postwar Decade
## 1919–29

The decade from 1919 is extremely significant in the history of the Curtiss companies, which were able to survive the disastrous early postwar years without new aeroplane orders, the competition of surplus war material, and various legal crises, to retain their position as the leading United States aeroplane manufacturers.

This decade also provides a convenient period of corporate history and design technology that fits logically into a single section of this book. 1929 saw the merger of the existing Curtiss companies and the Wright Aeronautical Corporation to form Curtiss-Wright. The aeroplanes designed up to 1929 reflect the design concepts established in World War I and are therefore all closely related.

Even before the war ended, a rosy postwar future was pictured for civil aviation. Aeroplane development had made great strides under the stimulus of wartime demand. Large bombers and flying-boats had been developed that could easily be adapted to transports, and smaller two-seaters had proved themselves as mail carriers. The war-trained pilots would be available to fly the new commercial air routes and to instruct at new flying schools. Both the former military pilots and the newly-trained civilians would want new aeroplanes for their personal use. These, and new designed-for-the-purpose commercial models, would keep the existing factories busy.

With the cancellation of most military contracts following the Armistice, the entire aviation industry was cut down to a fraction of its wartime size. Curtiss closed all but two of its nine plants, one in Buffalo and the Curtiss Engineering Corporation at Garden City. The Willys motor interests withdrew and the company was in effect returned to its prewar operators. Glenn Curtiss returned to an active role in management with the title of Chief of Engineering. The presidency was assumed by Clement M. Keyes, who had been part of the motor group. With a very small amount of aircraft business to preside over, Keyes spent much of his time testifying on behalf of Curtiss and the rest of the aircraft industry before the various boards and committees investigating the wartime and postwar 'scandals'.

What military business remained in 1919 was mostly the completion of experimental models under development at the time of the Armistice and some modification of military models transferred from the Army to the Post Office Department as mailplanes. In spite of the reduction, for a few months optimism prevailed in much of the industry while new commercial models were rushed to completion in anticipation of the promised boom. Curtiss revived the Curtiss Exhibition Company, opened new flying schools, established dealerships throughout the United States, and even set up the Curtiss Export Company to handle anticipated foreign sales. It also bought the Army's Hazelhurst Field, adjacent to the Garden City plant, and renamed it Curtiss Field. When the boom failed to materialize, work on new civil models was abandoned in June 1920.

The immediate postwar military picture was no better. In spite of the charge that the US Air Services were equipped only with obsolete aeroplanes at war's end, there was no pressure from the taxpayers or the Congress to replace them with up-to-date equipment. 'The War to End Wars' had been won and there was no longer a need for large standing armies. The very junior air arm could get along on what it had. With their new models unable to compete with war-surplus machines in the commercial market and unable to obtain a share of the small military business that remained, many of the wartime firms were forced out of business by the early 1920s. A few survived on military orders for the rebuilding of wartime Service models, but Curtiss did not participate in this programme.

Thanks to its enormous resources, Curtiss was able to survive this critical period, but not by means of the originally planned programmes, which had been developed without consideration of competition from surplus war material. Surplus, in fact, can be credited with saving the company at this time.

In a move that became the subject of further scandals in the continuing investigation of wartime and subsequent military-civilian aircraft transactions, Curtiss bought some $20,000,000 worth of surplus aeroplanes, engines, and equipment from the War and Navy Departments for $2,700,000, or approximately thirteen percent of the original cost. One facet of the 'scandal' was that this huge deal, made in mid-1919, took place well before direct sales of surplus aircraft from the government to the public began. This was not an accusation against Curtiss. The reasoning behind such sales was that most surplus military aeroplanes were not in condition to be safely flown away by a new civil owner; they needed more refurbishment than the government was willing to undertake. Consequently, the government invited bids from the original manufacturers and other firms qualified to handle the work.

While Curtiss bought back many of its own aeroplanes and engines, most of them never used and needing nothing more than removal from the crate and subsequent assembly, it also bought several hundred standard SJ-1s. These were two-seat trainers very similar to Curtiss's own JN-4.

While Curtiss was able to dispose of most of the surplus aeroplanes by the end of 1920, the stockpile of OX-5 engines lasted into 1930. The K-6 (later C-6) engine, like the new commercial aeroplanes, couldn't compete with surplus types in the civil market and quickly went out of production.

Unused OX-5s, which had cost $1,800 new, were sold by Curtiss for $1,000 in 1919 but dropped to $550 by early 1921. The going price for a new surplus OX-5 was $250 in the late 1920s. The initial Curtiss sale prices for refurbished JN-4As, JN-4Ds and MF flying-boats were $4,000 for the trainers and $10,000 for the flying-boats. The JN-4 price, while nearly equal to that of some late OX-5 powered versions but below the overall average that the government paid for JN-4s, was still about half that of a new 1919 Curtiss Oriole.

Even with its early lead in the sale of surplus material, Curtiss ran into competition from its own products. There had been no anticipation of wholesale dumping of surplus aeroplanes by the government; initial re-sales to the manufacturers had been on a continuing basis and at a rate that fairly well matched the manufacturers' ability to sell them. This stable arrangement was upset in 1920 when serious efforts were made by the Aircraft Disposal Company in the United Kingdom to unload large quantities of surplus British aircraft in the United States. Industry tried every trick to resist this invasion, and even urged the government to ban them on the grounds that they were in poor condition and therefore unsafe. For once, the unsettled Wright patent suit was an asset to American industry, particularly Curtiss. The licence sold to Britain was for wartime use in Europe; surplus machines imported into the States were therefore subject to litigation.

The British threat did force the US Government to accelerate sale of its own surplus, however, and largescale advertizing campaigns were directed to the public by both the Army and the Navy, starting in May 1920. This, of course, forced the manufacturers to lower prices on the models then on hand. Again, Curtiss was able to draw on its reserves to survive the additional setback.

The patent situation was still a major headache. The controversial Wright patents had been transferred to Wright-Martin's successor company, The Wright Aeronautical Corporation, in October 1919. With the wartime need for co-operation over, Wright renewed litigation in September 1920. In later testimony before a Congressional Committee, Curtiss President Keyes declared that because of the unsettled patent situation, the Curtiss Company was seriously considering liquidation in mid-1920. Not only the Wright patent was involved; Curtiss had approximately 200 in its own name, some of them quite basic. One major legal matter that was finally resolved at this time was the Janin suit. On 15 December, 1921, the US Circuit Court of Appeals settled this in favour of Glenn Curtiss, finally establishing him as the inventor of the flying-boat.

To the benefit of the industry worldwide, the original Wright patent was quietly allowed to expire in 1923. The war-born patent pool, The Manufacturers' Aircraft Association, continued to operate, however, and embraced most US manufacturers. Curtiss sued several non-members for infringement of Curtiss patents but dropped the suits when these firms joined the Association.

In 1921, Glenn Curtiss removed himself from active participation in company affairs. Although retaining his position on the Board of Directors, he took extended vacation starting in the spring of 1921 and moved to Florida. There he became involved in ranching and profited enormously from Miami real estate transactions at the very beginning of the Florida land boom. With some irony he later remarked that he made more money in five years in Florida than he had in his entire career in aviation.

Following the 1920 decision to remain in operation, the Curtiss Company had only military business to look forward to, and a very peculiar business it was at this time. While there was a demonstrated need for new types, there was no rush on the part of industry to design and build new military prototypes of either aeroplanes or engines. If the Army liked a new test model well enough to want it produced, the originating firm had no assurance that it would get the order. In buying the prototype, the Government also bought the rights to the design. Bids for the desired number of production articles were then invited from the entire industry including the originator, who might or might not be the successful bidder.

Curtiss, with no prototypes of its own up for bids at this time, benefited from this policy. When the Army wanted 50 production versions of the Orenco (Ordnance Engineering Company) Model D fighter, designed late in 1918 and tested in 1919, Curtiss underbid Orenco and got the order in 1920. Orenco struggled on in search of other business for a while but closed down in 1922.

The following years saw continuation of this policy of Government ownership of purchased designs. When it became desirable to augment the night bomber force with an additional 110 Martin NBS-1 twin-engined bombers in 1921, the Government decided to help the ailing industry by awarding small orders to several companies. Curtiss was successful bidder for 50. Martin had only built 20 of its own design on an earlier order and was not in on the re-order.

Partly due to industry reluctance to invest its meagre funds in the development of new models that it might see others produce, the Army and Navy both expanded their wartime practice of developing new models of their own design and actually building prototypes. In this case, industry could bid on the production orders. Curtiss built production quantities of two Navy-designed models, the TS-1 fighter and the CS Scout, under this procedure (these two models bridged the times when delegated designs were built under the original Naval designations and when the designation of the actual manufacturer was used). A variation of this government-design policy was for the Army or Navy to work up a basic design on paper and then turn it over to industry for final detailing and the construction of a prototype. Curtiss came in for a share of this work, too, notably with the PN-1 night pursuit for the Army and the CT torpedoplane and the F4C-1 fighter for the Navy.

Although procurement policies were modified over several years to the increasing advantage of the designers, retention of proprietary rights in their own designs was not guaranteed to the companies concerned until passage of the Kelly Act in 1925. This legislation brought a degree of stability to the industry, opened up new markets, and helped prepare the industry for the 'Lindbergh Boom' of 1927–29.

Thanks to its excellent research and manufacturing facilities and its experienced staff of designers, Curtiss was able to maintain its wartime position as the leading US aircraft manufacturer throughout the 1919–29 period. However, all new aeroplane and engine business from late 1920 to 1925 was military. The main Curtiss contributions to the state-of-the-art in the early 1920s were the magnificent D-12 engine, the record-setting military racers, and the PW-8, the first of the postwar-designed pursuits to go into production. It took a combination of events to open up a significant commercial market in 1926. By that time, the majority of cheap war-surplus types in civil use were worn out, the Kelly Act laid the groundwork for the transfer of air mail operations from the Post Office Department to private contractors, and the country had recovered from the postwar economic slump to the point where interested private owners and commercial flying organizations could afford to buy newly-built aero-planes in sufficient numbers to support an industry.

The new Curtiss Flying Service, replacing the old Curtiss Exhibition Company, expanded the Curtiss-owned flying schools into a national chain and served as a demonstration and sales organization for the new commercial aeroplanes.

One notable addition to the Curtiss product line at this time was the Reed metal propeller. Dr Sylvanus Albert Reed developed a forged metal propeller in 1921 after obtaining Curtiss backing for the project. Curtiss manufactured this, starting in 1923. It was in wide use by the military until replaced by the ground-adjustable Standard (later Hamilton-Standard) of the late 1920s but remained in production for lower-powered fixed-pitch installations up to the Second World War.

There was nothing basically new about the aeroplanes of this period, however. They stayed close to the basic design concepts standardized in the First World War and showed only detail refinement. The most significant structural change was the replacement of the wartime wood-truss fuselage with welded steel or bolted aluminium tubing. Wings were still wooden frame into the 1930s. The basic military aeroplane was still an open-cockpit wire-braced biplane, and rear-cockpit armament on 1929 designs was still a pair of ·30-calibre Lewis machine-guns on a World War I Scarff mounting. It was in the commercial field, where the dollar advantages of more efficient monoplane designs had a significant and much more immediate effect on procurement policy, that the initial advances in new design were made. From the late 1920s into the mid-1930s, commercial models led the military into new design and structural concepts, notably monoplanes and all-metal construction.

All of the aeroplanes described in this section are presented in sequence of Curtiss model designation under the 1935 system, which matches the actual chronology very closely. The several non-Curtiss designs built by Curtiss between 1920 and 1924 are included in their proper sequence. Three notable aircraft series of this period are described in separate sections devoted to those particular models: The Curtiss Racers, the Hawk Biplane and the Falcon Biplane.

Three other models, the commercial Robin, Thrush, and Kingbird, are dealt with later. Although the prototypes were built at Garden City within this period, production was at the St Louis plant.

War-surplus Standard Aero Corporation Model J remodelled by Curtiss with JN-4B type nose and Curtiss OX-5 engine. The fuselage bears the former Army serial 22693 but the number on the rudder is 22677.

### Rebuilt Standard

Among the surplus aeroplanes that Curtiss bought from the US Government in 1919 were numerous model J-1s designed by the Standard Aero Corporation. These were also built under licence by the Fisher Body Division of General Motors, Wright-Martin, and Dayton-Wright. Since one of the major deficiencies of this model was the original 100 hp Hall-Scott A-7A engine, Curtiss reconditioned the J-1s to nearly-new and sold them for $3,500, approximately half the cost of a new machine. Wing area varied depending on whether the original ailerons or larger ones built by Curtiss to improve controllability were fitted.

#### OX-5 powered version

Trainer. Two pilots. 90 hp Curtiss OX-5.

Span 44 ft $10\frac{3}{32}$ in (13·68 m); length 27 ft $1\frac{1}{2}$ in (8·26 m); height 10 ft $4\frac{5}{8}$ in (3·16 m); wing area 429 sq ft (39·85 sq m).

Empty weight 1,448 lb (657 kg); gross weight 2,025 lb (918 kg).

Maximum speed 68 mph (109·43 km/h); cruising speed 54 mph (86·9 km/h); climb 410 ft/min (2·08 m/sec); service ceiling 9,250 ft (2,819 m); range 344 miles (553 km).

### C-6 powered version

Trainer. Two pilots. 150 hp Curtiss C-6.

Span, length and height as OX-5 version. Wing area (with large ailerons) 436 sq ft (40·5 sq m). Empty weight 1,500 lb (680 kg); gross weight 2,275 lb (1,032 kg).

Maximum speed 79·3 mph (127·61 km/h); cruising speed 63·4 mph (102·03 km/h); climb 710 ft/min (3·60 m/sec); service ceiling 9,750 ft (2,972 m); range 264 miles (425 km).


## Night Mail

The Curtiss Night Mail of 1922 was a quick attempt at adapting existing war-surplus aircraft to low-cost mailplanes for the Post Office Department. The aeroplane used was not a Curtiss, but the Standard J. It was given engineering Model Number L-411-1 but was overlooked on the 1935 redesignation list.

Other than the conversion of the front cockpit to a mail pit and the installation of a 160 hp Curtiss C-6 engine, the major change to the Standard was the fitting of entirely new wings. These were shorter than the 44 ft 10 in (13·66 m) of the Standard, were of equal span, with only one bay of struts, and used the new thick-section USA-27 aerofoil.

Approximately six were delivered and at least one was used by the Post Office as a two-cockpit utility aircraft rather than a single-seat mailplane.

Span 33 ft (10·05 m); length 26 ft 11 in (8·2 m); height 10 ft 3 in (3·12 m); wing area 364 sq ft (33·81 sq m).

Empty weight 1,704 lb (773 kg); gross weight 2,524 lb (1,145 kg).

Maximum speed 106 mph (170·58 km/h); cruising speed 85 mph (136·79 km/h); climb 800 ft/min (4·06 m/sec); service ceiling 12,000 ft (3,658 m); range 538 miles (866 km).

Curtiss Night Mail of 1922 fitted new Curtiss-design wings and Curtiss C-6 engine to the fuselage and tail of a war-surplus Standard J.

Big sales were expected for the OX-5 powered Oriole after World War I, but the new design could not compete with cheap surplus models using the same engine.

## Model 17—Oriole

The Oriole, also called Experimental 519 and Design L-72, was a new three-seat light commercial and sports aeroplane developed early in 1919 for the mass market that the aircraft industry optimistically expected to blossom right after the war. The Oriole was also the first of the new production Curtiss aeroplanes to be marketed under a bird's name rather than a model number, as was to be the Curtiss custom into the 1930s.

The first Oriole appeared in June 1919 and early sales seemed to bear out the builder's optimistic expectations even at the price of $9,850. Unfortunately, as war-surplus models came on the market, their enormous price advantage easily overcame the appeal of the Oriole's improvements and production was soon terminated. In 1921, Curtiss slashed prices to $3,000 for new OX-5 powered Orioles and $4,800 for the C-6 models to clear them out of the factory.

The Oriole was still a significant design, however. Its seating arrangement, pilot in the rear cockpit and two passengers sitting side by side in the front, with their entrance enhanced by anchoring the centre section struts ahead of the cockpit and adding a small door at the side, became the standard for practically all American three-seat biplanes built up to the mid-1930s. To achieve comfortable shoulder room without widening the fuselage unnecessarily, the front seats of the Oriole were staggered slightly. The added luxury of an electric starter, advertized as a standard feature of the Oriole, was an innovation that did not catch on with other light commercial aeroplanes for many years.

174

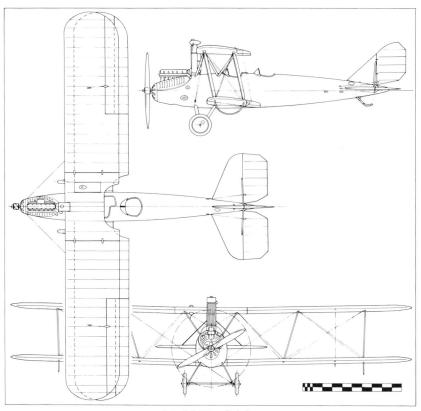

Model 17—Oriole.

Performance of the Oriole was improved by installing the 160 hp Curtiss C-6 engine and increasing the wing span by four feet. Earlier model did not have the sloping inner struts and rounded wingtips.

Designed by William Gilmore, the Oriole had the laminated wood veneer fuselage of the 1918 Model 18s and very JN-like two-bay wings with traditional thin aerofoil. Early Orioles were fitted with the surplus Curtiss OX-5 engine but this was quickly replaced with the 150 hp Curtiss K-6 and the 160 hp C-6. Even with this increased power the performance was short of expectations so the wing span was increased from the original 36 ft (10·97 m) to 40 ft (12·19 m). Long-wing Orioles can be recognized by the outward slope of the inner interplane struts and the rounded wingtips; the short-wing model had vertical struts and square wingtips.

Orioles with clipped wings and uprated engines did well in stockplane races of the early 1920s. This one, flown by Curtiss Flying Service manager 'Casey' Jones, introduced the wing surface radiators developed by Curtiss in 1922.

Although faring poorly in sales, the Oriole achieved a degree of fame at the hands of Curtiss test pilot C. S. 'Casey' Jones, who won numerous prizes in early postwar air races with his personal model. He constantly refined this and it ended up with clipped wings and revised strutting.

The exact number of Orioles built is unknown and only a few survived to 1927 when US civil aircraft were required to be licensed. Although never issued an Approved Type Certificate, some Orioles were licensed for commercial operation after 1927 on the basis of individual aircraft inspection.

### Oriole (short-span)
Utility aircraft. Pilot and two passengers. 90 hp Curtiss OX-5.

Span 36 ft (10·97 m); length 25 ft (7·62 m); height 10 ft 1 in (3·07 m); wing area 326 sq ft (30·28 sq m).

Empty weight 1,428 lb (648 kg); gross weight 2,036 lb (923 kg).

Maximum speed 86·3 mph (138·88 km/h); cruising speed 69 mph (111·04 km/h); initial climb 500 ft/min (2·54 m/sec); service ceiling 8,000 ft (2,438 m); range 582 miles (937 km).

### Oriole (long-span)
Utility aircraft. Pilot and two passengers. 160 hp Curtiss C-6.

Span 40 ft (12·19 m); length 26 ft 1 in (7·95 m); height 10 ft 3 in (3·12 m); wing area 399 sq ft (37·06 sq m).

Empty weight 1,732 lb (786 kg); gross weight 2,545 lb (1,154 kg).

Maximum speed 97 mph (156·1 km/h); cruising speed 77·6 mph (124·88 km/h); initial climb 700 ft/min (3·55 m/sec); service ceiling 12,850 ft (3,917 m); range 388 miles (624 km).

## Oriole Conversions

With the supply of cheap war-surplus aeroplanes exhausted by 1925, two firms sought to undercut the price of entirely new machines by fitting available components of unfinished short-wing Curtiss Orioles to new structure.

Curtiss-Ireland Comet—Mr G. S. Ireland, a Curtiss salesman at the time, acquired a supply of Oriole fuselages and obtained the assistance of Curtiss engineers in developing new wings for them. These used a later thick aerofoil, had the same 36-ft span but an area of 366 sq ft (34 sq m), and required only one bay of struts. This improvement raised the top speed to 99 mph (159·32 km/h) with the OX-5 engine and allowed a gross weight increase to 2,163 lb (981 kg). Alternate engines were the 150–160 hp Curtiss K-6 and C-6 and the 150–180 hp Wright-Hispano A, I, and E.

To produce this hybrid that he named Comet, Ireland established a small plant near the Curtiss Garden City factory. While the Curtiss company had nothing to do with the Comet, enough examples appeared in subsequent records as Curtiss-Ireland to establish a Curtiss identity.

Pitcairn Orowing—Harold Pitcairn, later of autogyro fame, established his own firm in 1923. In 1925 he took the opposite course to Ireland and fitted short-span Oriole wings, tail surfaces, and undercarriage to a new light-weight three-seat steel-tube fuselage and marketed the result as the Pitcairn PA-2 Orowing in open acknowledgement of the origin of the wings.

The Ireland Comet, erroneously referred to as Curtiss-Ireland Comet, was a short-wing Oriole with OX-5 engine fitted with new wings by G.S. Ireland in 1925. The wing roots were thinned to mate with the original Oriole fuselage and centre-section fittings.

177

The Curtiss Seagull was a civil version of the wartime MF flying-boat fitted with the 160 hp Curtiss C-6 engine.

## Model 18—Seagull

This was a refurbished wartime MF Navy flying-boat sold commercially in 1920. In spite of such improvements as the 160 hp Curtiss C-6 engine, sales were poor, approximately 16, because of direct competition from surplus Navy models and from other firms that offered their own rebuilt versions of the MF. Technical data as for MF except:

Empty weight 1,191 lb (540 kg); gross weight 2,726 lb (1,236 kg). Maximum speed 76·5 mph (123·11 km/h); cruising speed 60 mph (96·55 km/h); climb 260 ft/min (1·32 m/sec); service ceiling 5,900 ft (1,798 m); range 288 miles (463 km).

## Model 19—Eagle

The Eagle was a 1919 effort to produce a potential airliner for the anticipated postwar aviation boom that never materialized. Also designed by Gilmore, the Eagle used essentially the structural concept of the earlier Oriole expanded to airliner size.

The first Curtiss Eagle was a three-engined transport with 150 hp Curtiss K-6.

178

Many innovations were incorporated. Six to eight passengers were seated in a properly-designed cabin with adequate windows and built-in conveniences. The two pilots were also within the cabin, a distinct departure from the converted wartime bombers and Navy flying-boats then in use as passenger carriers. A bogie type undercarriage was used, featuring two sets of tandem wheels. An unusual feature of this gear was the use of a large streamlined metal fairing to cover most of each wheel, anticipating the use of the speed-enhancing pants that came into use in 1930.

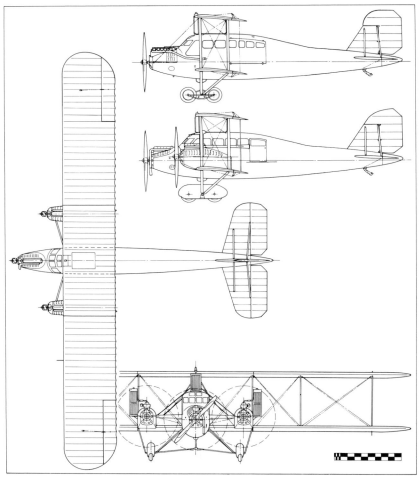

Single- and three-engined Eagle.

The second Eagle had two 400 hp Curtiss C-12 engines but made only one flight in that configuration. (*Courtesy Maumo Salo*)

Three-engined Eagle—The first Eagle was built as a trimotor powered with 150 hp Curtiss K-6 engines and the few production models used these or the 160 hp C-6.

Twin-engined Eagle—One twin-engined Eagle, powered with 400 hp Curtiss C-12s, was built. After the near loss of this version on its first flight due to loss of power on one engine at take-off, it was decided that 800 hp was too much for the Eagle airframe.

Single-engined Eagle—A single-engined version was developed to use the 400 hp wartime Liberty engine. The US Army Air Service bought three of these for ambulance and personnel transport work and assigned Army serial numbers 64241-64243.

The US Army bought three Eagles each fitted with single 400 hp Liberty engines. This one was specially equipped as an ambulance.

### Eagle I

Transport. Two pilots and six passengers. Three 150 hp Curtiss K-6 or three 160 hp Curtiss C-6.

Span 61 ft 4 in (18·69 m); length 36 ft 9 in (11·2 m); height 12 ft 4 in (3·75 m); wing area 900 sq ft (83·61 sq m).

Empty weight 5,130 lb (2,327 kg); gross weight 7,450 lb (3,379 kg).

Maximum speed 107 mph (172·19 km/h); climb in 10 min—4,075 ft (1,242 m); range 475 miles (764 km).

### Eagle II

Transport. Two pilots and six passengers. Two 400 hp Curtiss C-12.

Span 64 ft 4⅛ in (19·61 m); length 36 ft 7 in (11·15 m); height 12 ft 11 in (3·93 m); wing area 937 sq ft (87·04 sq m).

Empty weight 5,310 lb (2,408 kg); gross weight 8,690 lb (3,942 kg).

Maximum speed 124 mph (199·55 km/h); range 750 miles (1,207 km).

### Eagle III

Transport. Pilot and nine passengers. One 400 hp Liberty 12.

Span 64 ft 4⅛ in (19·61 m); length 37 ft $2\frac{9}{16}$ in (11·34 m); height 13 ft $6\frac{1}{16}$ in (4·11 m); wing area 937 sq ft (87·04 sq m).

Empty weight 4,245 lb (1,925 kg); gross weight 7,425 lb (3,368 kg).

Maximum speed 100 mph (160·93 km/h); climb in 10 min—5,000 ft (1,524 m).

The Crane was an amphibious version of the Seagull flying-boat.

## Model 20—Crane Amphibian

Introduced in 1924, this was an amphibious version of the Model 18 Seagull and an improvement over an amphibious version of an MF that the Elias Aircraft Co had developed for the US Navy in 1920.

181

The PN-1 Night Pursuit was a US Army design, the prototypes of which were built by Curtiss.

## Model 21—PN-1 Night Pursuit

This was not a Curtiss design but was built to details laid down by the Engineering Division of the US Army Air Service. The design was heavily influenced by the wartime German Fokker D.VII, particularly in wing structure and bracing and the welded steel-tube fuselage that became a first for Curtiss.

As originally completed, the PN-1 (P for Pursuit, N for Night) was not fitted with interplane struts. After it was determined that the cantilever wings were not torsionally stiff, the struts were added.

Of two PN-1s ordered, serials 63276 and 63277, only one was completed. This was statically tested at McCook Field without being flown.

### PN-1

Single-seat Night Pursuit. 230 hp Liberty 6.

Span 30 ft 10 in (9·39 m); length 23 ft 6 in (7·16 m); height 10 ft 3 in (3·12 m); wing area 300 sq ft (27·87 sq m).

Empty weight 1,631 lb (740 kg); gross weight 2,311 lb (1,048 kg).

Maximum speed 108 mph (173·8 km/h); climb to 6,500 ft (1,981 m) $5\frac{1}{2}$ min; service ceiling 23,900 ft (7,284 m); range 255 miles (410 km).

Armament—two ·30-in Browning machine-guns.

US Army serial numbers: 63276, 63277

## Model 24—CT Torpedoplane

This design was laid out by the US Navy Bureau of Aeronautics, and Curtiss completed only one of eight ordered (Navy serial A5890). The layout was quite unconventional, with a crew pod and engine nacelles built onto a fabric-covered wooden cantilever wing; the tail surfaces were supported by booms connected to the twin floats and the wing.

Fitted initially with two 300 hp Wright-Hispano H engines, the CT (Curtiss Torpedoplane in the emerging Navy designation system) was delivered to the Rockaway Naval Air Station near the Garden City plant on 1 May, 1921. It was returned to Curtiss in March 1922 for refitting with 435 hp Curtiss D-12 engines. The CT was struck from the Navy list on 9 November, 1923.

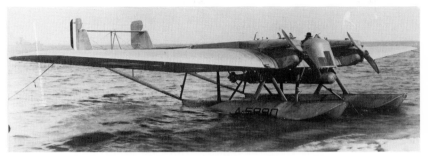

The CT was designed by the US Navy and built by Curtiss in 1921. This is the single example after being refitted with Curtiss D-12 engines in 1922.

### CT (Wright-Hispano)
Torpedoplane. Three crew. Two 300 hp Wright-Hispano H.

Span 65 ft (19·81 m); length 46 ft (14·02 m); height 14 ft 6 in (4·41 m); wing area 830 sq ft (77·1 sq m).

Empty weight 6,489 lb (2,943 kg); gross weight 9,884 lb (4,483 kg).

Maximum speed 100 mph (160·93 km/h); range 350 miles (563 km).

Armament—one or two ·303 Lewis machine-guns.

### CT (Curtiss D-12)
Torpedoplane. Three crew. Two 435 hp Curtiss D-12.

Span, length, height, wing area and armament as Wright-Hispano version.

Empty weight 7,684 lb (3,485 kg); gross weight 11,208 lb (5,084 kg).

Maximum speed 107 mph (172·19 km/h); climb 2,600 ft (792 m) in 10 min; service ceiling 5,200 ft (1,585 m); range 350 miles (563 km).

US Navy serial number: A5890

## Model 25—Seagull

Another civil modification of the wartime MF flying-boat marketed, like the Model 18, as Seagull. No information is available as to detail differences.

## Model 26—Orenco D

In 1918, the Army bought four examples of an experimental fighter developed by the Ordnance Engineering Co (Orenco) of Baldwin, NY. This design, Orenco's Model D, proved desirable as a production model for the postwar Air Service, so the Army, which owned the design under prevailing

Curtiss won the 1920 order for fifty production models of the Orenco Model D that had been developed by the Ordnance Engineering Company in 1918.

policies, invited bids from the industry for a lot of 50. Curtiss won the order; Orenco was unable to sell other designs and soon shut down.

The Orenco D, modified only slightly by Curtiss to have a longer upper wing and horn-balanced ailerons, was an all-wood single-seater featuring a ply-covered fuselage and the American version of the 300 hp French Hispano-Suiza engine built by Wright as its Model H. It was, in fact, the only single-seat fighter with plywood fuselage ever to serve in the Army. Some were diverted to test work with French Lamblin 'Pineapple' radiators and turbo-superchargers, but the nose radiator installation of the prototypes was standard.

### Orenco D

Single-seat Pursuit. 300 hp Wright-Hispano H.

Span 33 ft (10·05 m); length 21 ft 5½ in (6·54 m); height 8 ft 4 in (2·53 m); wing area 273 sq ft (25·36 sq m).

Empty weight 1,908 lb (865 kg); gross weight 2,820 lb (1,279 kg).

Maximum speed 139 mph (223·69 km/h); cruising speed 133 mph (214 km/h); climb 1,140 ft/min (5·79 m/sec); service ceiling 12,450 ft (3,795 m); range 340 miles (547 km).

Armament—two ·30-in Browning machine-guns.

US Army serial numbers: 40107/40110 (Orenco), 63281/63330 (Curtiss)

## Model 28—Navy TS-1

In 1921, the US Navy designed an all-wood fighter specifically for operation from its soon-to-be-commissioned aircraft carrier the USS *Langley*. Bids for production were invited from industry and Curtiss won the order for 34 examples. As a check on costs, the Naval Aircraft Factory built five TS-1s plus four experimental versions. Their serial numbers are presented with those of the Curtiss-built TS-1s for identification purposes.

The TS-1 had several odd features. Most notable were the raising of the fuselage above the lower wing, the longer span of the lower wing, and the

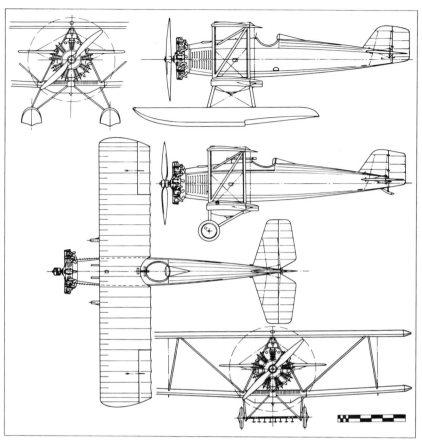

Model 28—Navy TS-1.

The TS-1 was designed by the US Navy. These were the Navy's first carrier-based fighters and could also operate as twin-float seaplanes.

185

use of diagonal struts to eliminate wing rigging wires. A droppable fuel tank was built into the lower wing centre section. Also, the TS-1 was the first production US fighter to use the new air-cooled radial engine (the Lawrence J-1) even though 200 hp was low by the fighter standards of the time. Cost less GFE was $9,569 each for the first eleven and $9,975 for the remainder.

### TS-1 (landplane)

Single-seat shipboard fighter. 200 hp Lawrence J-1.

Span 25 ft $0\frac{5}{16}$ in (7·62 m); length 22 ft $1\frac{3}{16}$ in (6·73 m); 8 ft $11\frac{15}{16}$ in (2·74 m); wing area 227·8 sq ft (21·16 sq m).

Empty weight 1,239 lb (562 kg); gross weight 1,927·5 lb (874·29 kg).

Maximum speed 131 mph (210·82 km/h); cruising speed 104·8 mph (168·65 km/h); climb 1,280 ft/min (6·5 m/sec); service ceiling 14,400 ft (4,389 m); range 468 miles (753 km).

Armament—two ·30-in machine-guns.

### TS-1 (seaplane)

As landplane except: Length 24 ft $9\frac{3}{16}$ in (7·54 m); height 9 ft $6\frac{13}{16}$ in (2·91 m).

Empty weight 1,443 lb (654·5 kg); gross weight 2,153 lb (976·58 kg).

Maximum speed 121 mph (194·72 km/h); cruising speed 96·8 mph (155·78 km/h); climb 930 ft/min (4·72 m/sec); service ceiling 13,500 ft (4,115 m); range 420 miles (674 km).

US Navy serial numbers: A6248/6270 (Curtiss), A6300/6304 (NAF)

The SX4-1 water glider was Glenn Curtiss's last direct effort at aircraft design.

## Model 29—SX4-1 Water Glider

In 1922, Glenn Curtiss initiated the development of a single-seat flying-boat type glider for use on the extensive water areas near his new home in Florida. Resembling a scaled-down NC flying-boat, the glider was to be towed into the air behind a speedboat. The original factory designation of SX4-1 does not conform to any known Curtiss designating system.

Span 28 ft (8·53 m); length 22 ft 11 in (6·79 m); wing area 280 sq ft (26 sq m). Empty weight 150 lb (68 kg). Towing speed 30 mph (48·27 km/h).

186

In 1921–22 Curtiss built fifty Martin MB-2 bombers under the US Army designation NBS-1.

## Model 30—NBS-1 Night Bomber

Curtiss's experience with large aircraft structures was limited to flying-boats during World War I and early 1919. Curtiss got into the landplane bomber business in a roundabout way when it underbid the Glenn L. Martin Co for a production lot of 50 Martin-designed NBS-1s (Night Bomber Short-Range) in 1921. The Army had originally ordered 20 from Martin under Martin's designation of MB-2. Duplicates ordered later were given the NBS-1 designation adopted under the new Army aircraft designation system of 1920.

Since the design was owned by the Army under prevailing policy, bids were invited from industry for further production. Because of the depressed state of the industry in the early postwar years, the splitting up of big orders was officially encouraged in order to give work to firms that needed it. Aeromarine Plane and Motor Co of Keyport, NJ, built 25 NBS-1s and L.W.F. of College Point, LI, built 35. However, this work did not save either company; both closed down soon after completing their NBS-1s. Aeromarine reopened in 1929, but L.W.F. went out of business permanently.

The NBS-1 was a thoroughly conventional bomber of the period, with all-wood framework and fabric covering. An advanced feature was the use of a single-wheel undercarriage unit under each engine. To simplify housing such a large machine, the wings folded aft just outboard of the engines.

187

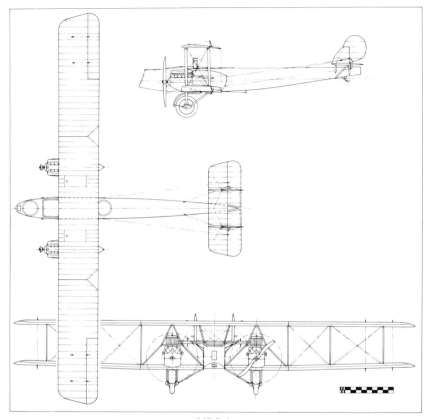

NBS-1.

The last 20 Curtiss-built NBS-1s, all of which were built at Garden City, were fitted with the new General Electric turbo-superchargers and were the first aeroplanes to use the devices in production quantities. Some NBS-1s remained in service into 1928.

### NBS-1

Short-range night-bomber. Four crew. Two 420 hp Liberty.

Span 74 ft 2 in (22·6 m); length 42 ft 7¾ in (12·99 m); height 14 ft 8 in (4·47 m); wing area 1,121 sq ft (104·14 sq m).

Empty weight 7,268 lb (3,296 kg); gross weight 12,064 lb (5,472 kg).

Maximum speed 98·7 mph (158·83 km/h); cruising speed 79 mph (127·13 km/h); climb 193 ft/min (0·98 m/sec); service ceiling 8,500 ft (2,591 m).

Armament—five ·30-in machine-guns, 1,334 lb (605 kg) bombs.

US Army serial numbers: 64195/64214 (Martin-20), 68437/68471 (L.W.F.-35), 68478/68527 (Curtiss-50), 22-201/225 (Aeromarine-25)

The CS-1 was a US Navy design built by Curtiss in 1922. The Naval torpedo recessed into the underside of the fuselage.

### Model 31—CS Scout

The CS was a multi-purpose scout-bomber-torpedoplane designed by the US Navy Bureau of Aeronautics. As with the Navy-designed TS, Curtiss won competitive bidding for a production order. In this case, however, Curtiss was recognized as the manufacturer in the aircraft designation, the letters CS identifying the aeroplane as Curtiss Scout in the initial Naval designation system of 1922–23.

The basic design of the CS was inspired by the earlier Douglas DT landplane or twin-float torpedoplane, improved primarily by the use of the later 530 hp Wright T-2 engine. Several features of the CS influenced subsequent Curtiss designs—the fuselage was welded steel-tubing and the unique feature of a bottom wing longer than the upper, previously seen at Curtiss on the TS fighter, was to reappear in the Curtiss Carrier Pigeon and Lark. The folding wing of the CS was not new, being a feature of the Martin-designed NBS-1. A unique design feature was a channel in the belly to receive the standard Naval torpedo, which was too long for complete internal stowage. Standard crew was three—a pilot and rear gunner in two tandem cockpits and a torpedoman/bomb-aimer inside the fuselage where he also had access to a machine-gun firing through a port in the belly.

CS-1 (Model 31)—Six were ordered in June 1922 with Navy serial numbers A6500/6505; first flight was in November 1922. One CS-1, A6502, was converted to the CS-2 prototype.

The Glenn L. Martin Co, mindful of how Curtiss had underbid it for a 50-aircraft Army order for Martin's own MB-2 bomber, underbid Curtiss for additional CS-1s; 35, serials A6801/6835, were built by Martin under the Curtiss designation but with the letters reversed as SC-1 in the post-1923 designation system. Unit costs were $25,200 less GFE. CS-1 A6501 was sent to Martin as a sample.

189

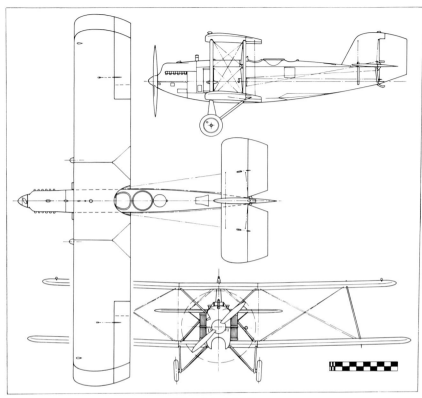

CS-1 (Model 31).

This CS-2 tested the new Curtiss wing surface radiators on a Navy Service aeroplane. The engine starting handle can be seen.

CS-2 (Model 31A)—Two improved CS-2s, featuring 600 hp Wright T-3 engines, were ordered as such (A6731, 6732) and CS-1 A6502 was converted by engine change. A6502 also featured the first application of the famous Curtiss wing surface radiators to a US Navy Service aeroplane. A6731 was converted to CS-3.

As with the CS-1, Martin underbid Curtiss for further CS-2 orders; 40 were built under the designation of SC-2 (A6928/6967), at unit costs of $19,863 less GFE.

**CS-1 (landplane)**

530 hp Wright T-2.

Span 56 ft 6 in (17·22 m); length 38 ft 5⅜ in (11·71 m); height 15 ft 2½ in (4·63 m); wing area 856·4 sq ft (79·55 sq m).

Empty weight 4,690 lb (2,127 kg); gross weight 7,908 lb (3,587 kg).

Maximum speed 105 mph (168·97 km/h); cruising speed 84 mph (135·18 km/h); climb 450 ft/min (2·6 m/sec); service ceiling 7,200 ft (2,195 m); range 570 miles (917 km).

Armament—two ·30-in machine-guns, one 1,618 lb (734 kg) torpedo.

**CS-1 (seaplane)**

As landplane except: Length 40 ft 3½ in (12·28 m); height 16 ft 0½ in (4·88 m).

Empty weight 5,390 lb (2,445 kg); gross weight 8,670 lb (3,933 kg).

Maximum speed 102 mph (164·15 km/h); cruising speed 81·5 mph (131·15 km/h); climb 435 ft/min (2·2 m/sec); service ceiling 5,250 ft (1,600 m); range 557 miles (896 km).

CS-3—CS-2 A6731 was redesignated CS-3 by the Navy following the change to a geared T-3 engine in November 1924. Martin then refined the design and produced 124 as the T3M-1 and T3M-2.

CS-4—Converted by Navy, details unknown.

CS-5—Converted by Navy, details unknown.

XSC-6—Martin SC-1 A6835 with 730 hp Packard 1A-2500 engine.

SC-6—Martin SC-1 A6834 with Packard 1A-2500 engine.

XSC-7—Conversion of CS-1 A6503 operated as a torpedo-bomber with T-3A engine at a gross weight of 8,609 lb (3,905 kg) on wheels and 9,343 lb (4,238 kg) on floats.

## Model 36—NBS-4 Night Bomber

In 1922, Curtiss received an experimental contract from the Army to develop two examples of a night bomber intended to replace the Martin-designed NBS-1 that was then the Army's only twin-engined bomber in squadron service. These were designated NBS-4 (XNBS-4 by time of delivery). Other manufacturers were also given contracts to develop new bombers.

The Curtiss effort, undertaken at Garden City, was essentially a refined NBS-1 using a welded steel-tube fuselage instead of wood but the same Liberty engines. The major aerodynamic change was adoption of the new and much thicker Curtiss C-72 aerofoil in place of the 1915-vintage RAF 15 of the NBS-1. One innovation was to build the bomb-aimer's window into

The NBS-4 was Curtiss's own improved version of the Martin-designed NBS-1 and had a welded steel-tube fuselage in place of wood.

an offset on the port side of the fuselage instead of under the nose gunner's station as in traditional installations.

The defensive armament of the XNBS-4 was originally like that of the NBS-1, with nose, top aft fuselage, and belly positions for single or double Lewis machine-guns. One NBS-4 was modified to extend each engine nacelle to a point well aft of the wing trailing edge to form a cockpit for a gunner who was provided with a standard World War I type Scarff machine-gun mounting. The idea was not new, having been tried on both British and German experimental bombers during the war.

The NBS-4s did not win a production order but they provided Curtiss with design experience that culminated with the successful Condor bomber and transport series of 1927–29. The first NBS-4 was delivered in May 1924 and was surveyed in July 1930 with 717 hours.

### NBS-4

Short-range night bomber. Four crew. Two 435 hp Liberty 12.

Span 90 ft 2 in (27·48 m); length 46 ft 5 in (14·14 m); height 15 ft 9 in (4·8 m); wing area 1,524·4 sq ft (141·6 sq m).

Empty weight 7,864 lb (3,567 kg); gross weight 13,795 lb (6,257 kg).

Maximum speed 100·2 mph (161·25 km/h); cruising speed 82·9 mph (133·41 km/h); climb 283 ft/min (1·43 m/sec); service ceiling 11,100 ft (3,383 m); range 728 miles (1,171 km).

Armament—five ·30-in machine-guns, 2,100 lb (952 kg) bombs.

US Army serial numbers: 68571, 68572

## Model 39—Curtiss-Hall F4C-1

Recognizing that the wood-and-wire type of construction was becoming outmoded, the US Navy encouraged the development of metal airframes. For comparative purposes, Curtiss was given a contract to produce two aluminium-frame versions of the established TS-1 shipboard fighter. Engineer Charles Ward Hall then developed the model designated

F4C-1 by the Navy but made some minor configuration changes in the process, the most notable being to raise the lower wing to the bottom of the fuselage.

Because of Hall's role in the project, the F4C-1 was sometimes referred to as a Curtiss-Hall rather than a plain Curtiss. Hall soon left Curtiss and gained further fame as a builder of aluminium airframes. Although it was purely an experimental design, the F4C-1 did not carry an X-prefix because the Navy did not identify experimentals as such until 1927.

The F4C-1 was an experimental metal-frame version of the Navy-designed TS-1 developed by Curtiss.

The designation is a bit confusing. Although it was the first actual Curtiss fighter design for the Navy under the new designation system, it was given the designation F4C because the earlier Curtiss racers, CR, R2C, and R3C, had equivalent fighter designations in their Navy paperwork. The next Curtiss fighter design skipped the F5C designation and became F6C. This was because of the large number of wartime F-5L flying-boats, some built by Curtiss, still in service under their original designations; the presence of two different F-5 models in the inventory would have been confusing.

### F4C-1

Single-seat fighter. 200 hp Lawrence J-1.

Span 25 ft (7·62 m); length 18 ft 4 in (5·58 m); height 8ft 4½ in (2·55 m); wing area 172·7 sq ft (16·04 sq m).

Empty weight 1,029 lb (467 kg); gross weight 1,703 lb (772 kg).

Maximum speed 125 mph (201·16 km/h); cruising speed 100 mph (160·93 km/h); climb 1,520 ft/min (7·72 m/sec); service ceiling 19,900 ft (6,065 m); range 470 miles (756 km).

Armament—two ·30-in machine-guns.

US Navy serial numbers: A6689, 6690

Illustrated is the prototype built for the Post Office mailplane competition of 1925. The Carrier Pigeon was Curtiss's first commercial design effort after 1919.

## Model 40—Carrier Pigeon

The Carrier Pigeon was developed at Garden City as the Curtiss entry in the 1925 US Post Office competition for a single-seat mailplane to be powered with the Liberty engine. The Post Office bought most of the prototypes entered, including the Curtiss. Ten improved models were built for National Air Transport (NAT) after the government mail routes began to be turned over to private contractors in 1926.

Wings were wooden framed, with welded steel-tube fuselage and aluminium frame tail. The most unusual design feature was the interchangeability of upper and lower wings. With no centre section and the lower wings separated by the fuselage, the lower wing had greater span. Ailerons, rudder, and elevators were also interchangeable as were the fin and tailplane. Aerofoil was the thick USA-27.

No licence numbers were assigned to the Carrier Pigeons when they were built, but the prototype was given Post Office Fleet Number 602. This became C27 after sale to NAT, and those built for NAT became C28/37 when licensing was adopted in 1927. C30 became R9344 and C35 became NR354. C/ns K-5015-1/K-5015-11.

### Carrier Pigeon

Single-seat mail and express carrier. 400 hp Liberty 12.

Span 41 ft 11 in (12·77 m); length 28 ft 9½ in (8·77 m); height 12 ft 1 in (3·68 m); wing area 505 sq ft (46·91 sq m).

Empty weight 3,603 lb (1,634 kg); gross weight 5,620 lb (2,549 kg).

Maximum speed 125 mph (201·16 km//h); cruising speed 105 mph (168·97 km/h); initial climb 800 ft/min (4·06 m/sec); service ceiling 12,800 ft (3,901 m); range 525 miles (845 km).

Payload 1,000 lb (454 kg).

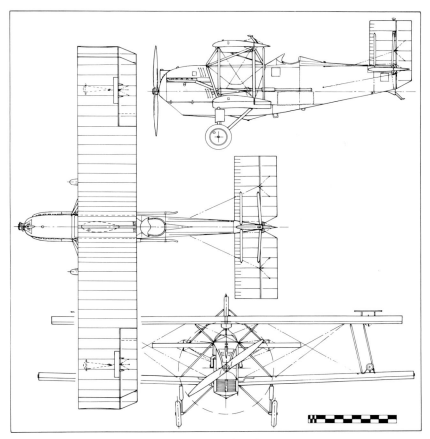

Model 40—Carrier Pigeon.

## Carrier Pigeon II

Three new mail/express aircraft were built at Garden City in 1929 as Carrier Pigeon II, also known as Carrier Pigeon CO. Using the geared water-cooled Conqueror engine, these were entirely new designs but were overlooked in the redesignations of 1935. Wooden framed wings with Curtiss C-72 aerofoil and box spars, aluminium frame tail surfaces, and aluminium fuselage with sheet monocoque structure forward and riveted aluminium tubing aft. The main fuel supply (175 US gallons—662·4 litres) was carried in a belly tank and pumped to a gravity tank in the upper port wing.

ATC No.237 was issued on 25 September, 1929, and all three aeroplanes were delivered to National Air Transport.
Registrations: 958A, 311N, 369N. C/ns: G-1/G-3.

195

The Carrier Pigeon II was a 1929 design that resembled the 1925 model only in being a single-seat mail and cargo carrier. The NC registration prefix meant that the aeroplane had a full commercial licence and could fly internationally.

### Carrier Pigeon II (CO)

Single-seat mail and express carrier. 600 hp Curtiss G1V-1570.

Span 47 ft 5⅜ in (14·46 m); length 34 ft 6¼ in (10·52 m); height 13 ft 5 in (4·08 m); wing area 550 sq ft (51·09 sq m).

Empty weight 4,235 lb (1,921 kg); gross weight 7,600 lb (3,447 kg).

Maximum speed 150 mph (241·39 km/h); cruising speed 128 mph (205·99 km/h); initial climb 780 ft/min (3·96 m/sec); service ceiling 14,200 ft (4,328 m); range 650 miles (1,046 km).

## Model 41 — Lark

The Lark was a companion 1925 design to the Carrier Pigeon and was essentially a scaled-down version of it intended for the private owner market. The parts interchangeability feature was retained. Two passengers were seated side by side in the front cockpit with another to the left of the pilot in the rear cockpit. The front cockpit could be converted quickly to a mail-cargo compartment and provision was made for an attachable belly cargo container. Initially powered with the then out-of-production 160 hp Curtiss C-6 engine as an economy measure, the Lark was also tried with the 180 hp war-surplus Wright-Hispano E, also out of production. These were both unacceptable to the commercial market, so the new 200 hp Wright J-4 air-cooled radial engine was installed. The J-4 version was also tested as a single-float seaplane. No sub-model designations were issued as a result of these changes and no c/ns are on record.

Competition from still-plentiful war surplus types and lighter contemporary designs with engines ranging from the OX-5 to the J-4 was too strong and only three Larks were built. One J-4 model saw brief service as a mailplane on the New York–Boston route of Colonial Air Transport; its 1926 letter registration N-AABC was changed to the 1927 number 1052 before the aeroplane was destroyed in a hangar fire in March 1927.

The Curtiss Lark was a scaled-down Carrier Pigeon for private and sporting use. The prototype with 160 hp Curtiss C-6 engine is seen at the 1925 National Air Races.

### Lark

Utility biplane. Pilot and up to three passengers or mail/cargo. 160 hp Curtiss C-6.

Span 30 ft 7½ in (9·33 m); length 22 ft 2½ in (6·76 m); height 8 ft 11 in (2·71 m); wing area 264·3 sq ft (24·55 sq m).

Empty weight 1,579 lb (716 kg); gross weight 2,449 lb (1,111 kg).

Maximum speed 114 mph (183·46 km/h); cruising speed 97 mph (156·1 km/h); climb 860 ft/min (4·36 m/sec); service ceiling 12,500 ft (3,810 m); range 440 miles (708 km).

Weights and performance with 200 hp Wright J-4: Empty weight 1,526 lb (692 kg); gross weight 2,708 lb (1,228 kg).

Maximum speed 117 mph (188·29 km/h); cruising speed 101 mph (162·54 km/h); climb 800 ft/min (4·06 m/sec); service ceiling 13,100 ft (3,993 m); range 380 miles (611 km).

The Lark could be fitted with a variety of engines. This seaplane version has the 200 hp Wright J-4 Whirlwind.

The Curtiss Seahawk was developed at company expense for a Navy fighter competition in 1927. The prototype shown was bought as the first of a contract for eighteen designated F7C-1.

## Model 43—F7C-1 Seahawk

The Seahawk prototype was built as a Curtiss-owned entry in a 1927 Navy fighter competition and first flew in February 1927. Powered with the 450 hp Pratt & Whitney R-1340B Wasp engine of the F6C-4, the Model 43 drew heavily on Hawk design experience with a touch of Falcon shown in the sweptback three-piece upper wing. A feature new to Curtiss was the installation of fuel tanks in each side of the fuselage outboard of the main structure, where they formed part of the streamlining.

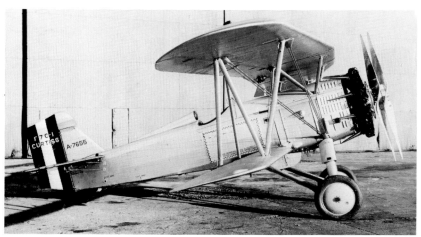

This production F7C-1 was used for experimental work, including the testing of a unique 'biplane' propeller.

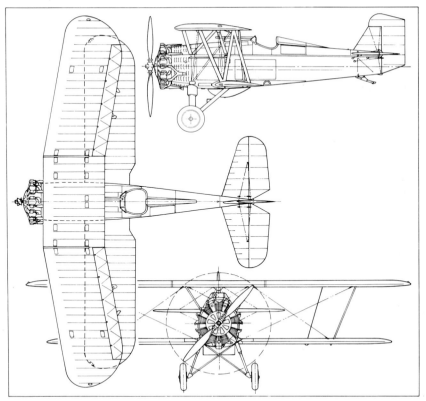

F7C-1 Seahawk.

XF7C-1—The prototype was tested by the Navy as a landplane and a single-float seaplane under the unofficial designation of XF7C-1 while Curtiss called it the Curtiss Navy Fighter. When the production orders were placed, the Navy purchased the prototype, designated it F7C-1 (later XF7C-1) and assigned the Navy serial number immediately preceding those of the production models. Following a crash, the original wings with 242 sq ft (22·48 sq m) of area were replaced with production F7C-1 wings having 275 sq ft (25·54 sq m). Published statements to the effect that the XF7C-1 flew originally with a straight upper wing cannot be verified through photographs. Cost of the XF7C-1 less GFE was $82,450.

F7C-1—The seventeen production F7C-1s ordered for the US Marines were equipped only as shore-based landplanes. These differed from the prototype principally in the use of a redesigned undercarriage and omission of the prototype's large propeller spinner. Deliveries began in December 1928 at unit prices less GFE of $17,111.

Single-seat fighter. 450 hp Pratt & Whitney R-1340.

Span 30 ft 8 in (9·34 m); length 22 ft 7¼ in (6·88 m); height 9 ft 8½ in (2·95 m); wing area 275 sq ft (25·54 sq m).

Empty weight 2,053 lb (931 kg); gross weight 2,768 lb (1,255 kg).

Maximum speed 155·5 mph (250·24 km/h); cruising speed 150 mph (241·39 km/h); climb 1,860 ft/min (9·44 m/sec); service ceiling 22,100 ft (6,736 m); range 355 miles (571 km).

Armament—two ·30-in machine-guns.

US Navy serial numbers: A7653 (XF7C-1), A7654/7670 (F7C-1)

## Models 48, 51—Navy N2C-1, Civil Fledgling

The Fledgling was designed late in 1927 as the Curtiss entry in a US Navy primary trainer competition. With the expansion of the Curtiss Flying Service and a subsequent need for civil trainers, lower-powered versions of the military prototypes were also developed. After Navy needs were supplied, an export version was marketed under the name of Guardsman.

Design philosophy followed that of military trainers since World War I; a large two-seater with light wing loading. The wings, with Curtiss C-72 aerofoil, were wood frame construction with routed spars; tail surfaces aluminium frame, and fuselage welded steel-tube. The design advance of the Fledgling over the Jenny of 1914–18 might seem doubtful due to the fact that the Fledgling had more wing struts!

Large Navy and export orders were placed for the Fledgling but civil sales other than to Curtiss Flying Service were limited; the aeroplane was not only considerably larger and less versatile than competing models, but the onset of the depression virtually wiped out the market for all civil biplane trainers.

The Curtiss Fledgling was developed for a 1928 US Navy trainer competition and delivered under the designation XN2C-1.

200

XN2C-1 (Model 48)—Three prototypes (A7650/7652) were built at Garden City for the 1928 Navy trainer competition. These, like most of the other competitors, were built under Navy contract rather than being builders' speculations. Although it was the first Curtiss trainer submitted to the Navy since the adoption of standardized designations in 1922–23, the fame of the NC-flying-boats of 1919 precluded the use of the logical NC-1 designation; hence N2C-1.

Powered with the 220 hp Wright J-5 engine, the XN2C-1s could operate as landplanes or single-float seaplanes. In July 1930, A7650 was fitted with a 170 hp Curtiss Challenger engine without a designation change and retained it to the end of its Service life in 1936, the only US Navy aeroplane to use this unique powerplant. In an unusual move, the Navy removed the X status of all three XN2C-1s on 1 July, 1928.

The production N2C-1s differed little from the three prototypes except for being fitted with balanced elevators.

N2C-1—Thirty-one production examples (A8020/8050) of the long-wing landplane XN2C-1s built at Buffalo but still using the J-5 engine which had just gone out of production. Colour was orange-yellow all over, the standard colouring for Navy primary trainers. Unit cost less GFE was $6,550. The first, A8020, was tested both on wheels and floats with short-span wings similar to the civil Fledgling Junior.

### N2C-1/Fledgling

Two-seat primary trainer. 220 hp Wright J-5.

Span 39 ft 2 in (11·93 m); length 27 ft 4 in (8·33 m); height 10 ft 4 in (3·14 m); wing area 365 sq ft (33·9 sq m).

Empty weight 2,135 lb (968 kg); gross weight 2,832 lb (1,285 kg).

Maximum speed 108·7 mph (174·93 km/h); cruising speed 87 mph (140 km/h); climb 695 ft/min (3·53 m/sec); service ceiling 15,100 ft (4,602 m); range 366 miles (589 km).

N2C-2 (Model 48A)—Twenty additional Navy Fledglings (A8526/8545), c/ns 1/20, delivered as N2C-2 because of an engine change to the new 240 hp Wright J-6-7 (R-760-9A). Identical to N2C-1 except that

Additional Fledglings for the Navy were designated N2C-2 and fitted with 240 hp Wright J-6-7 engines because the J-5 was no longer in production.

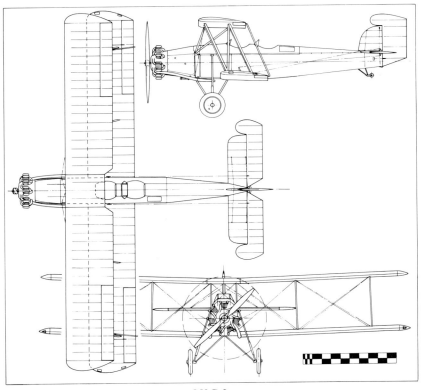

N2C-2.

Some obsolete N2C-2s were fitted with tricycle undercarriages, increased dihedral, and radio controls for use as pilotless aerial targets for live gunnery training.

gross weight was 2,860 lb (1,297 kg), maximum speed 116·2 mph (187 km/h), and service ceiling 17,800 ft (5,425 m).

A few N2C-2s surviving in the late 1930s were modified extensively with tricycle undercarriages and extra dihedral and were operated as radio-controlled anti-aircraft gunnery targets.

Civil and Export Fledglings (Model 51)—The commercial Model 51 was similar to the military version except for the omission of Navy standard items and the use of a 170 hp Curtiss Challenger engine. One hundred and nine were built for the Curtiss Flying Service and painted in the standard colours with yellow wings and horizontal tail and orange fuselage. ATC-191 was issued in August 1929. Data as N2C-1 except:

The majority of civil Fledglings were powered with the unique six-cylinder twin-row Curtiss Challenger.

203

Empty weight 1,991 lb (903 kg); gross weight 2,637 lb (1,196 kg).

Maximum speed 104 mph (167·36 km/h); cruising speed 88 mph (141·62 km/h); climb 670 ft/min (3·4 m/sec); service ceiling 14,100 ft (4,298 m); range 346 miles (557 km).

C/ns and registrations: B-1 7992 (formerly c/n G-3); B-2/11 8660/8669 (8663 to J-1); B-12/20 8671/8679 (8677 to J-1); B-21/30 8690/8699 (8690, 8691 to J-1, 8691 to NS-39); B-31/35 250H/254H; B-36/45 259H/268H; B-46 295H; B-47 269H; B-48 270H; B-49 CF-ACA (to NC 264V); B-50 CF-ACB (to China); B-51 868N (to CF-ACC); B-52/54 271H/273H; B-55/59 290H/294H*; B-60/63 296H/299H; B-64/93 460K/489K (463K to J-2, 465K to J-1 Special); B-94/96 650M/652M; B-97/99 no record of registrations; B-100 653M; B-101 966M; B-102 274H (to 965M, to J); B-103 967M; B-104/106 no record of registrations; B-107/109 654M/656M.

* B-55 (290H) was converted to Fledgling Jr.

The Fledgling Jr was an otherwise standard Fledgling fitted with shorter wings to increase its speed. The alteration had more disadvantages than advantages.

Fledgling Jr—In an attempt to get more speed and manoeuvrability from the Fledgling, a short-wing version known as the Fledgling Jr was converted from Fledgling c/n B-55 (290H). Although receiving ATC-182 in July 1928, this version did not go into production. While maximum speed was increased, so was the landing speed, and all other performance suffered as well. Wright J-6-5 and J-6-7 engines were also tried.

Data for Challenger powered version:

Span 27 ft 10 in (8·48 m); wing area 289 sq ft (26·84 sq m).

Empty weight 1,921 lb (871 kg); gross weight 2,567 lb (1,164 kg).

Maximum speed 107 mph (172·19 km/h); stalling speed 50·1 mph (80·62 km/h); climb 575 ft/min (2·92 m/sec); service ceiling 10,600 ft (3,231 m).

Fledgling Guardsman—A convertible civil-military version of the Challenger-powered Fledgling intended for export. Licensed under Memo 2-59 in July 1929. Garden City prototype No.1 and Buffalo serial Nos.B-1 and up were eligible for this designation.

Fledgling J-1—The Challenger engine had certain shortcomings that made a replacement desirable for use in the hard-working Fledgling. When the new Wright J-6 Whirlwind engine series appeared in 1929, the five-cylinder J-6-5 model was tried. Producing only 165 hp, this was no improvement, and only four Fledgling J-1s used this engine. One (NC8691) was later converted to J-1 Special under Memo 2-472 when fitted with an old Wright J-5.

Maximum speed 102 mph (118·41 km/h); climb 545 ft/min (2·76 m/sec); service ceiling 11,650 ft (3,551 m).

Serial numbers: B-5, B-18, B-21, B-22. Registration numbers NC8663, 8677, 8690, 8691.

The Fledgling J-2 was similar to the Navy N2C-2 and received a civil type certificate but the only sales were to Colombia (*illustrated*), Czechoslovakia and Brazil. (*Courtesy Thomas S. Cuddy Jr*)

Fledgling J-2—As the J-6-5 engine was not a satisfactory substitute for the Challenger, the 245 hp Wright J-6-7 was tried in the J-2 version of the Fledgling licensed under ATC-269 in November 1929. Two existing Challenger-powered models (NC463K and 274H) were converted for the test programme, but no commercial production was undertaken. Several J-2s were built for export to Colombia and Brazil.

### Model 49, F8C/O2C/XF10C/XS3C Helldiver

Other than the Hawks and Falcons, the principal Curtiss military production model of the late 1920 period was the two-seat fighter-bomber known as the Helldiver. Although this was the first production Navy aircraft designed specifically for dive-bombing, it was originally given the fighter designation XF8C-2, which gave the impression that it was a variant of the F8C-1 Falcon when it was actually an entirely new design. Production versions served briefly in the fighter role but were soon withdrawn from the fleet and assigned to Naval Reserve units, where they stayed to the mid-1930s. Some F8C-5s on order were completed as O2C-1 observation models while others were ordered as observation aircraft. An attempt to prolong the production life of the basic model by detail refinement and the installation of more powerful engines in later prototypes was not successful.

205

The XF8C-2 of 1928 was the prototype of a long series of production Helldivers. Initial fame was achieved as a dive-bomber but principal use was for observation.

XF8C-2 (Model 49)—The Helldiver prototype was the third aeroplane on a $73,008 (less GFE) Navy contract for three experimental two-seat fighters. The first two were Naval versions of the Army's XA-4 Falcon ordered as XF8C-1, while the third was an entirely new design ordered as XF8C-2 and identified by Curtiss as L-117-1. Built at Garden City, the XF8C-2 clearly showed its origins in the Falcon line combined with details of the F7C-1.

A unique feature, inspired by the Vought O2U Corsair and the XF7C-1, was the use of main fuel tanks built into each side of the fuselage alongside the front cockpit. Fuselage structure was welded steel-tube, wings were wooden framed and the tail surfaces were aluminium framed. Armament consisted of two forward-firing ·30 calibre machine-guns in the centre section of the upper wing outboard of the propeller arc, two flexible guns on a Scarff ring around the rear cockpit, plus underwing bomb racks. Powerplant was the same 450 hp Pratt & Whitney R-1340 Wasp used in the F8C-1/OC-1 Falcon and the F6C-4 Hawk.

The original XF8C-2, which first flew in November 1928, was lost on a maker's test flight on 3 December, 1928. It was replaced without cost to the Navy by a duplicate carrying the same Navy serial number, A7673, in August 1929.

XF8C-4 (Model 49A)—A second Helldiver prototype, delivered in April 1929, was designated XF8C-4. The principal outward difference from the XF8C-2 was a cutout at the bottom of the rudder to accommodate a new and relocated oleopneumatic tailskid assembly. Navy serial number was A8314 and cost less GFE was $61,894.

F8C-4 (Model 49B)—Twenty-five production versions of the XF8C-4 were built at Buffalo, early examples going into service with VF-1B aboard

The XF8C-4 was the second prototype Helldiver and was followed by twenty-five production examples.

the USS *Saratoga* in 1930. Although not fitted with engine ring cowlings when delivered, many F8C-4s were so equipped in later years. Unit cost $15,450 less GFE, Navy serial numbers A8421/8445.

### F8C-4

Two-seat fighter/dive-bomber. 450 hp Pratt & Whitney R-1340-88.

Span 32 ft (9·75 m); length 25 ft 11⅞ in (7·92 m); height 10 ft 2 in (3·09 m); wing area 308 sq ft (28·61 sq m).

Empty weight 2,506 lb (1,137 kg); gross weight 3,776 lb (1,713 kg) fighter, 4,038 lb (1,832 kg) bomber.

Maximum speed 137 mph (220·47 km/h); cruising speed 116 mph (186·68 km/h) at 6,000 ft (1,829 m); climb 1,030 ft/min (5·23 m/sec); service ceiling 19,800 ft (6,035 m); range 452 miles (727 km) at 6,000 ft (1,829 m).

Armament—four ·30-in machine-guns, 500 lb (226 kg) bombs.

Production F8C-4 with under-fuselage auxiliary fuel tank, bomb racks, and markings of Navy Fighter Squadron VF-1 serving aboard USS *Saratoga* in 1930.

207

F8C-5—Although carrying fighter designations, the sixty-three F8C-5s ordered were intended primarily for land-based observation duties and were delivered without deck arrester gear. Because of this, they were soon redesignated as O2C-1. Curtiss-designed anti-drag rings around the radial engines were standard initial equipment. Navy serial numbers A8446/8456, A8589/8597, A8748/8790.

Sixty-three production F8C-5s were intended primarily for observation duties from shore bases and were not equipped to operate from carriers. The designation was soon changed to O2C-1.

XF8C-6—The first two F8C-5s (A8446, 8447) were fitted with wing flaps and leading-edge slats for test work and were known to Curtiss Engineering as L-117-5. They were reconverted to standard and redesignated F8C-5 (later O2C-1) after the test programme.

Cyclone Helldivers (Model 49C)—Two prototypes of improved Helldivers were introduced at Garden City in August and September 1930 as company-owned demonstrators carrying civil registrations but with Navy colouring and markings. The major change was the use of a 575 hp Wright R-1820 Cyclone engine and the addition of closed canopies to the cockpits. On the first Cyclone-powered model, later to become the F8C-7 and XO2C-2, the aft turtledeck was raised to streamline the canopy into the fuselage contours. Later, streamlining was improved still further by the addition of cuffs to the terminals of the flying wires. The Navy bought both prototypes.

XF8C-7—As a civil aeroplane, Curtiss identified this as Helldiver Cyclone Command. It was registered as Helldiver A-4 984 V and had c/n 1. The Navy designated it XF8C-7 in November 1930, then XO2C-2 and O2C-2 with Navy serial A8845. Cost less GFE was $19,934. It was used as the personal transport of the then Assistant Secretary of the Navy for

The Helldiver A-4 with Wright Cyclone engine was developed at Curtiss expense and eventually sold to the US Navy as the XF8C-7. It was redesignated XO2C-2 and O2C-2 before reverting to XF8C-7. Figures on rudder (984V) are civil registration used while the aeroplane was company-owned. Absence of prefix letters means that it was only registered or 'identified', not licensed.

Aviation, David S. Ingalls, the Navy's only World War I ace. Maximum speed was 178·6 mph (287·42 km/h), climb was 1,840 ft/min (9·34 m/sec), and service ceiling was 10,800 ft (3,292 m). This aeroplane reverted to XF8C-7 before being surveyed in March 1934, with 377 hr flying time.

XF8C-8—The second Curtiss-owned Cyclone Helldiver had standard armament and was identified by Curtiss as the Cyclone Military Helldiver. It was registered as Helldiver A-3, also with c/n 1, and carried registration

The Helldiver A-3, also with Cyclone engine, was another Curtiss private venture and was sold to the Navy as the XF8C-8 before becoming O2C-2, XF10C-1, and XS3C-1. Civil registration suffix V has no significance.

983V. This was acquired by the Navy as XF8C-8, serial A8847. The Navy also ordered two other examples at the same time under the designation O2C-2 with serials A8848 and A8849. Price for all three, less GFE, was $59,866. The additional two were temporarily redesignated as XF8C-8 while A8847 later became O2C-2, XF10C-1, and XS3C-1.

XF10C-1—The former XF8C-8, 8847, first of the three O2C-2s, was returned to the factory for further testing but crashed. Curtiss replaced it with an extensively modified airframe using newly designed tail surfaces, a single-strut undercarriage, and a 650 hp R-1820E Cyclone, in a further attempt to improve the design, and delivered it under the same Navy serial number. It was then redesignated as a scouting type, XS3C-1, but was temporarily considered for the fighter role as XF10C-1 and became known as such without having actually used the designation. See XS3C-1 for performance.

O2C-1—The sixty-three F8C-5s became O2C-1 observation types and a further thirty O2C-1s were ordered as such with Navy serial numbers A8941/9870.

XO2C-2—The second designation for the first Cyclone Helldiver, A8845. Became O2C-2 and eventually reverted to XF8C-7.

O2C-2—The second Cyclone Helldiver demonstrator was bought by the Navy as XF8C-8 but became O2C-2 along with two duplicates. With a later Cyclone engine in a replacement airframe, the second prototype became XF10C-1 and XS3C-1 (*which see*). The third was returned to the factory and became a test bed for the new 650 hp twin-row Wright R-1510 engine in June 1933, but it caught fire in the air and crashed in July 1933. With 575 hp

The first sixty-three O2C-1 Helldivers were the F8C-5s redesignated. Together with an additional thirty built as observation aircraft, most of these ended their service in Reserve Training Squadrons. (*Gordon S. Williams*)

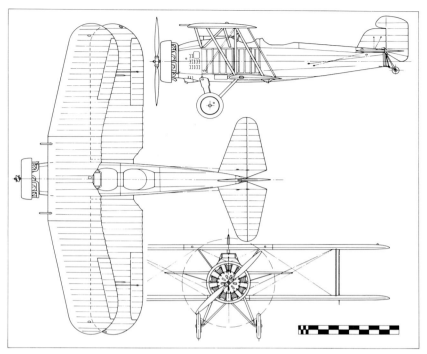

O2C-1 (Model 49)

The XO2C-2, used as an executive transport by the Assistant Secretary of the Navy for Air, was the first XF8C-7 redesignated. This aeroplane was the first to have blue fuselage, struts, and undercarriage for identification of high Navy rank.

The second Cyclone-powered O2C-2 had a canopy over the forward cockpit only and served briefly on aircraft carriers as a Command aeroplane.

R-1820-64 Cyclone, O2C-2's gross weight was 4,755 lb (2,157 kg), maximum speed 171 mph (275·19 km/h) and climb 1,600 ft/min (9·28 m/sec). Navy serial numbers were A8847/8849.

XS3C-1 (Model 61)—Scout designation assigned to XF8C-8/O2C-2 A8847 replacement with extensive airframe modification. *See* XF10C-1. With the 620 hp R-1820E Cyclone, gross weight was 5,014 lb (2,274 kg), maximum speed 180 mph (289·67 km/h) and service ceiling 18,700 ft (5,700 m). Finally crashed in February 1932.

After fleet service, the third O2C-2 was returned to Curtiss and served as a testbed for the new 650 hp twin-row Wright R-1510 engine.

The second Cyclone Helldiver, the XF8C-8, was later extensively modified to become the XF10C-1 and finally the XS3C-1, shown.

**XS3C-1**

Span 32 ft (9·75 m); length 26 ft 3⅞ in (8·02 m); height 10 ft 2 in (3·09 m); wing area 308 sq ft (28·61 sq m).

Empty weight 1,577 lb (715 kg); gross weight 4,941 lb (2,241 kg).

Maximum speed 180 mph (289·67 km/h); cruising speed 140 mph (225·3 km/h); rate of climb 1,600 ft/min (8·12 m/sec); service ceiling 18,700 ft (5,700 m); range 600 miles (966 km).

## Model 50—Robin

Prototypes of this commercial monoplane were built at Garden City but production was assigned to St Louis. (See page 377).

## Model 51—Fledgling

For detail continuity, the descriptions of the commercial Fledglings have been combined with those of the Model 48 US Navy N2C trainers and export Model 51 Fledglings. (See page 200).

## Model 52—B-2 Condor Heavy Bomber

Although designed two years before the commercial Robin as a refinement of the XNBS-4, the Condor heavy bomber received a higher sequential number in the 1935 model list. Principal differences from the XNBS-4 were a change to the new geared V-1570 Conqueror engines and increase of the crew to five. The unique outboard gunners' cockpits tested on one XNBS-4 were retained along with the archaic biplane tail. A significant change, resulting from the Curtiss association with Charles Ward Hall and his metal structure concepts, was the use of welded steel tube truss wing spars with riveted duralumin ribs.

The XB-2 Condor of 1927 evolved from Curtiss's experience with the NBS-1s and NBS-4s. This is the single prototype with two-blade propellers. The machine-gun position can be seen in the rear of the engine nacelle.

**XB-2**—One prototype, Army serial number 26-211, was ordered in 1926. Built at Garden City, it was delivered in July 1927 but was lost the following December after only 59 hours' flying.

**B-2**—Two production B-2s were ordered in 1928 and ten more in 1929 (serials 28-398, 399, 29-28/37). Deliveries began in June 1929. Notable external differences from the XB-2 were three-blade propellers and somewhat shorter and wider radiators. One B-2 was used to test an early automatic-pilot installation in 1930. The last B-2 was surveyed in July 1936, after accumulating, 1889 hours.

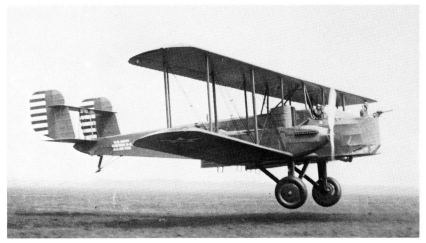

The twelve production B-2 Condors that followed the XB-2 formed the entire US Army heavy bomber force from 1929 until the early 1930s.

## B-2A—One B-2, 29-30, equipped with dual controls.

Two 600 hp Curtiss GV-1570s.
Span 90 ft (27·43 m); length 47 ft 4½ in (14·43 m); height 16 ft 6 in (5·02 m); wing area 1,496 sq ft (138·97 sq m).
Empty weight 9,300 lb (4,218 kg); gross weight 16,591 lb (7,526 kg).
Maximum speed 132 mph (212·43 km/h); cruising speed 105·5 mph (169·78 km/h); initial rate of climb 850 ft/min (4·31 m/sec); service ceiling 17,100 ft (5,212 m); range 805 miles (1,295 km).
Armament: six ·30-in machine-guns, 2,508 lb (1,138 kg) bombs.
US Army serials: 26-211 (XB-2), 28-398, 399, 29-28/37 (B-2).

### Model 53—Condor CO Transport

In 1928, following Army release of the B-2 design for the purpose, Curtiss developed a civil transport version. Called Condor 18 because of its 18-passenger capacity, six were built at Garden City in two separate batches of three in expectation of sales to the booming air transport industry. First flight was in June 1929.

The first three were little more than B-2s with the fuselage modified to carry 18 passengers in three rows of seats, plus three crew. The pilots were again enclosed, as in the 1919 Eagle, and were moved forward into the nose. Length was increased by stretching the fuselage ahead of and behind the wings. The nacelles were similar to those of the B-2 but with the gun stations faired over. ATC-193 was issued in August 1929.

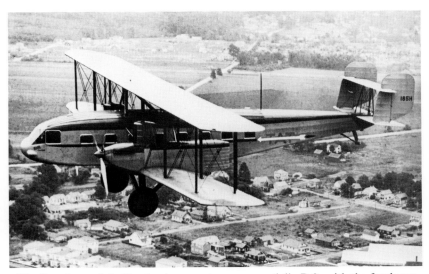

The first three of six Condor transports were essentially B-2s with the fuselages modified to carry 18 passengers. Wings and tail were identical to the B-2.

The final three civil Condors had enlarged tail surfaces, dihedral on both wings, and redesigned engine nacelles. (*Roger Besecker*)

The second three had notable differences; a two-foot reduction in length, dihedral on both wings instead of on the bottom wings only, higher vertical tail, and a wider horizontal tail. The nacelles were considerably revised, using monocoque metal construction forward, and were streamlined at the rear to a near-parabolic shape.

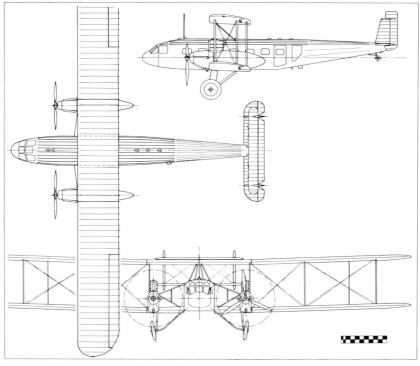

Condor CO (Configuration for final three).

Unfortunately, the new civil Condor had little appeal to the airlines, most of which were then using the well-established Ford and Fokker three-engined monoplanes. The only advantage that the converted bomber could offer was greater passenger capacity. One airline, Transcontinental Air Transport (TAT), tested NC725K and NC185H on its routes but did not buy. Curtiss then stored the unsold Condors at Garden City. All were eventually sold, at uneconomic prices, to Eastern Air Transport between January 1931 and July 1932. Before this sale, some underwent extensive rebuilding at the St Louis plant.

The most notable use of the Condors came after their retirement from the airline in 1934. Famed transatlantic pilot Clarence D. Chamberlin bought four between July 1935 and April 1936, stripped the luxury interiors to allow extra seating, and for several years used them on barnstorming tours of the United States to carry sightseeing passengers wherever such business could be found.

Two 625 hp Curtiss GV-1570s.

Span 91 ft 8 in (27·93 m); length 57 ft 6 in (17·52 m) and 55 ft 7 in (16·94 m); height 16 ft 3 in (4·95 m); wing area 1,510 sq ft (140·2 sq m).

Empty weight 12,426 lb (5,636 kg); gross weight 17,900 lb (8,119 kg).

Maximum speed 145·2 mph (233·67 km/h); cruising speed 125 mph (201·16 km/h); service ceiling 17,000 ft (5,182 m); absolute single-engine ceiling 3,500 ft (1,067 m).

C/ns G-1/G-6. Registrations NC185H, 725K, 984H (later 985V), 726K/728K.

## Model 54—Tanager

The unique Tanager was developed between October 1927 and October 1929 to fulfil the requirements of the Guggenheim Safe Airplane Competition, the object of which was to produce an aeroplane with a specific speed range for general civil use that would eliminate stall-spin accidents in the low speed range.

While safe flight at the required low speed of 35 mph (56·32 km/h) was

The unique Curtiss Tanager won the Guggenheim Safe Aeroplane competition in 1929 but its advanced features were too costly to incorporate in production civil aeroplanes of the time.

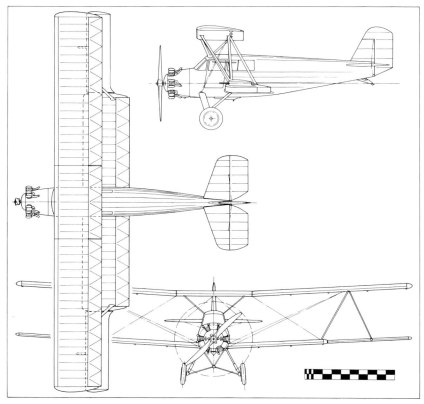

Model 54—Tanager.

relatively easy to attain, the maximum speed requirement of 110 mph (177 km/h) virtually dictated the use of what later came to be called variable geometry; the slow-speed devices had to be retracted or otherwise neutralized to allow achievement of the required maximum speed. Other requirements were the ability to clear a 35-ft (10 m) obstacle 500 ft (152 m) from the start of take-off, to carry two people for three hours, and have a payload of five pounds per horsepower (2·26 kg/hp) (the latter to rule out building a big 'floater' to meet the low-speed requirement and then putting in a big engine to achieve the speed and climb performance).

Curtiss quickly decided that no existing stock aeroplane could be adapted to cover the required speed range, much less meet the safety requirements, and that a new special design would have to be developed.

The low-speed requirements were met with a long-span cabin biplane using full-span trailing-edge flaps on both wings and full-span Handley Page automatic slots on the leading edges. These added 33 and 50 percent, respectively, to the overall lift coefficient. Major safety features were floating ailerons installed outboard of the lower wingtips that trimmed automatically to fair with the relative air flow regardless of the aeroplane's angle-of-attack, a long-stroke undercarriage to absorb the impact of hard landings, and a reinforced cabin structure. Improved controlability was a major safety feature; co-ordinated turns could be made with ailerons alone and high-rate descents right onto the ground could be made by holding the control stick fully back throughout the descent from any altitude.

The structure was conventional, with riveted aluminium tube fuselage and wood frame wings, all fabric covered. Aerofoil was the well-proven Curtiss C-72 and power was the 185 hp Curtiss Challenger.

First flight was on 12 October, 1929. The Tanager won the $100,000 prize, which just about equalled the development cost, and Curtiss was promptly sued for that sum by runner-up Handley Page for unauthorized use of the patented slots. The life of the Tanager was short; it was destroyed in 1930 when the grass on which it was parked caught fire.

Although some Tanager wing features (less the slots) were soon tried on a Curtiss-Wright Travel Air 4 biplane and on a Robin, the Tanager had no direct effect on subsequent Curtiss civil designs. The added features were expensive, and new designs of the early depression years were kept as simple as possible to minimize costs. The first application of wing flaps and slots to a subsequent Curtiss military design was on the XA-8.

### Tanager

Pilot and two passengers. 185 hp Curtiss Challenger.

Span 43 ft 10 in (13·35 m); length 26 ft 8 in (8·12 m); height 11 ft 4 in (3·45 m); wing area 333 sq ft (30·93 sq m).

Empty weight 1,959 lb (888 kg); gross weight 2,841 lb (1,289 kg).

Maximum speed 112 mph (180·24 km/h); cruising speed 95 mph (152·88 km/h); landing speed 37 mph (59·54 km/h); climb 700 ft/min (3·55 m/sec); service ceiling 12,500 ft (3,810 m); range 535 miles (861 km).

Registration 181M, c/n G-1.

## Model 55—Kingbird, US Navy RC-1

Prototypes of this twin-engined transport were built at Garden City but production was assigned to St Louis. The type is described on page 386.

## Model 56—Thrush

The prototype of this single-engined commercial monoplane was built at Garden City but production was assigned to St Louis. The type is described on page 390.

## Model 57—Teal

In 1929, the Garden City plant built two pusher monoplane amphibians, with cantilever wooden wings and metal hulls. While the layout was conventional for the time, the Teal did not win acceptance and further effort was stopped by the Depression.

The amphibious Teal was the unfortunate victim of poor timing; the worldwide economic depression killed the market for it.

A-1—The first Teal (G-1, 969V) was a three-seater powered with the 165 hp Wright J-6-5 Whirlwind engine and flew in March 1930. The J-6-5 was an inadequate powerplant and the A-1 was quickly modified to use the 225 hp J-6-7 and underwent modification to increase its wing area. Unfortunately, the increased weight nullified most of the performance gains.

B-1—The second Teal (G-2, 970V) was a four-seater powered with the 225 hp Wright J-6-7. At a gross weight of 3,647 lb (1,654 kg), the maximum speed was 110 mph (177 km/h), cruising speed was 93 mph (149·66 km/h) and ceiling was 11,200 ft (3,414 m).

### Teal A-1

Three-seat commercial amphibian. 165 hp Wright J-6-5.

Span 45 ft 6$\frac{3}{8}$ in (13·87 m); length 30 ft 3$\frac{11}{32}$ in (9·22 m); height 11 ft 6 in (3·5 m); wing area 248 sq ft (23·03 sq m).

Empty weight 2,135 lb (968 kg); gross weight 2,959 lb (1,342 kg).

Maximum speed 99·4 mph (159·96 km/h); cruising speed 85 mph (136·79 km/h); climb 400 ft/min (2 m/sec); service ceiling 10,400 ft (3,170 m); range 450 miles (724 km).

# XP-10

The unorthodox XP-10 was missed in the 1935 redesignation list. The aeroplane was designed and built under an Army contract dated 18 June, 1928, which called for a new pursuit design having good manoeuvrability and high speed at high altitude. The odd feature was the gull form of the upper wing, which was directly joined to the fuselage. By eliminating the centre section and its above-the-fuselage location, the traditional upward-and-forward blind spot for the pilot was eliminated. The major fault of the XP-10 lay in the readoption of the old PW-8 style wing surface radiators. These proved as troublesome as before and were the principal reason for the Army's rejection of the design. Performance was hardly better than contemporary Hawk models with the same Conqueror engine, so Curtiss confined its subsequent biplane pursuit efforts to further Hawk variants.

Delivered in April 1930, the XP-10 was scrapped in August 1931 with only 10 hours' total flight time.

## XP-10

Single-seat pursuit. 600 hp Curtiss V-1370-15.

Span 33 ft (10·05 m); length 23 ft 3 in (7·08 m); height 8 ft 8 in (2·64 m); wing area 270 sq ft (25·08 sq m).

Empty weight 3,040 lb (1,379 kg); gross weight 3,975 lb (1,803 kg).

Maximum speed 191 mph (307·38 km/h) at sea level, 215 mph (346 km/h) at 12,000 ft (3,658 m); cruising speed 153 mph (246·22 km/h); initial climb 1,650 ft/min (8·38 m/sec); service ceiling 26,500 ft (8,077 m); range 461 miles (742 km).

Armament—two machine-guns.

US Army serial number: 28-387.

The gull-winged XP-10 of 1930 was only marginally superior to the contemporary Hawk pursuits and was handicapped by the wing surface radiators.

The unique Curtiss-Bleeker SX5-1 helicopter of 1929 suffered a drive gear failure before making a successful free flight and was scrapped.

### Curtiss-Bleeker Helicopter

The most unconventional aircraft ever built by Curtiss was the Curtiss-Bleeker SX5-1 helicopter. This was not a Curtiss design, but carried a non-standard Curtiss designation similar to the water glider of 1922. Maitland B. Bleeker designed the helicopter while in college and then persuaded Curtiss to finance and build it.

At that time, one of the major problems of single-rotor helicopters was how to overcome the tendency of the fuselage to rotate in a direction opposite to the directly-driven rotor. Bleeker sought to correct this by having each rotor blade driven by its own propeller through shafts and gears from a single engine in the fuselage. Each blade, which was more like an aeroplane wing than the traditional narrow autogyro or helicopter rotor blade, also had its own trimming surface called a Stabovator and could almost be regarded as a separate captive aeroplane.

The rotor blades, or wings, were controllable from minus 12·5 deg angle of attack to plus 27·5 deg and could be operated collectively or cyclically in the manner of later successful helicopters by means of a conventional stick and auxiliary control in the cockpit.

The two-seat helicopter, which was built at Garden City, got off the ground in tethered flight at Curtiss's Valley Stream Airport late in 1929, but flying ended when the drive gear broke. Curtiss could not justify the cost of the special replacement part for such a questionable design in depressed times and terminated the project.

### SX5-1

420 hp Pratt & Whitney Wasp.
Rotor span 47 ft 4 in (14·42 m); rotor blade area 322 sq ft (29·91 sq m).
Gross weight 3,400 lb (1,542 kg).
Registration: 373N, c/n 2.

222

# The Racers,
# 1920–25

After the First World War, the popular prewar sport of air racing was revived on a worldwide scale. The 1919 races were largely flown with war-surplus aeroplanes or minor redesigns of them; by 1920, however, entirely new designs had been developed specifically for the major races, and the specialized unlimited racer category, that was to last until 1941, was established.

One of the most significant factors of these races is that they were recognized as valuable proving grounds for new high-performance equipment and as a result the manufacturers of racing aeroplanes and engines were backed by their governments. While Curtiss got off to an inauspicious start in the 1920 Gordon Bennett race (Glenn Curtiss had won the first one in 1909), subsequent races up to 1925 did much to improve the performance and reliability of Curtiss engines while the specialized racing aeroplanes made valuable contributions to subsequent US Service designs.

Actually, subterfuge was necessary at times to get development funds for racers past the budgetary watchdogs of the early 1920s; US Navy aeroplanes actually designed as racers were given fictitious fighter designations on some of the approval paperwork in the belief that the development of a new fighter would not be disputed while an apparently frivolous activity like racing would be rejected. US military support of Curtiss racers began in 1921, reached its peak in 1925, and then diminished, ending with the National Air Races of 1930.

Unlimited one-event racing was not the only type conducted. In the United States, a phenomenon known generally as the National Air Races quickly developed. These annual affairs and their lesser regional counterparts sometimes covered a period of up to ten days and featured many closed-course races for aeroplanes of different engine size as well as cross-country races from major cities to the race site. The Services participated in the unlimited events and in special events for their standard models. There were even pylon races for multi-engined bombers!

A separate military event was the Curtiss Marine Trophy Race for US military seaplanes. This was established by Glenn Curtiss in 1915 and continued annually, except for 1917, into 1930.

Modification of privately-owned aeroplanes for the lesser racing events was strictly up to the owners, and usually took the form of clipping the wings and hotting up the engines. Curtiss test pilot C. S. 'Casey' Jones was most successful at this, clipping the wings of an Oriole and adding refinements with Curtiss engineering assistance to become one of the most consistent winners of the early 1920s.

This section is concerned only with the Curtiss racers designed as such from 1920 to 1925, which are presented in the sequence of the 1935 model redesignation system. Racing adaptations of standard Service types like the Hawk and Falcon are covered in the sections devoted to those models.

### Model 22, The Cox Racers

In the spring of 1920, Texas oil millionaire S. E. J. Cox decided to have two racers built for the James Gordon Bennett race to be held in France the following September. Cox shopped around for a suitable builder and found that Curtiss was interested and well-qualified. The company was anxious to promote its new 400 hp C-12 engine and had the design skills and factory facilities to turn out a specialized racer quickly. Following Cox's evaluation of preliminary design studies, Curtiss was given a contract, on 19 June, for two C-12 powered monoplane racers, capable of reaching 200 mph (322 km/h). The world speed record at the time was 176·15 mph (283·48 km/h).

The two racers were named *Texas Wildcat* and *Cactus Kitten* by Mrs Cox, a pilot who owned a Curtiss Oriole and had flown it home to Texas from the factory.

Designed by Curtiss Chief Engineer W. L. Gilmore and assistant Arthur Thurston, the Cox racers were built at Garden City as Design L-19 and drew heavily on Gilmore's experience with low-drag laminated wooden fuselages from the 1918 Model 18s up to the postwar Oriole and Eagle. Tail shapes were similar on all of these. The special C-12 engine, delivering 427 hp at 2,250 rpm, was faired neatly into the pointed nose, and radiators were mounted on each side of the fuselage near the cockpit, which was located far aft for balance.

The Cox racers departed from traditional design in a number of ways. The cockpit had a canopy that rolled forward on tracks to allow pilot entry and was faired in between what would have been a normal windshield and an integral aft turtledeck. This new cockpit design, which was not developed further at the time, anticipated those of the 1931 Gee Bee world record racer and the standard military models of the late 1930s.

The high monoplane wing was unique in being strut-braced to the ends of the wheel axles. This wing had a new double camber aerofoil, essentially a symmetrical section of a type to become popular many years later.

*Texas Wildcat*—For the first test flight of the *Texas Wildcat*, made on 25 July, a 25-ft (7·62 m) wing with a thicker and more conventional aerofoil was fitted to lower the take-off and landing speeds and make them compatible with the small size of Curtiss Field. The aeroplane demonstrated a speed of 183 mph (294·5 km/h) with the 'slow' wing and it was

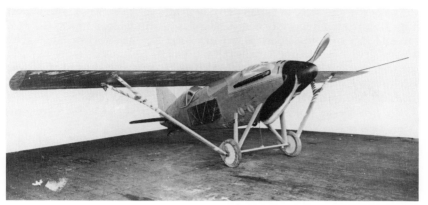

The Curtiss-Cox *Texas Wildcat* photographed in France with its original monoplane racing wing.

estimated that it would be capable of 214 mph (344·39 km/h) with the 'fast' one. With time running short, both racers were packed off to France without further testing; *Cactus Kitten* was not even flown.

After many delays due to French red tape, the *Texas Wildcat* was set up at the Morane factory field, some 30 miles (48 km) from the race site at Étampes. On its first flight with the racing wing, the *Texas Wildcat* showed how aptly it was named. After an excessively long take-off run because of the highly-pitched racing propeller, the aeroplane became unstable at high speed. Curtiss test pilot Roland Rohlfs declared the wing entirely unsuitable. Consequently, Curtiss racing team chief Mike Thurston designed new biplane wings and arranged for them to be built at the Morane-Saulnier factory.

*Texas Wildcat* after being fitted with biplane wings hastily built before the 1920 Gordon Bennett race.

The new wings were installed one day before the race. After a quick test hop, Rohlfs prepared to fly across 30 miles of strange country to the race site and did not put aboard a full fuel load for the short distance. The wheels hit an obstruction on take off, but Rohlfs continued on his way. He got lost, but finally found Étampes, where he landed just as his fuel was exhausted. Unfortunately, the damaged wheels gave way on landing and the racer was flipped on its back and damaged beyond repair.

### *Texas Wildcat* (biplane)

Single-seat racer. 427 hp Curtiss C-12.

Span 25 ft (7·62 m); length 17 ft 7¾ in (5·37 m); height 7 ft 10 in (2·38 m); wing area 145 sq ft (13·47 sq m).

Empty weight 1,816 lb (823·7 kg); gross weight 2,407 lb (1,091·8 kg).

Maximum speed 214 mph (344·39 km/h).

*Cactus Kitten*—The *Cactus Kitten* was not even uncrated in France because it was known that it too would be unstable with its original wing and there was no time to build a second replacement set. Returned to the United States, it was still owned by Cox when it was modified for entry in the 1921 Pulitzer Trophy Race.

With the lessons of the *Texas Wildcat* in mind and a maximum landing speed limitation of 75 mph (120·69 km/h) for Pulitzer racers, the *Cactus Kitten*, now identified as Design L-19-1, was fitted with a set of cut-down 18-T triplane wings and the enclosed cockpit was modified to the open type. Flown by Clarence Coombs under Racing Number 3, the *Cactus Kitten* lived up to its potential by achieving second place to the new Curtiss CR at a speed of 170·3 mph (274·06 km/h) for the 155-mile (250 km) closed course. The winning time of the 1920 Gordon Bennett race had been 168·5 mph (271·17 km/h).

The second Curtiss-Cox racer, the *Cactus Kitten*, was converted to a triplane before its first flight and came second in the 1921 Pulitzer Trophy Race.

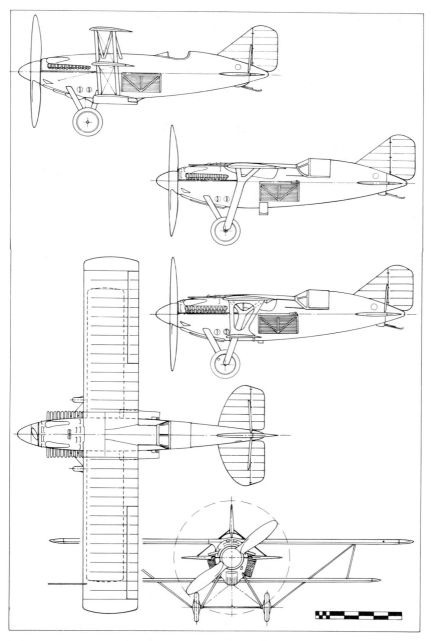

Curtiss Cox *Texas Wildcat* (as monoplane and biplane) and *Cactus Kitten* (top).

Cox subsequently sold the *Cactus Kitten* to the US Navy for one dollar for use as a trainer for the Navy's 1923 racing team. It bore neither Navy serial number nor designation.

**Cactus Kitten (triplane)**

Single-seat racer. 427 hp Curtiss C-12.
Span 20 ft (6·09 m); length 19 ft 3 in (5·86 m); wing area 210 sq ft (19·5 sq m).

## Model 23, Navy CR

In 1921, the US Navy decided to compete for the Pulitzer Trophy Race, which had been won by the Army in 1920 with a hotted-up experimental fighter. Curtiss, the only major US manufacturer with previous experience in unlimited racer design, was given a contract for two new racers on 16 June, 1921. In the absence of a Naval aircraft designation system at the time, these aeroplanes were identified simply as Curtiss Racer No.1 and Curtiss Racer No.2. The Curtiss Garden City plant where they were designed and built gave them the engineering numbers L-17-1 and L-17-2, but in early released photographs they were identified only as CR. In 1922, the new Naval designation system identified the pair as CR-1 and CR-2; C-for-Curtiss, R-for-Racer, and -1 and -2 for two slightly different configurations.

The CRs, designed by Mike Thurston and Henry Routh, drew heavily on the design of the Cox racers, but used more conventional biplane wings with a proven Sloan aerofoil section. The engines used were special 425 hp direct-drive developments of the 1920 Curtiss C-12 known as the CD-12 that operated on a mixture of 50 percent Benzol and 50 percent gasoline. As on the Cox machines, the nose contours were uninterrupted by radiators; novel French Lamblin units were fitted inside each pair of undercarriage struts.

The pilots sat in conventional open cockpits of which the size of the opening had been reduced by the addition of a 'horsecollar' coaming fitted in place after the pilot was seated. Further drag reduction was achieved by the use of streamlined flying wires; wing N-struts cross-laminated from wood produced a single unit without the traditional drag-producing end fittings.

CR-1—The first CR, Navy serial number A6080, became the CR-1 but the designation was not official until March 1922. With plenty of time until the race, scheduled for November, both CRs were tested and tuned to perfection. Shortly before the race, however, both the Army and the Navy withdrew their entries so the first CR was not raced in 1921.

In 1922, the Navy was back in racing along with the Army. The CR-1 was test flown in its 1921 configuration, with such minor refinements as streamlined wheels and slightly larger tail surfaces added before the races, but was converted to CR-2 configuration with new wing skin radiators by race time. Flown by Navy pilot Lt Alford J. Williams (Racing No.8), it came in fourth behind the two new Army Curtiss R-6 racers and the CR-2 at 188·8 mph (303·83 km/h). The CR-1 was converted to CR-3 in 1923.

**CR-1**

Single-seat racer. 425 hp Curtiss CD-12.

Span 22 ft 8 in (6·3 m); length 21 ft 0⅜ in (6·41 m); height 8 ft 4½ in (2·55 m); wing area 168 sq ft (15·6 sq m).

Empty weight 1,665 lb (755 kg); gross weight 2,095 lb (950 kg).

Maximum speed 185 mph (297·72 km/h); service ceiling 24,000 ft (7,315 m); range 235 miles (378 km) at full throttle.

CR-2—The second CR, Navy serial number A6081, was completed before the first. With no external designation or serial number applied, it could be distinguished from its sister only by the shape of the removable metal cowling on top of the nose. On CR-1 the bottom of the cowling formed a smooth curve from the centreline at the propeller to the top of the fuselage; on CR-2 the bottom and rear of the cowling formed a right angle. It was test flown by Curtiss pilot Bert Acosta on 1 August, 1921. All went well until the landing; an unseen depression during the landing run stood the racer on its nose but with only slight damage.

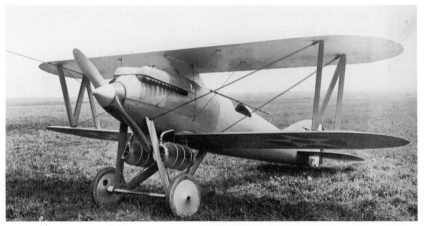

Original form of the Curtiss CR-2, ordered by the US Navy for the 1921 Pulitzer Race but flown to first place by Curtiss pilot Bert Acosta at 176·7 mph.

After the Navy withdrew from the 1921 race, Curtiss arranged to borrow the second CR and race it as a Curtiss entry with Acosta as the pilot. With the Army out of the race too, Acosta's only serious competition was the Curtiss-Cox triplane. Using Racing No.4, he won easily at a speed of 176·7 mph (284·36 km/h), a new closed-course record, even though holding back because of a broken flying wire. On 19 November, 1921, Acosta flew the same machine at 197·8 mph (318·32 km/h) to exceed the known world's record of 194·53 mph (313·06 km/h). It was not known at the time that France had just raised the record to 205·24 mph (330·29 km/h).

The CR-2 in its 1922 racing configuration with wing surface radiators, enlarged tail and streamlined wheels.

The Navy had Curtiss modify the second CR for the 1922 races and the CR-2 designation became official. The major change was to replace the Lamblin radiators with new Curtiss developed wing-surface radiators fitted to each of the upper wings. Other refinements were an increase in vertical tail area and the installation of streamlined wheels as on the CR-1. Flown by Lt H. J. Brow, the CR-2 (Racing No.40) was placed third in the 1922 Pulitzer behind the Army's two new Curtiss R-6s at a speed of 193·2 mph (310·92 km/h).

CR-3 (Model 23A, L-17-3)—In 1923, the Navy had Curtiss convert both CRs to CR-3 seaplanes for the Schneider Trophy Race to be held in England. New Curtiss D-12 engines boosted to 475 hp at 2,300 rpm were installed and the vertical tail area was increased again. A significant change was replacement of the original wooden propellers with new forged aluminium Curtiss-Reed propellers that allowed higher engine speeds. Piloted by Lt David Rittenhouse, CR-3 A6081 (Racing No.4) won at 177·4 mph (285·49 km/h), a new closed-course record, and A6080 (Racing No.3) piloted by Lt Paul Irvin came second at 173·5 mph (279·21 km/h).

All European entries withdrew from the 1924 Schneider, to be held in the United States. Rather than win by default, the United States cancelled the race but set up a series of record attempts during which Lt G. T. Cuddihy in CR-3 A6081 set a new world's closed-course seaplane speed record of 188·07 mph (302·66 km/h).

### CR-3 (seaplane)

Single-seat racer. 450 hp Curtiss D-12 5PL.

Span 22 ft 8 in (6·3 m); length 25 ft 0⅜ in (7·62 m); height 10 ft 9 in (3·27 m); wing area 168 sq ft (15·6 sq m).

Empty weight 2,119 lb (961 kg); gross weight 2,746 lb (1,245 kg).

Maximum speed 194 mph (312·2 km/h); service ceiling 22,000 ft (6,706 m); range 281 miles (452 km) at full throttle.

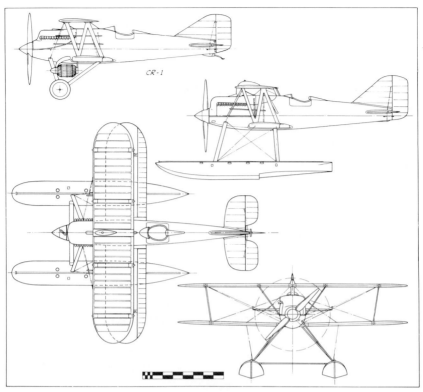

CR-1 and CR-3.

Both CRs were converted to CR-3 seaplanes for the 1923 Schneider Trophy
Race. This is the former CR-2, which came first at 177·4 mph.

CR-4—Not raced in 1925, A6081 was used as a test-bed and as a trainer for the 1926 racing teams under the designation of CR-4.

### Model 23, Army R-6

The winning of the 1921 Pulitzer by the Navy-owned CR inspired the Army to order nine brand-new racers for the 1922 race. Two of these were a new Curtiss design developed from the CR. Army designation was R-6 with Army serial numbers 68563 and 68564 (McCook Field P-Numbers 278 and 279). These were ordered on 27 May, 1922, and were built and delivered in 90 days.

Costing $71,000 plus $5,000 for spare parts, the R-6s used essentially the fuselage and tail of the CR but with a cleaner undercarriage, smaller wings with a new Curtiss C-27 aerofoil and I-struts, and a special 460 hp D-12 engine cooled by unique radiators built into both surfaces of the upper wings. This major advance in the reduction of cooling drag on high-speed aeroplanes had been intended for the 1920 racers but was first tried on an experimental racing Oriole in 1921.

The US Army wanted to beat the Navy in the 1922 Pulitzer Race, so ordered two R-6s from Curtiss. The second example (*illustrated*) won at 205·8 mph.

Contrary to normal procedure, the first flights of the R-6s were made at the Garden City factory by the Army pilots who were later to race the aeroplanes. Piloted by Lt Russell Maughan, 68564 (Racing No.43) won the 1922 Pulitzer at 205·8 mph (331·19 km/h), another new record, and Lt Lester J. Maitland was second at 198·8 mph (319·93 km/h) (Racing No.44). Four days later, 68564 set a new world's straightaway* speed record of

* A 2 km dash before official observers.

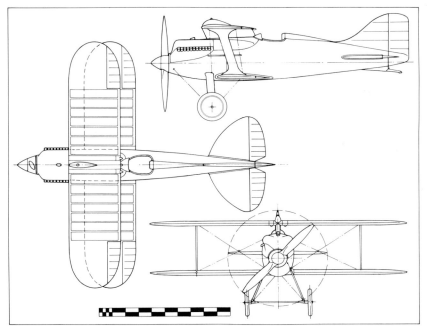

R-6 (Model 23).

224·28 mph (360·93 km/h) when flown by Brigadier-General William B. Mitchell. In March 1923, Maughan raised this to 236·587 mph (380·74 km/h).

The R-6s were placed fifth and sixth in the 1923 Pulitzer behind the Navy's new R2C-1s, 68563 (Racing No.49) at 218·9 mph (352·28 km/h) and 68564 (Racing No.50) at 216·5 mph (348·41 km/h). During a diving start for the 1924 Pulitzer, 68564 (Racing No.68) shed its wings, but 68563 (Racing No.69) was placed fifth at 218·9 mph (352·28 km/h), and was static tested to destruction in 1925.

### R-6

Single-seat racer. 460 hp Curtiss D-12 special.

Span 19 ft (5·79 m); length 18 ft 11 in (5·76 m); height 7 ft 11 in (2·41 m); wing area 138 sq ft (12·82 sq m).

Empty weight 1,454 lb (659 kg); gross weight 1,950 lb (884·5 kg).

Maximum speed 236 mph (379·79 km/h); range 283 miles (455 km) at full throttle.

## Model 32, Navy R2C/Army R-8

Since the Army won the 1922 Pulitzer Race with new Curtiss R-6 racers, the Navy sought redress in 1923 and again ordered two examples of a later model from Curtiss. Since the Naval Aircraft designation system was changed slightly in March 1923, these were given the designations of R2C-1.

The Navy set out to beat the Army in the 1923 Pulitzer and ordered two R2C-1s. The second (*shown*) won at 243·68 mph. (*Walter J. Addems*)

R2C-1—The two R2C-1s, Navy serial numbers A6691 and A6692, were logical developments of the CRs and R-6s and were fitted with the slightly enlarged Curtiss D-12A engines boosted to 507 hp. Surface radiators were installed on both wings and a shorter wire-braced undercarriage with shock-absorbing wheels was used. The major detail departure was the lowering of the upper wings to the top of the fuselage and use of a new Curtiss C-62 aerofoil.

On 6 October Lt Alford J. Williams won the Pulitzer in A6692 (Racing No.9) at 243·68 mph (392·15 km/h) with Lt H. J. Brow second in A6691

The Pulitzer-winning R2C-1 of 1923 was put on floats for the 1924 Schneider Trophy Race and redesignated R2C-2, but the event was cancelled.

(Racing No.10) at 241·77 mph (389·08 km/h). On 2 November, Brow raised the world straightaway speed record to 259·16 mph (417·07 km/h) in A6692; ten days later Williams topped it with 266·59 mph (429·02 km/h) for a new world's straightaway record. A6691 was sold to the Army in 1923 and A6692 was not raced in 1924.

R2C-2 (Model 32A)—The surviving R2C-1, A6692, was put on floats for the 1924 Schneider Trophy Race (which was cancelled) and was redesignated R2C-2. It was used as a trainer for the 1925 Schneider race, and crashed on 13 August, 1926, when being used as a trainer for that year's Schneider race.

The US Army R-8 was the first US Navy R2C-1 acquired for $1.00 after the 1923 Pulitzer Race.

R-8—After the 1923 Pulitzer race, the Navy sold R2C-1 A6691 to the US Army for the token price of $1.00. The Army assigned the designation R-8 and serial number 23-1235 (McCook P-354). The R-8 crashed on 2 September, 1924, on a test flight before that year's Pulitzer race.

### R2C-1/R-8
Single-seat racer. 507 hp Curtiss D-12A.

Span 22 ft (6·7 m); length 19 ft 8½ in (6 m); height 6 ft 10 in (2·08 m); wing area 148 sq ft (13·74 sq m).

Empty weight 1,677 lb (761 kg); gross weight 2,071 lb (939 kg).

Maximum speed 266 mph (428·07 km/h); range 173 miles (278 km) at full throttle.

## Model 42, Army/Navy R3C
For the 1925 racing season, the Army and Navy teamed up to buy three improved racers from Curtiss. Procured under Navy serial numbers A6978, A6979, and A7054, two were for the Navy and one for the Army. The Army model (A6979) was flown under the Navy designation of R3C-1 and the original Navy serial number.

Three R3C-1s were built for the 1925 Pulitzer, two for the Navy and one for the
Army. The Army model won at 248·99 mph.

R3C-1—The R3C-1s were landplanes virtually indistinguishable from
the R2C-1 except for larger Curtiss V-1400 engines, a wide foot to the
interplane I-struts, and a new Curtiss C-80 aerofoil.

Only two R3C-1s were entered in the Pulitzer race, which was won by
Army Lt Cyrus Bettis at a disappointing 248·99 mph (400·7 km/h) in A6979
(Racing No.43). Second place went to Navy Lt Alford J. Williams in A6978
(Racing No.40) at 241·7 mph (388·97 km/h).

### R3C-1

Single-seat racer. 565 hp Curtiss V-1400.

Span 22 ft (6·7 m); length 20 ft (6·09 m); height 6 ft 9½ in (2·07 m); wing area 144 sq ft (13·37
sq m).

Empty weight 1,792 lb (813 kg); gross weight 2,150 lb (975 kg).

Maximum speed 263 mph (423·25 km/h); range 216 miles (348 km) at full throttle.

The three R3C-1s were put on floats for the 1925 Schneider Trophy event and
became R3C-2s. Both Navy models (*the first is shown*) dropped out and the
Army model won at 232·57 mph.

236

R3C-2 (Model 42A)—Following the Pulitzer race, all three R3C-1s were fitted with twin floats for the 1925 Schneider Trophy race, held on 26 October. This was won by Army Lt James H. Doolittle in A6979 (Racing No.3), the same aeroplane that had just won the Pulitzer race. Both Navy models dropped out before the finish. Doolittle pushed the Army R3C-2 to a new straightaway seaplane speed record of 245·7 mph (335·4 km/h). In 1926, USMC Lt Christian Schilt came second in the Schneider race at 231·4 mph (372·39 km/h) in A6979 (Racing No.6).

This R3C-2 is preserved by the National Air Museum.

### R3C-2 (seaplane)

Single-seat racer. 565 hp Curtiss V-1400.

Span 22 ft (6·7 m); length 22 ft (6·7 m); height 10 ft 4 in (3·14 m); wing area 144 sq ft (13·37 sq m).

Empty weight 2,135 lb (968 kg); gross weight 2,738 lb (1,242 kg).

Maximum speed 245 mph (394·28 km/h); range 290 miles (467 km) at full throttle.

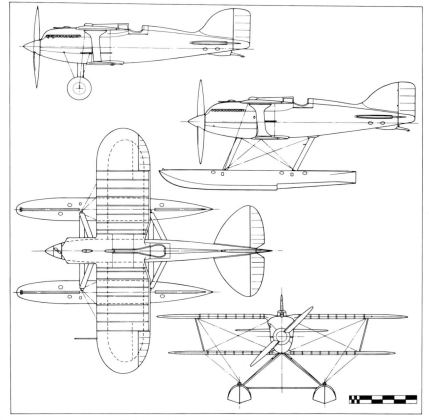

R2C-1 (Model 32) and R3C-2 (Model 42A).

237

The first R3C-2 was modified at Curtiss for the 1926 Schneider and was redesignated R3C-4. It did not complete the course.

R3C-3—For the 1926 Schneider race, the Naval Aircraft Factory reworked R3C-2 A7054 and fitted it with a 700 hp Packard 2A-1500 engine. It reached a top speed of 255 mph (410·37 km/h) as a seaplane but crashed on a pre-race test flight. Calculated top speed as a landplane was 314 mph (505·32 km/h).

R3C-4—R3C-2 A6978 was returned to Curtiss to be refurbished for the 1926 Schneider race. The major change was installation of a new Curtiss V-1500 engine; this was the faithful old D-12/V-1150 with more

For the 1926 Schneider event, the Naval Aircraft Factory installed a 700 hp Packard engine in the third R3C-2. As the R3C-3 it crashed before the race.

displacement and became the immediate predecessor of the famous V-1570 Conqueror. New floats of improved streamlined form were fitted, which, in photographs, can be distinguished from R2C-2 and R3C-2 floats by the downward curve of the top line at the bow. The R3C-4 (Racing No.4) was in second place when it was forced out on the last lap.

# The Hawk

The Curtiss Hawk, introduced in 1923 and produced through many variations until 1938, is probably the best-known United States single-seat fighter produced between the two World Wars. It opened the era of steel-tube construction in the USA and served to the end of the biplane fighter era.

Hawk was a trade name promoted by Curtiss to continue its policy of naming its aeroplanes after birds. This won wide acceptance by the public but never became official with the US Government even though there was some unofficial use of the name.

The Hawk line, then un-named, originated in 1922 as a private venture of the Curtiss Company, which was in desperate need of military business at that depressed time. While the US Army had no immediate requirements for a new fighter, Curtiss felt that a new design, using new structural concepts and the new 435 hp Curtiss D-12 engine, would create a demand by virtue of its superiority to the wartime designs then in service.

The Army was sufficiently impressed with the prototype Curtiss Model 33 to buy it in April 1923, under the designation PW-8, for Pursuit, Water-cooled, Model 8, and ordered the completion of two more. Price was $16,000 each less GFE. Following delivery of 25 production PW-8s, subsequent production models started the new P-for-Pursuit series with P-1. Equivalent Navy models appeared in 1925 as F6C-1. The sale of export models began in 1926 and continued into 1938.

Altogether, 717 Hawks were built by Curtiss; 278 for the Army, 132 for the Navy, and 307 demonstrators and export models. A further eight were built by Aviolanda in the Netherlands, and Curtiss had the doubtful satisfaction of seeing near-copies built in several other countries.

Construction was traditional but updated, the major changes in American practice being the use of wire-braced welded steel-tube fuselage and divided-axle undercarriage. Wings were of wood and the tail surfaces were aluminium frame. Armament was the US standard of the time, either two ·30-calibre machine-guns or one ·30 and one ·50-calibre synchronized to fire through the propeller. Variations are detailed in the appropriate aeroplane descriptions.

Because the various Hawks are usually identified by their Service designations, they are presented in this section first in sequence of US Army designation, then Navy designation, and finally civil/export designation. Curtiss model numbers under the 1935 redesignation system follow the military designations in paragraph headings.

Three experimental pursuits were designed and built at Curtiss expense in 1922 and were bought by the US Army as XPW-8s. This is the first example, with Army lettering but non-standard civil colour scheme.

## US Army Hawks

The Army Hawks were procured in two categories—Pursuits and Advanced Trainers, and are described in that order.

*Pursuits*

PW-8 (Model 33)—The original PW-8, company designation L-18-1, was an interesting mixture of traditional and new design concepts. The new metal structure of fuselage and tail was offset by wooden wings with a thin Curtiss C-62 aerofoil requiring two bays of interplane struts. The most distinctive feature of the design was the use of the unique Curtiss wing-surface radiators used on Curtiss racers from 1922. While these improved the streamlining they were troublesome from a maintenance standpoint and their area made them very vulnerable to gunfire. They proved undesirable for military aeroplanes and were not used on later production models.

While the three prototypes were procured as PW-8s (Army serials 23-1201/1203), they became XPW-8s in March 1924, when the X-for-Experimental prefix was adopted. To distinguish them from the production PW-8s, the X-designations are used here.

XPW-8 No.1.—This flew as a Curtiss-owned aeroplane in January 1923, and was purchased by the Army on 27 April and was used on 9 July, 1923, for an unsuccessful attempt to cross the United States in a dawn-to-dusk flight.

The Army converted the first XPW-8 to the CO-X to compete in two-seat racing events at the 1923 National Air Races but the Navy objected and the modified pursuit was withdrawn. (*John Underwood*)

CO-X—An unofficial conversion by Air Service engineers at McCook Field. They added a second cockpit to XPW-8 No.1, called it Corps Observation Experimental, and entered it in the 1923 Liberty Engine Builders Trophy race for military two-seaters. Because of protests, the CO-X was withdrawn before the race.

XPW-8 No.2—The second XPW-8 was a refinement of No.1 and was the prototype of the production versions. Most visible external improvement was the revised undercarriage.

PW-8—The twenty-five production PW-8s (serials 24-201/225) were ordered on 25 September, 1923, and deliveries began in June 1924. Several were diverted to McCook Field for experimental work, and 24-204 achieved fame by successfully completing the dawn-to-dusk crossing of the States on 23 June, 1924, when piloted by Lt Russell Maughan.

Twenty-five production PW-8s were ordered in the configuration of the second XPW-8.

The third XPW-8 was completed as the XPW-8A with shorter wings and a core-type radiator installed in the centre section of the upper wing. Large fuselage serial number preceded by A.S. for Air Service was standard for 1922–24 period.

XPW-8A (Model 34)—The third XPW-8 (23-1203) was held at the factory for the installation of new single-bay wings. These had a core-type radiator built into the centre section of the upper panel. While not as troublesome as the surface type, this radiator was still inadequate and was soon replaced at Army request by the tunnel type beneath the engine developed by Boeing on its PW-9. This was to become a trademark of all subsequent production Hawks and Falcons with liquid-cooled engines.

The XPW-8A was delivered on 4 September, 1924; its only notable public performance was when it won third place in the 1924 Pulitzer Trophy Race.

The XPW-8A became the XPW-8B when fitted with tapered wings based on those of the competing Boeing XPW-9. The change to tunnel radiator was made while still under the XPW-8A designation.

243

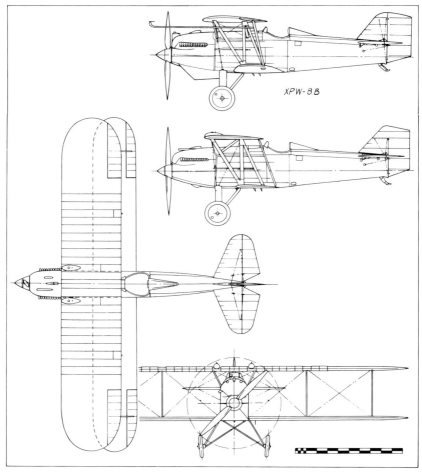

PW-8 and XPW-8B.

XPW-8B—Air Service officials at McCook Field had been impressed by the performance of the Boeing XPW-9, which was very similar to the PW-8 except for tapered wings inspired by the Dutch Fokker D-XI. McCook then asked Curtiss to try tapered wings on the XPW-8A and sent it back to the factory for conversion to XPW-8B.

Using photographs of the XPW-9 as a guide, Curtiss engineer George Page produced a wood-frame wing using two parallel box spars, reinforced plywood-web ribs, and the new Clark-Y aerofoil. The new wings were an outstanding success and the basic Hawk configuration was established.

## P-1 Series

The P-1s were the first tapered-wing Hawks in production and established some milestones in Army aviation. From 1918 and through to the P-1Bs, standard colouring for US combat aircraft was olive drab overall; but, starting with P-1Cs, wing and tail colouring was changed to high visibility chrome yellow.

In July 1926, the Army Air Service became the Army Air Corps and the serial numbers of the aeroplanes were preceded by the letters AC for Air Corps instead of AS for Air Service. A notable change introduced late in 1926, but not used universally until the end of 1927, was the new Army tail striping. When this was adopted, the words U.S. ARMY were added to the sides of the fuselage and to the undersides of the lower wing.

P-1 (Model 34A)—Fifteen production versions of the XPW-8 were ordered, with Army serial numbers 25-410/424. They were fitted with the D-12 engine but had provision for alternative installation of the slightly larger 500 hp Curtiss V-1400. Fuel capacity could be increased by installation of a 55-gallon (208 litre) auxiliary fuel tank under the belly. Deliveries started in August 1925 but the last five P-1s were completed as P-2s.

The first P-1 was fitted with an experimental inverted Allison air-cooled variant of the Liberty engine in 1926 and became the XP-17 in 1930 following another engine change.

P-1A (Model 34G)—Twenty-five improved P-1s were ordered in September 1925 with deliveries beginning the following April. Serial numbers 26-276/300. Engines were improved D-12Cs and the fuselage was lengthened three inches (7·62 cm). 26-296 was converted to the XAT-4 and 26-300 was delivered as the first XP-3A before becoming XP-21 and XP-21A. Three additional P-1As resulted from the installation of D-12 engines in P-2s 25-421, 422, and 424.

The ten Curtiss P-1s were production versions of the XPW-8B and were the first models in the long line of Curtiss Hawks.

245

The first P-1 was used as a testbed for an inverted Allison engine in 1926 but did not, as was customary, receive a revised designation. It later became XP-17 when fitted with still another experimental engine.

XP-1A—Not a prototype; P-1A 26-280 was diverted to test work.

P-1B (Model 34I)—Twenty-five improved Hawks, serials 27-63/87. Ordered on 17 August, 1926, deliveries began in December 1926.

XP-1B—Not prototypes; P-1Bs 27-71 and 27-73 were used for test work at Wright Field; 27-73 had machine-guns in the wings.

P-1C (Model 34O)—Thirty-three improved versions were ordered in October 1928, serial numbers 29-227/259. Cost with spares, less GFE, was $894,729.92. These had larger wheels fitted with brakes and the last two had hydraulic instead of rubber-block shock absorbers. The last P-1C was completed as XP-6B.

XP-1C—Not a prototype; P-1C 29-238 was diverted to test work. Other P-1Cs also underwent extensive test modifications but were not redesignated.

Curtiss P-1A of 1926, still with vertical tail stripes and large stars at the wingtips.

The sixth P-1B was delivered in November 1926 with vertical tail stripes but was quickly changed to have the new Army design adopted that month. U.S.ARMY was added to the fuselage at the same time.

The P-1C was the last of the P-1 line built as a pursuit aircraft.

The twelfth P-1C was assigned to Wright Field for experimental work and was redesignated XP-1C. A new radiator design was being tested.

P-1Ds were lower-powered AT-4 Advanced Trainers refitted with Curtiss D-12 engines and reclassified as Pursuits. Note new standardized data block on fuselage and older style identification on rudder.

Although carrying Pursuit designations, the former AT-5s that became P-1Es were used only as trainers. The large tube-and-wire-mesh mudguards over the wheels are for use on muddy or gravel aerodromes.

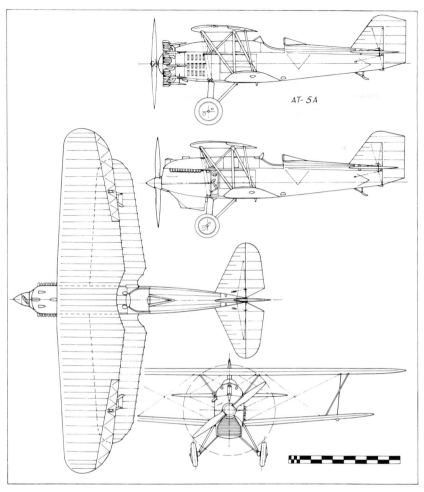

P-1A and AT-5A.

P-1D—Thirty-five AT-4s, serials 27-88/97 and 27-213/237, became P-1Ds when refitted with D-12 engines.

P-1E—All five AT-5s, serials 27-238/242, became P-1F when fitted with D-12 engines.

P-1F—All thirty-one AT-5As, serials 28-42/72, became P-1F when fitted with D-12 engines. One additional P-1F resulted from installation of a D-12 in the second XP-21, 28-189, formerly the second XP-3A.

This P-1F of the 43rd School Squadron at Kelly Field was originally an AT-5A.

The P-2s differed from the P-1 in having larger Curtiss V-1400 engines. This first example has an experimental turbo-supercharger installed.

The first XP-3A was converted from a P-1A by installation of a Pratt & Whitney Wasp radial engine.

## P-2 to P-5

P-2 (Model 34B)—The last five P-1s, serials 25-420/424, were redesignated P-2 when completed with 500 hp Curtiss V-1400 engines. This enlarged D-12 was not satisfactory, so 25-421, 422, and 424 were converted to P-1A. Only 25-420 remained a P-2; 25-423 became the XP-6.

XP-2—Not a prototype; P-2 25-420 diverted to test work with a turbo-supercharger.

XP-3—Designation assigned to P-1A 25-300, which was to be fitted with the new 390 hp Curtiss R-1454 air-cooled radial engine. This proved unsatisfactory before installation in the XP-3 so the designation was cancelled.

XP-3A No.1 (Model 34N)—The P-1A that was to have become XP-3 was completed in October 1927 with the new 410 hp Pratt & Whitney R-1340-1 Wasp air-cooled radial engine under the designation XP-3A. A later engine changed the designation to XP-21.

P-3A—Five Service test versions of the first XP-3A, serials 28-189/193. Deliveries began in October 1928. In spite of the Navy's switch from D-12 engines to the Wasps with the contemporary F6C-4, the Army didn't like the Wasp in its Hawks, leaving it to the new Boeing P-12s. With spares less GFE the five P-3As cost $58,964.91.

XP-3A No.2—Not a prototype; production P-3A 28-189 used for test work in development of the famous NACA cowling. It was placed second in the 1929 National Air Race Free-for-All at 186 mph (294·5 km/h), when the Army raced against civilians for the last time. Converted to XP-21 No.2, P-1F.

Ring cowlings were added to five Service test P-3As after delivery.

251

The first P-3A was used in the development of the NACA cowling and became the second XP-3A. Compare arrangement of fuselage lettering with that on P-1Ds and Fs.

P-5 (Model 34L)—Five Hawks similar to P-1As except that they were fitted with side-mounted turbo-superchargers on D-12F engines for improved altitude performance. Service ceiling was 31,900 ft (9,723 m) compared to the 21,350-ft (6,507 m) absolute ceiling of the P-1A. Maximum speed was only 142 mph (228·52 km/h) at sea level but increased to 166 mph (267·14 km/h) at 25,000 ft (7,620 m). Further development was curtailed by adoption of the larger V-1570 Conqueror engine for Army Hawks. Serials 27-327/331; cost for the five with spares, $181,802.95.

The five P-5s were similar to P-1As except for installation of turbo-superchargers.

|  | PW-8 | P-1C | P-3A | P-5 |
|---|---|---|---|---|
|  | 420 hp | 422 hp | 450 hp | 435 hp |
|  | Curtiss D-12 | Curtiss D-12C | P & W R-1340-3 (SR-1340B) | Curtiss D-12F |
| Span . . . | 32 ft 0 in (9·75 m) | 31 ft 6 in (9·6 m) | 31 ft 6 in (9·6 m) | 31 ft 6 in (9·6 m) |
| Length . . | 23 ft 1 in (7·03 m) | 23 ft 0 in (7·01 m) | 22 ft 11 in (6·98 m) | 23 ft 1 in (7·03 m) |
| Height . . | 9 ft 1 in (2·76 m) | 8 ft 9 in (2·66 m) | 8 ft 9 in (2·66 m) | 9 ft 0 in (2·74 m) |
| Wing area . | 279·3 sq ft (25·94 sq m) | 252 sq ft (23·41 sq m) | 252 sq ft (23·41 sq m) | 252 sq ft (23·41 sq m) |
| Empty weight . | 2,185 lb (991 kg) | 2,195 lb (996 kg) | 2,024 lb (918 kg) | 2,551 lb (1,157 kg) |
| Gross weight . | 3,155 lb (1,431 kg) | 2,973 lb (1,348 kg) | 2,730 lb (1,238 kg) | 3,340 lb (1,515 kg) |
| Maximum speed . | 171 mph (275·19 km/h) | 154·4 mph (248·47 km/h) | 153 mph* (246·22 km/h) | 171·8 mph** (276·48 km/h) |
| Cruising speed . | 136 mph (218·86 km/h) | 123 mph (197·94 km/h) | 137 mph (220·47 km/h) | 115 mph*** (185·07 km/h) |
| Initial climb . | 1,830 ft/min (9·2 m/sec) | 1,460 ft/min (7·4 m/sec) | 1,800 ft/min (9·1 m/sec) | 1,250 ft/min (6·35 m/sec) |
| Service ceiling . | 20,350 ft (6,203 m) | 20,800 ft (6,340 m) | 23,000 ft (7,010 m) | 31,900 ft (9,723 m) |
| Range . . | 544 miles (875 km) | 300 miles (483 km) | 342 miles (550 km) | 310 miles (499 km) |
| Armament . . | Two machine-guns in each type | | | |

\* 170·8 mph (274·87 km/h) with experimental NACA cowling.
\*\* at 20,000 ft (6,096 m)
\*\*\* at sea level

## P-6 Series (Model 34, 35)

The P-6 series resulted from installation of the new 600 hp V-1570 Conqueror engines in what were essentially P-1C airframes. The V-1570 was a direct development of the D-12 by way of the V-1400 engine.

P-6Es still in service in 1935–37, by then the only surviving Army Hawks, underwent the gradual change to the new Air Corps blue from the old olive drab fuselage colouring.

The XP-6 was the fourth P-2 fitted with the new Curtiss V-1570 Conqueror engine and became the prototype of the long P-6 line.

The eighteen Service test and production P-6s had more rounded nose contours and fuselage lines than the prototype XP-6.

XP-6 (Model 34P)—The fourth P-2, serial 25-423, became the prototype of the P-6 line when fitted with the Conqueror. Stripped of military equipment, it was placed second in the unlimited event of the 1927 National Air Races.

P-6/YP-6—Eighteen improved XP-6s with Prestone-cooled V-1570 engines for Service test, and Army serial numbers 20-260/273, 29-363/366. They differed noticeably from the XP-6 in having the fuselage rounded out to match the fatter engine cowling, which was itself more rounded in front and side elevations than the old P-1 type and the XP-6. Cost for the eighteen, including two engines for each, was $628,310.31.

The Y-for-Service-test designation was adopted just at this time but does not appear to have been applied to these aeroplanes although they are sometimes recorded as YP-6s. Since the new engines were not ready, nine aeroplanes, serials 29-269/273 and 29-363/366, were delivered in October 1929 with water-cooled V-1570-17 engines as P-6s; the others were completed later as P-6As.

A P-1A was fitted with the XPW-8A wings and surface radiators for the 1927 National Air Races and won at 201 mph. The XP-6A designation was assigned because it used the Conqueror engine.

The first nine P-6s were fitted with Prestone cooling systems in place of water, permitting smaller radiators, and were redesignated P-6As. (*Ben Heinowitz*)

Two additional P-6s resulted from conversion of P-11s 29-367 and 368. All the P-6s later became P-6Ds.

XP-6A No.1 (Model 34Q)—One P-1A, 26-295, was extensively modified as a racer for the 1927 National Air Races. With a boosted Conqueror in a PW-8 style nose, it was fitted with XPW-8A wings and PW-8 surface radiators. It came first in the unlimited event at 201 mph (323·47 km/h) on the closed course but crashed during preparations for the 1928 races.

P-6A—The first nine P-6s, serials 29-260/268, were completed with Prestone-cooled V-1570-23s and designated P-6A. After undergoing various cowling modifications and changes to three-bladed propellers, some P-1As became P-6Ds.

The fifth P-6A was used for test work and became the second XP-6A.

XP-6A No.2—Not a prototype; P-6A 29-263 was diverted to test work.

XP-6B—The last P-1C, 29-259, was delivered on 18 July, 1929, with a Conqueror engine as XP-6B. Fuselage lines and cowling were as the later P-6 and P-6A. Used for a flight from the eastern United States to Alaska by Captain Hoyt, it was known at Curtiss as *The Hoyt Special*.

The single XP-6B was the last P-1C completed with a Conqueror engine, extra fuel capacity, and the fuselage contours of the P-6.

P-6C—New designation assigned to forty-six Y1P-22s; but the designation was cancelled in favour of P-6E for the same aeroplanes. There was an advantage in applying lower designations to production versions of high-number experimental models differing from standard Service models mainly in powerplant because many parts common to both could then be carried in the spares inventory under the same model and parts number.

XP-6D—A new prototype created by installing a turbo-supercharged V-1570-C Conqueror in P-6A 29-260. Sea level top speed increased to 172 mph (276·8 km/h) and speed at 15,000 ft (4,572 m) increased to 197 mph (317 km/h). The aircraft reverted to P-6A.

P-6D—All of the P-6s and all P-6As except 29-67 were fitted with turbo-supercharged Conquerors in March and April 1932 and redesignated P-6D. The only outward difference from the XP-6D was the use of three-bladed propellers.

XP-6E (Model 35)—The third P-11, 29-374, was completed as YP-20. Later, when fitted with the Conqueror engine, new horizontal tail, and the single-strut undercarriage of the XP-22, it was redesignated XP-6E and became the prototype of the new Curtiss Model 35. It later became XP-6F.

P-6E—Forty-six production examples of the XP-22 with the 700 hp V-1570C Conqueror, first designated Y1P-22 then P-6E. Ordered on 8 July, 1931, deliveries began in December 1931 with serial numbers 32-233/278.

The first P-6A became the XP-6D when fitted with a turbo-supercharger.

All P-6s and all P-6As but one became P-6Ds when fitted with turbo-superchargers in 1932.

The extensively redesigned XP-6E was ordered as a P-11, delivered as a YP-20, and then rebuilt as a new pursuit prototype.

The 46 production P-6Es, most famous of the Hawk line, were originally ordered as Y1P-22s. The markings shown were unique to the 17th Pursuit Squadron of the 1st Pursuit Group, and were used only on their P-6Es.

Unit cost was $13,130 less GFE. The last was held at the factory for conversion to XP-23; 32-233 became the XP-6H, and 32-254 became the XP-6G and then P-6G before reverting to P-6E.

| | XP-6A | P-6A | XP-6B | P-6E |
|---|---|---|---|---|
| | 730 hp Curtiss V-1570HC | 600 hp Curtiss V-1570A | 600 hp Curtiss V-1570C | 700 hp Curtiss V-1570C |
| Span . | 30 ft 0 in (9·14 m) | 31 ft 6 in (9·6 m) | 31 ft 6 in (9·6 m) | 31 ft 6 in (9·6 m) |
| Length | 22 ft 2 in (6·75 m) | 23 ft 1 in (7·03 m) | 23 ft 1 in (7·03 m) | 22 ft 7 in (6·88 m) |
| Height | 8 ft 6 in (2·59 m) | 8 ft 9 in (2·66 m) | 8 ft 9 in (2·66 m) | 8 ft 11 in (2·71 m) |
| Wing area . | 253·6 sq ft (23·55 sq m) | 252 sq ft (23·41 sq m) | 252 sq ft (23·41 sq m) | 252 sq ft (23·41 sq m) |
| Empty weight | 2,927 lb (1,328 kg) | 2,389 lb (1,084 kg) | 2,698 lb (1,224 kg) | 2,715 lb (1,231 kg) |
| Gross weight | 3,204 lb (1,453 kg) | 3,172 lb (1,439 kg) | 3,483 lb (1,580 kg) | 3,436 lb (1,558 kg) |
| Maximum speed . | 210 mph (337·95 km/h) | 176 mph* (283·24 km/h) | 197 mph** (317·03 km/h) | 193 mph (310·59 km/h) |
| Cruising speed | 168 mph (270·36 km/h) | — | — | 165 mph (265·53 km/h) |
| Initial climb | — | 1,910 ft/min (9·7 m/sec) | 1,730 ft/min (8·78 m/sec) | 2,480 ft/min (12·59 m/sec) |
| Service ceiling | — | 27,200 ft (8,290 m) | 32,000 ft (9,754 m) | 23,900 ft (7,285 m) |
| Range | — | — | — | 244 miles (393 km) |
| Armament . | All except the unarmed XP-6A had two machine-guns | | | |

* at 5,000 ft (1,524 m)
** at 15,000 ft (4,572 m)

P-6E with side views of P-6, P-6D and XP-6F. ▶

258

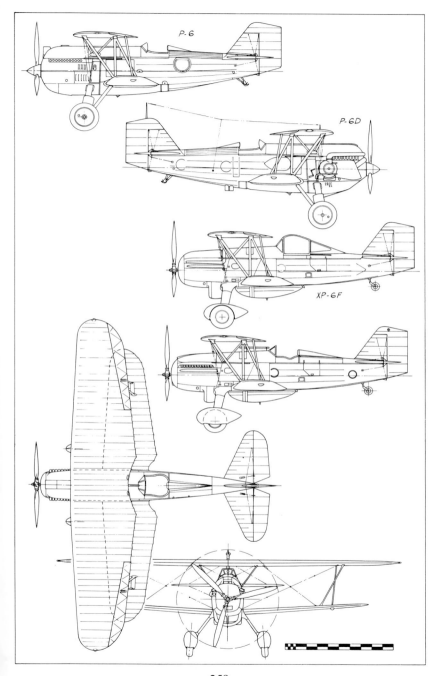

P-6

P-6D

XP-6F

259

The P-6Es rapidly became obsolete. Instead of being given expensive overhauls when they were needed, they were allowed to wear out in service and were not refurbished for continued service as were other types. One survived into 1942.

XP-6F (Model 35C)—The XP-6E, serial 29-374, was sent back to Curtiss for installation of a turbo-supercharged V-1570F (V-1570-55) engine delivering 675 hp at 2,450 rpm and was redelivered in March 1933 as the XP-6F. Gross weight increased by 389 lb (176 kg) and sea-level top speed decreased to 194 mph (312·2 km/h) but the speed at 15,000 ft (4,572 m) was 225 mph (362 km/h).

The XP-6E became XP-6F when fitted with a turbo-supercharger and cockpit canopy in 1933. The open-sided wheel fairings became common on P-6Es in their later years.

XP-6G—One P-6E, 32-254, was fitted with an unsupercharged V-1570F engine and redesignated XP-6G. When the experimental work was finished, the aeroplane retained the F engine but dropped the experimental prefix to become plain P-6G and finally P-6E again.

XP-6H—The first production P-6E, 32-233, returned to the factory for installation of four ·30-calibre guns in the wings. These increased the gross weight to 3,858 lb (1,750 kg) and reduced the top speed to 190 mph (305·77 km/h). Delivered on 20 April, 1933. The special wings were later removed and the aeroplane reverted to P-6E.

P-11—At the time the P-6s were ordered, the Army also ordered three identical airframes to be fitted with the new 600 hp Curtiss H-1640 Chieftain engine, a unique two-row twelve-cylinder air-cooled model. The engine proved unsatisfactory in other test aeroplanes before the P-11s were completed so they were given other designations; 29-367 and 368 became P-6s with Conqueror engines and 29-374 became the YP-20 with a Wright Cyclone before becoming XP-6E and XP-6F.

One P-6E was fitted with a V-1570F engine and redesignated XP-6G.

The first production P-6E was equipped with four ·30-in calibre machine-guns in the wings and redesignated XP-6H.

The first P-1 was not redesignated when fitted with a different engine in 1926 but became XP-17 when fitted with an experimental Wright V-1470 in 1930.

XP-17—Not a prototype; the first P-1 of 1925, 25-410, was used as a test-bed for the new Wright V-1470 inverted V-12 air-cooled engine in June 1930, and was redesignated XP-17.

YP-20—The third P-11, 29-374, was completed in October 1930 with a 650 hp Wright R-1870-9 Cyclone radial engine under the designation of YP-20. Fin and rudder were changed slightly by raising the division between the rudder balance area and the top of the fin by half a rib space.

The powerplant installation was unsatisfactory; 29-374 was then fitted with a V-1570-23 Conqueror and the new nose and undercarriage of the XP-22 and redesignated XP-6E.

The aeroplane that was to have been the third P-11 was completed as the YP-20.

XP-21—The two Hawk airframes that became XP-3A were used as test-beds for the new 300 hp Pratt & Whitney R-985 Wasp Junior engine. Following change to a D-12 engine, 28-129 became a P-1F while 26-300 became XP-21A.

XP-21A—The first XP-21, 26-300, became XP-21A when fitted with an improved R-975 Wasp Junior engine.

XP-22—The third P-6A, 29-262, was redesignated XP-22 when used to test new radiator and oil cooler installations for a V-1570-23 engine. The final modification was an entirely new nose, with belly radiator and oil cooler and the machine-guns lowered to troughs on the sides under the engine cylinder banks instead of between them as on previous installations. A new single-leg undercarriage was also installed.

The new features were soon removed and replaced by the original P-6A units and the aeroplane reverted to a P-6A.

Y1P-22—Original designation for 46 Service test versions of the XP-22. The figure 1 in the designation indicated the use of F-1 funds instead of the regular Air Corps appropriation and was not an indication of aeroplane

The third P-6A was rebuilt as the XP-22. In spite of the higher designation number, it was the prototype of the P-6E model.

detail or status. The designation was changed to P-6C and finally to P-6E before the aeroplanes were delivered.

XP-23 (Model 63)—The last P-6E, 32-278, was held at the factory for conversion to XP-23. This resembled previous Hawks only in the wings; the fuselage structure was a metal monocoque, new shape tail surfaces were used, and a turbo-supercharged and geared G1V-1570-C Conqueror drove a left-hand propeller.

The XP-23 was delivered on 16 April, 1932. While it had improved altitude performance, the Army recognized that it had reached the end of the line in biplane fighter development; the turbo-supercharger was removed and the XP-23 was redesignated YP-23.

The wings of the last production P-6E were fitted to a new-design fuselage, tail, and undercarriage to produce the turbo-supercharged XP-23.

263

YP-23—The XP-23 was redesignated YP-23 after removal of the supercharger and installation of a two-bladed propeller on a G1V-1570-C1 (V-1570-27) engine. This aeroplane was later used in an interesting test to determine the effect of radiator drag on fast aeroplanes by being flown briefly with no radiator at all; on a very short flight, water was pumped through the engine from an isolated fuel tank and discharged overboard.

With its turbo-supercharger removed, the XP-23 was redesignated YP-23.

*Trainers*

In 1924, the US Army decided to use up-to-date pursuit designs with lower-powered engines as advanced trainers. Boeing and Curtiss, the Army's only suppliers of Pursuit aircraft, were each given contracts for prototypes.

In spite of substantial production orders to Curtiss, the concept was not successful. Using the same structures as the pursuits, the low-powered trainers were vastly over-stressed for their missions and were over-weight for their power. After short service, they were fitted with D-12 engines and redesignated as pursuits, P-1D to P-1F.

XAT-4 (Model 34J)—Curtiss fitted P-1A 26-296 with a 180 hp Wright-Hispano E engine and delivered it on 1 July, 1926, as XAT-4.

AT-4—Forty production versions of XAT-4 were purchased for $590,799.44 less GFE, with deliveries beginning in April 1927. Serial numbers 27-88/97, 27-213/242. The last five were completed as AT-5. All the AT-4s were soon converted to P-1Ds.

AT-5 (Model 34K)—The last five AT-4s, serials 27-238/242, were fitted with the new 220 hp Wright J-5 Whirlwind engine and delivered as AT-5s before being converted to P-1Es.

AT-5A (Model 34M)—Thirty-one improved AT-5s, serial numbers 28-42/72, with the longer fuselage and other structural improvements of the P-1A. These all became P-1Fs.

At Army request, Curtiss installed a 180 hp Wright-Hispano E engine in a P-1A to produce the XAT-4 Advanced Trainer.

Although 35 production AT-4s were delivered in 1927, the concept of a pursuit aircraft with a lower-powered engine was not successful and all were refitted with Curtiss D-12 engines and redesignated P-1D.

Five Hawks ordered as AT-4s were completed with 220 hp Wright J-5 radial engines as AT-5s. All became P-1Es when re-engined with D-12s.

Using the same J-5 engine as the AT-5, the AT-5A had minor structural improvements. This one was used in NACA cowling development tests. All of the AT-5As were converted to P-1Fs.

| | YP-20 | XP-23 | AT-4 | AT-5 |
|---|---|---|---|---|
| | 650 hp Wright R-1870-9 | 600/700 hp Curtiss G1V-1570-C | 180 hp Wright E | 220 hp Wright J-5 |
| Span . | 31 ft 6 in (9·6 m) | 31 ft 6 in (9·6 m) | 31 ft 6 in (9·6 m) | 31 ft 6 in (9·6 m) |
| Length . | 23 ft 0 in (7·01 m) | 23 ft 9 in (7·23 m) | 23 ft 1¾ in (7·07 m) | 22 ft 8 in (6·9 m) |
| Height . | 9 ft 3 in (2·81 m) | 9 ft 6 in (2·89 m) | 8 ft 6½ in (2·6 m) | 8 ft 10 in (2·69 m) |
| Wing area . | 252 sq ft (23·41 sq m) | 252 sq ft (23·41 sq m) | 252 sq ft (23·41 sq m) | 252 sq ft (23·41 sq m) |
| Empty weight . | 2,523 lb (1,144 kg) | 3,274 lb (1,485 kg) | 1,847 lb (838 kg) | 1,802 lb (817 kg) |
| Gross weight . | 3,231 lb (1,465 kg) | 4,124 lb (1,871 kg) | 2,484 lb (1,127 kg) | 2,445 lb (1,109 kg) |
| Maximum speed . | 188·6 mph (303·51 km/h) | 180 mph* (289·67 km/h) | 133 mph (214·03 km/h) | 125·4 mph (201·8 km/h) |
| Cruising speed . | 150 mph (241·39 km/h) | 190 mph (305·77 km/h) | 107 mph (172·19 km/h) | 100 mph (160·93 km/h) |
| Initial climb . | 2,600 ft/min (13·2 m/sec) | 1,370 ft/min (6·95 m/sec) | 950 ft/min (4·82 m/sec) | 1,096 ft/min (5·56 m/sec) |
| Service ceiling . | 27,800 ft (8,473 m) | 30,000 ft plus (9,144 m plus) | 16,400 ft (5,000 m) | 16,330 ft (4,977 m) |
| Range . | 237 miles (381 km) | 435 miles (700 km) | 535 miles (861 km) | 488 miles (785 km) |

The YP-20 and XP-23 each had two machine-guns
* Sea level speed. 223 mph (358·87 km/h) at 15,000 ft (4,572 m)

266

## US Navy Hawks

The first US Navy Hawks were near-duplicates of the contemporary Army models, with only minor changes to meet Naval specifications. As the Navy made greater use of them, they adopted additional features peculiar to naval operations. The Navy continued to develop new Hawk models after the Army dropped the type and did not retire its last Hawks from the fleet until 1937.

### F6C Series

This started as a land-based fighter for the Marines that duplicated the Army P-1, but subsequent engine changes and special Navy features made it considerably different from late P-1s. Navy Hawks up to and including the F6C-3 could be fitted with twin floats.

F6C-1 (Model 34C)—Nine F6C-1s, Navy serials A6968/6976, were ordered in March 1925. While this was the first Curtiss Navy fighter after the F4C, it skipped the logical F5C designation at Navy request because of the large number of F-5L flying-boats still in service under their original designations. Reports that a Navy version of the PW-8 with a radial engine was designated F5C cannot be verified.

The first F6C-1 was delivered in August 1925, and the last four were converted to F6C-2 before delivery. The first F6C-1 was converted to the prototype F6C-4 and then to XF6C-5. Two others, A6970 and 6972 were converted to F6C-3; the final two served into 1932.

The US Navy F6C-1 of 1925 duplicated the Army P-1 except for minor details of the Navy specification. These were not equipped to fly from aircraft carriers.

The F6C-2s were the last four of nine F6C-1s and were modified for carrier operations. This one is aboard USS *Langley*, the Navy's only aircraft carrier until 1927. The hooks on the undercarriage engaged the fore-and-aft wires on the deck.

F6C-2 (Model 34D)—The last four F6C-1s (A6973/6976) were modified at the factory with reinforced fuselages, deck arrester hooks, and new high-impact undercarriages to suit them for carrier operations. Delivered in November 1925, the F6C-2s served until 1928.

F6C-3 (Model 34E)—Thirty-five improved versions of the F6C-2 (serials A7128/7162) were delivered starting in January 1927, unit price $12,938 less GFE. Originally, these had F6C-2 undercarriages but in 1928 these were changed to a revised spreader-bar type introduced on the first production F6C-4. When operated as land-based fighters by the Marines, eight F6C-3s reverted to the F6C-1 type of undercarriage.

Although F6C-1s and -2s could also be fitted with floats, F6C-3s were the only ones to use them in service. This one was assigned to *Red Ripper* Squadron VB-1

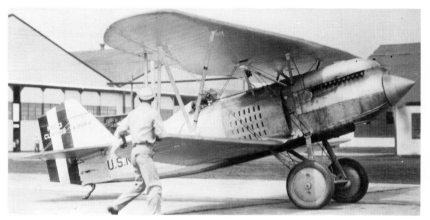

One F6C-3, A-7144, was modified for racing in 1928. The major change was installation of the radiator within the fuselage behind the engine.

In 1928, Navy Squadron VB-1 operated its F6C-3s on floats. One cleaned-up F6C-3, A7147, won the Curtiss Marine Trophy for 1930 before being converted to the XF6C-6. Shortly afterward, in keeping with the new Navy policy of using only air-cooled engined aircraft in the fleet, the F6C-3s were withdrawn from squadron service.

In 1928, A7144 was modified extensively for racing by having the radiator installed inside the fuselage and a low-drag undercarriage fitted. It was further refined in 1929 as the F6C-6.

XF6C-3—One F6C-3, A7136, was diverted to test work and given the X-for-Experimental prefix that the Navy adopted in 1927.

F6C-4 (Model 34H)—After the first F6C-1 was converted to the F6C-4 prototype in 1926, thirty-one production examples at $11,808 each less

The first F6C-1 was re-engined with the 420 hp Pratt & Whitney Wasp to match the contemporary Army XP-3A and was redesignated F6C-4. (*Arthur Price*)

269

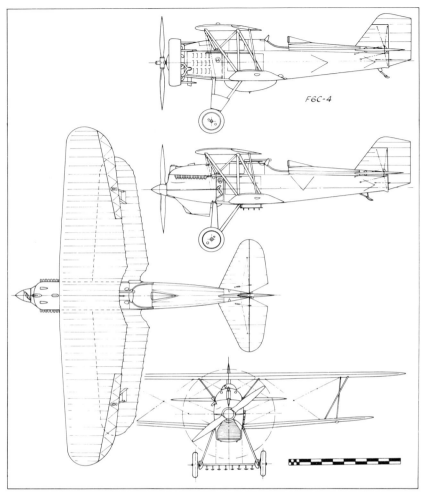

F6C-2 and F6C-4.

GFE were ordered (serials A7393/7423). The first of these, featuring the nose spinner of the prototype, was delivered in February 1927, but the second and following did not come until nearly a year later. These did not have the spinner but had the redesigned spreader-bar undercarriage of A7393, and were withdrawn from squadron service in 1930 and sent to Pensacola as trainers.

XF6C-4—The first production F6C-4, A7393, was used for test work under the designation of XF6C-4.

The thirty-one production F6C-4s had revised undercarriages for carrier operations. The engine ring cowlings were later additions. Application of the star insignia to the underside of the upper wing was most unusual.

XF6C-5—The first F6C-1, after conversion to F6C-4, was fitted with a 525 hp Pratt & Whitney R-1690 Hornet engine and production F6C-4 undercarriage and redesignated XF6C-5.

F6C-6—This was F6C-3 A7144 modified for 1929 racing. After being placed fourth in the unlimited free-for-all race, it was reconverted to F6C-3 with -4 undercarriage but retained the rounded-out rear fuselage of its racing configuration.

The prototype F6C-4 had its Wasp engine replaced by a 525 hp Pratt & Whitney Hornet and was redesignated XF6C-5.

The F6C-3 that was modified for 1928 racing was further modified for 1929 and was redesignated F6C-6. (*William F. Yeager*)

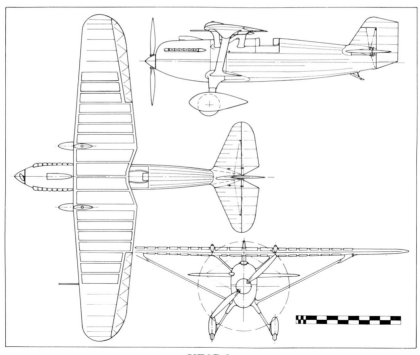

XF6C-6.

For the 1930 National Air Races, F6C-3 A-7147 was converted to a monoplane and fitted with a special 770 hp V-1570 Conqueror engine and wing surface radiators. It was given the designation XF6C-6.

XF6C-6—The winner of the 1930 Curtiss Marine Trophy, F6C-3 A7147, was returned to the factory in June 1930 for the most extreme modification performed on any Hawk—it was converted to a monoplane racer for the 1930 Thompson Trophy Race.

The upper wing was retained, but was moved aft several inches to maintain balance after removal of the lower wing. The conventional radiator was removed and the old Curtiss surface radiators of the early 1920s were fitted to the wing. Curtiss calculations showed a top speed of 250 mph (402·33 km/h). Marine Corps Captain Arthur Page was well on the way to proving this by leading the field with a best-lap speed of 219·6 mph (353·4 km/h) when he was overcome by fumes and crashed.

This F6C-4 was fitted with an inverted air-cooled Ranger engine at the Naval Aircraft Factory and redesignated XF6C-7 but the original designation on the rudder was not changed.

273

XF6C-7—One F6C-4, A7403, was converted at the Naval Aircraft Factory in 1932 to serve as a test-bed for the new 350 hp Ranger SGV-770 inverted air-cooled V-12 engine. The F6C-4 designation on the rudder was not changed.

### F11C Series (Model 64, 67)

XF11C-1 (Model 64)—The XF11C-1 ordered in April 1932 was an extensive revision of earlier Navy Hawks, having the new experimental 600 hp Wright R-1510 twin-row Whirlwind 14 engine and the single-strut undercarriage of the XF6C-6 and the Army P-6E. Wing gap was increased slightly, and the tail surfaces and ailerons were metal covered. The XF11C-1, serial 9217, was delivered in September 1932 (the A-prefix to Navy serial numbers ceased in 1930). As a new prototype, the cost was high—$65,306.18.

The XF11C-1 with twin-row Wright R-1510 engine was built under a 1932 Navy contract.

XF11C-2 (Model 64A)—The XF11C-2 was an existing civil Hawk II demonstrator with 700 hp Wright R-1820 Cyclone that was purchased by the Navy shortly before construction of the XF11C-1 was authorized, hence the lower serial of 9213. The XF11C-2 had fabric-covered tail surfaces and longer undercarriage legs. After minor modification, the XF11C-2 became the prototype of the production F11C-2s at a cost of $42,530.

F11C-2—Twenty-eight production examples of the XF11C-2 were ordered as dual-purpose fighter-bombers in October 1932, Navy serials 9265/9292 and 9331/9340. These were delivered to Squadron VF-1B in February 1933. After a year, the F11C-2s were redesignated BFC-2 and had the cockpits modified with partial canopies. Serial 9269 was held at the factory for conversion to XF11C-3. Unit costs, less GFE, were $13,108.

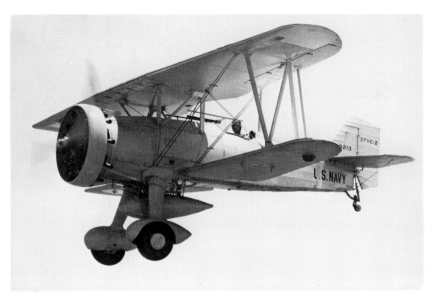

The XF11C-2 was an existing Hawk II or Goshawk demonstrator that the Navy bought before awarding the contract for the XF11C-1.

XF11C-3 (Model 67)—The fifth F11C-2, serial 9269, was delivered as a new Curtiss model and had a manually-retractable undercarriage inspired by that on the 1931 Grumman XFF-1, plus metal-frame wings. The top speed increased by 17 mph (27·35 km/h), but the weight increase of approximately 370 lb (168 kg) was a noticeable handicap. The twenty-seven production aircraft were delivered under a new designation, BF2C-1.

The twenty-eight production F11C-2s served for only a year with that designation before being modified and redesignated BFC-2. (*Courtesy William T. Larkins*)

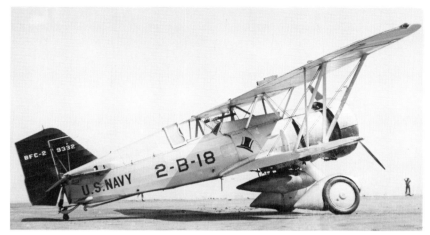

F11C-2 after cockpit changes and redesignation as BFC-2 Bomber-Fighter. *High Hat* Squadron VB-2 had been VF-1 when flying the same aeroplanes as F11C-2s. (*John C. Mitchell*)

XBFC-1—In March 1934 the Navy adopted a new designation, BF for Bomber-Fighter and the XF11C-1 was then redesignated XBFC-1.

BFC-2—The twenty-seven F11C-2s were redesignated BFC-2 after 13 months of service.

XBF2C-1—The XF11C-3 redesignated.

BF2C-1 (Model 67A)—Twenty-seven production examples of the XF11C-3, with metal-frame wings and the late BFC-2 cockpit canopies. Navy serial numbers 9586/9612. These were delivered to Squadron VB-5B

Production version of the XF11C-3 was designated BF2C-1. The undercarriage was weak and the new metal-frame wings had vibration problems. (*Fred Bamberger*)

in October 1934 but were withdrawn from service within a year because of serious mechanical problems, particularly with the undercarriage, and unsatisfactory vibration characteristics of the metal-frame wings. Unit costs less GFE, $17,995.

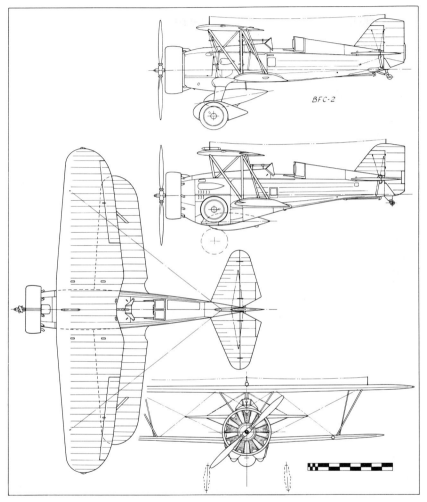

BF2C-1 and BFC-2.

## Civil and Export Hawks

The first Hawks to be exported had no specific Curtiss designations and were identified by their similarity to equivalent US Army models. By 1930 Curtiss began giving them sequential Hawk type numbers. The following models are presented as identified in Curtiss records.

P-1—Hawks with D-12 engines approved for export by the US Army.

P-1A—Eight went to Chile in 1926 and one to Japan in 1927.

P-1B—Eight to Chile in 1927. Others are believed to have been built in Chile.

P-6—Improved Hawks with water-cooled Conqueror engines; eight were sold to the Netherlands East Indies in September 1930, and eight more were built in the Netherlands. The export P-6s became Hawk Is in Curtiss records after the new Hawk II appeared in 1932.

Export Model P-6S was the basic US Army P-6 airframe with Wasp radial engine. This was one of three sold to Cuba.

P-6S—Basically P-6 airframes fitted with 450 hp Pratt & Whitney Wasp engines; three went to Cuba and one to Japan in 1930. Price complete $18,445.

Japan Hawk—One Conqueror-powered Hawk, US registration 42K, appears under this designation in 1930 factory photographs but does not appear in sales records. It is possible that it is the recorded Japanese P-6S using the Conqueror instead of the Wasp engine.

Hawk 1 (Model 35)—A Conqueror-powered company demonstrator built in 1930 and registered 9W with c/n 17. Following a crash, this was rebuilt and re-registered NR-9110, becoming known as the Doolittle Hawk because of being demonstrated by the famous Jimmy Doolittle. It was later sold to air show pilot Jesse Bristow and was used for that work until forced down at sea between Florida and Cuba during an air race in January 1940.

The water-cooled Japan Hawk carried US civil registration while under factory test.

Hawk I was the designation given to civil and export versions of US Army P-6. This privately-owned former Curtiss demonstrator was used for air show work until 1940. Letters NX preceding the registration number mean that the aeroplane is operating on an Experimental Licence. (*Roger Besecker*)

One Hawk 1-A demonstrator, here fitted with rare Bliss Jupiter engine, was sold to Gulf Oil Company and became the famous *Gulfhawk* when flown by aerobatic pilot Al Williams. (*Courtesy Al Bachmann*)

Hawk 1A—The most famous individual Hawk was the 1A flown by Alford J. Williams for the Gulf Oil Company from 1930 to 1936 as the *Gulfhawk*. It was a special demonstrator built in April 1929 for long-distance flights. It used the Conqueror engine and had extra fuel tanks fitted into the sides of the fuselage as on the Helldivers. Original registration was NR636E, c/n 1. After a crash, it was rebuilt as a Hawk 1A with a 575 hp Wright Cyclone engine and sold to Williams in August 1930 under registration NR982V. In August 1931 Williams installed a 575 hp Bliss Jupiter engine, which was the American-built version of the British Bristol Jupiter. Following another crash, 982V was again rebuilt with a 710

*Gulfhawk* underwent many modifications. Here it is with larger Wright Cyclone engine and a rounded-out and metal-skinned fuselage. (*Courtesy Roger Besecker*)

hp R-1820F-3 Cyclone. The side tanks were removed and the fuselage was metal-skinned. The engine was transferred to Williams's new Grumman *Gulfhawk II* in 1936 and 982V was placed in an aeronautical trade school. It was retrieved in 1958 by movie pilot Frank Tallman, who installed a 600 hp Pratt & Whitney Wasp engine. This last flying example of the long Hawk line is presently owned by the US Marine Corps Museum at Quantico, Virginia.

Hawk II (Models 35, 47)

The Hawk II, sometimes called Goshawk, was an extensively redesigned model with a Wright Cyclone radial engine and single-leg undercarriage that preceded the US Navy F11C/BFC design. In fact, a company-owned Hawk II demonstrator was sold to the Navy as the XF11C-2 before the contract for the previously-designated XF11C-1 was signed. Prices ranged from $11,825 to $15,700 less engines.

Model 35—One hundred and twenty-six exported to eight countries as follows:

    Bolivia—nine, c/ns H-23/26, H-64, H-65, SH-27/29; December 1923 to June 1934.

    Chile—four, c/ns SH-7/9, 11767; January 1935. Others built under licence in Chile.

    China—fifty, known c/ns H-47/63, H-66/79; March to September 1933.

    Colombia—twenty-six, twin-float seaplanes; c/ns SH-3/6, SH-10/25, SH-30/35; October 1932 to March 1934.

Colombia bought twenty-six seaplane versions of the Hawk II. The auxiliary vertical fin can be seen under the rear fuselage.

The Export Hawk II design preceded the US Navy F11C-2. Ernst Udet was so impressed with Al Williams's demonstrations of dive-bombing with *Gulfhawk* that he had the German Air Ministry buy two Hawk IIs to introduce dive-bombing tactics in Germany. (*Courtesy Heinz Nowarra*)

Nineteen Hawk IIs or Turkeyhawks were delivered to Turkey in 1932.

The Hawk III was the export version of the US Navy BF2C-1 that had wood-frame wings to eliminate the vibration problem. Shown here in Thai markings.

Cuba—four, Model 35B, c/ns H-19/22; January 1933.
Germany—two, H-80, 81; October 1933.
Thailand—twelve, H-85/96; August–September 1934.
Turkey—nineteen, c/ns unknown; August–September 1932.

The last biplane Hawk model was the export Hawk IV with enclosed cockpit and improved streamlining. Only one example was built.

Model 47—One improved Hawk II model, registration X13263, c/n DH-46, was sold to Norway in July 1934, following rebuild after use as a Curtiss demonstrator.

Hawk III (Model 68)

Export version of the US Navy BF2C-1. Since these aircraft had wooden wings, they did not have the vibration problems of the Navy's model. One hundred and thirty-eight were sold as follows:

Model 68A—One demonstrator, c/n 11894, registration NR-14703, delivered September 1934.

Model 68B—twenty-four to Thailand, c/ns 12061/12084; August 1935 to February 1936.

Model 68C—102 to China, c/ns 12095, 12175/12185, 12096/12155, 12726/12755; March 1936 to June 1938.

In addition, one Hawk III of unspecified model, c/n 11924, was sold to Turkey in April 1935; and ten to Argentina, c/n 12085/12094, in May and June 1936.

Hawk IV (Model 79)

One slightly refined Hawk III, c/n 12186, used as a demonstrator with registration NR188M. It was sold to Argentina in July 1936. Principal external difference from the Hawk III was the use of a completely enclosed cockpit.

| | XF6C-6* (racer) | F11C-2 (BFC-2, Hawk II) | BF2C-1 (Hawk III) | Hawk IV** |
|---|---|---|---|---|
| | 770 hp Curtiss V-1570 | 600 hp Wright SR-1820F-2 | 650 hp Wright R-1820-04 | 745 hp Wright R-1820 |
| Span . . . | 31 ft 6 in (9·6 m) | 31 ft 6 in (9·6 m) | 31 ft 6 in (9·6 m) | 31 ft 6 in (9·6 m) |
| Length . . | 23 ft 0 in (7·01 m) | 22 ft 7 in (6·88 m) | 24 ft 4 in (7·41 m) | 23 ft 6 in (7·16 m) |
| Height . . | 8 ft 11 in (2·71 m) | 9 ft 8⅝ in (2·96 m) | 9 ft 11½ in (3·03 m) | 9 ft 11½ in (3·03 m) |
| Empty weight . | 2,600 lb (1,179 kg) | 3,037 lb (1,378 kg) | 3,326 lb (1,509 kg) | 3,420 lb (1,551 kg) |
| Gross weight . | 3,130 lb (1,420 kg) | 4,132 lb (1,874 kg) | 4,552 lb (2,065 kg) | 4,614 lb (2,093 kg) |
| Maximum speed . | 250 mph (402·33 km/h) | 202 mph*** (325·08 km/h) | 225 mph (362·09 km/h) | 248·5 mph (399·91 km/h) |
| Cruising speed . | 200 mph (321·86 km/h) | 150 mph (241·39 km/h) | 157 mph (252·66 km/h) | 211·8 mph (340·85 km/h) |
| Initial climb . | — | 2,300 ft/min (11·68 m/sec) | 1,950 ft/min (9·9 m/sec) | — |
| Service ceiling . | — | 25,100 ft (7,650 m) | 27,000 ft (8,230 m) | 30,300 ft (9,235 m) |
| Range . . | 270 miles (435 km) | 522 miles (840 km) | 725 miles (1,167 km) | 577 miles (929 km) |
| Armament . . | All except the XF6C-6 racer had two machine-guns | | | |

* F6C-1/F6C-3 similar to Army P-1, F6C-4 similar to Army P-3A
** With constant-speed propeller
*** Speed at 8,000 ft (2,438 m)

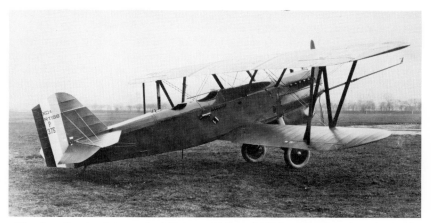

The first Curtiss Falcon, the US Army XO-1 of 1924, with original vertical tail and 420 hp Liberty engine.

# The Falcon Biplane

The two-seat Falcon series originated in 1923 as the Curtiss entry in a formal Air Service fly-off competition for new observation designs powered with the wartime Liberty engine. While the development and production life of the Falcon paralleled that of the Hawk, it is one of the forgotten aeroplanes of history, due mostly to the fact that it was a workhorse two-seater and did not have the glamour of the fighters. Actually, nearly as many Falcons were built for the US Armed Forces as Hawks—one hundred and seventy for the Army, twenty-seven for the Navy, twenty-one civil, plus undetermined export models. In 1933, the venerable Falcon was unique in being the only 1923 design still in production in the US.

Curtiss Falcons were procured for the US Army under eleven different designations using six different powerplants, while the Navy models had two designations and two powerplants. Export models added a seventh power option. The original Curtiss model designation was L-113, changed to Model 35 under the 1935 system (38, 44, 45, and 72 for later versions; some experimental variants were overlooked). The Army assigned the designation XO-1 to the prototype.

The Curtiss design took second place to the Douglas XO-2 in the observation design competition which took place in 1924, but the setback was only temporary. The Army decided that the ubiquitous Liberty was no longer suited to first-line military aeroplanes, so it scheduled a 1925 contest for observation types to be powered with the new Packard 1A-1500, a 510 hp V-12 engine very similar to the contemporary Curtiss D-12 (V-1150). All that Curtiss had to do was change engines in the XO-1. This time, Curtiss won and received an order for ten O-1s to be powered with the D-12 since the Army rejected the Packard at that time.

The Falcon had unique fuselage construction for the time—aluminium tubing bolted and riveted together with steel tie-rod bracing. The wings were wooden-framed with a wire trailing edge and the new Clark-Y aerofoil. The centre-section was placed well forward for improved pilot access and visibility, making it necessary to sweep the upper wing panels back nine degrees to achieve balance. This became the Falcon's principal recognition feature.

Armament followed the traditional World War I practice, with a single ·30 calibre Browning machine-gun for the pilot and twin Lewis guns on a Scarff ring around the rear cockpit. Bomb racks could be fitted under the lower wing. Armament improvements are covered in the aeroplane descriptions.

The Falcon name did not die out with the passing of the biplane—Curtiss assigned it to the SNC-1 monoplane trainer built for the US Navy in World War II.

The biplane Falcons are described here in sequence of US Army, then Navy, and finally civil and export designations.

### US Army Falcons

*Observation Types*

### O-1 Series (Model 37)

XO-1—No change of Curtiss model designation was involved in the change from Liberty to Packard engine in the XO-1, Army serial 23-1252. On this model alone, the fin/rudder combination resembled the PW-8s. As flown in the 1924 competition, the XO-1 was without armament but performance figures were corrected for the weight differential.

The XO-1 refitted with 510 hp Packard engine for 1925 Observation aircraft competition.

Production O-1s were fitted with Curtiss D-12 engines instead of the Packard. The small A.S. serial number on the fuselage and the manufacturer's name and Army model number on the rudder were standard for the 1925–26 period.

O-1 (Model 37A)—Ten production O-1s (25-325/334) were ordered as a result of the 1925 competition. The major difference from the prototype was the use of the Curtiss D-12 engine in place of the Packard and a revision of the vertical tail surfaces to increase the fin area and decrease the rudder balance area. Gross weight was increased from 3,857 lb (1,750 kg) to 4,165 lb (1,889 kg); maximum speed decreased from 154 mph (247·8 km/h) to 144 mph (231·7 km/h), and service ceiling dropped from 23,400 ft (7,132 m) to 17,500 ft (5,334 m). Range was increased by use of a 56-gallon (212 litre) auxiliary fuel tank under the belly. The first O-1 was evaluated in 1926 as a possible two-seat pursuit type.

O-1s converted to other designations: 25-325 to O-1 Special, an unarmed

Special unarmed O-1 for use by high government official (with four-star flag on rudder). A.S. prefix to serial number changed to A.C. for Air Corps in mid-1926, U.S. ARMY was added to the fuselage early in 1927.

One O-1 was completed with a Liberty engine and delivered as the O-1A.

transport for VIPs, in 1926; 25-331 and 332 to XO-13A and XO-13 racers, respectively, in 1927; 25-333 completed as O-1A.

O-1A—The ninth O-1, 25-333, was completed with a Liberty engine and improved rear cockpit appointments at Air Service direction. The lines were altered by deepening the aft fuselage to form a permanent fairing behind a 56-gallon (212 litre) auxiliary fuel tank between the rear undercarriage struts. There was no change in Curtiss designation. Although 223 lb (101 kg) heavier than the O-1, the O-1A was 4 mph (6·43 km/h) faster. Surveyed 10 October, 1930.

O-1B (Model 37B)—The first major production O-1 variant; forty-five, 27-243/287, were ordered in 1927. Improvements included wheel brakes, a droppable 56-gallon (212 litre) belly tank, and provisions for dumping the fuel in the 113-gallon (427 litre) main tank. One additional O-1B resulted from the conversion of O-11 28-207 to YO-13D and then to O-1B. Weights and performance were very close to those of the O-1.

The principal production O-1 was the O-1B, of which 45 were built. The droppable under-fuselage fuel tank can be seen.

Four O-1Cs were O-1Bs modified for executive use. There is a baggage compartment door aft of the rear cockpit. Star marking on the fin indicates use by a Brigadier-General.

Five O-1Bs converted to other designations as follows: 27-243 to A-3 and back to O-1B; 27-244 to XA-4; 27-263 to XO-18 and back to O-1B; 27-264, 266/268 to O-1C (27-266 reconverted to O-1B).

O-1C—Four O-1Bs, 27-264, 266/268, were modified in 1927 in the manner of the O-1 Special to serve as personal transports under the designation of O-1C for Presidential Cabinet officers and Air Corps general officers. Armament was removed, a baggage compartment with external starboard-side door was added, and the rear seat was widened. One, 27-266, was later converted to O-13B.

O-1D—This designation, to have been assigned to an improved O-1B with Curtiss V-1150F engine, was not used.

Only noticeable outward change on the O-1E was the addition of balance areas to the elevators. (*A.U. Schmidt*)

Standard O-1E fitted with experimental canopy over the pilot's cockpit. The letters M.A.D. on the rudder indicate assignment to Middletown Air Depot.

O-1E (Model 37I)—The forty-one O-1Es, 29-282/322, were improved O-1Bs with V-1150E engines. Refinements included Frise ailerons, horn-balanced elevators, oleo-pneumatic shock absorbers, E-4 gun synchronizer system, and a 36-gallon (136 litre) belly tank. One, 29-296, was fitted at the factory with a pilot's cockpit enclosure. Gross weight was increased to 4,532 lb (2,056 kg), maximum speed reduced to 140·8 mph (226·59 km/h) and the service ceiling to 15,300 ft (4,663 m). An additional O-1E resulted from the conversion of A-3B 30-1.

O-1Es converted to other designations: 29-288 to O-1F; 29-295 to XBT-4, XO-1G, and Y1O-1G; 29-319/321 to YO-13C and O-13C; 29-322 to XO-26, Y1O-26.

O-1F (Model 37J)—One O-1E, 29-288, was modified along the lines of the O-1Cs by removal of the armament, addition of a baggage

The single O-1F was an O-1E with the executive transport features of the O-1Cs.
(*Gordon S. Williams*)

The XO-1G was built as an O-1E which was then converted to XBT-4 before becoming a new experimental observation variant in 1930. Principal changes were new horizontal tail, revised rear cockpit, and relocated tailwheel.

compartment, and a more comfortable rear cockpit. Original powerplant was the V-1150F engine, later changed to a V-1150EM.

XO-1G (Model 38)—The XO-1G was a doubly converted aeroplane, having been built as O-1E 29-295 and then converted to XBT-4 for an Army Basic Trainer competition. Modification as a new observation aircraft prototype involved enough changes to justify a new Curtiss model number. Most noticeable were revision of the rear cockpit and change to a single post-mounted machine-gun, cut-out of the lower rudder to accommodate a new steerable tailwheel located well aft of the original tailskid position, and completely redesigned horizontal tail surfaces. A cut-out was added to the wing above the pilot. After delivery to the Army, this became Y1O-1G and eventually O-1G with V-1150EM engine.

The XO-1G was transferred from experimental to Service test status and became the Y1O-1G.

291

Thirty O-1Gs were production versions of the Y1O-1G. (*E.M. Sommerich collection*)

Y1O-1G—The XO-1G, 29-295, changed from experimental to Service-test status. Redesignated O-1G; destroyed in a crash on 6 June, 1932.

O-1G—Thirty production versions of the XO/Y1O-1G, 31-472/501, were ordered in 1931, and had a redesigned pilot's instrument panel and a new gunner's seat. Refinement of the design increased maximum speed to 143 mph (230·13 km/h) and the service ceiling to 17,000 ft (5,181 m) in spite of a gross weight increase to 4,426 lb (2,008 kg).

## O-11, 12, 13, 16, 18, 26 Series Falcons

XO-11 (Model 37C)—With the new D-12 engines in short supply because of pursuit aeroplane requirements, the plentiful supply of Liberty engines still owned by the Government was tapped to power additional Falcons intended for service with the National Guard.

The fourth O-1, 25-328, was fitted with a Liberty and given the lines of the O-1A by Curtiss at the direction of the Air Corps Observation Board and was redesignated XO-11. A second XO-11 resulted from the diversion of production O-11 27-98 to test work at Wright Field.

O-11—Sixty-six production O-11s, 27-1/35, 27-98/107, 28-196/217, were ordered for the National Guard. Except for details concerning the Liberty engine, the O-11 airframes were similar to the O-1B.

O-11s converted to other designations: One to O-11A; 27-35 to XO-12; 27-98 to XO-11 No.2; 27-207 to O-13D, O-13C, O-1B; 28-196 to XO-16.

O-11A—One unarmed O-11 modified with dual controls, a deepened belly, improved tail surfaces, and such O-1E features as oleo shock absorbers and a castoring tailskid.

XO-12—The last O-11 of the original order, N.G. 27-35, was fitted with a Pratt & Whitney R-1340 Wasp engine to evaluate this new air-cooled engine in a proven observation aeroplane. After test, the XO-12 remained

292

The O-11A was extensively modified for use by Treasury Department and US Customs officials in patrolling the US–Mexican Border. (*Ned Moore*)

The single XO-12 was an O-11 modified to test the Wasp radial engine for possible use in National Guard aeroplanes. (*Courtesy Thomas S. Cuddy II*)

in the service of the National Guard and retained its experimental designation until scrapped in April 1933, with a flight time of 748 hours.

XO-13—The eighth O-1, 25-332, was returned to Curtiss for a change to the new 600 hp Curtiss V-1570 Conqueror engine uprated to 730 hp at 2,600 rpm as one of the Army's entries in the Liberty Engine Builders Trophy event of the 1927 National Air Races. The new engine justified the change of designation. After achieving a top speed of 169 mph (271·97 km/h) in tests, the XO-13 came second in its closed-course race at 164 mph (263·92 km/h) using a mixture of 80 percent Benzol and 20 percent petrol. Scrapped in June 1928 with 272 flying hours.

The XO-13 was the eighth O-1 fitted with a special 730 hp Curtiss Conqueror engine for the 1927 National Air Races.

The XO-13A was also an O-1 refitted with a special Conqueror engine. Streamlining was improved by replacing the standard cooling system with wing surface radiators. This aeroplane came first in the military two-seater event of the 1927 National Air Races.

The three YO-13Cs were O-1Es modified to Service test the production Conqueror engine in observation aircraft.

XO-13A—The seventh O-1, 25-331, was modified more extensively than the XO-13 for the 1927 race. In addition to the special V-1570 engine giving 720 hp at 2,560 rpm, both wings were modified to accommodate surface radiators in the old PW-8 style as a drag-reduction measure. Best straightaway speed was 176·5 mph (284 km/h) and speed round a closed course to win the Liberty Engine Builders Trophy was 170·5 mph (274·38 km/h). Scrapped in March 1930 with 482 flying hours.

O-13B—One O-1C, 27-266, was converted to O-13B to evaluate the new 600 hp Curtiss V-1570-1 Conqueror engine in a standard observation aircraft. At 4,400 lb (1,996 kg) gross weight, the O-13B had a maximum speed of 165·2 mph (265·85 km/h).

YO-13C (Model 37K)—Three O-1Es, 29-319/321, were converted to YO-13C by the installation of 600 hp V-1570 Conqueror engines. Designation later changed to O-13C. One additional O-13C, 28-207, was created temporarily by replacing the supercharged SV-1570 engine of the YO-13D with the unsupercharged model of the O-13C. Gross weight 4,542 lb (2,060 kg), maximum speed 156·2 mph (251·37 km/h), service ceiling 19,750 ft (6,020 m).

The single YO-13D was an O-11 modified to test a Prestone-cooled Conqueror engine.

YO-13D—One O-11, 28-207, was converted to YO-13D by installing a supercharged Curtiss SV-1570 Conqueror engine and a modified radiator system. This aircraft became an O-13C with an unsupercharged V-1570-1 and then was converted to O-1B with a V-1150-5. At 4,600 lb (2,086 kg), the YO-13D had a maximum speed of 160 mph (257·49 km/h).

XO-16 (Model 37G)—O-11 28-196 became the XO-16 when completed at Buffalo with revised fuselage contours and cockpit arrangements and a V-1570-9 Conqueror engine. Curtiss records indicate that this was water-cooled and radiator size shown in the photograph confirms water; Army records say Prestone-cooled. Gross weight was less than the O-13s, 4,305 lb (1,953 kg), while maximum speed and service ceiling increased to 161·6

The XO-16 was an O-11 refitted with a Conqueror engine and embodying more fuselage modifications than used on the O-13s.

mph (260·06 km/h) and 23,300 ft (7,102 m), respectively.

XO-18—O-1B 27-263 was redesignated XO-18 when used as a flying test-bed for the experimental 610 hp Curtiss H-1640-1 Chieftain engine, a unique twelve-cylinder twin-row air-cooled radial. The engine proved unsuitable and the XO-18 reverted to O-1B.

Y1O-26 (Model 37L)—O-1E 29-322 was converted to a test-bed for a Prestone-cooled geared V-1570-11 Conqueror. Some Army records refer to this as XO-26. The smaller radiator required for Prestone resulted in an attempt to improve streamlining by grouping the coolant and oil radiators close to the raised thrust line of the geared engine. Gross weight 4,574 lb (2,075 kg), maximum speed 161·2 mph (259·42 km/h), service ceiling 20,500 ft (6,248 m). The aircraft, now designated 0-26, was surveyed in August 1934, with 511 flight hours.

The XO-18 was an O-1B modified as a testbed for the experimental Curtiss H-1640 Chieftain engine.

The Y1O-26, later O-26, was an O-1E used to test a geared Conqueror engine with experimental nose radiator. (*Gordon S. Williams*)

O-39 (Model 38A)—Ten O-39s, 32-211/220, were delivered in 1931. These were essentially O-1Gs with V-1570-25 Conqueror engines. The engine cowling and radiator design matched those of the contemporary Curtiss P-6E fighter. Some were modified with enclosed cockpits and all had the rudder area reduced later by cutting down the top of the rudder by about two inches (5 cm).

At a gross weight of 4,679 lb (2,122 kg), the O-39 was the fastest of the standard Army Falcons, with a maximum speed of 170·5 mph (274·38 km/h). This was increased to 173·3 mph (278·89 km/h) on the enclosed models. Service ceiling was 22,800 ft (6,949 m).

The ten O-39s were similar to O-1Gs except for Conqueror engines with P-6E type radiators. Rudders were shortened after delivery.

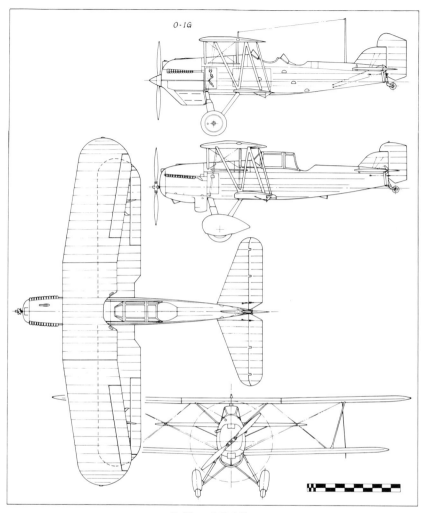

O-39 and O-1G.

## Attack and Trainer Falcons

A-3 (Model 44)—The O-1B observation model was easily adapted to the ground attack role under the designation of A-3. Minor changes consisted of adding bomb racks under the lower wings and installing a single ·30 calibre machine-gun in each lower wing just outboard of the propeller arc. Performance, with the D-12D (V-1150-3) engine was similar to that of the O-1B. A total of 66 was ordered on three contracts.

US Army serial numbers: 27-243/262 (20), 27-298/317 (20), 28-83/108 (26).

The A-3 was similar to the O-1B except for bomb racks and additional machine-guns in the lower wings for ground attack purposes.

Six A-3As were disarmed A-3s fitted with dual controls for training.

The seventy-eight A-3Bs incorporated the same structural improvements as the O-1E. Dice insignia identifies the 90th Attack Squadron. (*Courtesy Peter Westburg*)

299

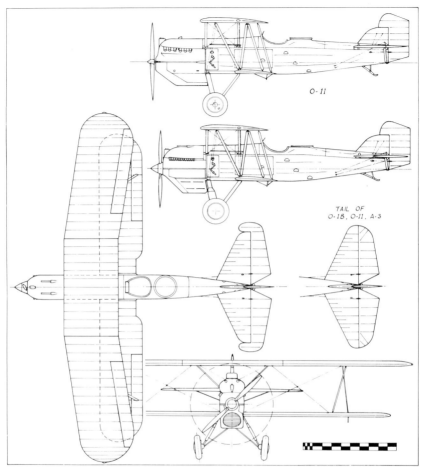

O-1E and O-11, with tailplane and elevators of O-1B, O-11 and A-3.

A-3A—Six A-3s, 27-306, 310, 315, 28-116/118, were redesignated A-3A
when fitted with dual controls for transition training of observers.

A-3B (Model 37H)—Seventy-eight attack equivalents of the O-1E,
Army serials 30-1/28, 30-231/280, with the same airframe and aerodynamic
improvements. When equipped for gunnery the gross weight was 4,458 lb
(2,022 kg); as a bomber, it was 4,476 lb (2,030 kg). Maximum speed was
139·4 mph (224·33 km/h) and service ceiling 14,400 ft (4,389 m). The high-
time A-3B had 2,850 hours and the last one in service was 30-13, scrapped
in October 1937. Serial 30-1 was converted to an O-1E.

The single XA-4 was an O-1B modified to test the Wasp engine in an attack aircraft.

XA-4—To evaluate the 440 hp Pratt & Whitney Wasp radial engine in an attack aircraft, A-3 27-244 was completed as the XA-4 with the R-1340-1 engine. Gross weight was reduced to 4,113 lb (1,866 kg); maximum speed was 137·4 mph (221·12 km/h), service ceiling 16,950 ft (5,166 m). Delivered in December 1927, the XA-4 was scrapped in March 1932, with 327 hours.

XBT-4 (Model 46)—O-1E 29-295 was completed in June 1930 as an experimental basic trainer at a time when the Army was reclassifying some other disarmed observation types to the new BT category. (Douglas O-2K to BT-1, Douglas O-32 to BT-2.) No orders were placed with Curtiss and the XBT-4 was quickly converted to the XO-1G. XBT-4 gross weight 4,156 lb (1,885 kg), maximum speed 140 mph (225·3 km/h).

The XBT-4 was an O-1E modified as the Curtiss entry in an Army Basic Trainer competition in 1929. It later became the XO-1G and Y1O-1G. The use of three-line data on US Army aeroplane fuselages ended in 1932.

301

| | XO-1 | O-39 | O-11 | A-3B |
|---|---|---|---|---|
| | 510 hp | 600 hp | 433 hp | 426 hp |
| | Packard 1A-1500 | Curtiss V-1570C | Liberty 12A | Curtiss D-12E |
| Span . . | 38 ft 0 in | 38 ft 0 in | 38 ft 0 in | 38 ft 0 in |
| | (11·58 m) | (11·58 m) | (11·58 m) | (11·58 m) |
| Length . . | 28 ft 4 in | 27 ft 7 in | 27 ft 3½ in | 27 ft 7 in |
| | (8·63 m) | (8·4 m) | (8·31 m) | (8·4 m) |
| Height . . | 10 ft 11 in | 10 ft 3 in | 10 ft 3 in | 10 ft 3 in |
| | (3·32 m) | (3·12 m) | (3·12 m) | (3·12 m) |
| Wing area . | 349·6 sq ft | 348 sq ft | 351 sq ft | 351 sq ft |
| | (32·47 sq m) | (32·32 sq m) | (32·6 sq m) | (32·6 sq m) |
| Empty weight . | 2,227 lb | 3,328 lb | 3,012 lb | 2,902 lb |
| | (1,010 kg) | (1,510 kg) | (1,366 kg) | (1,316 kg) |
| Gross weight . | 3,857 lb | 4,679 lb | 4,532 lb | 4,476 lb |
| | (1,750 kg) | (2,122 kg) | (2,056 kg) | (2,030 kg) |
| Maximum speed | 154 mph | 173·3 mph | 146·9 mph | 139·4 mph |
| | (247·83 km/h) | (278·89 km/h) | (236·4 km/h) | (224·33 km/h) |
| Cruising speed | 123 mph | 138 mph | 115 mph | 111 mph |
| | (197·94 km/h) | (222·08 km/h) | (185·07 km/h) | (178·63 km/h) |
| Initial climb . | 1,275 ft/min | 1,620 ft/min | 1,066 ft/min | 948 ft/min |
| | (6·47 m/sec) | (8·22 m/sec) | (5·41 m/sec) | (4·81 m/sec) |
| Service ceiling . | 23,400 ft | 22,800 ft | 16,630 ft | 14,400 ft |
| | (7,132 m) | (6,949 m) | (5,069 m) | (4,389 m) |
| Range . . | 595 miles | 760 miles* | 437 miles | 647 miles** |
| | (957 km) | (1,223 km) | (703 km) | (1,041 km) |
| Armament . | One fixed, two | One fixed and one | — | Four fixed, two |
| | flexible machine- | flexible machine- | | flexible machine- |
| | guns | gun, 250 lb | | guns, 200 lb |
| | | (113 kg) bombs | | (91 kg) bombs |

* With 142 gal (537 litres)
**With 100 gal (378·5 litres)

## US Navy Falcons

XF8C-1 (Model 37D)—Two XF8C-1s, A7671, 7672, were general-purpose models combining the features of the Army XO-12 and XA-4 Falcons. Fitted with bomb racks and the extra wing guns of the A-3, they were given a fighter designation because the Navy, which purchased them for the US Marines, did not have an attack designation at the time. With a gross weight of 3,918 lb (1,777 kg), maximum speed was 137·5 mph (221·28 km/h) and service ceiling 17,300 ft (5,273 m).

A7671 soon dropped its experimental status and became F8C-1. Shortly thereafter, it was designated OC-1 as an observation type. Delivered in February 1928, A7671 saw service with the Marine observation squadron VO-10M in China and with VO-8M on the US West Coast. A7672 became OC-1 briefly before becoming XOC-3 in October 1930.

F8C-1—Four production versions of the XF8C-1s for the Marine Corps. These were redesignated OC-1s soon after delivery in January 1928. Navy serials A7945/7948.

Two XF8C-1s were naval equivalents of the Army XA-4 for Marine Corps. The first example was later redesignated OC-1. (*Courtesy William T. Larkins*)

XF8C-2—A third aeroplane, A7673, was ordered on the XF8C-1 contract, but it was an entirely new design, the Helldiver.

F8C-3—Twenty-one later versions of the XF8C-1s delivered from February to April 1928. Navy serials A7949/7969. Additional military equipment increased gross weight to 4,175 lb (1,894 kg), decreased maximum speed to 136 mph (218·86 km/h), and service ceiling to 16,400 ft (4,999 m). They were soon redesignated OC-2s. Unit price less GFE was $12,800.

Four production F8C-1s were built for the Marines but were soon redesignated OC-1. The diagonal mark between the Squadron and aeroplane numbers identified Navy and Marine Corps observation aircraft before adoption of letter O. The circle around the symbol distinguished Marine aeroplanes from Navy aircraft into 1937.

Marine Corps' F8C-1 A-7945 after being redesignated OC-1.

OC-1—The four production F8C-1s and the two XF8C-1 prototypes redesignated as observation aircraft. The last one, A7947, was surveyed in April 1935.

OC-2—The twenty-one production F8C-3s redesignated. The last OC-2, A7952, was scrapped in October 1935, with 2,511 flying hours.

### OC-2

Two-seat observation aircraft. 425 hp Pratt & Whitney R-1340 Wasp.

Span 38 ft (11·58 m); length 27 ft 11 in (8·5 m); height 10 ft 3 in (3·12 m); wing area 351 sq ft (32·6 sq m).

Empty weight 2,512 lb (1,139 kg); gross weight 4,175 lb (1,894 kg).

Maximum speed 136 mph (218·86 km/h); cruising speed 109 mph (175·41 km/h); initial climb 1,000 ft/min (5·08 m/sec); service ceiling 16,400 ft (4,999 m); range 653 miles (1,051 km).

Armament—six machine-guns.

Twenty-one production F8C-3s were ordered for the Marines but were delivered as OC-2s. All Marine Corps aeroplanes carried the Marine Corps emblem on the fuselage.

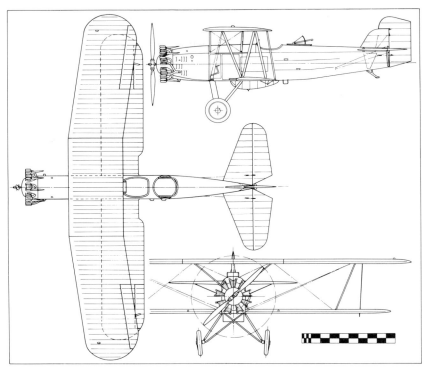

OC-2.

The second XF8C-1 was redesignated XOC-3 when used to test the Curtiss Chieftain engine.

305

XOC-3—The second XF8C-1, A7672, was redesignated XOC-3 for test of a 600 hp Curtiss Chieftain engine installation similar to that of the Army XO-18. The fuselage was rounded out with stringers in the manner of the XO-16 to match the engine cowling. Empty weight 2,842 lb (1,289 kg), gross weight 4,278 lb (1,940 kg), maximum speed 160 mph (257·49 km/h), service ceiling 20,400 ft (6,218 m). A7672 remained XOC-3 until struck off charge in April 1932.

### Civil and Demonstrator Falcons

A batch of twenty commercial Falcons, c/ns 1/20, was started in Buffalo in 1928. Details of seating and powerplant varied according to customer requirements. The differences resulted in the aeroplanes being licensed under a variety of ATCs and Category-2 Memo Approvals while some operated as demonstrators on straight experimental licences. All but c/ns 2 and 4 are accounted for in the following paragraphs.

Conqueror Mailplane—A Curtiss demonstrator similar to the O-1B but fitted with a Conqueror engine and having provision for mail but no passenger. On loan to Transcontinental Air Transport (TAT) when it crashed on 21 August, 1928.
Registration: X-5988. C/n 1

One Falcon demonstrator was fitted with a forward cabin for combined mail/passenger service.

Lindbergh Special—Listed in Curtiss records as a modified A-3B, one special Falcon was built in June 1928 and sold to Charles A. Lindbergh in June 1929 in connection with his survey work for Transcontinental Air Transport. This model, licensed under Memo 2-71 in May 1929, had a special D-12D engine and provision for a passenger in the rear cockpit. The

A used 1928 Falcon demonstrator was modified in 1929 for Charles A. Lindbergh and became known as the Lindbergh Special. (*Courtesy Robert L. Taylor*)

normal gross weight of 4,808 lb (2,181 kg) was increased to 5,148 lb (2,335 kg) and the payload to 1,000 lb (454 kg). The normal 135-gall (388 litre) fuel capacity was increased to 150 gal (567 litres). Maximum speed was 151 mph (243 km/h), cruising speed 135 mph (217·25 km/h), service ceiling 15,400 ft (4,694 m). Later it was converted to take a Wright Cyclone engine. Registration: 7455. C/n 3

D-12 Mailplane—One two-seat civil cargo Falcon appeared with the 435 hp Curtiss D-12D engine and an enclosed cabin in the front cockpit/mail compartment area. It was sold to TAT in May 1928 as a survey aircraft. It crashed in Chicago on 29 September, 1928, and its engine was then installed in the Lindbergh Special. Registration: 7431. C/n 5

Although carrying the civil markings NR310E, this Conqueror powered Falcon demonstrator was intended for the military market and was sent on a sales tour of Europe.

307

Conqueror Demonstrator—Essentially an O-1B airframe with O-1G type cockpits and Prestone-cooled Conqueror engine delivered in September 1928. Cooling changed to water for overseas sales tour. Sold to unknown foreign customer.
Registration: NR310E. C/n 6

Fourteen single-seat Falcon mailplanes with Liberty engines were sold to National Air Transport in 1928–29. (*Joseph P. Juptner collection*)

Liberty Mailplane—Advertized as the Curtiss Falcon Cargo, fourteen single-seat mailplanes, each with provision for approximately 820 lb (372 kg) of payload, were delivered to National Air Transport (NAT) between November 1928 and June 1929. Used on night mail flights, they were fitted with landing lights under each lower wing, and the exhaust stacks were extended aft of the pilot's seat so that the glare wouldn't interfere with his forward vision. Licensed under Memo 2-31, which was cancelled and replaced by ATC-103 in January 1929, the Falcon Cargos were unique in being the last US newly built commercial aeroplanes to use the Liberty engine. Empty weight varied from 3,179 to 3,341 lb (1,442–1,515 kg), gross weight from 5,110 to 5,265 lb (2,318–2,388 kg); maximum speed 146 mph (234·96 km/h); cruising speed 124 mph (199·55 km/h); service ceiling 14,000 ft (4,267 m).
Registrations and c/ns: 112E (7), 208E/214E (8/14), 301E (15), 8670 (16), 255H/258H (17/20)
NAT sold NC208E to Wright Aeronautical Corp, which installed a Conqueror engine and used the aeroplane for engine experiments until 1936. NC212E was also sold to Wright, who installed an F-series Cyclone radial engine. In this form it became the prototype of the Colombia Cyclone Falcon.
Two former NAT Falcons were caught by Treasury Department agents while involved in rum-running during the prohibition era. These (NC112E and 301E) were transferred to the US Coast Guard but did not get Service designations and were not used. One other ex-NAT Falcon, NC258H, was also involved in smuggling but was burned by its pilot to avoid capture.

### Falcon Mailplane (1928)

Single-seat mail/cargo aircraft. 425 hp Liberty 12A.

Span 38 ft (11·58 m); length 27 ft 5⅚ in (8·38 m); height 10 ft 11 in (3·32 m); wing area 351 sq ft (32·6 sq m).

Empty weight 3,179 lb (1,442 kg); loaded weight 5,110 lb (2,318 kg).

Maximum speed 146 mph (234·96 km/h); cruising speed 124 mph (199·55 km/h); initial climb 840 ft/min (4·26 m/sec); service ceiling 14,000 ft (4,267 m); range 728 miles (1,172 km).

Geared Conqueror Mailplane—In August 1929 a modified Falcon Cargo was licensed under ATC-213 for NAT with a 600 hp geared Conqueror engine. This had the same payload as the Liberty model but at 5,295 lb (2,402 kg) gross weight had a maximum speed of 160 mph (257·49 km/h), cruising speed of 136 mph (218·86 km/h), and service ceiling of 17,700 ft (5,395 m). This aeroplane was reconverted to take a Liberty engine in November 1930.
Registration: 301E. C/n 15

This Falcon mailplane, 301E, was identical to the Liberty-engined model except for the substitution of a geared Curtiss Conqueror.

PAA Cyclone Falcon—In October 1930 Curtiss modified the former Lindbergh Falcon and renamed it the Pan-American Falcon Mailplane for delivery to Pan American Airways for use on its Grace Division in South America. Powered with a 575 hp Wright Cyclone R-1820E, this now had a gross weight of 4,648 lb (2,108 kg) and a useful load of 1,709 lb (775 kg). Auxiliary fuel tanks and landing lights were not included in the normal gross weight. Maximum speed 154 mph (247·83 km/h), cruising speed 123 mph (197·94 km/h), service ceiling 22,100 ft (6,736 m), range 416 miles (669 km). This model was still flying in 1938.
Registration: NC7455. C/n 3

The former Lindbergh Special Falcon was rebuilt as a single-seat mailplane with Wright Cyclone engine for service in South America.

A former Liberty-engined Falcon was obtained from NAT by Wright Aeronautical Corporation and used as a testbed for a geared and turbo-supercharged Curtiss Conqueror.

The greatly revised Falcon II of 1934 was the last of the biplane Falcon line.

Wright Falcon—One of the NAT Liberty-powered Falcon mailplanes was acquired by the Wright Aeronautical Division of Curtiss-Wright in February 1932, and was used as a flying test-bed for various experimental versions of the V-1570 Conqueror engine that included steam-cooling and turbo-supercharging.
Registration: X-108E. C/n 8

1934 Falcon II (Model 72)—Final and fastest model in the original biplane Falcon series was the 1934 version powered with a 745 hp SR-1820F-53 Cyclone engine. Built in the Kenmore plant in July 1934, this was advertized as the Falcon II. Major outward changes from earlier Falcons were the single-strut undercarriage, NACA cowling, full canopy covering both cockpits, and a fold-down rear turtledeck that allowed traverse of the rear-cockpit machine-gun. This feature was to appear on subsequent Curtiss US Navy and US Army two-seaters to the end of the Second World War. The Falcon II was available for export in light bomber, long-range reconnaissance, and attack versions, with minor differences in gross weight and performance.

This was the last biplane Falcon built and was destroyed when the wings came off during a dive test on 6 November, 1934.
Registration: X-14369. C/n F-1-37

### Falcon II

Multi-purpose military two-seater. 745 hp Wright SR-1820F-53 Cyclone.

Span 38 ft (11·58 m); length 26 ft 6 in (8·07 m); height 10 ft 3 in (3·12 m); wing area 348 sq ft (32·32 sq m).

Empty weight 3,447 lb (1,563 kg); gross weight 4,770 lb (2,164 kg).

Maximum speed 205 mph (329·91 km/h) at 8,000 ft (2,438 m); initial climb 1,600 ft/min (8·12 m/sec); service ceiling 26,000 ft (7,925 m); range 560 miles (901 km).

Armament—three fixed and one flexible machine-gun, 500 lb (227 kg) bombs.

## Export Falcons

South American D-12 Falcon (Model 37F)—In March 1928 Curtiss sold one seaplane version of the O-1B to Colombia. This was followed by an order from Colombia for fifteen production aircraft also powered with the D-12 engine. The prototype, named *Ricautre* after a Colombian hero, was flown from New York to Colombia by Benjamin Mendez, a Colombian who had learned to fly just for this purpose. After a series of accidents, *Ricautre* reached Colombia. Ten additional D-12 Falcons were sold to Peru, a sale which was to put Falcons on both sides of the Colombia–Peru war of 1932–34.

Colombia Cyclone Falcon—One hundred Falcons powered with 712 hp Wright Cyclone engines were ordered by Colombia for use in its 1932–34 war against Peru. These were used both as landplanes and as twin-float seaplanes. The landplanes had open-side wheel pants and used the aft

311

In 1928, Colombia bought this seaplane version of the O-1B and then ordered fifteen more.

tailwheel location and revised horizontal tail introduced on the O-1G, and had canopies over the front cockpits.

### Colombia Cyclone Falcon

Two-seat military seaplane. 712 hp Wright SR-1820F-2 Cyclone.

Span 38 ft (11·58 m); length 28 ft 11 in (8·81 m); height 12 ft 8 in (3·86 m); wing area 351 sq ft (32·6 sq m).

Empty weight 3,617 lb (1,641 kg); gross weight 5,734 lb (2,601 kg).

Maximum speed 178 mph (286·45 km/h); initial climb 1,530 ft/min (7·77 m/sec); service ceiling 23,900 ft (7,285 m); range 680 miles (1,094 km).

Armament—three fixed and one flexible machine-gun, 400 lb (181 kg) bombs.

One hundred Cyclone Falcons for Colombia were essentially O-1G airframes with radial engines. Cockpits were enclosed, but some later had open cockpits with fixed windshields.

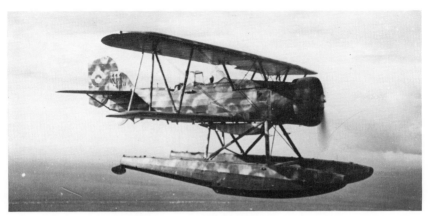
Colombia's Cyclone Falcons were used primarily as seaplanes during the 1932–34 war with Peru.

Chilean Falcon—At least ten O-1E Falcons were built in government factories in Chile, along with a number of P-1 Hawks. Between eight and ten of the O-1Es were hurriedly transferred to Brazil in September 1932 to help quell the revolt and secession of São Paulo Province. Some were lost in early action against the insurgents before the Brazilian military serials 1 to 7 were assigned to the survivors.

Moth Aircraft Corporation was formed in 1928 to manufacture the British de Havilland 60 Moth lightplane and the later 85 hp de Havilland Gipsy engine that was designed for it. Curtiss acquired the firm in 1929. Production of the aircraft continued as the Curtiss-Wright Moth 60GMW and the engine became the 90 hp Wright Gipsy. Moth production was transferred to St Louis in 1930 and ended in 1931. (*Peter M. Bowers*)

# Expansion,
# Merger and Depression

One of the major events in American aviation history was the merger of two old and antagonistic names in American aviation, Curtiss and Wright, which took place on 26 June, 1929; but since at the time neither organization was controlled by its founder and the product lines were complementary rather than competitive, the merger could not really be regarded as the wedding of old enemies.

From 1911 to 1929, the word Curtiss was a collective term covering the basic aeroplane manufacturer and a number of wholly-owned subsidiaries that manufactured supplemental products such as engines and propellers, sold or serviced Curtiss products, or provided fixed-base aeronautical services to the public and the military.

In the Lindbergh Boom of the late 1920s, Curtiss expanded its activities to include the establishment of new manufacturing firms in partnership, some to build established Curtiss designs, as Curtiss-Robertson, or Curtiss-Caproni, which was to supplement the Curtiss product range with Italian Caproni designs. Other established firms such as Travel Air of Wichita, Kansas, with a famous product line of its own, and Moth Manufacturing

Co of Lowell, Massachusetts, which built an Americanized version of the British de Havilland Moth, were purchased outright and made subsidiaries of Curtiss Aeroplane & Motor Co, as was Keystone Aircraft Corporation of Bristol, Pennsylvania. There was also Curtiss Reid Aircraft Co Ltd, resulting from Curtiss's acquiring a controlling interest in the Reid Aircraft Co of Montreal, manufacturers of a light trainer (not to be confused with Curtiss-Reed propellers dating from 1922). These were in addition to the Curtiss Flying Service and the sales organizations.

Reid Aircraft Company was formed early in 1928 by W. T. Reid to manufacture the Rambler lightplane that he had designed. In December, Curtiss acquired a one-third interest and the firm became Curtiss-Reid. Manufacture of the Rambler continued in Canada through 1931, after which the Curtiss affiliation was ended and the firm reorganized as Montreal Aircraft Industries Ltd.

In 1929, Curtiss Aeroplane & Motor Company employed 3,275 people, up from 2,175 in 1928.

Orville Wright (Wilbur died in 1912) sold his interest in the original Wright Company to New York financial interests in 1915 and served subsequently only as a consultant. The new Wright firm merged with Glenn L. Martin in 1916 to become Wright-Martin. One asset acquired with Martin was the Simplex Automobile Company of New Brunswick, NJ, controlled by Martin. Simplex held the American licence to manufacture the French Hispano-Suiza aero-engine, a modern powerplant far ahead of contemporary American models and in great demand by the Allies for combat aircraft. Production of this engine by Wright-Martin at New Brunswick started the engine-building career of what was to become the Wright Aeronautical Corporation after Martin dropped out and formed a new aeroplane manufacturing firm of his own in 1918.

Except for short excursions into aeroplane design from 1923 to 1926, Wright was exclusively an engine manufacturer. After acquiring the Lawrence Aero Engine Corporation and the services of its designer, Charles Lawrence (who eventually became president of Wright), Wright pioneered the production and further development of the air-cooled radial engine in the United States. The few high-powered liquid-cooled designs it developed were not notably successful and were abandoned. Wright's latter-day fame was built on the air-cooled radial, particularly as a result of the near-monopoly that Wright radials enjoyed on most of the long-distance flights, starting with Byrd's flight to the North Pole in 1926. By the time of the merger, Curtiss had a monopoly in the liquid-cooled field, since the other major supplier, Packard, had dropped out. Wright, however, was faced with stiff competition from Pratt & Whitney after some Wright officials and engineers left in 1925 to establish a new engine manufacturing company in facilities owned by the old established Pratt & Whitney Tool Company at Hartford, Connecticut.

After the Curtiss-Wright merger, the former Wright organization took over all engine and propeller manufacture and Curtiss concentrated on aeroplanes. Production of existing Curtiss engines was transferred to the new Wright plant at Paterson, NJ, and the new Curtiss Kenmore factory in Buffalo, built for engine production, was switched to aeroplane manufacture.

The merger was completed in the business sense by setting up two major divisions under their original names but under the direction of a corporate headquarters in New York City. However, there was a recognized separation of spirit as well as specialized facilities that was never completely

The Travel Air Manufacturing Company added the Model 6000 to its product line in 1928. After the firm became a division of Curtiss-Wright, the Travel Air models were redesignated, the 6000 becoming the Curtiss-Wright 6. The 6B version shown, with 300 hp Wright J-6-9 Whirlwind engine, was the only pre-merger Travel Air design to be built at St Louis after the Wichita plant was closed in 1930. This 1966 photograph shows the aircraft fitted with a 420 hp Wright R-975. (*Peter M. Bowers*)

316

resolved in succeeding years. The election of former Wright personnel to key corporate positions soon led to Wright becoming the dominant division.

At first, control was too tight from headquarters—the conduct of business was slowed in all plants by the delay involved in clearing everything with New York. In May 1930 control was loosened and the various companies attained a high degree of autonomy.

As the Lindbergh Boom continued after the Curtiss-Wright merger, the new firm continued the established Curtiss expansion policies. The former Curtiss Flying Service, renamed Curtiss-Wright, enlarged its existing schools throughout the country and opened new ones. Other aircraft manufacturers were brought into the fold and the prospects of Curtiss-Wright becoming a 'General Motors of the Air' were rosy until the worldwide depression that began in October 1929 very nearly destroyed the American aircraft industry. At the height of the boom, the Curtiss-Wright Corporation contained the following identified organizations: The Curtiss Aeroplane & Motor Company; The Curtiss-Caproni Corporation; The Curtiss-Robertson Airplane Manufacturing Co*; The Keystone Aircraft Corporation; The Moth Aircraft Corporation; The Travel Air Manufacturing Company*; The Wright Aeronautical Corporation; Curtiss-Wright Flying Service; The Curtiss-Wright Sales Corporation**; The Curtiss-Wright Export Corporation**.

Commercial sales of the established designs dropped to a trickle in the first year of the depression, forcing the closure of some of the satellite plants and transfer of their product lines to the St Louis facility. The Garden City experimental plant was also closed in 1930. Even the introduction of a new low-cost light aeroplane for the private pilot could not save the St Louis plant for long, and it, too, was shut down. Military sales dropped almost to zero with the completion of the Army and Navy five-year re-equipment programme adopted in 1926, and the Wright engines were getting heavy competition from Pratt & Whitney for the little airline and military business that remained. Shares of Curtiss-Wright stock dropped from $30.00 to seventy-five cents by 1932. Curtiss-Wright showed a financial loss of $450,000 in 1931, but sharp economies reduced the 1932 loss to $80,000.

It looked for a while as though even the Buffalo plants would have to close as well. Fortunately, an order from Colombia for Hawks and Falcons, larger than any single US military order to Curtiss since the war, was received at this time. Since these aircraft used Wright engines and Curtiss propellers, the Colombian sale can be credited with saving the Curtiss-Wright organization at this low point in its career. It kept the production lines going and the personnel together until new military and civil markets began to open up as the depression waned.

* Later became Curtiss-Wright Airplane Company
** From Curtiss-Wright Flying Service

Glenn Curtiss flew for the last time on 30 May, 1930, when he took the controls of civil Curtiss Condor No.5 during the 20th anniversary re-enactment of his historic Albany—New York City flight of 1910. He died soon after, on 23 July.

Although inactive in company affairs since his retirement in 1921, Glenn Curtiss retained his seat on the Board of his own Company and the later Curtiss-Wright organization. He visited Hammondsport regularly every summer, but he had two additional reasons for being in New York in 1930.

The first was for state and local celebration of the 20th anniversary of the historic Albany–New York flight of 29 May, 1910, and the second was a court appearance in Rochester in defence of the continuing Herring suit, now pressed by Herring's heirs.

On 30 May he retraced the 1910 flight route in a new Condor transport, actually taking the controls for a while (the flight was made a day later than the actual anniversary date to take advantage of the Memorial Day holiday). It is interesting to note that although he received US pilot's licence No.1 from the Aero Club of America in 1911, Curtiss never held the federal licence required after 1926. He was no longer an active pilot.

After giving testimony for five days at Rochester late in June, Curtiss suffered abdominal pains and was operated on for acute appendicitis. The trial was postponed. He seemed well on the way to recovery when he died suddenly of a pulmonary embolism on 23 July, 1930, at the age of 52.

The man who, perhaps, did more for United States aviation between 1907 and 1918 than any other individual is buried at Hammondsport, his birthplace. Appropriately, his grave is within a few hundred feet of the site of his triumphal 1908 flights in the *June Bug*.

# Entering a New Era,
# 1930–39

While the economic depression that began in October 1929 became a major milestone in aircraft economics and marketing, it also coincided with a period of significant structural and design change. Up to 1929, most aeroplane designs (particularly military) reflected the concepts established during World War I. While welded steel or bolted aluminium tubing had been substituted for wooden fuselage trusses in the early 1920s, the aeroplanes could at best be regarded merely as refined wartime types with more powerful engines.

The early 1930s saw the widespread adoption of entirely new concepts. All-metal structures began to replace wood, and fabric covering gave way to metal. At first, metal wings were merely a substitute for the traditional wood and fabric structures, and still required external bracing; soon, however, cantilever structures were adopted.

The increasing speed of the more powerful machines forced enclosure of the crews and made the drag of external fixtures such as the undercarriage and radial engine cylinders a severe handicap. Steps were taken first to fair the undercarriage and then to retract it. The radial engines were fitted at first with anti-drag rings and then were completely enclosed, with the fuselage contours being rounded out to match the engine diameter and improve the overall streamlining. Ethylene glycol replaced water as the coolant for liquid-cooled engines, thereby allowing smaller radiators with less drag. Much greater emphasis was placed on detail refinement and reduced interference drag by greatly increasing the use of wind-tunnel and qualitative flight testing of new designs.

Established models in production, of course, retained their original features but adopted such state-of-the-art advances as could be added easily: cowlings, cockpit enclosures, and single-strut undercarriage legs. In some, retractable undercarriages were adopted.

As performance increased, the last major handicap of the traditional biplane was the drag of the second wing and the interplane bracing; a change to the monoplane was inevitable. Civil aviation had recognized the aerodynamic and economic superiority of the monoplane as early as 1926; but the Services, citing greater manoeuvrability and structural strength, held to the biplane for tactical and training types. The Army acceded to progress first and allowed the development of tactical monoplanes as early as 1929; the Navy lagged by several years, citing the monoplane's higher landing speed as a serious handicap to carrier operations, until the adoption of flaps finally eliminated this objection.

Since the Army and Navy were Curtiss's principal customers in the 1930s, the new Curtiss designs were tailored closely to those customers' expressed wishes. While military aircraft development was to some extent retarded by the slowness of the Services of major nations to accept advances in the art, the all-metal cantilever monoplane with retractable undercarriage and fully enclosed crew became the world standard by 1937.

The aeroplanes in this section are arranged in sequence of the 1935 model designating system. Some that would normally be considered World War II subjects because of their extensive war service are correctly placed in this section because their development was essentially completed before the war began in 1939.

### Model 58—F9C Sparrowhawk

The first Curtiss military aeroplane of the new era was a small single-seat shipboard fighter developed to US Navy Specification 96 of 10 May, 1930. Named Sparrowhawk by Curtiss, the XF9C-1 was smaller and used less power than contemporary fighters as required by the specification. The small size and unique gull-wing configuration, plus the catchy name and the unique operation with airships, caught the public's fancy and was to give the F9C fame out of all proportion to its numbers or actual accomplishments.

The XF9C-1 was in competition with the General Aviation (formerly Fokker) XFA-1 and the Berliner-Joyce XFJ-1. The Navy's small fighter concept did not prove successful and the Sparrowhawk would have been

The Curtiss XF9C-1 Sparrowhawk was designed to a Navy specification for a small fighter to operate from carriers. All metal parts were painted light grey.

abandoned like its competitors had not an entirely new mission materialized. The Navy's rigid airships *Akron* and *Macon*, then under construction, were to carry aeroplanes. The F9C, best of the three small-fighter competitors, proved to be the only high-performance type that could be accommodated.

XF9C-1 (Model 58)—A single XF9C-1, Navy serial number A8731, was ordered from Curtiss on 30 June, 1930. First flown in March 1931, it had a metal monocoque fuselage and tail and fabric-covered metal-frame wings. Power was a 420 hp Wright R-975C (J-6-9) Whirlwind. After tests as a carrier-based fighter, it was fitted with airship hook-on gear at the Naval Aircraft Factory and first hooked-on to the airship *Los Angeles* on 17 October, 1931. It went into service as a spare aeroplane for *Akron* under its X-designation and retained such orginal design details as its balanced rudder and close-gap wings, but the original high-pressure tyres were replaced by the low-pressure type of the production F9C-2s with their open-sided fairings. Cost was $74,442 less GFE. After brief reassignment to *Macon* in 1933, the XF9C-1 was transferred to the Naval Aircraft Factory and was scrapped there in January 1935, with a total flight time of 213 hours.

The second Sparrowhawk prototype was company-financed and was unofficially designated F9C-2 before the Navy bought it as the XF9C-2.

XF9C-2 (Model 58A)—During Navy tests of the XF9C-1, Curtiss built a second prototype as a private venture and gave it the unofficial designation XF9C-2. This was painted on the tail along with the civil registration X986M. Since it was built as a civil aeroplane, Curtiss gave it c/n 1. The original colour scheme was the blue and silver of Navy Flag Officers' aeroplanes.

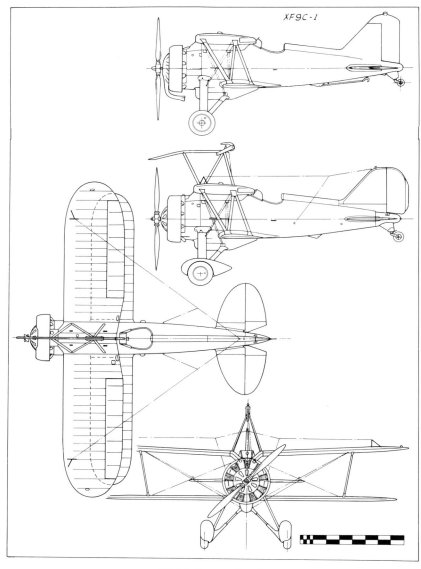

F9C-2 Sparrowhawk.

Principal differences from the XF9C-1 were the 438 hp R-975E-3 engine, the use of a single-leg wire-braced undercarriage, and a four-inch-higher location for the upper wing that resulted in a more noticeable gull-wing effect at the fuselage. Later, the fin and rudder were redesigned to eliminate the rudder balance area and the aeroplane was used by Curtiss to demonstrate a new controllable-pitch Curtiss propeller.

The Navy bought the XF9C-2 for $29,953 complete after ordering six production versions and the original designation became official after Navy serial number 9264 was assigned. The XF9C-2 was modified to production F9C-2 standard and so designated before going into service. The most notable change was replacement of the single-leg undercarriage with the tripod type of the XF9C-1 and the F9C-2s.

After the loss of the *Macon*, 9264 was stripped of its skyhook, redesignated XF9C-2, and assigned to the Naval Air Station at Anacostia. In 1939 it was given to the Smithsonian Institution, fitted with a replacement skyhook built for the purpose at the Naval Aircraft Factory, and put on display with a wholly inaccurate colour scheme and the erroneous Navy serial number of 9056, taken from an F9C-2. These errors were corrected when the twice-designated XF9C-2 was refurbished by the museum in 1975.

Two additional XF9C-2s, former F9C-2 9056 and one other, appeared in the records when they were redesignated XF9C-2 following the loss of the airship *Macon*.

F9C-2—Six production versions of the XF9C-2 were ordered in October 1931, with Navy serial numbers 9056/9061. Unit costs less GFE averaged $24,426. As first flown on 14 April, 1932, 9056 was fitted with the single-leg XF9C-2 undercarriage. This was immediately changed to the earlier XF9C-1 tripod type and the others were completed with the same type. After a short period in service, the vertical fin area of the F9C-2s was increased by adding a new rudder post eight inches aft of the original; rudder area was also increased slightly.

The first production F9C-2 had the single-leg undercarriage of the second prototype but quickly reverted to the XF9C-1 tripod design.

The small size of the Sparrowhawk suited it for hook-on operations from the US Navy airships *Akron* and *Macon*.

The fame of the Sparrowhawks is due mainly to their unique status as auxiliaries to Naval airships. The *Akron* and *Macon* could each carry up to four F9C-2s in an internal hangar with one more suspended from an external station called The Perch. The aeroplanes were fitted with the hook-on gear that enabled them to fly up under the airship and engage a trapeze at the bottom of an elevator assembly that could then hoist them into the hangar. While the F9C-2s were popularly regarded as defensive fighters, their principal mission was to act as scouts to extend the effective operating area of the airships, which were themselves used as scouts.

On a few occasions, in 1934, when the Sparrowhawks were operating exclusively from the *Macon* without using land bases, they were flown without undercarriages. This reduced both weight and drag and allowed the installation of a streamlined 30-gallon auxiliary fuel tank similar to that developed for the F11C-2 to extend their range still farther.

The F9C-2s assigned to an airship were not part of a regular Naval aeroplane squadron but were auxiliaries of the airship. Each F9C-2 pilot and aeroplane had the status and markings of a Section Leader in a regular squadron.

The XF9C-1 and all six F9C-2s were originally assigned to the *Akron*, which was based at Lakehurst. No aeroplanes were aboard when that airship was lost at sea on 4 April, 1933. All the Sparrowhawks were then transferred to the *Macon*, based at Moffett Field, Sunnyvale, California.

Four F9C-2s were lost at sea with *Macon* on 12 February, 1935. The three that were not aboard, including 9056 and the former XF9C-2 9264, were stripped of their hook-on gear and redesignated XF9C-2. Both former F9C-2s were scrapped at San Diego in 1936 and 9264 eventually reached the Smithsonian Institution as previously described.

### F9C Sparrowhawk
#### XF9C-1
420 hp Wright R-975C Whirlwind.

Span 25 ft 6 in (7·77 m); length 19 ft 5 in (5·91 m); height 7 ft 1 in (2·15 m); wing area 172·8 sq ft (16·05 sq m).

Empty weight 1,823 lb (827 kg); gross weight 2,482 lb (1,126 kg).

Maximum speed 176·5 mph (284·04 km/h); cruising speed 141 mph (226·91 km/h); initial climb 2,150 ft/min (10·92 m/sec); service ceiling 22,600 ft (6,888 m); range 328 miles (528 km).

#### XF9C-2
438 hp Wright R-975E-3 Whirlwind.

Span, length and wing area as XF9C-1. Height 7 ft 3 in (2·2 m).

Empty weight 1,946 lb (883 kg); gross weight 2,605 lb (1,182 kg).

Maximum speed 181·5 mph (292·09 km/h); cruising speed 140 mph (225·3 km/h); initial climb 2,150 ft/min (10·92 m/sec); service ceiling 22,600 ft (6,888 m); range 287 miles (462 km).

#### F9C-2
438 hp Wright R-975E-3 Whirlwind.

Span and wing area as XF9C-2. Length 20 ft 1½ in (6·13 m); height (with hook) 10 ft 7 in (3·22 m).

Empty weight 2,117 lb (960 kg); gross weight 2,779 lb (1,260 kg).

Maximum speed 176·5 mph (284·04 km/h); cruising speed 138 mph (222·08 km/h); initial climb 1,690 ft/min (8·58 m/sec); service ceiling 19,200 ft (5,852 m); range 297 miles (478 km).

Each type had two ·30-in machine-guns.

When operating entirely from airships, the performance of Sparrowhawks was increased by removing the undercarriage. (*Paul Matt collection*)

The first Curtiss tactical monoplane for the US Army was the XA-8 Shrike.

## Model 59—A-8, A-10 Shrike

In 1930 Curtiss developed a new two-seat ground attack aircraft to Army requirements as the XA-8. This was a major advance for Curtiss in several respects—the first Curtiss military monoplane, the first with both all-metal structure and covering, the first Curtiss to use trailing-edge flaps, full-span leading-edge slats, and enclosed cockpits and undercarriage that were designed-in instead of being added later. In spite of these advances, however, the XA-8 and its derivatives featured wire-braced wings which, with the exception of the contemporary Douglas O-31 and Boeing P-26, were an anachronism not seen on military monoplanes since early in the first World War.

The crew sat in two widely-separated cockpits. The pilot controlled four ·30-calibre machine-guns mounted in the undercarriage fairings where their rate of fire would not be slowed by synchronization gear. The rear cockpit was fitted with a single ·30-calibre flexible gun. Racks beneath the wings could carry up to 400 lb (181 kg) of bombs or chemical tanks.

Curtiss named the new model Shrike after that bird of prey, but the name was not used by the customers.

XA-8 (Model 59)—First flown in June 1931, the XA-8 (Army serial number 30-387) was fitted with a 600 hp liquid-cooled Curtiss V-1570C engine driving a fixed-pitch three-bladed propeller. The XA-8 was in competition with the General Aviation (Fokker) XA-7 and won an order for thirteen Service test models. It was scrapped in March 1937.

YA-8 (Model 59A)—Five Service test YA-8s (Army serials 32-344/348), similar to the XA-8 except for Prestone-cooled V-1570-31 engines and minor refinements, went into service in June 1932. The first YA-8 was held at the factory for conversion to YA-10 (Model 59B). The others were redesignated A-8 upon completion of Service testing. Unit cost less GFE was $32,298.

Five YA-8s were Service test versions of the XA-8. The arrowhead insignia of Wright Field appears on the fuselage.

Y1A-8—Eight duplicates of the YA-8 were procured with different funds and were designated Y1A-8 (Army serials 32-349/356) to indicate their purchase with F-1 funds rather than the regular appropriation. The last Y1A-8 became the Y1A-8A. The others became A-8 after Service test and thereby lost their budgetary distinction from the YA-8s.

Y1A-8A—No Curtiss designation change was involved in the conversion of the last Y1A-8 (32-356) to Y1A-8A with 675 hp geared V-1570-57 engine, a revised wing, and a quarter-ton gross weight increase to 6,287 lb (2,852 kg). In spite of the increased power, the top speed dropped 3 mph (4·82 km/h) to 181 mph (291·28 km/h). The Y1A-8A later became the A-8A.

Eight Y1A-8s were duplicates of the YA-8. The difference in designation was to indicate procurement with different funds. (*A.U. Schmidt*)

327

The last Y1A-8 was completed as the Y1A-8A with geared instead of direct-drive Conqueror engine. (*Fred Bamberger collection*)

A-8B—Forty-six A-8Bs with V-1570-57 engines were ordered after test of the Y1A-8A, but these were redesignated A-12 after tests of the YA-10 proved that air-cooled radial engines were preferable to liquid-cooled V-types for the attack mission.

YA-10 (Model 59B)—The first YA-8 (32-344) was refitted with a 625 hp Pratt & Whitney Hornet air-cooled radial engine. Other minor changes increased the gross weight to 6,135 lb (2,783 kg) and reduced the top speed to 175 mph (281·63 km/h). The advantages of the radial engine for attack aircraft were proved on the YA-10 and the forty-six A-8Bs on order were produced as A-12s. The Navy ordered a duplicate of the YA-10 as XS2C-1 (Model 69).

The first YA-8 was fitted with a Pratt & Whitney Hornet engine and redesignated YA-10. (*William T. Larkins*)

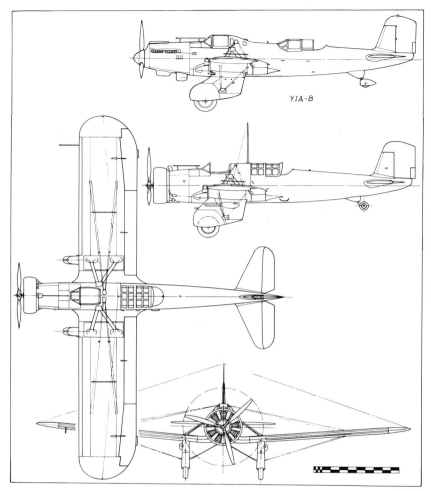

A-12 Shrike.

## Model 60—A-12, Export Shrike

A-12—The wide separation of the A-8s cockpits hindered co-operation by crew members and the YA-10 proved the advantages of the air-cooled radial engine. The resulting changes to the basic design, most noticeably in moving the rear cockpit forward and installing a 690 hp Wright R-1820-21 Cyclone engine, resulted in a new Curtiss model number, 60, and a new US Army designation. Forty-six A-12s, serial numbers 33-212/257, were delivered in 1934 at unit costs less GFE of $19,483.

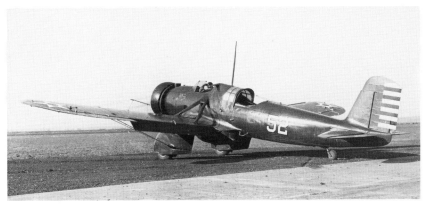

The Cyclone-powered A-12 was an improved version of the A-8s and A-10.
(*A. U. Schmidt*)

The last operational A-12s in the Army were at Pearl Harbor in
December 1941, but were not flown in combat.

Export Shrike—Twenty export versions of the A-12 were sold to China
in 1936. Delivered in May, the unit price was $24,328.45. C/ns
12155/12174.

**A-8/A-12 Shrike**

|  | XA-8 | YA-8 | A-12 |
|---|---|---|---|
|  | 600 hp Curtiss V-1570C | | |
| Span . . . | 44 ft 0 in (13·41 m) | 44 ft 0 in (13·41 m) | 44 ft 0 in (13·41 m) |
| Length . . . | 32 ft 8 in (9·95 m) | 32 ft 0 in (9·75 m) | 32 ft 3 in (9·82 m) |
| Height . . . | 9 ft 0 in (2·74 m) | 9 ft 0 in (2·74 m) | 9 ft 0 in (2·74 m) |
| Wing area. . . | 256 sq ft (23·78 sq m) | 256 sq ft (23·78 sq m) | 284 sq ft (26·38 sq m) |
| Empty weight . . | 3,672 lb (1,666 kg) | 3,910 lb (1,774 kg) | 3,898 lb (1,768 kg) |
| Gross weight . . | 5,400 lb (2,449 kg) | 5,888 lb (2,671 kg) | 5,756 lb (2,611 kg) |
| Maximum speed . | 196·8 mph (316·71 km/h) | 183 mph (294·5 km/h) | 176·7 mph (284·36 km/h) |
| Cruising speed . . | 167 mph (268·75 km/h) | 153 mph (246·22 km/h) | 151 mph (243 km/h) |
| Initial climb . . | 1,265 ft/min (6·42 m/sec) | 1,325 ft/min (6·73 m/sec) | 1,170 ft/min (5·94 m/sec) |
| Service ceiling . | 19,800 ft (6,035 m) | 18,100 ft (5,517 m) | 15,150 ft (4,618 m) |
| Range . . . | 472 miles (760 km) | 480 miles (772 km) | 521 miles (838 km) |
| Armament . . | Each type had five machine-guns and could carry ten 30 lb (13·6 kg) or four 122 lb (55·3 kg) bombs | | |

Twenty export versions of the A-12 were sold to China in 1936 as Model 60As.

## Model 62—O-40 Raven

In 1931 Curtiss designed a new observation model to Army requirements. Like the A-8/Model 59, this had metal monocoque fuselage
construction and metal-frame, metal-covered wings. A new advanced
feature for Curtiss was the use of a retractable undercarriage. Army
development funds were meagre in the early 1930s, and only one prototype
and four Service test O-40s were procured.

YO-40 (Model 62)—The single YO-40 (serial number 32-343) was
caught in the Army's transition from traditional biplane O-types to the new
monoplanes and had a narrow-chord lower wing that qualified it as a true
sesquiplane. To resolve the tail-heaviness problem resulting from the

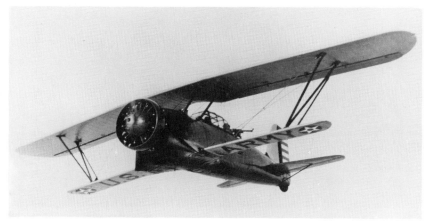

The YO-40 Raven was classified as a sesquiplane because of its small lower wing.

331

After a crash, the YO-40 was rebuilt with minor refinements as the YO-40A.

forward position of the lower wing and the forward position of the upper wing centre section necessitated by the cockpits, the outer wing panels were swept back 10 degrees.

The unique undercarriage was attached to structure projecting slightly from the lower fuselage, and retracted inward. Powerplant was a 653 hp Wright SR-1820E Cyclone fitted with a Curtiss anti-drag ring. Armament was a single ·30-calibre machine-gun mounted in the right upper-wing centre section and a flexible ·30 in the rear cockpit. Delivered in February 1932, the YO-40 crashed on 20 May, 1932. It was returned to the factory, rebuilt, and redelivered as the YO-40A.

The four Y1O-40Bs were monoplane adaptations of the YO-40A sesquiplane.
(*Gordon S. Williams*)

YO-40A (Model 62A)—The damaged YO-40 was rebuilt to the same configuration but with stronger wings and minor refinements and was redelivered as the YO-40A with the same serial number. The Service test designation was never removed; when obsolete, the YO-40A was operated as the ZYO-40A, the Z identifying it as obsolete. It was scrapped in March 1938.

Y1O-40A—This designation was assigned to four improved versions of the YO-40A but was not used because the aeroplanes were redesigned to a degree that required a new designation.

Y1O-40B—The four aeroplanes to have been Y1O-40A were delivered in June 1933 as monoplanes with 670 hp R-1820-27 (Y1R-1820F) engines, under the designation of Y1O-40B (serials 32-415/418). Unit costs were $45,845. Basically, these were YO-40As with the lower wing removed. The inward-retracting undercarriage installation was the same as on the sesquiplane. Following Service test, the aeroplanes became O-40B; the last one was surveyed in 1939.

### YO-40

653 hp Wright SR-1820E Cyclone.

Span 44 ft (13·41 m); length 27 ft 9¼ in (8·46 m); height 10 ft 6 in (3·2 m); wing area 314 sq ft (29·17 sq m).

Empty weight 3,393 lb (1,539 kg); gross weight 4,565 lb (2,071 kg).

Maximum speed 195·8 mph (315·1 km/h); cruising speed 170 mph (273·58 km/h); stalling speed 69 mph (111·04 km/h); initial climb 1,960 ft/min (9·95 m/sec); service ceiling 25,400 ft (7,742 m); range 349 miles (562 km).

Armament—two machine-guns.

### Y1O-40B

670 hp Wright R-1820-27 (Y1R-1820F).

Span 41 ft 8 in (12·69 m); length 28 ft 10 in (8·78 m); height 10 ft 8 in (3·25 m); wing area 266 sq ft (24·71 sq m).

Empty weight 3,754 lb (1,703 kg); gross weight 5,180 lb (2,350 kg).

Maximum speed 187·7 mph (302·06 km/h); cruising speed 160·5 mph (258·29 km/h); stalling speed 62 mph (99·77 km/h); initial climb 1,660 ft/min (8·43 m/sec); service ceiling 23,100 ft (7,041 m); range 324 miles (521 km).

Armament—two machine-guns.

## Model 66—XP-934, XP-31 Swift

Although it was an unsuccessful competitor against the Boeing XP-936/P-26 for the US Army's interim monoplane pursuit of 1933–36, the Model 66 Swift was still a significant design in that it brought Curtiss further into the new design era and revealed important new design problems associated with it.

Encouraged by the Army, Curtiss undertook the development of a new pursuit as a company-funded project for which the Army provided the powerplant and military equipment and assigned the experimental project number XP-934 for test under a bailment contract.

The Curtiss XP-934 Swift was originally fitted with a Wright Cyclone radial engine. The external side gun pods can be seen.

The all-metal Swift drew heavily on the design features of the A-8 Shrike, including a pilot's enclosed cockpit, wing flaps, and full-span leading-edge slats that opened automatically at 15 mph (22·6 km/h) above stalling speed. Four ·30-in calibre machine-guns were carried, two in troughs in the nose and two in external packages on each side of the cockpit. The aeroplane was designed for the 600 hp Conqueror engine but the Army, correctly believing that this liquid-cooled model was nearing the end of its usefulness for pursuit types, insisted on a change to the 700 hp F-series Wright Cyclone air-cooled radial.

The single Swift left the factory in July 1932 but its performance was disappointing. Within a month, the Cyclone was replaced with a G1V-1570F Conqueror. While the speed increased, other performance characteristics were handicapped by serious overweight. The Army bought the aeroplane in February 1933, assigning the designation XP-31 and Army serial number 33-178. The civil-type engine was replaced with an equivalent

When submitted to the Army for test, the XP-934 Swift had a geared Conqueror engine.

334

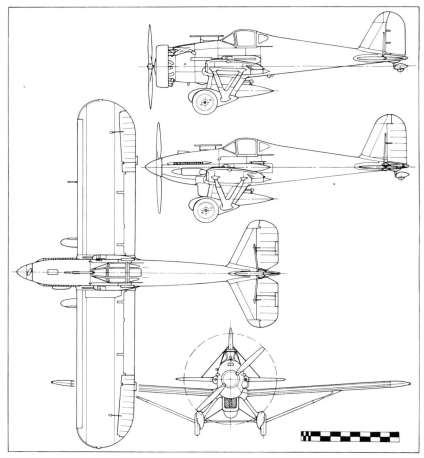

XP-31 Swift.

military V-1570-53. Purchase price was $40,000. Soon redesignated ZXP-31 (Z for Obsolete), it accumulated a total of 287 flying hours by July 1936 when it was retired to an Air Corps mechanics' school.

### XP-934/XP-31 Swift
Single-seat Pursuit. 600 hp Curtiss Conqueror G1V-1570 F.

Span 36 ft (10·97 m); length 26 ft 3 in (8 m); height 7 ft 9 in (2·36 m); wing area 203 sq ft (18·85 sq m).

Empty weight 3,334 lb (1,512 kg); gross weight 4,143 lb (1,879 kg).

Maximum speed 215 mph (346 km/h) at sea level; cruising speed 184 mph (296·11 km/h); climb 2,130 ft/min (10·82 m/sec); service ceiling 22,700 ft (6,919 m); range 396 miles (637 km) with 75 gal (284 litres), 642 miles (1,033 km) with 125 gal (473 litres). Armament—four ·30-in machine-guns.

335

The US Navy tested a single variant of the Army A-10 as the XS2C-1 scout.
Metal parts were painted light grey.

## Model 69—XS2C-1 Shrike

In December 1932 Curtiss delivered a development of the Army YA-10 Shrike to the Navy as the single XS2C-1. This was fitted with a 625 hp Wright R-1510-28 twin-row engine and carried Navy serial number 9377. This was evaluated as a land-based aeroplane only; arrester gear was not installed and the aircraft was unarmed.

Although the XS2C-1 was not accepted for service, it was significant as the first example of a two-seat combat monoplane to be evaluated by the Navy since the early 1920s.

### XS2C-1

625 hp Wright R-1510.

Span 44 ft (13·41 m); height 9 ft (2·74 m); wing area 256 sq ft (23·78 sq m).

Empty weight 3,677 lb (1,668 kg); gross weight 4,822 lb (2,187 kg).

Maximum speed 193 mph (310·59 km/h); cruising speed 162 mph (260·7 km/h); initial climb 1,720 ft/min (8·73 m/sec); service ceiling 21,100 ft (6,431 m); range 468 miles (753 km).

## Model 70—F13C Series

Curtiss Model 70 was a new and unnamed single-seat fighter caught squarely between the old and new structural concepts and the transition from monoplanes to biplanes. In its initial form it was a high-wing cabin monoplane generally similar to contemporary civil models. The principal advanced feature was an undercarriage that retracted into the fuselage. The XF13C was designed to incorporate this feature instead of it being adapted as in the Model 67/XF11C-3. Since the US Navy was still distrustful of monoplanes, the XF13C-1 could be converted to a biplane by the simple addition of a lower wing. Total cost to the Navy for the original aeroplane and two modifications was $124,661.

336

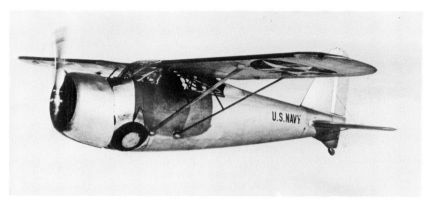

The XF13C-1 looked more like a commercial cabin monoplane than a Navy shipboard fighter.

XF13C-1—Ordered on 23 November, 1932, the single XF13C-1, Navy serial number 9343, was completed in December 1933. Powerplant was the new Wright XR-1510-A2 twin-row radial engine rated 600 hp at 10,000 ft (3,048 m). This was soon changed to an SGR-1510-12 rated at 700 hp at 7,000 ft (2,134 m). Armament consisted of one ·30 and one ·50-calibre machine-gun firing through the propeller disc. Standard deck arrester gear was fitted.

XF13C-2—The biplane (actually a sesquiplane) conversion of the XF13C-1 was designated XF13C-2 but served such a short period in this configuration that the original designation on the rudder was not changed.

When an optional lower wing was added, the XF13C-1 became the XF13C-2. Metal surfaces were painted silver.

Minor improvements including redesigned vertical tail surfaces changed the
XF13C-1 to the XF13C-3.

This aircraft actually flew first, in December 1933. The added lower wing
had a span of 24 ft 3 in (7·39 m), increasing the effective wing area from
204·3 to 281·7 sq ft (18·97 to 26·16 sq m). The gross weight was reduced to
4,092 lb (1,856 kg). Performance was inferior to the monoplane on almost
all counts and the XF13C-2 was quickly reverted to a monoplane.

XF13C-3—The monoplane Model 70 was tested further as the XF13C-3
with minor improvements, most notably a vertical tail of reduced height.
This was adopted when a Navy study showed that production quantities of
F13Cs could not be closely-packed on carrier decks because the high tail of
one F13C could not pass under the high wing of another.

### XF13C-1
Single-seat fighter. 700 hp Wright SGR-1510-12.
Span 35 ft (10·66 m); length 25 ft 8½ in (7·83 m); height 9 ft 9½ in (2·98 m); wing area 204·3 sq
ft (18·97 sq m).
Empty weight 3,241 lb (1,470 kg); gross weight 4,141 lb (1,878 kg).
Maximum speed 242 mph (389·45 km/h) at 10,000 ft (3,048 m); service ceiling 25,050 ft
(7,635 m).

### XF13C-2
As XF13C-1 except: Wing area 281·7 sq ft (26·16 sq m).
Empty weight 3,192 lb (1,448 kg); gross weight 4,092 lb (1,856 kg).
Maximum speed 210 mph (337·95 km/h) at 10,000 ft (3,048 m); service ceiling 28,000 ft
(8,534 m).

### XF13C-3
As XF13C-1 except: Length 25 ft (7·62 m); height 8 ft 9½ in (2·67 m).
Empty weight 3,412 lb (1,548 kg); gross weight 4,634 lb (2,102 kg).
Maximum speed 246 mph (395·89 km/h) at 7,000 ft (2,134 m); service ceiling 25,250 ft
(7,696 m).
Each version had two machine-guns.

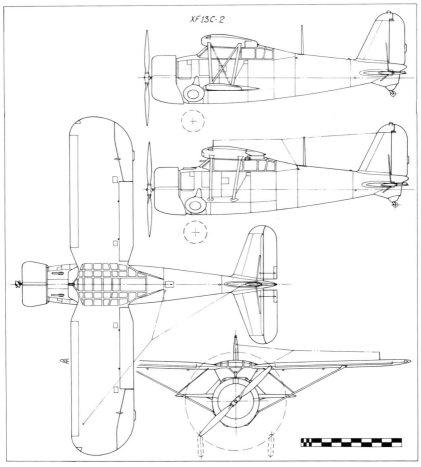

XF13C-1 and XF13C-2.

## Model 71—O3C, SOC, SO2C, SON Seagull

Built late in the new era that preceded the pre-World War II development period, the XO3C-1 Seagull was a throwback to the tube-and-fabric biplane of the middle 1920s but did not indicate regression of Curtiss technology. It was designed to a Navy specification and was in competition with equivalent Vought and Douglas designs. Its 'modern' features were relatively few—full-span leading-edge slats on the upper wing, trailing-edge flaps on the upper wing, and a cowling around the Pratt & Whitney Wasp radial engine as specified by the Navy.

The XO3C-1 of 1934 reverted to older operational and structural concepts but incorporated such refinements as slots and flaps. Metal parts were painted grey. The floats were of stainless steel.

This was Curtiss's second use of the name Seagull, which became official for the SOC/SON when the US Government adopted names for popular identification of military aircraft in October 1941.

The XO3C-1 won largescale production orders for the 1935–38 period under the designation SOC in the Navy's new Scout-Observation class established in 1934. By the late 1930s, the SOCs and their Navy-built SON duplicates had a monopoly of the US Navy's battleship and cruiser catapult seaplane roles. Although production was completed in 1938 and

The XO3C-1 was updated with cockpit enclosures before being redesignated XSOC-1.

the SOCs were due for replacement in 1941, these aeronautical anachronisms outlived their intended replacements and served with the fleet to the end of the war.

XO3C-1/XSOC-1 (Model 71)—Built at Buffalo, the XO3C-1, Navy serial number 9413, was originally an open-cockpit observation biplane with backward-folding wings. Structure was welded steel-tube fuselage and aluminium-frame wings and empennage, all fabric covered. Full-span

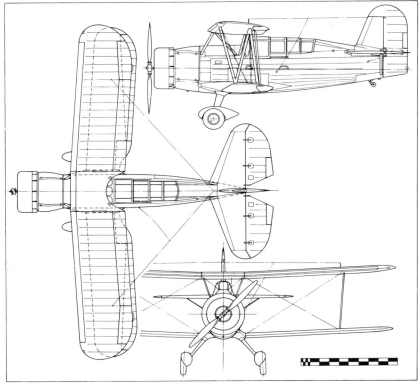

SOC-1 Seagull.

ailerons were fitted to the bottom wing and full-span flaps to the upper. Armament was a single fixed ·30-calibre machine-gun in the nose and a single ·30-calibre on a swivel mount in the rear cockpit. The single prototype cost $113,445 less GFE.

The XO3C-1 was originally tested in March 1934 as an open-cockpit seaplane with an amphibious single float. It was soon modified to production SOC standard with enclosed cockpits, upper-wing ailerons, and single-strut undercarriage, prior to being redesignated XSOC-1 on 23 March, 1935, the date the first production models were ordered.

For stowage aboard battleships and cruisers, the wings of SOCs could be folded.
This SOC-1 is a scout attached to a cruiser as indicated by the letters CS.
*(Peter M. Bowers)*

SOC-1 (Model 71A)—The production versions of the XO3C-1/XSOC-1
were designated SOC-1 and one hundred and thirty-five were ordered with
Navy serial numbers 9856/9990. Principal outward differences from the
prototype were a full NACA cowling around the 550 hp R-1340-18 engine,
small ailerons added to the top wing, and a large canopy enclosing both
cockpits. The canopy was streamlined into the tail by a collapsible
turtledeck that could be lowered to allow the rear-seat gunner a clear field
of fire, a feature developed on the last Falcon biplane.

Deliveries of SOC-1 landplanes from the Buffalo Kenmore plant began
on 12 November, 1935. Since this factory was some distance from the
aerodrome, the task of trucking dismantled SOCs from the factory and

This SOC-2 is part of the cruiser *Trenton*'s own aircraft complement, not part of
a scouting squadron assigned to several cruisers. Metal parts were painted silver.
*(Gordon S. Williams)*

This SOC-3 has the all-blue fuselage and tail of a Flag Officer's aircraft, in this case, the Commander-in-Chief of the United States Fleet. (*William T. Larkins*)

then re-assembling them was avoided by flying the factory-assembled aeroplanes from a makeshift airstrip set up alongside the factory parking lot.

US Navy serial numbers: 9856/9990. C/ns: 11926/12060.

SOC-2 (Model 71B)—Outwardly indistinguishable from the SOC-1, the forty SOC-2s, with serial numbers 0386/0425 in the second Navy serial number series, were given minor improvements and R-1340-22 engines. C/ns: 12200/12239.

XSO2C-1 (Model 71C)—The single XSO2C-1, Navy serial number 0950, was an improved SOC given a new Navy model designation although

The sixty-four SON-1s were Curtiss SOC-3s built by the Naval Aircraft Factory. (*Frank Shertzer*)

343

Three SOC-3s built to US Coast Guard requirements were designated SOC-4. The Coast Guard used this distinctive rudder marking from 1935 until the Japanese attack on Pearl Harbor. (*Gordon S. Williams*)

it was outwardly indistinguishable from the SOC. Production as a new model was not justified so the established SOC series was continued.

SOC-3/SON-1 (Model 71E)—Eighty-three SOC-3s, outwardly indistinguishable from earlier SOCs, were ordered with Navy serial numbers 1064/1146. At this time, the Navy had a policy of manufacturing 10 percent of its own aeroplanes, partly as a check on costs. When the SOC-3 order was placed, an additional forty-four were ordered to be built at the Naval Aircraft Factory under the designation of SON-1. These were given the immediately-following Navy serial numbers of 1147/1190. SOC-3 c/ns: 12329/12411.

SOC-3s fitted with deck arrester gear were redesignated SOC-3A. This one is making the 2,000th landing on USS *Long Island* on 20 April, 1942.

344

SOC-4 (Model 71F)—The US Coast Guard. a branch of the US Treasury Department in peacetime, operated mostly Naval aircraft types under Navy designations but under separate serial numbers and markings. In 1938 it accepted three improved SOC-3s modified to Coast Guard requirements as SOC-4s and assigned USCG serial numbers V171/173. In 1942 these were taken over by the Navy, modified to SOC-3A standard (*see below*), and given serial numbers 48243/48245 in the third Navy serial number series. C/ns: 12412/12414.

SOC/SON A Variants—The Seagulls operated as seaplanes at sea and were fitted with wheels when their ships were in port; none was originally fitted with deck arrester gear. Starting late in 1941, numbers of SOCs and SONs were modified to operate on wheels from small escort-carriers. Those so modified had the letter A added to their designations, as SOC-3A.

### XO3C-1 (amphibian)
Two-seat Observation biplane. 550 hp Pratt & Whitney R-1340-12.
Span 36 ft (10·97 m); length 30 ft 2⅝ in (9·21 m); height 14 ft 1 in (4·29 m); wing area 348 sq ft (32·32 sq m).
Empty weight 3,596 lb (1,631 kg); gross weight 5,250 lb (2,381 kg).
Maximum speed 159·3 mph (256·36 km/h); cruising speed 136 mph (218·86 km/h); initial rate of climb 820 ft/min (4·16 m/sec); service ceiling 15,000 ft (4,572 m); range 586 miles (943 km).

### SOC-1 (landplane)
550 hp Pratt & Whitney R-1340-18.
Span 36 ft (10·97 m); length 26 ft 10 in (8·17 m); height 13 ft 0⅞ in (3·98 m); wing area 342 sq ft (31·77 sq m).
Empty weight 3,442 lb (1,561 kg); gross weight 5,130 lb (2,327 kg).
Maximum speed 162 mph (260·7 km/h); initial rate of climb 1,055 ft/min (5·35 m/sec); service ceiling 16,200 ft (4,938 m); range 878 miles (1,413 km).

### SOC-3 (seaplane)
550 hp Pratt & Whitney R-1340-22.
Span 36 ft (10·97 m); length 31 ft 1 in (9·47 m); height 14 ft 7 in (4·44 m); wing area 342 sq ft (31·77 sq m).
Empty weight 3,633 lb (1,648 kg); gross weight 5,495 lb (2,492 kg).
Maximum speed 161 mph (259·1 km/h); initial rate of climb 915 ft/min (4·64 m/sec); service ceiling 14,400 ft (4,389 m); range 859 miles (1,382 km).
Each version had two ·30-in machine-guns.


## Model 73—F12C, S4C, SBC-1

The Curtiss Model 73, developed in Buffalo, was another transition model in which the biplane influence died hard. Although carrying a later Curtiss retroactive model number, the Model 73/F12C preceded the design of the Model 70/F13C. The two-seat Navy fighter prototype, ordered on 30 June, 1932, as the XF12C-1, was essentially a Navy version of the Army's O-40 Raven series (Model 62). The parasol wing feature made it in effect a biplane without a lower wing.

The original configuration of the XF12C-1 with twin-row Wright SGR-1510 engine.

The Navy was having difficulty in defining the roles of its new-era aeroplanes at this time and first classified the Model 73 as a fighter, then as a scout, and finally as a scout-bomber. While on a company test flight as a scout-bomber, the monoplane crashed. Curtiss built a new airframe with the same Navy serial number but completed it as an entirely new biplane that won sizeable production orders under a later Curtiss model number (*see* Model 77).

XF12C-1 (Model 73)—This was a two-seat monoplane fighter, Navy serial number 9225, and it first flew in July 1933. The structure was all metal except for fabric covering on the movable control surfaces and the flaps. Intended for use from carriers, the XF12C-1 was fitted with arrester gear and backward-folding wings. Full-span leading-edge slats were fitted. The powerplant was the new 625 hp twin-row Wright SGR-1510-92, but this was unsatisfactory and was soon changed to a 775 hp twin-row Wright

The XF12C-1 with modified engine cowling and wings folded, October 1933.

346

After the change to single-row Wright Cyclone engine, the XF12C-1 was redesignated XSBC-1. (*Courtesy John Underwood*)

R-1670 which was also a new and unproved engine. The wheels retracted into the lower fuselage as on the contemporary XF11C-3 Hawk. Forward armament reverted to a single ·30-calibre machine-gun in a trough in the nose. Rear-cockpit armament was a single ·30 on a swivel mount.

XS4C-1—The XF12C-1 was not accepted as a fighter. In December 1933 it was re-evaluated as a scout, the XS4C-1, following a further engine change to a 700 hp single-row Wright SR-1820-80 Cyclone. The scout designation was short-lived and the aeroplane was redesignated as a scout-bomber in January 1934.

XSBC-1—The final US Navy designation for the Model 73 monoplane was XSBC-1, identifying it as a Scout-Bomber in that new combined category established in 1934. The well-proved Cyclone engine was more reliable than the previous experimental models and aeroplane performance was improved.

The XSBC-1 crashed during a company test flight in September 1934, pilot Paul Hovgard parachuting to safety. The single aeroplane cost the Navy $100,739 less GFE.

### XF12C-1

625 hp Wright GR-1510-92.

Span 41 ft 6½ in (12·66 m); length 29 ft 1½ in (8·87 m); height 10 ft 4½ in (3·16 m); wing area 272·5 sq ft (25·31 sq m).

Empty weight 3,884 lb (1,762 kg); gross weight 5,485 lb (2,488 kg).

Maximum speed 217 mph (349·22 km/h); cruising speed 185 mph (297·72 km/h); service ceiling 22,500 ft (6,858 m); range 738 miles (1,188 km).

Armament—two fixed and one flexible machine-gun.

### XSBC-1

700 hp Wright SR-1820-80.

Span, height, wing area and armament as XF12C-1. Length 29 ft 9¹³⁄₁₆ in (9·08 m).

Empty weight 4,189 lb (1,900 kg); gross weight 6,060 lb (2,749 kg) Scout, 6210 lb (2,817 kg) Bomber.

Maximum speed 213 mph (342·78 km/h) at 13,000 ft (3,962 m); initial climb 1,600 ft/min (8·12 m/sec); service ceiling 24,000 ft (7,315 m).

The Model 75 was the Curtiss-owned entry in the 1935 US Army pursuit aircraft competition. Colouring was the standard Army blue fuselage and yellow wings of the time.

## Model 75—Export Fighter,
## US Army P-36 and P-37, RAF Mohawk

The Model 75 was originally developed as the Curtiss entry in a US Army pursuit aircraft competition scheduled for May 1935. The Curtiss lost the initial contest but was the real winner in the end, with 227 sold to the Army, 753 exported, and at least 25 built under licence in other countries from raw materials or Curtiss-supplied kits. These are described first in sequence of Curtiss model number and then by US Army designation.

Configuration and equipment of the completely new Curtiss were determined by the military specification to which it was designed and owed very little to previous Curtiss designs. The principal designer was Donovan A. Berlin, who had just come to Curtiss from Northrop, and the structure of the new model was heavily influenced by established Northrop designs. The Model 75 and its competitors ushered in a completely new era of American pursuit/fighter aircraft design concepts.

The competitors were all company-owned aeroplanes without military designation. Since all were experiencing teething troubles, the Army postponed the competition twice, finally to April 1936. Still suffering powerplant problems, the Model 75 lost out to the Seversky entry, which won an order for 77 examples to be designated P-35. Curtiss got a consolation order for three Y1P-36s powered, at Army direction, with the same Pratt & Whitney R-1830 engine used by the P-35. The Y1P-36 did so well with this engine that it won a 1937 Army competition and Curtiss was rewarded with an order for 210 P-36As, the largest single US military aeroplane order since the first World War. These became the principal US Army fighters until 1941, when they were replaced by the P-40. A few saw action at Pearl Harbor but the US combat career of the Curtiss Model 75 started and ended there.

After the P-36A order was placed, the US Government permitted Curtiss to sell equivalent models to France and later to Norway and the Netherlands. Nearly 200 served as the most effective French fighter until the fall of France in June 1940. Other Hawk 75s *en route* were diverted to Loyalist French ports and to French Africa. Britain took over the French 75s still in the factory plus some French escapees and named them Mohawk. While the RAF made little combat use of its Mohawks, many were reassigned to other nations and did well in less active war theatres.

The 75 fought on both sides. The Germans captured some still in their shipping crates in France and Norway and sold them to Finland, which used them against the Russians. Other 75s in Vichy-controlled French North Africa fought briefly against US forces during the Allied landings there.

Curtiss also developed a simplified version with non-retractable undercarriage for sale to lesser powers and did a brisk export business in all Model 75 variants. Licences to manufacture these were given to Argentina and China.

Although the letter suffixes of the Model 75 designation do not match the sequence of aeroplane development and production, the Model 75s are described in letter sequence in the following paragraphs.

Model 75—The prototype, carrying civil registration X-17Y and c/n 11923, was an all-metal low-wing monoplane initially powered with the unfortunate 900 hp Wright R-1670 twin-row radial engine with a full NACA cowling. The metal-frame movable control surfaces were fabric covered and streamlining was enhanced by an enclosed cockpit with the canopy faired into a high rear turtledeck. Both the main undercarriage units and the tailwheel retracted, the main legs rotating backward 90 degrees and turning 90 degrees on their axes simultaneously to lay the wheels flat in the thin rear portion of the wing.

The wing was built in two halves joined on the aeroplane centreline. Initial armament was a pair of machine-guns under the forward turtledeck firing through openings in the top of the cowling. No armour protection or self-sealing fuel tanks were provided.

The original Wright engine was unsatisfactory and was replaced temporarily by a 700 hp Pratt & Whitney R-1535. Since this model had passed its peak of development, a 675 hp Wright R-1820F Cyclone was used in the competition of April 1936. With this engine the aeroplane was designated Model 75B. The aeroplane/engine compatability problems were not fully resolved by then and the 75B lost out to the Seversky 1-XP. The airframe was then modified to become the XP-37 (Model 75I).

Model 75A—This designation, prefixed with the letter H, applied to the principal export version of the 75, which used several variants of both Wright Cyclone and Pratt & Whitney Twin Wasp engines. One company-owned demonstrator submitted to the US Army was also designated 75A (registration NX22028, c/n 12931).

The 75A was generally inferior in speed and armour to the German

H75A-1s for France were export versions of the US Army P-36A and were delivered in natural metal finish.

Messerschmitt Bf109 that was its principal adversary, but it was superior in manoeuvrability and the rugged airframe could absorb terrific punishment. Firepower was weak by European standards, with only two synchronized machine-guns in the nose and two in the wings. Although approaching obsolescence when it entered combat, the 75A gave an excellent account of itself in the hands of dedicated pilots.

H75-A1 (RAF Mohawk I)—One hundred, powered with 1,050 hp Pratt & Whitney R-1830-SC3G engines, delivered to France starting in December 1938. C/ns 12798/12897. France used the manufacturer's model designation and numbered the aircraft consecutively within the model. This information appeared in three lines on the rudder as: CURTISS H75-C1 No. 09. The C stood for Chasse (pursuit), and the 1 indicated a single-seater; 09 was the ninth H75 ordered by France.

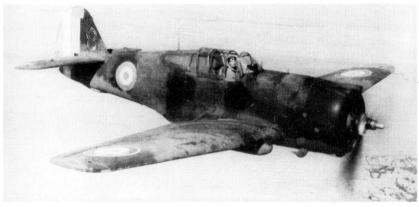

Although H75As had French insignia applied at the factory, markings were modified and camouflage paint applied in France. This is an H75A-2.

It is interesting to note that the throttles of French military aircraft operated in the reverse of the accepted standard; forward movement reduced power, and the French 75s were so equipped. Instrumentation and the four 7·5-mm machine-guns were French. After the fall of France, some H75-A1s 'escaped' to England and entered the RAF as Mohawk Is. Mohawk Is and Mohawk IIs were mixed in the RAF serial number blocks AX880/898, BJ876/878, RK876/879, BL220/223.

H75-A2 (RAF Mohawk II)—A further hundred for France, delivered from May 1939. C/ns 12932/13031. These had two additional wing guns and the 1,050 hp R-1830-S1C3G engine, which made them more like the US Army P-36D. French Air Force numbering continued from the H75-A1, the first H75-A2 being numbered 101. Some reached Britain and became Mohawk IIs.

H75A-2s for France had additional wing guns. Some, like the example illustrated, were taken over by Britain and designated Mohawk II.

H75-A3 (RAF Mohawk III)—One hundred and thirty-five for France, with improved 1,200 hp R-1830-S1C3G engines and A2 armament. Deliveries began in February 1940; C/ns 13671/13805. Approximately sixty reached France; others were diverted to French Morocco while more than 20 were taken over by Britain as Mohawk IIIs. RAF serials were BK569/588, plus some mixed with Mohawk IVs in serial number block AR630/694. Refitted with British equipment, these were transferred to Portugal, South Africa, and India.

H75-A4 (RAF Mohawk IV)—Two hundred and eighty-four A4s were built out of 795 ordered by France, c/ns 13806, 13808/14090. These were armed like the A3s but were fitted with 1,200 hp Wright R-1820-G205A Cyclone engines. Cyclone-powered 75s could be distinguished from Twin Wasp models by their short-chord cowlings of slightly greater diameter and the absence of engine cowling flaps and bulbous nose gun port covers.

Only six A4s reached France before the surrender, and some of those were impressed by the Luftwaffe. Four were lost at sea in transit, 23 were diverted to Martinique, where they sat out the war, and the remaining production was taken over by Britain as Mohawk IVs.

The German Luftwaffe took over this H75A-4 after the fall of France in 1940; 225 delivered to Britain became Mohawk IVs. (*H.J. Nowarra*)

Mohawk IV—The exact total of Mohawk IVs cannot be determined from RAF serial numbers since some blocks applied to both IIIs and IVs without distinction; the numbers appearing as IVs total 278, only six less than the total of H75-A4s built. However, some 75As other than A4s became Mohawk IVs, including the ten A9s for Persia and at least six of the former Chinese A5s assembled in India. Mohawk IV serials of record were: AR630/694, BB918/979, BJ531/550, BJ574/588, BK876/879, BL220/223, BS730/742, BS744/747, BS784/798, BT470/472, LA157, LA158.

H75-A5—This Cyclone-powered model was to be assembled in China by Central Aircraft Manufacturing Company following delivery of one complete aeroplane and kits of unassembled parts. This operation was not completed. After assembling some in China, the firm was reorganized as Hindustan Aircraft Ltd, in Bangalore, India, and at least six A5s are known to have been assembled there. These were absorbed into the RAF as Mohawk IVs.

Germany captured numbers of H75A-6s from Norway and sold eight to Finland. (*Courtesy Air International*)

The twenty H75A-7s ordered by the Netherlands were diverted to the Netherlands East Indies in 1940. NXC-1 on the rudder was a special civil registration used during factory testing of export military aeroplanes.

H75-A6—Norway ordered twenty-four A6s with 1,200 hp Pratt & Whitney R-1830-S1C3G Twin Wasp engines and four-gun armament in 1939, c/ns 13643/13654 and 13659/13670. Deliveries began in February 1940. The Germans captured most of those received in Norway and sold eight to Finland.

H75-A7—Twenty A7s with Cyclone engines were ordered by the Netherlands but all were diverted to the Netherlands East Indies starting in May 1940. C/ns 14424/14443. These saw intensive fighting before the territory fell to the Japanese.

H75-A8 (US Army P-36G)—Norway ordered an additional thirty-six A8s with 1,200 hp R-1820-G205A Cyclone engines just before the German occupation, c/ns 14546/14581. Six were delivered to Free Norwegian forces in Canada in February 1941 and the remaining 30 were requisitioned by the US Army as P-36G.

Thirty of the thirty-six H75A-8s for Norway were taken into the US Army as P-36Gs. (*Courtesy Gerry Beauchamp*)

353

Britain took over ten H75A-9s from Iran and designated them Mohawk IV.

The Curtiss-owned Model 75 prototype was refitted with a Wright Cyclone and designated 75B for the 1936 pursuit aircraft competition.

The first of two Model 75H demonstrators with non-retractable undercarriages and Cyclone engines was sold to China in 1937.

H75-A9—Ten for Persia (now Iran) used Wright R-1820-G205A engines and were designated A9. With c/ns 15252/15261, these were taken over by the British from that country and were transferred to India as Mohawk IVs.

75B—Final US Army competition version of the Model 75 prototype fitted with 850 hp Wright SGR-1820-G5 Cyclone engine.

75D ('XP-36')—Original form of Model 75 prototype with 900 hp Wright SCR-1670-G5 engine given retroactive designation. There was a tendency in later years to refer to this one aeroplane in its various configurations as the XP-36. This was a matter of historical convenience only; there was no such official designation. The aeroplane never became Army property as a P-36 but was rebuilt and delivered as the XP-37.

75E—US Army Y1P-36, which see.

75H—Two demonstrator models of the simplified Model 75 with non-retractable undercarriages were built as 75H and advertized as Hawk 75. Initial powerplant was the Wright R-1820 Cyclone but engine and armament could be changed to suit the customer's requirements. Wing bomb racks were added to this model.

The first 75H, which carried US civil registration NR-1276 (c/n 12327), was sold to China. The second, formerly registered NR-1277 (c/n 12328), was sold to Argentina.

75I—US Army P-37, which see.

The Model 75J was a second Curtiss-owned demonstrator, fitted with an experimental external supercharger.

75J—The Model 75A demonstrator, NX-22028 (c/n 12931), fitted with an external mechanical supercharger on the Pratt & Whitney R-1830.

75K—Study for a Model 75 to be powered with a 910 hp Pratt & Whitney R-2180 Twin Hornet engine; not known to have been built. Later modified to become 75R.

75L—US Army P-36A to P-36F, which see.

75M—China is reported to have had a total of 112 Model 75Ms, non-retractable undercarriage models with R-1820 Cyclone engines and two

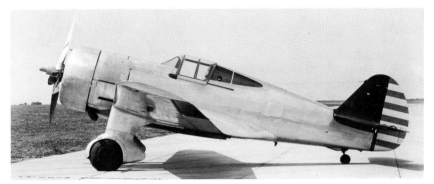

The Model 75M was the production version of the 75H; some were assembled in China from parts supplied by Curtiss.

wing-mounted machine-guns in addition to the standard nose armament. Only 30 are accounted for in Curtiss records, c/ns 12625/12654, with delivery beginning in May 1938. Tooling and kits for an unspecified number were delivered to Central Aircraft Manufacturing Company, however, for manufacture of 75Ms in China, where three full squadrons are known to have been operational.

H75N—Twelve non-retractable undercarriage H75Ns similar to 75Ms except for four wing guns were delivered to Siam (now Thailand) starting in November 1938. C/ns 12756/12767. These fought the Japanese briefly during the invasion of Siam; those not destroyed were taken over by the Japanese. The sole surviving example is now in the Royal Thai Air Museum at Bangkok.

In addition to twenty Model 75Os delivered to the Argentine by Curtiss, twenty were built in that country. Argentine-built model illustrated.
(*Dan P. Hagedorn via Gerry Beauchamp*)

356

H75O—Twenty-nine production examples of the non-retractable undercarriage 75H demonstrator with 875 hp Cyclone engines were delivered to Argentina starting in November 1939. C/ns 12769/12797. An additional 20 were built in Argentina in 1940. Some of the H75Os remained in service into the 1960s.

75P—Re-engined P-36A completed as the XP-40.

75Q—Two additional non-retractable undercarriage demonstrators with R-1820 engines. One, c/n 12898, was converted to have a retractable undercarriage and presented by Madame Chiang Kai-shek to General Claire Chennault, who was then reorganizing the Chinese Air Force. The other was flown as a demonstrator in China by American pilots but crashed after take-off on 5 May, 1939.

H75R—The 75A/75J demonstrator fitted with still another external supercharger arrangement and submitted to the US Army for test in January 1939, but the turbo-supercharged Seversky XP-41 (converted from the last P-35) was chosen instead and went into production as the P-43.

75S—US Army XP-42, which see.

| | 75 ('XP-36') | 75A-8 (P-36G) | 75M |
|---|---|---|---|
| | 900 hp Wright SCR-1670-G5 | 1,200 hp Wright R-1820-G205A Cyclone | 875 hp Wright GR-1820-G3 Cyclone |
| Span . . . | 37 ft 0 in (11·27 m) | 37 ft 0 in (11·27 m) | 37 ft 0 in (11·27 m) |
| Length . . . | 28 ft 3½ in (8·62 m) | 28 ft 6 in (8·68 m) | 28 ft 7 in (8·71 m) |
| Height . . . | 9 ft 1 in (2·76 m) | 9 ft 3 in (2·81 m) | 9 ft 3 in (2·81 m) |
| Wing area . . . | 237 sq ft (22 sq m) | 236 sq ft (21·92 sq m) | 236 sq ft (21·92 sq m) |
| Empty weight . . | 3,760 lb (1,705 kg) | 4,675 lb (2,121 kg) | 3,975 lb (1,803 kg) |
| Gross weight . . | 4,843 lb (2,106 kg) | 5,880 lb (2,667 kg) | 5,305 lb (2,406 kg) |
| Maximum speed . | 281 mph (452·21 km/h) at 10,000 ft (3,048 m) | 322 mph (518·2 km/h) at 15,200 ft (4,633 m) | 280 mph (450·6 km/h) at 10,000 ft (3,048 m) |
| Cruising speed . . | 250 mph (402·33 km/h) | 261 mph (420·03 km/h) | 240 mph (386·23 km/h) |
| Initial climb . . | — | 15,000 ft (4,572 m) in 6 min | — |
| Service ceiling . . | 30,000 ft (9,144 m) | 32,350 ft (9,860 m) | 31,800 ft (9,693 m) |
| Range . . . | 537 miles (864 km) | 650 miles (1,046 km) | 1,210 miles* (1,947 km) |
| Armament . . . | two machine-guns | four ·30 m-g two ·50 m-g | two–four m-g |

*With fuel overload

The Model H75R was the former 75J redesignated. Although carrying US Army markings here, the machine was still Curtiss-owned.

## US Army Curtiss Model 75s

As a result of the 1936 fighter competition, the Army gave Curtiss an order for three Service test Model 75s designated Y1P-36. These in turn won an order for 210 production P-36As with the same R-1830-12 engine on 7 July, 1937, but not all were delivered under that designation. Most went directly to Air Corps pursuit squadrons but a few were used for experimental work or underwent improvements prior to delivery and acquired new designations within the P-36 series. Two others were converted to new prototypes.

Y1P-36 (H75E)—Three Service test aircraft ordered as a result of the April 1936 fighter aircraft competition. Delivered in March 1937, these were fitted with the 1,050 hp Pratt & Whitney R-1830-13 engine and armament was the prevailing Army standard of one ·30 and one ·50-calibre machine-gun under the cowling. The Y1P-36s could be distinguished from the prototype by the R-1830 engine and modified view panels behind the cockpit, and from the following P-36As by the absence of engine cowling flaps and bulbous covers for the machine-gun ports.

The Y1P-36s were redesignated P-36 upon completion of Service testing. Each was carried on Army books at a different price—$48,432, $43,477, and $73,477, presumably less GFE.

US Army serial numbers: 37-68/70. C/ns: 12240/12242.

P-36A (75L)—The original $4,113,550 P-36A contract was for 210 aircraft, Army serials 38-1/210, c/ns 12415/12624. Deliveries began in April 1938 but only 176 of the first 178 were completed as P-36As. Before completion, 38-10 was converted to the XP-40 (75P) and 38-4 became the

Three Y1P-36s with P & W R-1830 engines were US Army Service test versions of the Cyclone-powered Model 75B. From 1937, all-metal US Army tactical aeroplanes were delivered in natural metal finish.

XP-42 (75S); 38-20 later became the P-36B and 38-85 became the prototype P-36C; 38-174 became the XP-36D, 38-147 became the XP-36E, and 38-172 became the XP-36F; 38-179 and on were completed as P-36Cs.

Principal points of distinction from the Y1P-36s were the addition of engine cowl flaps and bulging frog-eye covers over the machine-gun ports in the cowling. The P-36As had mostly been replaced by P-40s at the time of the Japanese attack on Pearl Harbor and only a few saw combat there.

Ten P-36As, 38-39, 43, 51, 53, 54, 60, 106, 158, 159 and 175 were transferred to Brazil in March 1942, and were assigned Brazilian Air Force serials 01 to 10.

An order for 210 P-36As resulted from the tests of Y1P-36s. Starting in February 1941, previously-silver tactical Army aeroplanes were camouflaged olive drab and grey. The 1940–41 style unit designation figures on the fin identify this as the ninth aeroplane of the 51st Pursuit Group. (*Peter M. Bowers*)

The single P-36B was P-36A 38-20 redesignated during tests of a revised supercharger.

P-36B—P-36A 38-20 was temporarily redesignated P-36B in November 1938 to evaluate 8:1 supercharger gearing.

P-36C—P-36A 38-85 was modified in December 1938 by the installation of a single ·30-calibre machine-gun in each wing in addition to the normal nose armament and became the prototype P-36C. An odd feature of the installation was that the ammunition boxes were carried beneath the wing in streamlined containers that became the distinguishing feature of this P-36 variant. The last thirty P-36As of the 210-aircraft order, 38-181/210, were completed as P-36Cs but differed from the prototype in having 1,200 hp R-1830-17 engines.

The last thirty P-36As, plus aircraft 38-85, were delivered as P-36Cs with two ·30-cal machine-guns added to the wings. Colouring shown was special camouflage applied to aeroplanes of the 27th Pursuit Squadron during 1939 War Games. (*Gordon S. Williams*)

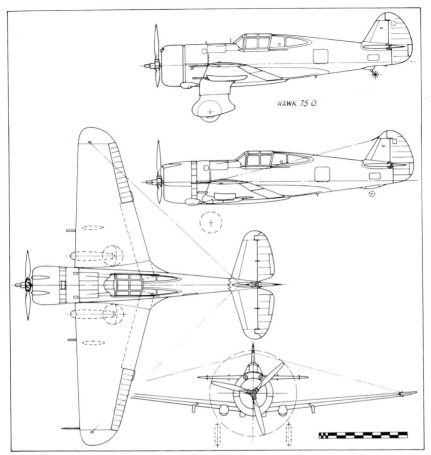

HAWK 75 O

P-36C.

XP-36D—P-36A 38-174 with standard nose armament was fitted with two pairs of ·30-calibre machine-guns, one in each wing panel in the manner of the H75A-2, and became the XP-36D.

XP-36E—P-36A 38-147 was fitted with six ·30-in calibre machine-guns in the wings and became the XP-36E. It was retired to an Army mechanics' school in August 1942.

XP-36F—P-36A 38-172 was fitted with two 23 mm Madsen cannon, one in a package mounted under each wing, and became the XP-36F. This experimental armament was soon removed and the aeroplane reverted to a P-36A. Surveyed in October 1944.

P-36G (H75A-8)—The thirty H75A-8s that the US Army requisitioned from the Norwegian contract received Army serial numbers

The XP-36D was P-36A 38-174 fitted with two ·30-cal machine-guns in each wing.

42-36305/36322 (18) and 42-108995/109006 (12) and their civil Wright Cyclone engines were redesignated R-1820-95. Useless as combat types and incompatible with the other P-36s because of their Wright engines, the P-36Gs were sent to Peru under Lend-Lease in 1943. One survived in 1977 in the Peruvian Air Force Museum.

P-37 Series (H75I)—Curtiss engineers realized that the Service life of the P-36 would be limited with the R-1830 air-cooled radial engine and adapted the prototype Model 75/75B airframe to the new twelve-cylinder liquid-cooled Allison V-1710-11 that delivered 1,150 hp at 20,000 ft (6,096 m) when fitted with a turbo-supercharger. The resulting aeroplane became the first US pursuit to exceed 300 mph (482·79 km/h).

Cannon-equipped XP-36F was P-36A 38-172 redesignated while the armament was being evaluated.

The US Army XP-37 was the Curtiss Model 75I fitted with an Allison V-1710 engine. The turbo-supercharger is visible beneath the nose. This aeroplane was finished with silver lacquer instead of having a natural metal finish.

XP-37—The rebuilt Model 75 prototype became Model 75I while retaining the same c/n (11923) and was delivered to the Army as a new airframe. It was designated XP-37 with Army serial number 37-375. It was first flown in April 1937, and after some necessary aerodynamic and mechanical adjustments, was delivered to the Army in June. Except for the cockpit, which was moved aft for balance, and the V-12 engine, the XP-37 was otherwise identical to the P-36. Cost of the single prototype, less GFE, was $104,352. The XP-37 was retired to an Army mechanics' school in August 1941 with a total of only 152 hours' flying time.

YP-37—Although the new engine/supercharger combination was quite troublesome in the XP-37, the Army was impressed by the potential and

Thirteen YP-37s were Service test versions of the XP-37. This example was delivered in natural metal finish.

The XP-42 was P-36A 38-4 fitted with a Pratt & Whitney R-1830 radial engine using a long propeller shaft in an attempt to impart the streamlining benefits of the V-type engine to the radial.

ordered 13 Service test versions as YP-37. These used V-1710-21 engines fitted with improved B-2 superchargers, had revised nose contours, a 25-in (63·5 cm) increase in fuselage length aft of the cockpit, and most of the aerodynamic improvements worked out on the XP-37. The YP-37s continued to suffer the supercharger problems of the X-model and did not live up to their potential; all but one were out of service or retired to mechanics' schools by early 1942. The highest-time aeroplane had only 212 hours. The last active example (38-474) was transferred to the National Advisory Committee for Aeronautics (NACA) for research in August 1942, and survived until January 1946. Unit costs less GFE were $34,481.

US Army serial numbers: 38-472/484. C/ns: 12655/12667.

XP-40 (75P)—The tenth P-36A, 38-10, was fitted with the Allison engine and delivered as the XP-40.

The nose of the XP-42 was progressively shortened until the aeroplane regained the appearance of a P-36A

XP-42 (75S)—The fourth P-36A, 38-4, was redesignated XP-42 and used for US Army and NACA research intended to overcome the aerodynamic drag handicap of large radial engines compared to equivalent liquid-cooled V-types. As delivered in March 1939, the XP-42 had a special 1,050 hp Pratt & Whitney R-1830-31 engine fitted with long extensions to the propeller shaft and nose casing to permit use of a streamlined nose with a large propeller spinner. The nose was progressively shortened until the XP-42 again resembled a P-36A. It retained the XP-42 designation until scrapped in January 1947.

|  | Y1P-36 | P-36C | YP-37 | XP-42 |
|---|---|---|---|---|
|  | 1,050 hp P&W R-1830-13 | 1,200 hp P&W R-1830-17 | 1,000 hp Allison V-1710-21 | 1,050 hp P&W R-1830-31 |
| Span . . . | 37 ft 3½ in (11·35 m) | 37 ft 3½ in (11·35 m) | 37 ft 3½ in (11·35 m) | 37 ft 3½ in (11·35 m) |
| Length . . | 28 ft 10 in (8·78 m) | 28 ft 10 in (8·78 m) | 32 ft 11½ in (10·04 m) | 28 ft 6 in (8·68 m) |
| Height . . | 9 ft 0 in (2·74 m) | 9 ft 3 in (2·81 m) | 11 ft 1 in (3·37 m) | 11 ft 1 in (3·37 m) |
| Wing area . | 236 sq ft (21·92 sq m) | 236 sq ft (21·92 sq m) | 236 sq ft (21·92 sq m) | 236 sq ft (21·92 sq m) |
| Empty weight . | 4,267 lb (1,935 kg) | 4,619 lb (2,095 kg) | 5,592 lb (2,536 kg) | 4,818 lb (2,185 kg) |
| Gross weight . | 5,414 lb (2,456 kg) | 5,829 lb (2,644 kg) | 6,700 lb (3,039 kg) | 6,260 lb (2,839 kg) |
| Maximum speed | 293 mph (471·53 km/h) at 10,000 ft (3,048 m) | — — — | 340 mph (547·16 km/h) at 10,000 ft (3,048 m) | 315 mph (506·93 km/h) at 15,000 ft (4,572 m) |
| Cruising speed | 261 mph (420·03 km/h) | — | 305 mph (490·84 km/h) | — |
| Climb . . | 10,000 ft (3,048 m) in 3 min 45 sec | — | 20,000 ft (6,096 m) in 8 min 30 sec | — |
| Service ceiling . | 31,500 ft (9,601 m) | — | 34,000 ft (10,363 m) | — |
| Range . . | 790 miles (1,271 km) | — | — | 730 miles (1,175 km) |
| Armament . . | two machine-guns | four machine-guns | two machine-guns | — |

## Model 76—A-14/A-18 Shrike

In 1934, parallel with the Model 75 fighter, Curtiss initiated a two-seat, twin-engined ground attack design for the Army which eventually became the XA-14 and was followed by a Service-test order for thirteen Y1A-18s. The designation change resulted from a change of powerplants.

The second-generation Shrikes were all metal, with fabric covering only on the movable control surfaces and on the wing aft of the front spar. All three undercarriage units retracted aft, leaving half of each wheel in the airstream. Four ·30-calibre machine-guns were concentrated in the extremely short nose, and a single flexible ·30-in machine-gun was in the rear cockpit, which was situated inconveniently far aft of the forward cockpit. Bombs were carried in a fuselage bomb bay on the XA-14 but the

The Curtiss Model 76 of 1935 was a company-owned prototype submitted to the Army for testing as a twin-engined ground attack aircraft.

Y1A-18s had bays in each wing holding 200 lb (90 kg) each. Chemical smoke tanks or additional bombs could be carried under the wings.

While the new Shrikes, the Army's first twin-engined models in the ill-defined Attack Series, performed well, no production orders resulted. The Y1A-18 experience proved the advantages of the twin-engined type, however, and established the Air Corps requirements that resulted in the larger and heavier Douglas A-20 and A-26 designs.

XA-14 (Model 76)—Flown initially as a company-owned aeroplane with civil registration X-15314 (c/n 11922), the Model 76 was fitted with the new and unproved Wright R-1670-5 twin-row engines under circular cowlings driving Curtiss two-position propellers. Following its first flight in September 1935 the Model 76 was tested by the Army at Wright Field and then returned to Curtiss.

Following modifications that included a notable change of engine cowling shape and new constant-speed propellers, the aeroplane was accepted by the Army in December as the XA-14, Army serial number

After modification, the Model 76 was purchased by the Army and designated XA-14.

Thirteen Y1A-18s were Service test versions of the XA-14 but with engines changed to Wright Cyclones. Tail lettering identifies Aeroplane No.16 of Third (C) Attack Group (A) in the 1938–39 Army unit designation system.

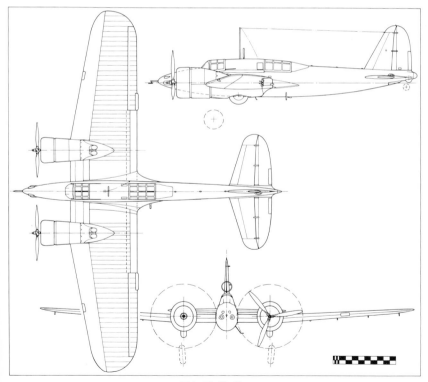

YA-18 Shrike

36-146. The XA-14 had a short military life; after being used to test 37-mm cannon installations, it was scrapped in August 1938 with a total of only 158 flying hours.

Y1A-18 (Model 76A)—On 23 July, 1936, the Army ordered thirteen Service test Y1A-18s at $104,640 each, complete. Deliveries began in July 1937 and were completed by October. The major difference from the XA-14 was the use of Wright R-1820-47 engines driving three-bladed propellers.

The Y1A-18s served initially with the 8th Attack Squadron of the Third Attack Group but were transferred to the Third Bombardment Group for operational training as plain A-18s in 1940. The last A-18 was withdrawn from service in 1943.

US Army serial numbers: 37-52/64. C/ns: 12187/12199.

Model 76 Projections—An improved Model 76B with Pratt & Whitney R-1830 engines was proposed to the Army but not accepted and a similar Model 76B was advertized for export but found no customers.

### XA-14

Two-seat Attack aircraft. Two 775 hp Wright R-1670-5.

Span 59 ft 6 in (18·13 m); length 40 ft 6 in (12·34 m); height 11 ft (3·35 m); wing area 530 sq ft (49·23 sq m).

Empty weight 8,875 lb (4,026 kg); gross weight 11,656 lb (5,287 kg).

Maximum speed 243 mph (391·06 km/h) at sea level; cruising speed 222 mph (357·26 km/h); initial climb 1,690 ft/min (8·58 m/sec); service ceiling 28,000 ft (8,534 m).

Armament—four ·30-in fixed and one ·30-in flexible machine-gun, twenty 30-lb (13·6 kg) bombs.

### Y1A-18

Two-seat Attack aircraft. Two 850 hp Wright R-1820-47.

Span, wing area and armament as XA-14.

Length 41 ft (12·49 m); height 11 ft 6 in (3·5 m).

Empty weight 9,580 lb (4,345 kg); gross weight 12,849 lb (5,828 kg).

Maximum speed 247 mph (397·5 km/h) at 2,500 ft (762 m); cruising speed 217 mph (349·22 km/h); service ceiling 25,000 ft (7,620 m); range 651 miles (1,048 km).


## Model 77—XSBC-2, SBC-3,
## SBC-4 Helldiver (RAF Cleveland)

Following the crash of the Model XSBC-1 on a company test flight, Curtiss built a replacement aeroplane for the Navy under the designation of XSBC-2. However, this was an entirely new design, a biplane dive-bomber that received the Curtiss model number 77 but used the XF12C/XSBC-1 Navy serial number 9552.

XSBC-2 (Model 77)—The XSBC-2 was a relatively conventional biplane of mixed construction. Fuselage and fixed tail surfaces were metal monocoque and the wings were metal frame with metal skin on the tapered upper wing and fabric on the straight-chord lower wing. The movable controls were fabric covered and full-span flaps were fitted to the lower wing. The stiff monospar construction of the one-piece upper wing allowed use of single I-struts instead of the traditional N-struts. Cockpit enclosures and a collapsible rear turtledeck similar to those of the SOCs were used.

The XSBC-2 was an entirely new biplane dive-bomber using the same Navy serial number as the crashed XSBC-1. Metal parts were painted light grey.

By the time the XSBC-2 flew on 9 December, 1935, the Wright R-1510 engine had been considerably improved and was ready for another trial; the 700 hp XR-1510-12 version was used but did not prove satisfactory.

XSBC-3—Because the Wright engine of the XSBC-2 proved unsatisfactory, a very similar 700 hp Pratt & Whitney R-1535-82 Twin Wasp Junior was substituted in March 1936. The aeroplane was then redesignated XSBC-3. Its performance in this configuration resulted in production models to which Curtiss reapplied the name Helldiver.

The engine change from Wright R-1510 to Pratt & Whitney R-1535 resulted in the XSBC-2 being redesignated XSBC-3. When a production order followed, Curtiss re-assigned the name Helldiver.

A production Curtiss SBC-3 based on the carrier USS *Saratoga* in 1940. Metal parts were painted silver. (*Peter M. Bowers*)

SBC-3 (Model 77A)—Eighty-three production SBC-3s with 750 hp R-1535-94 Twin Wasp Junior engines were ordered in August 1936. Deliveries began on 17 July, 1937, with one being held at the factory for conversion to the XSBC-4 prototype. All went to carrier-based units in the fleet, where some served into late 1941 before being relegated to training units.

US Navy serial numbers: 0507/0589. C/ns: 12243/12325.

XSBC-4 (Model 77B)—The eighth-from-last SBC-3, Navy serial number 0582, was kept at the factory and became the first of two XSBC-4s by change to the single-row 750 hp Wright R-1820-22 Cyclone engine that revised the nose contours considerably. A second XSBC-4 resulted from the diversion of the first production SBC-4, serial 1268, to test work.

One SBC-3 was completed with a Wright Cyclone engine and became the first of two XSBC-4s.

370

SBC-4 (RAF Cleveland)—Starting on 5 January, 1938, one hundred and twenty-four production SBC-4s with 850 hp Wright R-1820-34 Cyclone engines (900 hp for take off) were ordered under Navy serial numbers 1268/1325, 1474/1504, and 1809/1843. Fifty (4199/4248, c/ns 12668/12717) were added later but did not increase the total inventory. The first example, 1268, was used for test work as the second XSBC-4.

The SBC-4 was the last combat biplane produced for the US Navy. Although some were assigned to Navy fleet units and to the US Marines following the start of deliveries in March 1939, the Navy finally acknowledged the end of the combat biplane era and had many of the SBC-4s delivered directly to the reserve training squadrons.

An SBC-4 of Naval Reserve Squadron VS-12R over San Francisco. (*Courtesy William T. Larkins*)

Early in 1940, France ordered ninety export versions of the SBC-4. Soon afterward, the US Navy responded to US Government desire to aid France by releasing 50 of its SBC-4s to France to hasten French acquisition of the type. These were returned to the factory for refurbishment and application of French markings and were later replaced by 50 of the French models then under construction (*see* serials above).

Most of the French SBC-4s had been loaded aboard a French aircraft carrier when France fell in June 1940. The carrier was diverted to the French island of Martinique, where it sat out the war and where the SBC-4s were eventually scrapped. Five of the French SBC-4s not aboard the carrier reached the United Kingdom, where they were named Curtiss Cleveland and received RAF serials AS467/471. Found unsuitable for combat, the Clevelands became instructional airframes.

Two carrier squadrons of US Navy SBC-4s were in service at the time of the attack on Pearl Harbor and the Marines kept a squadron of land-based SBC-4s in service until June 1943.

One of fifty US Navy SBC-4s returned to Curtiss in 1940 to be refurbished for transfer to France. The civil registration NXC-27 on the rudder was assigned temporarily for local testing of a military model to be exported.
(*Courtesy Ray Wagner*)

| | XSBC-1 | SBC-3 | SBC-4 |
|---|---|---|---|
| | 700 hp Wright XR-1510-12 | 750 hp P & W R-1535-94 | 850 hp Wright R-1820-34 |
| Span. . . | 34 ft 0 in (10·36 m) | 34 ft 0 in (10·36 m) | 34 ft 0 in (10·36 m) |
| Length . . | 28 ft 5¾ in (8·69 m) | 28 ft 2 in (8·58 m) | 28 ft 1 9/16 in (8·57 m) |
| Height . . | 10 ft 5 in (3·17 m) | 10 ft 5 in (3·17 m) | 10 ft 5 in (3·17 m) |
| Wing area . . | 317 sq ft (29·44 sq m) | 317 sq ft (29·44 sq m) | 317 sq ft (29·44 sq m) |
| Empty weight . | 3,769 lb (1,710 kg) | 4,268 lb (1,936 kg) | 4,552 lb (2,065 kg) |
| Gross weight . | 5,651 lb (2,563 kg) | 5,951 lb (2,699 kg) | 7,080 lb (3,211 kg) |
| Maximum speed . | 229 mph (368·53 km/h) at 7,000 ft (2,134 m) | 219·5 mph (353·24 km/h) at 9,000 ft (2,743 m) | 234 mph (376·58 km/h) at 15,200 ft (4,633 m) |
| Cruising speed . | 172 mph (276·8 km/h) | 165 mph (265·53 km/h) | 175 mph (281·63 km/h) |
| Initial climb . | 2,000 ft/min (10·16 m/sec) | 1,560 ft/min (7·92 m/sec) | 1,630 ft/min (8·28 m/sec) |
| Service ceiling . | 27,500 ft (8,382 m) | 24,000 ft (7,315 m) | 24,000 ft (7,315 m) |
| Range . . | 500 miles (805 km) | 364 miles (586 km) | 405 miles (652 km) |
| Armament. . | One fixed ·30-in and one flexible ·30-in machine-gun and one 500 lb (227 kg) bomb (each type). | | |

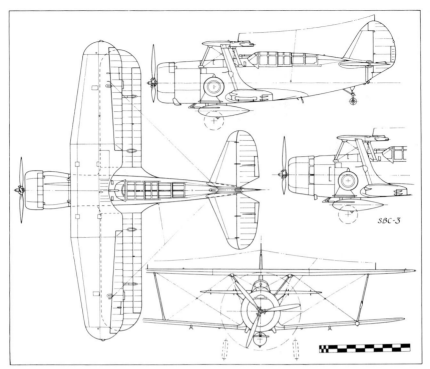

SBC-3

SBC-4 Helldiver.

Representative early Curtiss-St Louis products—a Robin refuels a Thrush during a record-breaking women's endurance flight of 196 hr 5 min in August 1932.

# St Louis Production

Early in 1928 the Curtiss Aeroplane & Motor Company acquired Robertson Airlines of St Louis, Missouri. Robertson, an air mail operator famed for having had Charles A. Lindbergh as its chief pilot, also operated a flying school and repair facility and had become a passenger airline.

A new Curtiss subsidiary was then established—Curtiss-Robertson Aircraft Corporation. Its purpose was to manufacture Curtiss aeroplanes in the midwestern United States, and a plant was established at Anglum, a suburb of St Louis.

Two separate production periods and product lines were involved at St Louis; one from 1928 into the depression year of 1931, when the plant was shut down, and the other from late 1932 to the end of World War II.

The first and major product was the Curtiss Robin, the prototypes of which had been built at Garden City. Other 'Eastern' designs were also produced at St Louis, but new designs were soon developed there under new CR and CW model numbers with constructor's numbers peculiar to that plant and the letters included in the model number. The 'Eastern' designs built in St Louis also used St Louis c/ns. After the Curtiss-Wright merger of 1929, Curtiss-Robertson Aircraft Corporation became the Curtiss-Robertson Division of Curtiss-Wright.

In 1929, Curtiss-Wright acquired the Travel Air (T-A) Manufacturing Co of Wichita, Kansas, as a subsidiary, and late in 1930, C-W bought out the Robertson interests and merged Travel Air and the former Curtiss-Robertson plant as Curtiss-Wright Airplane Company (note spelling) and the Wichita firm became its Travel Air Division. As an economy move, Curtiss-Wright soon shut down the Wichita plant and moved personnel and drawings to St Louis. To this combined product line was added the de Havilland Moth biplane formerly produced in Massachusetts by Curtiss-Wright's Moth subsidiary.

The second St Louis era began in 1932 when Curtiss-Wright sent George Page there to finalize and produce a biplane transport that had gone through preliminary design in Buffalo.

In 1936, further Curtiss-Wright corporate reorganization resulted in the Curtiss-Wright Airplane Company becoming the St Louis Airplane Division of Curtiss-Wright; the Buffalo plant became the Curtiss Aeroplane Division. Production of several St Louis-designed models continued on a relatively small scale until large orders were received from the US Army and Navy in 1940–41. The plant was then expanded to approximately eight times its former size.

It was shut down at the end of the war and was eventually acquired by the McDonnell Aircraft Company, now McDonnell-Douglas.

# St Louis Model Numbers

Early in 1930, Curtiss-Robertson sought to produce new models to be designed in St Louis as well as the established Robin, Thrush, and Kingbird lines that had originated in New York. Several designs were started under various designations beginning with the letters CR (for Curtiss-Robertson), but all except two were discontinued because of the Depression in spite of the fact that some had progressed to the point where c/ns and civil registrations were assigned. The only designs in this group to be completed were the Model CR-1 Skeeter and the CR-2 Coupe.

Following the cancellation of the above designs, the St Louis engineering staff was allowed to proceed with the new CW-1 (for Curtiss-Wright) Junior economy lightplane model for private owners. This designation did not actually start a new model series; new models developed at Wichita following the Travel Air Model 11 continued that numbering system but the number was prefixed with the letters CW for Curtiss-Wright to reflect the new order, so the first design to use the new-style designation was the CW-12. St Louis took advantage of the earlier unused numbers and applied CW-1 to CW-3 to new designs initiated there.

Not all of the CW numbers between -3 and -11 were used by new Curtiss-designed aeroplanes; most were applied retroactively for record purposes to pre-merger Travel Air designs. Designations other than CW were actually used, however, CA for the 1934 amphibian designed by Frank Courtney and CR for the Skeeter and Coupe models of 1930.

# St Louis Serial Numbers (C/ns)

Over the years, the c/ns assigned to aeroplanes built in St Louis were quite inconsistent. When Robin production started in 1928, c/ns were assigned sequentially starting with No.1. The Thrush line introduced a new c/n series starting with 1001. When Thrush production ended soon after, the second-series numbers were continued for the CW-1 Junior line starting with 1012. The Kingbird started another series at 2001 and the CR-2 Coupe established still another at 3001.

In the meantime, the former Travel Air plant in Wichita had switched from the straight numerical sequence of airframes regardless of model that was in use before the merger with Curtiss-Wright to a new system based on the actual numbers of each individual model. The Travel Air 6000A that became the Curtiss-Wright 6A started anew with c/n 6A-2001 while the 6000B/6B with a different engine started with 6B-2001.

This practice continued at St Louis with minor variations for most, but not all, CW models from CW-12. The CW-12 to CW-15 models were numbered consecutively within the basic model number regardless of powerplant while the CW-16 series started with 16-2001 but followed 16-2012 with plain 3501 and on.

The CW-19 models began to include the sub-designation in the c/n again, as 19R-14, but the CW-22 series introduced further departures of the CW-16 type. The series started logically with c/n 22-1 and carried this system part-way into US Navy SNC-1 production, after which it jumped to apparently random groups of numbers in the 2800, 3600, 3700, 3800, and 4200 ranges far beyond any possibility of meaningful continuity.

The single CW-20T transport of 1940 started another series at 101, but the relatively few derivative US Army C-46As built at St Louis followed different systems. The first two had c/ns 24 and 25, which preceded c/n 26 for the first C-46A built in the World War II plant at Louisville. This, in turn, followed the twenty-five C-76s (five of which were built in St Louis) that had c/ns 1/25. Ten C-46As built in St Louis on that particular contract had Louisville c/ns 376/385 while the seventeen C-46Es built in St Louis had c/ns 2929/2945 that did not fit into any other known C-46 c/n series. Other St Louis c/n variations will be found in the appropriate text in this section.

The St Louis aeroplanes are presented here first in chronological sequence of the original Eastern model numbers and then the St Louis originated Curtiss-Wright numbers. Former Travel Air Division models designed after the Curtiss acquisition are considered *bona-fide* Curtiss designs and are included. The military/export models produced after September 1939 are detailed in the next section, which covers Second World War production.

The prototype Curtiss Robins featured wide lift-strut fairings and rubber-cord shock absorbers in square housings. X-5049, illustrated, was the first OX-5 powered Robin. (*Courtesy Joseph P. Juptner*)

## Model 50 Robin

In the opening months of the Lindbergh Boom, Curtiss decided to produce a three-seat cabin monoplane for the expanding personal aeroplane market. With steel-tube fuselage and wood-frame wings using the thick Curtiss C-72 aerofoil, this was a conservative design; the pilot sat forward at stick-type controls and the two passengers sat side by side behind him.

The choice of powerplant was surprising for the time—the 12-year-old war-surplus Curtiss OX-5. It has been said that the Robin was produced specifically to use up Curtiss's stock of OX-5s. With its price of only $250.00, the OX-5 contributed to the Robin's popularity by keeping the initial price down to $4,000. Early Robins with the 185 hp Curtiss Challenger engine sold for $7,500 and those with the 165 hp Wright J-6-5 sold for $7,000. The new Curtiss Crusader engine, a 120 hp inverted six-cylinder air-cooled model intended to replace the OX-5, was test-flown in the Robin but was not produced.

An odd feature of a few early Robins was the strutting—circular-section steel tubing was used, and this was streamlined by the attachment of broad fairings that were supposed to act as aerofoils to produce lift. These were soon replaced with streamlined steel tubing. Early undercarriages used rubber cord shock absorbers housed in streamlined boxes; these were replaced by oleo-pneumatic shock struts.

Four Robin prototypes, with Curtiss engineering designations L-710, were built at Garden City but production was assigned to St Louis, where the first one flew on 7 August, 1928. Altogether, 769 Robins were built, making it the most numerous US civil aeroplane model of its day and the Curtiss model built in the greatest numbers between the two World Wars. Robins reached a production peak of 17 per week in mid-1929.

Robins were built under ten separate Approved Type Certificates, plus a few odd variants and later modifications under several of the lesser Category 2 or 'Memo' Certificates. Engine changes in existing models resulted in redesignation, so totals by models as originally built cannot be determined by registration records.

Serving mostly as private-owner types, Robins did little to win fame except for three separate occasions when they broke the world's refuelling endurance record—420 hr 21 min on 13–30 July, 1929; 553 hr 28 min on 21 July–17 August, 1930, by the same aircraft and crew; and 653 hr 34 min on 4 June–1 July, 1935. A Robin was also used to set the women's duration record at 123 hours in January 1930, later to be beaten by a Thrush. Perhaps the best-known Robin of all is the former OX-5 model converted to J-1 and flown from New York City to Ireland on 17–18 July, 1938. Pilot Douglas 'Wrong-Way' Corrigan had declared his intention to fly nonstop to Los Angeles, but turned east and crossed the Atlantic instead. He still owned this aeroplane in 1977.

Unfortunately for historical compilations such as this book, the registration numbers assigned to the 769 Curtiss Robins seldom involved space-saving parallel runs of registrations and c/ns as was often common to other major production models. Since it would be necessary to run over 300 individual registration/serial pairs under some Robin descriptions if all were to be covered, an obviously impractical procedure, such data are presented only for a few Robin variants. However, all known Robin registrations and c/ns will be found in the listings for all civil-registered Curtiss models presented in Appendices II and III.

Robin—The OX-5 powered prototypes and the earliest production models, issued ATC-40 in May 1928, were identified and marketed simply as the Curtiss Robin.

Challenger Robin (Model 50A)—Early Robins using the 165 hp version of that unique twin-row six-cylinder Curtiss engine were built under ATC-63 issued in August 1928. No letter designation was used, distinction from the contemporary OX-5 model being established by the naming of the engine. Like the early OX-5 version, this first Challenger variant used a tailskid and was not fitted with wheel brakes.

Comet Robin—A variant unknown either to Curtiss or the US Government appeared in 1937 when a private owner installed a 150 hp Comet radial engine in a J-1 Robin, c/n 693, registered 791M. This unauthorized act was performed in Oregon, the last of the American states in which aeroplanes could fly without federal licences or inspection.

Robin B—Built under ATC-68, this most popular Robin had such refinements as brakes and a steerable tailwheel. The actual differences between this and the OX-5 Robin certificated under ATC-40 were so slight that the FAA in later years combined the two in its own specifications. The price of a Robin B dropped to as low as $2,495 in an attempt to dispose of

X-6831 was the third Robin prototype built at Garden City and the first to have a Challenger engine. (*Smithsonian Institution*)

The production Robin B built in St Louis retained the OX-5 engine and had narrow streamlined steel-tube wing struts. (*Courtesy Robert Esposito*)

A few early Robins were fitted with war-surplus 150 hp Wright-Hispano engines and were designated Robin B-2. (*Emil Strasser*)

unsold models in the Depression year of 1930. Approximately 325 Robin Bs were built.

Robin B-2—Some Robins were fitted with the 150–180 hp Wright A, I, or E engine and licensed under Memo 2-132 issued in September 1929, to c/n 112, registered 259E.

Robin C—Approximately 50 improved Robin Cs with the 185 hp Curtiss Challenger engine were built in St Louis under ATC-69. Two special Cs with earlier 170 hp Challengers were built under Memo 2-91 issued in July 1929.
Registrations: 384E, 8337. C/ns: 180, 210.

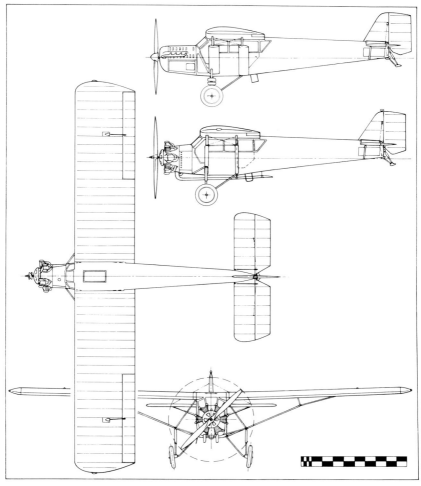

Robin C with side view of OX-5 Robin prototype.

The highest-powered production Robin was the C-1 model with 185 hp Curtiss Challenger engine. (*Gordon S. Williams*)

Robin C-1 (Model 50C)—The Robin C-1 was the principal Challenger-powered model; at least 200 were built under ATC-143. A C-1 named *St Louis Robin* twice set a world's endurance record, the last for 553 hr 28 min in July–August 1930. One special C-1, c/n 668, was fitted with a rigid undercarriage to test the new Goodyear air wheels; Memo 2-192 was issued for this aeroplane in March 1930.

Robin C-2 (Model 50D)—Six special C-2s with 170 hp instead of 185 hp Challenger engines were built under ATC-144. Additional fuel was carried in a tank built over the top of the cabin and projecting above the wing contour.

Registrations and c/ns: 9273 (338), 55H (420), 323K (480), 324K (482), 325K (484), 373K (536).

Robin CR—This was to have been a production model with the 120 hp six-cylinder inverted air-cooled Curtiss Crusader engine that was developed as an intended replacement for the ubiquitous OX-5. At least two converted Robins were used for flight tests of the Crusader, but the engine was not put into production.

The Robin CR used to test the short-lived Curtiss Crusader engine was similar in appearance to this converted Robin B used by Menasco Motors to test a new inverted air-cooled six-cylinder Menasco engine. (*Courtesy Dustin Carter*)

381

Robin W (Model 50J)—To use a lower-cost engine than the Challenger but still have more power than the OX-5, several Robins were fitted with the 110 hp Warner Scarab air-cooled radial engine and licensed under ATC-268 issued in November 1929. The Robin W was not a success. The apparent increase in power was illusory; 1918 horsepower and 1929 horsepower were simply not the same. The old OX-5 engine had a displacement of 502 cu in and turned a 104-in propeller at 1,400 rpm to deliver its rated 90 hp. The later 110 hp Warner, with 422 cu in, turned a smaller-diameter propeller at 1,850 rpm but delivered significantly less thrust in spite of its higher rating. The weight advantage of the Warner could not offset the decreased thrust. The Robin was too big for the Warner engine, which later proved to be very successful in smaller aeroplanes.

The light weight of the 110 hp Warner Scarab engine made necessary a very long nose to maintain proper balance in the Robin W. (*Courtesy National Air and Space Museum*)

At least four Robin Ws existed; NC8376 converted from B c/n 252, former C-1 NC13H c/n 384, unknown c/n VH-UJE exported to Australia, and the XC-10 built with Warner engine for the US Army.

Robin J-1 (Model 50H)—A change to the 165 hp Wright J-6-5 Whirlwind engine in 1929 resulted in the Robin J-1 starting at c/n 382, which was otherwise similar to previous models. ATC-220 was issued in September 1929. At least 40 were built as J-1s while other models were converted to J-1 standard by their owners. The most famous of these was the former B-model flown across the Atlantic by Douglas 'Wrong Way' Corrigan. Any Robin from c/n 39 on was eligible for conversion to a J-1 provided the manufacturer certified the conformity.

Robin J-2 (Model 50I)—This was a J-6-5 Robin similar to the J-1 except for an increase of fuel capacity from 50 to 80 gallons. Two were built under

The Robin J-1 had the 165 hp Wright J-6-5 Whirlwind engine. This one was converted by Douglas 'Wrong Way' Corrigan from a Robin B. (*Robert Esposito*)

ATC-221 issued the same day as for the J-1.

Registrations: 12H, 790M. C/ns: 382, 691.

Robin J-3—FAA records list Robin 12H c/n 382, the first J-2, as a temporary J-3 model, but the detail differences are unknown. This aeroplane existed in 1977 as a J-1.

Robin M—Several Robin Bs had their OX-5 engines replaced by the 115 hp Milwaukee Tank V-502 engine, which was an air-cooled rebuild of the OX-5 developed in the late 1920s. Robin Ms were licensed under Memo 2-345 issued on 13 May, 1931.

Robin 4C (Model 50E)—The Robin was a large aeroplane for only three people, and the logical expansion to four seats was made with the Model 4C, which was simply a production Robin C (c/n 208, registration X-8336) fitted with an extra seat alongside of and slightly aft of the pilot, who had been moved to the left as far as possible. After testing at Garden City in September 1929, ATC-270 was issued in November. No production of this original four-seat Robin was undertaken.

The Robin M had the 115 hp Milwaukee Tank V-502 engine, an air-cooled conversion of the OX-5. (*A. U. Schmidt*)

383

The Robin 4C-1 was the wide-fuselage four-seat model with the seating reduced to three. X-544N, shown here, was c/n 769, the last Robin built. (*Courtesy James Dilonardo*)

Robin 4C-1—The production four-seat Robin had the forward fuselage widened and deepened, but three were produced as special three-seat versions with the Challenger engine and a gross weight of only 2,600 lb (1,179 kg). These received Memo 2-198 approval in April 1930. The third 4C-1 was also the last Robin built.

C/ns: 700, 767, 769. Registrations: 508N, 625V, 554N.

Robin 4C-1A (Model 50G)—At least eleven production Robin 4C-1A four-seaters were built under ATC-309 issued on 3 April, 1930. To obtain increased cabin room, the forward part of the cabin was made 4 in (10·16 cm) wider, the belly was deepened, and the windshield was enlarged. Because of this added bulk forward, the vertical tail was also enlarged. Initial price was $7,995.

Registrations and c/ns: 509N (702), 510N (704), 512N (706), 514N (708), 516N (710), 563N (712), 564N (714), 565N (716), 566N (718), 567N (720), 606V (730).

The four-seat Robin 4C-1A had noticeably different proportions to the three-seat models. (*Gordon S. Williams*)

384

# Robin

| | B | C-1 | J-1 | 4C-1A |
|---|---|---|---|---|
| | 90 hp Curtiss OX-5 | 185 hp Curtiss Challenger | 165 hp Wright J-6-5 | 185 hp Curtiss Challenger |
| Span | 41 ft 0 in (12·49 m) | 41 ft 0 in (12·49 m) | 41 ft 0 in (12·49 m) | 41 ft 4 in (12·59 m) |
| Length | 25 ft 8½ in (7·83 m) | 25 ft 1 in (7·64 m) | 25 ft 1 in (7·64 m) | 25 ft 5 in (7·74 m) |
| Height | 7 ft 9½ in (2·37 m) | 8 ft 0 in (2·43 m) | 8 ft 0 in (2·43 m) | 8 ft 0 in (2·43 m) |
| Wing area | 223 sq ft (20·71 sq m) | 223 sq ft (20·71 sq m) | 223 sq ft (20·71 sq m) | 225 sq ft (20·9 sq m) |
| Empty weight | 1,472 lb (668 kg) | 1,700 lb (771 kg) | 1,641 lb (744 kg) | 1,811 lb (821 kg) |
| Gross weight | 2,440 lb (1,107 kg) | 2,440 lb* (1,107 kg) | 2,361 lb (1,071 kg) | 2,850 lb (1,293 kg) |
| Maximum speed | 100·5 mph (161·73 km/h) | 120 mph (193·11 km/h) | 118 mph (189·89 km/h) | 115 mph (185·07 km/h) |
| Cruising speed | 84 mph (135·18 km/h) | 102 mph (164·15 km/h) | 100 mph (160·93 km/h) | 98 mph (157·71 km/h) |
| Initial climb | 400 ft/min (2·03 m/sec) | 640 ft/min (3·25 m/sec) | 750 ft/min (3·81 m/sec) | 505 ft/min (2·56 m/sec) |
| Service ceiling | 10,200 ft (3,109 m) | 12,700 ft (3,871 m) | 13,000 ft (3,962 m) | 11,200 ft (3,414 m) |
| Range | 480 miles (772 km) | 300 miles (483 km) | 338 miles (544 km) | 481 miles (774 km) |

* From c/n 228 on 2,600 lb (1,179 kg).

Robin 4C-2—A change to the 225 hp Wright J-6-7 Whirlwind engine in the second Robin 4C-1A, c/n 704, resulted in the designation 4C-2, but the new model was not certificated.

Robin XC-10—One much modified Robin W was delivered to the US Army as the XC-10 with Army serial number 29-452. With increased

With increased dihedral and a raised thrust line, the US Army XC-10 used for early experiments in radio-controlled flight was an adaptation of the Robin W.

dihedral and enlarged vertical tail surfaces for improved stability, the XC-10 was used for early experiments in the radio control of unpiloted aeroplanes. Delivered in October 1929, the XC-10 accumulated only 100 flight hours before being scrapped in March 1935.

Surviving Robins—The Robin was the most numerous example of the few pre-war Curtiss designs still flying in 1977. Most of those that survived to the beginning of the Vintage Aeroplane or Antique boom that began in the early 1950s did so by being involved in useful work like crop dusting and bush flying, where their obsolescence and slow-flying characteristics were an asset rather than a handicap. At first, postwar attrition was high as more suitable aeroplanes became available as economical replacements— there were 182 on the US register in 1947 but only 50 in 1952.

The survivors were rescued by the antique movement. Relatively few were restored 'Pure' with their original (and orphan) engines; these were mainly for show. Those used as regularly active recreational aeroplanes are mostly fitted with war-surplus 220 hp Continental R-670 and 220–300 hp Lycoming R-680 radial engines. Oddly, while an engine change changed the designation of the Robin in its early years, such is not now the case. A Robin B re-engined with a Challenger is now just a modified B. Similarly, a B and a C both refitted with R-680 engines that make them identical are still a B and a C.

The Robin population has been more stable since the aircraft became valuable and pampered antiques. The number dropped to 42 in 1964, and while only 34 were listed as active in 1975, several are known to have been retired to museums, not lost to crashes or scrapping.

### Model 55 Kingbird

The Kingbird was essentially an enlarged twin-engined version of the Model 56 Thrush that was under simultaneous development. Seating was for eight and there was increased baggage and fuel capacity. The unique design feature was the close placement of the propellers ahead of a short

The sole Curtiss Kingbird C with Curtiss Challenger engines.

The Kingbird D-1 with 225 hp Wright J-6-7 Whirlwind engines. Note the large cutouts in the twin rudders to allow elevator movement.

nose to minimize engine-out control problems. The timing of the Kingbird was poor; it appeared in May 1929, but production models were not available until mid-1930, after the Depression was under way. Three prototypes were built at Garden City but production was at St Louis.

Kingbird C—The first prototype, c/n G-1, registration 3133, was originally powered with two 185 hp Curtiss Challenger engines, but was so underpowered that it was quickly converted to the higher powered J-model without being certificated as a C-model.

Kingbird D-1—The second and third prototypes were completed with 225 hp Wright J-6-7 Whirlwind engines and received ATC 347 in August 1930. However, these were soon converted to D-2 models; there were no production D-1s. C/ns: G-2, G-3. Registrations: 310N, 374N.

Kingbird D-2—Fourteen production models built at St Louis with 300 hp Wright J-6-9 Whirlwind engines. ATC 348 also issued in August 1930. All but the two converted from D-1s served Eastern Air Transport as airliners. Unit cost was $25,555. C/ns: 2001/2012, 2014, 2015. Re-

The principal Kingbird model was the D-2. Fifteen were built with 300 hp Wright J-6-9 engines. (*A. U. Schmidt*)

gistrations: 585N, 586N, 588N, 589N, 599N, 600V/602V, 620V/622V, 626V, 628V, 629V.

Kingbird D-3—The last production Kingbird was the single D-3 model, c/n 2016, registration 11816, powered with 330 hp Wright J-6-9s; ATC 440 was awarded in August 1931. Seating was reduced to five passengers and one pilot but space was provided for 259 lb (117 kg) of baggage or mail plus toilet facilities and increased fuel capacity.

Kingbird J-1—The first prototype, c/n G-1, was converted to J-1 by change to 240 hp Wright J-6-7 engines. Memo Approval 2-122 was issued in September 1929; the aircraft crashed on 23 July, 1930.

Kingbird J-2—The third prototype, c/n G-3, became the J-2 model (for J-6-7 engines) and served as the prototype for the D-1 model to which it was converted before becoming D-2.

Kingbird J-3—The second prototype, c/n G-2, became the J-3, a six-seat mailplane with 300 hp J-6-9s, and received Category 2 Approval 2-196 in March 1930.

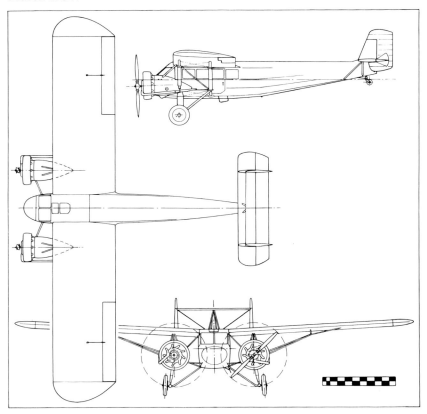

Kingbird D-2.

One Kingbird D-2 served the US Marines as the RC-1.

JC-1/RC-1—The US Navy ordered one D-2 Kingbird, c/n 2013, for the Marines under the designation JC-1 (J for Utility). By the time the machine was delivered in March 1931 the designation had been changed to RC-1 in the R-for-Transport category. This use of the single C and R in combination did not duplicate the CR-1 racer of 1921 because the sequence of the letters was now reversed. Carrying US Navy serial number 8846, the single RC-1 served into 1936.

### Kingbird C
Seven-seat light transport. Two 185 hp Curtiss Challengers.
Span 54 ft 6 in (16·61 m); length 34 ft 5⅛ in (10·5 m); height 10 ft (3·04 m); wing area 405 sq ft (37·62 sq m).
Empty weight 3,442 lb (1,561 kg); gross weight 5,202 lb (2,360 kg).
Maximum speed 113 mph (181·85 km/h); cruising speed 96 mph (154·49 km/h); initial climb 790 ft/min (4·01 m/sec); service ceiling 12,900 ft (3,932 m); range 378 miles (608 km).

### Kingbird D-2
Eight-seat light transport. Two 300 hp Wright Whirlwind J-6-9s.
Span, height and wing area as Kingbird C. Length 34 ft 9 in (10·59 m).
Empty weight 3,877 lb (1,759 kg); gross weight 6,115 lb (2,774 kg).
Maximum speed 142 mph (228·52 km/h); cruising speed 112 mph (180·24 km/h); initial climb 1,000 ft/min (5·08 m/sec); service ceiling 16,000 ft (4,877 m); range 415 miles (668 km).

### Kingbird D-3
Six-seat light transport. Two 330 hp Wright Whirlwind R-975E (J-6-9).
Dimensions and wing area as D-2. Empty weight 4,215 lb (1,312 kg); gross weight 6,600 lb (2,994 kg).
Maximum speed 142 mph (228·52 km/h); cruising speed 122 mph (196·33 km/h); initial climb 1,000 ft/min (5·08 m/sec); service ceiling 16,000 ft (4,877 m); range 550 miles (885 km).

The first Thrush, with original rudder configuration. The engine cowling was added in attempt to improve performance.

## Model 56 Thrush

Three prototypes of the Thrush, essentially a six-seat enlargement of the Robin with Challenger engine, were built at Garden City before production was started in St Louis. The Thrush was built in two versions, with a total of thirteen.

Challenger Thrush—Fuselage construction of the Thrush differed from the Robin in using mostly riveted aluminium tubing instead of welded steel. Awarded ATC 159 in June 1929, the Challenger model was somewhat underpowered. Extensive cowling tests were made in an effort to improve the front-end streamlining and improve performance. The third prototype, with minor refinements, received ATC 160 at the same time. Intended price

Ten production Thrush J models were built with J-6-7 engines and two of the three prototypes were converted to this configuration.

of a Challenger Thrush in 1929 was $10,000, but all three prototypes were converted to higher-powered J-models.

C/ns: G-1, G-2, G-3. Registrations: 7568, 9787, 9142.

Thrush J—The first two Thrush prototypes were converted to the J-model with 225 hp Wright J-6-7 Whirlwind engines and received ATC 236 in September 1929. Ten production versions were built at St Louis under ATC 261, awarded in October. Even with the larger engine, the Thrush was underpowered since its principal competition, the Ryan Brougham and the Travel Air 6000 had both gone to 420 hp by this time. The major shortcoming of the Thrush, however, was poor timing; its market vanished with the onset of the depression.

C/ns: 1001/1010. Registrations: 522N, 523N, 542N, 552N, 553N, 562N,* 580N/582N.

Thrush J Special—One J-model, c/n 1005, was converted to J-Special under Memo Approval 2-210 by installation of a 240 hp J-6-7 engine in May 1930.

**Thrush J**

Pilot and five passengers. 225 hp Wright J-6-7 Whirlwind.

Span 48 ft (14·63 m); length 32 ft 7½ in (9·34 m); height 9 ft 3 in (2·81 m); wing area 305 sq ft (28·33 sq m).

Empty weight 2,260 lb (1,025 kg); gross weight 3,678 lb (1,668 kg).

Maximum speed 122 mph (196·33 km/h); cruising speed 104 mph (167·36 km/h); initial climb 650 ft/min (3·3 m/sec); service ceiling 13,200 ft (4,023 m); range 493 miles (793 km) (60 gal/227 litres), 905 miles (1,456 km) (110 gal/416 litres).

### T-32 'Condor II'

For a project with which to reopen the Depression-closed St Louis plant, Curtiss sent engineer George Page there to finalize his twin-engined biplane transport design, started in Buffalo in 1931, and get it into production.

Designated T-32 for a transport (T) with a 3,200 lb (1,451 kg) payload, (32) it was named Condor to benefit from the reputation of the earlier Condor 18 that had been developed from the B-2 bomber. Although universally referred to as the Condor II, the II was never the official title for the new model.

The aeroplane was an anachronism when it first flew on 30 January, 1933. Including the Garden City Condors, it was the only biplane airliner since the last Boeing 80-A was delivered in April 1930. The new generation of sleek all-metal monoplanes with retractable undercarriages, spearheaded by the revolutionary Boeing 247, were just coming on the scene. The only 'Condor II' feature that matched the Boeing was the retractable undercarriage. However, Curtiss knew that there was an immediate market for sleeper transports, in which speed was not such an important factor and the Condor's bulky fuselage was an asset. The simplicity of the old-

* C/n 1006, 562N, crashed on its first flight and its registration was transferred to c/n 1007.

fashioned frame-and-fabric construction, including the tubular wing spars inherited from the earlier Condors, allowed quick production and delivery and the antiquated 'Condor II' was able to pioneer night sleeper travel for Eastern Air Transport and American Airways in 1933. Airline service was short, however, and the biplanes were all replaced within three years. Others were built for non-airline customers and military service; the last 'Condor II' to fly was in the Peruvian Air Force and was scrapped as late as September 1956.

Altogether, 45 'Condor IIs' were delivered up to October 1934, with c/ns starting arbitrarily at 21 and ending at 65. Initial price was $60,000.

### Civil 'Condor IIs'

T-32—Twenty-one twelve-passenger sleepers were built as T-32s under ATC 501, issued in March 1933. These had ground adjustable propellers and narrow anti-drag rings around the engines; c/ns 21/41. Two were supplied to the US Army as YC-30s. There was one special aircraft for the 1933 Byrd Antarctic Expedition (c/n 41, registration NR12384) with extra tankage. Wheel undercarriage for c/n 41 was rigid since it was intended to operate mainly on floats or skis.

The Condor T-32 for the Byrd Antarctic Expedition could be fitted with floats or skis. It is seen over Manhattan. (*Fred Bamberger collection*)

This Condor T-32 has been modified and brought up to AT-32 standard under the designation T-32C. (*Gordon S. Williams*)

C/ns 28, 29, 30, and 36, formerly NC12366/12368 and NC 12374, went to the United Kingdom as G-AEZE, AEWD/F and were drafted into the RAF as P5723/5726.

Registrations and c/ns: NC12353, 12354 (21, 22), NC12363/12365 (23/25), NC12366/12369 (28/31), NC12371/12378 (32/39), NC12383, 12384 (39, 40).

Subsequent changes of 'Condor II' nationality and registration are too numerous to list here.

T-32C—Ten T-32s brought up to later AT-32 standards and issued new ATC 547. C/ns: 21, 23/25, 31/33, 38/40.

AT-32—Improved model with controllable-pitch propellers, full NACA cowlings on the engines, and the nacelles extended aft of wing for better streamlining. New ATC 534 applied to all five variants listed below:

AT-32A—Sleeper or day transport with SGR-1820-F3 Cyclones rated 710 hp at 7,000 ft (2,134 m). Three built, registrations NC12390/12392, c/ns 42/44.

AT-32B—As AT-32A except F2 Cyclones rated 720 hp at 4,000 ft (1,219 m). Three built, registrations NC12393/12395, c/ns 45/47.

AT-32C—Day transport for 15 passengers, engines as AT-32B. C/n 53 was sold to Swissair, original registration CH-170 changed to HB-LAP.

AT-32D—As AT-32C with standard engines. Four built, registrations NC12396/12399; c/ns 48/51, c/n 49 converted to sleeper.

AT-32E—Deluxe day transport for twelve passengers, F-3 engines. Two delivered to US Navy and Marines as R4C-1s.

393

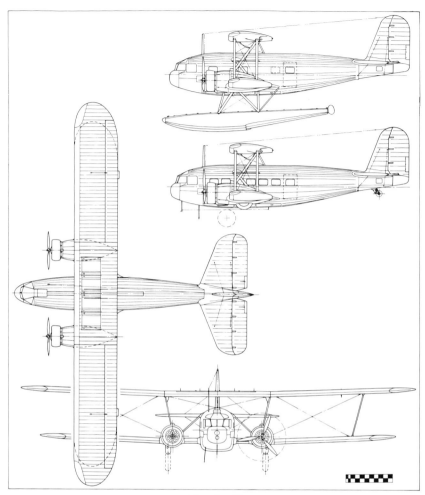

Condor II.

### Export 'Condor IIs'

It was easy to adapt the boxy 'Condor II' to bomber (BT-32) and heavy-cargo (CT-32) versions, all of which were sold outside the United States.

BT-32—Eight built, with provision for up to 1,680 lb (762 kg) of bombs in the fuselage and under the wings. Manual machine-gun turrets were on top of the nose and mid-fuselage, plus one in the aft cabin floor, for a total of five guns. The prototype, c/n 52, was sold to China; three seaplane versions, c/ns 54/56, went to Colombia; and four landplanes, c/ns 59/62, eventually went to the Peruvian Air Force as OB-11A/OB-11D.

Three float-equipped Condor BT-32 bombers were sold to Colombia.
(*Edgar Deigan collection*)

CT-32—Three cargo carriers with large three-segment loading door on the starboard side. Three built for Argentine Army, Argentine serials I-E-31, 2-Gt-11, 3-Gt-1; c/ns 63/65.

### US Military 'Condor IIs'

YC-30—Two T-32s, c/ns 26 and 27, were delivered to the US Army under Army serial numbers 33-320 and 321 in May 1933. At unit costs of $44,030 less GFE, these served in routine transport work into 1938.

The two US Army YC-30s were early T-32 Condors equipped as executive transports. (*E.M. Sommerich collection*)

R4C-1—Two AT-32Es, c/ns 57 and 58, were delivered to the Navy under Navy serials 9584 and 9585 and were used by both the Navy and the Marines. Although only the second Curtiss transport for the Navy, the logical R2C and the R3C designations in the R-for-Transport category were skipped because of their previous use by the 1923–25 Curtiss racers. After service with the Marines, both R4C-1s were used by the US Antarctic Service and were abandoned in Antarctica in 1941.

Two AT-32E Condors delivered to the US Navy as R4C-1s were among the last Condors built. Compare the redesigned engine nacelles to those of earlier models.

### AT-32 'Condor II'

Sleeper transport. Two pilots, cabin attendant, 12 passengers. Two 720 hp Wright R-1820F Cyclones.

Span 82 ft (24·99 m); length 48 ft 7 in (14·8 m); height 16 ft 4 in (4·97 m); wing area 1,208 sq ft (112·22 sq m).

Empty weight 12,235 lb (5,550 kg); gross weight 17,500 lb (7,938 kg).

Maximum speed 190 mph (305·77 km/h); cruising speed 167 mph (268·75 km/h); initial climb 1,200 ft/min (6·09 m/sec); service ceiling 23,000 ft (7,010 m); range 716 miles (1,152 km).

### Courtney Amphibian CA-1

This unique design resulted from the Curtiss-Wright directors' 1933 decision to build an amphibian. British test pilot Frank Courtney, then a consultant to Curtiss-Wright, convinced the board that he could design one better than any then existing. The board gave him approval but stipulated that the aeroplane had to be a biplane with a pusher engine. Development funds were found in the assets of the inactive Curtiss-Caproni Division and three prototypes were built in St Louis.

The Curtiss-built Courtney CA-1 amphibian was an example of how an innovative designer could be held back by obsolete requirements.

With metal hull and wooden wings, the five-seat CA-1 re-introduced the tricycle landing gear to aviation. The inherent tail-heaviness problem of pusher designs was overcome by moving the 365 hp Wright R-975E-1 (J-6-9) Whirlwind engine forward yet keeping the propeller behind the trailing edge of the upper wing by means of an extension shaft. When Wright told Courtney that this couldn't be done, he had an independent machine shop successfully build the assembly to his design.

Although c/n 101 received Memo Approval 2-497 in January 1935, and along with c/n 102 it received ATC 582 in September, the CA-1 was not put into production. Both American-registered aeroplanes and the unregistered third, along with the design data, were sold to Japan.

C/ns 101/103. Registrations: 13298 (101), 11780 (102).

**CA-1**

Commercial amphibian. Pilot and four passengers. 365 hp Wright J-6-9 Whirlwind.
Span 40 ft (12·19 m); length 31 ft (9·44 m); height 12 ft (3·65 m).
Empty weight 2,980 lb (1,352 kg); gross weight 4,650 lb (2,109 kg).
Maximum speed 151 mph (243 km/h); cruising speed 125 mph (201·16 km/h); initial climb 835 ft/min (4·24 m/sec); service ceiling 14,000 ft (4,267 m); range 550 miles (885 km).

## CR-1 Skeeter

This was an ultra-light two-seat sportplane based on the configuration of a powered glider, the Snyder MG-1 (for Motor Glider) Buzzard that was owned by Curtiss test pilot Lloyd Child and some associates. Curtiss-Wright was impressed by the capability of the design and acquired the manufacturing rights in July 1930.

Preferring two seats and a steel-tube fuselage to the original wood, the St Louis engineering staff worked up the preliminary design of an improved version, the CR-1 (for Curtiss-Robertson) and named it Skeeter, a

The CR-1 Skeeter was developed from a powered glider design and was the prototype of the mass-produced CW-1 Junior of 1931. (*Courtesy Paul Matt*)

colloquialism for mosquito. The chief engineer of the Curtiss-Wright Moth Division, Karl White, went to St Louis when Moth production was transferred there, and was given the job of finalizing the CR-1 design. Because of the Depression, he was cautioned to keep the selling price below $1,500.

The CR-1, which flew in October 1930, had too many structural and aerodynamic short-cuts to be a marketable product, and only one was built, c/n 3001, registration 607V. One major drawback was the efficient but costly 24 hp British ABC Scorpion engine. The performance was good, however, so White revised the design for production as the CW-1 Junior.

The two-seat CR-2 Coupe was an intended replacement for the Moth biplane but did not go into production.

398

## CR-2 Coupe

The Coupe, which appeared late in 1930, was a light two-seat cabin monoplane with side-by-side seating that was developed as a potential replacement for the obsolescent open-cockpit Moth biplane. The original powerplant was the same Wright-built version of the British de Havilland Gipsy engine. Fuselage and tail were welded steel tubing with fabric covering while the wood-frame wings were unusual for a low-wing monoplane in being strut-braced from above. A second CR-2 had the 125 hp Kinner B-5 radial engine.

The Depression eliminated the market for the Coupe and only the two prototypes were built.
C/ns: 3001, 3002. Registrations: 627V, 637V.

### CR-2 Coupe

90 hp Wright Gipsy.

Span 38 ft (11·58 m); length 25 ft (7·62 m); height 8 ft (2·43 m); wing area 188 sq ft (17·46 sq m). Empty weight 1,136b lb (515 kg); gross weight 1,747 lb (792 kg).

Maximum speed 110 mph (177·02 km/h); cruising speed 90 mph (144·83 km/h); initial climb 600 ft/min (3·04 m/sec); range 450 miles (724 km).

## CW-1—CW-12

CW-1 St Louis designed Junior lightplane.

CW-2 Low-wing two-seat monoplane with Kinner engine; not built.

CW-3 Duckling amphibious version of CW-1 Junior.

CW-4 St Louis designation for Buffalo-designed T-32 'Condor II' transport. Also applied for record purposes to former Travel Air 4000/4 series.

CW-5 St Louis freighter design, not built.

CW-6 Former Travel Air Model 6000 of 1928, later Curtiss-Wright Model 6. Four 6B versions built at St Louis after Wichita plant closed; four others built from left-over parts by Air-Tech of San Diego, California, after St Louis plant closed.

CW-7 Former Travel Air Model 7000 of 1927.

CW-8 Former Travel Air Model 8000 of 1928.

CW-9 Former Travel Air Model 9000 of 1928.

CW-10 Former Travel Air Model 10 of 1929.

CW-11 Former Travel Air Model 11 of 1929.

CW-12 Wichita-designed Sport Trainer; production continued at St Louis.

There was no CW-13; Curtiss preferred to avoid possible sales resistance to the controversial number 13. The CW numbers resumed at CW-14.

The CW-1 Junior was Curtiss-Wright's last effort to sell light commercial aeroplanes during the Depression. This one was used for a clown act in air shows in the late 1930s. (*Gordon S. Williams*)

## CW-1 Junior

The Junior was an improved CR-1 Skeeter with structural and aerodynamic refinements and more comfortable passenger accommodation. A major change was replacement of the ABC Scorpion engine with the American 45 hp Szekely SR-3. In spite of the changes, the price was kept below the initial target—the Junior sold for $1,490.

Since the corporate identity had changed since the design of the CR-1, the Junior that followed it was identified as a Curtiss-Wright design (CW) rather than a Curtiss-Robertson (CR). The serial numbering system also changed; instead of starting another series or continuing from the Skeeter's c/n 3001, the Juniors followed the last Thrush, c/n 1010, with c/n 1012 for the first production Junior. There may have been an intermediate unregistered prototype that was assigned c/n 1011.

The Junior, first flown in December 1930, was pleasant to fly because pilot and passenger were placed ahead of the cantankerous and oil-throwing Szekely engine. Most Juniors surviving past 1950 have undergone changes to later flat-four engines such as the 50/65 hp Lycoming O-145 and the 65 hp Continental A-65.

C/ns and registrations: 1012 632V, 1013/1019 630V/636V, 1020/1081 638V/699V, 1082/1107 10900/10925, 1108/1119 10929/10940, 1120/1177 10942/10999, 1178/1182 11800/11804, 1183/1190 11808/11815, 1191/1234 11817/11860, 1235/1268 11865/11894 and 11896/11899, 1269 12299, 1270 12300, 1271 12301, 1272 12305.

CW-1A—Other engines were tried in Juniors in an attempt to overcome the many problems of the Szekely. One such experiment involved the unique four-cylinder 40 hp Augustine rotary engine. Memo Approval 2-442 was issued to Junior c/n 1225 on 18 March, 1933.

CW-1S—Further attempts to improve the powerplant of the Junior involved the 40 hp French Salmson AD-9 nine-cylinder radial. Two conversions were made to CW-1S (for Salmson); Memo Approval 2-525 was issued to c/ns 1164 and 1224 on 26 September, 1936.

## CW-1 Junior

45 hp Szekely SR-3.

Span 39 ft 6 in (12·03 m); length 21 ft 3 in (6·47 m); height 7 ft 4 in (2·23 m); wing area 176 sq ft (16·35 sq m).

Empty weight 570 lb (259 kg); gross weight 975 lb (442 kg).

Maximum speed 80 mph (128·74 km/h); initial climb 600 ft/min (3·04 m/sec); service ceiling 12,000 ft (3,658 m); range 200 miles (322 km).

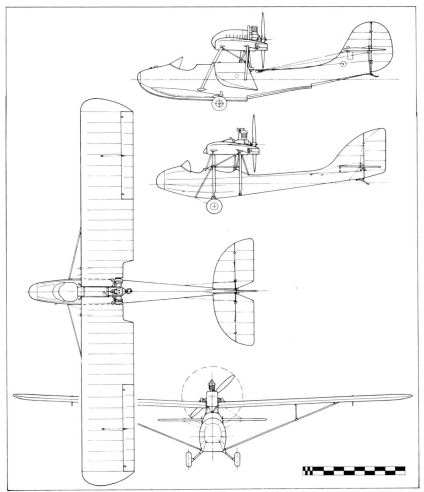

CW-1 Junior with side view of CW-3 Duckling.

## CW-3 Duckling

The CW-3 was basically a CW-1 Junior redesigned as an amphibian with heavier structure and a more powerful engine. Marketed unsuccessfully under the name Duckling, one of the three CW-3s built was named *Teal* in duplication of the 1929 Garden City amphibians. Original powerplant was the Velie M-5 of 60 hp which was quickly changed to the more powerful Lambert and Warner models.

CW-3W—Duckling powered with 90 hp Warner radial engine.
CW-3L—Duckling powered with 90 hp Lambert radial engine.
Registrations: 12306, 12325, 12326. C/ns: 1501/1503.

The CW-3 Duckling, also called Teal, was an amphibious version of the CW-1 Junior. Company officials pose here for publicity pictures; the man with the shotgun was Curtiss-Wright's vice-president Walter Beech.

## CW-12 Sport Trainer

The CW-12 was a new generation light two-seat biplane designed in 1930 by former Travel Air engineers Ted Wells and Herb Rawdon for the private-owner market and using a variety of late-model small-displacement engines. Designed and built in Wichita, these are often referred to as Travel Airs but are legitimately Curtiss designs because of their timing.

CW-12K—The high-performance version, powered with the 125 hp Kinner B-5; two built under ATC 406 issued in March 1931. Initial selling price of $4,288.
C/ns: 12-2003, 12-2011. Registrations: 437W, 445W.

CW-12Q—The most popular of the CW-12s because of the lower price of $3,500 resulting from use of the 90 hp Curtiss-Wright Gipsy engine. Price was further reduced as the depression hampered sales. ATC 401 issued in February 1931.
C/ns: 12-2001, 12-2004/2010, 12-2022/2039. Registrations: X430W, 438W/444W, 495W/498W, 352M (c/n 12-2026), 414W/419W, 11708/11714.

CW-12W—This variant used the seven-cylinder 110 hp Warner Scarab engine under a Curtiss low-drag cowling. Twelve examples were built; ATC 407 issued in March 1931.
C/ns: 12-2002, 12-2012/2020, 12-2040, 12-2041. Registrations: 434W, 493W, 494W, 410W/413W, 408W, 11700, 11701, 11815, 11716.

Sales of CW-12Q Sport Trainers with 90 hp Wright Gipsy engines were hampered by the Depression. Since they were designed and built in the Wichita plant, formerly Travel Air, the CW-12s and 16s are often identified as Curtiss-Wright Travel Airs.

### CW-12Q

90 hp Curtiss-Wright Gipsy.

Span 28 ft 10 in (8·78 m); length 21 ft 5 in (6·52 m); height 8 ft 10 in (2·69 m); wing area 206 sq ft (19·13 sq m).

Empty weight 1,071 lb (486 kg); gross weight 1,725 lb (782 kg).

Maximum speed 105 mph (168·97 km/h); cruising speed 88 mph (141·62 km/h); initial climb 600 ft/min (3·04 m/sec); service ceiling 12,000 ft (3,658 m); range 390 miles (628 km).

### CW-12W

110 hp Warner Scarab.

Span, height and wing area as CW-12Q. Length 20 ft 10 in (6·34 m).

Empty weight 1,186 lb (538 kg); gross weight 1,800 lb (816 kg).

Maximum speed 117 mph (188·29 km/h); cruising speed 99 mph (159·32 km/h); initial climb 780 ft/min (3·96 m/sec); service ceiling 15,000 ft (4,572 m); range 480 miles (772 km).

The CW-12W with 110 hp Warner engine did not sell as well as the CW-12Q because of its higher price.

403

## CW-14 Sportsman, Speedwing and Osprey

Designed by Fred Landgraf, the CW-14 was a development of the Travel Air 4000/4 series. The three-seat civil versions initially carried on the old Travel Air Speedwing designation and the two-seat export military models were called Osprey. Approximately 15 were built, starting in 1931 and resuming after the St Louis plant reopened in 1933.

CW-14C—Prototype of the series, powered originally with the 185 hp Curtiss Challenger engine. Category 2 Approval 2-351 issued June 1931. Converted to A14D model; sold to Argentine Government and given serial number E-439.
C/n: 14-2001. Registration: X433W.

CW-A14D—Civil three-seat Sportsman with 240 hp Wright R-760E (J-6-7) Whirlwind. Issued ATC 442 in August 1931; initial price $10,895.
C/ns: 14-2001, 14-2006/2009. Registrations: 449W, 12307, 12310, 12323, 12329.

The CW-A14D Sportsman was a three-seat biplane developed from earlier Travel Air designs. (*Courtesy Joseph P. Juptner*)

CW-B14B—Speedwing Deluxe similar to A14D except for 300 hp Wright R-975E (J-6-9) Whirlwind. Issued ATC 485 in June 1932; initial price $13,500.
C/ns: 14-2010, 2011. Registrations: NC12332, NS-1A (to NC68261 after World War II).

CW-B14R—Special Speedwing Deluxe, a single-seater powered with a supercharged 420 hp Wright SR-975E. Issued Memo Approval 2-403 in March 1932.
C/n: 14-2003. Registration: NC12311.

CW-C14B—Osprey two-seat militarized model with cockpits moved slightly aft and centre section strut arrangement revised. Single synchronized machine-gun for pilot, flexible gun for observer, racks for light bombs under wings. Powered by 300 hp Wright R-975E.

CW-C14R—Osprey as CW-C14B except for J-6-9 Whirlwind engine.

This CW-B14B Speedwing Deluxe, NS-1A, for the US Department of Commerce is shown with the front cockpit covered. NS prefix to registration meant that the aeroplane was government-owned. (*Paul Matt collection*)

The Osprey was a militarized export version of the CW-14. This is the CW-C14R with 420 hp Wright R-975E (J-6-9) engine.

| | 14C | A14D | C14R |
|---|---|---|---|
| | 185 hp Curtiss Challenger | 240 hp Wright J-6-7 | 420 hp Wright R-975E |
| Span . . . | 36 ft 0 in (10·97 m) | 31 ft 0 in (9·44 m) | 31 ft 0 in (9·44 m) |
| Length . . | 23 ft 10 in (7·26 m) | 23 ft 6½ in (7·17 m) | 23 ft 6½ in (7·17 m) |
| Height . . | 9 ft 7½ in (2·93 m) | 9 ft 1½ in (2·78 m) | 9 ft 1½ in (2·78 m) |
| Wing area . | 266·8 sq ft (24·78 sq m) | 248 sq ft (23·03 sq m) | 248 sq ft (23·03 sq m) |
| Empty weight . | 1,569 lb (712 kg) | 1,772 lb (804 kg) | 2,186 lb (992 kg) |
| Gross weight . | 2,600 lb (1,179 kg) | 2,870 lb (1,302 kg) | 3,250 lb (1,474 kg) |
| Maximum speed . | 120 mph (193·11 km/h) | 155 mph (249·44 km/h) | 174 mph (280·02 km/h) |
| Cruising speed . | — | — | 157 mph (252·66 km/h) |
| Initial climb . | 740 ft/min (3·75 m/sec) | 1,000 ft/min (5·08 m/sec) | 1,700 ft/min (8·63 m/sec) |
| Service ceiling . | 14,500 ft (4,420 m) | 16,000 ft (4,877 m) | 18,500 ft (5,639 m) |
| Range . . | 600 miles (966 km) | 600 miles (966 km) | 580 miles (933 km) |
| Armament . . | — | — | One fixed and one flexible machine-gun, 500 lb (227 kg) bombs |

## CW-15 Sedan

A four-seat monoplane designed by former Travel Air engineer Walter Burnham and strongly reminiscent of the Travel Air Model 10. Fifteen were built. Some engine changes were made long after production ended.

The CW-15N Sedan with the rare 210 hp Kinner C-5 engine. (*A.U. Schmidt*)

The first prototype of the CW-15 Sedan series, a further development of the old Travel Air line. This is the CW-15C model with Curtiss Challenger engine.

CW-15C—The prototype and eight production aircraft built under ATC 426 of June 1931 with 185 hp Curtiss Challenger engines. Then fitted with a Wright R-760 engine, the prototype was being used in 1977 as a jump aircraft for sport parachutists. Initial price $6,370, reduced to $4,595.

C/ns: 15-2001, 15-2203/2207, 15-2210/2212. Registrations: 436W, 10928, 11805–11807, 11861, 11864 (to XB-DEE), 12302, 12303 (to NS-4Y, NS-58).

CW-15D—A higher-powered Sedan with 240 hp Wright J-6-7 engine; ATC 444 issued in August 1931. Initial price $9,600. Three were built as CW-15Ds, some others converted by engine changes.

C/ns: 15-2209, 15-2213, 15-2214. Registrations: NS-34, 12304, 12314.

CW-15N—An intermediate-powered version with the little-used 210 hp Kinner C-5 engine. Three built at an intermediate price of $6,950, later reduced to $5,100 to overcome slow sales.

C/ns: 15-2002, 15-2202, 15-2208. Registrations: 448W, 10927, 11862.

### CW-15C

185 hp Curtiss Challenger.

Span 43 ft 5 in (13·23 m); length 30 ft 5 in (9·27 m); height 8 ft 10 in (2·69 m); wing area 240 sq ft (22·29 sq m).

Empty weight 2,083 lb (945 kg); gross weight 3,281 lb (1,488 kg).

Maximum speed 115 mph (185·07 km/h); cruising speed 97 mph (156·1 km/h); initial climb 600 ft/min (3·04 m/sec); service ceiling 12,000 ft (3,658 m); range 525 miles (845 km).

### CW-15N

210 hp Kinner C-5.

Dimensions and wing area as CW-15C.

Empty weight 2,081 lb (944 kg); gross weight 3,279 lb (1,487 kg).

Maximum speed 125 mph (201·16 km/h); cruising speed 105 mph (168·97 km/h); initial climb 700 ft/min (3·55 m/sec); service ceiling 13,000 ft (3,962 m); range 475 miles (764 km).

The CW-16E Light Sport with 165 hp Wright J-6-5 engine was a three-seat development of the CW-12 series. (*E. M. Sommerich*)

## CW-16 Light Sport

Essentially a three-seat version of the CW-12 series developed by Wells and Rawdon; but its greater utility could not overcome the depressed market.

CW-16E—The highest-powered and final model of the 16 series, with 165 hp Wright J-6-5 engine; ATC 463 issued in February 1932. Ten built at bare-minimum price of $4,600 each.

C/ns: 3501/3508, 3519, 3520. Registrations: 12331, 12335/12337, 454W/456W, 12352, 12379, 12380.

### CW-16E

165 hp Wright R-540E (J-6-5).

Span 28 ft 10 in (8·78 m); length 21 ft 1 in (6·42 m); height 8 ft 10 in (2·69 m); wing area 206 sq ft (19·13 sq m).

Empty weight 1,320 lb (599 kg); gross weight 1,950 lb (885 kg).

Maximum speed 131 mph (210·82 km/h); cruising speed 111 mph (178·63 km/h); service ceiling 18,900 ft (5,761 m); range 336 miles (541 km).

CW-16K—Eleven 16K models were powered with the 125 hp Kinner B-5 engine. Issued ATC 411 in April 1931; price $4,488.

C/ns: 16-2001, 16-2003/2012. Registrations: 446W, 421W, 422W, 407W, 409W, 11703/11707, 11718.

CW-16W—One minor variant with 110 hp Warner Scarab engine. Issued ATC 429 in June 1931.

C/n: 16-2002. Registration: 420W.

The CW-16K was similar to the CW-16E except for its 125 hp Kinner B-5 engine. (*E. M. Sommerich*)

The small diameter of the 110 hp Warner Scarab engine allowed the NACA cowling on the CW-16W to fair smoothly into the fuselage. (*E.M. Sommerich*)

### CW-17R Pursuit Osprey
An improved export version of the B-14B Osprey with 420 hp J-6-9 engine was advertized in 1932 but there is no evidence that one was built.

### CW-18
Intended for a US Army trainer competition but not built.

The all-metal CW-19W Coupe of 1935 was Curtiss-Wright's first truly modern civil aeroplane. (*Gordon S. Williams*)

## CW-19

The CW-19 was designed at the specific request of the Bureau of Air Commerce. In 1934–35, that government agency was encouraging the industry to develop light private-owner aeroplanes that would capitalize on the latest construction techniques. For the CW-19, all-metal construction was decreed by Curtiss management.

Although developed as a private-owner type and type-certificated as such, the characteristics of the basic design suited it better to military training and light attack work and the aeroplane was redesigned to take on these missions. The degree of initial structural over-design is reflected by the fact that the basic CW-19 wing was used with little change on later Curtiss-Wright military models of up to 900 hp. Altogether, twenty-six CW-19s were built, c/ns 1/26.

CW-19L—One low-wing cabin monoplane with side-by-side seating for two was built in 1935 and was the second CW model to be named Coupe. It also appears in some records as the Sparrow. Powerplant was the 90 hp Lambert R-266 driving a Curtiss-Reed fixed-pitch propeller. A distinctive feature was the fitting of large fairings known as spats to the fixed undercarriage.

The single example was bought by the Government, which assigned registration NS-69 from the special Government low-number block. Approved Type Certificate A-589 was issued on 2 December, 1935.

CW-19W—Ninety horsepower was rather marginal for the weight of the aeroplane. It should be pointed out that 90 hp from a 503 cu in (8,243 cc) engine like the OX-5 which turned a large propeller at 1,400 rpm delivered

410

considerably more thrust than 90 hp from the 266 cu in (4,359 cc) Lambert turning at 2,375 rpm. The Lambert was replaced by a 145 hp Warner Super Scarab without affecting the ATC. The subsequent performance was much too 'hot' for the average private pilot and development of the CW-19 for that market was discontinued.

CW-19R—For military use, the CW-19 fuselage was altered to change the coupé-type cabin seating to tandem seating under a sectioned sliding canopy. Power was increased with options for the 350 hp Wright R-760E2 (J-6-7) Whirlwind and the 450 hp R-975E3 (J-6-9). Armament installations varied. A single machine-gun could fire through the propeller disc and/or a pair of guns could be mounted on the outboard sides of the undercarriage fairings. Provision was made for a flexible gun in the rear seat position and bomb racks under the fuselage. Twenty CW-19Rs were sold to China and South American countries and three to Cuba.

CW-A19R—An unarmed version of the CW-19R with the same engine options corresponded to US Army Basic Training models. Since it also had potential as a high-performance sports model, the CW-A19R was put on

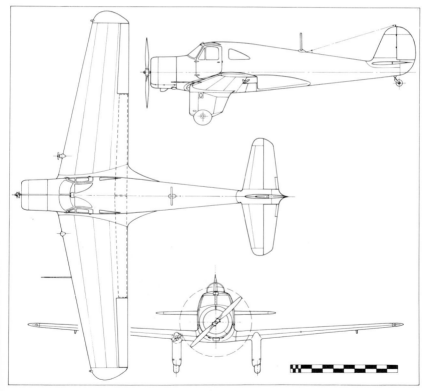

CW-19W Coupe.

411

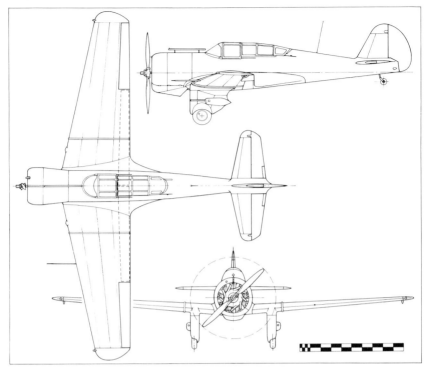

CW-19R.

The CW-19R was a higher-powered development of the CW-19 with tandem seating and light armament for the export military trade. The tube above the nose is a gunsight; forward-firing guns are attached to the undercarriage.
(*Courtesy Joseph P. Juptner*)

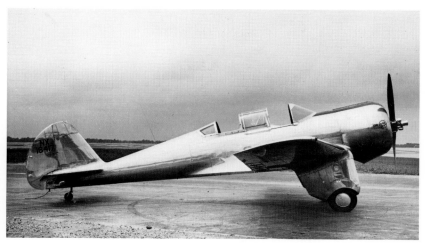

The CW-A19R was a civil development of the militarized CW-19R. (*Gordon S. Williams*)

the civil market under ATC A-629. Besides the company-owned demonstrator (NX11781, c/n 14926) one CW-A19R (16421, c/n 19R-14) found a private owner, and another, NX 16417, was rebuilt as a CW-22.

CW-B19R—Returning to the cabin configuration, the B19R was a four/five-seat civil version of the A19R that was advertized but not built.

### CW-19W
Two-seat sports aircraft. 145 hp Warner Super Scarab.

Span 35 ft (10·66 m); length 26 ft 4 in (8·02 m); height 7 ft 2 in (2·18 m); wing area 174 sq ft (16·16 sq m).

Empty weight 1,400 lb (635 kg); gross weight 2,100 lb (953 kg).

Maximum speed 154 mph (247·83 km/h); cruising speed 132 mph (212·43 km/h); initial climb 850 ft/min (4·31 m/sec); service ceiling 17,600 ft (5,364 m); range 1,100 miles (1,770 km).

### CW-19R
Two-seat light fighter and attack aircraft. 350 hp Wright R-760E2 (J-6-7) Whirlwind.

Span, length and wing area as CW-19W.

Empty weight 1,992 lb (904 kg); gross weight 3,500 lb (1,588 kg).

Maximum speed 185 mph (297·72 km/h); cruising speed 164 mph (263·92 km/h); initial climb 1,890 ft/min (9·6 m/sec).

Armament—one-to-three fixed and one flexible machine-gun and bombs.

### CW-23
The single CW-23 was a company-owned prototype developed from the CW-19R. It featured a 600 hp Pratt & Whitney R-1340 Wasp engine, the inward-retracting undercarriage of the CW-21B, and a rigid roof over the two tandem seats with car-type doors for entry. It was intended to meet the Army's new requirement for a Basic Combat aeroplane, an advanced training type with armament. With civil registration NX19427 and c/n

The single CW-23 with 600 hp Wasp engine combined features of the CW-19 and CW-21 into an experimental Basic Trainer for evaluation by the US Army.

7033, the CW-23 was tested by the Army in 1939, but no orders were placed.

### CW-23

Two-seat advanced trainer. 600 hp Pratt & Whitney R-1340 Wasp.

Span 35 ft (10·66 m); length 27 ft 7 in (8·4 m); height 8 ft 11 in (2·71 m); wing area 174 sq ft (16·16 sq m).

Empty weight 3,500 lb (1,588 kg); gross weight 5,000 lb (2,268 kg).

Maximum speed 330 mph (531·07 km/h); cruising speed 267 mph (429·68 km/h); initial climb 4,000 ft/min (20·32 m/sec); service ceiling 31,500 ft (9,601 m).

Armament—one fixed and one flexible machine-gun.

# World War II

Although the actual period of World War II was from September 1939 to 14 August, 1945, for aviation it must be considered as having started in 1934 and continuing to the early 1950s. 1934 can generally be regarded as the year in which the specifications were formulated for the new generation of aircraft that became the principal aircraft of the war. Some of these, such as the German Messerschmitt Bf 109 fighter, had a proving period in the Spanish civil war of 1936–39. Aircraft constructed during the war to the basic prewar specifications formed the backbone of the world's air powers up to the Korean action of 1950–53. Also, some models that served throughout the war, such as the SOC Seagull, were out of production before the war started.

This relatively long period of use for single military aircraft models resulted from the complexity of modern aircraft. Several years, nearly the period of a major war, are required to design, build, test, and then tool up for mass production of a new model. It therefore became common practice to stretch the production of an accepted model well past its date of obsolescence. The Curtiss P-40, adapted from a 1935 design, was in production from late 1939 to November 1944, and the SB2C Helldiver, flown in prototype form in 1940, was being produced by three manufacturers at the war's end.

American industry also built military aircraft to the post-1934 concepts although these were considerably behind equivalent European types in armament and armour. Because of a strict US arms embargo, new American equipment did not fight in Spain but the principal Curtiss production design of the 1936–40 period, the Model 75, saw combat in China before the Second World War.

The American aviation industry began to get on a war footing in 1938, when the government permitted military aircraft sales to France and Britain, who were then building up their forces. Significant build-ups of US forces did not get under way until 1940, but the Curtiss-Wright Corporation played a major role in both the French and US programmes. Significant deliveries of Curtiss aircraft to Britain resulted from that country's taking over existing French contracts after the fall of France in June 1940. Official US concern for the welfare of the Allied cause is shown by the fact that fifty US Navy Curtiss SBC-4 scout-bombers were recalled from service in 1940 and then sent to Curtiss-Wright for refurbishment and delivery to France.

The obsolescent SOCs served with the US Fleet throughout the Second World War. In February 1941, the Navy adopted overall light grey camouflage, deleted the upper starboard and lower port wing stars, and added stars to the fuselage. The grey, as on this SOC-1 from the cruiser *Astoria*, was used into early 1942. (*Peter M. Bowers*)

During the US build-up prior to the attack on Pearl Harbor, all existing Curtiss-Wright plants were expanded and new aircraft factories were built at Colombus in Ohio and Louisville in Kentucky. Although many new Curtiss aircraft were designed and flight-tested, mass production of significant Service aircraft was limited to three models during the war period—the Model 81/87 (P-40 Tomahawk, Kittyhawk and Warhawk), the C-46 Commando, and the SB2C Helldiver. The wartime manufacture of two Curtiss-Wright designs, the C-46 Commando Army transport and the SB2C Helldiver, Navy dive-bomber, was licensed to other manufacturers. Curtiss-Wright, on the other hand, built 354 P-47G fighters designed by Republic Aviation Corp.

While most of the Curtiss aeroplanes were built in Curtiss factories during the war, Wright undertook an extensive licensed-production programme in which established motor car manufacturers built Wright engines in their own plants. One unforeseen result of this programme was that the large number of Curtiss engineers and inspectors needed at the car plants resulted in a shortage of essential personnel at the home plant, seriously affecting the development and perfection of critical new engine models, particularly the 2,200 hp R-3350 Cyclone used in the Boeing B-29.

Curtiss-Wright received severe criticism in the famous Truman Report investigating US military procurement during the war. In addition to criticizing the prolonged production of the obsolete P-40, particular mention was made of the large number of experimental Curtiss models and their slow development. Curtiss-Wright was not entirely at fault here; the designs were requested by the military, but changing military requirements for the aircraft often necessitated extensive redesign while development was further hampered by changing priorities.

# Curtiss World War II Military Service Test and Production Models by Plant, 1935–46

Taken by plant in order of Curtiss model number, the production quantities of military aircraft delivered by the Aeroplane Division of Curtiss-Wright from 1936 into 1946 are as follows:

**Buffalo Plant**

| | | |
|---|---|---:|
| Model 71 | SOC Seagull II | 261 |
| Model 75 | P-36/Mohawk | 1,206 |
| Model 75I | YP-37 | 13 |
| Model 76A | Y1A-18 Shrike II | 13 |
| Model 81/87 | P-40/Tomahawk/Kittyhawk/Warhawk | 13,920 |
| Model 77 | SBC Helldiver II | 257 |
| Model 85 | O-52 Owl | 203 |
| Model CW-20 | C-46/R5C Commando | 2,711 |
| Republic P-47G Thunderbolt | | 354 |
| | | 18,938 |

**St Louis Plant**

| | | |
|---|---|---:|
| Model 84 | A-25 Shrike/Helldiver III | 900 |
| Model CW-20 | C-46 Commando | 29 |
| Model CW-21 | Demon | 24 |
| Model CW-22 | SNC-1 Falcon II | 441 |
| Model CW-25 | AT-9 Jeep | 791 |
| Model CW-27 | C-76 Caravan | 5 |
| | | 2,190 |

**Columbus Plant**

| | | |
|---|---|---:|
| Model 84 | SB2C Helldiver III | 5,516 |
| Model 82 | SO3C Seagull III/Seamew | 795 |
| Model 97 | SC Seahawk | 576 |
| | | 6,887 |

**Louisville Plant**

| | | |
|---|---|---:|
| Model CW-20 | C-46/R5C Commando | 438 |
| Model CW-27 | YC-76, YC-76A Caravan | 20 |
| | | 458 |

Total Curtiss Production and Service Test
(Including licence-built Republic P-47s but excluding CW-19s) 28,473

417

# Curtiss Models Built by Other Manufacturers

| | | |
|---|---|---:|
| Model 71 | SOC Seagull by Naval Aircraft Factory, as SON-1 | 44 |
| Model 84 | SB2C Helldiver III by Canadian Fairchild, as SBF | 300 |
| | SB2C Helldiver III by Canadian Car & Foundry, as SBW | 835 |
| Model CW-20 | C-46 Commando by Higgins (498 cancelled) | 2 |
| | | 1,181 |

# Curtiss World War II Prototypes*, 1935–46

| | | |
|---|---|---:|
| Model 71 | XSO2C-1 Seagull | 1 |
| Model 75 | 'XP-36', converted to Model 75I (XP-37), plus Second Demonstrator | 2 |
| Model 76 | XA-14 | 1 |
| Model 82 | XSO3C-1 Seagull | 1 |
| Model 84 | XSB2C-1 Helldiver | 1 |
| Model 86 | XP-46, XP-46A | 2 |
| Model 90 | XP-60 (To XP-60D) | 1 |
| Model 91 | XP-62 | 1 |
| Model 94 | XF14C-2 | 1 |
| Model 95 | XP-60A/YP-60E | 4 |
| Model 96 | XBTC-2 | 1 |
| Model 97 | XSC Seahawk** | 2 |
| Model 98 | XBT2C-1 | 9 |
| Model 20 | Airliner; to Army as C-55 | 1 |
| Model 21 | Demon Export Fighter | 5 |
| Model 22 | Falcon II | 1 |
| Model 23 | Advanced Trainer | 1 |
| Model 24 | XP-55 (3), Flying Mockup (1) | 4 |
| | | 39 |

| | |
|---|---:|
| Grand Total Curtiss-Designed or Built Aeroplanes, 1935–46, including 26 CW-19s: | 29,693 |

* Unlisted prototypes such as XP-40 and XP-42 are conversions of production aeroplanes, not true design prototypes.

** Additional XSCs are early production models redesignated for test work.

All of the Second World War Curtiss aeroplanes except the Models 71, 75 (P-36), 76, 77, 81/87/P-40, and the Model 19 are presented in this section, first in sequence of Curtiss-Buffalo model numbers and then by St Louis CW model numbers.

The XSO3C-1 Seagull of 1939.

## Model 82—SO3C Seagull/Seamew

The SO3C was intended to replace the obsolescent SOC. The third model to be called Seagull by Curtiss, it was the first to use it as an official US Service name. The British named their version Seamew. The SO3C was an entirely new mid-wing monoplane design operable on wheels or floats. It was plagued with aerodynamic problems plus those of the troublesome inverted air-cooled Ranger V-770 engine and by excessive weight caused by additional Navy equipment requirements. There were 795 production aircraft but the type was retired by March 1944; some were actually replaced in the fleet by SOCs, the model the SO3C was designed to replace. Delivery of SO3Cs had only been completed in January 1944. A projected SOR-1, the SO3C-1 to be built by Ryan, and the SO3C-4, a deck-landing version, were not built.

XSO3C-1 (Model 82)—The prototype XSO3C-1, Navy serial 1385 in the second series, was ordered on 9 May, 1938. Built at Buffalo, it first flew on 6 October, 1939. It was a conservative mid-wing two-seat monoplane designed to the same general specification as the competing Vought XOS2U-1 and XSO2U-1. Powerplant was the 450 hp Ranger V-770-6, an inverted air-cooled V-12 that obtained high power from small displacement through greater crankshaft speed.

Armament was a single fixed ·30-calibre machine-gun and a flexible ·30-in in the rear cockpit. Wing racks could carry two 100 lb (45 kg) bombs or two 325 lb (147 kg) depth-charges.

SO3C-1 (Model 82A)—The production SO3Cs were built at Columbus, and 141 SO3C-1s were delivered under the initial contract for 300, Navy serials 4730/4783 and 4793/4879 in the second series. Deliveries began in July 1942.

419

Production SO3C-1s had redesigned wingtips and added vertical tail area. A portion of the vertical fin slid forward with the rear cockpit canopy.

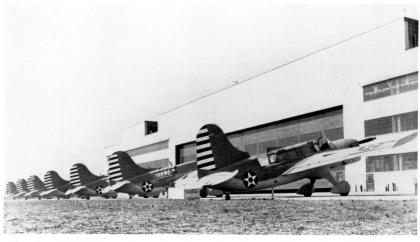

Curtiss SO3C-1 Seagulls at the Columbus factory. Camouflaged US Navy, Marine, and Coast Guard aeroplanes had red and white rudder stripes from January to May 1942. The camouflage shown was the short-lived 1941–42 scheme of grey-green top and sides and light grey undersides. The stars readopted for both wings of camouflaged Navy types after Pearl Harbor were retained into 1943. (*Courtesy Harold Andrews*)

The aerodynamic problems of the prototype were somewhat alleviated in the production models by redesigned wingtips and tail surfaces. The early SO3C-1s were soon retired and some were converted to expendable radio-controlled aerial targets.

SO3C-1B (Model 82C)—Two hundred and fifty SO3C-1s were to be built for the Royal Navy as SO3C-1B, but these were delivered as SO3C-2C, which see.

SO3C-2 (Model 82B)—Fitted with 520 hp V-770-6 engines and 24-volt electrical systems, the last 150 aeroplanes of the initial SO3C order, plus 50 others, were completed as SO3C-2, Navy serials 4880/5029 in the second series and 04149/04198 in the third.

SO3C-2C (Royal Navy Seamew)—SO3C-2s fitted with arrester gear for deck landings were designated SO3C-2C. When operating on wheels, these could carry a 500 lb (227 kg) bomb under the fuselage.

Two hundred and fifty Seamews for the Royal Navy, to have been SO3C-1Bs, were designated SO3C-2C. These were built under US Navy serials 22007/22256 and also carried RN serials FN450/649, JW550/599. Seventy went to Canada.

Thirty additional Seamews ended up as radio-controlled targets called Queen Seamews, including serials JX663/669, JZ771/774.

SO3 C-2 Seagull.

This SO3C-2C, named Seamew by the Royal Navy, carries British camouflage and fin flash but US stars on wing and fuselage. The red centre was deleted from the star marking in May 1942.

SO3C-3 (Model 82C)—The 150 SO3C-3s, Navy serials 04199/04348, were essentially SO3C-2s put through a weight-reduction programme in an attempt to improve performance.

### XSO3C-1 seaplane

Two-seat Scout Observation seaplane. 450 hp Ranger V-770-6.

Span 38 ft (11·58 m); length 35 ft 11⅞ in (10·96 m); height 15 ft 3 in (4·64 m); wing area 290 sq ft (26·94 sq m).

Empty weight 3,955 lb (1,794 kg); gross weight 5,365 lb (2,434 kg).

Maximum speed 190 mph (305·77 km/h); initial climb 860 ft/min (4·36 m/sec); service ceiling 19,000 ft (5,791 m); range 825 miles (1,328 km).

Armament—one fixed and one flexible ·30-in machine-gun, two 100 lb (45 kg) bombs.

### SO3C-2C landplane

Two-seat Scout Observation landplane. 520 hp Ranger V-770-6.

Span and wing area as XSO3C-1. Length 35 ft 8 in (10·87 m); height 14 ft 6 in (4·41 m).

Empty weight 4,800 lb (2,177 kg); gross weight 7,200 lb (3,266 kg).

Maximum speed 172 mph (276·8 km/h) at 8,100 ft (2,469 m); cruising speed 125 mph (201·16 km/h); initial climb 720 ft/min (3·65 m/sec); service ceiling 15,800 ft (4,816 m); range 1,150 miles (1,851 km).

Armament—one fixed ·30-in and one flexible ·50-in machine-gun, two 100 lb (45 kg) bombs or two 325 lb (147 kg) depth-charges or one 500 lb (227 kg) bomb.

## Model 84—SB2C Helldiver/A-25 Shrike

The Model 84 was the third Curtiss design to bear the names Helldiver and Shrike but the first to use either as an official Service name. The model originated in 1938 in response to a tight US Navy specification leading to a Navy dive-bomber competition. After evaluation of preliminary design studies, the Navy ordered a single prototype as XSB2C-1 on 15 May, 1939. Where past policy had always decreed the testing of a prototype before placing production orders, the Navy was so anxious to obtain new designs for its 1940 expansion programme that it pinned its faith on design studies and wind-tunnel tests and placed an initial order for 370 production SB2C-1s on 29 November, 1940, several weeks before the prototype flew.

Getting the SB2C into action proved to be a major production, test, and debugging effort for both Curtiss and the Navy. While none of the major features of the SB2C were entirely new—all but the Pratt & Whitney R-2800 engine having been well-proven on other designs—some were new to Curtiss. In addition, the aeroplane incorporated many internal systems that were new to the state of the art and ended up as probably the most complex single-engined design of its time. Getting everything to work together, plus overcoming aerodynamic and structural deficiencies plus production problems, produced many headaches that delayed the combat debut of the SB2C to a degree that brought severe criticism of both the design and its production from Congressional Committees. The early -1 model carried many of its problems into combat and earned the nickname of 'The Beast' from flight and maintenance crews. Even at that date, serious recommendations were made to abandon the SB2C as a combat type.

Blame for the Helldiver's problems is largely due to the Navy's requirements for military load, equipment, and structural features, and its limitation on the size of the airframe that carried them.

With other war orders building up, Curtiss could not build the SB2C at Buffalo or St Louis so the Navy built a new plant for Curtiss at Columbus. The US Army developed a sudden interest in dive-bombers after the initial success of the German Junkers Ju 87 in 1940 and ordered duplicates of the SB2C from Curtiss. To avoid interference with Navy production, these were built at St Louis.

Production was soon under way but the first SB2C-1 did not fly until June 1942. Various problems delayed delivery to the Navy until December. Combat debut of the Helldiver was over Rabaul on 11 November, 1943, and the type went on to replace the Douglas SBD and become the only dive-bomber in the Fleet. The Army did not use its version, the A-25, operationally but did turn some over to Australia.

In spite of continuing problems, the SB2C was ordered in still greater numbers, and Curtiss was again unable to meet the demand. Consequently, the Navy ordered licensed production by the Canadian plant of Fairchild and by the Canadian Car & Foundry Company. The last of 5,516 Navy Helldivers was delivered in October 1945, and the type remained in fleet service until 1 June, 1949.

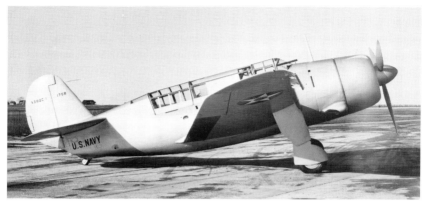

Curtiss XSB2C-1 Helldiver in December 1940. The wingtip slots are open.

### US Navy Helldiver

XSB2C-1 (Model 84)—The XSB2C-1, Navy serial number 1758, was a conventional-looking two-seat all-metal low-wing monoplane that most impartial observers considered to be unusually close-coupled for a dive-bomber, which needed good directional stability. The short length was dictated by the size of the lifts on current aircraft carriers.

The crew sat in tandem under a long canopy that faired into a collapsible rear turtledeck as on the SOCs and SBCs. To reduce storage space aboard ship, the outer wing panels folded hydraulically upward, outboard of the inward-retracting undercarriage. Powerplant was the new 1,700 hp Pratt & Whitney R-2800-8 Double Wasp, an eighteen-cylinder, twin-row radial. Split trailing-edge dive-brakes were fitted to the centre section and automatic leading-edge slats were fitted to the outer two-thirds of each outer wing panel.

Initial armament was a pair of ·30-calibre machine-guns in the nose and a pair of ·50-calibre machine-guns on a power-driven mount in the rear cockpit. An internal bomb bay could carry a 1,000 lb (454 kg) bomb. Displacement mechanism moved this bomb clear of the propeller arc before release during near-vertical dive bombing.

The XSB2C-1 made its first flight on 18 December, 1940. It suffered a major crash in February 1941, but was rebuilt. Never released from manufacturer's trials, the XSB2C-1 was never tested by the Navy before it suffered an in-flight wing failure and was destroyed on 21 December, 1941.

SB2C-1 (Model 84)—Although the production SB2C-1s differed considerably in internal detail from the prototype, they did not carry a revised Curtiss model number. Of the 370 on the initial order, only 200 were completed as plain SB2C-1s. Serial numbers were 00001/00200 in the Navy's third series.

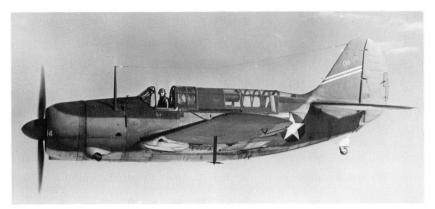

A production SB2C-1 Helldiver with 1943–44 blue and white camouflage. The diagonal stripes on the fin were reference marks for the Landing Signal Officer during landings aboard aircraft carriers.

Forward armament was changed from two ·30-in guns on the nose to four ·50-in guns in the centre section outside of the propeller arc. A marking oddity of the SB2C's was the application of top-surface camouflage to the underside of the outer wing panels. This was done to camouflage the aeroplanes on the deck of aircraft carriers when the wings were folded, thereby exposing their under-surfaces to observation from above.

The first flight of a production SB2C-1 was on 30 June, 1942, and the first few aeroplanes were used as test vehicles. Like the prototype, SB2C-1 00001 suffered wing failure during a dive test in January 1943. The first delivery of SB2Cs to a fleet squadron was in December 1942 but the type did not see combat for almost a year. Aerodynamic problems continued to plague the SB2C-1s and they were restricted from making high-speed dives in the clean configuration.

SB2C-1As were former US Army RA-25As transferred to the US Marines as trainers. (*Frank Shertzer*)

425

The SB2C-1C was identical to the SB2C-1 except for installation of cannon armament. White rectangles and a short-lived red border were added to the US star insignia in July 1943. This is the prototype, converted from SB2C-1 00243. A Helldiver with folded wings is in the background. (*Courtesy Harold Andrews*)

SB2C-1A—The US Marines acquired 410 A-25As from the Army, redesignated them SB2C-1A (A to indicate their Army origins and equipment differences) and used them as advanced trainers.
US Navy serial numbers: 75218/75588 (371), 76780/76818 (39).

SB2C-1C (Model 84A)—The SB2C-1C was identical to the SB2C-1 except for the substitution of two 20 mm wing-mounted cannon in place of the four ·50 calibre machine-guns. The cannon version was identified by the letter C appended to the designation.

Of the 778 SB2C-1Cs delivered, the first 170 were part of the original SB2C-1 order completed as SB2C-1Cs. Navy serial numbers were 00201/00370 (170), 01008/01208 (201), and 18192/18598 (407).

XSB2C-2 (Model 84C)—Before the XSB2C-1 flew, the Navy became interested in a twin-float seaplane version and planned to fit newly-

The fifth SB2C-1 Helldiver was tested on floats as the XSB2C-2. Upper surface colouring was used on the underside of the upward-folding wing.

designed Edo floats to the prototype late in its test programme. A total of 350 SB2C-1 seaplanes (Curtiss Model 84D) was planned. Destruction of the prototype postponed the seaplane tests, which were finally made with the fifth production SB2C-1, 00005. By the time the tests were completed, Navy interest in combat seaplanes had passed and the production order was cancelled.

The XSB2C-2 did contribute to Helldiver development, however. It was the test vehicle for a new free-moving rear gun mount with two ·30 calibre guns in place of the previous power-driven ·50s.

XSB2C-3 (Model 84E)—The eighth SB2C-1, 00008, was returned to Curtiss after test by the Navy for conversion to the experimental prototype of the SB2C-3.

The eighth SB2C-1 was converted to XSB2C-3 and became the prototype of the -3 series. The red border of the insignia was replaced by blue in August 1943.

SB2C-3 (Model 84E)—The 1,112 SB2C-3s, Navy serial numbers 18599/19710, incorporated many improvements over the SB2C-1s as developed on the XSB2C-3, including 1,900 hp R-2800-20 engines and four-blade propellers. Performance and bomb load were both improved and SB2C-3s began replacing -1s early in 1944. These, too, were relegated to training roles by the end of the war.

SB2C-4 (Model 84F)—The 1,985 SB2C-4s, Navy serial numbers 19711/21191, 64993/65286, and 82850/83127, featured greatly improved combat effectiveness. Wing racks were added for up to eight 5-in (127 mm) rockets or an additional 1,000 lb (454 kg) of bombs. Handling characteristics during dives were improved by perforating the surfaces of the trailing-edge dive flaps.

SB2C-4E—An unspecified number of SB2C-4s were fitted with radar for night operations. This was carried in a radome on the starboard centre section between the undercarriage and the wing hinge.

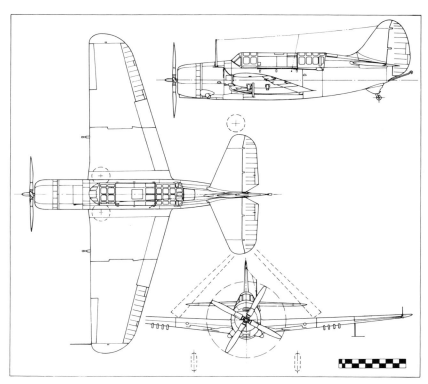

SB2C-4 Helldiver.

The SB2C-4E was fitted with a radome beneath the starboard wing for night operations. Overall 'Midnight Blue' became the standard Navy camouflage in 1944. (*E.M. Sommerich collection*)

The SB2C-5 had increased internal tankage and could also carry external fuel tanks.

XSB2C-5 (Model 84G)—One SB2C-4, Navy serial 65286, was held at the factory for conversion to the experimental SB2C-5 prototype.

SB2C-5 (Model 84G)—The 970 SB2C-5s, Navy serial numbers 83128/83751 and 89120/89465, differed from the SB2C-4 mainly in increased fuel capacity.

XSB2C-6 (Model 84H)—Two SB2C-3s, serials 18620 and 18621, were modified at the factory to incorporate 2,100 hp R-2600-22 engines, more fuel, and had their fuselages lengthened and wingtips squared in an attempt to overcome directional stability problems.

| | XSB2C-1 | SB2C-1, -1C | SB2C-5 |
|---|---|---|---|
| | Wright XR-2600-8 1,500 hp at 2,400 rpm at 7,000 ft (2,134 m) | Wright R-2600-8 1,700 hp at 2,600 rpm at sea level | Wright R-2600-20 1,900 hp at 2,800 rpm at sea level (take-off) |
| Span . . . | 50 ft 0 in (15·24 m) | 49 ft 8⅝ in (15·15 m) | 49 ft 8⅝ in (15·15 m) |
| Length . . . | 35 ft 5 in (10·79 m) | 36 ft 8 in (11·17 m) | 36 ft 8 in (11·17 m) |
| Height . . . | 10 ft 4 in (3·14 m) | 13 ft 1½ in (4·01 m) | 13 ft 1½ in (4·01 m) |
| Wing area . . | 422 sq ft (39·2 sq m) | 422 sq ft (39·2 sq m) | 422 sq ft (39·2 sq m) |
| Empty weight . . | 7,030 lb (3,189 kg) | 10,114 lb (4,588 kg) | 10,580 lb (4,799 kg) |
| Gross weight . . | 10,189 lb (4,622 kg) | 16,607 lb* (7,533 kg) | 15,918 lb*** (7,220 kg) |
| Maximum speed . | 325 mph (523·02 km/h) at 15,000 ft (4,572 m) | 273 mph (439·34 km/h) at 13,400 ft (4,084 m) | 260 mph (418·42 km/h) at 16,100 ft (4,907 m) |
| Cruising speed . | 244 mph (392·67 km/h) | — | 148 mph (238·17 km/h) |
| Climb . . . | 15,000 ft (4,572 m) in 5·6 min | 10,000 ft (3,048 m) in 11·4 min* | 10,000 ft (3,048 m) in 8·9 min |
| Service ceiling . . | 30,000 ft (9,144 m) | 21,200 ft (6,462 m) | 26,400 ft (8,047 m) |
| Range . . . | 1,330 miles (2,140 km) | 1,375 miles at 157 mph (2,213 km at 252·66 km/h) | 1,805 miles at 150 mph (2,905 km at 241·39 km/h) |
| Armament . . | Two fixed ·30-in m-g, two flexible ·50-in m-g, 1,000 lb (454 kg) bombs | Four flexible ·50-in m-g (two 20 mm cannon)**, two flexible ·30-in m-g, 2,000 lb (907 kg) bombs or Mk.13 torpedo | Two 20 mm cannon, two flexible ·30-in m-g |

* Bomber with two 1,000 lb (454 kg) bombs and two external fuel tanks
** SB2C-1C
*** Scout with one bomb-bay tank and one external tank

A surplus SB2C-5 modified for NACA research programmes after the Second World War. (*Gordon S. Williams*)

### Licence-Built Helldivers

With the Curtiss factories unable to meet the Navy's increased requirements for the still unproven SB2C, additional production was assigned to the Canadian branch of the Fairchild Aircraft Corporation which built 300 as SBF, and to the Canadian Car & Foundry Company, which built 835 of an initial order for 1,000 as SBWs. The dash number of each indicated essential similarity to the equivalent SB2C variant.

SBF-1—Fifty equivalents of the SB2C-1C ordered in 1942 under Navy serial numbers 31636/31685. One designated XSBF-1 for test.

SBF-3—One hundred and fifty equivalents of the SB2C-3 with Navy serials 31686/31835 following the SBF-1s.

The Canadian branch of Fairchild built the SB2C-4E under the designation SBF-4E. (*Courtesy Harold Andrews*)

430

SBF-4E—One hundred equivalents of SB2C-4E with Navy serial numbers 31836/31935 following the SBF-3s.

SBW-1—A total of forty SBW-1s, equivalent of the SB2C-1C, was delivered. The US Navy serials 21192/21231 immediately followed the first SB2C-4 order.

SBW-1B (Royal Navy Helldiver I)—Four hundred and fifty SBW-1s on a separate order were intended for the Royal Navy as Helldiver Is, but only 26, with Navy serials 60010/60035 and corresponding British serials JW100/125, were delivered. These were designated SBW-1B, the letter B identifying British use. These reached Britain in 1944 but never became operational.

Canadian Car & Foundry built the Curtiss SB2C-4E as the SBW-4E. An N-prefix added to the designation on the rudder indicates postwar use as a trainer. The yellow band and number, and absence of the fuselage star, was a short-lived marking of Naval Reserve squadrons just after the Second World War. (*Gordon S. Williams*)

SBW-3—Four hundred and thirteen equivalents of the SB2C-3 with Navy serial numbers 21233/21645 following the forty SBW-1s.

SBW-4E—Ninety-six equivalents of the SB2C-4E with Navy serials 21646/21741 followed the SBW-3 serials. One hundred and seventy-four of the original SBW-1B order were completed as SBW-4Es for the US Navy with Navy serials 60036/60209.

SBW-5—The last 86 aeroplanes built on the original SBW-1B order were completed as SBW-5 equivalents of the SB2C-5 with Navy serials 60210/60295.

The US Army adopted the SB2C-1 as the A-25A Shrike. The Army version dispensed with folding wings and arrester gear. The full serial was 42-79942. (*John C. Collins*)

## US Army Shrike

A-25A Shrike, Australian Helldiver (Model S84)—The US Army became interested in dive-bombers in 1940 and acquired some existing Navy designs with very little modification. An initial order was placed for one hundred SB2C-1s under the Army designation A-25A and the total eventually reached 900 out of a planned 3,000.

One of ten US Army A-25A Shrikes transferred to Australia. The rear turtledeck folded down to allow traverse of the rear gun. There was a similar feature on the SBC, SOC, O-52 and SO3C as well as the Helldiver series. (*Courtesy Harold Andrews*)

432

The first order was made part of the Navy production contract. The Navy foresaw interference with its own production at Columbus, so the Army versions were built at the Curtiss St Louis plant and subsequent orders were on Army contract. The Army originally named the A-25A Shrike, but later adopted the Navy's name, Helldiver.

The A-25As differed from the SB2C-1 mainly in having no arrester gear and in using larger wheels, Army radio equipment, and revised armour. The wing-folding feature was to be dispensed with as well, but the first ten A-25As had folding wings. The differences justified a revised Curtiss model designation of S84 (later 84B).

The first A-25A flew on 29 September, 1942. Of 150 intended for Lend-Lease to Australia, only ten were delivered (Australian serial numbers A-69-1/A-69-10). The Army soon lost interest in dive-bombers and never used the A-25A in combat. The remaining 890 were used by the Army as RA-25A trainers and target tugs and 410 were eventually turned over to the US Marines, who used them as operational trainers under the designation SB2C-1A. The R (for Restricted) prefix to Army aeroplanes in World War II meant that they were not to be used for their designated purpose.

US Army serial numbers:

| | | | |
|---|---|---|---|
| A-25A-1-CS | 41-18774/18783 (10) | A-25A-15-CS | 42-79673/79732 (60) |
| A-25A-5-CS | 41-18784/18823 (40) | A-25A-20-CS | 42-79733/79972 (240) |
| A25A-10-CS | 41-18824/18873 (50) | A-25A-25-CS | 42-79973/80132 (160) |
| | 42-79663/79672 (10) | A-25A-30-CS | 42-80133/80462 (330) |

### Model 85—O-52 Owl

The classic two-seat heavy observation aircraft still figured in US Army thinking in the late 1930s. In 1939, without testing a prototype, the Army ordered 203 from Curtiss as the O-52. Unit cost complete was $50,826.

First flown in February 1941, these proved to be the last of their breed—the tactical observation role was soon given to low-powered lightplanes of the Cub class and the long-range work went to light bombers or camera-carrying fighters.

The Curtiss O-52 Owl of 1941 ended the era of high-powered two-seaters as US Army observation aircraft. (*John C. Collins*)

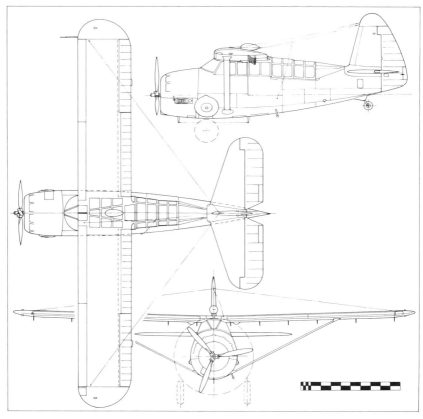

O-52 Owl.

The O-52 was a straightforward and uncomplicated design that could almost be regarded as a monoplane development of the established SBC line (Model 77) with 600 hp Pratt & Whitney R-1340-51 Wasp engine. The undercarriage and rear fuselage/gun arrangements were very similar.

A contemporary of the Model 84/XSB2C-1, the O-52 did not share its complexities. Its only fault lay in being an aeroplane without a purpose—the mission it had been designed for ceased to exist soon after its delivery. A few O-52s were sent overseas prior to the attack on Pearl Harbor and presumably saw action; the remainder served in training roles in the United States. Ten appeared on the post-war civil register under 'Limited' Type Certificate LTC-16 but only three survived in 1977, one in the EAA (Experimental Aircraft Association) museum, one in the Air Force Museum, and one in a private collection.

US Army serial numbers: 40-2688/2890. C/ns: 14221/14423.

## O-52 Owl

Two-seat Observation monoplane. 600 hp Pratt & Whitney R-1340-51.

Span 40 ft 9 in (12·42 m); length 26 ft 4¾ in (8·04 m); height 9 ft 11½ in (3·03 m); wing area 210 sq ft (19·5 sq m).

Empty weight 4,231 lb (1,919 kg); gross weight 5,364 lb (2,433 kg).

Maximum speed 220 mph (354·05 km/h); cruising speed 192 mph (309·98 km/h) at 75 per cent power; climb 10,000 ft (3,048 m) in 8·2 min; service ceiling 21,000 ft (6,401 m); range 700 miles (1,127 km) at 50 per cent power.

Armament—one fixed and one flexible ·30-in machine-gun.

## Model 86—CP-39-13/XP-46

With the P-40 just getting into production, Curtiss began to develop a potential replacement for it that reflected early British and French war experience. The original Curtiss designation was CP-39-13 because it was designed to Army Circular Proposal 39-13. The Army designation of XP-46 was used after a contract for two prototypes was signed on 29 September, 1939.

The XP-46 was an intended P-40 replacement but was not enough of an improvement to justify production. (*Peter M. Bowers*)

XP-46—The first XP-46, Army serial 40-3053, made its first flight on 15 February, 1941. It bore a general resemblance to the P-40 but was smaller and featured an inward-retracting undercarriage. Armour and fuel tank protection were improved and the armament was increased to two ·50-calibre machine-guns in the nose below the cylinder banks and four ·30-calibre machine-guns in each wing, making it the most heavily-armed US fighter up to that time. Powerplant was the 1,150 hp Allison V-1710-39. Automatic leading-edge slats were installed on the outer portions of the wing.

XP-46A—To save time, the second XP-46, 40-3054, was delivered without armament or radio for aerodynamic testing and was redesignated XP-46A. The XP-46s had no significant advantage over the P-40 except in firepower and the design was not developed further.

The XP-46A was delivered without armament to accelerate the test programme.

**XP-46**

Single-seat Pursuit. 1,150 hp Allison V-1710-39.

Span 34 ft 3¾ in (10·45 m); length 30 ft 2 in (9·19 m); height 10 ft 1 in (3·07 m); wing area 208 sq ft (19·32 sq m).

Empty weight 5,625 lb (2,551 kg); gross weight 7,665 lb (3,477 kg).

Maximum speed 355 mph (571·3 km/h) at 12,200 ft (3,719 m); climb 12,300 ft (3,749 m) in 5 min; range 325 miles (523 km).

Armament—two ·50-in and eight ·30-in machine-guns.

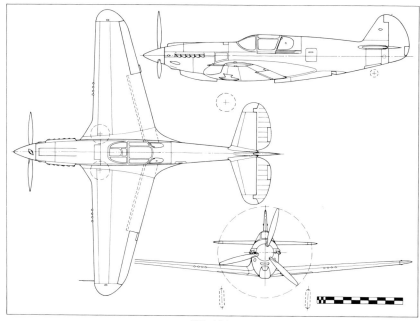

XP-46A.

436

## Model 90—XP-60, XP-60D

Following the failure of the XP-46 to win production orders, Curtiss sought another design as the eventual replacement for the P-40. This started as Model 88, an improved XP-46 that the Army designated XP-53 with the yet-to-be-built Continental XIV-1430-3 engine. Curtiss quickly dropped this in favour of Model 90, which the Army designated XP-60.

The design started late in 1940 as a modified P-40D; the improvements did result in a faster aeroplane and 1,950 production versions were ordered on 31 October, 1941. All were cancelled in January 1942 when the Army decided that Curtiss production facilities should be used for increased production of the existing P-40 and licence-manufacture of the Republic P-47.

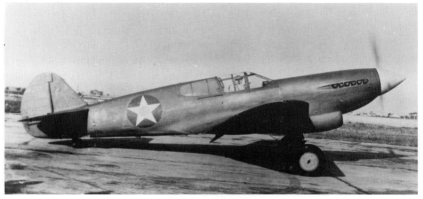

The XP-60 of 1941 was a quick experiment that married a laminar-flow wing to a P-40D fuselage with a Packard-Rolls Merlin engine.

Subsequent changes in Army requirements for the design, plus low priorities by the Army and by Curtiss, dragged out the development of another acceptable model to such a late date that production was no longer justified. So many changes were made, in fact, that Curtiss assigned a new model number to the XP-60A, B, C, and E versions (*see* Model 95).

XP-60 (Model 90, 90A)—One XP-60, Army serial 41-19508, was ordered on 1 October, 1940. This used a P-40D fuselage and tail assembly fitted with a new wing that featured a laminar-flow aerofoil and inward-retracting undercarriage. The powerplant was the 1,300 hp Packard-built Rolls-Royce V-1650-1 Merlin as used in the XP-40F then under development. The firepower increase over the P-40 was impressive—eight ·50-in calibre machine-guns in the thick-section wings. Armour protection was provided for the pilot and the fuel tanks were self-sealing.

After test flights began on 18 September, 1941, it was found necessary to enlarge the vertical tail and make minor modifications that resulted in redesignation as Curtiss Model 90A. The XP-60 was later redesignated XP-60D.

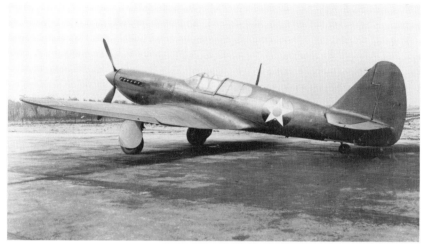

The XP-60 was modified with a larger tail and improved engine features to become the XP-60D.

XP-60D (Model 90B)—Further changes to the XP-60, including a two-stage V-1650-3 (Merlin 61) engine and four-blade propeller, resulted in redesignation as XP-60D and Curtiss Model 90B in August 1942. By the time these changes were made, the intervening Army designations had been assigned to improved versions then being designed. The XP-60D crashed on 6 May, 1943.

### XP-60

Single-seat Pursuit monoplane. 1,300 hp Packard Merlin V-1650-1.

Span 41 ft 5¼ in (12·62 m); length 33 ft 7 in (10·23 m); height 10 ft 8½ in (3·26 m); wing area 275 sq ft (25·54 sq m).

Empty weight 6,951 lb (3,153 kg); gross weight 9,277 lb (4,208 kg).

Maximum speed 387 mph (622·8 km/h) at 22,000 ft (6,706 m); cruising speed 314 mph (505·32 km/h); climb 15,000 ft (4,572 m) in 7·3 min; service ceiling 29,800 ft (9,083 m); range 800 miles (1,287 km) at 365 mph (587·4 km/h) at 8,500 ft (2,591 m).

Armament—eight ·50-in machine-guns.

## Model 91—XP-62

On 27 June, 1941, the Army ordered a new heavy-weight fighter from Curtiss, the XP-62, with serial number 41-35873. This was to use the heaviest engine ever mounted in a single-engined fighter to that time, the 2,300 hp Wright R-3350-17, the same as used in the Boeing B-29 bomber then under development. The XP-62 was intended to operate at high altitude and was fitted with a turbo-supercharger; the cockpit designed for pressurization was a design first for single-seat fighters, the earlier Lockheed XP-38A being an adaptation.

By the time the XP-62 flew on 21 July, 1943, the US fighter programme had been fixed and there was no longer a requirement for the XP-62.

The pressurized XP-62 of 1943 was the heaviest Curtiss single-seater and used co-axial propellers to absorb the power of the 2,300 hp Wright R-3350 engine.

### XP-62

Single-seat Pursuit monoplane. 2,300 hp Wright R-3350-17.

Span 53 ft 8 in (16·35 m); length 39 ft 6 in (12·03 m); height 16 ft 3 in (4·95 m); wing area 420 sq ft (39·01 m).

Empty weight 11,775 lb (5,341 kg); gross weight 16,650 lb (7,552 kg).

Maximum speed 448 mph (720·97 km/h) at 27,000 ft (8,230 m); climb 15,000 ft (4,572 m) in 6·6 min; service ceiling 37,500 ft (11,430 m); range 1,300 miles (2,092 km).

Armament—four 20 mm cannon.

## Model 94—XF14C-2

On 30 June, 1941, the Navy ordered two experimental shipboard fighters from Curtiss with serials 03183 and 03184 in the second series. One, designated XF14C-1, was to be powered with the yet untried Lycoming H-2470-4 engine, the other was to use the existing Wright XR-3350-16. Structurally, these were mid-way between the XP-60 and the XP-62. They featured an armament of four 20 mm cannon and upward-folding wings for shipboard storage.

The cannon-equipped XF14C-2 was a lighter Navy equivalent of the XP-62. The all-white finish was non-standard.

439

Because of the late development of the Lycoming, only the Wright-powered model was completed. Designated XF14C-2 and carrying Navy serial number 03183, this was completed in September 1943 but was not delivered until July 1944. The Navy by this time had standardized on the Grumman F6F and the Vought F4U as carrier fighters and the Curtiss was abandoned.

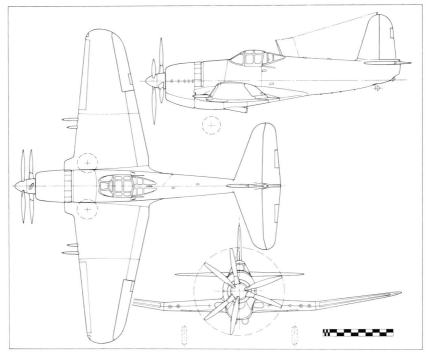

XF14C-2.

### XF14C-2

Single-seat Navy Fighter. 2,300 hp Wright XR-3350-16.

Span 46 ft (14·02 m); length 37 ft 9 in (11·5 m); height 17 ft (5·18 m); wing area 375 sq ft (34·83 sq m).

Empty weight 10,531 lb (4,777 kg); gross weight 14,950 lb (6,781 kg).

Maximum speed 418 mph (672·69 km/h) at 32,000 ft (9,754 m); cruising speed 172 mph (276·8 km/h); climb 2,700 ft/min (13·71 m/sec); service ceiling 39,800 ft (12,131 m); range 1,530 miles (2,462 km).

Armament—four 20 mm cannon.

The XP-60A (Curtiss Model 95) was a later design than the XP-60 and combined a new fuselage and Allison V-1710 engine with the basic XP-60 (Model 90) wing.

## Model 95—XP-60A, B, C, E

Changing Army requirements for the Curtiss Model 90/XP-60 resulted in extensive changes to the original design and the adoption of a new Curtiss model number—95. Actually, the original Model 95 was a study for a new design that was discontinued and the XP-60A developments started as Model 95A. Where the Model 90/XP-60 could be regarded as a P-40D with a new wing, the Model 95A/XP-60A and its successors could be regarded as the XP-60 wing fitted to a variety of new fuselages and powerplants.

XP-60A (Model 95A)—In 1942, extensive redesign was undertaken to adapt the XP-60 design to the 1,425 hp Allison V-1710-75 engine fitted with a General Electric turbo-supercharger. In normal Army and Curtiss practice, a change of engine manufacturer or even model would justify a new aeroplane model number; such was not the case here. Nose and fuselage contours of the XP-60A (Army serial 42-79423) were extensively revised to accommodate the new installations and armament was reduced to six ·50-in calibre guns.

The XP-60A first flew on 11 November, 1942, after the supercharger was removed because it was a fire hazard. The aircraft was soon dismantled and some of its parts were used in the XP-60C and XP-60E.

YP-60A—In October 1941 the Army ordered 1,950 P-60As fitted with turbo-supercharged Allison V-1710-75 engines. The first 26 aeroplanes on this contract, Army serials 43-32762/32787, were to be delivered as Service test models designated YP-60A. Following cancellation of the production order in favour of P-40Ks and Ls plus Curtiss-built P-47Gs in January

1942, the YP-60As were cancelled on 19 July, 1943. One YP-60A, 43-32763, was completed as the YP-60E.

P-60A-1—The last 474 aeroplanes of the P-60A order were to be completed as P-60A-1, Army serials 43-32789/33262, but all were cancelled in June 1943.

XP-60B (Model 95B)—The single XP-60B, Army serial 42-79425, was to have been similar to the XP-60A except for a Wright instead of a General Electric supercharger on the V-1710-75 engine. The aeroplane was not completed in this configuration but fitted with a Pratt & Whitney R-2800 it was delivered as the XP-60E.

XP-60C (Model 95C)—The XP-60C, Army serial 42-79424, was originally to have been an airframe similar to the XP-60A and XP-60B fitted with the new and still experimental 2,300 hp Chrysler XIV-2220 engine. Since this engine was having development troubles, an order was given in September 1942 to complete the aeroplane with a 2,000 hp Pratt & Whitney R-2800-53 engine driving a six-bladed counter-rotating propeller. Armament was reduced further to a total of four ·50-in calibre guns. First flight was on 27 January, 1943.

XP-60E (Model 95D)—The XP-60B, 42-79425, was completed with an R-2800 engine in place of the original V-1710 and was redesignated XP-60E. Principal outward difference from the XP-60C was the use of a single-rotation propeller. The four-gun armament matched the XP-60C. First flight of the XP-60E was on 26 May, 1943.

The XP-60C was an XP-60A type airframe fitted with a 2,000 hp Pratt & Whitney R-2800.

442

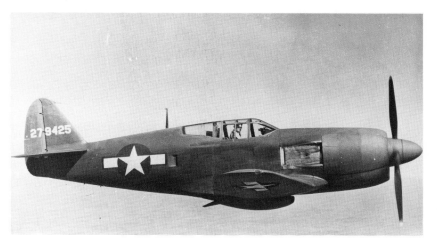

This aeroplane was begun as the XP-60B with an Allison V-1710 engine but was completed as the XP-60E with Pratt & Whitney R-2800 and single-rotation propeller that distinguished it from the XP-60C.

YP-60E—The single YP-60E, Army serial 43-32763, was the second YP-60A completed with a 2,000 hp Pratt & Whitney R-2800-18 engine. Major appearance changes resulted from the use of a bubble canopy over the cockpit and revised fuselage and vertical tail shapes. Armament remained four ·50-in calibre guns. First flight was on 15 July, 1944.

The YP-60E was sold as surplus after the war. Purchased by James DeSanto, it was entered in the 1947 National Air Races with Race No.80 and civil registration NX21979, but crashed on a qualifying flight.

This aeroplane was ordered as the YP-60A with Allison V-1710 engine but was completed as the YP-60E with Pratt & Whitney R-2800. (*Courtesy Harold Andrews*)

443

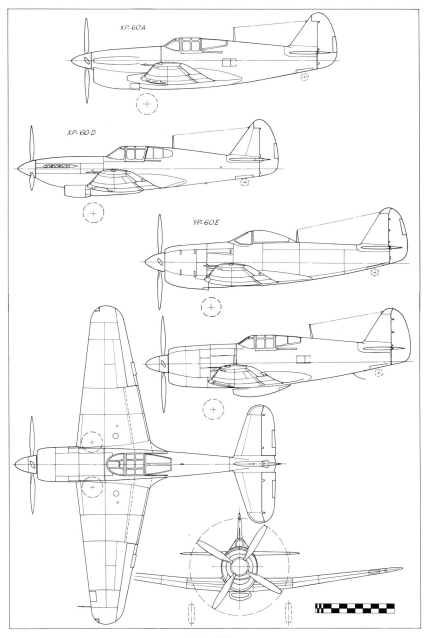

XP-60E.

444

|  | XP-60A | XP-60C | XP-60E |
|---|---|---|---|
|  | 1,425 hp Allison V-1710-75 | 2,000 hp P & W R-2800 | 2,000 hp P & W R-2800 |
| Span . . . | 41 ft 4 in (12·59 m) | 41 ft 4 in (12·59 m) | 41 ft 4 in (12·59 m) |
| Length . . . | 33 ft 8 in (10·26 m) | 33 ft 11 in (10·33 m) | 33 ft 11 in (10·33 m) |
| Height . . . | 10 ft 9 in (3·27 m) | 10 ft 9 in (3·27 m) | 10 ft 9 in (3·27 m) |
| Wing area . | 275 sq ft (25·54 sq m) | 275 sq ft (25·54 sq m) | 275 sq ft (25·54 sq m) |
| Empty weight . . | 7,800 lb (3,538 kg) | 8,600 lb (3,901 kg) | 8,285 lb (3,758 kg) |
| Gross weight . . | 10,160 lb (4,608 kg) | 11,835 lb (5,368 kg) | 11,520 lb (5,225 kg) |
| Maximum speed . | 420 mph (675·91 km/h) at 29,000 ft (8,839 m) | 414 mph (666·25 km/h) at 20,350 ft (6,203 m) | 405 mph (651·77 km/h) at 15,000 ft (4,572 m) |
| Climb . . . | 15,000 ft (4,572 m) in 6·5 min | 30,000 ft (9,144 m) in 6 min | 15,000 ft (4,572 m) in 4·8 min |
| Service ceiling . . | 32,500 ft (9,906 m) | 35,000 ft (10,668 m) | 34,800 ft (10,607 m) |
| Range . . . | 375 miles (603 km) | 315 miles (507 km) | 315 miles (507 km) |
| Armament . . | six ·50-in m-g | four ·50-in m-g | four ·50-in m-g |

## Model 96—XBTC-2

On 31 December, 1943, the Navy ordered two single-seat bomber-torpedo aircraft from Curtiss under the designation XBTC-1. With serials 31401 and 31402, these were pioneers in the new BT class and were in competition with the Douglas XBT2D, Martin XBTM, and Fleetwings XBTK.

The Curtiss XBTC-2 Bomber-torpedo prototypes did not fly until July 1946, and lost out to competitors that had flown much earlier.

445

In spite of increased performance that would seem to encourage the carriage of stores internally, the BTs could carry a great variety under the wings. Armament was four 20 mm cannon in the wings. A change in dash number on the 3,000 hp Pratt & Whitney R-4360 Wasp Major engine resulted in redesignation of the aeroplane to XBTC-2, in which form the first one flew in July 1946, more than sixteen months after the XBT2D and eight after the XBTM. These won the postwar production orders and the Curtiss was not developed further.

### XBTC-2

3,000 hp Pratt & Whitney XR-4360-8A Wasp Major.

Span 50 ft (15·24 m); length 39 ft (11·88 m); height 12 ft 11 in (3·93 m); wing area 425 sq ft (39·48 sq m).

Empty weight 13,410 lb (6,083 kg); gross weight 19,830 lb (8,995 kg) with one 1,000 lb (454 kg) bomb, 20,830 lb (9,448 kg) with two 1,000 lb bombs, 21,660 lb (9,825 kg) with one Mk.13-2 torpedo.

Maximum speed 347 mph (558·43 km/h) at sea level, 374 mph (601·88 km/h) at 16,000 ft (4,877 m); cruising speed 188 mph (302·55 km/h); initial climb 2,250 ft/min (11·43 m/sec); service ceiling 26,200 ft (7,986 m); range 1,835 miles (2,953 km) at 188 mph (302·55 km/h).

Armament—four 20 mm cannon, 2,000 lb (907 kg) bombs or one torpedo.

## Model 97—SC Seahawk

In June 1942 the US Navy solicited design proposals for an improved scouting seaplane to operate from cruisers. Curtiss submitted studies of its single-seat Model 97. The Navy issued a letter of intent in October and followed with a contract for two XSC-1s on 31 March, 1943.

Named Seahawk, the SC, of conservative design, was a low-wing monoplane with Wright R-1820 Cyclone engine and folding wings. It profited from the problems of the Model 84/SB2C by stressing both

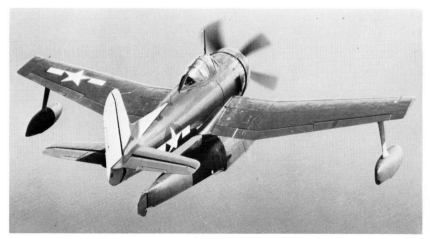

The prototype of the single-seat XSC-1 Seahawk flew in February 1944 and was intended to replace SOC and SO3C scouts based on cruisers.

The XSC-1, showing method of wing folding.

structural and systems simplicity. Although designated as a scout, the SC had good strike capability and could carry extra personnel. The Seahawk entered service in October 1944, replacing SOCs and SO3Cs, and served into 1949, when fixed-wing scouts were replaced by helicopters.

XSC-1 (Model 97A)—The first of two XSC-1s with 1,350 hp Wright R-1820-62 engines flew on 16 February, 1944. Armament was a pair of forward-firing ·50-in calibre machine-guns and up to 325 lb (147 kg) of bombs under each wing.

A production SC-1 Seahawk being launched from a shipboard catapult.

Serial numbers of the prototypes were 34095 and 34096. The first three aeroplanes on the initial SC-1 production order were also designated XSC-1, serials 35298/35300.

SC-1 (Model 97B)—Five hundred production SC-1s were ordered in June 1943, eight months before the prototypes flew. Navy serial numbers were 35298/35797, with the first three used as production prototypes designated XSC-1. A second order for 450 was terminated after 66 were delivered up to VJ Day under Navy serial numbers 93302/93367. One was designated XSC-2.

Although operated as a single-seater, the SC-1 could carry an air-evacuation patient on a litter in the fuselage and had two compartments in the central float for additional bombs. While the SC-1s operated primarily as seaplanes, Curtiss built and delivered them as landplanes. The Navy

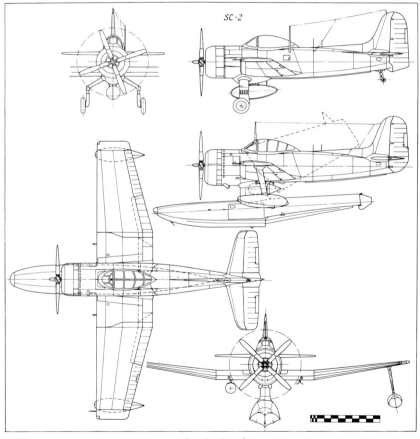

SC-1 Seahawk.

448

Distinguishing features of the SC-2 were the circular throat of the engine cowling and the moulded clear-plastic cockpit canopy. (*Peter Troop*)

negotiated a separate contract with Edo (Earl D Osborne Co) for manufacture of the floats.

XSC-1A—Became XSC-2 before completion.

XSC-2 (Model 97C)—One SC-1, Navy serial 35202, modified and redesignated with a 1,425 hp R-1820-76 engine. This was temporarily designated XSC-2A due to installation of arrester gear.

SC-2 (Model 97D)—Only ten of a projected 450 SC-2s were completed, due to VJ Day cancellations. Serials 119529/119538. The engine was the R-1820-76. Distinguishing features were the completely circular engine cowling (as viewed from the front) and the clear-blown instead of segmented cockpit canopy.

### SC Seahawk

1,350 hp Wright R-1820-62 Cyclone.

Span 41 ft (12·49 m); length 36 ft 4½ in (11·08 m); height (on beaching gear) 16 ft (4·87 m); wing area 280 sq ft (26·01 sq m).

Empty weight 6,320 lb (2,867 kg); gross weight 9,000 lb (4,082 kg).

Maximum speed 313 mph (503·71 km/h) at 28,600 ft (8,717 m); cruising speed 125 mph (201·16 km/h); climb 2,500 ft/min (12·7 m/sec); service ceiling 37,300 ft (11,369 m); range 625 miles (1,006 km).

Armament—two ·50-in machine-guns, two 325 lb (147 kg) bombs.

### Model 98—XBT2C-1

On 27 March, 1945, the Navy gave Curtiss a contract for ten XBT2C-1 bomber-torpedo aircraft, serial numbers 50879/50888. While generally similar to the XBTC, these had the smaller 2,500 hp Wright R-3350-24 engine with single-rotation propeller and could carry a second crewman in the aft fuselage. Armament was reduced to two 20 mm wing guns but the

Although ordered later, the single-seat XBT2C-1 Bomber-torpedoplane was completed and flown before the XBTC-2.

bomb load increased to 4,000 lb (1,814 kg). Search radar was carried in a pod under the starboard wing.

In spite of being ordered later than the XBTC, the XBT2C-1 flew first, in January 1946; only nine of the ten ordered were completed.

### XBT2C-1

2,500 hp Wright R-3350-24.

Span 47 ft 7$\frac{1}{8}$ in (14·5 m); length 39 ft 2 in (11·93 m); height 12 ft 1 in (3·68 m); wing area 416 sq ft (38·64 sq m).

Empty weight 12,268 lb (5,565 kg); gross weight 19,022 lb (8,628 kg).

Maximum speed 297 mph (477·96 km/h) at sea level, 330 mph (531·07 km/h) at 17,000 ft (5,182 m); initial climb 1,890 ft/min (9·6 m/sec); service ceiling 26,300 ft (8,016 m); range 1,310 miles (2,108 km).

Armament—two 20 mm cannon, eight 5 in (127 mm) wing rockets and one 2,000 lb (907 kg) bomb or two 500 lb (227 kg) or four 250 lb (113 kg) bombs.

The wings of the XBT2C-1 folded in the manner of the SB2C. The doors of the long internal bomb bay are open and the perforated wing flaps are lowered.

## Model CW-20—C-46, C-55, R5C Commando

Design studies for CW-20, a proposed 'New Era' civil transport inspired by the Boeing 247 and the Douglas DC-2, were begun at St Louis in 1935. The design was settled in 1936 to be a 36-passenger all-metal pressurized airliner with capacity for an additional 8,200 lb (3,719 kg) of cargo. Entirely conventional in appearance by contemporary standards, the outstanding feature of the CW-20 was its size for a twin-engined design, its wingspan of 108 ft 1 in (32·94 m) was 4 ft 2 in (1·26 m) greater than that of the contemporary four-engined Boeing B-17 bomber, and the wing area was only 60 sq ft (5·57 sq m) less.

The circumstances of history changed the role of the CW-20. Instead of being produced as an airliner, the basic design was militarized as the US Army C-46 and the Navy R5C and served US forces in all theatres of World War II and took part in the Korean War and the early years of the Vietnam War. While the early Service models had a high degree of mechanical problems, these could not be laid to faulty design. The new aeroplanes were rushed into heavy duty with minimum maintenance in harsh environments that were unforeseen by the designers, particularly the 'Hump' run from India to China. Subsequent improvements made the C-46 one of the most reliable military aircraft of the Second World War.

The sole CW-20T of 1940 in its original configuration with twin fins and rudders.

Not counting the prototype, 3,182 C-46/R5C Commandos were delivered from 1942 to 1945. After discussion of the prototype, these are described in sequence of their US military designations in the following paragraphs.

CW-20T—As completed in 1940, the prototype CW-20 was a twin-finned transport (T) powered by two Wright R-2600 Twin Cyclone engines each developing 1,700 hp for take off. The civil registration number was NX-19436 and the c/n was 101 under the St Louis plant system. Intended for cabin pressurization that was not used, the fuselage cross-section was of double-lobe type, with two circular sections intersecting at the level of the cabin floor. The 'crease' caused by the intersection was faired over with

451

After being fitted with single fin and rudder, the CW-20T was sold to the US Army as the C-55. The Curtiss P-36 and P-40 are used for comparison in this July 1941 Curtiss publicity photograph.

aluminium skin. The nose was exceptionally well streamlined by aligning the pilots' windows with the overall fuselage lines instead of using the stepped windshield of contemporary designs.

First flight was on 26 March, 1940, at the hands of famed engineering test pilot Edmond T. Allen, loaned by Boeing.

C-55/*St Louis* (Model CW-20A)—Following early flights, the CW-20 prototype was laid up for improvements, the most notable of which was removal of the twin fins and rudders and dihedral tailplane in favour of a new single fin and rudder and a straight horizontal tailplane located lower on the fuselage.

Thanks to its new expansion programme, the US Army was very interested in the CW-20. It ordered 46 modified cargo versions as C-46 in July 1940 and then bought the prototype for $361,556 in June 1941, assigning it the later designation of C-55 and Army serial number 41-21041. The civil Wright engines became R-2600-17s.

In an unusual move, the Army soon returned the C-55 to Curtiss and allowed it to be sold to British Overseas Airways (BOAC) in September 1941, in whose hands it received the British registration G-AGDI and was named *St Louis* after the city in which it was built. It was scrapped in Britain on 29 October, 1943.

### CW-20/C-55 *St Louis*

Personnel transport. Four crew and 36 passengers. Two 1,700 hp Wright R-2600-17A.

Span 108 ft 1 in (32·94 m); length 76 ft 4 in (23·26 m); height 21 ft 9 in (6·62 m); wing area 1,360 sq ft (126·34 sq m).

Empty weight 27,600 lb (12,519 kg); gross weight 40,000 lb (18,144 kg).

Maximum speed 254 mph (408·76 km/h) at 7,000 ft (2,134 m); cruising speed 222 mph (357·26 km/h) at 10,000 ft (3,048 m); initial climb 1,500 ft/min (7·62 m/sec); service ceiling 26,900 ft (8,199 m); range 1,500 miles (2,414 km).

C-46 (Model CW-20B)—The initial US Army order was for 46 cargo versions to be built at Buffalo and powered with 2,000 hp (take off) Pratt & Whitney R-2800-43 engines. The first 25 were delivered as C-46-CU personnel transports with accommodation for 50 troops or 33 litter patients and four attendants. Alternatively, they could carry up to 10,000 lb (4,536 kg) of cargo. They differed little in outward detail from the modified CW-20T; most of the airliner windows were removed in favour of only four on the port side and five on the starboard. Since it was determined that the fairing over the fuselage crease line had no aerodynamic advantage, this feature was abandoned except for a small portion at the very rear. Curtiss four-bladed electric propellers were fitted. The first C-46 rolled out of the factory in May 1942 and was delivered to the Army in July. Cost complete was $354,714.

C-46A (CW-20B)—The C-46A had significant military improvements over the C-46, including reinforced floor for 15,000 lb (6,804 kg) of cargo, large two-segment cargo door on the port side at the rear of the cabin, and later 2,000 hp (take off) R-2800-51 engines. The final twenty-one aeroplanes of the original C-46 order were completed as C-46A-1-CU. The last C-46As cost only $271,127 complete.

Demand for the type became so great that the Army placed additional orders. A total of 1,039 C-46A-CUs was built at Buffalo, and continued Buffalo c/ns; 438 C-46A-CKs were built in a new Curtiss plant at Louisville, under St Louis c/ns; two C-46A-CSs were built at St Louis; and two of a planned total of 500 C-46A-HIs were built by the new Aircraft Division of the Higgins Boat Co, New Orleans, Louisiana. Camouflage was not applied to C-46A-50 and on.

Minor differences between different batches or blocks of C-46As led to use of the Army's new block number system of identification, already in use on the P-40. (*See page 476 for explanation*).

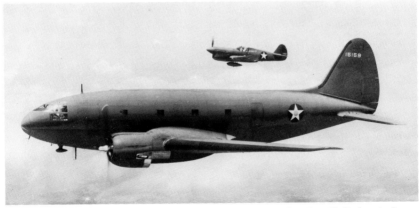

The first production C-46 Commando was completed in May 1942, just before the red centre was removed from US star insignia. The escort is a P-40F.

C-46As had a heavier structure and increased power for heavy cargo. This is
C-46A-60 347204 photographed in India. From C-46A-50 camouflage was not
used. (*Peter M. Bowers*)

| Model | Army Serials | | C/ns |
|---|---|---|---|
| C-46A-CU . . | 41-5159/5183 | (25) | 26361/26385 |
| C-46A-1-CU . . | 41-5184/5204 | (21) | 26386/26406 |
| | 41-12280/12283 | (4) | 26407/26410 |
| C-46A-5-CU . . | 41-12284/12333 | (50) | 26411/26460 |
| C-46A-10-CU . | 41-12334/12383 | (50) | 26461/26510 |
| C-46A-15-CU . | 41-12384/12433 | (50) | 26511/26560 |
| C-46A-20-CU . | 41-24640/24689 | (50) | 26561/26610 |
| C-46A-25-CU . | 41-24690/24739 | (50) | 26611/26660 |
| C-46A-30-CU . | 41-24740/24775 | (36) | 26661/26696 |
| | 42-3564/3577 | (14) | 26697/26710 |
| C-46A-35-CU . | 42-3578/3683 | (106) | 26711/26816 [7] |
| C-46A-40-CU . | 42-60942/61091 | (150) | 26817/26966 [8] |
| | 42-107318/107373 | (56) | 27005/27060 |
| C-46A-41-CU . | 42-107280/107317 | (38) | 26967/27004 |
| C-46A-45-CU . | 42-107374/107399 | (26) | 27061/27086 |
| | 42-96529/96802 | (274) | 30191/30464 [1], [2] |
| C-46A-50-CU . | 42-96803/96805 | (3) | 30465/30467 [1] |
| | 42-96806/96828 | (23) | 30468/30490 [1], [2] |
| | 42-101036/101201 | (166) | 30491/30656 [1], [2] |
| C-46A-1-CS . | 43-46953, 46954 | (2) | 24, 25 [3] |
| C-46A-1-CK . | 43-46955/46972 | (18) | 26/43 [4] |
| C-46A-5-CK . | 43-46973/47032 | (60) | 44/103 |
| C-46A-55-CK . | 43-47033/47202 | (170) | 104/273 [5] |
| C-46A-60-CK . | 42-47203/47304 | (102) | 274/375 |
| C-46A-60-CS . | 42-47305/47314 | (10) | 376/385 [9] |
| C-46A-60-CK . | 42-47315/47402 | (88) | 386/973 |
| C-46A-HI . | 43-43339, 43340 | (2) | Unknown [6] |

[1] Note the oddity of lower Army serials and higher c/ns.
[2] Mixture of C-46A-45-CU, C-46A-50-CU, C-46D-1-CU, and C-46D-5-CU.
[3] Note c/ns lower than CW-20T prototype (101).
[4] Continuation of St Louis c/ns at Louisville.
[5] C-46A-10 to -50 blocks were not used.
[6] Civil registration N46575 for 43-43340 postwar, then to Bolivia as CP-749.
[7] 42-3658, 3666, 3668, 3671, 3673, 3675, 3676, 3680, 3682, 3683 to C-46A-36-CU.
[8] Many to C-46A-41-CU.
[9] Built at St Louis with Louisville c/ns.

The single XC-46B, 346953, was the first St Louis built C-46A fitted with stepped windshield. (*William T. Larkins*)

XC-46B (CW-20B-1)—In 1944 the first C-46A-1-CS, 43-46953, was converted to the single XC-46B. This received the revised Curtiss designation of CW-20B-1. Principal outward change was adoption of a stepped windshield as used on contemporary bomber and transport designs. Engines were 2,100 hp (take off) R-2800-34Ws with water-injection to boost take-off power.

XC-46C—The aeroplane to have carried this designation was completed as the first C-46G and was subsequently converted to the XC-113.

C-46D (CW-20B-2)—All of the 1,410 C-46Ds were built at Buffalo. These were primarily personnel transports, but with one additional cargo door on the starboard side of the fuselage. These were phased into the end of C-46A-CU production and used the same R-2800-51 engines. In fact, C-46D-1s and -5s were mixed on the production line with C-46A-45s and

All C-46Ds were built at Buffalo and served primarily as personnel transports. This is C-46D-15, with open paratroop door. Camouflage was not used on C-46Ds from part-way through the -15 block. (*Courtesy Harold Andrews*)

-46s in the serial number ranges of 42-96803/96828 and 42-101036/101236. Serials and c/ns for later C-46D-5-CUs and subsequent blocks are listed here:

| Model | Army Serials | | C/ns |
|---|---|---|---|
| C-46D-5-CU . . | 42-101202/101235 | (34) | 30657/30690 |
| C-46D-5-CU . . | 44-77295/77443 | (149) | 32691/32839 |
| C-46D-10-CU . | 44-77444/77893 | (450) | 32840/33289 [1], [2] |
| C-46D-15-CU . | 44-77894/78344 | (451) | 33290/33740 |
| C-46D-20-CU . | 44-78345/78544 | (200) | 33741/33940 |

[1] 44-77444 was C-46A-55-CU.
[2] 44-77446 was C-46A-55-CU.

### C-46/R5C Commando

| | C-46 | C-46A |
|---|---|---|
| | Two 2,000 hp<br>P & W R-2800-43 | Two 2,000 hp<br>P & W R-2800-51 |
| Span . . . | 108 ft 0 in<br>(32·91 m) | 108 ft 0 in<br>(32·91 m) |
| Length . . . | 76 ft 4 in<br>(23·26 m) | 76 ft 4 in<br>(23·26 m) |
| Height . . . | 21 ft 9 in<br>(6·62 m) | 21 ft 9 in<br>(6·62 m) |
| Wing area . . | 1,360 sq ft<br>(126·34 sq m) | 1,360 sq ft<br>(126·34 sq m) |
| Empty weight . . | 29,485 lb<br>(13,374 kg) | 30,000 lb<br>(13,608 kg) |
| Gross weight . . | 40,000 lb<br>(18,144 kg) | 45,000 lb<br>(20,412 kg) |
| Maximum speed . | 264 mph<br>(424·86 km/h)<br>at 13,000 ft<br>(3,962 m) | 270 mph<br>(434·51 km/h)<br>at 15,000 ft<br>(4,572 m) |
| Cruising speed . | — | 173 mph<br>(278·41 km/h) |
| Climb . . . | 10,000 ft<br>(3,048 m)<br>in 8·7 min | 10,000 ft<br>(3,048 m)<br>in 17·4 min |
| Service ceiling . . | 27,600 ft<br>(8,412 m) | 24,500 ft<br>(7,468 m) |
| Range . . . | 2,300 miles<br>(3,701 km) | 3,150 miles (5,069 km) at<br>173 mph (278·41 km/h),<br>1,000 miles (1,609 km) at<br>237 mph (381·4 km/h) |

C-46E (CW-20B-3)—The seventeen C-46E-1s were built at St Louis. These had later R-2800-75 engines but reverted to the single port-side cargo door of the C-46A. Most noticeable outward difference was the use of a stepped windshield as on the XC-46B. Army serials 43-47403/47419, c/ns 2929/2945.

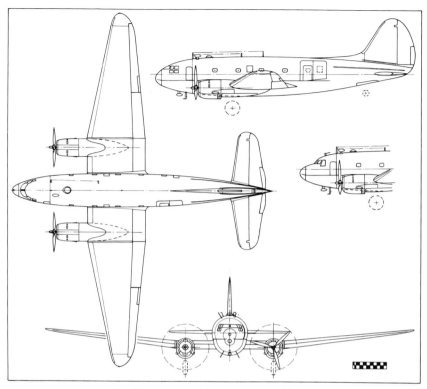

C-46D Commando, with nose of C-46E.

Seventeen C-46Es were built in St Louis and were essentially C-46A airframes with the stepped windshield of the XC-46B. (*Peter M. Bowers*)

457

Distinguishing features of Buffalo-built C-46F were square wingtips and three-blade propellors. This is C-46F-1. (*Peter M. Bowers*)

C-46F (CW-20B-4)—The 234 C-46F-1s were built at Buffalo and continued the C-46D-20 serials but used lower c/ns. The remaining 166 on the order for 400 were cancelled after VJ Day. The C-46Fs used the same R-2800-75 engine as the C-46E, three-blade propellers, squared wingtips, and had cargo doors on both sides. Army serials 44-78545/78778, c/ns 22368/22601.

C-46G (CW-20B-5)—Of three hundred C-46G-1-CUs intended to follow the 400th C-46F-1, only the first was completed. Army serial 44-78945, c/n 22768. This had the double cargo doors of the C-46D and F, squared wingtips, and the stepped windshield of the XC-46B and C-46E. Engines were 2,100 hp (take off) R-2800-34W. Following delivery, the C-46G-1 was flown to Columbus where it was converted to the XC-113.

C-46H—Designation assigned for improved version with dual tail-wheels, cancelled after VJ Day. Some postwar Air Force modifications of C-46s were later redesignated C-46H.

C-46J—Designation not assigned.

The original C-46H series was cancelled; this is a C-46A-41-CU redesignated C-46H after the war. Note red bars added to white rectangles of US insignia in January 1947. (*William T. Larkins*)

The single C-46G-1-CU was fitted with a General Electric propeller-turbine in the starboard nacelle and was redesignated XC-113.

XC-46K (CW-20E-2)—To have been a late 1945 project with 2,500 hp Wright R-3350-BD engines, it was cancelled.

XC-46L (CW-20H)—Three aeroplanes fitted with 2,500 hp Wright R-3350-BD engines and delivered in 1945.

XC-113 (CW-20G)—The single C-46G-1-CU, 44-78945, was sent to the Curtiss Columbus plant and converted to the XC-113, a flying test-bed for the new General Electric TG-100 propeller-turbine. The engine arrangement was unusual; where most high-power experimental engines of the type were installed on the aeroplane centreline, the TG-100 was installed in the starboard nacelle of the XC-113 while the original R-2800-34W was retained in the port nacelle.

The different power of the two engines, plus their different acceleration characteristics and reaction time to throttle movement, made the XC-113 almost unmanageable. The test programme was ended by a ground accident soon after it began in October 1946, and the aeroplane never flew.

Some C-46As were transferred directly to the US Navy and Marines from the factory and served them as R5C-1s into postwar years. (*Peter M. Bowers*)

R5C-1 (CW-20B, Army C-46A)—Starting in 1944, random batches of C-46A-CUs and CKs were diverted to the US Marines to a total of 160 under the naval designation of R5C-1. These were used mainly in support of the Marines' island-hopping campaigns in the Pacific, but R5Cs remained in service for several years after the war. A complete correlation of Navy serial numbers to c/ns and former Army serials is not available. Navy serials 39492/39611 (120) and 50690/50729 (40).

Fitted with stair-door and windows, this war-surplus C-46 shows the most extensive modification of a Commando for passenger work. (*E.M. Sommerich*)

## Civil C-46s

Curtiss plans to produce the CW-20 as a postwar civil transport were frustrated both by the availability of many C-46s on the surplus market and the availability of later model and much more suitable transport designs. The civil C-46 conversions, made by firms other than Curtiss (*see* Appendix I), did not win a place on US trunk airlines along with the mainstay surplus Douglas DC-3s (C-47), DC-4s (C-54), and Lockheed Constellations (C-69). They did serve foreign passenger airlines and some US feeder lines, however. The principal civil work of the C-46 under US registry was as a freighter. Not all of these were surplus; the US Air Force retained title to many into the 1960s and leased them to the operators for use as civil aeroplanes.

Thirty-one were on the US civil register in 1948, 218 in 1952, and 183 remained there in 1969; 126 were in scheduled airline service outside the United States in 1973.

## Model CW-21 Demon

In 1938, Curtiss St Louis adapted the basic wing of the CW-19 to a new light-weight single-seat interceptor design, the Model CW-21. With simple structure and minimum equipment, the Demon was intended as an economical yet high-performance design for small-country air forces. No armour or fuel tank protection was provided; armament was light by European standards, with two guns in the nose and one in each wing. The first CW-21 flew in September 1938.

CW-21—Four* CW-21s were built, and all carried US civil registrations during their test periods before foreign sales. These were conventional in appearance but their small size resulted in an abrupt change of fuselage lines behind the big 850 hp Wright R-1820-G5 Cyclone engine. The pilot sat well aft for balance and the rear-fuselage turtledeck sloped abruptly to a narrow cross-section just ahead of the tail. The undercarriage retracted backward, with the vertically-aligned wheels and their struts enclosed in clamshell fairings. The wing was too thin to allow these to lay flat in the rear portion as on the P-36.

The first CW-21, NX19431, was sold by the St Louis Airplane Division to the Curtiss-Wright Export Sales Division in February 1939, and was sent to China as a demonstrator. It was eventually sold to the Chinese, who promptly crashed it. Three others, built in March 1940, and fitted with 1,000 hp Cyclone engines, were then sold to China but all were lost on the ferry flight from Rangoon to their base in China.

US registrations: 19431, 19941/19943. C/ns: 21-1/21-4.

CW-21A—This was a proposal only to use the Allison V-1710 engine in the CW-21 airframe. The redesigned flush inward-retracting undercarriage was used on the CW-21B.

* An erroneous impression exists that there were five Curtiss-Wright 21s. An Experimental licence was issued to a private individual, Mr Curtis Wright, for his Model CW-21, c/n 0001, registration NX37601, in November 1946.

The first of four CW-21 Demon interceptor fighters.

461

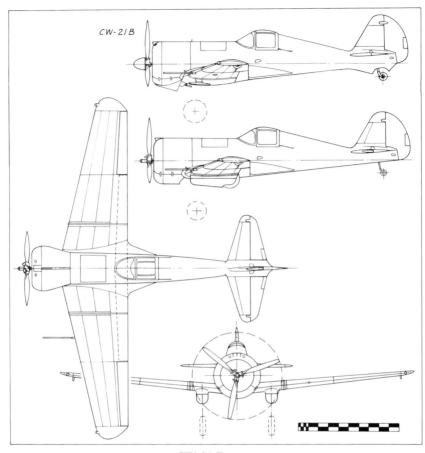

CW-21 Demon.

Twenty-four CW-21Bs for the Netherlands East Indies were similar to the
CW-21 except for inward-retracting undercarriages.

CW-21B—Twenty-four examples of an improved CW-21B were sold to the Netherlands East Indies in 1941. These differed from the CW-21s mainly in having an undercarriage that retracted inward and flush with the lower wing surface.

The CW-21Bs saw brief but intensive action following the Japanese invasion of Java in April 1942, and some were captured by the Japanese. C/ns: including 2853/2872 (20). NEI serials: CW-344/CW-363.

### CW-21B

Single-seat interceptor fighter. 850 hp Wright R-1820-G5 Cyclone.

Span 35 ft (10·66 m); length 27 ft 2½ in (8·29 m); height 8 ft 2 in (2·48 m); wing area 174·3 sq ft (16·19 sq m).

Empty weight 3,382 lb (1,534 kg); gross weight 4,500 lb (2,041 kg).

Maximum speed 314 mph (505·32 km/h) at 12,200 ft (3,719 m); cruising speed 282 mph (453·82 km/h); service ceiling 34,300 ft (10,455 m); range 630 miles (1,014 km).

Armament—four machine-guns of various calibres and arrangement.

The CW-22 combined features of the CW-19R and CW-21 in a military Falcon trainer. This is CW-A22, the 1939 prototype with post World War II change of registration. (*Thomas M. Barnett*)

### Model CW-22—SNC-1 Falcon

In 1940 the Curtiss St Louis plant introduced the CW-22, a military basic trainer and light attack model that was a direct development of the CW-19B and incorporated some features of the CW-21.

Named Falcon, the CW-22 was a conventional all-metal two-seater with 420 hp Wright R-975 Whirlwind engine and an undercarriage identical to that of the CW-21. Armament was one synchronized ·30-in calibre machine-gun and one flexible ·30-in calibre for the observer/gunner.

CW-A22—One prototype built and demonstrated as a civil aeroplane under Memo Approval 2-549; registration number NX18067, c/n 1. This was still flying in 1977 under registration N500G.

This uncamouflaged CW-22B was one of fifty sold to Turkey.

CW-22—The Netherlands East Indies received thirty-six Model 22s as part of a large re-equipment order for Buffalo-built Model 75s and St Louis-built 21s and 22s placed before the fall of the Netherlands in 1940. These were diverted to the Netherlands East Indies but were delivered in Australia in March 1942 due to the fall of Java. They saw extensive action against the Japanese, with approximately twelve being attached to the US 49th Pursuit Group. A few captured examples were used by the Japanese. NEI serial numbers CF464/499. One, c/n 22-57, rebuilt from a CW-A19R, flew under civil registration as X-16417 while being used as a demonstrator.

The major production version of the CW-22 was the CW-22N Scout-trainer delivered to the US Navy as the SNC-1. (*E. M. Sommerich*)

464

CW-22B—Many improved CW-22As were exported; 50 to Turkey, 25 to the Netherlands East Indies, and 25 to various Spanish-speaking countries. One, c/n 3604, flew under the civil registration NX19446.

CW-22N—Following evaluation of the A22 prototype, the US Navy placed an initial order for 150 Falcons in 1940 under the designation of SNC-1 (SN for Scout Trainer). These were followed by two other orders to a total of 305. Navy serials were 6290/6439 in the second series and 05085/05234 and 32987/32991 in the third series. A higher cockpit canopy was adopted starting with serial 05085. War surplus Falcons could be licensed as civil aircraft under the 2-549 certificate.

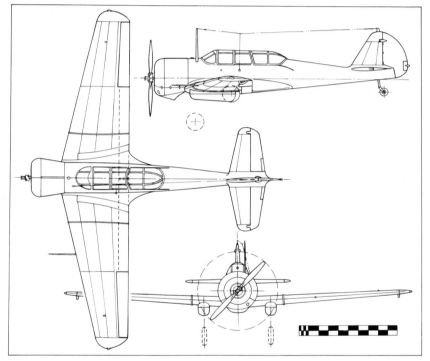

SNC-1 Falcon.

### SNC-1 Falcon

Two-seat scout trainer. 420/450 hp Wright R-975-28 Whirlwind.

Span 35 ft (10·66 m); length 27 ft (8·22 m); height 9 ft 11 in (3·02 m); wing area 173·7 sq ft (16·13 sq m).

Empty weight 2,736 lb (1,241 kg); gross weight 3,788 lb (1,718 kg).

Maximum speed 198 mph (318·64 km/h) at sea level; climb 1,650 ft/min (8·38 m/sec); service ceiling 21,800 ft (6,645 m); range 780 miles (1,255 km).

Armament—one fixed and one flexible ·30-in machine-gun.

465

The CW-24B was a lightweight flying mock-up of the proposed Ascender pursuit.

## Model CW-24—XP-55 Ascender

In 1940, the US Army decided to break away from its traditional evolutionary approach to the development of fighter aircraft and invited the industry to submit unorthodox design proposals. Curtiss-St Louis responded with studies of the Model CW-24, a swept-wing pusher with canard elevators, the new 2,200 hp Pratt & Whitney X-1800 (H-2600) engine, and the first application of tricycle undercarriage to a Curtiss military aeroplane.

It should be pointed out that the canard design had serious aerodynamic shortcomings and had even been rejected by the Wright brothers, who in 1910 converted to designs with all the elevating and stabilizing surfaces behind the wing. While sporadic attempts were made subsequently by other designers to capitalize on some of the canard's known advantages, the inherent disadvantages outweighed them every time. The Curtiss proposal of a canard fighter under these circumstances was a daring move indeed and was accepted with misgiving by the Army. A contract for further data, a wind-tunnel test model, and an option for one prototype aeroplane was awarded on 22 June, 1940.

Since the Curtiss entry was rated below some of the others, the Army soon lost interest and withdrew support. Curtiss then decided to develop the design on its own and built a simplified full-scale flying mock-up under the designation CW-24B.

CW-24B—The CW-24B was a light-weight low-powered mock-up of the proposed fighter built quickly of wood and fabric and powered with a commercial 275 hp Menasco C-6S-5 engine. This was shipped to the Army flight-test centre on Muroc Dry Lake in California, where it made its first flight on 2 December, 1941. Performance was low with only 275 hp, but the CW-24B proved the feasibility of the unorthodox design. After various modifications that included addition of dorsal and ventral fins, enlargement of the original vertical fins and their relocation 4 ft (1·21 m) farther outboard, plus the lengthening of the wingtips, the CW-24 flight programme was completed in May 1942. The aeroplane, with Army serial number 42-39347 assigned, was then shipped to Langley Field, for further study by the NACA laboratories.

XP-55 (Model 24)—During the flight programme of the CW-24B, design work went ahead on the proposed fighter version and a contract for three XP-55s was received on 10 July, 1942. Since the Pratt & Whitney X-1800 engine did not materialize, the engine chosen was the 1,275 hp Allison V-1710-95.

The first XP-55, Army serial 42-78845, was essentially like the finalized CW-24B. First flight was on 19 July, 1943, from the Army's Scott Field near the St Louis plant. Some of the inherent stability problems of canards, amplified by the high fighter wing loading, soon appeared. The first XP-55 was lost on 15 November, 1943, when the pilot could not recover from a stall and took to his parachute after falling out of control for 16,000 ft (more than 4,800 m).

The second XP-55, 42-78846, was too far on to be conveniently modified in the light of No.1's experience so was flown under restrictions (including prohibition of stalls below 20,000 ft (6,096 m)) starting on 9 January, 1944. The third aircraft, 42-78847, was modified to include greater forward elevator travel and had the wing span increased by 4 ft (1·21 m), and was fitted with the designed complement of four forward-firing machine-guns and used for gunnery and performance tests. First flight was on 25 April, 1944. Maximum level-flight speed was 390 mph (627·63 km/h).

The XP-55 Ascender was developed from the wooden CW-24B. 278845, illustrated, was the first of three. (*Courtesy Harold Andrews*)

467

This view of the second XP-55 shows the unusual configuration and the covers over the nose machine-gun muzzles.

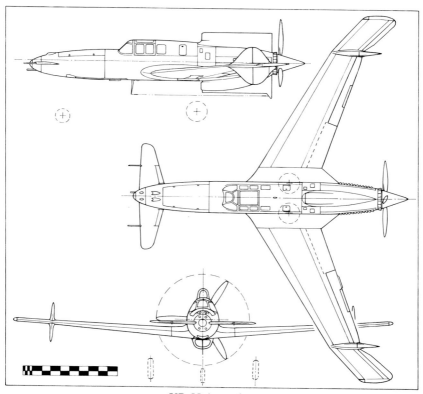

XP-55 Ascender.

468

The official name, Ascender, originated in jest by a Curtiss engineer, was not new with the XP-55, having been applied for obvious reasons to earlier designs that flew tail first.

**XP-55 Ascender**

Single-seat Pursuit. 1,275 hp Allison V-1710-95.

Span 40 ft 7 in (12·36 m); length 29 ft 7 in (9·01 m); height 11 ft 7 in (3·53 m); wing area 209 sq ft (19·41 sq m).

Empty weight 5,325 lb (2,415 kg); gross weight 7,710 lb (3,497 kg).

Maximum speed 390 mph (627·63 km/h) at 19,300 ft (5,883 m); climb 20,000 ft (6,096 m) in 7·1 min; service ceiling 34,600 ft (10,546 m); range 635 miles (1,022 km).

Armament—four ·50-in machine-guns.

## Model CW-25—AT-9 Jeep

Under the expansion programme of 1940, the Army Air Corps developed a requirement for a fast twin-engined trainer to familiarize pilots with the handling characteristics of new medium bombers then going into production, such as the North American B-25 and Martin B-26. Curtiss lengthened the basic Model 19 wing for a new two-seat twin-engined model that was produced from 1941 to 1943 as the AT-9. This was named Jeep after a fictitious comic strip animal of the time but the name achieved its greatest fame after it was given to the Army's ubiquitous little utility car that appeared at the same time as the AT-9. It also appears on some listings of wartime named aeroplanes as another Curtiss Fledgling.

The prototype of the AT-9 Jeep advanced trainer had steel-tube fuselage structure with fabric covering.

The AT-9 was a special-purpose trainer with side-by-side seats only for the student pilot and the instructor. While still in the design stages, future production was jeopardized by an impending aluminium shortage so the prototype was built with a welded steel-tube fuselage. The 791 production aircraft were all-aluminium, however.

469

Production AT-9s, used for twin-engined transition training, were of all-metal construction. (*Peter M. Bowers*)

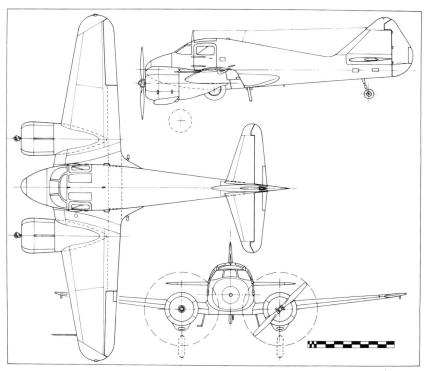

AT-9 Jeep.

470

Service use of the AT-9 was curtailed after B-25s and B-26s were on hand in sufficient numbers to allow some to be diverted to training duty. With a full complement of crew stations, these could double as crew integration trainers as well as pilot transition trainers, a versatility not shared by the single-purpose AT-9. Limited utility kept the AT-9 from finding a useful place in the postwar surplus market although it did receive Limited Type Certificate No. L-31-2.

AT-9—Four hundred and ninety-one AT-9s with 295 hp Lycoming R-680-9 engines were delivered. Initial unit costs complete were $44,965. US Army serial numbers: 41-5745/5894 (150), 41-11931/12271 (341).

AT-9A—Three hundred improved models, US Army serials 42-56853/57152 (300), differing mainly in having R-680-13 engines and revised undercarriage retraction hydraulics. Unit costs dropped to $40,286.

### AT-9 Jeep

Advanced trainer. Two pilots. Two 295 hp Lycoming R-680-9s.

Span 40 ft 4 in (12·29 m); length 31 ft 8 in (9·65 m); height 9 ft 10 in (2·99 m); wing area 233 sq ft (21·64 sq m).

Empty weight 4,494 lb (2,011 kg); gross weight 6,060 lb (2,749 kg).

Maximum speed 197 mph (317·03 km/h); cruising speed 175 mph (281·63 km/h); climb 10,000 ft (3,048 m) in 8·6 min; service ceiling 19,000 ft (5,791 m); range 750 miles (1,207 km).

### Model CW-27—C-76 Caravan

In 1941–42, the impending aluminium shortage threatened to curtail the production of some conventional all-aluminium military aeroplanes then on order. With the metal allocated to high-priority tactical types, lower-priority transports and trainers were expected to suffer. Consequently, the government encouraged the development of new models that would use a minimum of critical materials.

This all-wood YC-76 Caravan was the first aeroplane built at the Curtiss Louisville plant.

471

The five production C-76 Caravans, one of which is illustrated, were built in St Louis. The twenty Service test models were built in Louisville.

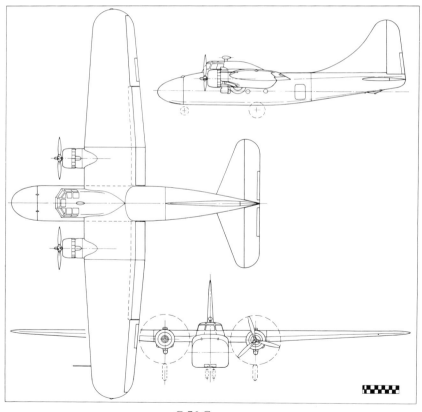

C-76 Caravan.

472

Curtiss responded to this requirement with the Model CW-27 Caravan, a wooden twin-engined transport that the Army designated C-76. Orders were placed with Curtiss for 200, to be built principally in the new Curtiss Louisville plant, and Higgins was to build an unspecified number in New Orleans. However, with the aluminium shortage overcome, increased orders were placed for established all-metal transports such as the C-46, and the C-76 programme was cancelled after 25 aeroplanes had been built at a cost of $144,977 each.

YC-76-CK—Eleven Service test YC-76s, Army serials 42-86918/86928 (c/ns 1/11), were the first aeroplanes built in the Louisville plant. These were twin-engined types in the size/weight category of the Douglas DC-3/C-47 and used the same 1,200 hp Pratt & Whitney R-1830-92 engines. The C-76 departed from current cargo aircraft practice in being a high-wing monoplane with tricycle undercarriage. The low-level cabin could be loaded directly from truck beds through both a hinge-up nose and conventional side doors. The pilots' compartment was well above the top fuselage line to avoid interference with the cargo compartment.

C-76-CS—Five production examples of the YC-76, Army serials 42-86913/86917, c/ns 21/25, were built at the St Louis plant. These were quickly reclassified as ZC-76, that is, obsolete.

YC-76A-1-CK—Nine further Service test versions (42-86929/86937, c/ns 12/20) built at Louisville with revised fuselage details.

### C-76 Caravan

Cargo and troop transport. Three crew and 45 troops. Two 1,200 hp Pratt & Whitney R-1830-92s.

Span 108 ft 2 in (32·96 m); length 68 ft 4 in (20·82 m); height 27 ft 3 in (8·3 m); wing area 1,560 sq ft (144·92 sq m).

Empty weight 18,300 lb (8,301 kg); gross weight 28,000 lb (12,701 kg).

Maximum speed 192 mph (308·98 km/h) at 7,300 ft (2,225 m); climb 10,000 ft (3,048 m) in 12·5 min; service ceiling 22,600 ft (6,888 m); range 750 miles (1,207 km).

### Republic P-47G Thunderbolt

Following cancellation of the P-60A contract in January 1942, Curtiss was given additional P-40 orders and was also requested to build 354 Republic P-47s in the Buffalo plant. The Curtiss-built Thunderbolts, serial numbers 42-24920/25273, were similar to the P-47D but were given a higher series letter because of the different manufacturer. Two P-47Gs were converted to two-seat TP-47Gs. First delivery of a P-47G was in December 1942.

US Army serial numbers:

| | |
|---|---|
| 42-24920/24939 | P-47G-CU |
| 42-24940/24979 | P-47G-1-CU |
| 42-24980/25039 | P-47G-5-CU |
| 42-25040/25119 | P-47G-10-CU |
| 42-25120/25273 | P-47G-15-CU |

P-40Es of 20th Pursuit Group carrying the white cross markings of the 1941 War Games.

# The P-40

The P-40 is by far the best-known Curtiss-Wright aeroplane of World War II. Between designated P-40s delivered to the US Army and the duplicate Model 81s and 87s purchased by Britain, it was also the Curtiss-Wright model built in the greatest quantities.

Britain operated its direct-purchase and Lend-Lease P-40 variants under the names of Tomahawk and Kittyhawk. It did not use the name Warhawk applied by Curtiss to variants powered with the Merlin engine. While attempts were made to apply these names to the US models, they did not catch on very well with either the Army or the public. Although the designation of P-40 actually applied only to the 11,995 examples delivered to the Army for its own use or for Lend-Lease to Britain, China, and elsewhere, it has since been applied as historical convenience to the entire production of 13,738 Curtiss-Wright Model 81/87 aeroplanes.

Although it was on hand in greater quantities than any other US Army fighter from 1941 into 1943, the P-40 design was obsolete by European standards before the prototype ever flew. In fact, no aeroplane design was laid out from scratch as the P-40; the XP-40 prototype was a production P-36A fitted with a liquid-cooled V-12 engine in place of the original air-cooled radial. The prototype of the P-36 flew in 1935 and the XP-40 flew in October 1938. Production P-40s only began to leave the factory in 1940.

The P-40 was behind the times when it first appeared and never did catch up. Its initial inadequacies, such as light firepower, non-sealing fuel tanks, and lack of protective armour, were not the result of poor Curtiss design work. Rather, they reflected the customer's requirements as spelled

474

out in Army Air Corps specifications which were themselves outmoded and were responsible for similar criticism being directed at other US military aeroplanes besides the P-40. Similarly, the poor showing made by the P-40 against Axis fighters early in the war does not reflect inferior design. The P-40 had been developed to be basically a low-altitude fighter under mid-1930s US tactical concepts that envisioned more ground support operations than high-altitude intercept missions. Its initial combat operations were in an entirely different environment and against later types of aircraft.

As the combat lessons of Europe and North Africa were brought to the attention of US aircraft manufacturers and the Army, the necessary improvements were made to aeroplanes already in production. While more guns and armour made the P-40 a more effective weapon, its performance suffered from the added weight. A drastic programme of weight reduction helped to some extent, but even then the P-40 was never able to match its major adversaries.

The P-40 was severely criticized in the Truman Report on several counts—particularly the original volume purchase of an inadequate and obsolete design and its continued production long after later designs were in full production.

The P-40 was put into largescale production because it was the best fighter available to the US Army at the time. Also, early deliveries were assured by its structural similarity to the P-36—the same production line and tooling could be used with little change. It was kept in production after later and more combatworthy designs were developed by other manufacturers because it was in production and far down the learning curve at a time when production lines had yet to be established for the new models. Its

Tomahawk II airframe c/n 17816 was fitted with a radial engine and used as a civil-registered flying testbed by Pratt & Whitney. (*Courtesy Warren M. Bodie*)

This P-40E-1 remained at the factory for test work. Here it is seen fitted with experimental 225-gallon auxiliary fuel tanks. (*Courtesy Harold Andrews*)

strong point then was its availability; what it may have lacked in quality it more than made up in quantity. However, this rationalization was not valid for long and could not justify the continuation of P-40 production to the end of 1944.

Before the inauguration of Lend-Lease in March 1941, 'P-40' sales were made to two customers under separate designation and serial number systems. The US Army Air Corps bought under the Army designation of P-40 with Army serial numbers while Britain, which placed orders on its own and took over the initial French orders, bought similar Curtiss 81s and 87s under the RAF names Tomahawk and Kittyhawk with RAF serials. After Lend-Lease was in effect, all procurement was through the Air Corps (Army Air Forces after 20 June, 1941) as P-40s with Army serials. Even though a particular Kittyhawk was intended for Britain, was equipped to meet British requirements, and also carried British markings and serial numbers, it also had a P-40 designation and a US Army serial number.

As an example of recalling loaned equipment, the US Army took over some of the P-40s delivered to Britain and used them in North Africa. The only changes made were to paint American star insignia over the British roundels and add the US serial number to the tail.

By late 1941, detail changes to US military aircraft were being made so fast that they were hard to keep track of. Consequently, a Block Designation system was set up, with the P-40F the first to use it (the P-40E-1 was in a different situation). All P-40Fs built in the -1 block,* identified as P-40F-1, were identical in detail. A change to the next aeroplanes at the factory would result in another block number 5 digits higher, as P-40F-5. The intervening digits were for possible use by field modifications, a certain change to a P-40F-1 making it a P-40F-2, etc. This procedure is still in use today.

*Cited as an example of the system; there was no P-40F-1 model but there was a P-40F-5.

For all its publicized shortcomings, the P-40 was still a very effective fighting machine when used properly. The enormous losses of the type at Pearl Harbor and in the Philippines on 7–8 December, 1941, were mainly the result of faulty command decisions in the matter of aircraft dispersal on the ground at a time of potential attack. Although obviously outclassed by the attacking Japanese fighters, the few P-40s that got into the air acquitted themselves well.

While Tomahawks provided most of the British fighter support in the North African campaigns of 1941–42, by far the most famous 'P-40' operations were those of the American Volunteer Group (AVG) in China. Called *The Flying Tigers*, the AVG was certainly one of the most unique as well as effective fighting organizations of the Second World War. From 20 December, 1941, to 4 July, 1942, it operated with an initial supply of 100 Curtiss 81A-2s diverted from a British Tomahawk II order. Because of the primitive bases from which they operated and the difficulty in obtaining fuel, ammunition, and particularly spare parts, no more than 55 fighters were available to the three AVG squadrons at any given time. Yet, in that six-month period, the Tigers destroyed 286 Japanese aeroplanes with the loss of only 12 of their own in combat. However, they lost 61 in accidents and Japanese air raids.

This record was achieved by using tactics carefully calculated to exploit the known weak points of the enemy while capitalizing on the Tomahawk's strong points and avoiding exposure of its own weaknesses to enemy action. The most effective tactic against more manoeuvrable Japanese fighters was a diving pass followed by a fast departure from the scene. Dogfighting between Tomahawks and the best Japanese fighters was carefully avoided but a P-40 could beat a Messerschmitt Bf 109 at low altitude. The weight that handicapped the performance of the P-40 had one

P-40F-20s, repossessed by the US Army from British Kittyhawk II orders, were flown from aircraft carriers for the invasion of North Africa in January 1943.

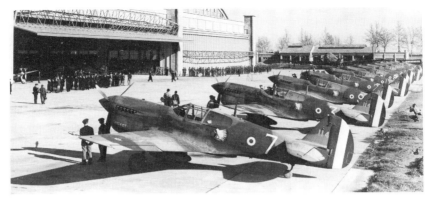

P-40F-5s handed over to Free French Forces in Algiers in 1943.

very tangible benefit—the rugged structure could absorb terrific punishment from enemy gunfire and allow the aeroplane to return to base when a lesser structure would have been destroyed.

Throughout the 1939–45 period, 20 US pursuit groups (excluding the AVG which was absorbed into the 14th US Air Force) used the P-40. Britain had 13 squadrons equipped at various times and Australia and New Zealand had eight and seven respectively. While Canada used many at home in defence and training roles, four Canadian squadrons flew Tomahawks overseas and three used Kittyhawks in Alaska and the Aleutians. While the French never got any of the early Tomahawks that they ordered in 1939, Free French forces were well-supplied with Lend-Lease P-40s and operated three squadrons in North Africa after November

British P-40M Kittyhawk III transferred to the Soviet Union, captured by Finland, and then used against the Russians.

1942. Other P-40s were supplied through Lend-Lease or diverted from British direct-purchase and Lend-Lease orders for China, the USSR, South Africa, Netherlands East Indies, neutral Turkey, Brazil, and Egypt. The one Dutch P-40 squadron fought the Japanese in the East Indies throughout the war and then fought the Indonesian rebels until February 1949, to end the combat career of the P-40.

Costs of P-40s varied considerably between models as detailed in the following descriptions, but the cost breakdowns of three representative production models are presented here:

| Item | | | P-40 | P-40E | P-40N |
|---|---|---|---|---|---|
| Airframe | . | . | $24,889 | $28,482 | $27,189 |
| Engine | . | . | 17,126 | 16,855 | 10,702 |
| Propeller | . | . | 3,425 | 2,481 | 3,110 |
| Electronics. | | . | 1,360 | 3,160 | 7,154 |
| Ordnance | . | . | 1,922 | 5,940 | 2,646 |
| Other | . | . | 2,816 | 2,700 | 2,068 |
| Grand Total | | . | $51,538 | $59,618 | $52,869 |

The last of the 13,738 P-40 types, a P-40N-40, left the factory on 30 November, 1944.

In the following descriptions of P-40/81/87 models, the US Army P-40s are listed in sequential order of Army designations regardless of Curtiss designation but are referenced to the Curtiss designation. This is followed by a listing of sequential marks of Tomahawks and Kittyhawks with British and Commonwealth serial numbers where available. The final listing cross-references both to the sequential Curtiss model numbers.

Existing Curtiss documents are contradictory in the presentation of the model numbers, sometimes showing H-81A-2, H81-A2, or H81-A-2. The style here is the author's choice.

## US Army P-40 Series

XP-40 (Model 75P)—Realizing that the radial-engined P-36A was at the limit of its growth, Curtiss engineer Donovan Berlin got Air Corps approval to install a 1,150 hp Allison V-1710-19 liquid-cooled engine in the 10th P-36A (c/n 12424), and submitted it as a new fighter prototype, the XP-40.

First flight was on 14 October, 1938, with the radiator under the fuselage and aft of the wing. Later, it was gradually moved forward until located at the extreme nose. Armament was two ·50-in calibre machine-guns in the nose. Wing racks could be fitted for six 20-lb (9 kg) bombs. The cost of engineering and shop changes to the basic P-36A airframe brought the unit cost of the XP-40 less GFE to $36,266.

The XP-40, converted from a P-36A airframe, with original aft radiator installation.

The XP-40 with intermediate radiator installation.

This final configuration of the XP-40 was used on the subsequent production models.

480

P-40 (Model 81)—On 26 April, 1939, the Army ordered 524 production P-40s similar to the final XP-40 configuration except for V-1710-33 engines and one ·30 calibre machine-gun in each wing, but only 200 were to be plain P-40s. Armour, bullet-proof windshields, and leakproof fuel tanks were added in service. Bombing provisions were not used. One, 39-221, was converted before completion to P-40G and is sometimes referred to as XP-40G.

Deliveries began in June 1940, after first flight on 4 April. The first three were unpainted, but the remainder were the first US Army fighters since the P-1B to be delivered in full camouflage—olive drab on top and sides and grey undersides. The standard rudder stripes and star insignia on both wings were retained and the plain P-40s were the only fighters produced with that combination. One P-40 became P-40A and 16 were sent to the Soviet Union. The P-40s were restricted from duty as fighters on 22 October, 1942, and were redesignated RP-40.

US Army serial numbers: 39-156/289 (134), 40-292/357 (66). C/ns: 13033/13232 (200).

P-40A—The P-40A designation was skipped in the initial assignments to P-40F but was applied retroactively to P-40 number 40-326 when it was converted to a camera-carrying photographic-reconnaissance model at Bolling Field in March 1942.

P-40B (Model H81-B)—The 131 P-40Bs differed from the P-40s mainly in having an extra ·30-in calibre gun in each wing. Deliveries began in January 1941, just before the Army deleted the tail stripes and upper right and lower port wing star from camouflaged aeroplanes and added a star to each side of the fuselage.

US Army serial numbers: 41-5205/5304 (100), 41-13297/13327 (31). C/ns: 15973/16103 (131).

Production P-40s of 1940 were the only US Army Pursuits to have the new camouflage colouring while retaining the rudder stripes and star insignia on both wings. (*Peter M. Bowers*)

481

The P-40B had two ·30-calibre guns in each wing instead of one as on the P-40. This one had no rudder stripes and the fuselage star of the early 1941 markings transition period had not yet been added. (*Peter M. Bowers*)

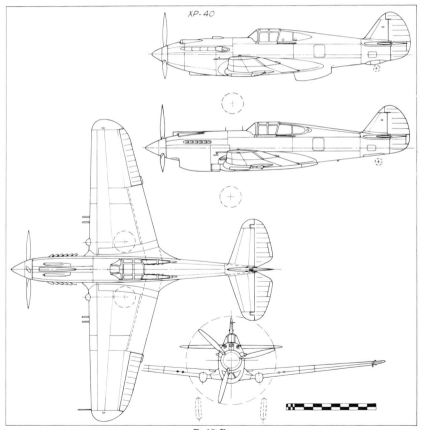

XP-40

P-40 B.

482

The P-40C was similar to the P-40B except for leak-proof fuel tanks. Markings were standardized with the star on each side of the fuselage, one on upper port wing surface, one on lower starboard. (*Peter M. Bowers*)

P-40C (Model H81-B)—The initial P-40 order was completed with 193 P-40Cs delivered from March to May 1941. Engines were still the V-1710-33, the main difference from the P-40B being internal leak-proof fuel tanks instead of tanks with external covers plus a droppable external tank. First flight was on 10 April, 1941.

US Army serial numbers: 41-13328/13520. C/ns: 16104/16296.

P-40D (Model H87-A2)—Twenty-three improved P-40s with enough changes to justify a new Curtiss model number. The 1,150 hp V-1710-39 engine had spur gear reduction that raised the thrust-line and resulted in a new shorter nose design that was retained by all subsequent P-40s. Nose guns were omitted and two ·50-in calibre guns were installed in each wing, along with provision for two 20 mm cannon that were never used. Shackles were added under the belly to carry a 52-gal (197 litre) auxiliary fuel tank or a 500 lb (227 kg) bomb, and wing bomb rack attachment points were added for six 20-lb (9 kg) bombs as on the XP-40. Fuel tanks were self-sealing and 175 lb (79 kg) of protective armour were used.

US Army serial numbers: 40-359/381. C/ns: 13234/13256.

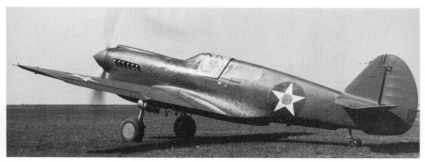

The P-40D had a redesigned nose and four ·50-calibre guns in the wings only.

483

The P-40E had six wing guns and provision for bombs. This one from the 20th Pursuit Group carries the circular marking of the 1941 War Games.

P-40E (Model 87-B2)—The 820 P-40Es were similar to the P-40Ds except for six ·50-in calibre guns, alternate provision for six 20-lb (9 kg) bombs or one 500-lb (227 kg) bomb, and deletion of the cannon mounts.

US Army serial numbers: 40-358 (c/n 13233), 40-382/681 (300, c/ns 13257/13556), 41-5305/5744 (440), 41-13521/13599 (79, c/ns 16737/16815).

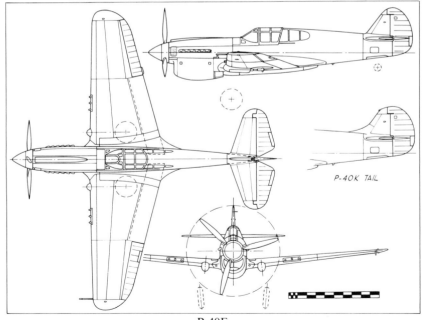

P-40E.

484

P-40E-1 (Model 87-A4)—This designation was adopted slightly in advance of the Block Designation system to identify the 1,500 Kittyhawk IAs supplied to Britain early in the Lend-Lease programme. Because they were procured with US funds, the aeroplanes had to have standard US Army designations. Since the British equipment installed made them different to the Army P-40Es, the -1 suffix was added to formalize the difference. Many of these were retained for US service but flew with British camouflage; six went to Brazil and received Brazilian serial numbers 01/06.

US Army serial numbers: 41-24776/25195 (420, c/ns 18795/19214), 41-35874/36953 (1,080, c/ns 18395/19474).

P-40E-1s were Kittyhawk IAs procured for Britain with Lend-Lease funds. This one, retained for US use, is seen with American markings applied over British camouflage.

XP-40F (Model 87-B3)—The single XP-40F was P-40D 40-360 (c/n 13235) fitted with a 1,300 hp British Rolls-Royce Merlin 28 engine and it flew on 30 June, 1941. This engine did much to overcome the limitations imposed by the Allison, and a total of 1,311 production P-40Fs was ordered, with American-made Merlin engines built by Packard as the V-1650-1 and the six-gun P-40E wing armament. Principal recognition feature was the absence of the top-mounted carburettor air scoop.

YP-40F—Unofficial designation for a second P-40F prototype developed from the third production aircraft, 41-13602, with the coolant system moved aft in several different configurations including inside a thickened wing-root section. Also used for test of additional vertical tail area.

P-40F—The first 699 of 1,311 P-40Fs had no dash numbers. The P-40F-5s and later models had the aft fuselage extended 20 in (50·8 cm) to improve directional stability. The P-40F-10s had manual instead of electric cowl flap controls, the -15s were winterized, and the -20s had revised oxygen systems. Some of the 150 delivered to Britain as Kittyhawk IIs were repossessed by US Forces for use in North Africa in 1942–43.

485

The XP-40F was the second P-40D refitted with a British Rolls-Royce Merlin engine. Distinguishing feature was the removal of the carburettor air scoop on top of the nose.

The third P-40F was diverted for test work and redesignated YP-40F. An experimental radiator installation is shown here.

Directional control problems resulted in the first P-40F being used for tests of revised tail shapes and lengthened rear fuselage. P-40F-10s and later aircraft had the fuselage lengthened by 20 in.

US Army serial numbers:

P-40F     41-13600/14299  (699, 41-13696 cancelled)   42 to P-40R-1
P-40F-5   41-14300/14422  (123)   9 to P-40R-1
P-40F-10  41-14423/14599  (177)   4 to P-40R-1
P-40F-15  41-19733/19932  (200)   11 to P-40R-1
P-40F-20  42-19933/20044  (112)   4 to P-40R-1

A P-40F Kittyhawk II repossessed from Britain and used by US forces in North Africa. (*Howard Levy*)

XP-40G (Model 81-AG)—Unofficial designation for P-40 39-221 fitted with H81-A2 Tomahawk IIA wings having four ·30-in calibre guns. Official designation was P-40G but status as an experimental variant resulted in frequent use of the improper X prefix. It was shipped to the USSR in 1943.

P-40G—The 43 additional P-40Gs were existing P-40s refitted in August and September 1941, with Tomahawk IIA wings. Sixteen, including 39-221, were shipped to the USSR starting in October 1941. All examples remaining in the United States were redesignated RP-40G in October 1942.

US Army serial numbers: 39-162, 176, 182,* 187, 190, 191, 196, 197, 204, 206, 209, 217, 220, 226, 235, 238, 243, 248, 257, 263, 267, 275, 276, 279, 288; 40-292, 297, 299/301, 303, 309, 315, 318, 320, 323, 331/333, 335/338**.

* Rebuilt as 42-14269.
** 40-338 rebuilt as 42-14261.

P-40H—Designation cancelled.

P-40J—To have been a turbo-supercharged P-40E; cancelled 18 May, 1942.

P-40K*—The 1,300 P-40Ks through to P-40K-15, ordered 28 October, 1941, with deliveries beginning in August 1942, were improved P-40Es with altitude-rated V-1710-73 engines and alternate provision for bombs or belly tanks. The P-40K-1s and -5s had revised engine controls, the -10s and later aircraft had the 20-in fuselage extension, and the -15s were winterized. All short-fuselage versions were fitted with a dorsal fin for improved directional stability.

* Curtiss model number unavailable.

The P-40K-1 (illustrated) and -5 had short fuselages with added dorsal fins. P-40K-10s and subsequent aircraft had increased length and the standard vertical tail of other late P-40s. (*Peter M. Bowers*)

One P-40K was redesignated XP-40K, two (42-9987, 45722) were redesignated XP-40Q, and 352 were Lend-Leased to Britain as Kittyhawk IIIs. Of these, some were repossessed for US operations in North Africa. Twenty-five P-40Ks were diverted to Brazil.

| US Army serial numbers: | | | C/ns |
|---|---|---|---|
| P-40K-1* | 42-45722/46321 | (600) | 15523/16122 |
| P-40K-5 | 42-9730/9929 | (200) | 21114/21313 |
| P-40K-10 | 42-9930/10264 | (335) | 21314/21648 |
| P-40K-15 | 42-10265/10429 | (165) | 21649/21813 |

XP-40K—One P-40K-10, 42-10219, with Allison V-1710-43, used to develop P-40 improvements. Experiments with cowling and relocated cooling systems altered the appearance from time to time.

* P-40K-1 originally assigned serials 42-65902/66501, P-40K-5/15 assigned 42-64502/65201; all cancelled and reassigned as shown.

The XP-40K was a standard P-40K-10 used for cooling system experiments.

P-40L (Model 87-B3)—The 700 P-40Ls to the P-40L-20 were similar to the Merlin-powered P-40F-5s except for minor equipment changes. The first P-40Ls were redesignated P-40L-1; the -5s had two wing guns removed; the -10s had electrical aileron trim tabs and engine control changes; the -15s had revised carburettor air filters and inter-aircraft signal lights; and the -20s had radio and electrical changes and provision for an incendiary (destruct) grenade. One hundred went to Britain as Kittyhawk IIs with no mark distinction from P-40Fs. Some repossessed for US operations in North Africa. Fifty-three were converted to P-40R-2 trainers in 1944.

The P-40L was similar to the P-40F except for minor equipment differences. This P-40L-20 has Air Transport Command insignia on the fuselage.
(*John C. Collins*)

US Army serial numbers 42-65202/65901 cancelled and replaced as follows:

| P-40L-1  | 42-10430/10479 | (50)  |                |
|----------|----------------|-------|----------------|
| P-40L-5  | 42-10480/10699 | (220) | 6 to P-40R-2   |
| P-40L-10 | 42-10700/10847 | (148) | 1 to P-40R-2   |
| P-40L-15 | 42-10848/10959 | (112) | 10 to P-40R-2  |
| P-40L-20 | 42-10960/11129 | (170) | 36 to P-40R-2  |

P-40M*—The 600 P-40Ms to the P-40M-10 were essentially P-40K-20s except for Allison V-1710-81 engines. The P-40M-1s had reinforced ailerons; the -5s had improved carburettor air filters and further aileron improvements; the -10s had revised undercarriage warning systems and fuel system changes. 364 went to Britain as Kittyhawk IIIs and 19 to Brazil.

US Army serial numbers:

| | | | C/ns |
|----------|-------------|-------|---------------|
| P-40M-1  | 43-5403/5462 | (60)  | 27091/27150  |
| P-40M-5  | 43-5463/5722 | (260) | 27151/27410  |
| P-40M-10 | 43-5723/6002 | (280) | 27411/27690  |

* Curtiss model number unavailable.

489

The P-40M was similar to the P-40K-20 except for its Allison engine. This one was photographed in New Guinea. (*E. M. Sommerich*)

P-40N (Models 87V, 87W)—The 5,220 P-40Ns were the major and final production model built under the P-40 designation. The first 1,500 were to have been P-40Ps with Merlin engines but were redesignated P-40N-1 and P-40N-5 with the 1,200 hp (war emergency power) Allison V-1710-81. The P-40N-1s were lightened airframes similar to the E, K, and M models with four-gun armament, no wing bomb racks, decreased fuel, increased armour, manually-operated undercarriage and flaps, and revised radio and oxygen systems.

The P-40N-5s had revised pilot's seats and rear-view windows, revised radio, readopted wing bomb racks and fuel tanks, and used 27-in (68·58 cm) magnesium wheels. The -6s were -5s fitted with reconnaissance cameras in the fuselage. The -10s were winterized; the -15s had electrical revisions

Distinguishing feature of the P-40N was the squared-off rear panel of clear-view windows behind the pilot. The air scoop on top of the nose identified the Allison engine installation. (*Courtesy Harold Andrews*)

490

and the -16s were -15s with cameras; the -20s and later models used the V-1710-99 engine, essentially a -81 with automatic control; the -25s had revised instrumentation and the -26s were -25s with cameras. Three RP-40N-26s were converted to two-seat trainers and the -30 had revised oil systems. Seventy were converted to P-40R-1 trainers in 1944.

Twenty-two P-40N-31s were P-40N-30s converted to two-seat trainers. The -35s had changes in carburettor, instruments, and lighting. The final P-40N-40 variants dispensed with the camouflage finish starting with 44-47860 and used 30-in (76·2 cm) wheels and metal-covered ailerons. One P-40N fitted with an experimental bubble canopy was unofficially called XP-40N. Five hundred and eighty-six were to be Kittyhawk IVs for Britain but the first 130 were diverted to the USSR. A further 41 were sent to Brazil, where some served until 1958. One still survived there as a monument (USAAC serial 44-7700; Brazilian serial 4064). All Brazilian P-40s were re-serialled in 1945 in the range 4020/4100.

One P-40N was fitted with a bubble canopy and unofficially designated XP-40N.
(*Courtesy Air International*)

| US Army serial numbers: | | | C/ns |
|---|---|---|---|
| P-40N-1 | 42-104429/104828 | (400) | 28191/28590 |
| P-40N-5 | 42-104829/105928 | (1,100) | 28591/29690 |
| P-40N-10 | 42-105929/106028 | (100) | 29691/29790 |
| P-40N-15 | 42-106029/106405 | (377) | 29791/30167 |
| P-40N-20 | 42-106406/106428 | (23) | 30168/30190 |
| | 43-22752/24251 | (1,500) | 30691/32190 |
| P-40N-25 | 43-24252/24751 | (500) | 32191/32690 |
| P-40N-30 | 44-7001/7500 | (500) | 32741/33240 |
| P-40N-35 | 44-7501/8000 | (500) | 33241/33740 |
| P-40N-40 | 44-47749/47968 | (220) | 33741/33960 |

An additional 780 P-40N-40s, 44-47969/48748 (c/ns 33961/34740) were cancelled.

P-40P-1—To have used the V-1650-1 engine; designation cancelled and 1,500 aeroplanes built as P-40N-1 and -5 with the V-1710-81.

The first XP-40Q was P-40K-10 42-9987 fitted with a new cooling system.

XP-40Q (Model 87X)—Two P-40Ks (42-9987, 42-45722) and one P-40N (43-24571), were extensively modified with revised cooling systems, two-stage superchargers, and structural changes that altered their appearance. When coolant radiators were moved into the wing roots, the two inboard guns were removed.

The most prominent XP-40Q feature, used on 42-45722 and 43-24571, was the addition of a bubble canopy as on the 'XP-40N'. Later, the wingtips were clipped. Speed increased to 422 mph (679·13 km/h) at 20,500 ft (6,248 m) making it the fastest of all the P-40s.

Registered NX300B, the second XP-40Q was an unauthorized starter in the 1947 Thompson Trophy; it was in fourth place when it caught fire.

P-40R—A US Army document reports that 600 P-40Rs were random P-40F and P-40L airframes relegated to training duties and fitted with Allison V-1710-81 engines in place of their original Merlins. However, only 70 P-40R-1s and 53 P-40R-2s can be confirmed by serial number.

US Army serial numbers: P-40R-1 (seventy P-40F conversions) 41-13600, 13615, 13640, 13641, 13651, 13659, 13662, 13663, 13666, 13682, 13691, 13715, 13722, 13747, 13794, 13818, 13822, 13825, 13830, 13834, 13842, 13853, 13916, 13976, 13977, 13982, 13992, 14046, 14051, 14071, 14078, 14124, 14129, 14132, 14150, 14167, 14168, 14189, 14190, 14256, 14268, 14293, 14304, 14332/14335, 14382, 14383, 14387, 14420, 14497, 14499, 14500, 14561, 19733, 19782/19784, 19788, 19845, 19880, 19886, 19889, 19919, 19935, 19939, 19971, 19990, 20039.

P-40R-2 (fifty-three P-40L conversions) 42-10513, 10616, 10642, 10648, 10669, 10676, 10712, 10864, 10873, 10874, 10883, 10903, 10913, 10924, 10944, 10953, 10954, 10964, 10974, 10983, 10991, 10992, 11010, 11026, 11037, 11039, 11053, 11055, 11058, 11060, 11064, 11065, 11068/11070, 11075, 11076, 11078, 11080, 11083, 11085, 11090/11092, 11105, 11109, 11110, 11112/11116, 11120.

492

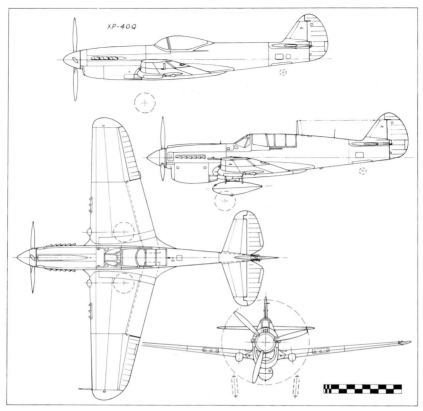

P-40N, with side view of XP-40Q No. 2.

The second XP-40Q was the first P-40K-1 with lengthened fuselage, bubble canopy, squared and shortened wingtips, and revised nose.

493

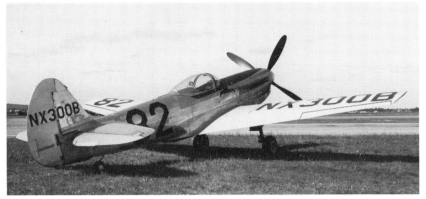

The second XP-40Q was briefly used for postwar racing. (*Peter M. Bowers*)

This P-40R-1 was a former short-tail P-40F with the Merlin engine replaced by an Allison. (*Peter M. Bowers*)

This P-40R-2 was a P-40L-20 with the Merlin engine replaced by an Allison. (*Peter M. Bowers*)

Some P-40Ns were converted to dual-control trainers and redesignated TP-40N. This is a TP-40N-30.

## Modified P-40s

TP-40—A few P-40Ns were converted to two-seat pilot transition trainers by adding a second cockpit behind the original installation. No new designation resulted, the letter T merely being added to the normal designation. This was in conflict with some single-seat models that were assigned to training schools and also given the T-for-Trainer prefix.

Twin-Engined P-40—In 1942, P-40C 41-13456 was modified to become the mock-up of an undesignated twin-engined fighter. Packard-Merlin engines and nose cowling from P-40Fs or Kittyhawk IIs were adapted to nacelles fitted to the top of the P-40C wing. No further information is available.

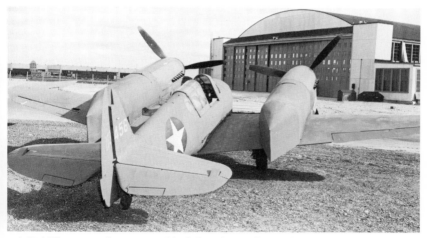

A P-40C was used to create this full-scale mock-up of a twin-engined Curtiss pursuit. (*National Air and Space Museum*)

495

| | XP-40* | P-40B* | P-40E* | P-40F* | P-40N-1** | XP-40Q-3** |
|---|---|---|---|---|---|---|
| | 1,150 hp Allison V-1710-19 | 1,090 hp Allison V-1710-33 | 1,150 hp Allison V-1710-39 | 1,240 hp Packard V-1650-1 | 1,200 hp Allison V-1710-81 | 1,425 hp Allison V-1710-121 |
| Span | 37 ft 3½ in (11·36 m) | 37 ft 3½ in (11·36 m) | 37 ft 3½ in (11·36 m) | 37 ft 3½ in (11·36 m) | 37 ft 3½ in (11·36 m) | 35 ft 3 in (10·74 m) |
| Length | 31 ft 9 3/16 in (9·68 m) | 31 ft 8½ in (9·67 m) | 31 ft 8½ in (9·66 m) | 31 ft 7 2/3 in (9·64 m) | 33 ft 4 in (10·15 m) | 35 ft 4 in (10·76 m) |
| Height | 9 ft 2¼ in (2·8 m) | 10 ft 8 in (3·25 m) | 10 ft 8 in (3·25 m) | 10 ft 7¾ in (3·24 m) | 12 ft 4 in (3·75 m) | — |
| Wing area | 236 sq ft (21·92 sq m) | 236 sq ft (21·92 sq m) | 236 sq ft (21·92 sq m) | 236 sq ft (21·92 sq m) | 236 sq ft (21·92 sq m) | — |
| Empty weight | 5,194 lb (2,356 kg) | 5,622 lb (2,550 kg) | 5,922 lb (2,686 kg) | 6,190 lb (2,808 kg) | 6,000 lb (2,722 kg) | |
| Gross weight | 6,280 lb (2,849 kg) | 7,610 lb (3,452 kg) | 8,515 lb (3,862 kg) | 8,674 lb (3,934 kg) | 7,740 lb (3,511 kg) | 9,000 lb (4,082 kg) |
| Maximum speed | 327 mph (526·24 km/h) at 12,000 ft (3,658 m) | 351 mph (564·87 km/h) at 15,000 ft (4,572 m) | 334 mph (537·51 km/h) at 15,000 ft (4,572 m) | 370 mph (595·44 km/h) at 22,000 ft (6,706 m) | 350 mph (563·26 km/h) at 16,400 ft (4,999 m) | 422 mph (679·13 km/h) at 20,500 ft (6,248 m) |
| Cruising speed | 294 mph (473·14 km/h) | 303 mph (487·62 km/h) | 308 mph (495·67 km/h) | 300 mph (482·79 km/h) | — | — |
| Climb | 12,000 ft (3,658 m) in 3·2 min | 15,000 ft (4,572 m) in 5·65 min | 15,000 ft (4,572 m) in 6·25 min | 15,000 ft (4,572 m) in 6·9 min | 14,000 ft (4,267 m) in 6·7 min | 20,000 ft (6,096 m) in 4·8 min |
| Service ceiling | 31,000 ft (9,449 m) | 30,000 ft (9,144 m) | 29,100 ft (8,870 m) | 32,000 ft (9,754 m) | 31,000 ft (9,449 m) | 39,000 ft (11,887 m) |
| Range (at 70% power) | 470 miles (756 km) | 606 miles (975 km) | 716 miles (1,152 km) | 752 miles (1,210 km) | 360 miles (579 km) | — |
| Armament | Two ·50-in m-g | Two ·50-in and four ·30-in m-g | Six ·50-in m-g | Six ·50-in m-g, one 500 lb (227 kg) bomb | Four ·50-in m-g, one 500 lb (227 kg) and two 100 lb (45 kg) bombs | Four ·50-in m-g |

* Curtiss figures    ** US Army figures

## Tomahawks and Kittyhawks—
## The Export Models 81 and 87

France was the first customer other than the US Army for the Model 81. The first export aircraft was completed in French markings in April 1940, but could not be delivered. Britain then took over the French contracts and accepted the aeroplanes under the name Tomahawk. The later Model 87, also ordered by France, was used by Britain as the Kittyhawk.

When Curtiss introduced the P-40F with the Merlin engine, the new name Warhawk was applied to distinguish it from the Allison-engined P-40Ds and Es. Britain did not adopt this name for the re-engined model but retained the name Kittyhawk for both versions of the Model 87.

Although P-40s were used by many nations during the war, Britain was the only actual purchaser other than the US Army. Many RAF models were released to other countries from the original direct purchase orders of 1939–40. Those ordered after March 1941 were Lend-Lease models delivered with Army P-40 designations and serial numbers in addition to RAF serial numbers and markings.

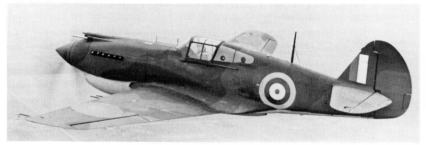

The British Tomahawk I was the equivalent of the US Army P-40B. Some were obtained by direct purchase, others were taken over from French contracts.

Some discrepancies and contradictions exist in Curtiss records matching Tomahawk and Kittyhawk designations to RAF serials and equivalent US Army P-40 models. The following RAF designations, serial numbers and correlations to P-40s are from British official records.

Tomahawk (Model 81)—A total of 1,180 Model 81 Tomahawks was delivered under British direct-purchase contracts. In addition, Britain took over ten P-40Cs from the US Army (41-13389, 13390, 13396/13401, 13406, and 13407) and operated them as Tomahawks of unspecified mark and without RAF serial numbers.

Tomahawk I (Model H81-A)—A total of 140 equivalents of the US Army P-40, except for four wing guns, were ordered on two contracts with deliveries beginning in April 1940. Britain quickly decided that these were unsuitable for combat and relegated them to training roles. Three were used by Canada with RAF serials.

RAF serials: AH741/840 (100); AH841/880 (40). C/ns: 14446/14545 (100); 14091/14130 (40).

The Tomahawk IIA was the Curtiss Model H81A-2 purchased by Britain in 1940.

AH774, 793, 840 to Canada as instructional airframes.

Tomahawk II—Designation was not used officially for specific aircraft but was a generalization for Improved Tomahawks delivered in October and November 1940.

Tomahawk IIA (Model H81-A2)—Protective armour and externally-covered self-sealing fuel tanks on 110 aircraft equivalent to the P-40B. Twenty-three transferred to the USSR and one to Canada.

RAF serials: AH881/990 (110). C/ns: 14131/14220 (90), 14582/14601 (20).

AH938 to Canada as an instructional airframe.

Tomahawk IIB (Model H81-A2, -A3)—A total of 930 in four lots. These were generally equivalent to the US P-40C and were used extensively by the RAF and South African Air Force in North Africa starting on 16 June, 1941. Of these, 100 unofficially designated H81-A3 were released to China

Britain released one hundred H81A-2 Tomahawk IIAs to the 'Flying Tigers' in China and Curtiss recorded them as H81A-3s. The famous shark's teeth marking did not originate with the Tigers but was copied from British Tomahawks used in North Africa in 1940.

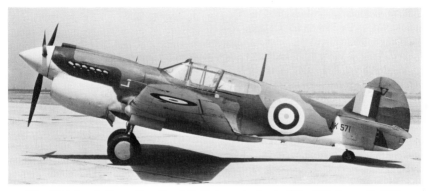

The Kittyhawk I was the direct British equivalent of the US Army P-40D.

and used by the AVG; 23 went to the USSR, and unspecified numbers went to Turkey and Egypt.

RAF serials: AH991/999 (c/ns 14658/14666) (9)*, AK100/570 (c/ns 14582/14951, 15423/15522) (471)**, AM370/519 (c/ns 15823/15972) (150)***, AN218/517 (c/ns 17817/18116) (300).

Kittyhawk—The French contract for Model 87s was taken over by Britain before construction began. The airframe and engine changes justified the new name of Kittyhawk; Britain bought 560 on direct-purchase contracts and a further 2,432 were supplied by the US Lend-Lease programme for a total of 2,992 Kittyhawks.

Kittyhawk I (Model A87-A2)—Fitted with four ·50-in calibre wing guns, these 560 aeroplanes were comparable to the P-40D. Britain took over the initial French order and deliveries began in August 1941; with 72 diverted to Canada and 17 to Turkey.

    * All to Russia    ** 36 to China    *** 64 to China

The Kittyhawk IA was the Lend-Lease P-40E-1 for Britain. This one is seen with 1941-style Australian markings and Australian serial number A29-82.
(*Royal Australian Air Force*)

499

RAF serials:                         C/ns
AK571/870 (300; 5 to Turkey)        14952/15251
AK871/950 (80; 3 to Turkey)         15342/15421
AK951/999 (49; 4 to Turkey)         18695/18743
AL100/230 (131; 5 to Turkey)        18744/18874
Canadian serials: 1028/1099 (72)

Kittyhawk IA (Model H87-A3, -A4)—The 1,500 Kittyhawk IAs were direct equivalents of the P-40E and were delivered under the US Army designation P-40E-1 to distinguish their British equipment and details from those for US service. Many of these were diverted to Canada, Australia, and New Zealand.

| RAF serials | Equivalent USAAC serials | | |
|---|---|---|---|
| ET100/999 (900) | 41-24776/25195 (420), 35874/36353 (480) | | |
| EV100/699 (600) | 41-36354/36953 (600) | | |
| Australian serials: | Canadian serials | New Zealand serials (62) | |
| A29-1/163 (163) | 720/731 (12) | NZ3001/3044 (44), | |
| | | NZ3091/3098 (8), | |
| | | NZ3100/3108 (9), NZ3271 | |

Instead of using the US Army name Warhawk, Britain called the Model H87B-3/P-40F the Kittyhawk II.

Kittyhawk II (Model H87-B3)—Wartime British sources identify the 330 British P-40Fs and P-40Ls as Kittyhawk IIs; later records list the first 230 as Kittyhawk IIAs. Eighty-one were transferred to the US Army overseas and seven (FL263, 270, 276, 280, 283, 305, and 307) were given to the Free French. New Zealand had one P-40L, serial NZ3074.

RAF serials: P-40F FL219/368 (150), FL369/448 (80); P-40L FS400/499 (100).

Kittyhawk III*—Of 616 Kittyhawk IIIs, the first 192 were P-40K-1s, the next 160 were P-40Ls, and the final 264 were P-40Ms. The last 170 were diverted to the USSR. Nine P-40K-1s were used by Canada under US Army serial numbers 42-45921, 45944, 45945, 45951, 45952, 45954, 45977, 46003, 46004.

* Curtiss model number unavailable

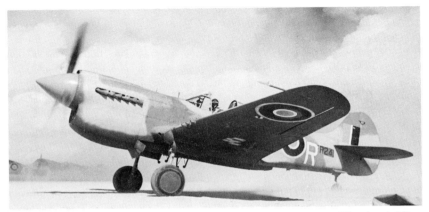

This Kittyhawk III is a short-tail P-40K-1 with dorsal fin. Later Kittyhawk IIIs were long-tail P-40Ls and Ms.

RAF serials (614)
P-40K-1: FL875/905 (31), FR111/115 (5), FR210/361 (152), FL710/713 (4)
P-40L: FL714/730 (17), FR116/140 (25), FR385/392 (8), FR412/521 (110)
P-40M: FR779/872 (94), FS100/269 (170)
Australian serials (210)

| | | P-40M-5, -10: | A29-400/414 (15) |
|---|---|---|---|
| P-40K-10: A29-164/202 (39) | | | A29-420/434 (15) |
| P-40K-15: A29-203/205 (3) | | | A29-443/460 (18) |
| P-40M-10: A29-300/389 (90) | | | A29-473/502 (30) |

The Kittyhawk IV was the P-40M which was widely used by Britain, Australia, New Zealand, and the Soviet Union. This white-tailed example was used by No.80 Squadron, RAAF, in New Guinea. (*E. M. Sommerich*)

Canadian serials
831/845 (15)
New Zealand serials (58)

| P-40K | NZ3045/3065 (21) | P-40M | NZ3066/3073 (8) |
|---|---|---|---|
| | NZ3090 (1) | | NZ3075/3089 (15) |
| | NZ3099 (1) | | NZ3109/3119 (11) |
| | | | NZ3180 (1) |

Kittyhawk IV (Model H87V, W)—The final 586 Kittyhawks were US Army P-40Ns delivered from March 1943 to January 1944. 130 of these were diverted to the USSR.

RAF serials (586)
FS270/399 (130; to Russia), FT849/954 (106), FX498/847 (350)
Australian serials (468)

| P-40N-1 | A29-415/419 | (5) | P-40N-20 | A29-600/704 (105) |
|---|---|---|---|---|
| | A29-435/442 | (8) | P-40N-25 | A29-800/811 (12) |
| | A29-461/472 | (12) | | A29-819/828 (10) |
| | A29-503/541 | (39) | P-40N-30 | A29-900/928 (29) |
| | A29-559/563 | (5) | P-40N-35 | A29-1000/1079 (80) |
| | A29-577/587 | (11) | P-40N-40 | A29-1100/1221 (122) |
| P-40N-15 | A29-542/558 | (17) | | |
| | A29-564/576 | (13) | | |

Canadian serials
846/880 (35)
New Zealand serials (172)

| P-40N | NZ3120/3179 (60) |
|---|---|
| | NZ3181/3270 (90) |
| | NZ3272/3293 (22) |

## Models 81 and 87—Export Model Designations

Model 81—General identification for the early sharp-nosed models and specifically the first 200 aeroplanes of the original P-40 order for 524 for the US Army.

Model H81-A1—Two French orders for 100 and 85 equivalents of the P-40 except for French instruments and equipment and the unique reverse-movement French throttles. The first few were completed in French markings but none was delivered to France; Britain took them all as Tomahawk Is.

Model 81-A2—Improved 81As equivalent to the P-40B. Britain ordered 865 on direct-purchase orders as the Tomahawk I and IA and released 100 identified as 81-A3s to China for the AVG.

Model 81-A3—Unofficial designation for one hundred aircraft from the British 81-A2 contract diverted to the AVG; Curtiss 'paper' designation.

Model 81-AC*—Forty conversions of P-40C type airframes to British requirements; new Tomahawk mark unspecified.

* Special Curtiss designations to indicate conversion rather than originally-designated model.

502

Model 81-AG —Forty-four conversions of early P-40s to P-40G.

Model H81-B—One hundred and thirty-one US Army P-40Bs and 193 P-40Cs.

## Model 87

Significant revision of Model 81 resulting in new model number; 22 to US Army as P-40Ds.

Model 87-A1—Unspecified number ordered by France but not delivered; designation cancelled.

Model 87-A2—Twenty equivalents of the P-40D for Britain as Kittyhawk Is.

Model 87-A3—Five hundred and forty equivalents of the P-40E to Britain as Kittyhawk IIs.

Model 87-A4—P-40Es with British equipment provided under Lend-Lease as P-40E-1s (British Kittyhawk IAs).

Model 87-A5—Unspecified number made as part of 87-A4 order.

Model 87-B2—US Army P-40E.

Model 87-B3—1,311 US Army P-40Fs; 230 intended for Britain as Kittyhawk IIAs; -B3 designation retained for 700 P-40Ls.

Model 87-V, 87-W—5,220 US Army P-40Ns, 456 British Kittyhawk IVs.

Model 87X—Three conversions of the P-40K and P-40N to XP-40Q.

\* \* \*

### Dummy P-40s

Numerous non-flyable reproductions of 'P-40' aeroplanes have been built for various purposes. Serious consideration was given in 1941 to the production of wooden dummy P-40s to use as airfield decoys to draw enemy fire away from real P-40s hidden nearby or to cause confusion as to the actual number on hand. In China, wood-and-straw dummies were actually constructed and deployed on airfields used by the AVG.

Non-flyable dummy P-40 built of wood and evaluated for possible quantity production of airfield decoys. This one was photographed at Wright Field in April 1942.

503

The acute shortage of pursuit aeroplanes early in 1942 forced motion picture studios to construct dummy aeroplanes for scenes involving damage to or complete destruction of the aeroplane. The armed forces were quite co-operative in providing flyable military machines for action scenes but had nothing available for destruction.

Dummy P-40Es were virtually mass-produced for the spectacular Pearl Harbor attack scene of the film *Tora Tora Tora!* Since the few surviving P-40 models were too valuable to destroy, a cast was made from a complete Kittyhawk 1A (P-40E) and fibreglass shells were made up from it to fit over internal structure adapted from other more expendable aircraft.

# The End of the Line

Like the rest of the major US aeroplane builders, Curtiss-Wright was hit by the massive contract cancellations that followed the unexpected early end of the Second World War. None of the major military producers had civil designs ready for the postwar market, but some were producing military transports that had commercial potential or had straight military models that figured in the government's postwar planning. Such firms were able to stay in production, albeit on a greatly reduced scale; Curtiss-Wright had nothing available other than the CW-20/C-46 Commando. Plans were made for civil adaptations of this, but with easily-convertible examples available to the potential users directly from war-surplus stocks, this plan was dropped.

With only two experimental military models in hand for postwar delivery and no assurance of production orders, in 1946 Curtiss-Wright shut down all aeroplane plants except Columbus and transferred all units of the Aeroplane Division to the government-owned Columbus plant. A new four-engined civil freighter was developed there to the point of demonstrating a full-scale mock-up, but no aeroplanes were built.

After the unique semi-jet XF15C lost out to the Ryan FR-1 for a postwar Navy fighter order and the order for 87 four-jet F-87s was cancelled in favour of the Northrop F-89, Curtiss-Wright shut down the Aeroplane Division and sold its assets to North American, which soon reopened the plant for the production of F-86 Sabres.

The sale of the Aeroplane Division to North American included design rights to the former Curtiss and Curtiss-Wright aeroplanes. This resulted in some confusion in government paperwork relating to the aeroplanes for a while. Just as existing Travel Air aeroplanes had become Curtiss-Wrights in 1930, so did all Curtiss-Wrights become North Americans. In some postwar government records they actually appeared this way. Current airworthiness and registration papers, technical specifications, and statistical inventories identify all Curtiss and Curtiss-Wright designs as Curtiss-Wright but also identify 1929 and earlier Travel Air designs as Curtiss-Wright as well.

The last two Curtiss-Wright aeroplane designs completed were delivered after the war and are sufficiently different from previous designs in concept as well as in timing to justify separate presentation as representatives of the postwar era of design.

The first Curtiss aeroplane to have jet propulsion was the XF15C-1. It was a mixed-power aircraft with a piston engine in the nose and the turbojet behind the wing.

### XF15C-1 (Model 99*)

The US Navy approached the Jet Age cautiously, realizing that the poor acceleration characteristics of the early jet engines made them unsuitable for operation from aircraft carriers. Desiring both the speed advantages of jets and the short takeoff capability of piston-powered types, the Navy ordered unique composite-powered fighter prototypes from two companies, Ryan (XFR-1) and Curtiss (XF15C-1). These were of conventional configuration and construction except that a turbojet was buried in the fuselage aft of the cockpit.

The jet in the XF15C-1 was an Americanized version of the British de Havilland H1-B Goblin built by Allis-Chalmers and delivering 2,700 lb

* Last of the Buffalo design numbers.

The T-tail of the modified XF15C-1 was an aerodynamic innovation that was fifteen years ahead of its time. (*Warren M. Bodie*)

XF15C-1.

(1,225 kg) static thrust (one pound of thrust is equal to one horsepower at an airspeed of 375 mph (603 km/h) ). The nose engine was a 2,100 hp Pratt & Whitney R-2800-34W.

Three XF15C-1s were ordered in April 1944, using the designation and serial numbers of an earlier design that had been cancelled. The XF15C-1s were built at Buffalo with Navy serial numbers 01213/01215, but no popular name was assigned. A unique feature, compared to other jets, was that the jet exhausted a short distance behind the wing and under the fuselage instead of through a long tailpipe down the centre of the fuselage to a point behind the tail surfaces. The wings folded upward and the armament of four 20 mm cannon was in the centre section outboard of the propeller. The first aircraft was flown without the jet installed on 27 February, 1945, but crashed in May after installation of the engine.

During the succeeding test programme with the other two aircraft, the horizontal tail was converted to the T-type that was to become popular more than a decade later. On propeller power alone, the XF15C-1 had a top speed of 373 mph (600·27 km/h) at 25,300 ft (7,711 m). With the jet thrust added, the speed at this altitude increased to 469 mph (754·77 km/h).

The two surviving prototypes had development problems and were not delivered to the Navy until November 1946.

### XF15C-1

Single-seat fighter. One 2,100 hp Pratt & Whitney R-2800-34W and one 2,700 lb (1,225 kg) thrust Allis-Chalmers/de Havilland H1-B Goblin turbojet.

Span 48 ft (14·63 m); length 44 ft (13·41 m); height 15 ft 3 in (4·64 m); wing area 400 sq ft (37·16 sq m).

Empty weight 12,648 lb (5,737 kg); gross weight 16,630 lb (7,543 kg) or 18,698 lb (8,481 kg) overload.

Maximum speed (both engines) 469 mph (754·77 km/h) at 25,300 ft (7,711 m); initial climb (both engines) 5,020 ft/min (25·5 m/sec); service ceiling 41,800 ft (12,741 m); range 1,385 miles (2,229 km).

Armament—four 20 mm cannon.

## XP-87 Blackhawk (Model 29A)

XP-87 Blackhawk (Model 29A)—Curtiss-Wright stepped further into the dawning Jet Age with the all-jet XP-87, an all-weather and night interceptor powered by four 3,000 lb (1,360 kg) static thrust Westinghouse XJ34-WE-7 turbojets paired in two pods under the wings. The XP-87 carried on the St Louis numbering system but was built at Columbus. This two-seater evolved from the unbuilt Model 29, a similarly-configured attack type designed for the Army in 1945 as the XA-43. This was cancelled and the funds and Army serial numbers were transferred to the later XP-87 Blackhawk.

Armament was initially to be automatically-operated nose and tail turrets, each containing a pair of ·50-in calibre machine-guns, plus internally-mounted rockets. This was all changed before completion to

The XP-87 was taken by road to Muroc Dry Lake, California, for its first test flights.

508

The first all-jet Curtiss was the XP-87 Blackhawk, delivered in 1948.

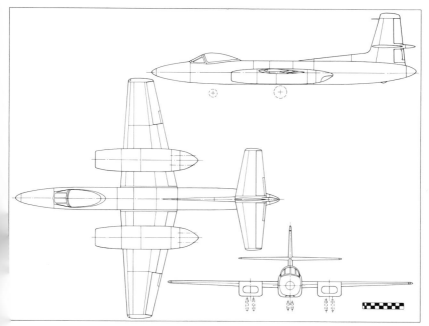

XP-87 Blackhawk.

four fixed 20 mm forward-firing cannon. Although it carried only a two-man crew, the XP-87 at 49,900 lb (22,634 kg) was very nearly the heaviest Curtiss or Curtiss-Wright aeroplane ever built, being exceeded only by some variants of the CW-20/C-46 series.

The first flight was at the Army Test Center at Muroc Dry Lake on 5 March, 1948. The aeroplane was trucked there over a very carefully surveyed route to ensure that the high load would pass safely under all bridges and overpasses. Initial performance of the XP-87, soon rede-signated XF-87, was promising, and an order for 57 F-87A fighter and 30 RF-87A photographic versions was placed on 10 June, 1948. However, the new Northrop XP-89 (XF-89) showed much more potential, so the F-87A order was cancelled in October and the funds were transferred to F-89 contracts. Work on the second XF-87 airframe, then in the process of conversion to the twin-engined XF-87A with 5,200 lb (2,359 kg) static thrust General Electric J-47 engines, was halted and the machine scrapped.

### XP-87 Blackhawk

Two-seat night fighter. Four 3,000 lb (1,360 kg) thrust Westinghouse XJ34-WE-7s.

Span 60 ft (18·28 m); length 62 ft 10 in (19·15 m); height 20 ft (6·09 m); wing area 600 sq ft (55·74 sq m).

Empty weight 25,930 lb (11,762 kg); gross weight 49,900 lb (22,634 kg).

Maximum speed 600 mph (965·59 km/h) at sea level; climb 35,000 ft (10,668 m) in 13·8 min; service ceiling 41,000 ft (12,497 m); range 1,000 miles (1,609 km).

Armament—four 20 mm cannon.

US Army serial numbers: 45-59600 (XP-87 No.1), 46-522 (XP-87 No.2 cancelled).

Curtiss-Wright had built its last aeroplane. Other Curtiss-Wright 'Flying Machines' illustrated here were built and flown, but they were not to be part of the illustrious Curtiss aeroplane legend. . . .

The jet-propelled KD2C-1 was a radio-controlled gunnery target, not a true aeroplane.

The four-propeller X-19 of 1963 was powered with two 2,200 hp Lycoming T-55 turbines and participated in government vertical-flight research programmes.

# Unverified Curtiss Aircraft Designations

The following information has been obtained from US Federal Aviation Agency records of aircraft identified as Curtiss, but the models and designations listed cannot be verified from presently available Curtiss technical data or period aviation publications. While it is possible that some are projects that were cancelled before completion, others are known to have been completed and flown. Some are known to be used models modified by owners who gave them revised designations that still reflect their Curtiss origins.

This incomplete information, listed alphabetically, is presented separately from the regular aircraft descriptions so that the coverage of actual and implied Curtiss or Curtiss-Wright model designations in this volume will be as complete as possible despite the lack of detail.

| Model | C/n | Registration | Remarks |
|---|---|---|---|
| A | 10 | 403V | Glider |
| Aircoach | CW-1H | 3436 | Hispano-Suiza engine |
| Alco Curtiss Allison | F-100 | 239K | OX-5 engine |
| Bird Wing | 1 | 1783 | |
| Bunting | — | 259Y | Single-seat open cockpit monoplane built by students at Curtiss-Wright Technical Institute, Glendale, California, in 1935. 36 hp Aeronca E-113 engine |
| Comet | 4 | 1347 | Not completed |
| Coupe | CW-1A | 3435 | Anzani engine, different aeroplane from CR-2 Coupe 627V, c/n 3001 |
| CW-2P | 2P-101 | 179M | Two-seat open cockpit monoplane, Anzani engine |
| Grasshopper | 1 | 981V | Glider |
| Pursuit | T.L.100 | 471 | |
| Scout EC-1 | — | 2120 | |
| Special | U-5442 | 1221 | |
| Temple Curtiss | A-1 | 6525 | Possibly Canadian-built |
| 2 Sport Trainer | 1-C | X-9741 | Anzani engine |
| 4 Commercial | 2-C | X-9742 | High wing 'full vision' cabin monoplane, Siemens-Halske engine |
| 5 Junior Transport | 3-C | X-9743 | High wing 'full vision' cabin monoplane, three 80 hp Anzani engines |

# APPENDIX I

# Type Certificates Issued to Commercial Curtiss Aeroplanes, 1927–46

## APPROVED TYPE CERTIFICATE (ATC)

Issued to aircraft that meet full licensing requirements for unlimited commercial operation. Approval usually granted as a result of manufacturer's test programme confirmed by government inspectors before the first article is delivered to the customer.

| ATC No. | Curtiss Model | Date Issued |
|---|---|---|
| 40 | OX-5 Robin | 28 May, 1928 |
| 63 | Challenger Robin | 15 Aug, 1928 |
| 68 | Robertson Robin (OX-5) | 29 Aug, 1928 |
| 69 | Robertson Robin (Challenger) | 29 Aug, 1928 |
| 103 | Falcon Mail (Liberty) | 22 Jan, 1929 |
| 143 | Robin C-1 | 17 June, 1929 |
| 144 | Robin C-2 | 16 May, 1929 |
| 159 | Thrush (Challenger) | 10 June, 1929 |
| 160 | Thrush (Challenger) | 10 June, 1929 |
| 182 | Fledgling Junior | 26 June, 1929 |
| 191 | Fledgling | 2 Aug, 1929 |
| 193 | Condor CO | 23 Oct, 1929 |
| 213 | Falcon Mail (Geared Conqueror) | 26 Aug, 1929 |
| 220 | Robin J-1 | 5 Sept, 1929 |
| 221 | Robin J-2 | 5 Sept, 1929 |
| 236 | Thrush J | 25 Sept, 1929 |
| 237 | Carrier Pigeon II | 25 Sept, 1929 |
| 261 | Thrush J | 24 Oct, 1929 |

| 266 | Fledgling J-1 | 14 Nov, 1929 |
| 268 | Robin W | 4 Nov, 1929 |
| 269 | Fledgling J-2 | 6 Nov, 1929 |
| 270 | Robin 4C | 6 Nov, 1929 |
| 309 | Robin 4C-1A | 3 April, 1930 |
| 347 | Kingbird D-1 | 16 Aug, 1930 |
| 348 | Kingbird D-2 | 16 Aug, 1930 |
| 397 | CW-1 Junior | 31 Jan, 1931 |
| 401 | CW-12Q | 12 Feb, 1931 |
| 406 | CW-12K | 23 Mar, 1931 |
| 407 | CW-12W | 23 Mar, 1931 |
| 411 | CW-16K | 7 April, 1931 |
| 425 | CW-15N Sedan | 4 June, 1931 |
| 426 | CW-15C Sedan | 10 June, 1931 |
| 440 | Kingbird D-3 | 6 Aug, 1931 |
| 442 | CW-A14D Sportsman | 13 Aug, 1931 |
| 444 | CW-15D Sedan | 22 Aug, 1931 |
| 463 | CW-16E Sport | 26 Feb, 1932 |
| 485 | CW-B14B Speedwing | 1 June, 1932 |
| 501 | T-32 Condor (CW-4) | 16 Mar, 1933 |
| 534 | AT-32 Condor | 16 April, 1934 |
| 547 | T-32C Condor | 16 July, 1934 |
| 582 | Courtney CA-1 Commuter | 3 Sept, 1935 |
| 589 | CW-19L Coupe | 3 Dec, 1935 |
| 629 | CW-19R, A-19R | 19 Feb, 1937 |

Postwar ATCs issued for conversion of
war-surplus C-46 models to civil use.

| ATC No. | Curtiss Model | ATC issued to | Date |
|---------|---------------|---------------|------|
| 772 | C-46A, D<br>C-46E<br>C-46F | Flying Tiger Line | 30 Sept, 1948<br>3 April, 1947<br>30 Sept, 1948 |
| 786 | C-46E | Curtiss-Wright Corp | 25 April, 1947 |
| 789 | C-46A, D<br>C-46F | L.B. Smith Aircraft Corp | 15 April, 1948<br>31 Jan, 1949 |
| 808 | C-46F | Skyways International Trading and Transport Corp | 23 Sept, 1948 |
| 2A-5 | C-46/CW-20T<br>Super C-46, C-46E | Tempo Design Corp | 20 Mar, 1956<br>28 May, 1958 |
| 3A-2 | C-46A, D<br>C-46F<br>C-46R | Airlift International | 6 May, 1953<br>23 Sept, 1949<br>12 Mar, 1957 |

CATEGORY 2 APPROVAL (MEMORANDUM APPROVAL)

Issued to some aircraft on an individual basis when they do not meet full ATC requirements but are satisfactory for limited commercial operation. Frequently assigned to ATC'd models that have been modified for special purposes to a degree that compromises full ATC compliance.

| Memo No. | Curtiss Model | Date Issued |
|---|---|---|
| 2-31 | Falcon Mail (Liberty) | Dec, 1928 superseded by ATC 103 |
| 2-37 | Falcon Cargo, c/n 5, D-12 engine | 2 Feb, 1929 |
| 2-59 | Fledgling, c/n 1 and on, B-1 and on | 9 July, 1929 |
| 2-71 | Falcon, c/n 6, Conqueror engine | 31 May, 1929 |
| 2-91 | Robin 'Spl.C', c/n 180, 210 | 8 July, 1929 |
| 2-122 | Kingbird J (Ex-C, c/n G-1) | 6 Sept, 1929 |
| 2-132 | Robin c/n 112, Hispano engine | 26 Sept, 1929 |
| 2-192 | Robin C-1 c/n 668, rigid undercarriage | 13 Mar, 1930 |
| 2-196 | Kingbird J-3 c/n G-2 | 26 Mar, 1930 |
| 2-198 | Robin 4C-1  c/n 769 | 3 April, 1930 |
| 2-210 | Thrush Special J c/n 1005 | 9 May, 1930 |
| 2-287 | Falcon Mail, c/n 3, Cyclone engine | 16 Oct, 1930 |
| 2-345 | Robin, Tank engine | 13 May, 1931 |
| 2-357 | CW-14C | 12 June, 1931 |
| 2-403 | CW-B14R c/n 2956, 1-seat c/n 2003, 2-seat | 9 Mar, 1932 |
| 2-442 | CW-1A c/n 3, Augustine engine | 11 Mar, 1933 |
| 2-472 | Fledgling J-1 Special, c/n B-22, Wright J-5 engine | 1 Mar, 1934 |
| 2-497 | Courtney CA-1 | 1 Jan, 1935 |
| 2-525 | CW-1S Salmson engine | 26 Sept, 1936 |
| 2-549 | CW-A22, 22B, Navy SNC-1 | 17 July, 1939 |

## CATEGORY III APPROVAL

Issued to pre-1927 designs for licensed commercial operation
in 1927 and later on basis of individual aircraft inspection
rather than conformance to requirements of an ATC or Memorandum
certificate.

| | |
|---|---|
| JN-4 series | Oriole |
| MF Seagull | Carrier Pigeon |
| HS-2L | Lark |

## LIMITED TYPE CERTIFICATE

Issued to surplus World War II and subsequent military aircraft
for limited commercial use that does not involve carriage of
persons or property for hire.    Issued to individuals, not to
the manufacturer.

| No. | Curtiss Model | Issued to | Date |
|---|---|---|---|
| LTC-16 | O-52 | Holmberg Aerial Survey Washington, DC | 6 May, 1947 |
| LTC-18 | P-40L, P-40N | Boardman C. Reed Pasadena, Cal | 8 May, 1947 |
| LTC-31 | AT-9, AT-9A | L. S. Rehr, Coral Gables, Florida | 14 Jan, 1948 |

## RESTRICTED CERTIFICATE

Similar to Limited Certificate, usually issued to surplus military models used for dusting and spraying, firefighting, skywriting, etc.

| | | | |
|---|---|---|---|
| AR-1 | P-40 series | Rogue River Valley Traffic Association | 21 May, 1951 |
| AR-19 | SB2C | Clayton V. Curtiss | 12 Oct, 1955 |

Introduction to
Appendices II to VI

# Identification of Aircraft
# Designed or Built by Curtiss

The following tables have been compiled to permit detailed identification of any Curtiss-designed or built aeroplane from knowledge of the civil registration or military serial number painted on the machine. Once this number is known, the tables provide the corresponding Curtiss or military model number, the Curtiss factory serial number (also called constructor's number, or c/n), reference to former or subsequent civil registrations, and changes of designation when appropriate.

Because of the lack of c/ns before 1927, the inconsistency of their application to 1934, and the incomplete records of subsequent assignments, c/ns are presented only for those aeroplanes where such information is complete for that model or is verified by registration records. Because of the extensive gaps, c/n columns are not included in the tables of military serial numbers, Appendices IV, V, and VI. Available c/ns will be found in the corresponding text.

Since the civil registrations or military serial numbers and the c/ns of most series-produced aeroplanes usually correspond sequentially, it has been possible to group some of the entries in these tables. For example, 261 Curtiss CW-1 Juniors were built, but unfortunately, the registration numbers were not consecutive for the entire run. The largest block of consecutive numbers for that model covered only 62 aeroplanes. These registrations were NC638V to NC699V and the corresponding c/ns were 1020 to 1081. These are presented in the appropriate columns as 638V/699V and 1020/1081, respectively. From such a parallel listing it is a matter of simple arithmetic to determine that the c/n of Junior NC650V is 1032.

While Curtiss was frequently issued blocks of consecutive civil registration numbers by the government, those were often scattered among different models in progress at the same time, so some aeroplane models are covered on a nearly individual basis. The Remarks column indicates significant changes to individual aeroplanes.

The reciprocal function of these tables, determining the identification numbers and c/ns assigned to various Curtiss models, is performed by the listings to be found in each aeroplane description in the text.

# United States Civil
# Registrations of Curtiss Aircraft, 1927–77

This appendix lists all of the US civil registration numbers applied to Curtiss-built civil aircraft at the factory and the civil registrations assigned to surplus Curtiss military models under private ownership except the C-46/R5C Commando. Coverage dates from 1927 since there was no prior requirement for the registration of US civil aircraft. Wherever possible, changes of registration are shown, as are the temporary US registrations assigned for use during the testing of Curtiss military aeroplanes built for other countries.

Because of frequent changes in their application, the current national identification prefix letter N and the second letters of pre-1948 registrations are not included in the identification column. Straight numerical registrations are arranged in ascending sequence; registrations with suffix letters are grouped alphabetically according to the suffix letter and then arranged numerically.

When US civil aircraft had to be registered, starting in 1927, many surplus World War I models kept their former military serial numbers as the required c/n. Some had entirely arbitrary c/ns while others had none at all. This number, when confirmed by registration records, appears in the c/n column.

Although Curtiss has delivered no civil aeroplanes since 1940, many World War II surplus models appeared on the civil register after the war. Also, because of the current popularity of antique aeroplanes, derelict military models and previously unregistered civil models are being sought out, restored to flying condition, and added to the civil register in the 1970s.

It will be noted that some aeroplanes appear in this listing with more than one US civil registration. This is particularly true of JN-4s and Robins that have been inactive for many years. When brought out of storage for restoration, the owners found that the original registrations had long since been cancelled and reissued to other aeroplanes as is the normal procedure. Latter-day numbers therefore had to be used. The same is true for exported models brought back into the US and given new registrations. There are other valid reasons for changing registration numbers, but these are the principal ones.

| Registration | Model | c/n | Remarks |
|---|---|---|---|
| 27/31 | Carrier Pigeon | 1/5 | C30 to 9344 |
| 33 | Carrier Pigeon | 7 | |
| 34 | JN-4D | - | |
| 35 | Carrier Pigeon | 9 | Also NR35 and 35Y |
| 37 | Carrier Pigeon | 11 | |
| 38 | JN-4D | - | |
| 39 | Fledgling J-1 | B-22 | Was NC8691 |
| 42 | JN-4C | 5010 | OXX-6 |
| 43 | JN-4 | - | |
| 45 | JN-4D | 3138 | |
| 51 | JN-4C | 6150 | |
| 52 | JN-4C | - | JN-4D wings |
| 53 | JN-4D | - | |
| 54 | JN-4D | - | |
| 56 | JN-4D, F-boat | - | To JN-4D Special C2044, 56 reissued to F-boat. |
| 58 | CW-15D | 15C-2212 | Was 15-C NC12303, NS-4Y. |
| 61, 62 | JN-4D | - | Also in FAA records as Orioles |
| 63 | Lark | 10 | Formerly 1052 |
| 66 | JN-4D | 6000 | To 383 |
| 68 | JN-4D | - | |
| 69 | CW-19L Coupe | 19L-1 | To CW-19W |
| 73 | MF | 5553 | |
| 74 | JN-4D | 7623 | Hispano-Suiza |
| 82 | JN-4C, JN-4D | - | At different times |
| 90 | JN-6H-E | - | Hispano-Suiza E |

| 92  | JN-4D, Oriole          | -          | C-6 engine in Racing Oriole |
|-----|------------------------|------------|-----------------------------|
| 102 | JN-4C                  | 10875      |                             |
| 109 | JN-4C                  | -          |                             |
| 111 | JN-4C                  | 444        | Ex-US Army 39158 now in Canadian museum as RCAF C227 |
| 121 | JN-4D                  | -          |                             |
| 122 | JN-4C                  | -          |                             |
| 124 | MF-2 Seagull           | -          | Packard A engine            |
| 141 | Seagull Amphibian, JN-4D | 1535 (JN) | C-6 engine in Seagull       |
| 147 | JN-4D                  | -          |                             |
| 159 | JN-4D                  | 5063       |                             |
| 169 | JN-4D                  | -          |                             |
| 177 | JN-4C                  | -          |                             |
| 182 | JN-4D                  | -          |                             |
| 183 | JN-4D                  | 2443       |                             |
| 189 | JN-4D                  | 3161       |                             |
| 190 | JN-4C                  | -          |                             |
| 194 | JN-6H                  | 5222       | OXX-6                       |
| 204 | JN-6H                  | -          |                             |
| 212 | Model unknown          | -          | K-6 engine                  |
| 215 | R-4L                   | -          | Gates Flying Service        |
| 220 | JN-4C                  | -          |                             |
| 221 | MF Seagull             | -          |                             |
| 224 | MF Seagull             | 16         | C-6A engine                 |
| 225 | JN-4C                  | -          |                             |
| 238 | JN-4C                  | C-459      |                             |
| 244 | JN-4C                  | -          | OXX-6 Special               |

| 249 | MF Seagull | - | C-6 engine |
| 250 | Standard J-1 | - | Curtiss rebuild, K-6 engine |
| 255 | JN-4C | - | |
| 257 | MF Seagull | - | Henry Ford Museum |
| 266 | JN-4D | - | |
| 271 | JN-6H | - | Changed to OX-5 |
| 273 | JN-4D | - | |
| 283 | JN-4D | 435 | |
| 297 | JN-4D | 388 | Hispano-Suiza A |
| 298 | JN-4D | - | Hispano-Suiza |
| 304 | F-boat | A4395 | OXX-6 |
| 308 | JN-4D | 3046 | |
| 318 | HS-2L | A1191 | LWF-built: to 3732 |
| 322 | JN-4D | 33932 | |
| 326 | JN-4D | 117-A | |
| 328 | JN-4C | - | |
| 352 | JN-4D | 33967 | Hispano-Suiza |
| 374 | JN-4C | 34153 | |
| 383 | JN-4D | 6000 | Formerly 66 |
| 471 | Curtiss Pursuit | T.L.100 | |
| 518 | JN-4C | 1203 | |
| 519 | JN-4D | 1394 | |
| 540 | Fledgling | B-1 | Formerly 7992 c/n G-3 |
| 601 | JN-4C | 250 | |
| 604 | JN-4D | 1673 | |
| 611 | JN-6H | 1 | |
| 652 | HS-2L | A1373 | LWF-built; Western Air Express |
| 653 | JN-4D | - | |

| | | | |
|---|---|---|---|
| 685 | JN-4C | 884 | |
| 686 | JN-4C | - | |
| 695 | JN-4D | - | |
| 711 | JN-4C | - | |
| 720 | JN-4D | - | |
| 721 | JN-4D | - | JN-4C wings |
| 723 | JN-4D | - | |
| 724 | JN-4D | 34050 | |
| 739 | JN-4D | - | |
| 741 | JN-4C | - | |
| 742 | JN-4D | - | |
| 745 | JN-4D | - | |
| 753 | JN-4D | 51928 | |
| 778 | JN-4D | - | |
| 780 | JN-4D | D4-1166 | |
| 788 | JN-4D | - | |
| 810 | JN-4C | C-476 | |
| 816 | JN-4D | - | |
| 818 | JN-6H or JN-4H | - | |
| 819 | JN-4D | - | OXX-6 |
| 823 | JN-4D | - | |
| 826 | JN-4D | 100 Sub | |
| 833 | JN-4D | - | |
| 853 | X-100 | 1 | |
| 859 | Oriole | - | C-6 engine, long wings |
| 860 | JN-4D | 577 | |
| 862 | JN-4D | 652100 | |
| 863 | JN-4D | - | |
| 895 | JN-4D | - | |

| | | | |
|---|---|---|---|
| 903 | MF Seagull | A5543 | Crawford Museum, Cleveland, Ohio. |
| 908 | JN-4C | - | |
| 923 No.1 | JN-4C | - | |
| 923 No.2 | TP-40N | 33915 | Ex-Army 44-47923 |
| 946 | JN-4D | - | |
| 954 | JN-4D | - | |
| 957 | JN-4D | - | |
| 965 | JN-4D | 3634 | |
| 966 | JN-4D | - | |
| 971 | JN-4C | - | |
| 985 | JN-4D | - | |
| 1028 | JN-4D | - | |
| 1039 | JN-4C | 108 | |
| 1040 | JN-4D | 44411 | |
| 1041 | JN-4D | - | |
| 1042 | JN-4D | 44326 | |
| 1043 | JN-4D | 44348 | |
| 1044 | JN-4D | - | |
| 1052 | Lark | 10 | To 63 |
| 1056 | MF Seagull | RAL 29 | Rogers Airlines rebuild |
| 1063 | Lark | - | |
| 1078 | JN-4D | - | |
| 1104 | JN-4D | - | Ontario, Canada museum |
| 1128 | JN-4C | 2727 | |
| 1134 | JN-4C | - | |
| 1135 | MF Seagull | - | Hispano-Suiza |
| 1143 | JN-4C | - | |
| 1147 | JN-4D | - | |

| 1149 | JN-4D | 1250 | |
|---|---|---|---|
| 1152 | JN-4D | 3676 | Anzani radial |
| 1153 | JN-4D | - | |
| 1154 | JN-4D | 1125 | |
| 1168 | Johnson-Curtiss | - | JN-4C wings on home-built fuselage |
| 1170 | JN-4C | 11915 | |
| 1176 | JN-4D | - | |
| 1190 | JN-4D | 5366 | |
| 1202 | JN-4D | - | |
| 1213 | JN-4D | - | |
| 1217 | JN-4D | 34135 | |
| 1219 | JN-4D | 35973 | |
| 1221 | Curtiss Special | U-5442 | OX-5, built 1916 |
| 1234 | JN-4D | 2435 | |
| 1247 | JN-4C | - | High-lift wings |
| 1271 | JN-4D | - | |
| 1274 | JN-6H | 44264 | |
| 1276 | Hawk 75 | 12327 | Fixed undercarriage demonstrator |
| 1277 | JN-4C | F.G.1 | Frank Gerbino rebuild |
| 1277 | Hawk 75 | 12328 | Fixed undercarriage demonstrator |
| 1295 | JN-4D | - | |
| 1298 | JN-4D | 835543 | |
| 1302 | JN-4D | 352 | |
| 1350 | JN-4D | 3044 | Pioneer village museum |
| 1371 | JN-4D | 3334 | |
| 1401 | JN-4D | 1401 | |

| 1414 | N-9 | - | JN-4D wings |
|------|-----|---|-------------|
| 1442 | JN-4D | 103 | |
| 1446 | JN-4D | M-843 | |
| 1461 | JN-4C | 1461 | |
| 1481 | JN-4C | - | |
| 1495 | JN-4D | 47391 | |
| 1500 | JN-4D | 33986 | |
| 1501 | JN-4D | 4002 | |
| 1506 | JN-4 | - | |
| 1508 | JN-4D | - | |
| 1510 | JN-4D | - | |
| 1518 | JN-4D | - | |
| 1522 | JN-4C | - | |
| 1537 | MF Seagull | 5520 | NAF-built, C-6A engine |
| 1575 | JN-4C | - | |
| 1580 | JN-4C | - | |
| 1581 | JN-4C | 2000 | Rebuilt 1926 |
| 1583 | JN-4D | - | |
| 1593 | JN-4D | - | |
| 1627 | JN-4D | 3603 | |
| 1639 | JN-4C | 4048 | Rebuilt 1927 |
| 1660 | Oriole | 189 | K-6 engine, restored 1970s |
| 1666 | JN-4H | 386 | |
| 1703 | JN-4C | - | |
| 1739 | JN-4D | - | |
| 1744 | JN-4D | 5220 | |
| 1783 | Curtiss Bird Wing | 1 | |

| | | | |
|---|---|---|---|
| 1786 | JN-4C | 11338 | |
| 1789 | Oriole | - | Hispano-Suiza |
| 1793 | JN-4H | - | Hispano-Suiza |
| 1800 | JN-4H | - | |
| 1801 | JN-4D | 560 | |
| 1803 | R-4 | - | German BMW engine |
| 1812 | JN-4D | - | |
| 1821 | JN-4D | 11741 | |
| 1834 | JN-4D | 3898 | |
| 1839 | JN-6H | - | |
| 1849 | HS-2L | A1145 | LWF-built |
| 1870 | JN-4D | 5001 | |
| 1872 | MF-2 Seagull | 505 | 1923 rebuild, C-6 engine |
| 1881 | JN-4D | 108 | |
| 1882 | MF Seagull | - | |
| 1883 | JN-4D | 44350 | OXX-6 |
| 1884 | JN-4D | - | |
| 1887 | JN-4C | - | |
| 1947 | JN-4C | M708 | |
| 1961 | JN-4D | AL-14 | |
| 1964 | JN-4D | 427 | |
| 1966 | JN-4C | 33788 | |
| 2000 | JN-4D | - | |
| 2001 | JN-6H | - | |
| 2002 | JN-6H | - | |
| 2009 | JN-4H | 101 | |
| 2014 | MF Seagull | 1 | K-6 engine |
| 2022 | JN-4C | 335 | |
| 2044 | JN-4D Special | 3 | Sikorsky monoplane wing; was 56 |

| | | | |
|------|--------------------|--------|----------------------------|
| 2060 | HS-2L | - | |
| 2066 | MF Seagull | - | Hispano or OXX-6 |
| 2110 | JN-4D | - | |
| 2120 | Curtiss EC-1 | | |
| | Scout | - | |
| 2139 | JN-4D | | |
| 2147 | JN-4D | 34133 | |
| 2151 | JN-4H | - | |
| 2172 | MF Seagull | A5483 | Hispano-Suiza, US Naval |
| | | | Aviation museum |
| 2188 | JN-4D | 44305 | |
| 2202 | JN-4C | - | |
| 2206 | JN-4C | - | Aeromarine 39 wings |
| 2221 | JN-4D | 105 | Remodelled 1928 |
| 2222 | JN-4D | - | |
| 2224 | JN-4C | - | Remodelled |
| 2226 | JN-4D | - | |
| 2287 | JN-4F (Special) | 4 | Sikorsky monoplane |
| | | | wing - 3 seat |
| 2283 | JN-4D | - | |
| 2310 | JN-4D | 1072 | |
| 2320 | MF Seagull | 5500 | Hispano-Suiza A |
| 2323 | MF Seagull | 5495 | Hispano-Suiza |
| 2324 | MF Seagull | 5493 | Hispano-Suiza |
| 2338 | JN-4D | - | |
| 2351 | JN-4D | - | |
| 2360 | JN-4D | - | |
| 2361 | MF Seagull | - | C-6 engine |
| 2373 | JN-4D | - | High-lift wings |
| 2374 | JN-4H | 42 | |

| 2382 | MF Seagull | - | Hispano-Suiza E-2 |
|---|---|---|---|
| 2383 | MF Seagull | 5536 | Wright J-5B |
| 2400 | JN-4D | - | Hispano-Suiza, High-lift wings |
| 2404 | JN-4D | 5360 | Restored 1968 |
| 2416 | JN-4D | 44407 | |
| 2420 | HS-2L (6 seat) | A-1981 | Western Air Express |
| 2421 | JN-4D | 553 | Chicago Museum |
| 2440 | JN-4D | - | |
| 2511 | JN-4C | - | |
| 2552 | JN-4D | 120 | |
| 2591 | JN-4D | - | |
| 2603 | MF Seagull | - | |
| 2611 | JN-4D | - | |
| 2613 | JN-4D | - | |
| 2620 | JN-4D | 1564 | |
| 2623 | JN-4D | - | |
| 2631 | JN-4D | 2535 | |
| 2688 | Oriole | - | OX-5 |
| 2711 | JN-4C Special | - | Remodel |
| 2723 | JN-4C | - | Special clipped wing |
| 2758 | JN-4D | 10 | |
| 2810 | JN-4D | - | |
| 2821 | HS-2L | A2222 | Gallaudet-built |
| 2822 | JN-4D | - | OXX-6 |
| 2831 | JN-4C | - | OXX-6 |
| 2877 | Oriole | - | Hispano-Suiza, short wings |
| 2889 | JN-4D | - | |
| 2926 | JN-4H | 34044 | Change to OX-5 |

| | | | |
|---|---|---|---|
| 2932 | HS-2L | A2021 | |
| 2939 | JN-4D | - | Engine changes for post World War II airshows |
| 2947 | MF Seagull | - | |
| 2970 | JN-4D | - | Extended lower wing |
| 2975 | JN-4D | - | |
| 2978 | MF Seagull | - | |
| 2980 | JN-4D | 33847 | |
| 2992 | JN-4D | - | |
| 3089 | Oriole | - | Sikorsky monoplane wing |
| 3098 | JN-4C | 117 | |
| 3112 | JN-4C | - | |
| 3121 | JN-4C | 1450 | |
| 3133 | Kingbird C | G-1 | Prototype; to J by engine change |
| 3231 | MF Seagull | RAL-20 | Rogers Airline rebuild, C-6 engine |
| 3236 | JN-4C | - | |
| 3240 | JN-4D | - | |
| 3271 | JN-4D | - | |
| 3302 | JN-4D | - | |
| 3324, 3325 | JN-4D | - | |
| 3333 | JN-4C | - | |
| 3346 | JN-4D | - | |
| 3354 | JN-4D | - | |
| 3356 | JN-4C | - | |
| 3358 | JN-4D | - | |
| 3365 | JN-4C | - | |
| 3378 | F-Boat | - | OX-5. Also Pusher replica by Timm. |

531

| | | | |
|---|---|---|---|
| 3383 | JN-4C | - | |
| 3386 | JN-4C | - | |
| 3387 | HS-2L | A-1162 | LWF-built, 6-seat |
| 3397 | JN-4C | 20 | |
| 3406 | JN-4D | - | |
| 3420 | JN-4D | - | |
| 3426 | JN-4D | - | |
| 3433 | JN-4C | - | |
| 3434 | JN-4C | - | |
| 3435 | Coupe | CW-1A | |
| 3436 | Aircoach | CW-1H | |
| 3471 | JN-4C | - | |
| 3482 | JN-4C | - | |
| 3484 | JN-4D | - | |
| 3485 | JN-4C | - | |
| 3486, 3487 | JN-4D | - | |
| 3489 | JN-4C | - | |
| 3492 | JN-4D | - | |
| 3541 | JN-4D | - | |
| 3544 | JN-4D | - | |
| 3554 | JN-4C | - | |
| 3563 | MF Seagull | 30 | K-6 engine |
| 3564 | JN-4D | - | |
| 3575 | JN-4C | - | |
| 3576 | JN-4D | - | |
| 3578 | JN-4D | - | |
| 3582, 3583 | JN-4D | - | |
| 3589 | JN-6H | - | |
| 3590 | JN-4D | - | |
| 3591 | JN-4D | 3801 | |

| | | | |
|---|---|---|---|
| 3630 | JN-4D | - | OXX-6 |
| 3636 | JN Special | - | |
| 3645 | JN-4D | - | |
| 3677 | JN-4D | - | |
| 3678, 3679 | JN-4C | - | |
| 3681 | JN-4D | - | |
| 3683 | JN-4D | - | |
| 3691 | JN-4D | - | |
| 3693 | JN-4D | 438 | |
| 3719 | JN-4D | - | |
| 3732 | HS-2L | A-1191 | LWF-built; was 318 |
| 3742 | JN-4D Special | - | |
| 3760 | JN-4D | - | |
| 3768 | JN-4D | - | |
| 3769 | JN-4D | - | |
| 3770 | F-Boat | 5 | Union 6 engine |
| 3811 | JN-4D | - | |
| 3812 | JN-4C | 999 | |
| 3813 | JN-4D | - | |
| 3816 | JN-4D | - | |
| 3868 | JN-4D | - | |
| 3871 | JN | - | |
| 3872 | JN-4D | - | |
| 3883 | JN-4D | - | With C-wings |
| 3896 | JN-4D | 3610 | Hall-Scott A-7A engine |
| 3897 | JN-4D | - | |
| 3918 | JN-6H | 3919 | |
| 3935 | JN-4D | - | |
| 3937 | JN-4D | - | |
| 3940 | JN-4D | - | |

| | | | |
|---|---|---|---|
| 3974 | JN-4D | – | |
| 3975 | JN-4C | C-1289 | |
| 4032 | JN-4D | – | |
| 4033 | JN-4D | – | |
| 4052 | JN-4D | – | |
| 4059 | JN-4D | 5365 | |
| 4061 | JN-4D | – | |
| 4063 | JN-6H | – | |
| 4067 | JN-4C | – | |
| 4069 | JN-4D | – | |
| 4093 | JN-4D | 113 | |
| 4100 | JN-4D | – | |
| 4153 | JN-4C | – | OXX-6, JN-4D wings |
| 4159 | JN-4D | – | |
| 4199 | JN-4D | 3809 | |
| 4210 | JN-4C | – | |
| 4217 | JN-4C | – | |
| 4222 | JN-4C | – | |
| 4230 | JN-4H or 6H | 81755 | |
| 4236 | JN-4D | – | |
| 4249 | JN-4C | – | |
| 4284 | JN-4D | – | OXX-6 |
| 4292 | JN-4D | 3327 | Gates Flying Circus |
| 4294 | JN-4C | – | |
| 4295 | JN-4D | – | |
| 4296 | JN-4D | – | |
| 4362 | JN-4H | – | |
| 4363 | P-40K-5 | – | Ex-US Army 42-9733 |
| 4435 | JN-4C | – | |
| 4436 | JN-4D | – | |

| 4439 | JN-4C | - | |
|---|---|---|---|
| 4490 | JN-4D | - | |
| 4491 | JN-4D | - | |
| 4492 | JN-4D | - | |
| 4565 | JN-4D | 212 | |
| 4652 | JN-4D | - | |
| 4726 | JN-6H | - | |
| 4727 | JN-4D | - | |
| 4754 | MF Seagull | 27 | C-6 engine |
| 4757 | JN-4D | 3725 | |
| 4790 | JN-4D | 1 | |
| 4802 | JN-4D | 44340 | |
| 4819 | MF Seagull | - | Hispano-Suiza |
| 4875 | JN-4D | - | |
| 4927 | JN-4D | - | |
| 4972 | JN-4C | - | |
| 4973 | JN-4C | - | |
| 4978 | MF Seagull | - | Hispano-Suiza |
| 4984 | JN-4D | - | OXX-6, de Havilland 6 wings |
| 5049 | Robin | G-1 | 1st prototype, OX-5 |
| 5073 | JN-4C | 990 | |
| 5094 | JN-4D | 44387 | |
| 5096 | JN-4D | - | |
| 5097 | JN-4D | - | |
| 5114 | JN-4D | 3034 | Curtiss Flying Service 1928 |
| 5145 | JN-4D | - | |
| 5151 | JN-4C | - | |
| 5154 | JN-4C | - | |

| | | | |
|---|---|---|---|
| 5158 | JN-4D | 585UB | |
| 5160 | JN-4C | - | |
| 5162 | JN-4D | 278 | |
| 5190 | JN-4D | 3030 | 3-seat |
| 5193 | JN-4C | - | |
| 5251 | JN-4D | - | |
| 5260 | JN-4D | - | OXX-6 |
| 5268 | JN-4H | - | |
| 5269 | JN-4D | - | |
| 5271 | JN-4C | - | |
| 5324 | JN-6H | 183 | Hispano-Suiza |
| 5331 | JN-4C | - | |
| 5332 | JN-4C | - | OXX-6 |
| 5356 | JN-4C | - | |
| 5362 | JN-4C | - | |
| 5377 | JN-4D | - | |
| 5391 | JN-4D | 396 | |
| 5419 | HS-2L | 111 | LWF rebuild - Western Air Express 6-seat |
| 5446 | Robin | G-2 | 2nd prototype; OX-5 |
| 5449 | JN-4D | - | |
| 5450 | MF Seagull | A-4408 | K-6 engine |
| 5451 | JN-4C | VC-51 | |
| 5599 | JN-4D | - | |
| 5620 | JN-4D | 2 | |
| 5627 | JN remodelled | - | Hall-Scott A-7A engine |
| 5647 | JN-4C | - | |
| 5648 | N-9 | - | OX-5 |
| 5649 | JN-4D | 1525 | |

| | | | |
|---|---|---|---|
| 5653 | JN-4D | - | |
| 5662 | JN-4D | - | |
| 5705 | MF Seagull | 24 | C-6 engine, 4-seat |
| 5792 | MF Seagull | 400 | Hispano-Suiza, 5-seat |
| 5826 | JN-4D | - | |
| 5931 | JN-4D | - | Post WWII rebuild, Ranger engine |
| 5988 | Falcon Mail | 1 | Conqueror engine |
| 6602 | JN-4D | 136 | |
| 6604 | JN-4D | 5219 | |
| 6703 | JN-4D Special | - | Sikorsky monoplane wing |
| 6812 | JN-4D | 3720 | Gnome |
| 6831 | Robin | G-3 | Third prototype, Challenger engine |
| 6845 | HS-2L | A-1301 | LWF-built |
| 7142/7145 | Robin | 3/6 | OX-5. 7145 restored with Continental R-670 |
| 7276 | Standard J | 22787 | Curtiss rebuild |
| 7431 | Falcon Mail | 5 | D-12 engine |
| 7455 | Falcon | 3 | D-12E to Cyclone |
| 7464 | JN-6H | 5514 | Packard A engine |
| 7496/7510 | Robin | 7/21 | OX-5 |
| 7568 | Thrush | G-1 | 1st prototype; engine change to Wright J-6-7 and sold to Venezuela |
| 7670 | JN-4D | 44262 | |
| 7682 | JN-4D | GWR-1 | Hispano-Suiza; G. W. Rogers rebuild |
| 7697 | JN-4C | B2937 | |

537

| | | | |
|---|---|---|---|
| 7701 | Oriole | 3309 | |
| 7748/7754 | Robin | 22/28 | OX-5. 7752 to Hispano-Suiza |
| 7804 | MF Seagull | - | Hispano-Suiza |
| 7903/7908 | Robin | 29/34 | OX-5 |
| 7909/7913 | Robin B | 35/39 | OX-5 |
| 7915 | Robin | 41 | OX-5 |
| 7917 | JN-4C | 100-A | |
| 7947 | MF Seagull | A-122 | C-6 engine |
| 7992 | Fledgling | G-3 | To 540  c/n B-1 |
| 8300, 8301 | Robin | 175, 173 | OX-5 |
| 8302/8304 | Robin | 177/179 | OX-5 |
| 8305/8307 | Robin B | 181, 183, 185 | |
| 8308/8310 | Robin B | 187/189 | |
| 8311/8319 | Robin B | 191/199 | 8319 to C-1 |
| 8322 | Robin | 190 | OX-5 |
| 8323/8326 | Robin | 200/203 | OX-5 |
| 8327/8329 | Robin B | 205, 207, 209 | |
| 8330/8332 | Robin B | 211/213 | |
| 8333 | Robin B | 215 | |
| 8334, 8335 | Robin C | 204, 206 | |
| 8336 | Robin 4C | 208 | |
| 8337 | Robin C Special | 210 | Challenger |
| 8338 | Robin C | 214 | |
| 8339, 8340 | Robin B | 216, 217 | |
| 8341/8343 | Robin B | 219/221 | |
| 8344/8346 | Robin B | 223/225 | |
| 8347/8349 | Robin B | 227/229 | |

| | | | |
|---|---|---|---|
| 8350 | Robin C | 230 | |
| 8351/8353 | Robin B | 231/233 | |
| 8354/8356 | Robin B | 235/237 | 8356 rebuilt as 3277G |
| 8357/8359 | Robin B | 239/241 | |
| 8360/8362 | Robin B | 243/245 | |
| 8363 | Robin B | 247 | Tank V502 engine |
| 8364 | Robin C-1 | 218 | To CF-AHF |
| 8365 | Robin C | 222 | |
| 8366/8368 | Robin C | 226, 234, 238 | |
| 8369/8372 | Robin C | 242, 246, 250, 254 | |
| 8373/8375 | Robin B | 248, 249, 251 | |
| 8376 | Robin B | 252 | To W with Warner engine |
| 8377/8379 | Robin B | 253, 255, 256 | 8379 to Menasco engine |
| 8381/8383 | Robin B | 257/259 | |
| 8387/8389 | Robin B | 261/263 | |
| 8390 | Robin C | 260 | |
| 8391 | Robin C | 264 | |
| 8392/8394 | Robin B | 265/267 | |
| 8395 | Robin C | 268 | |
| 8396/8398 | Robin B | 269/271 | |
| 8399 | Robin C | 272 | |
| 8660/8669 | Fledgling | B-2/B-11 | 8663, 8667 converted to J-1 |
| 8670 | Falcon Mail | 16 | Liberty engine |
| 8671/8679 | Fledgling | B-12/B-20 | |

539

| | | | |
|---|---|---|---|
| 8690, 8691 | Fledgling J-1 | B-21, B-22 | J-6-5 engines; 8691 to NS39 |
| 8692/8699 | Fledgling | B-23/B-30 | |
| 9110 | Hawk P-6 | 17 | Demonstrator, was NR9W |
| 9142 | Thrush J | G-3 | Challenger engine to Wright J-6-7 |
| 9200/9202 | Robin B | 273/275 | |
| 9203/9205 | Robin B | 277/279 | |
| 9206, 9207 | Robin C | 276, 280 | 9206 to C-1 |
| 9208/9210 | Robin B | 281/283 | |
| 9211 | Robin C | 284 | |
| 9212/9214 | Robin B | 285/287 | |
| 9215 | Robin C | 288 | |
| 9216/9218 | Robin B | 289/291 | |
| 9219 | Robin C | 292 | |
| 9220/9222 | Robin B | 293/295 | |
| 9223 | Robin C | 296 | Restored with Lycoming R-680 |
| 9224/9226 | Robin B | 297/299 | |
| 9227 | Robin C | 300 | |
| 9228 | Robin B | 301 | |
| 9229 | Robin C | 302 | |
| 9241 | Robin B | 303 | |
| 9242 | Robin C | 304 | |
| 9243 | Robin B | 305 | To Corrigan's J-1 |
| 9244 | Robin C | 306 | |
| 9245 | Robin B | 307 | |
| 9246 | Robin C | 308 | |
| 9247/9249 | Robin B | 309, 313, 311 | |

| | | | | |
|---|---|---|---|---|
| 9250 | Robin C-1 | 312 | | |
| 9251 | Robin C | 314 | | |
| 9252 | Robin C-1 | 316 | | |
| 9253 | Robin B | 317 | | |
| 9254 | Robin C | 318 | | |
| 9255 | Robin B | 319 | | |
| 9256 | Robin C-1 | 320 | | |
| 9257 | Robin B | 321 | | To M with Tank engine |
| 9258 | Robin C | 322 | | |
| 9259 | Robin B | 323 | | |
| 9260, 9261 | Robin C | 324, 326 | | |
| 9262 | Robin C-2 | 327 | | |
| 9263 | Robin C | 328 | | |
| 9264, 9265 | Robin B | 325, 329 | | |
| 9266 | Robin C-2 | 330 | | |
| 9267 | Robin B | 331 | | |
| 9268 | Robin C | 332 | | |
| 9269 | Robin B | 333 | | |
| 9270 | Robin C-1 | 334 | | |
| 9271 | Robin B | 335 | | |
| 9272 | Robin C | 336 | | |
| 9273 | Robin C-2 | 338 | | Seaplane |
| 9274/9276 | Robin C-1 | 340, 344, 360 | | 9275, 9276 to C-2 |
| 9277, 9278 | Robin C | 348, 350 | | |
| 9279/9281 | Robin C-1 | 352, 354, 356 | | |
| 9282 | Robin C-1 | 358 | | |
| 9283 | Robin B | 337 | | Restored as C-1 |
| 9284/9286 | Robin B | 339, 341, 343 | | |

| | | | |
|---|---|---|---|
| 9287/9290 | Robin B | 345, 347, 349, 351 | |
| 9291 | Robin C-1 | 362 | Restricted licence |
| 9292/9294 | Robin C-1 | 364, 366, 368 | |
| 9296/9299 | Robin B | 353, 355, 357, 359 | |
| 9344 | Carrier Pigeon I | K-5015-4 | was C-30 |
| 9741 | Sport Trainer | 1C | |
| 9742 | Commercial | 2C | |
| 9743 | Jr. Transport | 3C | |
| 9787 | Thrush J | G-2 | Second prototype |
| 9950 | P-40N-35 | 26149 | Ex-Army 44-7983, restored 1977 (c/n doubtful) |
| 10044 | MF Boat | A1204 | K-6 engine |
| 10059,10060 | Robin | 43, 44 | |
| 10260 | Oriole | JK-1101 | Hispano-Suiza |
| 10362 | Pusher | 1 | Replica 1912 Pusher, built in 1930 by private individual |
| 10389 | JN-4C | 1898 | |
| 10492 | HS-2L | A9816 | |
| 10626 | P-40N-30 | - | Under restoration 1977 |
| 10900/10925 | CW-1 Junior | 1082/1107 | |
| 10926,10927 | CW-15N Sedan | 15N-2201, 2202 | |
| 10928 | CW-15C Sedan | 15C-2203 | |
| 10929/10940 | CW-1 Junior | 1108/1119 | |
| 10942/10999 | CW-1 Junior | 1120/1177 | |

| | | | |
|---|---|---|---|
| 11122 | Kittyhawk I | 15286 | Ex-RAF AK905, RCAF 1052, CF-OGZ; to N40PE |
| 11700, 11701 | CW-12W | 12W-2019, 2020 | |
| 11703/11707 | CW-16K | 16K-2007/ 2011 | |
| 11708/11712 | CW-12Q | 12Q-2033/ 2037 | |
| 11713 | CW-12W | 12W-2038 | |
| 11714 | CW-12Q | 12Q-2039 | |
| 11715, 11716 | CW-12W | 12W-2040, 2041 | |
| 11718 | CW-16K | 16K-2012 | |
| 11729/11732 | BT-32 Condor II | 59/62 | To Peruvian Air Force OB-11A/OB-11D |
| 11756 | CT-32 Condor II | 63 | Argentine Navy I-E-301 |
| 11780 | CA-1 Courtney | 102 | Amphibian |
| 11781 | CW-19R | 19R-1 | |
| 11800/11804 | CW-1 Junior | 1178/1182 | |
| 11805/11807 | CW-15C Sedan | 15C-2205/ 2207 | 11807 to CW-15D |
| 11808/11815 | CW-1 Junior | 1183/1190 | |
| 11816 | Kingbird D-3 | 2016 | To CF-BVG |
| 11817/11860 | CW-1 Junior | 1191/1234 | |
| 11861 | CW-15C Sedan | 15C-2207 | |
| 11862 | CW-15N Sedan | 15N-2208 | |
| 11864 | CW-15C Sedan | 15C-2210 | To Mexico as XB-DEE |
| 11865/11899 | CW-1 Junior | 1235/1268 | |

| 12299, 12301 | CW-1 Junior | 1269, 1271 | |
| 12302 | CW-15C Sedan | 15C-2211 | |
| 12303 | CW-15C Sedan | 15C-2212 | To ISD NS-4Y, NS-58 |
| 12304 | CW-15D Sedan | 15D-2213 | |
| 12305 | CW-1 Junior | 1272 | |
| 12306 | CW-3 Teal | 1501 | Amphibian; also Duckling |
| 12307 | CW-A14D | 14-2006 | |
| 12310 | CW-A14D | 2007 | |
| 12311 | CW-B14R | 2003 | |
| 12314 | CW-15D Sedan | 15D-2214 | |
| 12323 | CW-A14D | 2008 | |
| 12324 | CW-3W | 1502 | Warner engine |
| 12325 | CW-3L | 1503 | Lambert engine |
| 12329 | CW-A14D | 2009 | |
| 12331 | CW-16E | 3501 | |
| 12332 | CW-B14B | 2010 | |
| 12335/12337 | CW-16E | 3502/3504 | |
| 12352 | CW-16E | 3508 | |
| 12353, 12354 | T-32 Condor II | 21, 22 | 12354 to C-35, C-100, AN-ABJ, XA-FAJ, XB-GIT |
| 12363/12365 | T-32 Condor II | 23/25 | All to T-32C, 12365 to XA-BDS |
| 12366/12369 | T-32 Condor II | 28/31 | 12366 to G-AEZE, RAF P5724; 12367 to G-AEWD, RAF P5723; 12368 to G-AEWE, RAF P5725; 12369 to T-32C Special, C-36, C-101, AN-AAV. |

| | | | |
|---|---|---|---|
| 12371/12378 | T-32 Condor II | 32/39 | 12371 to T-32C, CF-BQN, XA-DOA; 12372 to T-32C; 12375 to G-AEWF, RAF P5726 |
| 12380 | CW-16E | 3520 | |
| 12383, 12384 | T-32 Condor II | 40, 41 | 12383 to T-32C, XA-BDV, China; 12384 to Byrd Antarctic Expedition. |
| 12390/12392 | AT-32A Condor II | 42/44 | 12390 to XY-AAI; 12391 to XA-BDR, China |
| 12393/12395 | AT-32B Condor II | 45/47 | |
| 12396/12399 | AT-32D Condor II | 48/51 | 12396 to XA-BDP, China 12398 to XA-BDU, China 12399 to XA-BDT, China |
| 13233 | Pusher replica | C-530 | |
| 13263 | Hawk II (Goshawk) | DH-46 | Demonstrator |
| 13298 | CA-1 Courtney | 101 | Amphibian |
| 13604 | 1912 Replica | - | Steel tube, radial engine for air show |
| 13634 | JN-4D | 1000 | Rebuilt 1933 |
| 14369 | Falcon | F-37-1 | Last Falcon biplane |
| 14703 | Hawk III | 11894 | To Argentina |
| 15315 | Model 76 | 11922 | To US Army XA-14 36-146 |
| 16417 | CW-22 | 22-57 | |
| 16421 | A-19R | 19R-14 | |
| 18067 | A-22 | 22-1 | Prototype SNC-1, 1938; to N500G |

| | | | |
|---|---|---|---|
| 19427 | CW-23 | 23-1 | |
| 19431 | CW-21 | 21-1 | |
| 19436 | CW-20/C-55 | 101 | To US Army C-55 41-21041, to UK as G-AGDI |
| 19441/19443 | CW-21 | 21-2/21-4 | |
| 19446 | CW-22B | 3604 | Postwar racing No.28 |
| 21549 | P-40N | - | |
| 21979 | P-40M or N | 27691 | |
| 22028 | 75-R | 12931 | Military test |
| 22584 | CW-D14B | 2038 | |
| 24034 | 1912 original | - | Restored for flight, OX-5; now in EAA Museum, c/n 12 |
| 28990 | 81-A Special | 17816 | Radial engine |
| 31686 | A-22 | 3707 | To N888U |
| 41806 | SO3C-1 | - | |
| 41997 | SNC-1 | 4219 | |
| 41998 | SNC-1 | 3688 | |
| 47074 | P-40K | | Records incomplete |
| 50063 | O-52 Owl | 14320 | Ex-Army 40-2787 |
| 50079 | O-52 Owl | 14324 | Ex-Army 40-2791 |
| 50143 | O-52 Owl | 14337 | Ex-Army 40-2804 |
| 50160 | O-52 Owl | 14242 | Ex-Army 40-2709 |
| 50323 | O-52 Owl | 14301 | Ex-Army 40-2768 |
| 52203 | P-36A | 12415 | Ex-Army 38-1 |
| 52723 | SNC-1 | 7871 | Ex-Navy 05208 |
| 61241 | O-52 Owl | 14302 | Ex-Army 40-2769 |

| | | | |
|---|---|---|---|
| 62435 | Kittyhawk IV/ P-40N-1 | 28370 | Ex-US Army 42-104608, RCAF 847 |
| 64583 | O-52 Owl | 14276 | Ex-Army 40-2743 |
| 67253, 67254 | P-40K | | Records incomplete |
| 67905 | SNC-1 | 4255 | Ex-Navy 05194; to N121E |
| 68261 | CW-B14B | 2011 | Was NS1A |
| 75234 | JN-4D | 490 | Post WW II restoration |
| 88917 | P-40F | | Ex-US Army 41-13781, restored 1977. |
| 92879 | SB2C-5 Helldiver | 83589 | Ex-Navy 83725 |
| 94466 | Kittyhawk I | 15314 | Ex-RAF AK933, RCAF 1057 |
| 94500 | P-40N-30 | - | Ex-Army 44-7369, to C-CTGR |
| 95459 | O-52 Owl | 14245 | Ex-Army 40-2712 |
| 96045 | Kittyhawk I | 15133 | Ex-RAF AK752, RCAF 1028 |

NXC-    Special registration series issued to Curtiss for test and ferrying of export Curtiss military aircraft in 1940. N for United States, X for experimental status, and C for Curtiss. Similar procedure for other manufacturers; NXG- Grumman, NXD- Douglas, etc.

| | | | |
|---|---|---|---|
| NXC-1 | H75A-7 | 14546 | First for Netherlands East Indies. |
| 5/54 | Model 77 | | Former US Navy SBC-4s refurbished by Curtiss for transfer to France. |

| | | | |
|---|---|---|---|
| 4124A | 1911 Model D Pusher | 2 | Replica by Cole Palen, 1957 |
| 300B | XP-40Q No.2 | - | Ex-US Army 42-45722, race No.82 |
| 3865B | Robin C | 469 | Ex-NC345K restored |
| 101OC | Pusher | 113 | Replica |
| 6699C | Robin | 7 | Ex-NC7496 restored, OX-5 |
| 6898C | JN-4D | 34135 | Restoration |
| 7890C | Robin | 45 | Ex-NC76E restored, OX-5 |
| 999CD | P-40N-30 | - | Ex-US Army 44-7084 |
| 2821D | JN-4D | 400 | Restoration |

| | | | |
|---|---|---|---|
| 39E | Seagull | 3 | K-6 engine |
| 46E,47E | Robin C | 80,81 | |
| 48E/53E | Robin B | 51/56 | |
| 76E/81E | Robin B | 45/50 | 76E to 7890C, 78E to NC74H No.2 |
| 103E/108E | Robin B | 57/62 | |
| 112E | Falcon Mail-plane | 7 | Liberty engine |
| 121E No.1 | Robin B | 63 | |
| 121E No.2 | Falcon 22 (SNC-1) | 4255 | Ex-Navy 05194, NC67905 |
| 122E/126E | Robin B | 64/68 | |
| 142E | JN-4D | 3887 | |
| 153E | Robin C | G-4 | |
| 156E/166E | Robin B | 69/79 | 163E to 168E No.2 |
| 167E/177E | Robin B | 82/92 | 168E No.2 was 163E, c/n 76 |
| 208E/214E | Falcon Mail-plane | 8/14 | Liberty engine |
| 217E/220E | Robin B | 93/96 | |
| 225E/230E | Robin B | 97/102 | 230E also listed as C-1 |
| 250E/265E | Robin B | 103/118 | NC259 to Hispano-Suiza |
| 273E | Robin B | 163 | |
| 283E/294E | Robin B | 121/132 | |
| 296E, 297E | Robin B | 119, 120 | |
| 301E | Falcon Mail-plane | 15 | Conqueror engine |

| | | | |
|---|---|---|---|
| 310E | Falcon Mail-plane | 6 | Conqueror engine |
| 313E/326E | Robin B | 133/146 | c/n 134 & 136 with Tank V-502 engine |
| 356E | Robin B | 147 | |
| 357E | Robin C | 148 | |
| 358E/360E | Robin B | 149/151 | |
| 361E | Robin Special | 152 | Kinner engine |
| 362E/368E | Robin B | 153/159 | |
| 369E | Robin C | 160 | |
| 370E/372E | Robin B | 161/163 | |
| 373E | Robin C-1 | 164 | |
| 374E/378E | Robin B | 165/169 | |
| 379E | Robin C | 170 | |
| 380E, 381E | Robin M | 171, 172 | Tank V-502 engine |
| 382E, 383E | Robin C | 174, 176 | |
| 384E | Robin C Special | 180 | 170 hp Challenger |
| 385E | Robin C-1 | 182 | |
| 386E, 387E | Robin C | 184, 186 | |
| 488E | JN-4D | 3811 | |
| 507E | JN-4D | 7327 | |
| 636E | Long-Distance Hawk | 1 | To NR-982V Gulfhawk 1A |
| 864E | JN-4D | 103A | Mercedes engine |
| 8639E | CW-1 Junior | | Was NC673V |
| | | | |
| 500G | A22 Falcon | A22-1 | Prototype; originally NX18067 |

| | | | |
|---|---|---|---|
| 1H/4H | Robin B | 361, 363, 365, 367 | |
| 5H/7H | Robin C-1 | 370, 372, 374 | |
| 8H/10H | Robin C-1 | 376, 378, 380 | |
| 12H, 13H | Robin J-1 | 382, 384 | 12H to J-3 temporarily 13H to Warner engine |
| 19H/21H | Robin C-1 | 386, 400, 390 | |
| 22H/25H | Robin C-1 | 392, 394, 396, 398 | |
| 26H | Robin B | 369 | |
| 27H/30H | Robin B | 371, 373, 375, 377 | |
| 32H/35H | Robin B | 379, 381, 383, 407 | |
| 36H | Robin B | 409 | |
| 37H/40H | Robin B | 389, 402, 404, 406 | |
| 41H/43H | Robin C-1 | 408, 410, 412 | |
| 44H, 45H | Robin B | 391, 393 | |
| 46H/48H | Robin B | 395, 397, 399 | 46H to CR, Crusader engine; 47H to B-2, Hispano-Suiza |
| 49H | Robin B | 401 | |

| | | | |
|---|---|---|---|
| 50H | Robin B | 403 | To M with Tank V-502 engine, to B-2 |
| 51H/53H | Robin C-1 | 405, 414, 416 | 51H restored as N6394T |
| 54H | Robin C-1 | 418 | |
| 55H | Robin C-2 | 420 | |
| 56H/59H | Robin C-1 | 422, 424, 426, 428 | 59H is 'St Louis Robin' 647 hr endurance record |
| 60H | Robin B | 429 | |
| 61H | Robin C-1 | 496 | |
| 62H/64H | Robin B | 411, 413, 415 | |
| 65H | Robin B | 417 | |
| 66H | Robin J-1 | 419 | |
| 67H | Robin B-2 | 421 | |
| 68H/70H | Robin B | 423, 425, 427 | |
| 71H/74H | Robin C-1 | 436, 438, 440, 442 | |
| 75H | Robin C-1 | 470 | Also as 75M |
| 76H/79H | Robin C-1 | 446, 448, 430, 452 | |
| 80H | Robin | 431 | |
| 81H, 82H | Robin C-1 | 432, 434 | |
| 83H/86H | Robin B | 433, 435, 437, 439 | |
| 87H | Robin C-1 | 456 | |
| 88H | Robin J-1 | 458 | |

| | | | |
|---|---|---|---|
| 92H/96H | Robin C-1 | 460, 462, 464, 466, 468 | |
| 97H | Robin C-1 | 470A | |
| 98H | Robin C-1 | 472 | |
| 99H | Robin B | 441 | |
| 185H | Condor CO | G-1 | |
| 190H | Robin C-1 | 428 | |
| 250H/254H | Fledgling | B-31/B-35 | |
| 255H/258H | Falcon Mail-plane | 17/20 | Liberty engine |
| 259H/268H | Fledgling | B-36/B-45 | |
| 269H, 270H | Fledgling | B-47, B-48 | |
| 271H/273H | Fledgling | B-52/B-54 | 271H to 271Y |
| 274H | Fledgling J-2 | B-102 | Also as 965M |
| 290H/294H | Fledgling | B-55/B-59 | 290H to Fledgling Jr |
| 295H | Fledgling | B-46 | |
| 296H/299H | Fledgling | B-60/B-63 | |
| 358H | JN-4D | 34 | |
| 362H | JN-4D | 440 | |
| 984H | Condor CO | G-3 | To 985V |
| 985H | Carrier Pigeon II | G-1 | |
| | | | |
| 72K | Hawk 1 | | Japanese Hawk |
| 300K/304K | Robin B | 443, 445, 447, 449, 451 | |

| | | | |
|---|---|---|---|
| 316K/319K | Robin B | 453, 455, 457, 459 | |
| 320K/323K | Robin C-1 | 474, 476, 478, 480 | |
| 324K/327K | Robin C-1 | 482, 484, 486, 488 | |
| 328K/330K | Robin C-1 | 490, 492, 494 | |
| 333K/336K | Robin C-1 | 498, 502, 504, 506 | |
| 337K/340K | Robin C-1 | 508, 510, 512, 514 | |
| 341K/344K | Robin B | 461, 463, 465, 467 | |
| 345K/348K | Robin B | 469, 471, 473, 475 | 348K restored with Continental R-670 |
| 354K/357K | Robin C-1 | 516, 518, 520, 542 | |
| 358K, 359K | Robin C-1 | 524, 526 | |
| 364K/367K | Robin B | 477, 479, 481, 483 | |
| 368K, 369K | Robin C-1 | 485, 528 | |
| 370K | Robin B | 530 | |
| 371K, 372K | Robin C-1 | 532, 534 | |
| 373K | Robin B | 536 | |
| 374K, 375K | Robin C-1 | 538, 540 | |
| 386K | Robin C-2 | 544 | |
| 387K/391K | Robin C-1 | 546, 548, 550, 552, 554 | |

| | | | |
|---|---|---|---|
| 392K | Robin C-2 | 556 | Restored with Continental R-670 |
| 393K/395K | Robin C-1 | 558, 560, 562 | |
| 396K/399K | Robin B | 487, 489, 491, 493 | |
| 460K/489K | Fledgling | B-64/B-93 | 463K to J-2, 469K to J-1 Special |
| 507K | JN-4D | 7318 | |
| 725K | Condor CO | G-2 | Also called Condor B-20 |
| 726K/728K | Condor CO | G-4/G-6 | |
| 900K, 901K | Robin B | 495, 497 | |
| 904K/908K | Robin B | 499, 501, 503, 505, 507 | |
| 909K/911K | Robin C-1 | 564, 566, 608 | |
| 916K/919K | Robin C-1 | 572, 574, 576, 578 | |
| 920K/922K | Robin C-1 | 580, 582, 584 | |
| 923K/926K | Robin B | 509, 511, 513, 515 | |
| 927K/929K | Robin B | 517, 519, 521 | |
| 930K/933K | Robin C-1 | 586, 588, 590, 592 | |
| 934K/937K | Robin C-1 | 594, 596, 598, 600 | 935K restored with Continental R-670 |

555

| | | | |
|---|---|---|---|
| 938K/940K | Robin C-1 | 602, 604, 606 | |
| 941K/943K | Robin B | 523, 525, 527 | |
| 944K/947K | Robin B | 529, 531, 533, 535 | |
| 948K/950K | Robin B | 537, 539, 541 | |
| 971K/973K | Robin C-1 | 610, 612, 614 | |
| 974K/977K | Robin C-1 | 618, 620, 622, 624 | |
| 978K/981K | Robin C-1 | 626, 628, 630, 632 | 979K restored with J-6-7 engine |
| 982K, 983K | Robin C-1 | 634, 636 | |
| 984K | Robin J-1 | 616 | |
| 985K/988K | Robin C-1 | 629, 631, 633, 635 | 987K as C-2 |
| 992K/994K | Robin B | 543, 545, 555 | |
| 995K/997K | Robin B | 549, 551, 553 | |
| 998K, 999K | Robin C-1 | 637, 638 | |
| 4161K | P-40N | – | |
| | | | |
| 67M | JN-4C | 919 | |
| 75M | Robin C-1 | 470 | Was 75H |
| 179M | CW-2P | 2P-101 | |
| 181M | Tanager | G-1 | Guggenheim winner |

| | | | |
|---|---|---|---|
| 182M | Robin J-1 | – | |
| 188M | Hawk IV | 12186 | To Argentina |
| 296M | Robin J-1 | – | |
| 352M | CW-12Q | 12Q-2026 | To NC370N |
| 560M | JN-4D | M-3233 | |
| 565M | N-9H | 46-105 | |
| 650M/652M | Fledgling | B-94/B-96 | |
| 653M | Fledgling | B-100 | |
| 654M/656M | Fledgling | B-107/B-109 | |
| 700M | Robin C-1 | 639 | |
| 701M/705M | Robin J-1 | 640/644 | |
| 711M | Robin C-1 | 724 | |
| 742M/744M | Robin C-1 | 645/647 | |
| 745M | Robin J-1 | 648 | |
| 746M, 747M | Robin C-1 | 649, 650 | |
| 748M | Robin J-1 | 651 | |
| 749M | Robin B | 652 | |
| 750M | Robin J-1 | 653 | |
| 751M | Robin C-1 | 654 | |
| 752M | Robin J-1 | 655 | |
| 753M | Robin C-1 | 656 | |
| 754M | Robin J-1 | 657 | |
| 755M | Robin C-1 | 658 | |
| 756M | Robin J-1 | 659 | |
| 757M | Robin C-1 | 660 | |
| 758M | Robin J-1 | 661 | |
| 759M | Robin C-1 | 662 | |
| 762M | Robin J-1 | 663 | |
| 763M | Robin C-1 | 664 | To CF-ALY |
| 764M | Robin J-1 | 665 | |

557

| | | | |
|---|---|---|---|
| 765M | Robin C-1 | 666 | To CF-ALZ |
| 766M | Robin J-1 | 667 | |
| 767M | Robin C-1 | 668 | |
| 768M | Robin J-1 | 689 | |
| 769M | Robin C-1 | 670 | To CF-AMA |
| 770M | Robin J-1 | 671 | |
| 771M | Robin C-1 | 672 | |
| 772M | Robin J-1 | 673 | |
| 773M/775M | Robin C-1 | 674/676 | |
| 776M | Robin J-1 | 677 | |
| 777M | Robin C-1 | 678 | |
| 778M | Robin J-1 | 679 | |
| 779M | Robin C-1 | 680 | |
| 780M | Robin J-1 | 681 | To Sprayer with Continental R-670 |
| 781M | Robin C-1 | 682 | |
| 782M | Robin J-1 | 683 | |
| 783M | Robin C-1 | 684 | |
| 784M | Robin J-1 | 685 | |
| 785M | Robin C-1 | 686 | |
| 786M | Robin J-1 | 687 | |
| 787M | Robin C-1 | 688 | |
| 788M | Robin J-1 | 689 | |
| 789M | Robin C-1 | 690 | |
| 790M/793M | Robin J-1 | 691, 693, 695, 697 | 790M to J-2 |
| 794M/796M | Robin J-1 | 699, 701, 703 | |
| 797M/799M | Robin B | 557, 559, 561 | |

| | | | |
|---|---|---|---|
| 849M | JN-4D | 36129 | |
| 965M | Fledgling J-2 | B-102 | Also NR274H |
| 966M, 967M | Fledgling | B-101, B-102 | |
| 986M | XF9C-2 | 1 | Became Navy 9264 |

| | | | |
|---|---|---|---|
| 310N | Kingbird J | G-2 | To J-3 |
| 311N | Carrier Pigeon II | G-2 | |
| 369N | Carrier Pigeon II | G-3 | |
| 370N | CW-12Q | 12Q-2036 | Was NC352M |
| 373N | Bleeker | 2 | Helicopter |
| 500N | Robin B | 563 | |
| 509N, 510N | Robin 4C-1A | 702, 704 | 510N to 4C-2 |
| 511N | Robin J-1 | 705 | |
| 512N | Robin 4C-1A | 706 | |
| 513N | Robin J-1 | 707 | |
| 514N | Robin 4C-1A | 708 | |
| 515N | Robin J-1 | 709 | |
| 516N | Robin 4C-1A | 710 | |
| 517N | Robin J-1 Deluxe | 711 | To Sprayer with Continental R-670 |
| 518N/521N | Robin J-1 | 713, 715, 717, 719 | |
| 522N, 523N | Thrush J | 1001, 1002 | 523N to Cuba |
| 524N | Robin B | 565 | |
| 515N/527N | Robin J-1 | 721, 723, 725 | |

559

| | | | |
|---|---|---|---|
| 529N/532N | Robin J-1 | 727, 729,<br>731, 733 | 532N restored; identi-<br>fied as J-1D |
| 533N, 534N | Robin J-1 | 735, 737 | |
| 535N | Robin J-1 Special | 739 | Experimental Chevrolet<br>engine |
| 537N/540N | Robin J-1 | 743, 745,<br>747, 749 | |
| 541N | Robin C-1 | 751 | |
| 542N | Thrush J | 1003 | |
| 551N | Robin B | 567 | |
| 552N, 553N | Thrush J | 1004, 1005 | |
| 554N | Robin 4C-1 | 769 | Last Robin built |
| 562N No.1 | Thrush J | 1006 | Crashed, 562N trans-<br>ferred to c/n 1007 |
| 562N No.2 | Thrush J | 1007 | |
| 563N/567N | Robin 4C-1A | 712, 714,<br>716, 718,<br>720 | |
| 579N | Robin B | 569 | |
| 580N/582N | Thrush J | 1008/1010 | |
| 584N | Robin J-1 | 755 | |
| 585N, 586N | Kingbird D-2 | 2001, 2002 | To Colombia K-1, K-2 |
| 588N, 589N | Kingbird D-2 | 2003, 2004 | 588N to Costa Rica T1-8 |
| 599N | Kingbird D-2 | 2005 | |
| 1008N | Kittyhawk IV/<br>P-40N-5 | 29640 | Ex-US Army 42-105878,<br>RCAF 870 |
| 1009N No.1 | Kittyhawk IV/<br>P-40N-20 | 31423 | Ex-US Army 43-23484,<br>RCAF 877 |
| 1009N No.2 | Kittyhawk III/<br>P-40M-10 | 27490 | Ex-US Army 43-5802,<br>RCAF 840; to N1233N |

| | | | |
|---|---|---|---|
| 1048N | Kittyhawk I | 15256 | Ex-RAF AK875, RCAF 1047 |
| 1151N | Kittyhawk IV/ P-40N-15 | 30158 | Ex-US Army 42-106396, RCAF 880* |
| 1195N | Kittyhawk IV/ P-40N | 30158 | Ex-US Army, RCAF* |
| 1197N | Kittyhawk IV/ P-40N-5 | 28954 | Ex-US Army 42-105192, RCAF 858 |
| 1223N | Kittyhawk I | 15208 | Ex-RAF AK827, RCAF 1038 |
| 1226N | Kittyhawk IV/ P-40N-15 | 29629 | Ex-US Army 42-105876, RCAF 867 |
| 1228N | Kittyhawk III/ P-40M-10 | 27466 | Ex-US Army 43-5788, RCAF 832 |
| 1230N | Kittyhawk I | 18730 | Ex-RAF AK968, RCAF 1067 |
| 1232N | Kittyhawk III/ P-40M-10 | 27483 | Ex-US Army 43-5795, RCAF 845 |
| 1233N | Kittyhawk III/ P-40M-10 | 27490 | Ex-US Army 43-5802, RCAF 840; to N1009N No.2 |
| 1236N | Kittyhawk IA/ P-40E-1 | 1323 | Ex-RAF ET862, RCAF 729 |
| 1237N | Kittyhawk I | 18731 | Ex-RAF AK987, RCAF 1068; to N5673N |
| 1251N | Kittyhawk I | 18757 | Ex-RAF AL113, RCAF 1073; to N222SU |
| 1252N | Kittyhawk III/ P-40M-10 | 27498 | Ex-US Army 43-5810, RCAF 844 |
| 4689N | O-52 Owl | 14270 | Ex-US Army 40-2737 |
| 5672N | Kittyhawk I | 18723 | Ex-RAF AK979, RCAF 1064; to N151U |

* Records confused

561

| | | | |
|---|---|---|---|
| 5673N | Kittyhawk I | 18731 | Ex-RAF AK987, RCAF 1068; To N1237N |
| 5704N | Bullock-Curtiss 1912 | 1 | Replica built 1947 |
| 40PE | Kittyhawk I | 15286 | Ex-RAF AK905, RCAF 1052, CF-OGZ, N11122 |
| 40PN | P-40N-30 | - | Ex-US Army 44-7369, N94500, C-CTGR |
| 222SU | Kittyhawk I | 18757 | Ex-RAF AL113, RCAF 1073, N1251 |
| 4644T | CW-1 Replica | EHS-1 | By Eldon H Sorenson, 1964 |
| 6394T | Robin C-1 | 405 | NC51H restored |
| 151U | Kittyhawk I | 18723 | Ex-RAF AK979, RCAF 1064, N5672N |
| 888U | A22 Falcon | 3707 | Ex-N31686 |
| 1048U | Kittyhawk I | - | Ex-RAF AK875, RCAF 1047 |

| | | | |
|---|---|---|---|
| 403V | A | 10 | Glider |
| 600V/602V | Kingbird D-2 | 2006/2008 | 2006 to K-3, 2007, 2008 to Turkey |
| 606V | Robin 4C-1A | 730 | |
| 607V | CR-1 Skeeter | 3001 | Prototype of CW-1 Junior |
| 608V, 609V | Robin J-1 | 757, 759 | |
| 620V/622V | Kingbird D-2 | 2009/2011 | |
| 623V | CW-1 Junior | 1012 | |
| 625V | Robin 4C-1 | 767 | |
| 626V | Kingbird D-2 | 2012 | |
| 627V | CR-2 Coupe | 3001 | Wright Gipsy |
| 628V, 629V | Kingbird D-2 | 2014, 2015 | 628V to Costa Rica T1-6 |
| 630V/636V | CW-1 Junior | 1013/1019 | |
| 637V | CR-2 Coupe | 3002 | Kinner B-5 engine |
| 638V/688V | CW-1 Junior | 1020/1070 | 673V to 8639E |
| 689V, 690V | CW-1 Junior | 1072, 1071 | |
| 691V/699V | CW-1 Junior | 1073/1081 | |
| 901V | HS-1L | 266 | |
| 969V | Teal A-1 | G-1 | |
| 970V | Teal A-2 | G-2 | |
| 981V | Grasshopper | 1 | Glider |
| 982V | Hawk 1A | 1 | Gulfhawk, ex-NR636E |
| 983V | Helldiver A-3 | 1 | To Navy XF8C-8 A8847 |
| 984V | Helldiver A-4 | 1 | To Navy XF8C-7 A8845 |
| 985V | Condor CO | G-3 | Was NC984H |

| | | | |
|---|---|---|---|
| 1207V | Kittyhawk I | 18796 | Ex-RAF AL152, RCAF 1082 |
| 5038V | P-40N | 22786 | Ex-US Army 44-7619; possible registration switch with N1251N |
| 9W | Hawk 1 | 17 | Conqueror engine; to NR9110 |
| 359W | JN-4D | 74 | Seaplane, Hi-Lift wings |
| 407W | CW-16K | 16K-2005 | |
| 408W | CW-12W | 12W-2018 | |
| 409W | CW-16K | 16K-2006 | |
| 410W/413W | CW-12W | 12W-2014/ 2017 | |
| 414W/417W | CW-12Q | 12Q-2027/ 2030 | |
| 418W | CW-12W | 12W-2031 | |
| 419W | CW-12Q | 12Q-2032 | |
| 420W | CW-16W | 16W-2002 | |
| 421W, 422W | CW-16K | 16K-2003, 2004 | |
| 430W | CW-12Q | 12Q-2001 | |
| 433W | CW-14C | 14C-2001 | Sold to Argentina |
| 434W | CW-12W | 12W-2002 | |
| 436W | CW-15C | 15C-2001 | Flying as 15D in 1978 |
| 437W | CW-12K | 12K-2003 | |
| 438W/444W | CW-12Q | 12Q-2004/ 2010 | |
| 445W | CW-12K | 12K-2011 | |

| | | | |
|---|---|---|---|
| 446W | CW-16K | 16K-2001 | |
| 447W | CW-6B | 6B-2040 | |
| 448W | CW-15N | 15N-2002 | |
| 449W | CW-A14D | A14-2001 | |
| 454W/456W | CW-16E | 3505/3507 | |
| 493W, 494W | CW-12W | 12W-2012, 2013 | |
| 495W/497W | CW-12Q | 12Q-2022/ 2024 | |
| 498W | CW-12W | 12W-2025 | |
| 608W | JN-4D | 241 | Rebuilt 1930 |
| 724W | JN-4D | 1313 | Le Rhône |
| | | | |
| 4Y | CW-15D Sedan | 15C-2212 | Was 15C NC12303; to NS-58 |
| 8Y | 1912 Pusher replica | 101 | Cut down JN-4 wings; built by Billy Parker for movies |
| 16Y | Hawk III | 11924 | |
| 17Y | Hawk 75 'XP-36' | 11923 | To 75B, 75I (Army XP-37) |
| 73Y | Seagull | – | |
| 259Y | Bunting | 1 | |
| 271Y | Fledgling | B-52 | Was 271H |

# APPENDIX III

# Civil Registrations of
# Exported Curtiss Aircraft, from 1920

This appendix lists the registrations applied at the factory to Curtiss civil aircraft built for sale outside the United States and the registrations issued by other governments to surplus military or former US civil Curtiss aeroplanes except C-46/R5C Commandos.

The registrations are arranged in alphabetical sequence of national registration symbols, as CF for Canada, D for Germany, G for Great Britain, etc. In those cases where national symbols have changed within the coverage of this listing, cross-reference is made from one to the other for a single grouping. All of the pre-1929 Canadian registrations beginning G-CA, for example, will be found following the later Canadian symbol CF.

AN-   NICARAGUA

| Registration | Model | c/n | Remarks |
|---|---|---|---|
| AAV | Condor T-32C | 31 | Was NC12369; C-36, C-101 |
| ABB | Condor T-32C | 39 | Was NC12378; to XA-FEC |
| ABG | Condor T-32C Special | 21 | Was NC12353, C-35, C-100; to XA-FAJ, XB-GIT |

C-   COLOMBIA

| | | | |
|---|---|---|---|
| 35 | Condor T-32C Special | 21 | Was NC12353; to C-100, AN-ABG, XA-FAJ, XB-GIT |
| 36 | Condor T-32C Special | 31 | Was NC12369; to C-101, AN-AAV |

566

| 100 | Condor T-32C Special | 21 | Was NC12353, C-35; to AN-ABG, XA-FAJ, XB-GIT |
|---|---|---|---|
| 101 | Condor T-32C Special | 31 | Was NC12369, C-36; to AN-AAV |

CF-    CANADA    (Originally G-CA  which follows the CF- listing)

The G-CY  series is military and will be found in Appendix VI.
The CF-  prefix was used from January 1929 until January 1974,
when it was changed to C-F  with 10 years allowed for transition from the old style to the new with the same letter combin-
ations.   In this presentation, former Empire military serial
numbers are referenced as RAF even though that title did not
originate until April 1918, as the result of amalgamating the
RFC and RNAS.  Curtiss-Reid aeroplanes and World War II Curtiss
Commandos are not listed.   Canadian-built Curtiss JN-4s are
listed as JN-4C.

| ACA/ACC | Fledgling | B-49/51 | |
|---|---|---|---|
| ACF | Robin C-1 | 454 | |
| ACG | Robin B | 385 | |
| ACH | Robin B | 387 | Registered as B-2 |
| ACJ | Robin C-1 | 450 | |
| ACK | Robin C-1 | 388 | |
| ACL | Robin C-1 | 342 | |
| ACM | Robin C-1 | 346 | |
| ACP | Robin C-1 | 310 | |
| ACQ | Robin B-1 | 315 | |
| AEA | HS-2L | 243 | LWF-built; USN A1145 |

| | | | |
|---|---|---|---|
| AFC | JN-4C | - | |
| AFU | Oriole | - | Hispano-Suiza |
| AFW | JN-4D | - | EX-US Army 3545 |
| AHE | Robin C-1 | 522 | |
| AHF | Robin C-1 | 218 | |
| AHH | Robin C-1 | 568 | |
| AHI | Robin C-1 | 570 | |
| AHJ | Robin B-1 | 547 | |
| ALE | JN-4C | - | |
| ALY | Robin C-1 | 664 | Was NC763M |
| ALZ | Robin C-1 | 666 | Was NC765M |
| AMA | Robin C-1 | 670 | Was NC769M |
| ARD | CW-1 Junior | 1141 | Was NC10963 |
| BQN | Condor T-32 | 32 | Was NC12371; to XA-DOA |
| BVG | Kingbird D-3 | 2016 | Was NC11816 |
| OGZ | Kittyhawk I | 15286 | Ex-RAF AK905, RCAF 1052 |

## G-CA    CANADA

Used from 1920 to 1928, with gradual phasing out following adoption of CF-  in January 1929.  Some G-CA  registrations remained in use after World War II.

| | | | |
|---|---|---|---|
| CAAA | JN-4C | - | RAF C210 |
| CAAB | JN-4C | - | RAF C1457 |
| CAAC | HS-2L | - | Curtiss-built; USN A1876 |

| | | | |
|------|-------|-------|---------------------------|
| CAAD | HS-2L | – | Curtiss-built; USN A1878 |
| CAAF | JN-4C | – | |
| CAAG | JN-4C | – | RAF C206 |
| CAAH | JN-4D | M3100 | |
| CAAI | JN-4C | – | RAF C1347 |
| CAAJ | JN-4C | 19 | Ericson |
| CAAK | JN-4C | – | RAF C122 |
| CAAL | JN-4C | 11 | Ericson |
| CAAM | JN-4C | – | RAF C590 |
| CAAN | JN-4C | – | RAF C197 |
| CAAO | JN-4C | – | RAF C282 |
| CAAP | JN-4C | 3291 | RAF C291 |
| CAAS | JN-4C | – | RAF C437 |
| CAAT | JN-4C | – | RAF C626 |
| CAAU | JN-4C | – | RAF C1350 |
| CAAV | JN-4C | – | RAF C118 |
| CAAW | JN-4C | – | RAF C290 |
| CABA | JN-4C | – | |
| CABB | JN-4C | 2884 | |
| CABC | JN-4C | – | |
| CABE | JN-4C | 162 | |
| CABF | F-Boat | – | |
| CABG | JN-4C | – | |
| CABH | JN-4C | – | Ericson |
| CABI | JN-4C | 5002 | Ericson |
| CABJ | JN-4C | – | RAF C187 |
| CABK | JN-4C | – | RAF C122 |
| CABL | JN-4C | – | RAF C109 |
| CABN | JN-4C | – | RAF C1353 |

| | | | |
|------|------------|--------|-----------------------------|
| CABO | JN-4C | – | RAF C144 |
| CABQ | JN-4C | – | RAF C1303 |
| CABR | JN-4C | – | RAF C1022 |
| CADA | JN-4C | 5006 | Ericson; to G-CADN |
| CADM | HS-2L | – | LWF-built; USN A1271 |
| CADN | JN-4C | 5006 | Ericson, was G-CADA |
| CADO | JN-4C | 5015 | Ericson |
| CADU | HS-2L | – | Gallaudet-built; USN A2261 |
| CADW | JN-4C | 5020 | Ericson |
| CADY | HS-2L | – | Origin unknown |
| CAEC | JN-2 | 3505 | |
| CAEF | MF Seagull | 833-3 | |
| CAEG | MF Seagull | 538 | Different wings |
| CAEI | JN-4C | – | |
| CAEJ | JN-4C | 5021 | Ericson |
| CAEP | JN-4A | – | Seaplane |
| CAEQ | JN-4C | – | |
| CAEX | JN-4C | 5061 | 3-seat Ericson |
| CAEY | HS-2L | – | Origin unknown |
| CAFB | Lark | 179-1-1 | |
| CAFH | HS-2L | – | LWF-built; USN A1274 |
| CAFI | HS-2L | – | LWF-built; USN A1258 |
| CAFP | HS-2L | – | Origin unknown |
| CAFQ | HS-2L | 212 | Curtiss-built |
| CAFR | JN-4C | 5062 | Ericson |
| CAFS | JN-4C | 5063 | 3-seat Ericson |
| CAFV | JN-4C | 5064 | 3-seat Ericson |
| CAFX | JN-4C | 5065 | 3-seat Ericson |
| CAFY | JN-4C | 5066 | Ericson |
| CAGT | HS-2L | – | Curtiss-built |

570

| | | | |
|---|---|---|---|
| CAHP | JN-4D | - | |
| CAHQ | HS-2L | - | Curtiss-built |
| CAIJ | JN-4C | 5067 | Ericson |
| CAJA | JN-4C | - | Modified |
| CAJF | JN-4C | - | Assembled from parts |
| CAJL | JN-4C | 2850 | Parasol monoplane wing |
| CANZ | HS-2L | - | LWF-built; USN A1152 |
| CAOA | HS-2L | 487 | Curtiss-built |
| CAOB | HS-2L | - | Gallaudet-built |
| CAOC/CAOM | HS-2L | - | Curtiss-built |
| CABT | JN-4C | 5005 | Ericson |
| CABU | JN-4C | - | RAF 1293 |
| CABW | JN-4C | 148 | Ericson |
| CABX | JN-4C | 77832 | To G-CATE |
| CABY | JN-4C | 5004 | Ericson |
| CABZ | JN-4C | - | |
| CACB | JN-4D | 8708 | |
| CACF | JN-4C | 5014 | Ericson |
| CACJ | JN-4C | - | RAF C574; seaplane |
| CACK | JN-4C | - | RAF C945 |
| CACM | HS-2L | - | Boeing-built; USN A4248 |
| CACO | JN-4C | - | Seaplane |
| CACP | JN-4C | 5018 | Ericson |
| CACQ | JN-4C | - | RAF C426 |
| CACR | JN-4C | 5061 | Ericson |
| CACS | HS-2L | 10064 | Aeromarine rebuild |
| CACT | HS-2L | - | Gallaudet-built; USN A2260 |

| | | | |
|---|---|---|---|
| CACU | HS-2L | - | Gallaudet-built; USN A2267 |
| CACV | HS-2L | - | Gallaudet-built; USN A2266 |
| CACW | HS-2L | - | Gallaudet-built; USN A2276 |
| CACX | HS-2L | - | Gallaudet-built; USN A2272 |
| CACY | HS-2L | - | Gallaudet-built; USN A2275 |
| CACZ | HS-2L | 514 | Curtiss-built |
| CADA | JN-4C | 5006 | Ericson; to G-CADN |
| CADB | HS-2L | - | Curtiss-built; USN A1727 |
| CADC | JN-4C | - | RAF C249 |
| CADD | JN-4C | - | RAF C434 |
| CADE | JN-4C | - | RAF C120 |
| CADF | JN-4C | - | RAF C123 |
| CADH | JN-4C | 5010 | Ericson |
| CADI (1) | JN-4C | - | RAF C437 |
| CADI (2) | MF Seagull | 210-17 | Curtiss-built |
| CADJ | JN-4C | - | |
| CADK | JN-4C | 5012 | Ericson |
| CADL | MF | 736-1 | Curtiss-built |
| CADN | JN-4C | 5006 | Ericson; was G-CADA |
| CAON | HS-2L | - | LWF-built |
| CAOP | HS-2L | - | LWF-built |
| CAOQ, CAOR | HS-2L | - | Curtiss-built |
| CAOS | HS-2L | - | LWF-built; USN A1250 |
| CAPE | HS-2L | - | LWF-built; USN A1300 |
| CAPF | HS-2L | - | LWF-built; USN A1342 |

572

| CARO | HS-2L | - | Curtiss-built; reg-istered as HS-3L |
|------|-------|---|-------------|
| CASA | JN-4D | - | |
| CATE | JN-4C | 77832 | Was G-CABX |
| CAVM | JN-4C | 11 | |
| CAWA | JN-4C | 5061 | Ericson |

CH-   SWITZERLAND   (Changed to HB- approximately 1935, see following)

| 170 | Condor AT-32 | 53 | To HB-LAP |
|-----|--------------|-----|-----------|

D-   GERMANY

| 3165 | Hawk II | H-81 | To D-IRIS |
|------|---------|------|-----------|
| IRIK | Hawk II | H-80 | |
| IRIS | Hawk II | H-81 | Formerly D-3165 |

G-   GREAT BRITAIN

| AEZE | Condor T-32 | 28 | Ex-NC12366, to RAF P5724 |
|------|-------------|-----|-------------|
| AEWD | Condor T-32 | 29 | Ex-NC12367, to RAF P5723 |
| AEWE | Condor T-32 | 30 | Ex-NC12368, to RAF P5725 |
| AEWF | Condor T-32 | 36 | Ex-NC12375, to RAF P5726 |
| AGDI | CW-20 | 101 | Ex-NX19436, US Army C-55 41-21041 |

<u>G-AU  AUSTRALIA</u>  1919-1929 (Replaced by VH-  and the same

last three letters, 1929)

| AUCN | MF Seagull | 419/29 | |
|------|------------|--------|---|
| AUGV | MF Seagull | 419/28 | |
| AUEV | JN-4D | 10074 | To VH-UEV |
| AUFG, AUFH | Curtiss-Ireland Comet | - | Improved Orioles |
| AUGB | JN-4D | 2885 | Converted to enclosed cabin with Hispano-Suiza; to VH-UGB |
| AUJE | Robin W | AB-34 | Substitute c/n; to VH-UJE |


<u>HB-  SWITZERLAND</u>  (Formerly CH-  )

| LAP | Condor AT-32 | 53 | Formerly CH-170 |
|-----|--------------|-----|-----------------|


<u>VH-  AUSTRALIA</u>  (1929 and on, formerly G-AU)

| UEV | JN-4D | 10074 | Was G-AUEV |
|-----|-------|-------|------------|
| UGB | JN-4D | 2885 | Was G-AUGB |
| UJE | Robin W | AB-34 | Substitute c/n; was G-AUJE |


<u>R-  ARGENTINA</u>  (later LV-  )
C/ns not given in available records.

| 2, 8, 11, 13 | JN | | OX-5 |
|--------------|-----|---|------|
| 21 | Oriole | | C-6 |
| 33, 34, 36 | JN | | OX-5 |
| 38 | JN or Robin | | OX-5 per different lists |

574

| | | |
|---|---|---|
| 39 | Robin | Challenger |
| 103 | Lark | C-6, to LV-AAA |
| 110 | Oriole | C-6 |
| 163 | JN | OX-5 |
| 164 | Robin | Challenger |
| 166 | Oriole | C-6 |
| 167 | JN | OX-5 |
| 197 | Oriole | C-6 |
| 204 | Robin | Challenger, to LV-ZAA |
| 216 | Curtiss | Model not specified |
| 220, 221 | JN | OX-5 |
| 228 | Oriole | C-6 |
| 254 | Robin | Challenger |
| 259 | Robin | Challenger, to LV-SBA |
| 260 | JN | OX-5, to LV-TBA |
| 264 | JN or Robin | OX-5 |
| 268 | JN | OX-5 |
| 273 | Robin | |

## LV-    ARGENTINA

| | | |
|---|---|---|
| AAA | Lark | C-6, was R-103 |
| AAC | Robin | |
| BAC | Robin | |
| FIB | Curtiss | Model not specified, listed as Kelito, ex-Navy |
| SBA | Robin | Challenger, was R-259 |
| TBA | JN | OX-5, was R-260 |
| ZAA | Robin | Challenger, was R-204 |

575

(became X- , later XA- and XB-   )

| SCOG | JN-4 | - | Probably JN-4D |
| SCOJ | JN-4 | - | Probably JN-4D |

X-    MEXICO    (Changed to XA- and XB- with the same three
last letters to distinguish between commercial
(XA) and privately-owned aircraft (XB))

| ABDB | Robin | - | To XA-BDB |
| BACJ | JN-4D | 4-D | |
| BADJ | Robin C-1 | 686 | Was NC785M |
| BADO | Robin C-1 | 649 | Was NC746M |
| BADZ | Robin C-2 | 556 | Was NC392K |
| BAEN | CW-1 Junior | 1080 | Was NC698V |
| BAES | CW-1 Junior | 1238 | Was NC11868 |
| BAEU | CW-1 Junior | 1239 | Was NC11869 |
| BAGA | Robin J-1 | 699 | Was NC794M; to XB-AGA |

XA-    MEXICO    Commercial aircraft

| AIV | Robin J-1 | 644 | Was NC705M |
| BAR | Robin J-1 | 729 | Was NC530N |
| BDB | Robin | - | Was X-ABDB |
| BDP | Condor AT-32D | 48 | Was NC12396 |
| BDR | Condor AT-32A | 43 | Was NC12391 |
| BDS | Condor T-32C | 25 | Was NC12365 |
| BDT | Condor AT-32D | 51 | Was NC12399 |
| BDU | Condor AT-32D | 50 | Was NC12398 |
| BDV | Condor T-32C | 40 | Was NC12383 |
| DOA | Condor T-32C | 32 | Was NC12371, CF-BQN |

| | | | |
|---|---|---|---|
| FAJ | Condor T-32C Special | 21 | Was NC12353, C-35, C-100, AN-ABG; to XB-GIT |
| FEC | Condor T-32C | 39 | Was NC12378, AN-ABB |

<u>XB-</u>  <u>MEXICO</u>  Privately-owned aircraft

| | | | |
|---|---|---|---|
| AGA | Robin J-1 | 699 | Was NC794M, X-BAGA |
| GIT | Condor T-32C Special | 21 | Was NC12353, C-35, C-100, AN-ABG, XA-FAJ |

<u>XY-</u>  <u>BURMA</u>

| | | | |
|---|---|---|---|
| AII | AT-32A | 42 | Was NC12390; destroyed by Japanese in World War II. |

# Serial Numbers of US Army
# Aircraft Designed or Built by Curtiss, 1909–46

This appendix lists the US Army serial numbers assigned to military aircraft built by Curtiss or associate contractors to the end of Curtiss military aeroplane deliveries.

Two numbering systems are presented; the straight numerical sequence system of 1908–21 and the Fiscal Year system of 1922 to date under which the serial numbers are assigned in sequence of aeroplane contract or procurement within a particular fiscal year (24-201/225 for the 201st to 225th procured in Fiscal Year 1924). Because of changes over the years, the prefix letters SC for Signal Corps, AS for Air Service, AC for Air Corps, etc, are not used.

As in the other appendices, the serial numbers are grouped by blocks whenever possible. Many of the JN-4s and JN-6s built with pre-1921 sequential numbers were rebuilt between 1922 and 1926, mostly as JNS, and were assigned new Fiscal Year serials. A few that were rebuilt a second time received still later numbers, which are listed individually. Where possible, cross-reference is made between the several serials for one aeroplane.

It should be noted that all US Army aeroplanes were identified by the builder's own designation until late 1920, just prior to adoption of the Fiscal Year serial numbering system in July 1921. In the case of Curtiss, all aeroplanes procured after 1920 are identified in this appendix by their standard Army designations.

The JN-4Can Canuck aeroplanes procured from the Canadian flying schools in the US in World War I and operated under their Canadian serials are not listed here, nor are several Curtiss flying-boats and seaplanes obtained from the Navy but not assigned regular Army serial numbers.

*Note on Conversions*—Often, one aeroplane of several on an Army order was modified before completion and given a revised or entirely new designation. This is indicated in the Remarks column. When the aeroplane was delivered with a designation other than the original, the remark will state 25-333 *as* O-1A for an aeroplane ordered as an O-1 but *delivered as* an O-1A. If the change was made after the aeroplane was delivered, the remark will be 25-331 *to* XO-13 for an in-service O-1 *converted to* XO-13.

| US Army Serial Number | Aeroplane Designation | Remarks |
|---|---|---|
| 2 | D | 60 hp pusher |
| 6 | E | 40 hp single-seat pusher changed to 60 hp two-seater |
| 8 | E | |
| 15 | F | Flying-boat |
| 21,22 | G | Fuselage tractor |
| 23 | E | |
| 29,30 | J | |
| 34 | F | Flying-boat |
| 35 | N | |
| 41/48 | JN-2 | |
| 49 | F | Flying-boat |
| 52,53 | JN-3 | |
| 60/63 | N-8 | No. 60 delivered with long wings, later shortened |
| 64/75 | R-2 | |
| 76/81 | JN-4 | |
| 102/107 | Twin JN | |
| 120/125 | JN-4 | |
| 130/135 | JN-4 | |
| 141/176 | JN-4B | |
| 177/192 | R-4 | |
| 229/264 | JN-4B | |
| 281/316 | R-4 | |
| 318, 319 | JN-4 | |

| | | |
|---|---|---|
| 322/325 | S-3 | Triplane Scout |
| 396/411 | H-14 | Cancelled and transferred to US Navy as HS-1 |
| 428 | Twin JN | |
| 433/446 | N-9 | |
| 468 | JN-4 | |
| 469 | R-4 | |
| 470 | Twin JN | |
| 471, 472 | JN-4C | Experimental Curtiss |
| 473 | L-1 | Sociable triplane |
| 474 | X-1 | Tandem-seat triplane |
| 475 | L-2 | Triplane seaplane |
| 492/503 | S-6 | Triplane Scout, last 11 cancelled |
| 504/521 | R-6 | |
| 541/556 | JN-4A | Four in this range |
| 1057/1656 | JN-4A | |
| 2157/2192 | R-4 | Last 35 cancelled |
| 2265, 2266 | JN-4 | |
| 2405/2454 | JN-4D | Built by Fowler |
| 2525/3924 | JN-4D | Built by Curtiss |
| 3925 | JN-4A | |
| 3976/4075 | JN-4D | Built by Liberty Iron Works |
| 4976/5375 | JN-4D | Built by Springfield |
| 12876 | JN-4D | Built by Curtiss |
| 33775/34224 | JN-4D | Built by St Louis |
| 34232/34257 | Bristol Fighter | (USAO-1)974 cancelled |
| 37932 | R-4 | |
| 37933/38332 | JN-4H | 38124 to JN-5; re-serialled 41358, reverted to JN-4H with serial 41358. |

580

| | | |
|---|---|---|
| 38333/38432 | JN-4HG | |
| 38433/38532 | JN-4HB | |
| 38533/38632 | JN-4 Can | Canadian-built Canuck |
| 39033/39042 | R-9 | From US Navy |
| 39062/39361 | JN-4 Can | Canuck |
| 39362/39367 | R-4L | |
| 39868/39917 | JN-4D | Built by US Aircraft |
| 39954/39959 | R-4L | |
| 40054 | 18-T | Wasp triplane |
| 40058 | 18-B | Hornet biplane |
| 40059 | 18-T | |
| 40064 | 18-B | |
| 41358 | JN-5H | Reverted to JN-4H but retained this serial |
| 41411/41735 | JN-4HG | |
| 41736/41885 | JN-6HB | |
| 41886/41985 | JN-6HO | |
| 41986/42110 | JN-6HP | |
| 42122/42125 | JN-4H, JN-4HG | |
| 43153 | S.E.5 | Following 999 cancelled |
| 44153/44242 | JN-6HG-2 | |
| 44243/44246 | JN-6HB | |
| 44257/44531 | JN-4D | Built by Springfield |
| 44728/45287 | JN-6HG-1 | |
| 47340/47414 | JN-4D | Built by Howell & Lesser |
| 47415/47514 | JN-4D | Built by Liberty Iron |
| 47816 | JN-4D-2 | Following 399 cancelled |
| 49117/49122 | JN-6HO | |
| 63276, 63277 | PN-1 | Engineering Division Design |

| | | |
|---|---|---|
| 63281/63330 | Orenco D* | Ordnance Engineering Co. design built by Curtiss |
| 64241/64243 | Eagle* | Converted civil transport |
| 68478/68527 | NBS-1 | Martin Model MB-2 |
| 68563, 68564 | R-6** | 1922 Racers |
| 68571, 68572 | NBS-4** | Curtiss improvement of NBS-1 |

* Since these models existed before the adoption of Army aeroplane designations, they were procured under their builder's designations.

** A few procurements were made under the cumulative serial number system after the Fiscal Year System was adopted on 1 July, 1921.

| US Army Serial Number | US Army Model | Remarks |
|---|---|---|
| 22-529/571 | JN-4H | Rebuilds |
| 23-473/480 | JNS-I | JN-4/6 rebuilt and redesignated with Wright-Hispano I engine |
| 23-485, 486 | JNS-I | |
| 23-488/490 | JNS-I | |
| 23-492 | JN-4H | 1923 rebuild |
| 23-493,494 | JNS-I | |
| 23-532/551 | JNS-I | |
| 23-554/556 | JN-6H | |
| 23-557 | JN-4H | |
| 23-605/650 | JN-4H, 6H, JNS-I | 22-606/625, 631/636 JNS-I; others JN-4H, JN-6H. 23-640 was 42098; to 26-17. |
| 23-937 | JN-4H or 6H | |
| 23-1201/1203 | XPW-8 | 23-1203 to XPW-8A, B |
| 23-1235 | R-8 | Army Racer; ex-Navy R2C-1 A-6691 |
| 23-1252 | XO-1 | Liberty engine for 1924 observation competition, Packard for 1925. |
| 24-41/48 | JN-6H | |
| 24-57/59 | JNS-I | |

583

| | | |
|---|---|---|
| 24-92, 93 | JNS | |
| 24-101/108 | JNS | |
| 24-134, 135 | JNS | |
| 24-140/150 | JN-6H | |
| 24-152/161 | JN-4H | |
| 24-164/180 | JN-6H | |
| 24-186/195 | JN-6H | |
| 24-201/225 | PW-8 | |
| 24-226,227 | JNS | |
| 24-231/245 | JNS | |
| 24-255/274 | JNS | |
| 25-1/44 | JNS | Mixed JNS-I, JNS-A2, JNS-E (engine variations) |
| 25-51 | JN-6H | Ex-45125 |
| 25-53 | JNS-I | Ex-45106 |
| 25-56/68 | JNS | |
| 25-74/77 | JNS-I | 25-77 is JNS-A2, Ex-44955 |
| 25-84 | JNS-I | |
| 25-90 | JNS-I | Ex-41598 |
| 25-127 | JNS-I | Ex-JN-4D 4944 |
| 25-129 | JNS-I | Ex-45120 |
| 25-134/160 | JNS-I | 25-141 is JNS-A2 |
| 25-165/200 | JNS-I | 25-199 is JNS-A2 |
| 25-325/334 | O-1 | 25-333 as O-1A, 25-328 as XO-11 No.1, 25-331 to XO-13, 25-332 to XO-13A |
| 25-410/419 | P-1 | 25-410 to XP-17 in 1929 |

584

| | | |
|---|---|---|
| 25-420/424 | P-2 | Last 5 P-1s, V-1400 engines 25-420 to XP-2, 25-421, 25-422, 25-424 to P-1A, 25-423 to XP-6 |
| 25-447 | JNS | Ex-41795 |
| 26-1, 2 | JNS | |
| 26-4/14 | JNS | |
| 26-16 | JNS-I | Ex-JN-4D 1070 |
| 26-17 | JNS-I | Ex-42098, 23-640 |
| 26-18 | JNS-I | Ex-45225 |
| 26-19 | JNS-I | Ex-JN-4D 3161 |
| 26-20 | JNS-I | Ex-JN-6H 41932 |
| 26-22 | JNS-I | Ex-JN-6H,45243 |
| 26-23/25 | JNS-I | Ex-JN-4Ds 1067, 3352, 3373 |
| 26-26 | JNS-I | Ex-JN-4D 3375 |
| 26-27, 28 | JNS-I | Ex-JN-6Hs 44808, 44894 |
| 26-31/35 | JNS-I | |
| 26-211 | XB-2 | Prototype Condor bomber |
| 26-276/300 | P-1A | 26-280 to XP-1A, 26-295 to XP-6A, 26-296 as XAT-4 to P-1A, 26-300 as XP-3A to XP-21 No.1, XP-21A |
| 27-1/35 | O-11 | 27-35 as XO-12 |
| 27-63/87 | P-1B | 27-71 to XP-1B |
| 27-88/97 | AT-4 | All to P-1D |
| 27-98/107 | O-11 | |
| 27-213/237 | AT-4 | All to P-1D |
| 27-238/242 | AT-5 | All to P-1E |

| | | |
|---|---|---|
| 27-243/287 | O-1B | 27-243 as A-3 prototype, 27-244 as XA-4, 27-263 as XO-18 to O-1B, 27-264, 266/268 as O-1C; 27-266 to O-13B |
| 27-298/317 | A-3 | 27-306, 310, 315 to A-3A |
| 27-327/331 | P-5 | 27-327 to XP-5 |
| 28-42/72 | AT-5A | 28-42/44, 46/51, 55/64, 66, 70/72 to P-1F |
| 28-83/118 | A-3 | 28-116/118 to A-3A |
| 28-189/193 | P-3A | 28-189 to XP-3A No.2, XP-21 No.2, P-1F |
| 28-196/217 | O-11 | 28-196 as XO-16; 28-207 as O-13D to O-1B |
| 28-387 | XP-10 | |
| 28-398, 399 | B-2 | |
| 29-28/37 | B-2 | |
| 29-227/259 | P-1C | 29-238 as XP-1C, to P-1C; 29-259 as XP-6B |
| 29-260/273 | P-6 | 29-260 to XP-6D, P-6A. 29-262 to P-6A, XP-22, P-6A 29-263 to XP-6A No.2, P-6A 29-264, 265, 267, 268 to P-6A. 29-266, 269/273 to P-6D in 1932. |
| 29-282/322 | O-1E | 29-288 to O-1F. 29-295 as XBT-4 to XO-1G, Y1O-1G. 29-319/321 to YO-13C, O-13C. 29-322 to Y1O-26, O-26. |
| 29-363/366 | P-6 | All to P-6D in 1932 |
| 29-367, 368 | P-11 | Delivered as P-6, to P-6D |

| | | |
|---|---|---|
| 29-374 | P-11 | Delivered as YP-20; to XP-6E, P-6E, XP-6F |
| 29-452 | XC-10 | Commercial Robin W |
| 30-1/28 | A-3B | |
| 30-231/280 | A-3B | |
| 30-387 | XA-8 | |
| 31-472/501 | O-1G | |
| 32-211/220 | O-39 | |
| 32-233/278 | YIP-22 | Delivered as P-6E. 32-278 as XP-23; to YP-23 |
| 32-343 | YO-40 | Rebuilt as YO-40A |
| 32-344/356 | YA-8 | 32-344 to YA-10, A-10. 32-349/355 as YIA-8. 32-356 as YIA-8A, A-8A. all but 32-344, 356 to A-8. |
| 32-415/418 | YIO-40B | |
| 33-178 | XP-31 | Originally XP-934 |
| 33-212/257 | A-12 | |
| 33-320, 321 | YC-30 | To C-30 |
| 36-146 | XA-14 | Civil registration X-15315 prior to Army purchase. |
| 37-52/64 | YIA-18 | To A-18 |
| 37-68/70 | YIP-36 | To P-36 |
| 7-375 | XP-37 | Former model 75, 75B proto. |
| 38-1/210 | P-36A | 38-4 as XP-42; to P-36A. 38-10 as XP-40. 38-20 to XP-36B, P-36B. 38-85 as P-36C prototype. 38-147 to XP-36E. 38-172 to XP-36F. 38-174 to XP-36D. 38-181/210 as P-36C |

| | | |
|---|---|---|
| 39-156/289 | P-40 | c/ns 13033/13166. 39-162, 176, 182, 187, 190, 191, 196, 197, 204, 206, 209, 217, 220, 235, 238, 243, 248, 257, 263, 267, 275, 276, 279, 288 to P-40G. |
| 40-292/357 | P-40 | c/ns 13167/13232. 40-292, 297, 299/301, 303, 309, 315, 318, 320, 323, 331/333, 335/ 358, 340, 348 to P-40G. |
| 40-358 | P-40E | |
| 40-359/381 | P-40D | 40-360 as XP-40F. |
| 40-382/681 | P-40E | |
| 40-2688/2890 | O-52 | |
| 40-3053, 3054 | XP-46 | 40-3054 as XP-46A |
| 41-140 | XP-53 | Cancelled |
| 41-5159/5183 | C-46 | |
| 41-5184/5204 | C-46A-1-CU | |
| 41-5205/5304 | P-40B | |
| 41-5305/5744 | P-40E | |
| 41-5745/5894 | AT-9 | |
| 41-11939/12279 | AT-9 | |
| 41-12280/12283 | C-46A-1-CU | |
| 41-12284/12333 | C-46A-5-CU | |
| 41-12334/12383 | C-46A-10-CU | |
| 41-12384/12433 | C-46A-15-CU | |
| 41-13297/13327 | P-40B | |
| 41-13328/13520 | P-40C | 41-13389, 13390, 13396/ 13401, 13406, 13407 (10) to RAF as Tomahawk I. |

588

| | | |
|---|---|---|
| 41-13521/13599 | P-40E | |
| 41-13600/14299 | P-40F | 41-13696 to P-40D, cancelled |
| 41-14300/14222 | P-40F-5 | |
| 41-14423/14599 | P-40F-10 | 41-14497, 14499, 14500, |
| | | 14561 to P-40R in 1944 (4). |
| 41-18774/18783 | A-25A-1 | Most to USMC as SB2C-1A |
| 41-18784/18823 | A-25A-5 | |
| 41-18824/18873 | A-25A-10 | |
| 41-19508 | XP-60 | |
| 41-19733/19932 | P-40F-15 | |
| 41-19933/20044 | P-40F-20 | |
| 41-21041 | C-55 | Ex civil CW-20 NX-19436; to |
| | | United Kingdom as G-AGDI |
| 41-24640/24689 | C-46A-20-CU | |
| 41-24690/24739 | C-46A-25-CU | |
| 41-24740/24775 | C-46A-30-CU | |
| 41-24776/25195 | P-40E-1-CU | Kittyhawk IA for RAF, |
| | | ET-100/519 |
| 41-35873 | XP-62 No.1 | |
| 41-35874/36953 | P-40E-1 | Kittyhawk IA for RAF, |
| | | ET-520/999, EV-100/699. |
| 42-3564/3577 | C-46A-30-CU | |
| 42-3578/3683 | C-46A-35-CU | 42-3658, 3666, 3668, 3671, |
| | | 3673, 3675, 3676, 3680, |
| | | 3682, 3683 to C-46A-36. |
| 42-9727/9729 | P-40K | Cancelled |
| 42-9730/9929 | P-40K-5 | |

589

```
42-9930/10264        P-40K-10              42-9987 to XP-40Q No.1

                                           42-10219 to XP-40K

42-10265/10429       P-40K-15

42-10430/10479       P-40L-1

42-10480/10699       P-40L-5

42-10700/10847       P-40L-10

42-10848/10959       P-40L-15

42-10960/11129       P-40L-20

42-11130/11676       P-40L-25             Cancelled

42-14237/14296       P-40L-30             Cancelled

42-24920/24939       P-47G-CU    )
                                 )
42-24940/24979       P-47G-1-CU  )        Republic P-47D built
                                 )
42-24980/25039       P-47G-5-CU  )        under licence by Curtiss
                                 )
42-25040/25119       P-47G-10-CU)
                                 )
42-25120/25273       P-47G-15-CU)

42-39347             XP-55

42-43258, 43259      XP-71               Cancelled

42-45722/46321       P-40K-1             42-45722 to XP-40Q No.2

42-56853/57152       AT-9A

42-60942/61091       C-46A-40/41-CU

42-78845/78847       XP-55

42-79423             XP-60A

42-79424             XP-60C

42-79425             XP-60E

42-79663/79672       RA-25A-10-SL )
                                  )
42-79673/79732       RA-25A-15-SL )       Most to US Marines as
                                  )
42-79733/80052       RA-25A-20-SL )       SB2C-1A;
                                  )
42-80053/80132       RA-25A-25-SL )       10 to RAAF
                                  )
42-80133/80462       RA-25A-30-SL )

42-86913/86917       C-76 -CS
```

| | | |
|---|---|---|
| 42-86918/86928 | YC-76-CK | |
| 42-86929/86937 | YC-76A-1-CK | |
| 42-86938/87112 | C-76A | Cancelled |
| 42-96529/96828 | C-46A-45/50-CU | |
| | mixed with | |
| | C-46D-5-CU | |
| 42-101036/101235 | C-46D-5 and | |
| | C-46A-20-CU mix | |
| 42-104429/104828 | P-40N-1 | |
| 42-104829/105928 | P-40N-5 | |
| 42-105929/106405 | P-40N-10 | |
| 42-106406/106428 | P-40N-15 | |
| 42-107280/107317 | C-46A-41-CU | |
| 42-107318/107373 | C-46A-40-CU | |
| 42-107374/107399 | C-46A-45-CU | |
| 42-108995/109006 | P-36G | Ex-Norwegian H75A-8 |
| 43-5403/5462 | P-40M-1 | |
| 43-5463/5722 | P-40M-5 | |
| 43-5723/6002 | P-40M-10 | |
| 43-22752/24251 | P-40N-20 | |
| 43-24252/24751 | P-40N-25 | 42-24571 to XP-40Q No.3 |
| 43-32763 | YP-60E | |
| 43-43339, 43340 | C-46A-1-HI | Built by Higgins |
| 43-46953, 46954 | C-46A-1-CS | |
| 43-46955/46972 | C-46A-1-CK | |
| 43-46973/47032 | C-46A-5-CK | |
| 43-47033/47202 | C-46A-55-CK | |
| 43-47203/47304 | C-46A-60-CK | |
| 43-47305/47314 | C-46A-60-CS | |
| 43-47315/47402 | C-46A-60-CK | |

591

| | | |
|---|---|---|
| 43-47403/47419 | C-46E-1-CS | |
| 44-7001/7500 | P-40N-30 | |
| 44-7501/8000 | P-40N-35 | |
| 44-47749/47968 | P-40N-40 | |
| 44-77295/77443 | C-46D-5-CU | |
| 44-77444/77893 | C-46D-10-CU | 44-77444, 77446 to C-46A-55 |
| 44-77894/78344 | C-46D-15-CU | |
| 44-78345/78544 | C-46D-20-CU | |
| 44-78545/78778 | C-46F-1-CU | |
| 44-78945 | C-46G-1-CU | To XC-113 |
| 45-59600, 59601 | XP-87 | 59601 cancelled |
| 46-522 | XP-87 | To XF-87A; cancelled before completion |

# APPENDIX V

# Serial Numbers of US Navy Aircraft Designed or Built by Curtiss, 1917–45

This appendix lists all the US Navy serial numbers assigned to US Navy, US Marine Corps, or US Coast Guard aircraft built by Curtiss or associated contractors from the standardization of the Navy serial numbering system in 1917 to the end of World War II procurement.

Aeroplanes existing before 1921 are identified by Curtiss designations; standard Naval designations are used for identification of subsequent designs. Because of the confusion of numbers that results from Navy use of three separate series of serial numbers, each series is identified in sequence by its own calendar period. The prefix letter A used in connection with Navy serial numbers until 1931 is not included.

| US Navy Serial numbers | Designation | Remarks |
|---|---|---|
| 60/65 | N-9C | |
| 66, 67 | R-3 | |
| 85/90 | N-9C | |
| 93 | JN | Erroneously called JN-1, TW |
| 96/125 | N-9C | |
| 145, 146 | H-14 | |
| 149 | S-4 | |
| 150 | S-5 | |
| 152 | H-12 | |
| 157/159 | JN-4B | |
| 162/197 | R-3 | Completed as R-6 |
| 198 | JN | |
| 201/234 | N-9C | |
| 291/293 | L-2 | Triplanes |
| 294/301 | N-9C | |
| 302/341 | R-9 | |
| 342/373 | N-9C | 365 to N-10 |
| 386, 387 | F-Boat | |
| 388, 389 | JN-4A | |
| 390/393 | F-Boat | |
| 408 | F-Boat | |
| 409/438 | N-9C | Built by Burgess |
| 445/449 | GS-2 | Gnome Scout biplane |
| 752/756 | F-Boat | |
| 765/783 | H-12 | |

| | | |
|---|---|---|
| 784/799 | H-16 | |
| 800/815 | HS-1, HS-2 | No. 815 cancelled |
| 818/867 | H-16 | |
| 868 | GS-1 | Gnome Scout triplane |
| 873/994 | R-6 | Most to R-9 |
| 995/997 | JN-4A | |
| 999/1028 | N-9C | Built by Burgess |
| 1031/1048 | H-16 | |
| 1049/1098 | H-16 | Built by Naval Aircraft Factory |
| 1099/1398 | HS-1L, HS-2L | By L.W.F., 50 cancelled. HS-2Ls start at 1223 |
| 1399/1548 | HS-2L | By Standard, 1479/1548 cancelled |
| 1549/2207 | HS-1L, HS-2L | HS-2Ls start at 1820 |
| 2217/2276 | HS-2L | By Gallaudet |
| 2277 | BT | Flying lifeboat |
| 2278 | HA | Crashed, parts to 4110 |
| 2279, 2280 | F-Boat | One by Verville |
| 2281 | F-Boat | By Burgess |
| 2285/2290 | N-9C | 2286/2290 as N-9H |
| 2291/2294 | NC-1/NC-4 | |
| 2295/2344 | F-Boat | |
| 2345/2350 | MF | |
| 2351/2650 | N-9C | 2410/2572, 2574/2650 as N-9H; 2473 to N-10 |
| 3205/3234 | JN-4H | |
| 3245/3324 | N-9H | |
| 3325, 3326 | 18-T | With long wings, 18T-2 |
| 3328/3332 | F-Boat | |

| | | |
|---|---|---|
| 3333/3382 | F-5L | By Canadian Aeroplanes. 3363/3382 cancelled. |
| 3459/3558 | H-16 | By NAF |
| 3559/4038 | F-5L | By NAF. 3618/3658, 3684/3783, 3801/3858, 3881,3883/3935, 3941/4008, 4014/4035 cancelled; 4036, 4037 to F-6L. |
| 4039/4078 | H-16 | |
| 4079/4108 | F-Boat | |
| 4110, 4111 | HA-1 | 4111 as HA-2 |
| 4112/4117 | JN-4B | |
| 4128/4217 | JN-4HG | |
| 4228, 4229 | HS-2L | By Loughead |
| 4231/4280 | HS-2L | By Boeing, 4256/4280 cancelled |
| 4281/4340 | F-5L | |
| 4349/4402 | F-Boat | |
| 4403/4449 | MF | 4419/4449 cancelled |
| 4470/4819 | F-5L | Cancelled |
| 4820/5019 | N-9 | Burgess, cancelled |
| 5258 | F-Boat | |
| 5259/5458 | F-5L | NAF, cancelled |
| 5459/5462 | HS-3 | |
| 5470, 5471 | JN-6HG-I | |
| 5483/5562 | MF | By NAF |
| 5564/5569 | HS-2L | NAS Miami * |
| 5581/5586 | JN-6HG-I | |
| 5590, 5591 | HS-3 | By NAF |

*This type of entry means that the aeroplanes were assembled from spare parts at the named Naval Air Station (NAS)

| 5615/5619 | HS-2L | NAS Hampton Roads |
| 5630 | HS-2L | A1171 rebuilt by L.W.F. |
| 5632/5635 | NC-5/NC-8 | By NAF |
| 5787 | HS-2L | NAS Key West |
| 5808 | HS-2L | NAS Anacostia |
| 5830/5833 | JN-6H | |
| 5859 | JN-6H | |
| 5885, 5886 | NC-9, NC-10 | By NAF |
| 5890/5898 | CT-1 | Last eight cancelled |
| 6002/6004 | XSA | Cancelled |
| 6080, 6081 | CF-1 | To CR-1, CR-2, CR-3 |
| 6193/6247 | JN-4H | |
| 6248/6270 | TS-1 | US Navy design |
| 6271/6288 | JN-4H | |
| 6316/6325 | JN-4H | From NAF spares, cancelled |
| 6500/6505 | CS-1 | Navy design, 6502 to CS-2, 6503 to XCS-7 |
| 6506 | HS-2L | NAS Coco Solo |
| 6507/6513 | HS-2L | From spares at NAF |
| 6528/6542 | N-9H | NAS Pensacola |
| 6545 | JN-4HG | From salvage of JN-4H and N-9H |
| 6553/6556 | HS-2L | NAS San Diego |
| 6557/6559 | F-5L | NAS Hampton Roads |
| 6618/6632 | N-9H | NAS Pensacola |
| 6689, 6690 | F4C-1 | Redesigned TS-1 |
| 6691, 6692 | R2C-1 | 6691 to Army R-8, 6692 to R2C-2 seaplane |
| 6697 | F-5L | NAS San Diego |
| 6731, 6732 | CS-2 | Navy design, 6731 to CS-3 |
| 6733/6742 | N-9H | NAS Pensacola |

| | | |
|---|---|---|
| 6801/6835 | SC-1 | Built by Martin, 6834 to SC-6, 6835 to XSC-6 |
| 6928/6967 | SC-2 | By Martin, to SC-5 |
| 6968/6976 | F6C-1 | 6968 to F6C-4 proto, XF6C-5, 6970, 6972 to F6C-3, 6973/6976 to F6C-2. |
| 6978, 6979 | R3C-1 | 6978 to R3C-2, R3C-4, 6979 to R3C-2 (US Army) |
| 7054 | R3C-1 | to R3C-2, R3C-3 |
| 7091/7100 | N-9H | NAS Pensacola |
| 7128/7162 | F6C-3 | 7136 to XF6C-3, 7144 to F6C-6, 7147 to XF6C-6 |
| 7393/7423 | F6C-4 | 7393 to XF6C-4, 7403 to XF6C-7 |
| 7650/7652 | XN2C-1 | |
| 7653/7670 | F7C-1 | |
| 7671, 7672 | XF8C-1 | 7671 to OC-1, 7672 to OC-1, XOC-3 |
| 7673 | XF8C-2 | |
| 7945/7948 | F8C-1 | To OC-1 |
| 7949/7969 | F8C-3 | To OC-2 |
| 8020/8050 | N2C-1 | |
| 8314 | XF8C-4 | |
| 8421/8445 | F8C-4 | |
| 8446/8456 | F8C-5 | To O2C-1 |
| 8526/8545 | N2C-2 | |
| 8589/8597 | F8C-5 | As O2C-1 |
| 8731 | XF9C-1 | |
| 8748/8790 | O2C-1 | |
| 8845 | XF8C-7 | To XO2C-2, O2C-2, XF8C-7 |
| 8846 | JC-1 | As RC-1 |

| | | |
|---|---|---|
| 8847 | XF8C-8 | To O2C-2, XS3C-1, XF1OC-1, O2C-2 |
| 8848, 8849 | O2C-2 | To XF8C-8 |
| 8941/8970 | O2C-1 | |
| 9056/9061* | F9C-2 | Survivors to XF9C-2 |
| 9213 | XF11C-2 | |
| 9219 | XF11C-1 | |
| 9225 | XF12C-1 | To XS4C-1, XSBC-1; crashed, new airframe with same serial became XSBC-2, -3 |
| 9264 | XF9C-2 | |
| 9265/9282 | F11C-2 | 9269 as XF11C-3, XBF2C-1, others to BFC-2 |
| 9331/9340 | F11C-2 | To BFC-2 |
| 9343 | XF13C-1 | To XF13C-2, XF13C-3 |
| 9377 | XS2C-1 | |
| 9413 | XO3C-1 | To XSOC-1 |
| 9584, 9585 | R4C-1 | |
| 9586/9612 | BF2C-1 | |
| 9856/9990 | SOC-1 | 9866 to SOC-3, some others to SOC-1A with arrester gear during World War II. SOC-1s were last Curtiss aeroplanes ordered in first US Navy serial number series, which ended at 9999 in 1934 to avoid going into five numerals. |

*End of A-prefix assignments for Curtiss.   F9C-2s ordered with it, delivered without it.

598

| US Navy Serial numbers | Designation | Remarks |
|---|---|---|
| 0386/0425 | SOC-2 | 0392, 0415 to SOC-2A |
| 0507/0589 | SBC-3 | 0582 as XSBC-4 No.1 |
| 0950 | XSO2C-1 | |
| 1064/1146 | SOC-3 | Some to SOC-3A in World War II |
| 1268/1325 | SBC-4 | 1268 as XSBC-4 No.2 |
| 1385 | XSO3C-1 | |
| 1474/1504 | SBC-4 | |
| 1758 | XSB2C-1 | |
| 1809/1843 | SBC-4 | |
| 4199/4248 | SBC-4 | |
| 4730/4783 | SO3C-1 | |
| 4784/4792 | SO3C-2C | |
| 4793/4879 | SO3C-1 | |
| 4880/5029 | SO3C-2 | |
| 6290/6439 | SNC-1 | |

Because of the rapid buildup for World War II, the second Navy serial number series was ended at 7303 to avoid duplicating serials then in use by aeroplanes ordered near the end of the first series.

US Coast Guard

| V171/173 | SOC-4 | To US Navy as SOC-3A 48243/48245 |
|---|---|---|

Third Series - from 1940

To avoid duplicating the serial numbers of practically all of the aeroplanes ordered in the quickly-filled second series, the third Navy serial number series was started with five figures; this was allowed to expand to six figures in 1945, shortly before the Navy's last procurement of Curtiss aeroplanes.

| US Navy Serial numbers | Designation | Remarks |
|---|---|---|
| 00001/00200 | SB2C-1 | 00005 as XSB2C-2, 00008 to prototype SB2C-3 |
| 00201/00370 | SB2C-1C | |
| 01008/01208 | SB2C-1 | All but 01008 cancelled |
| 01213/01215 | XF15C-1 | Reassigned serials |
| 03183, 03184 | XF14C-1 | 03183 to -2, 03184 cancelled |
| 04149/04198 | SO3C-2 | |
| 04199/04348 | SO3C-3 | |
| 05085/05234 | SNC-1 | |
| 18192/18598 | SB2C-1C | |
| 18599/19710 | SB2C-3 | Some to -3E; 18620, 18621 to XSB2C-6 |
| 19711/21191 | SB2C-4 | Some to -4E |
| 21192/21232 | SBW-1 | Canadian Car & Foundry. 21198 to SBW-3; 21232 to SBW-5, cancelled. |
| 21233/21645 | SBW-3 | 21234 as SBW-1 |
| 21646/21741 | SBW-4E | |
| 22007/22256 | SO3C-3 | |

| | | |
|---|---|---|
| 30297, 30298 | XF14C-3 | Cancelled |
| 31399/31402 | XBTC-1 | 31400, 31401 as XBTC-2, 31399, 31402 cancelled |
| 31636/31685 | SBF-1 | Canadian Fairchild |
| 31686/31815 | SBF-3 | |
| 31836/31935 | SBF-4E | |
| 32987/32991 | SNC-1 | |
| 34095, 34096 | XSC-1 | |
| 35298/35797 | SC-1 | 35298/35300 as XSC-1 |
| 39492/39611 | R5C-1 | C-46As from US Army |
| 48243/48245 | SOC-3A | SOC-4s from Coast Guard |
| 50690/50739 | R5C-1 | Army C-46As; 50730/50739 cancelled |
| 50879/50888 | XBT2C-1 | Cancelled; serials reassigned |
| 60010/60035 | SBW-1B | To RAF JW100/125 |
| 60036/60209 | SBW-4E | |
| 60210/60459 | SBW-5 | 60210, 60296/60459 cancelled |
| 64993/65286 | SB2C-4E | 65286 to prototype SB2C-5 |
| 75218/75588 | SB2C-1A | A-25As from US Army |
| 76780/76818 | SB2C-1A | A-25As from US Army |
| 82858/83127 | SB2C-4, 4E | |
| 83128/83751 | SB2C-5 | 83128 temporary XSB2C-5 |
| 89120/90019 | SB2C-5 | 89466/90019 (554) cancelled |
| 93302/93651 | SC-1 | 93368/93651 (284) cancelled |
| 119529/119778 | SC-2 | 119539/119778 (240 of 250) cancelled |

# Serial Numbers of British and Commonwealth Military Aircraft Designed or Built by Curtiss, 1914–45

This appendix lists the RNAS, RFC, RAF, RAAF, RNZAF and RCAF serial numbers assigned to aircraft built by Curtiss and associate contractors and to former US military and civil Curtiss aircraft acquired by Britain and Canada for military use. RAF serials are listed numerically within groupings by alphabetical prefix. Prefixed and unprefixed serials are listed separately.

In the case of World War II Lend-Lease aircraft built with US military serial numbers even though intended for Commonwealth use and carrying Commonwealth military markings and serials, the US serials are presented when known.

| Serial Number | | Curtiss Model | Remarks |
|---|---|---|---|
| 882, 883 | (2) | H-4 Small America | Austro-Daimler engines |
| 950, 951 | (2) | H-4 Small America | 950 with 125 hp Anzani |
| | | | 951 with 100 hp Anzani |
| 1228/1231 | (4) | H-4 Small America | Built by Airco & Saunders |
| 1232/1239 | (8) | H-4 Small America | American built. 1232/1235 90 hp Curtiss engines changed to 100 hp Anzani, 1238 to 150 hp Sunbeam, 1239 to 100 hp Anzani. |
| 1323/1334 | (12) | R-2 | Cancelled |
| 1362/1367 | (6) | JN-3 | March 1915 |
| 3073/3092 | (20) | T Triplane Boat | Only 3073 built |
| 3345/3423 | (79) | JN-3 | 3345 to French, 3384, 3386, 3393 rebuilt by Fairey. |

| | | | |
|---|---|---|---|
| 3424/3444 | (21) | JN-4 | 3425, 3432, 3434, 3436, 3438, 3440, 3442, 3444 to dual control trainers. |
| 3445/3544 | (100) | R-2 | 160 hp Curtiss engines replaced by 200 hp Sunbeam. |
| 3545/3594 | (50) | H-4 Small America | 3580 converted to Felixstowe F.1 |
| 3700 | | Twin Canada | Accepted 11 Nov, 1916 |
| 5624/5639 | (16) | JN-3/JN-4 | Transfers from RNAS to RFC |
| 5722/5728 | (7) | JN-3/JN-4 | "        "        "        "        " |
| 5910/5915 | (6) | JN-3/JN-4 | "        "        "        "        " |
| 6116/6135 | (20) | JN-3/JN-4 | "        "        "        "        " |
| 7308/7320 | (13) | JN-3/JN-4 | "        "        "        "        " |
| 8338/8343 | (6) | H-4 Small America | Built by Norman Thompson as NT-4 |
| 8392/8403 | (12) | JN-3 | Canadian-built. 8403 to French |
| 8650/8699 | (50) | H-12 Large America | 160 hp Curtiss engines replaced by Rolls-Royce Eagle |
| 8802/8901 | (100) | JN-4 | 8881/8900 not delivered; 8901 to RFC, 8852, 8856, 8858 to French. |
| 9500/9600 | (101) | Twin Canada | Cancelled |
| A614/625 | (12) | JN-3/JN-4 | Transfers from RNAS to RFC |
| A898/903 | (6) | JN-3/JN-4 | "    "    "     "      " |

| | | |
|---|---|---|
| A1254/1260 (7) | JN-3/JN-4 | Transfers from RNAS to RFC |
| A3276/3280 (5) | JN-4 | "    "    "    "    " |
| A4056/4060 (5) | JN-4A | "    "    "    "    " |
| A5160/5168 (9) | JN-3/JN-4 | "    "    "    "    " |
| A5215/5224 (10) | JN-3/JN-4 | "    "    "    "    " |
| A5492/5496 (5) | JN-3/JN-4 | "    "    "    "    " |
| B1901/1950 (50) | JN-4/JN-4A | Admiralty contract |
| C101/500* (400) | JN-4C | |
| C501/1450* (950) | JN-4C/JN-4A | 501/560, 1015/1051 JN-4A, 1060/1260 and 1401/1450 on JN-4D contracts. |
| C1451/1500* (50) | JN-4C | 1451/1457 ambulance conversions. No higher numbers con-firmed. |
| N1160/1179 (20) | H-12 Large America | Cancelled |
| N1510/1519 (10) | H-12/H-16 Large America | Cancelled; to have been built by Airco. |
| N2140/2159 (20) | H-4 Small America | Built by Norman Thompson as NT-4A. |
| N4060/4074 (15) | H-16 Large America | Delivered March, 1918; Rolls-Royce Eagle VIII installed in Britain. |

* Special block for procurement of training aircraft in Canada which duplicated numbers assigned to combat and trainer types for use in Europe.

N4330/4353 (24)     H-12B Large America     Delivery starting
                                            January, 1918; Rolls-
                                            Royce Eagle. 4351/4353
                                            cancelled.

N4890/4999 (110)    H-16 Large America      4950/4999 cancelled;
                                            4900/4949 delivered
                                            in 1919 and put into
                                            storage.

N5660/5709 (50)     JN-4                    Some cancelled

Procurement of Curtiss aeroplanes by the RAF began with the impressment of four T-32 Condors from the British civil register. These were followed by direct purchases from Curtiss of Tomahawk equivalents of the US Army P-40 and the takeover of French Model 75 contracts after the fall of France in 1940.

All procurement was by direct purchase with British funds until the advent of Lend-Lease in March 1941. From this time, American aeroplanes were provided by US Army or Navy channels and funds and carried US designations and serial numbers in addition to the assigned RAF serials, markings, and colouring. These aeroplanes were operated by the RAF under the British Name system, ie, Kittyhawk IA instead of P-40E-1.

| RAF Serial Number | | RAF/US Military Model | Remarks |
|---|---|---|---|
| P5723/5726 | (4) | Condor II | Ex-civil G-AEWD, ZE, WE, WF |
| AH741/880 | (140) | Tomahawk I | |
| AH881/990 | (110) | Tomahawk IIA | 936, 952, 965/971, 974/985, 987, 989/990 to USSR. |
| AH991/999 | (9) | Tomahawk IIB | |

606

| | | | |
|---|---|---|---|
| AK100/570 | (471) | Tomahawk IIB | 210/224, 226/241 lost at sea. Some to AVG; 254, 434, 440, 448, 470, 561 to Egyptian Air Force. |
| AM370/519 | (150) | Tomahawk IIB | Many to AVG |
| AN218/517 | (300) | Tomahawk IIB | 469/517 to USSR, others to Turkey and Egypt. |
| AR630/694 | (65) | Mohawk III/IV | Ex-French order. 642, 643, 652, 664, 666, 668, 671, 673, 679, 680 to Portugal; 648, 657, 659, 660, 683, 684, 686, 688, 689, 692/694 to South Africa. |
| AS467/471 | (5) | Cleveland I | Ex-US Navy SBC-4 via French |
| AX799 | | Hawk | Type not identified but probably Mohawk IV since it was acquired in India. |
| AX880/898 | (19) | Mohawk | Ex-French; sent to India, Portugal and South Africa. |
| BB918/979 | (62) | Mohawk IV | Most to India, South Africa and Portugal. |

| | | | |
|---|---|---|---|
| BJ434/453 | (20) | Mohawk IV | Ex-French; most to India and South Africa. |
| BJ531/550 | (20) | Mohawk IV | Most to India, South Africa and Portugal. |
| BJ574/588 | (15) | Mohawk IV | |
| BK569/588 | (20) | Mohawk III | Most to India and South Africa. |
| BK876/879 | (4) | Mohawk | 876, 878 to South Africa, 879 to India. |
| BL220/223 | (4) | Mohawk | 220 to Portugal, 221/223 to South Africa. |
| BS730/747 | (18) | Mohawk IV | Most to India and South Africa. |
| BS784/798 | (15) | Mohawk IV | Eight to South Africa, six to India, one to Portugal. |
| BT470/472 | (3) | Mohawk IV | Ex-French; all to India. |
| ET100/999 )<br>EV100/699 ) | (1500) | Kittyhawk I/IA | Many to Australia and New Zealand. |
| FL219/448 | (230) | Kittyhawk IIA/P-40F | FL273, 369/448 returned to USAAF, 263, 270, 276, 280, 282, 305, 307 to Free French. |
| FL710/730 | (21) | Kittyhawk III/P-40M | Received Sept/Oct 1942; to Middle East. |
| FL875/905 | (31) | Kittyhawk III/P-40M | |

608

| | | | |
|---|---|---|---|
| FN450/649 | (200) | Seamew I/SO3C-2 | Only 453, 463, 467, 472/475, 483, 489, 573, 608, 622 and 631 known deliveries to RAF, 53 to Canada. |
| FR111/140 | (30) | Kittyhawk III/P-40M | Nov 42/Feb 43; to Middle East |
| FR210/361 | (152) | Kittyhawk III/P-40M | |
| FR385/392 | (8) | Kittyhawk III/P-40M | Nov 42/Aug 43 |
| FR412/521 | (110) | Kittyhawk III/P-40M | |
| FR779/872 | (94) | Kittyhawk III/P-40M | |
| FR884, 885 | (2) | Kittyhawk IV/P-40N | Oct 43. |
| FS100/269 | (170) | Kittyhawk III | To USSR |
| FS270/399 | (130) | Kittyhawk IV/P-40N | |
| FS400/499 | (100) | Kittyhawk II | |
| FT849/954 | (106) | Kittyhawk IV/P-40N | 898/904 lost at sea. |
| FX498/847 | (350) | Kittyhawk IV/P-40N | |
| JW100/125 | (26) | Helldiver I/SBW-1B | Built by Canadian Car & Foundry |
| JW550/669 | (120) | Seamew I/SO3C-2C | Seventeen to Canada |
| JX663/669 | (7) | Queen Sewmew/SO3C-2C | Radio-controlled targets |
| JZ771/774 | (4) | Queen Seamew/SO3C-2C | "    "      " |
| LA157/165 | (9) | Mohawk | All but 159/162 assembled in India. |

609

Australian serial numbers use the letter A and a number to identify the individual model of aeroplane, followed by sequential numbers to the total of that model procured. A29 identified all Curtiss Kittyhawk variants and A69 was assigned to former US Army Curtiss A-25A Shrikes. Some gaps occur in Kittyhawk listings.

| Australian Serial Number | | Curtiss/US Army Model |
|---|---|---|
| A29-1/163 | (163) | Kittyhawk IA/P-40E-1 |
| A29-164/202 | (39) | Kittyhawk III/P-40K-10 |
| A29-203/205 | (3) | Kittyhawk III/P-40K-15 |
| A29-206/299 | (94) | Not listed |
| A29-300/389 | (90) | Kittyhawk III/P-40M-10 |
| A29-390/399 | (10) | Not listed |
| A29-400/414 | (15) | Kittyhawk III/P-40M-5, 10 |
| A29-415/419 | (5) | Kittyhawk IV/P-40N-1 |
| A29-420/434 | (15) | Kittyhawk III/P-40M-5, 10 |
| A29-435/442 | (8) | Kittyhawk IV/P-40N-1 |
| A29-443/460 | (18) | Kittyhawk III/P-40M-5, 10 |
| A29-461/472 | (12) | Kittyhawk IV/P-40N-1 |
| A29/473/502 | (30) | Kittyhawk III/P-40M-5, 10 |
| A29-503/541 | (39) | Kittyhawk IV/P-40N-1 |

```
A29-542/558          (17)      Kittyhawk IV/P-40N-15

A29-559/563          (5)       Kittyhawk IV/P-40N-1

A29-564/576          (13)      Kittyhawk IV/P-40N-15

A29-577/587          (11)      Kittyhawk IV/P-40N-1

A29-588/599          (12)      Not listed

A29-600/704          (105)     Kittyhawk IV/P-40N-20

A29-705/799          (95)      Not listed

A29-800/811          (12)      Kittyhawk IV/P-40N-25

A29-812/818          (7)       Not listed

A29-819/828          (10)      Kittyhawk IV/P-40N-25

A29-829/899          (71)      Not listed

A29-900/928          (29)      Kittyhawk IV/P-40N-30

A29-929/999          (71)      Not listed

A29-1000/1079        (80)      Kittyhawk IV/P-40N-35

A29-1080/1099        (20)      Not listed

A29-1100/1221        (122)     Kittyhawk IV/P-40N-40

A69-1/10             (10)      Shrike I/A-25A
```

| New Zealand Serial Numbers | | Curtiss/US Army Model |
|---|---|---|
| NZ3001/3044 | (44) | Kittyhawk IA/P-40E-1 |
| NZ3074 | | Kittyhawk II/P-40F |
| NZ3091/3098 | (8) | Kittyhawk IA/P-40E-1 |
| NZ3100/3108 | (9) | Kittyhawk IA/P-40E-1 |
| NZ3271 | | Kittyhawk IA/P-40E-1 |
| NZ3045/3065 | (21) | Kittyhawk III/P-40K |
| NZ3066/3073 | (8) | Kittyhawk III/P-40M |
| NZ3075/3089 | (15) | Kittyhawk III/P-40M |
| NZ3090 | | Kittyhawk III/P-40K |
| NZ3099 | | Kittyhawk III/P-40K |
| NZ3109/3119 | (11) | Kittyhawk III/P-40M |
| NZ3120/3179 | (60) | Kittyhawk IV/P-40N |
| NZ3180 | | Kittyhawk III/P-40M |
| NZ3181/3270 | (90) | Kittyhawk IV/P-40N |
| NZ3272/3293 | (22) | Kittyhawk IV/P-40N |

Several different serial numbering systems have been used by
the Canadian Forces and are presented separately under this
heading.


## WORLD WAR I

Canada did not have air forces of its own in World War I.
Aeroplanes procured for use by Britain or in Canada were
mostly issued numbers in the current British series. However,
Canadian-built Curtiss JN-4s and 4As procured for use in
Canadian training programmes were assigned a special block
of serials, C101/1500. These duplicated C-series numbers
assigned to combat and training aeroplanes built in England.
Since these were painted on both sides of the rudder only and
the aeroplanes seldom carried the standard roundels or rudder
stripes, contemporary photographs seen many years later
created the impression that the aeroplanes carried US civil
markings.


## RCAF G-CY SYSTEM 1919-29

The Canadian Air Force was established in 1919 and became the
Royal Canadian Air Force in 1923. Originally, Canadian Government aeroplanes, combat and peaceful types alike, were
identified by civil-type lettering instead of serial numbers.
The initial letter was G (for Great Britain) followed by a

dash and the two letters CY preceding two more letters that
identified the individual aeroplane.   Canadian civil aeroplanes were similarly marked G-CA in this same period.   The
G-CY  system was shortened after 1929 to use only the last two
letters on the aeroplane.   This practice overlapped the
adoption of sequential numbers for military aeroplanes and
was soon phased out.

| RCAF Serial Number | Curtiss Model | Remarks |
|---|---|---|
| AE | HS-2L | LWF-built, US Navy A1248 |
| AF | HS-2L | Hull built by Niagara Boat Co, US Navy A1875 |
| AG | HS-2L | Curtiss-built |
| AH | HS-2L | Curtiss-built |
| BA | HS-2L | Curtiss-built |
| BB | HS-2L | Curtiss-built |
| BD | HJ-2L | Curtiss-built |
| CN | JN-4C | |
| CO | JN-4C | |
| CP | JN-4C | |
| DC/DG | JN-4C | |
| DR/DU | HS-2L | Curtiss-built |
| DV, DW | JN-4C | |
| DX, DY | HS-2L | Curtiss-built |
| EA, EB | HS-2L | Curtiss-built |
| ED | HS-2L | Curtiss-built |
| EF | HS-2L | Curtiss-built |
| EJ | HS-2L | Gallaudet-built |
| EK, EL | HS-2L | Curtiss-built |

| EP | H-16 | |
| GA | HS-2L | Curtiss-built |
| GL/GV | HS-2L | Curtiss-built |

## SEQUENTIAL NUMBERING SYSTEM FROM 1929

In 1929, the RCAF adopted a sequential numbering system for military aeroplanes, but the preceding two-letter system remained in simultaneous use for several years.  In World War II, some of the RAF aeroplanes turned over to Canada while carrying RAF serial numbers were renumbered in the Canadian system.  Most US Army aeroplanes delivered to Canada under Lend-Lease after 1941 were also given Canadian numbers.

| RCAF Serial Number | | Model Name/US Army Designation | Remarks |
| --- | --- | --- | --- |
| 720/731 | (12) | Kittyhawk IA/P-40E-1 | From RAF ET845/866 range |
| 831/845 | (15) | Kittyhawk III/P-40M | From US Army 43-5706/5795 range |
| 846/880 | (35) | Kittyhawk IV/P-40N | From US Army 42-104568/106396 and 43-22885/23493 ranges |
| 1028/1099 | (72) | Kittyhawk I | From RAF AK752/996 and AL109/228 ranges |

Many of the aeroplanes acquired by Canada during the war years
through British procurement channels were operated under their
original RAF serials instead of being assigned new Canadian
serials.

| RAF Serial Number | Model Name/US Military Designation | Remarks |
|---|---|---|
| AH774 | Tomahawk I | To instructional airframe |
| AH793 | Tomahawk I | To instructional airframe A-314 |
| AH840 | Tomahawk I | To instructional airframe A-315 |
| AH938 | Tomahawk IIA | To instructional airframe |
| FN480/486 (7) | Seamew I/SO3C-2C | |
| FN489/496 (8) | Seamew I/SO3C-2C | |
| FN498, 499 | Seamew I/SO3C-2C | |
| FN600/608 (9) | Seamew I/SO3C-2C | |
| FN610/613 (4) | Seamew I/SO3C-2C | |
| FN615, 616 | Seamew I/SO3C-2C | |
| FN618/620 (3) | Seamew I/SO3C-2C | |
| FN622, 623 | Seamew I/SO3C-2C | |
| FN625 | Seamew I/SO3C-2C | |
| FN627 | Seamew I/SO3C-2C | |
| FN629/642 (14) | Seamew I/SO3C-2C | |

JW576/578 (3)   Seamew I/SO3C-2C
JW581/583 (3)   Seamew I/SO3C-2C
JW614/618 (5)   Seamew I/SO3C-2C
JW621, 622      Seamew I/SO3C-2C
JW624           Seamew I/SO3C-2C
JW638           Seamew I/SO3C-2C
JW640           Seamew I/SO3C-2C
JW642           Seamew I/SO3C-2C

The RCAF obtained some aeroplanes on loan from the US Army (as distinguished from Lend-Lease programmes) and operated them under their original US Army designations and serial numbers instead of assigning RAF names and serial numbers.    The only Curtiss models involved were the following nine P-40K-1s:

42-45921, 45944, 45945, 45951, 45952, 45954, 45977, 46003 and 46004.

When the RCAF grounded an unserviceable aeroplane and assigned it to a school as an instructional airframe, it was given a new serial number in a special A-series that identified these non-flying models.

| Instructional Airframe Number | Model | Previous Identification |
|---|---|---|
| A289 | Kittyhawk III | US Army 43-5691, RCAF 834 |
| A314 | Tomahawk I | RAF AH793 |
| A315 | Tomahawk I | RAF AH840 |
| A389 | Kittyhawk I | RCAF 1071 |
| A390 | Kittyhawk I | RAF AL110; to A433 |
| A391 | Kittyhawk I | RAF AL113 |
| A392 | Kittyhawk I | RAF AL124 |
| A433 | Kittyhawk I | RAF AL110; former A390 |
| Unknown | Tomahawk I | RAF AH774 |
| Unknown | Tomahawk IIA | RAF AH938 |

# US Army McCook Field and Wright Field P-Numbers applied to Curtiss Aeroplanes

The reader will note that many Curtiss aeroplanes of the US Army carried on their rudders the letter P followed by a number. These were applied sequentially to aeroplanes assigned for test to the US Army Air Service Engineering Center at McCook Field, Dayton, Ohio, starting in 1917. Originally, the letter P was an abbreviation of the contracted word Plane for Aeroplane. The practice continued at nearby Wright Field after McCook was closed in 1927 and ended early in 1930 with P-599, a Curtiss A-3B.

Some of the marked aeroplanes were actual prototypes with permanent Experimental designations, some were standard production models diverted for test work, while others were standard models given temporary X-designations for the duration of the testing. These temporary designations are identified in the following table by (T).

The system was changed in 1930 to identify design studies (projects) as well as flyable aeroplanes starting at XP-900 and was preceded by the letter X for Experimental. The P-for-Plane was replaced by a letter indicating the type of aeroplane; P then came to mean Pursuit. The letters were used to identify experimental aeroplanes still on paper or flyable articles on Bailment contract that had not yet been assigned official Army designations.

The only Curtiss aeroplane to carry such a designation was the Swift, which was identified as XP-934 while being tested as Curtiss property before purchase and the assignment of the official US Army designation of XP-31.

| P-Number | Aeroplane Model | US Army Serial numbers | Remarks |
|---|---|---|---|
| P-1 | JN-4B | - | |
| P-2 | JN-4A | 1621 | |
| P-3 | JN-4A | 1555 | |
| P-4 | JN-4D | 12876 | |
| P-5 | JN-4A special | 1262 | 100 hp, Hall-Scott A-7A engine |
| P-6 | JN-4H | 37935 | |
| P-15 | R-4L | 39954 | |
| P-19 | JN-4A special | 1527 | 100 hp, Hall-Scott A-7A engine |
| P-20 | R-4L | 39957 | |
| P-24 | JN-5H | 41358 | To 180 hp  JN-4H |
| P-27 | R-4L | 39958 | |
| P-29 | JN-4H | 37936 | |
| P-57 | JN-4C | 39349 | |
| P-63 | JN-6HG-2 | 44219 | |
| P-86 | 18-B | 40058 | Hornet |
| P-100 | JN-4D-2 | 47816 | |
| P-101 | Orenco D | 40109 | Prototype sent to Curtiss in June 1920 |
| P-103 | JN-4H | 41795 | |
| P-111 | JN-6H-I | 45010 | |
| P-112 | JN-6HG-1 | 44941 | |
| P-114 | JN-6HG-E | 44944 | |
| P-115 | JN-6HG-1 | 44954 | |
| P-116 | JN-6HG-I | 44913 | |
| P-117 | JN-6HG-1 | 44936 | |
| P-161 | Orenco D | 63282 | Curtiss-built, later with turbo-supercharger |
| P-186 | JN-4HG-1 | 44246 | Double elevators, wing flaps, air brakes |
| P-198 | PN-1 | 63276 | Army design built by Curtiss |

| | | | |
|---|---|---|---|
| P-199 | JN-4H | 38096 | |
| P-209 | JN-4HG | 41616 | |
| P-254 | NBS-1 | 68482 | Martin design built by Curtiss |
| P-278 | R-6 | 68564 | Winner 1922 Pulitzer Race |
| P-279 | R-6 | 68563 | 1922 Racer |
| P-293 | NBS-1 | 68508 | Curtiss-built, turbo-supercharger test |
| P-295 | XPW-8 No.1 | 23-1201 | To CO-X 2-seat racer, 1923 (T) |
| P-314 | JNS-I | 23-538 | Army rebuild |
| P-316 | NBS-1 | 68519 | Curtiss-built |
| P-322 | NBS-1 | 68526 | Curtiss-built |
| P-333 | XPW-8 No.2 | 23-1202 | |
| P-352 | XNBS-4 No.1 | 68571 | |
| P-354 | R-8 | 23-1235 | Ex-US Navy R2C-1 A6691 |
| P-357 | PW-8 | 24-201 | |
| P-358 | PW-8 | 24-202 | Turbo-supercharger test |
| P-361 | PW-8 | 24-204 | Dawn-to-Dusk Flight, June 1924 |
| P-364 | XPW-8A | 23-1203 | To XPW-8B |
| P-372 | JNS-I | 24-93 | Automatic pilot, supercharger |
| P-375 | XO-1 | 23-1252 | Liberty engine 1924, Packard engine 1925 |
| P-399 | NBS-1 | 68523 | Curtiss-built |
| P-400 | P-1 | 25-410 | To inverted Allison engine in 1926; to XP-17 in 1929 |
| P-431 | P-2 | 25-420 | To XP-2 with turbo-supercharger |
| P-434 | XNBS-4 No.2 | 68572 | |
| P-437 | O-1 Special | 25-325 | Curtiss D-12 engine, no armament |

621

| | | | |
|---|---|---|---|
| P-440 | O-1 | 25-334 | |
| P-444 | XAT-4 | 26-296 | From P-1A; to P1-D |
| P-449 | O-1A | 25-333 | From O-1; Liberty engine |
| P-451 | XP-3A No.1 | 26-300 | From P-1A;to XP-21 No.1, XP-21A |
| P-457 | P-1B | 27-68 | |
| P-460 | P-1B | 27-82 | |
| P-461 | P-1B | 27-87 | |
| P-462 | P-1B | 27-80 | |
| P-473 | AT-5 | 27-239 | To P-1E |
| P-476 | XO-11 No.1 | 25-328 | From 4th O-1 |
| P-477 | XB-2 | 26-211 | Condor heavy bomber |
| P-478 | O-11 | - | |
| P-484 | O-1B | - | |
| P-487 | XO-11 No.2 | 27-98 | From production O-11 |
| P-488 | XP-6A No.1 | 26-295 | Modified P-1A; 1927 race winner |
| P-489 | XO-13A | 25-332 | Modified O-1, 1927 race winner |
| P-493 | A-3 | 27-243 | |
| P-494 | XP-6 | 25-423 | Modified P-2, V-1570 Conqueror engine |
| P-495 | XO-13 | 25-331 | Modified O-1, V-1570 Conqueror engine |
| P-497 | O-1C | 27-268 | From O-1B; unarmed VIP transport |
| P-500 | XA-4 | 27-244 | Attack model from O-1B; Wasp engine |
| P-502 | XP-5 (T) | 27-327 | Service test of turbo-supercharger |
| P-508 | XP-1A (T) | 26-280 | Production P-1A for test work |
| P-511 | A-3 | 27-246 | |
| P-515 | XO-18 | 27-263 | From O-1B to O-1B |
| P-517 | AT-5A | 28-42 | To P-1F |

| | | | |
|---|---|---|---|
| P-518 | O-11 | – | |
| P-523 | XP-1B No.1 (T) | 27-71 | Production P-1B diverted to test |
| P-524 | XP-3A No.2 (T) | 28-189 | From P-3A; NACA cowling test. To XP-21 No.2, P-1F |
| P-526 | P-1A | 26-296 | |
| P-532 | O-1B Special | 27-276 | |
| P-537 | P-1C | 29-227 | |
| P-541 | P-3A | – | |
| P-542 | P-5 | 27-330 | |
| P-552 | B-2 | 28-398 | |
| P-558 | O-1C | 27-267 | VIP transport |
| P-572 | XP-1B No.2 (T) | 27-73 | Production P-1B to test wing guns |
| P-573 | P-1B | 27-82 | |
| P-574 | P-1A | 26-288 | |
| P-578 | XC-10 | 29-452 | Commercial Robin W; radio control test |
| P-579 | XP-1C (T) | 29-238 | Production P-1C for cooling tests |
| P-580 | P-6 | 29-260 | |
| P-582 | B-2 | 29-29 | |
| P-583 | O-11 | 28-216 | |
| P-585 | O-11 | 28-200 | |
| P-586 | XP-6A No.2 (T) | 29-263 | From production P-6A; to P-6D |
| P-587 | O-1E | 29-282 | |
| P-590 | XP-6B | 29-259 | From last production P-1C; V-1570 engine |
| P-595 | A-3B | 30-1 | To O-1E |
| P-596 | O-1B | 27-277 | |
| P-599 | A-3B | 30-246 | |
| XP-934 | Swift | No Army serial | Purchased as XP-31 serial 33-178 |

# INDEX

The index of this book has been compiled in a special form to serve a double function. In addition to being listed by page number for the purpose of locating specific aeroplanes in the book, all Curtiss aeroplanes have been placed on one or more of five separate lists that group them according to Popular Name, Curtiss Model Number, Curtiss Letter Designation, US Army Designation, and US Navy Designation. While these lists contain page numbers and serve as indices, each also stands alone as a complete compilation of the Curtiss aeroplanes covered by that particular designation system.

## Curtiss Aeroplanes Identified by Name, either Officially Assigned by Curtiss or Originated by Others and Accepted for Common Usage

Curtiss named many of its aeroplanes (Hawk, Falcon, etc) but some models operated under names given to them by others (Tomahawk, Seamew, etc). All known names are listed. Where differences are significant, as between Kittyhawk I and Kittyhawk IV, each is listed separately. Where the same name has been used on several different models, the numerical designation appears in parentheses for clarification, as Seahawk (Model 43) and Seahawk (Model 97). Some early models had no specific names or designations. These were identified in the factory by customer name (Stinson Special) or by configuration (Freak Boat), and are so listed.

Scout EC-1, 512
Scout, S-series, 130–4
Seagull (Model 18), 178
Seagull (Model 25), 183
Seagull (Model 71), 339–45
Seahawk (Model 43), 198–200
Seahawk (Model 97), 446–8
Seamew, 421
Sedan, 406, 407
Shrike (Model 59, 60), 326–30
Shrike (Model 69), 336
Shrike (Model 76), 364–8
Shrike (Model S84), 423, 432, 433
*Silver Dart*, 21, 28
Skeeter, 397, 398
Small America, 60, 84, 90
Sparrow, 410
Sparrowhawk, 320–5
Special, 512
Speed Scout, 133
Speedwing, 404, 405
Sport Trainer, 402, 403
Sportsman, 404
*St Louis*, 452

Stinson Special, 136
Swift, 333–5

*Tadpole*, 52
Tanager, 217–19
Teal (Model 57), 220
*Teal* (Model CW3), 401–2
Temple Curtiss, 512
*Texas Wildcat*, 224–6
Thrush, 172, 374, 390, 391
Tomahawk I, 474, 497
Tomahawk II, IIA, IIB, 498
Tractor Hydro, 1911, 46
Travel Air 6000, 316
Turkeyhawk, 282

Wanamaker Triplane, 136, 137
Warhawk, 474
Wasp, 139, 140
Water Glider, 186
Whistling Benny, 140
*White Wing*, 27
Wireless Scout, 131

## Curtiss Aeroplanes Listed by Curtiss Numerical Model Designation System of 1935

All of the Curtiss aeroplanes given numeric designations by the factory are listed here in strict numerical order regardless of the particular system under which that number was applied. Where letter prefixes are added to basic numerical designations, as S84, the letter does not affect the numerical progression. Where letters are used as suffixes to a given number, the sequence is alphabetical (84, 84A, etc).

Since mere numbers are in themselves meaningless, a popular name or commonly-used military designation appears with the number wherever possible (Model 34P matched to US Army designation XP-6). The numerical designation list of 1935, which was made up to be retroactive to 1916, overlooked many models and is not always chronologically accurate. However, it is 'Official' and is published here in its entirety for the first time outside of Curtiss documents.

| | | | | |
|---|---|---|---|---|
| 1 | (JN-4A), 152 | | 5 | (N-9), 111–14 |
| 1A | (JN-4B), 153 | | 6 | (H), 90 |
| 1C | (JN-4D), 156–8 | | 6A | (H-12), 92 |
| 1D | (N-8), 111 | | 6B | (H-12A), 92 |
| 1E | (JN-4H), 159 | | 6C | (H-16), 94–6 |
| 1F | (JN-6), 158, 162 | | 6D | (H-12B), 92 |
| 2 | (R/R-4), 120–6 | | 7 | (FL), 106 |
| 2 | (Sport Trainer), 512 | | 8 | (HS series), 100–5 |
| 2A | (R-6/R-9), 126–30 | | 9 | (L series), 107, 108 |
| 3 | (T), 136, 137 | | 10 | (S/S-3), 130–4 |
| 4 | (Commercial), 512 | | 10A | (S-4), 133 |
| 4 | (K), 106 | | 10B | (S-5), 133 |
| 5 | (Junior Transport), 512 | | 10C | (S-6), 133 |

628

H75-A2, 350, 351
H75-A3, 351
H75-A4, 351, 352
H75-A5, 352
H75-A6, 352, 353
H75-A7, 353
H75-A8, 353, 357, 361
H75-A9, 354, 355
75B   (prototype), 354, 355
75D   ('XP-36'), 355, 357
75E   (Y1P-36), 358, 365
75H, 354, 355
75I   (P-37), 362–4
75J   (demonstrator), 355
75K   (demonstrator), 355
75L   (P-36A), 358
75M, 355–7
H75N, 356
H75O, 356, 357, 361
75P   (XP-40), 364, 474, 479, 480, 496
75Q   (demonstrator), 357
H75R (demonstrator), 357, 358
75S   (XP-42), 359, 364
76    (A-14, A-18), 365–8
77    (XSBC-2, -3), 368
77A   (SBC-3), 370
77B   (SBC-4), 370–3
81    (P-40 series), 474–83, 497, 498
H81-A1, 502
81-A2, 502
81-A3, 502
81-AC(conversion), 502
81-AG(conversion), 503
H81B (P-40B, C), 503
82    (XSO3C-1), 419
82A   (SO3C-1), 419, 420
82B   (SO3C-2), 421
82C   (SO3C-3), 421

84    (SB2C/A-25 series), 424–33
84    (SB2C-1), 424–5
84A   (SB2C-1C), 426
84C   (XSB2C-2), 426
84E   (XSB2C-3), 427
84F   (SB2C-4), 427
84G   (SB2C-5), 429
84H   (XSB2C-6), 429
S84   (A-25A), 432, 433
85    (O-52), 433–5
86    (XP-46), 435–6
87    (P-40 series), 499–503
87A-1, 503
87A-2, -3, -4, 503
87B-2 (P-40E), 474, 484, 496
87B-3 (P-40F, L), 477, 478, 485–7, 496
87V   (P-40N), 490, 493, 496
87W   (P-40N), 502
87X   (XP-40Q), 492–6
90    (XP-60), 437
90A   (XP-60), 437
90B   (XP-60D), 438, 444
91    (XP-62), 438
94    (XF14C-2), 439–40
95    (XP-60A, B, C, E), 441–2, 444
95A   (XP-60A), 441
95B   (XP-60B), 442
95C   (XP-60C), 442
95D   (XP-60E), 442, 444
96    (XBTC-2), 445, 446
97    (SC series), 446–9
97A   (XSC-1), 447
97B   (SC-1), 447, 448
97C   (XSC-2), 449
97D   (SC-2), 449
98    (XBT2C-1), 449, 450
99    (XF15C-1), 506–8


## Curtiss Aeroplanes Listed by Curtiss Letter Designation

Curtiss identified some of its aeroplanes by various letter systems over the years. All are presented here in strict alphabetical sequence regardless of system or chronology. Single letters appear first, as H, followed by numbered and lettered variants (H-4, H-12A) and then a second letter (HA, HA-1). Sometimes a specific configuration is spelt out, as JN-6H Ambulance, R-Pusher and R-Twin for two separate R identifications, etc.

A (Glider), 512
AT-32/AT-32E Condor, 393

BA, 76
BAP, 77, 109
BAT, 77

BT, 79, 80
BT-32, 394, 395

CA-1, 396, 397
CB, 81
CP-39-13, 435–6

## Curtiss Aeroplanes with US Army Designations in the 1920–1948 Systems

All Curtiss aeroplanes identified in the basic US Army alpha-numeric system of 1920 and its later variations are listed in sequence of type, model, and series. The type is identified by letter in alphabetical sequence, as A-for-Attack, B-for-Bomber. The consecutive model within the type is identified by number, as AT-4, AT-5, and the series by a suffix letter (AT-5A). Status prefixes (X for Experimental, Y for Service Test) are presented first for each model in order to keep them together by type regardless of whether the aeroplane is an actual prototype (XO-1) or a production model diverted for test work after delivery (XP-1B). Where some specific aeroplanes have been redesignated, both designations are presented in their alphabetical sequence, as AT-5As becoming P-1F and the YP-20 becoming the XP-6E.

# Curtiss Aeroplanes with US Navy Designations in 1911–1961 Systems, including Curtiss Designs Built by Others under Different Designations

The Naval listing of Curtiss aeroplanes was similar to the Army, mostly covering them in sequence of type, model and series in the standardized 1922–1962 system. A few designations from the 1911–1916 systems appear in their proper alphabetical positions regardless of system or chronology.

Naval designations for Curtiss designs built by other manufacturers are given, with parenthetical reference to the Naval designation of the equivalent Curtiss model, as the Canadian Fairchild SBF-1 being paired with the Curtiss SB2C-1C. In the rare case of duplicate Naval designations for different Curtiss models, the Curtiss model number is given for each, as SC-2 (Model 31A) and SC-2 (Model 97D).

| | |
|---|---|
| A-1, 47–9 | F6C-3, 267–9 |
| A-2, 52, 53 | XF6C-4, 270 |
| A-3, 4, 49 | F6C-4, 267–71 |
| AB-1, 51–3 | XF6C-5, 267, 271 |
| AB-2/5, 53 | XF6C-6, 272, 273 |
| AH-3, 54 | F6C-6, 269–72, 284 |
| AH-8, 49 | XF6C-7, 273, 274 |
| AH-9, 49 | XF7C-1, 199 |
| AH-11, 12, 49 | F7C-1, 198–200 |
| AH-13, 49 | XF8C-1, 302, 303, 305 |
| AH-14/18, 49 | F8C-1, 302, 304 |
| AH-62, 123 | XF8C-2, 206 |
| AX-1, 52 | F8C-3, 206 |
| | XF8C-4, 206, 207 |
| XBFC-1, 276 | F8C-4, 206, 207 |
| BFC-2, 274, 276, 277 | F8C-5, 208 |
| XBF2C-1, 276, 284 | XF8C-6, 208 |
| BF2C-1, 275–7 | XF8C-7, 208 |
| XBTC-2, 445, 446 | XF8C-8, 209 |
| XBT2C-1, 449, 450 | XF9C-1, 320, 321, 325 |
| | XF9C-2, 321, 325 |
| C-1, 51, 53 | F9C-2, Frontispiece, 322–5 |
| C-2, 53 | XF10C-1, 210 |
| C-3/5, 53 | XF11C-1, 264 |
| CR, 228 | XF11C-2, 264 |
| CR-1, 228, 229, 231 | F11C-2, 274–6, 284 |
| CR-2, 228–30 | XF11C-3, 274 |
| CR-3, 230, 231 | XF12C-1, 345–7 |
| CR-4, 232 | XF13C-1, 336–9 |
| CS-1, 189, 190 | XF13C-2, 337–9 |
| CS-2, 190, 191 | XF13C-3, 338 |
| CS-3/5, 191 | XF14C-2, 439–40 |
| CT-1, 170, 182 | XF15C-1, 506–8 |
| | |
| E-1, 52 | JC-1, 389 |
| | |
| F4C-1, 170, 192, 193 | KD2C-1, 511 |
| F5C-1, 267 | |
| F-5L, 83–6 | XN2C-1, 200 |
| F-6, 84 | N2C-1, 201 |
| F6C-1, 267 | N2C-2, 201, 202 |
| F6C-2, 267, 268, 270 | |
| XF6C-3, 269 | OC-1, 302, 304 |

# Aeroplanes of Other Designers or Manufacturers, Including Curtiss Designs Manufactured, Modified, or Assembled by Others

This list and index covers all aeroplanes of non-Curtiss design that are mentioned in this book. Some have influenced Curtiss designs or have been derived from them and some have been competitors for US civil or military business or have been wartime adversaries. In some cases, other designs have been built by Curtiss while Curtiss designs have been built by others, either under Curtiss model designations or differing manufacturer or military designations. Some listed aeroplanes are Curtiss aeroplanes modified or merely assembled from spare parts by other organizations to become new aeroplanes. Some of these retained their original Curtiss identities while others acquired new names and product identification.